MARSHAL PÉTAIN

By the same author

The Reactionary Revolution: The Catholic revival in French literature 1870–1914
(1966)

« Je fais à la France le don de ma personne

Ph. Pétain

Juin 1

Marshal Pétain, June 1940

MARSHAL PÉTAIN

Richard Griffiths

CONSTABLE LONDON

First published 1970
by Constable & Company Ltd
10 Orange Street, London WC2
Copyright © 1970 by Richard Griffiths

ISBN 0 09 455740 3

Printed in Great Britain
by Ebenezer Baylis & Son Ltd
The Trinity Press, Worcester, and London

To the memory of
Pierre Lambert

CONTENTS

ILLUSTRATIONS

PREFACE

THIS book is not a biography in the usual sense of the term. Indeed, apart from a very small number of pages, it is entirely concerned with thirty years of its subject's life, starting moreover at the age of fifty-eight. This is explained by the fact that before 1914 there is little in Pétain's life to interest us, and that all that is of any significance is crammed into the two wars and the inter-war period. Within these thirty years, though the book on the whole follows a chronological course, there are places where the discussion of the problems raised by Pétain's activities disturbs the strictly chronological plan. It might, indeed, be called 'a biography with pauses for thought'.

I was first attracted to a study of this man by the problem which the disparity between his reputation in the First World War and that in the Second appeared to present. An additional attraction, to someone interested in French politics (and particularly in French politics of the Right), was the whole question of the policies of the National Revolution of 1940, and their political antecedents. Pétain is an important figure for study not only because of his personal fate, but also because through him, as an important public figure and therefore a mouthpiece, the political attitudes of a whole section of the French nation can be examined.

In the study of Pétain's own fate, researches produced a significant change of opinion on my part. The problem which had seemed to exist disappeared from view. The events of 1940 had originally seemed inexplicable in relation to Pétain's former career, unless the 'senility' theory were to be produced; but a close examination of his life up to that time eventually shows us that he would hardly have been expected to act in any other way. His 1940 actions were the natural product of his views and actions in previous years, and he does not appear to have been affected by senility at this stage.

Pétain has seemed to many a tragic figure; but he had not the stature for this. A figure of pathos, certainly. And, as will be realised by any reader of this book, it is in the years immediately succeeding 1940 that the author has felt the greatest sympathy for his subject. The Pétain of the inter-war period had been a man with a good reputation as a soldier, who had subsequently been given an adulation out of all proportion to his merits, and had been believed to be competent in a great many areas of which he had no experience. The result of this had been a certain vanity and self-sufficiency. Convinced that he alone, as an 'incarnation' of France, could save his country, he acted on this basis, and in accordance with many of the *simpliste* pre-conceptions of which he had shown himself capable in the preceding years. It is only when stripped of this vanity, and faced by the consequences of the actions he had taken, that Pétain, behaving at times with courage and dignity, deserves a little more of our sympathy.

As will have been seen already, I fall into none of the accepted Pétain camps. I do not see him as a villain; I do not see him as hero, saint or martyr; I do not even excuse him on grounds of senility. It is not the duty of historian or biographer to accuse or to justify, but to describe and to attempt to explain.

In explaining Pétain, one is led also to try to explain much that happened around him: the military tactics and strategy of the First World War, and the political and military intrigues of the same period; the bases of military preparation in the inter-war period, and Pétain's share of any blame that is going; the political background, and Petain's involvement in it; and the political basis of the Vichy Government. This last problem is one of the most fascinating, in particular when the policies of 1940 are taken in relation to the permanent demands of a certain Right which was particularly active in the inter-war period, but which claimed the allegiance of a large number of inarticulate Frenchmen, including military men such as Pétain.

In the biography of such a controversial figure, many have been the works which quote evidence which may well be unreliable: unauthenticated conversations with witnesses, or autobiographical writings produced long after the event, and yet pronounced worthy of belief. It has been my aim to rely as much as possible on contemporary evidence; where less reliable sources have had to be used, I have on the whole referred to this fact in the text. In the process, a certain amount of fairly colourful 'material' has had to be omitted; but the reliable texts themselves provide more than enough colour for any one work. My practice has been to supply references in footnotes where I actually quote from a document, or where expert opinions have been divided on a question, or where a new document has brought new facts to the common store of knowledge. Apart from this, however, (and particularly in relation to the Second World War, where the same facts are often quoted in a multitude of sources) I have not felt it necessary to specify sources more fully for the authenticated facts.

In such a many-sided subject, there have been many works which have been of value for giving an understanding of the background. As well as being mentioned in the bibliography, most of these are mentioned at the points where they have been of particular use. I would like, however, to name here a few that have been of the greatest value to me: for inter-war politics, Denis Brogan's *The Development of Modern France*, René Rémond's *La Droite en France* and Eugen Weber's *Action Française;* for Vichy France, Robert Aron's *Histoire de Vichy*, Henri Michel's *Vichy: Année 40* and André Brissaud's *La Dernière Année de Vichy*; and, for both these periods, Geoffrey Warner's *Pierre Laval and the Eclipse of France*, a magnificent piece of work to which I am indebted for much of my information about the Pétain-Laval relationship.

Many people have helped me, either by putting me on the track of documents or by giving me excellent advice. I would like particularly to thank M. Robert Aron, Mme Catherine Backès, Mme Hélène Bouvard, M. Pierre Claudel, Mr Patrice Charvet, M. Jacques Deschanel, General Maurice Durosoy, General Sir John Evetts, the late Maître Maurice Garçon, M. René Gillouin, Mme Anne Heurgon-Desjardins, Maître Jacques Isorni, General Henri Jauneaud, Miss Annette Kahn, Dr Leo Kahn, Mme Clara Malraux, M. Gabriel Marcel, M. Henri Massis, Mme Renée Nantet, Mme Jeannine Quillet, M. Pierre Quillet, M. Pierre Roland-Lévy, Mme Madeleine Sabine, General Max von Viebahn, Colonel Wemaere, and Mr Sam White.

I should like to thank the following publishers and authors for permission to quote from their work: Éditions Berger-Levrault for General E. Laure's *Pétain* (1941); Eyre & Spottiswoode (Publishers Ltd) for *The Private Papers of Douglas Haig, 1914–1919* edited by Robert Blake (1952); Librairie Plon for Fayolle's *Cahiers secrets de la Grande Guerre* (1964); and La Guilde du Livre for Benoist-Mechin's *Lyautey L'Africain, ou le rêve immolé* (1966).

The staffs of the libraries of the Institut für Zeitgeschichte, Munich, and of the Bibliothèque de l'Institut, Paris, must be singled out above all other institutions for their unfailing kindness and help. In both these places one has felt that nothing could be too much trouble when helping a reader.

My thanks are also due to the Master and Fellows of Selwyn College, Cambridge, and the Principal and Fellows of Brasenose College, Oxford, for enabling this book to be written.

INTRODUCTION

UNTIL the age of fifty-eight, Pétain's career had little to distinguish it. He was a colonel in 1914, with two years to go to the retiring age. None of the later opinions which were to be held on him, whether favourable or adverse, seem to have bearing on this career soldier, unknown outside military circles, whose career appeared to be ending in semi-obscurity. There were, however, certain aspects of his military thought which were to have great bearing on the war to come. By his courageous defence of these theories, which ran counter to those which were fashionable at the time, Pétain perhaps prevented his own peacetime advancement, but the war was to prove him right. He was one of the only French military figures to see the important changes that had been created in the balance of military power by the new weapons (machine-guns, barbed wire, and heavy artillery), and to try to devise new tactics to cope with them. In abstract, his views were shunned; in practice, after 1914, they were accepted; though even he had not foreseen the extraordinary situation that was to be created by the continuous front of trench warfare.

His military advancement was also hindered by certain personal traits, including a biting irony and a refusal to suffer fools gladly, even if they were his superiors. These traits continue throughout his later career and they, too, are important in any assessment of Pétain's character and career.

Philippe Pétain was born on 24 April 1856, of peasant stock, at Cauchy-la-Tour, near Béthune, in the Pas-de-Calais. His mother died when he was one and a half years old, and in 1859 his father married again. From 1867 to 1875 Pétain was a boarder at the Collège St Bertin at St Omer, and he then spent a year at the Dominican college in Arcueil. In 1876, he entered the military school of St Cyr, which he left, in 1878, as a *sous-lieutenant*. In the entry to St Cyr, he was listed 403 out of 412; he left as 229 out of 386.

St Cyr was perhaps one of the strongest influences in Pétain's later life. He learned there not only a respect for military virtues but also the military contempt for politicians and civilians, the mistrust for Republican education and the doctrines of the left, and the respect for tradition, which were to mark his later thought. He also developed that straight-faced irony which was to be one of his most effective methods of communication.

It took Pétain twelve years to reach the rank of captain. He had spent five years as *sous-lieutenant* in the 24th Battalion of Chasseurs at Villefranche-sur-mer (1878–83), and five as *lieutenant* in the 3rd Battalion of Chasseurs at Besançon (1883–8), before entering the *École de Guerre* in 1888. Here he was taught by some of the foremost military thinkers of his time. When he left, in 1890, however, he only received the grade of '*Bien*', which was not of the highest. He joined the XVth Corps at Marseilles, as a captain.

In peacetime France, promotion was slow. One of the swifter ways to advancement was in the colonial army, yet there was, in military circles in metropolitan France, something of a contempt for the colonial military, and for the enemies they had to fight. Be that as it may, Pétain (unlike Joffre, Galliéni, Lyautey or Mangin) was to remain in France for the whole of his military career, until the Riff War in 1925, when his continental preconceptions about warfare proved, as we shall see, unsuited to the colonial field.

Pétain's promotion was, however, slow even by peacetime standards. He was now, after twelve years in the army, a captain. After two years with the 15th Corps, he took over command of a company in the 29th Battalion of *Chasseurs*, garrisoned at Vincennes. This brought him nearer to the centre of military things, and in just over a year he had been brought onto the staff of General Saussier, the military governor of Paris. He continued on this staff, having been promoted to *officier d'ordonnance*, under Saussier's successors Zurlinden and Brugère.

For further promotion above the rank of captain to be possible, Pétain had to fulfil the condition of a certain amount of time in command of troops, and so he soon joined the 8th Battalion of *Chasseurs*, stationed near Amiens. With these troops he did a great deal of instruction, and also became noted, at the time of manoeuvres, by senior officers who observed him. It was not until 1900 that he reached the rank of major.

In this year a former teacher of his from the *École de Guerre*, General Millet, had him appointed to the *École normale de tir* (Rifle School) at Châlons. Within a short time of starting to teach there, Pétain found himself in opposition to the policy of the authorities, and in particular of the Director, Colonel Vonderscherr. This policy was one of providing a 'field' of fire, for which purpose the riflemen would be trained to fire as a group, and would not be encouraged to develop individual accuracy. Pétain insisted, on the contrary, that each man must be trained for individual accuracy above all. When Pétain was asked to modify his teachings, he refused. Finally Vonderscherr succeeded in getting him removed by the authorities.

This incident shows us two things about Pétain: his concern for the accuracy and power of fire, and his refusal to modify his opinions in face of opposition from his superiors. The first is important in relation to his eventual military opinions, the second in relation to the slowness of his advancement, and his later personal attitudes.

Pétain's removal was done in a civilised manner. He was asked to request a change of post; this he agreed to do, on condition that he could choose his own new position, and that it should be Paris. Laure tells us that the official request had a pencilled marginal note on it, which read: 'To be placed as well as possible'.[1] He was, in fact, put in charge of a battalion of the 5th Infantry Regiment, in Paris.

Six months later, he was called away again, to another post as instructor.

This time it was at the *École de Guerre*, to lecture on infantry tactics. The man in charge of this was General Bonnal, who had noted Pétain during manoeuvres of the 8th Battalion of *Chasseurs* in 1900, and had singled him out for special praise.

Pétain's lectures were very favourably noticed, and he was a definite success. Nevertheless, in accordance with normal army policy, he had to leave the *École de Guerre* in 1903, to take over command of a battalion once more, this time in the 104th Infantry Regiment, where he remained for a year, before returning to the place that had been kept for him at the *École de Guerre*. Here he had definitely become accepted as one of the few experts upon the teaching of shooting. It took until 1907, however, for him to reach the rank of lieutenant-colonel.

His teachings were already in some senses unusual, and the Director soon had him transferred to the 118th Infantry Regiment at Quimper; with the advent of a new director, General Maunoury, he was however recalled to the *École de Guerre*, where from 1908–10 he held the chair of infantry tactics, and from 1910–11 was director of infantry tactics.

The rest of his pre-war career seemed merely the prelude to retirement. In 1910 he became a colonel, and in 1911 took over command of the 33rd Infantry Regiment, at Arras. Here, during the next couple of years, his regiment's manoeuvres were to be over the same ground on which he was to fight in late 1914 and early 1915. In early 1914, he took over command of the 4th Infantry Brigade.

Pétain's advancement, in the last ten years of his pre-war career, had definitely been retarded. Much of the blame for this must be laid on the unorthodox theories he was putting forward; much, also, may rest on his own attitudes towards his superiors. It is clear, however, that the powers that be became opposed to his advancement. His moves back and forth to the *École de Guerre* depended very much on who was in direct charge at the time; in a letter written to his nephew Paul Pomart, during his exile at Quimper in 1907, he said: 'It is possible that I will not be remaining too long here. The *École* is calling for me again, but as I have a bad press at the Ministry, I do not know which will win: the betting is open.'[2]

The 'bad press at the Ministry' was not a figment of Pétain's imagination. In 1914 General Franchet D'Esperey, feeling that Pétain had not received the promotion he deserved, approached General Guillaumat, head of the War Minister's 'Cabinet', about the possibility of his being made a general 'divisionnaire', but got the reply that Pétain would never become a general.[3] He was, by 1914, clearly destined to retire as a colonel in two years' time.

We have little evidence of any political attitudes on Pétain's part; the reasons for his non-acceptability must therefore have been almost certainly military. And the obvious aspect through which he must have given offence was his teachings at the *École de Guerre* during his three periods there as a lecturer. What were these teachings, and why did they cause such feelings?

They were revolutionary. In the same way in which de Gaulle has been seen (far less justifiably) as a man swimming alone against the tide of French military opinion before the Second World War, and producing theories which matched the new military situation, Pétain rejected in his lectures the principles which lay at the foundation of French contemporary military thought.

The war of 1870, in which French defensive attitudes had been part of the reason for the defeat, had impressed French military thinkers with the value of the offensive. Military instruction began once more to be based on the examples of the Napoleonic Wars, and the offensive became the only true tactic. French military thought revolved round the idea of the charge, the impetuous onslaught by which, with bayonets fixed, the French soldiers, imbued with *furia francese*, would overrun the enemy positions; the enemy, frightened and bewildered, morally beaten by the courage of their assailants, would give in or retreat.

Pétain's theories were not, as has often been suggested, the exact opposite of this. He never, now or during the experiences of the war, set up the defensive as the be-all and end-all of warfare. He saw clearly that a war could eventually only be won in terms of the offensive. But he reinstated the defensive as a part of the tactics leading to this larger strategy, and he set realistic limits to the powers of a tactical offensive.

His lectures were reproduced in roneo-typed form, and are preserved in the Army History Library at Vincennes. This text enables us to see exactly where his originality lay. The course was based on a historical outline of French military tactics. In the second part, which dealt with the 1870 war, Pétain made the important comment: 'The fundamental fact to be gathered from the 1870 war is the bringing to light of the considerable importance that has been acquired by fire-power; this importance has exceeded all forecasts. The progress in arms will impose on infantry new combat procedures.'[4]

This was the basis for Pétain's new view of tactics; the importance of fire-power. Throughout his life he was to repeat the simple dictum: '*le feu tue*.' An obvious enough statement, but one that was ignored by most of his contemporaries before 1914. In the third part of the course, which dealt with the period from 1870 to 1902, he again returned to the question of fire-power, and its 'preponderant power' in modern warfare. This condition meant that soldiers must seek invulnerability as far as possible, and use the ground as a shield. They must hide themselves from the view of their opponents.

According to Pétain, this had been very clear just after 1870, but had been forgotten thereafter, as the enthusiasm for Napoleonic methods took over. Despite the lessons of the Boer War and the Manchurian War, where the devastating effects of machine guns had been shown, French military methods had not adapted themselves.

Pétain's views were anathema to those who saw war as a heroic business. For the soldier to *hide* himself was beneath contempt. A frontal attack, a charge that would carry all before it, was the only true tactic. The official line continued in this direction. Headquarters continued to produce offensive directives, and Colonel Grandmaison, head of the 3rd (Operational) Bureau of the General Staff, (whose name has become forever associated with this policy), even suggested that, with the right moral fervour, it was possible to advance under a hail of enemy bullets.

Pétain's views were therefore, tactically, completely opposed to the official line. One must not overstress his foresight as to the new conditions of war, however. Fire-power was the important thing he foresaw, in its transformation of the field of battle; but he did not mention barbed wire, the other main instrument in the creation of strength for defence; nor did he foresee the completely static nature of the warfare to come. He saw that the new conditions created an advantage for the defensive, but his tactics were meant to show how, with care, to overcome this. The offensive remained the way to win a battle, but it was an offensive tempered with caution, which had perhaps been prepared by an initial defensive action. We shall see how, as the war proceeded, these ideas were gradually changed under the force of events. Pétain was, until 1918, probably the most adaptable of French military minds, starting always from facts and not from abstract theories.

It may have been these views that held Pétain back. He was certainly well thought of by some, or he would not have been a lecturer at the *École de Guerre* (or, as one story has it, have been offered at one stage the directorship of the *École Normale de Tir*, after Vonderscherr's retirement); but he obviously incurred the disapproval of others, as his perpetually changing life had shown, and his moves to and from the *École de Guerre*. Another factor may have been his ill-disguised contempt for some of his superiors, of which there are many stories, the best of them being his public words to his troops, on manoeuvres in 1913, after the General in command had commented on their tactics: 'I am certain that General Le Gallet has intended, in order to strike your minds more forcibly, to present a synthesis of all the faults which a modern army should no longer commit.'

A cold irony, which was the counterpart of a cold assessment of any military situation, these are the salient characteristics of the Pétain we see in 1914, at the outbreak of war. He was a man prepared for retirement, convinced that his career was at an end; yet there was no sign of emotion, of impatience at lost opportunities. He was aware of his own worth, and of the foolishness of others; he did not need events to prove him right, even though this is what they were about to do.

PART I

Fire-Power

IN 1914, at the age of fifty-eight, Pétain was a colonel; in 1918, at the age of sixty-two, he was a Marshal of France. Had the war not occurred, his career would have ended in obscurity, and he would have lived for thirty-five years of retirement undisturbed by national affairs. As it was, he was to remain in positions of national eminence, military, political or diplomatic, for another twenty-six years. Four years thus changed the course of this man's life, and started a new and more brilliant career for him at a time when other men were finishing theirs. These four years of his life have often been described; controversies have grown up around them, legends have been made and destroyed. Our task, in these chapters, will not only be to trace those steps which led Pétain to the reputation and honours which he eventually achieved, but also to examine the views which he held both on matters of military strategy and tactics, and upon wider matters of national interest. We shall find much which explains aspects of his later career.

The Battle of the Frontiers, the Battle of Guise, and the Battle of the Marne

On the outbreak of war, Colonel Pétain was in command of the 4th Infantry Brigade, at St Omer. As part of General Lanrezac's 5th Army, the Brigade's first move was to Belgium, which it entered on 13 August 1914. This was the month of the worst French losses of the whole war. In Lorraine, thousands of Frenchmen, valiantly attacking the enemy according to the instructions of Plan XVII, were mown down by the enemy machine guns. Already Pétain's views of the effectiveness of fire-power and of the necessity for new tactics were being borne out.

Pétain's own brigade's movements have been accurately conveyed to us by the short-lived *Journal de Route* which Pétain kept until late October of this year.[1] In this Belgian campaign, one of Pétain's main observations was that of the fatigue of his troops. On one night march (14–15 August) he notes: 'From three o'clock onwards, groups of men begin not getting up after halts, and one is obliged to strike them to make them get up.' Admittedly, the demands were enormous; over forty kilometres in twelve hours, with every soldier bowed beneath the usual immense load. The forced march in question had been necessary, however. It had enabled the brigade to race the Germans to the left bank of the Meuse, near Dinant, where they took up a defensive position on the right of the 5th Army. In Pétain's *Journal*, during this stage of the campaign, certain things of interest are noted. He becomes aware of some of the drawbacks in the traditional defensive system, particularly in the topographical situation in which he find himself, and sets about a reorganisation;* and, when a reserve division shows weakness, he confides to his diary his convictions as to the responsibility of those who have been ruling the country for the state of the army: 'They will probably wish once more to blame military men for what is happening to us, whereas the entire responsibility lies on the country's representatives. A nation has the army it deserves.'

Soon the French army in Belgium was in full retreat. On the night of 27–28 August, Pétain had reached the village of Iviers, in the Aisne department. And it was here that he heard of his promotion to the rank of *général de brigade*. His comment on this is typically ironic: 'I have just learnt of my promotion to general. It even seems that they want to put me in command of a division. Are they already reduced to using such revolutionary measures?'

This was the first step in Pétain's rapid advancement. And unlike the subsequent ones, it does not seem to have been caused by any awareness on the part of his superiors of any outstanding qualities on his part. Indeed, he had hardly been tried as yet. The explanation is simple, and Pétain's irony was justified. The French army just did not have enough senior officers. Some had died, but far more had proved incapable of filling their posts. In just over a months, Amouroux tells us,[2] the commander-in-chief, Joffre, had got rid of two *généraux d'armée*, nine *généraux de corps d'armée* (out of twenty-one), thirty-three *généraux de division d'infanterie* (out of forty-seven), and five *généraux de division de cavalerie* (out of ten). Amid the general indecision and incompetence, Pétain had shown the virtues of organisation and carefulness. His brigade had, before and during the retreat, acquitted itself well.

Pétain was not to take over his new division for some days, however; and meanwhile, on the very morning of the announcement of his promotion, the 28th, the 4th Brigade was ordered with the rest of the 5th Army under Lanrezac into the Battle of Guise, a counter-attack mainly aimed at slowing the German advance, to help the Allied armies, particularly the British, to reorganise themselves. This battle, which has sometimes been seen as a prelude to the Marne, was in fact something completely different. The Marne was a moment of supreme military opportunism, combined with sound tactical sense; an operation which was completely to change the course of the war. Guise was, on the other hand, a limited operation, with far less ambitious aims or consequences. Yet there is no denying the achievement of this short action, and the incredible spirit which must have fired those who, in full retreat, managed to carry out this counter-attack. Pétain was later to describe these men and their achievement in the following words:

Only those who commanded them in those tragic days can fully measure the valour of their efforts! Worn out with fatigue, deprived of food and sleep,

* See later in this chapter

4

shaken by the memory of bloody engagements, separated from so many friends with whom they had received the baptism of fire, and to whom they had not been able to give any last rites, drowned in the flood of refugees, they were still able, when their commander watched them pass by, to raise their heads with pride and turn their eyes to him, which is the mark of accepted discipline.

So do not be astonished at what they did at Guise, for otherwise you will not understand the Marne! Guise was a localised offensive about-turn; a block-busting blow delivered by a boxer who had seemed to be almost knocked out, and who suddenly bounded back, ready for the attack.

It was too soon, however . . .[3]

Too soon for a complete victory, but soon enough to slow down the German advance, which was the main object of this action. On the 29th, Pétain's *Journal* contains the words 'The enemy is retreating'. But the respite was short, and on the next day the French were forced once more to continue their retreat. As Correlli Barnett puts it: 'Lanrezac, abandoned by the British, whose retreat was at this stage of an impressive rapidity, and after having struck his dislocating blow, now fell swiftly back.'[4]

On 1 September Pétain went to take over his new command, the 6th Infantry Division, at Fismes. His predecessor, General Bloch, had been removed by Joffre. The division, still in retreat, was not in the best of form as far as discipline was concerned. Crossing the Marne at Verneuil, Pétain was even forced to round up some of his men, revolver in hand. On the 5th, reaching new headquarters at Louau, he received the order 'Tomorrow, attack northwards.' The Battle of the Marne had begun.

The Battle of Guise had been of more use than it had at first seemed. For one result of it had been to deflect von Kluck's advance, with the German 1st Army, (the right wing of the German advance) eastwards. Von Kluck had already shown some disagreement with the Commander-in-Chief, Moltke, on his line of advance. Moltke's plan would have brought the 1st Army to the west of Paris. Von Kluck, believing the B.E.F. (British Expeditionary Force) to be out of action and Maunoury's French 6th Army to be unimportant, thought that the best plan would be for the German 1st and 2nd Armies, under himself and Bülow, to turn in eastwards and out-flank the rest of the French army, separating it from Paris. Orders were orders, and von Kluck had in principle to obey Moltke; but the Commander-in-Chief was far distant, and, as Corelli Barnett says, 'it would not require much of an excuse for the bullheaded Kluck to swing eastwards out of the axis of advance prescribed by Moltke. Lanrezac's French 5th Army provided that excuse on August 29 by striking back strongly at Bülow round Guise . . .'[5] Kluck turned inwards to help Bülow, leaving Maunoury's 6th Army and the B.E.F. to the west of him.

It was this change of direction that had provided the French with their opportunity. Opinions are divided as to who first saw the advantage that had been handed to the Allies, but it was certainly Joffre, as Commander-in-Chief, who so organised things as to enjoy that advantage to the full. The attack by the French forces on 6 September came as a complete surprise to the German command.

The French plan was for the armies to the south of the main German force to stand firm, while those to the east and west should attack the sides of the salient formed by the German advance. Franchet d'Esperey's 5th Army (he had replaced Lanrezac), in which was Pétain's 6th Division, was one of the attackers from the west, with on its left the B.E.F., and beyond them Maunoury's 6th Army. The advance was slow, and the 5th Army soon dug itself in, but, as Barnett points out, the main effect of the day was on German morale, as their advance was first stopped, and then reversed.

For some days the Battle of the Marne, though fierce, was indecisive. On the 9th came the German retreat to the line of the Vesle and the Aisne, between Reims and Soissons. Pétain's division, as part of the 5th Army, reached and crossed the Vesle west of Reims on 12 September, and reached the Aisne canal on the 13th. Here the enemy stopped, and counter-attacked in some strength; the French advance was checked, and Pétain settled down to the building of a defensive system to withstand further attacks. His methods were unusual at this date, both in the depth of the defences and in the fact that he was prepared to give ground (the village of Loivre) if it was in the best interests of the defence;* an attitude which seems reasonable enough to us, but which was almost unthinkable at the time. The strength of his defences was put to its greatest test on 27 September, when despite a violent attack, his division remained firm.

These achievements, which had aided the operations of the 5th Army around Reims, were rewarded by a citation, in which he was described as having 'by his example, his tenacity, his calmness under fire, his constant intervention at difficult moments, obtained from his division, during fourteen consecutive days of the Battle of Reims, a magnificent effort, resisting repeated attacks by night and day, and, on the fourteenth day, despite the losses undergone, warded off a furious attack by the enemy.'[6]

In that fortnight, Pétain's efforts had not been purely defensive. He had also executed various attacks of his own, strongly supported by artillery. But it was already becoming clear that the war was reaching a new phase. The war of movement was over, the '*course à la mer*' ('rush to the sea') had begun. On each side, the armies tried to outflank each other, in vain, until the network of trenches and of defensive positions stretched from Switzerland to the sea. The lessons which Pétain had preached before the war, about the importance of fire-power and the new situations created by new weapons, had proved true, but had produced results which even he had not foreseen. For, important as had been his stress on the defensive, it had been as a preparation for the counter-offensive which was to follow; nowhere had he given any hint of the possibility of the gigantic stalemate which now faced the European armies. Indeed, who could have foreseen it? Even now, it seems to us like some appalling nightmare. That two opposed forces should remain stagnant, at such a short distance from each other, for such a length

* See later in chapter

of line, for such a length of time, would have seemed the wildest fantasy to anyone, before the time that it actually happened. The defensive had shown its strength; even though most generals continued, for much of the rest of the war, not to believe it.

Years later, Pétain was to say of late September and early October 1914:

> The glorious epoch was over, in which combatants had dared to face each other openly, and in which audacity and spontaneous reactions had retained for the struggle its character of improvisation: the lessons of fire-power could no longer be ignored.
>
> From this moment onwards, war was to change in character. Munitions were to take a more and more important part, as the factories multiplied their quantity and their power.
>
> Artillery and machine-guns were to become the masters of the field of battle. People were to realise the value of shelter and the necessity for communications....[7]

Pétain himself was one of the first to realise the import of the new situation. After launching some unsuccessful attacks on the German lines, from 12–16 October, he wrote to his army corps commander on the 16th: 'The Germans are using the techniques of siege warfare. Faced with this method, I have gained the conviction that any offensive carried out by ordinary methods is doomed to certain failure, whatever the forces and means of action which are used. One must come to employ against them the techniques of attack of siege warfare.'[8]

The same day he received the rosette of Officer of the Légion d'Honneur; and four days later, the 20th, he was appointed to the command of the 33rd Army Corps. He was to move to a new region, where he was to face the full implications of the new style of warfare. Above all, he was to find himself in command of immeasurably more men than ever before. From a brigade to an army corps in under three months: the swift ascent had begun.

Artois

In the 'rush to the sea', as each side tried to outflank the other, the fate of the town of Arras, an important communications centre, had been very much in the balance. It was in this sector that some of the fiercest fighting of October had taken place.[9] The German attacks had reached their height in the three days 21–23 October. On the 23rd Pétain came to take over his new command: 'It was on 23 October, the day of the last German attack, that I took over the command of the 33rd Army Corps, whose headquarters was at Aubigny. Thus the fortunes of war brought me back to this region which I knew well, from having held manoeuvres for my regiment, the 33rd Infantry, there for several years ...'[10]

Knowledge of the ground must certainly have been useful; but the experience of pre-war manoeuvres, even those of Pétain with their concentration on fire-power, can hardly have been of much use in the new situation, the new style of warfare which was emerging.

The new commander made a very good impression on his officers and

7

men, perhaps the more so because of the contrast he made with General d'Urbal, his predecessor, who was going to a new command in Flanders. An officer of the *état-major*, Commandant Serrigny, who was to become Pétain's constant companion throughout the war, noted: 'Although very cold, the newcomer is not solemn like his predecessor. He seems to have a completely different idea of his role as commander. Hardly had he arrived before he went to visit his divisional generals, a thing which d'Urbal had never done.'[11]

Mordacq, too, noted the difference between Pétain and d'Urbal, and the immediate effect which Pétain's personality had on his men:

> ... The impression, both for officers and men, was quite different from that produced by his predecessor, General d'Urbal.
> Indeed he was a quite different type of commander, of a completely different temperament. When they saw the General, tall as he was, moving from parapet to parapet observing the enemy positions without even bothering to bend down to protect himself, asking questions simply, but remaining nevertheless very cold and talking little; starting no conversations, yet showing in his eyes a look of great kindness, the *Alpins* [alpine regiment] were rather amazed. Yet they immediately gained the impression of a leader, a very great leader....[12]

Here, already, we have the picture of Pétain which was to make his popularity at the time of Verdun, and was to stand him in such good stead at the time of the 1917 mutinies: the commander who visits his men, who cares about his men, yet who retains their respect by remaining aloof from them, cold and reserved. Above all, the impression is already being formed of a leader who is the opposite of the 'embusqués' hidden in their châteaux behind the lines; a leader who is prepared to share the dangers of his men, and who knows their preoccupations. Indeed, during his time on the Artois front Pétain did much to improve the morale of his men, particularly in the period just before the offensive of May 1915. He improved the *lieux de repos* behind the lines, helped to organise tours of the 'Théâtre des Armées', and managed to obtain permission for his men to have regular leave in Amiens. Far more than most of his fellow-generals, Pétain appears to have concerned himself with the welfare of his troops. For him they were not mere cannon-fodder; they were men like himself. His experience as a front-line colonel had taught him more than most of his colleagues were ever likely to learn. Mordacq describes him, on the first day of his command, as saying that he had come to assess the situation and 'the morale of his men.'* Mordacq may, of course, have been imagining this precise statement; he was writing twenty years afterwards, for the last seventeen or so of which the word 'morale' had rarely been absent from Pétain's lips. But the concrete facts of Pétain's Artois command show that, whether he had forumlated it in the terms he was later to use, he already had a great concern for his men's welfare.

* Mordacq, op. cit. p. 203 'So one sees that, from the very beginning of the war, this was always his *idée fixe*, his great preoccupation.'

Pétain's army corps, the 33rd, was part of the 10th Army under General de Maud'huy, which was under the general command of Foch, Commander of the Armies of the North. Its task was the defence of Arras, which it covered to the east. Its three divisions were deployed as follows: to the north, the 70th, under General Fayolle; in the centre, the 77th, under General Barbot, mainly Alpins; to the south, the 45th (zouaves) under General Drude.

In October 1914, following the most violent of the German attacks, the main task, despite orders to the contrary, was nevertheless to consolidate the defence of Arras.* Pétain organised the construction of sound defensive lines, against which the German attacks foundered. Gradually the line quietened down, until by the end of October it was clear that the immediate danger was past.

Hardly was this so, than the High Command began to clamour again for offensives. Few, at this stage, were those who, like Pétain, realised the turn which the war had taken. Already Pétain's difficulties with the partisans of the offensive were beginning, difficulties which were to continue right until the end of the war. He was even accused of writing reports that were too 'flat'; that is to say, he did not indulge in the hyperbole of some of his colleagues.† Counter-attacks against enemy onslaughts on his own positions he performed with alacrity; (one such occurred on 26 November); properly prepared offensives he was prepared to envisage; but the offensive for its own sake appeared to him madness in a war that was now effectively ruled by artillery (of which the French were sorely short), machine guns and barbed wire.

For the moment, the obsession of High Command was the *percée*, or breakthrough, the swift attack which would pierce the opposing line, and permit once more the war of movement which they believed to be natural to war. At the end of November Foch came to discuss, with Maud'huy and his generals, the project of an attack. Early November was filled with Maud'huy's hesitations as to the scope of the attack.‡ On 27 December it took place. Fayolle, whose division took the main part in the attack on Carency, one of the small villages which the Bavarian forces opposite them had converted into veritable fortresses, had foreseen the futility of such an attack even at the time of Foch's November discussions:

'I've never heard so many stupid things said . . . I wonder whether those great leaders who push themselves forward in this war are not those who take no account whatsoever of the human lives which are entrusted to them.

* Serrigny wrote on 29 October: 'We are always told to attack, but Pétain is beginning to realise the futility of such operations.' Serrigny, op. cit. p. 4

† Serrigny, op. cit. p. 13, 30 November 1914: 'I did not hesitate to tell [Pétain] that the 33rd Corps is judged rather badly by our superiors because we seem unable to recount our great deeds. Our neighbours send off every day magnificent accounts, and are quoted as models.'

‡ Maud'huy, in fact, seemed at this time more convinced of the futility of an attempt at breakthrough than did Serrigny (Serrigny, op. cit. pp. 14–18). It was certainly the latter who stood out for a large-scale attack.

Attack! Attack! Easily said. You might just as well try, at Carency and Ablain, knocking down a brick wall with your fist or your head. And when I have taken Carency, at the cost of five hundred dead and the same number of wounded, will matters have improved in any way? No.'[13]

The failure of this attack has been blamed on the weather and the conditions, which were indeed abominable, and on the French tactics. But it was the strength of the enemy positions, the power and precision of their machine-gun fire, which were the true destroyers of the offensive. Gains of ground were few and slight; and they were lost again overnight.

The next day, therefore, the orders which had been given the night before, to continue the attack, appeared useless. Pétain, with Barbot, the commander of the 77th Division, went to see Maud'huy, with whom was Foch. Foch declared that, as the new objectives were once more out of reach, an attack must be made again on the same objectives as the day before. Pétain declared that under present conditions, further attack was impossible. So the attack was indefinitely postponed.

But not put out of mind. Three months later, on 24 March 1915, Foch wrote to Joffre that the capture of ridge 140–132, north of Arras, 'will doubtless have a great effect and lead to a *percée* of the enemy line.' A new offensive had already been set on foot.

D'Urbal, who had come back to this sector to command the whole 10th Army in replacement of Maud'huy,* took great care in the preparation of this attack. Joffre was convinced that this was to be the great breakthrough. The forces amassed were impressive: 5 army corps (18 divisions), 293 heavy guns, 780 field guns were to attack on a front of twelve kilometers.

It must not be thought that, because of Pétain's growing realisation of the advantages enjoyed by the defensive in modern war, he was entirely against the offensive. Everything goes to show that, given the new circumstances, he was searching as much as the others for the methods of attack suitable to them. The offensive for its own sake was not a virtue to him, as it so patently was for many of his colleagues and superiors. But a properly prepared attack, with adequate artillery support, and with forces large enough to overcome the initial advantage of the defence, seemed to him at this stage to be a quite acceptable venture. His concern with the need for overwhelming force, whether of munitions or men (which was to be so clear in his relations with headquarters at a later date) is shown in an anecdote often told about him at this time. Before the attack, d'Urbal asked his corps commanders how many grenades they needed. One replied: 'Five thousand'; Pétain replied 'Fifty thousand.'[14]

Pétain's preparations for the attack were meticulous; and they were crowned, at first, with tremendous success. The attack took place on 9 May preceded by a four-hour artillery barrage. Of the whole line, it was Pétain's 33rd Corps which effected the only real breakthrough. Within an hour, the

---

* Fayolle noted on 3 April: 'Maud'huy has gone to the Vosges Army and been replaced by d'Urbal. I think that Pétain was disappointed, and had hoped to take over command of the Army.' Fayolle, op. cit. p. 97

Moroccan division on the right and the 77th Division in the centre had reached their objective, ridge 119–140, while the 70th Division, on the left, under Fayolle, was encircling from the south the strongpoint of Carency, which had cost them so dear in December. The enemy was retreating fast, and the advance troops found themselves on the east slopes of Vimy ridge, with the plain of Lens before them. It looked as though the hoped-for breakthrough had occurred. They were through the German lines.

But all was not as well as it seemed. Firstly, the breakthrough had been on a very narrow front, that of the 33rd Corps. Their neighbours had not done half so well, and the troops could now be fired upon by the enemy artillery from either side. Secondly, the men were themselves physically exhausted. Thirdly, French artillery ammunition was running out. Fourthly, d'Urbal had neglected to supply the reserve divisions which had been asked for before the battle, and which would have been needed to take advantage of the breakthrough. By evening the enemy reserves had come up and closed the breach, and the 33rd Corps had retired some way.

Serrigny lays most of the blame on d'Urbal and the question of the reserves, claiming that he thus showed himself to be as incompetent in charge of an army as he had been in charge of an army corps.[15] Not all blame can be laid on him, however. It might have seemed that the great breakthrough had occurred; and, indeed, at this stage of the war the German defences were thin enough (as opposed to Champagne later in the year) for them to be 'pierced' completely; but, as Pétain was clearly to see, and state in a later report, as long as the enemy had available reserves behind the lines, such a 'breakthrough' could always be brought to a halt at new defensive positions. The 'breakthrough' was a myth. 'The fleeting moment of the breakthrough had passed', sighs Laure;[16] but it was bound to pass. The moment had merely come sooner because of the lack of French reserves.

Nevertheless, Pétain's success of the 9th was received with joy. On the 10th he was made Commander of the Légion d'Honneur. D'Urbal called out for more attacks, counting on the exploitation of the surprise of the 9th. He wrote to Pétain on the 11th: 'It's on your attack that I count . . . The 33rd Corps has the honour of striking the shattering blow.' Joffre and Foch too, took the same line, feeling that this was the beginning of the victory.

Pétain, however, was not so happy. His army now formed a salient, and any further attack to the east would make its position even more dangerous. On the 10th, he told his divisions that their main job was to make sure of the positions they had taken, while helping the divisions on either side of them to go forward. On d'Urbal's insistence, Pétain's corps attacked ridge 119–140 again on the 11th, without success. After this failure, Pétain wrote to d'Urbal: 'A new attack on these heights seems to me to be doomed to the same failure. Even if it succeeded, we would have no chance of staying there, as the enemy could fire down both our flanks.'[17]

Nevertheless d'Urbal wished to continue these frontal attacks, until convinced by a personal meeting with Pétain on the 12th. From now on more reasonable attacks were made, to ease the flanks, though pressure for attacks went on.*

For a few weeks things on this front went slowly, while, under pressure from Foch, a new major attack was prepared. It finally took place on 16 June. Again, it was only the 33rd Corps which made any gains, and these were only partly successful. The offensive was called off on 18 June, though as Serrigny tells us, futile minor attacks were to continue on this front, with great loss of life.[18]

Despite the eventual failure of the Artois offensive, in it Pétain had made his name. His had been the only successes of importance, and in his preparation and execution of them he had shown a tactical grasp superior to that of those around him, including his commanders. On 21 June he was appointed to the command of the 2nd Army, though he remained a while, at d'Urbal's request, to deal with a new and dangerous position, a German counter-attack which had almost surrounded his Moroccan division. Pétain, in the course of dealing with this, decided (horror of horrors to those who believed in never giving up ground!) to evacuate the dangerous salient which had formed on ridge 119. Pétain's own explanation of this unusual action was as follows: 'Obviously the abandoning of the position presents disadvantages from the point of view of morale. It is always bad to give ground to the enemy. But these disadvantages cannot be compared with those which could result, at a given moment, from the capture by the enemy of three or four battalions, and from the consequential loss of several thousand men.'[19]

On this typical note Pétain left the 33rd Corps to join his new Army, the 2nd, which was also in the region of Artois, but with which he was soon to move to the front in Champagne.

In a 'Note on the operations in the region of Arras' which he addressed to the *Grand Quartier Général* (General Headquarters) on 29 June, Pétain showed the lessons he had learned from the Artois campaign. These lessons were of general import. Unlike Serrigny, he did not blame this or that circumstance for the lack of success: he had learned that the whole concept of the 'breakthrough' was ill-advised, and doomed to failure, in that the affluence of enemy reserves, which could arrive faster than the attacking infantry, would block the breach: 'The present war has taken the form of a war of attrition. There is no decisive battle, as there used to be. Success will belong finally to the side which possesses the last man.'[20]

Instead of a centralised battle, he adds, one should have a decentralised battle, which would be more effective both in destruction of the enemy and in raising morale. One must, oneself, keep a last reserve for the end of

* Fayolle notes in his diary, on 13 June: 'I could not go to Mass, because Pétain arrived. He is furious with d'Urbal and Foch. They are idiots, he says. Attack, says Foch, without bothering about the state of preparation. Attack, repeats d'Urbal. And it's as easy as that. The attack on 9 May cost us, counting subsequent deaths, forty or fifty thousand men. That on the 15th will cost us just as many. 100,000 men to gain what? At most, ridge 140.' Fayolle op. cit. p. 111

King George V decorating General Pétain, July 1917

Foch and Weygand at 4th Army H.Q. August 1918

the war; and for this purpose it was necessary to limit the expenditure of one's own troops.

This report shows how near, in one sense, Pétain was to his colleagues; and in another sense, how far. Like them, and before most of them, he saw the war as one of attrition. Unlike them, he saw the necessity for sparing one's own troops in the process; and for this purpose he declared the need for new and less costly methods. In the cause of attrition, the Allied armies were to fling men into costly and murderous attacks in 1916; in 1917, as Commander-in-Chief, Pétain was to show on several occasions the virtues of his own methods. But it must be made clear that, despite these more reasonable methods, Pétain was never (*pace* most of his biographers) an enemy of the concept of attrition, in the sense that he saw the depletion of enemy reserves as a prime object of the war.

Champagne

A new offensive was, in the opinion of the Commander-in-Chief, not only possible, but necessary. The lessons of Artois had been, for him, different from those seen by Pétain. The attempted breakthrough had, he thought, almost succeeded. A new offensive on the same basis, but with stronger forces, was called for.

After some indecision about the place where the attack was to take place, Joffre finally decided, on 11 July, that it would be in Champagne, supported by a secondary action around Arras by French and British forces. The Champagne attack would be made by two complete armies, Pétain's 2nd and De Langle de Cary's 4th. Surprise has occasionally been expressed that Pétain, whose views in his June report had been so completely opposed to the concept of this kind of attack, should have been chosen; but it is quite clear that (1) he was the man who had had most success in the Artois campaign, and had shown beyond all doubt his capability for this kind of attack, (2) Joffre took little notice of reports which contained theories as opposed to facts, and had probably forgotten Pétain's, if he had ever read it.*

We know that Pétain expressed his views to Castelnau, Commander of the Central Army Group, but whether they reached Joffre is another matter. Joffre's statement in a letter to the Minister of War on 29 August 1915 is a statement of his own views, rather than a refutation of anyone else's:

'We have the right to conclude from the events of Arras that, with the powerful artillery forces we possess, it is possible to make a breakthrough in the enemy front which can be exploited, but on condition that powerful attacks are made simultaneously in different regions, each of them on a wide front.'[21]

So more powerful artillery will fill one of the lacks shown by the Artois offensive. And the enemy will be kept from pouring in his reserves by having

* Joffre, as one of his subordinates put it, 'is not a martyr to work; he never writes, and rarely consults a dossier, but much prefers one of his collaborators to make a succinct exposé of it.'

them kept busy on other fronts. Joffre has seen some of the same dangers as Pétain; but he sees them as soluble in the short term. For him, it will be enough to keep the reserves busy. Pétain has seen more clearly the advantage of those on the defensive, and realises the need for extensive depletion of those reserves in the long term.

The date of the attack was originally to have been the beginning of September. But Pétain, with his usual care for complete preparation, insisted on the date being put back, just as he had had the second Artois offensive put back from the end of May to 16 June. In one sense, this shows his sense in wishing all to be perfect. In another, it is senseless in its wasting of any element of surprise.

For it is quite clear that surprise was not one of the things this attack could eventually count on. Pétain, arriving in Champagne on 2 August, had, it is true, taken for secrecy's sake the title of 'Adjutant to the General commanding the Central Army Group', but contemporary accounts show that the September offensive was one of the worst-kept secrets of the war. Auguste Terrier, writing to General Lyautey on 9 September, said: 'People are talking also, a great deal, far too much, about the coming offensive. They say that General de Castelnau has come round to the idea. The publicity given to General Joffre's journey to Italy has, so they say, partly the object of making people believe that there is going to be a French offensive in south Alsace, so as to hide the true attack. Everyone is talking about this offensive, and they have full details of it! German espionage can hardly be starving for lack of food.'*

Louis Marcellin, a journalist, notes in his book *Politique et Politiciens*: 'From 4 September onwards, people have been talking publicly about an imminent great offensive. I can read in my notes, taken on the 6th: "The rumour is confirmed of a great offensive soon on our front." The information is precise: it will be on the 25th. Everyone seems to know, including no doubt the Germans, who have so many spies among us.'[22]

Unlike the German High Command, whose offensives at Verdun and in March 1918 were to be prepared with such care and secrecy, the Allied armies appear to have found great difficulty in keeping anything secret. As with the Nivelle offensive in 1917, the Germans had plenty of time in September 1915 to reinforce their defences at the point of attack, though

---

* Terrier to Lyautey, Paris, 9 September 1915. B. Inst., MS 5903. Terrier's correspondence with Lyautey, who was in Morocco for most of the war, is invaluable for the insight it gives not only into the conduct of public affairs (Terrier, as Director of the Moroccan Office in Paris, mixed in Government circles), but also for the assessments he makes of public opinion. Lyautey, cut off from all but official bulletins, asked him on several occasions to write about everything: 'Have no scruples in sending me what you describe as "potins", which are, in my eyes, indispensable for understanding anything at all of the official news' (Lyautey to Terrier, 19 June 1916). 'It is precious to me that you should continue to write to me all you know about Paris, without fearing to go on too long or to repeat what others may be telling me, for, if you do not, I will know nothing, as nobody writes to me any more.' (Lyautey to Terrier, 29 August 1917). This correspondence will be used at various points in this book.

their whole line was already being provided with defences in depth which were far more efficacious than those in Artois in May had been. Apart from this, French stocks of munitions were not high enough for anything but a limited tactical success to be possible.

The attack eventually took place on 25 September, and was a dismal failure. Initial success in overrunning the German first line was followed by a full stop in front of the second line positions. The methods of Artois were even less successful than before; with the new strengthening of the German lines, even the hope of a breakthrough was absent. And by continuing the action for some days, the attacking forces made their own situation, and losses, even worse. On the evening of the 29th, the attack was stopped.

Castelnau, convinced that a new attack of the strength of that of the 25th was needed to take the second line, sent for more munitions and fresh troops The new attack was made on 6 October and was again unsuccessful.

The method was wrong; this was clear. Castelnau, in his report (27 October 1915) declared that the breaking of the enemy front became, after each attempt, more difficult to achieve. He did not believe the failure to be due to lack of material or men. The preparation had been perfect, artillery and munitions had been enough. Perhaps the importance was speed in overrunning the successive positions. Pétain, however, saw the impossibility of the aim as well as the method: 'The Battle of Champagne shows us the difficulty, if not the impossibility of carrying in one rush the successive enemy positions, in the present state of armaments, of methods of preparation, and of the forces opposed to us.'[23]

His report on the offensive, sent in on 1 November, stresses once again the importance of attrition: 'Before thinking of renewing attacks as costly as those of September, it seems that there would be good reason to proceed methodically with attrition of the enemy. Our plan would thus comprise two successive phases: attrition of the enemy; the attempt at decisive action.'[24]

Attrition's aim would be to use up the enemy's reserves so that one would no longer have to fear their intervention. It would happen in repeated attacks on different fronts, followed by one big push in a suitable area. In the initial attacks, there would be no need for large forces, or for reserves to take advantage of any success. The main need would be an immense about of heavy artillery, and unlimited munitions. Guns and machines would take the principal role, not infantry.

This lesson, an extension of Pétain's original belief in the value of fire-power, was to be his watchword throughout the rest of the war. The guns should clear the ground, the infantry occupy it.

The other lesson of Champagne, for Pétain, was the necessity for overwhelming superiority in any attack. Few other officers really believed this; lying figures from headquarters kept many believing, right to the end of the war, that the defence tended to lose more men than the attack. Pétain's view was categorical: 'If the attacking forces are not superior to the defence in the ratio of three to one, then the moment for the definitive effort has not come, and attrition of the enemy has not been enough.'

Pétain at the end of 1915

In the first year and a half of the war, Pétain showed himself to be, as he had been in his pre-war theories, a realist. It may seem to us to require little realism to conceive that a headlong rush into enemy machine-gun fire is unrealistic; yet this is what many pre-war theorists, and 1914 generals, had failed to realise. Pétain had always been convinced, by the examples of the Balkan and Russo–Japanese wars, of the strength of modern fire-power; and this in turn had led him to a realisation of the strength of defensive positions. Unlike General Pellé, who in late 1917 could still write, 'The experience of trench warfare has shown us that in this war the adversary who is attacking has less in the way of casualties, and uses up less forces than he who is being attacked',[25] Pétain realised very early on that any attack needed three times as many forces as the defenders, and that only if it were properly prepared could any hope of advantage be gained from it.

Pétain's realism showed itself quite clearly in his quick acceptance of the lessons of war. His pre-war theories, while assessing certain changes that had come to warfare, had certainly not foreseen the stagnation of trench warfare. Faced by it, he was the first, after his experience near Reims in October 1914, to realise that new methods for attack were needed.

This must be stressed; Pétain remained a man of attack, even though convinced of the power of the defensive. The defensive could serve its purpose; but it was only attack which would win the war. This attack must not be blind and wasteful, new methods were needed. Like many others, Pétain at first saw the most hope in the idea of the strongly-supported breakthrough, or *percée*, on a narrow front.

His experiences on the Artois front, however, speedily convinced him of the futility of this theory. While others were finding excuses for what they saw as a narrow failure, Pétain was condemning the method, and formulating a new one, the drainage of enemy reserves by attrition, to prepare for the final thrust which would succeed because of the enemy's inability to call up support to close the breach.

Pétain was, here as elsewhere, ahead of his contemporaries, though coming to the same conclusions as them. One lesson only was needed to show him the dangers of a policy; for most of his commanders, it took two or three attempts.

'Attrition' has become an ugly word to our generation. It seems to sum up most of the horrors of the First World War. Yet in itself it was a reasonable policy, given the facts of the situation. War consists, in large part, of killing the enemy. Because a theory is based on weakening the enemy by killing his men, it should not immediately be condemned. What was to be condemned, in the carrying-out of this theory, was the inefficiency and blindness which led to as many men of one's own side being killed as those of the other. Attrition has come to mean blind attacks, in which each side appeared to be bleeding the other to death, and in which a whole generation of Europe's manhood was destroyed for what appeared to be the futile exchange of a few furlongs of territory. It means, to us, the first day of the Somme, or Nivelle's 1917 offensive. To Pétain it meant carefully-constructed attacks, in which artillery did much of the damage, in which enemy losses were far superior to one's own, and in which certain fixed and restricted objectives were reached. The first real examples of this policy were those he achieved when Commander-in-Chief in late 1917. They show that for Pétain, the general who cared for his men, who unlike some other generals never saw them as canon-fodder, to be a believer in 'attrition' was no paradox.

In the details of his tactics, too, Pétain had shown more realism than most generals at this time. Instead of defending every inch of territory that had been gained, he was prepared to make tactical withdrawals. Examples of this are the evacuation of the village of Loivre, on the Reims front in September 1914, and the evacuation of ridge 119 in June 1915. He was prepared, too, to see the danger of further attack along a dangerous salient, as in May 1915, and to convince his superiors of the wisdom of consolidating rather than advancing. He became aware of the moments to stop attacks that had become merely wasteful. For this carefulness and sense he was to become a figure of suspicion to members of the attacking school.

In the defensive, he had shown himself to be a master. Near Reims, in front of Arras, and elsewhere, he had by careful preparation, been able to resist heavy German attacks. Already he had started creating defence in depth. Even in August 1914, in his defensive position near Dinant in Belgium, he had seen the dangers of putting too many people in the front line: 'In the present state of affairs, there are too many people in the front line, continually on the watch; and it is impossible for this line easily to be reinforced or to retreat. The consequence: great expenditure of men and great fatigue. I have ordered for tomorrow, not a change of positions, but a redeployment of forces . . .'[26]

In September, on the Aisne canal, he created three lines of trenches, and eventually put most of his division in the second line. In front of Arras in October he organised similar defence in depth to ward off the German onslaughts. He had already formulated the defensive policy which was to receive so much opposition even in 1918.

We, from our historical viewpoint, can thus see that at the end of 1915 Pétain had proved himself to be a great general of care and foresight, a man unwilling to undertake foolhardy operations. By the very nature of this war, he was something of a pessimist, believing that little could be done that was decisive in the short run, and that success in the long run depended upon prudence and care for the lives of the French soldiers, and upon full use both of the advantages of defence and those of prepared and limited attack.

A mention must be made of Serrigny. This brilliant soldier was to remain at Pétain's side throughout the war, and afterwards. Of great intellectual calibre, it is possible that he drafted many of Pétain's later documents. But, drafted by him or not, they were accepted by Pétain, in whose line of thought they clearly were. So for the rest of this chapter documents emanating from

Pétain are treated as accurate indications of his thought (influenced or no by Serrigny).

By the end of 1915, French High Command thought highly of Pétain, too. But not for the same reasons as we have just given. They admired his results rather than his methods or his theories, of which they were on the whole unaware. He was the man who had successfully defended at Reims and Arras, who had had violent success compared with all others in the Artois offensive, and who had not failed too miserably in Champagne. Their confidence in him was shown by his rapid rise from command of a brigade to that of an army.

Pétain's rapid rise was accompanied, as we can see from contemporary accounts, by an increasing conviction of his own superiority, and of the stupidity of others. His poker-faced wit, which had already been in evidence before the war, became more and more astringent; later in the war we shall see examples of it being used on politicians (a procedure which earned him as much mistrust from them as he had received from his military superiors before the war). And his self-esteem was already dangerously high. Fayolle, whose admiration for Pétain was at this stage very strong ('He is one of the best of the younger men. He understands, and knows how to proceed. His energy verges on brutality, but this excess is for the best . . .'[27]), nevertheless felt bound to criticise this side of him:

> He is convinced of his own importance, with remarkable lack of self-consciousness. He is nevertheless the best general I have met so far in the war.[28]
>
> Pétain and Serrigny came to lunch. I noted Pétain's bad characteristics; he detracts from his good qualities by the superficiality of his conversation and by the way in which he lets one see too clearly just how full he is of his own importance. He is worth much more than appears on the surface. . . .[29]

His disappointment at not getting an army in April shows this conviction of his own worth. His actual appointment to an army in June showed that this conviction was shared by his superiors. The politicians, who had small knowledge of tactics, admired him too, for his success. That he was not admired by them for his prudence and defensive policy is shown by the criticisms that were showered on Joffre, who in comparison with Pétain was a man of the offensive.

For Joffre had been under constant criticism throughout the year. His famed imperturbability was now believed to be incapability, and he was criticised for being too far from the front. Above all, parliamentary opinion, trained by the military to believe in offensives, blamed Joffre for waiting too long to attack (a criticism which would hardly have been levelled by Pétain!). As early as February 1915, Terrier notes the parliamentary unrest: 'There is a campaign, as you know, in progress against the temporisations of Joffre. It is led above all by M. Paul Doumer, not only at the Senatorial Army Commission, but also in corridors and meetings. René Millet . . . tells me that Doumer has been making his remarks even on tramcar platforms!'[30] The name of Galliéni had been mentioned as a possible successor. Above all,

Terrier was worried that the general public might get to hear these things.

On 20 June 1915, Terrier mentions the controversy over the respective roles of Joffre and Galliéni at the Marne, and suggests that Joffre's supporters may be trying to silence all the criticisms of his inactivity: 'Is it a reply to the criticisms of Joffre's over-long defensive? People are blaming the Generalissimo for waiting too long, and for remaining himself too far from the front.'[31]

In December, criticism of Joffre reached new heights. Names of successors were suggested because they might be more *active* than him. Again, Parliament was clamouring for offensives.

As it was, Joffre was not to depart for another year, though the Briand Government did its best to limit his powers, and place someone else in command, by 'kicking him upstairs'. On 3 December a decree was discussed in the Chamber which would make him commander-in-chief of all French armies, not only those in France. The aim of this was seen by some, says Marcellin, as being 'to smother Joffre under flowers by giving him an honorific post and at the same time a successor.'[32] The fact that this successor might be the Catholic Castelnau worried parliamentary anticlericals so much that Briand had to promise not to create a successor to Joffre. He did, however, make what Marcellin calls a 'secret generalissimo' by eventually making Castelnau Joffre's adjutant, under the title of Chief of Staff. The intention was that Castelnau should rule; in the event, the G.Q.G. made it possible for Joffre to carry on almost as before, with Castelnau's powers far less than the Government had wished and expected.

All this was to be of importance in 1916, the year of Pétain's first great test, Verdun.

Chapter Two

Verdun

LOCAL actions had continued on the Champagne front till early November, mainly to safeguard and ameliorate positions. Pétain remained on this front, with his 2nd Army, until 5 January 1916, when he left to go, 'in reserve', to Noailles, to instruct and manoeuvre four army corps on relief from the front.

Meanwhile the Allies were making plans for 1916. On 5 December Joffre held a conference at his headquarters in Chantilly. An all-out offensive for 1916 was agreed, on all fronts. In France, the 'successes' of 1915, which had 'so depleted the German reserves', were to be repeated on a larger scale, by both French and British forces, on the Somme. There would be forty French divisions, and twenty-five British, and the attack would not be undertaken until there was enough heavy artillery to support it, which would mean that it would take place in a few months' time. Later, in early February, the date was moved to July.

The Germans too were making their plans for 1916. Falkenhayn, the Commander-in-Chief, describes in his memoirs the memorandum he sent to the Kaiser in December 1915. It was a longish document, taking in the world situation, but its conclusions were simple: France has been greatly weakened, and England is beginning to be the more dangerous opponent. England, however, is difficult to get at; the only way really to hit England is to destroy one of its allies. Of these, France is the most vulnerable: 'France . . . is at the limits of endurance. If we succeed in showing the French people clearly, that it has militarily nothing more to hope, then the limits will have been crossed, and England will have had its best sword knocked out of its hand.'[1] A mass breakthrough is impossible and unnecessary. Unnecessary, because there are objectives behind the French front for whose defence the French Command will be forced to fight to the last man: 'If it does so, France's forces will bleed to death . . . whether we reach our goal or not. If it does not, and we reach our goal, the moral effect in France will be enormous.'[2] Falkenhayn saw this as a limited commitment as far as German forces were concerned. The objectives concerned were Belfort and Verdun, both of them close to the front line. Verdun was the one he chose.

The view of 'attrition' stated in this memorandum is near to that of Pétain, not only in its realisation of the impossibility of a breakthrough. Its stress on the limited nature of such exercises is Pétain's, too. But the method chosen, that of a continued onslaught on one objective, is not. Falkenhayn should have realised that such a plan would eventually have the result of bleeding both armies nearly to death—though he could not, perhaps, have foreseen the stubborn resistance that was to be put up under Pétain. Pétain's concept of 'attrition' was of surprise attacks, on limited objectives, at various points of the line, in which the defenders would be pulverised more by artillery than by men. A large-scale and lengthy onslaught on one objective was far from his ideas.

German preparations for the Battle of Verdun were kept amazingly secret —particularly when compared with the general publicity which seemed to prepare every French offensive. The French were unprepared. Not only that, but the line of fortresses defending the town of Verdun had been gradually dismantled over the months. The roster of incompetence and unawareness has been discussed in many books, and there is little place for it here. Enough to say that much blame must be laid at Joffre's door, for ignoring warnings which seemed to him to come 'from the wrong quarter', i.e. from soldiers via the Government.

Gradually the French began to realise that an attack was likely, though no one was convinced that the main blow would be in this quarter. Castelnau came on 24 January to supervise the creation of some new defensive positions. Better still, reinforcements arrived. But everything was still essentially in a state of unpreparedness.

The details of the battle have been brilliantly described in Alistair Horne's book, *The Price of Glory—Verdun 1916*,[3] and from now on I shall be going into detail only on those aspects particularly connected with Pétain.

On 21 February the German attack began, after the heaviest preliminary bombardment yet seen in the war. Initial successes were not as swift or as great as had been expected, but by the 24th it appeared that Verdun was about to fall. Castelnau came urgently to see Joffre. Castelnau's position was by now very odd. Abel Ferry describes it in his *Carnets secrets*: 'Castelnau, appointed Joffre's Chief of Staff by the Government, found himself in a completely false position. He had the responsibility and title of second-in-command, but his subordinates had the power and the right of signature.'[4] The G.Q.G. had closed its ranks, and far from being commander-in-chief in all but name, as the Government had hoped, Castelnau did not even have the full powers of second-in-command.

Now Castelnau arrived, insisting on the necessity of large reinforcements at Verdun, to safeguard the left bank of the Meuse. The force to be sent, he suggested, was the 2nd Army, under its commander General Pétain, who would replace General Herr. To this Joffre agreed.

Much has been made by biographers of the choice of Pétain, and Castelnau's brilliant assessment of him as 'the man for the job.' A much more likely reason for the choice, at this date, was the fact that Pétain's army, and Pétain himself, were currently in reserve. An army was needed, so the 2nd Army was sent for.

Later on the evening of the 24th, having received news that the situation was even worse than he had thought, and that defence of the right bank was in collapse, Castelnau went back to see Joffre. According to a story later published in *Le Matin*—and denied by Joffre—Joffre was already in bed: 'He was asleep. "He sleeps so soundly", as the newspapers say. A ridiculous scene took place at the door, with the orderly officer preventing the Chief of Staff from entering the Commander-in-Chief's bedroom. Finally, Castelnau succeeded in getting a message passed. Joffre, woken up, turned over, saying "Let him do as he likes." Then he went back to sleep.'[5]

Castelnau rushed to Verdun, arriving there are breakfast time on the 25th, and visited the front on the right bank. At 3.30 p.m. he telephoned to G.Q.G. his conviction that the right bank could be saved after all, and that Pétain should now be put in charge of both banks of the Meuse. Without waiting for Joffre's reply, he sent the order to Pétain. (After all, Joffre had said: 'Let him do as he likes.') It is important to realise that this was Castelnau's decision, and not Joffre's, particularly in view of certain Joffre-Pétain situations which we will come to later.* Joffre had been prepared to give up the right bank, and thus Verdun itself; indeed, in the months before the attack he had established a line of withdrawal behind Verdun, on the left bank. Verdun, for him, was not an essential feature of the French line. In this he may well have been right, but his later attitudes should not be taken as having been his from the start.†

The telegram telling Pétain of his appointment had reached Noailles at 10 p.m. on the 24th, and produced one of the serio-comic situations which abound in the history of these few days. For Pétain could not be found. Luckily Serrigny had an idea where to find him, and after a swift drive to Paris, arrived at the Hotel Terminus-Nord. The proprietress denied that Pétain was there, but eventually Serrigny found himself outside the General's door, where Pétain's boots lay decorously beside a pair of lady's slippers.‡ He knocked, and after a hasty discussion with a half-clad Pétain in the corridor, was told by the General to find himself a room. They would depart for Chantilly, Joffre's headquarters, in the morning.

Leaving Paris at seven the next morning, they reached Chantilly at eight. The apparently imperturbable Joffre greeted Pétain with the words: 'Well Pétain, you know it's not going too badly.' From Chantilly, they set off for Verdun. It was while they were *en route* that the great fort of Douaumont, the lynch-pin of the Verdun defensive system, fell. Owing to inefficiency, it had not even been properly manned, and a ridiculously small force of Germans, to their own surprise, had succeeded in taking it. When they reached General Herr's headquarters at Dugny, all was in chaos. Serrigny, who shared Pétain's

---

* In June of this year, Henry Bordeaux, the official historian, was made by G.Q.G. to add, at this point, that Castelnau had acted 'on the orders of the Commander-in-Chief.' In the margin, however, Castelnau himself wrote on 2 July: 'I received no such orders. The truth must be told.'

† Horne writes: 'Although later, as the salvation of Verdun seemed assured, the Joffre coterie claimed the honours, there is nothing to suggest that, at the moment of de Castelnau's departure from Chantilly, Joffre had definitely made up his mind not to retreat to the Left Bank'. Horne, op. cit. pp. 141–2

‡ We now know that this was the future Mme Pétain. See letter of 22 February 1916, in Amouroux, op. cit. p. 140

dislike of politicians, describes it thus: 'I had the clear impression that we had come into a madhouse, unless it was Parliament at question time.'[6]

Castelnau informed Pétain that he was to take over at midnight, and Pétain retired to the small town of Souilly, where he took up his headquarters.

Castelnau's decision stubbornly to defend the right bank, and thus Verdun, may well have been wrong, as Horne points out. A strategic withdrawal may well have been the correct policy at this time, though later, of course, it became impossible, for questions of morale. Joffre's imperturbability may have masked an unconcern for the fate of this particular strongpoint; a much misunderstood man, he continually showed a far greater grasp of the overall situation of the war than most other army men. But French policy of the time was not to lose ground unless you could not help it; the French had, in a sense, fallen into Falkenhayn's trap, though it soon became clear that the Germans had fallen into it too.

The irony of fate had put Pétain, the apostle of strategic withdrawal, in charge of the French forces. But he had his orders, and he was going to do his best to carry them out. His order of the day on 26 February reads: 'Beat off at all costs the attacks of the enemy, and retake immediately any piece of land taken by him.' [7]

The main thing was to stand firm; and here Pétain's experience of the defensive stood him in good stead. Though sick with double pneumonia immediately on his arrival, Pétain directed operations from his sickbed, convinced that if they could hang on for another two or three days, until reinforcements arrived, all would be well.

Castelnau had ordered Douaumont to be retaken, but after one attempt, which was naturally a failure, Pétain set down to organising the defence. While the front line continued desperately to resist the onslaught, Pétain had new defensive lines constructed behind it. The forts (which had been almost completely disarmed in the period before the attack) were rearmed, new lines of trenches were dug. A 'Line of Resistance' was formed. Against the new defensive system the Germans flung themselves in vain.

The difficult thing about the defence of Verdun, stuck as it was in a salient partly encircled by the Germans, was going to be the problem of communications. The enemy held the main railway line; a secondary one was under perpetual bombardment. All that was left was one narrow-gauge railway and the second-class road from Bar-le-Duc. This road, which was seven yards wide, was to be the sole source of supply for Verdun. There was just room for vehicles to pass, but at the moment the road was chaos.

Pétain set about the organisation of a proper railway link; but this was a long-term solution, and for present needs a complete re-organisation of road transport was necessary. Aided by Major Richard the engineer, Pétain set about this: the road was reserved for motor transport, with all infantry having to march on each side of it; any vehicle that broke down was to be pushed into the ditch. Workshops were set up in the six areas into which the road had been divided, each capable of servicing the transport. For the massive supplies to be carried, Richard had collected together an unheard-of number of vehicles. Pétain had at his service 175 automobile sections, consisting of 300 officers, 3,500 men, and 3,900 vehicles. Thanks to superb organisation, about 1,700 vehicles went each way every day, at the rate of one every 25 seconds. From 27 February to 6 March, 190,000 men, 23,000 tons of munitions, and 2,500 tons of military equipment were transported over this road. This was the 'Sacred Way', as the author Maurice Barrès was to baptise it; it became for many the symbol of the fortitude of the defence of Verdun, and years later another author, Paul Valéry, was to devote one of the most moving passages of his speech, welcoming Pétain to the French Academy, to a superb and evocative description of this road.

The whole thing almost broke down, however, on 28 February, the day of a disastrous thaw; the lorries sank into the mud almost up to the axles. Richard summoned up manpower, however, to throw gravel under the wheels of the trucks as they passed. The road was lined on both sides by these workers, and the method succeeded; the vehicles continued to roll.

Gradually Pétain's defence had ground the Germans to a standstill. For the date of 27 February, German archives have recorded that it was the first day of the battle on which German forces had no success anywhere.[8]

One of the causes, from now on, of Pétain's success was to be his reorganisation of the French artillery, over which he exercised very close control. Horne describes his policy thus: 'Again and again he insisted that the artillery "give the infantry the impression that it is supporting them and that it is not dominated." While the infantry was still too weak to wrest the initiative from the enemy, carefully prepared artillery "offensives" were directed by Pétain, to cause maximum loss to the enemy at minimum cost to himself.'[9]

By early March, this first attack of the enemy seemed spent. But a new one, supported by reinforcements, was in preparation on both banks of the river. (The reason for the new choice of terrain was that the Germans had realised that the only way to continue any advance on the right bank was to put out of action the positions on the left bank, in particular the *Mort Homme* ridge, which were providing enfilading fire.) The attack took place on 6 March; but thanks to Pétain's new systems of defence, it was on the whole unsuccessful. Joffre's premature rejoicings were unfounded, however: on the 14th, another violent German attack took place on the left bank, and for the rest of the month the fighting was bloody, if inconclusive. Further heavy German attacks took place in April and May, leading to the final capture of the *Mort Homme* at the end of May, which left the way open for the continuation of the right bank offensive.

Throughout this period, from March till the end of May, Pétain, as well as fighting one battle with the Germans, was fighting another with his Commander-in-Chief. The main problem was that of reserves.

The positions of the two men were quite clear. Pétain needed continual reserves because of the tremendous losses being inflicted by the German attack; he also needed them in large numbers because of the system he eventually perfected, whereby divisions were perpetually replaced in the front line, and sent to rest far from the front until they were needed again.

His observation of the troops as they passed his headquarters at Souilly had shown him that in this, even more than in the other battles of the war, the horrors of the front line were not to be endured for too long by the same men. The Germans kept the same forces in the line, replacing casualties; the French forces were perpetually replaced in their entirety. 'The main difference', as Laure says, 'between these two systems is on the question of morale.'[10] Pétain, as he was to show on many occasions, never underestimated morale as a factor in the conduct of war.

Nevertheless, even without this system his needs would have been enormous. Which makes it difficult to understand Joffre's apparently niggling attitude, until we realise his other commitments, and until we place Verdun in perspective in Allied strategy. Joffre had just agreed, with Haig, the plan for the Battle of the Somme. The first phase had been planned as a series of secondary actions to use up enemy reserves, followed by the big push on the Somme itself. Joffre had thought at first that Verdun might well serve as one of these secondary actions; but he was alarmed at the thought that he might be using up his own reserves there. And it must be admitted that, viewed objectively, Joffre's attitude seems reasonable. Verdun was just one point on the line: he had shown that by his unconcern about it at first. But the French High Command had taken a decision on Verdun; and by now the morale of the nation depended on its defence. Joffre was himself to show, in June, an insistence on its retention. So his attitude, though understandable and even commendable strategically, must have been infuriating to the General who was forced to carry out the High Command's will at this one point.

That Joffre was not the only person, however, to be worried at this draining of French resources (the 'bleeding' which Falkenhayn had intended) is shown by a letter from Terrier to Lyautey written in May: 'I have found, in many of our military leaders, the idea that Verdun has devoured the best forces in the army, notably those which we wanted to use in the common offensive. . . . The resistance at Verdun has been very fine, but no offensive has been possible there, and even if the Germans have missed their main objective, the triumphant and publicised occupation of Verdun, they have achieved the second, which was to hinder, if not completely to prevent, our offensive.'[11]

The Pétain-Joffre running battle was continual. On 9 March Pétain asked for an uninterrupted supply of reserves. Joffre stated that the 2nd Army would have to be sufficient unto itself (on the German system). The next day Pétain sent a telegram: 'The enemy attacks are more and more violent; we cannot face up to them unless the influx of reserves is continuous.'[12] Joffre gave in. Between then and the end of March, five new divisions and nine heavy artillery groups were sent, and two reserve divisions placed at Pétain's disposal. In April, even more reserves were demanded. At every moment that Joffre thought that enough had been sent, a telephone call or telegram would make him give more. Finally, he accepted the principle of replacement of any division which had lost fifty per cent of its force.

Both men were exasperated by this. Pétain was to say continually that 'the

G.Q.G. gave him more trouble than the Boche.' Joffre was later to write of Pétain that, while his role at Verdun had been immense, and indispensable, nevertheless 'the very great qualities of this great leader were counter-balanced by a state of mind which made him give an exaggerated importance to the events at Verdun. If I had given in to all his requests, the French army in its entirety would have been absorbed by the battle.'[13]

There is enough truth in this to make it uncomfortable. Pétain, perhaps because his training had on the whole been tactical, was unable to think in strategic terms, even when he later became Commander-in-Chief. His ascent had perhaps been too swift.

Nevertheless, it was now to go one stage further. On 19 April Joffre promoted Pétain to the command of Army Group Centre. In his place at the head of the 2nd Army in Verdun would go General Nivelle, a dashing man of the offensive, who had attracted attention to himself by a brilliant counter-offensive on the right bank, in early April. Joffre, who clearly wanted more offensive tactics, later claimed that he had wished to give Pétain the opportunity to see things in greater perspective (though Poincaré states that it was Briand who initiated the promotion); but certainly Pétain was not pleased. And, though he moved to his new command at Bar-le-Duc in early May, his requests for forces for Verdun still continued, on behalf of Nivelle.

The plans for a French participation in the Somme offensive still continued. Terrier notes, on 2 May, that the French forces were to be placed under General Micheler: 'Why, people are asking, General Micheler and not General Pétain? Ah, they say, that's because too much glory must not crown the same head. . . . What *is* certain, is that they are tending to give up the anonymity, so depressing for the troops and their commanders, which was the rule in the army up till now. It's because morale must be raised in many of the soldiers, who are fed up at the idea of a third winter campaign . . .'[14]

Pétain was one of the first public heroes of the war. This must be remembered in any assessment of public opinion of him later. He was the saviour of Verdun, and was to remain so for the rest of his life. Incidentally, considering Pétain's views on French chances at an offensive on the Somme, people's desire to see him at the head of that offensive is rather ironic.

The new, offensive attitudes of G.Q.G. with regard to Verdun are shown by one of the first orders given to Pétain in his new command, on 28 April: 'The mission of General Pétain is to ensure, on the whole front of Army Group Centre, the inviolability of our positions, and, as far as Verdun is concerned, to take possession of the fort of Douaumont.'[15]

So a large-scale attack was to be mounted on the right bank even while the desperate battle was heaving on the left bank! Pétain, while envisaging an eventual recapture of the fort, had never done so under such conditions. It was already clear to him that both sides were destroying each other, but that the Germans had more reserves; he was already calling for the support of France's allies, a cry he was to repeat more than once before the English Somme attack finally took place and took the pressure off Verdun. In such conditions, how could one waste men in a futile attack on a stronghold?

Nevertheless, orders were orders, as always for Pétain, and the attack was prepared. Nivelle, and General Mangin his subordinate, were both extremely keen on it. It was Mangin, the brutal yet recklessly brave colonial officer, who directed the attack on 22 May. It was a dismal failure. Pétain, who had felt that the time was inopportune, the troops too few, and the front too narrow, nevertheless assumed responsibility, and never blamed Nivelle or Mangin.

Verdun June–December 1916

The taking of the *Mort Homme* at the end of May had aroused alarm among the French generals at Verdun—and not only in the case of Pétain. Contemporaries inimical to Pétain, and subsequent historians, have played up strongly the 'pessimistic' or 'defeatist' side of Pétain in the second half of the war, and have produced accounts of a series of incidents which go to support this view; we will examine these incidents in the chronological order in which they occurred. But it is quite clear that at the end of May 1916 the outlook seemed bad not only to Pétain but also to the man who is so often described as an incorrigible optimist, General Nivelle. Haig, in his diaries, records the following statement by Poincaré: 'Poincaré said that he had just returned from Verdun where he had seen the senior Generals—Pétain, Nivelle and another General. They told him "Verdun sera prise" and that operations must be undertaken without delay to withdraw pressure from that part.'*

This attitude, while partly one of concern, was also quite clearly aimed at advancing the British offensive on the Somme, which was one of Pétain's constant requirements—justifiably so, as the effect produced on Verdun by the eventual offensive was to show. During May Pétain had written to a friend, Colonel Des Vallières, a liaison officer with the British: 'Will your British do nothing to relieve me? Are they capable of a great effort? . . . If not, I would almost prefer them to refrain: the unknown quantity of their forces will keep more men facing them than a weak offensive. . . . Do everything you can to speed it up. . . . They talk of 15 June. That's very late! The latest possible date seems to me to be the 1st, and I will not hide from you the fact that if it was even sooner, I would give a sigh of relief.'[16] The Somme offensive was not, of course, to take place till 1 July.

Meanwhile, on 1 June what Horne has described as 'the most massive assault on the right bank since the initial onslaught in February'[17] had started. The forces were almost as strong as those of February, attacking on a much narrower front. Initial successes were tremendous, and by the 7th

---

* *The Private Papers of Douglas Haig 1914–1919*, Blake ed. London 1952. Entry for 31 May 1916. The same day's entry shows that Foch's subsequent reputation of being always unthinkingly for the offensive at all costs is also somewhat over-simplified: 'Foch came in for a reprimand from M. Briand because he had stated to the politicians that he was against the offensive this year. His excuses seemed very lame, he ate humble pie, and I thought he looked untrustworthy and a schemer. He had evidently spoken very freely to Clemenceau recently.'

the Germans had captured Vaux, the other great fort which, with Douaumont, had been the strongpoint of the defensive system of Verdun. Nivelle ordered an immediate attack to recapture the fort, which was futile and bloodily repulsed; Pétain intervened over the head of Nivelle, to order no further such attempts to be made.

The reductions in French artillery, and the shortage of replacements of men, both caused by Joffre's concern with the Somme offensive and France's part in it, had put the defenders of Verdun in an almost impossible situation. On 11 June Pétain wrote to Joffre: 'We are fighting, from the point of view of artillery, in the ratio of one to two; this situation cannot continue indefinitely without danger to the security of our front.'[18]

The same day, he wrote: 'Verdun is menaced and Verdun must not fall. The capture of this city would constitute for the Germans an inestimable success which would greatly raise their morale and correspondingly lower our own. A tactical success by the English, however great it might be, would not compensate in the eyes of public sentiment for the loss of this city, and at this moment sentiment possesses an importance that it would be inexpedient to disregard.'[19]

This shows quite clearly that, whatever Pétain or Joffre may have thought about the defence of Verdun when it started, by now Pétain had realised its enormous importance, not for military reasons, but for reasons of national morale, which would not have been so strongly affected in the earlier stages. This importance which he laid upon the defence of Verdun must be taken into account when we discuss the charges of pessimism laid against him in this month of June.

These charges have come mainly from Joffre, whose memoirs were to appear in 1932. The most important ones concern the days of 23–24 June; before considering them, we must realise that these were the days when the Germans came nearest to finally capturing Verdun. Horne, whose chapter on these days is entitled 'The Crisis', describes the immense effect that German use of a new kind of gas, phosgene, had had on the evening of the 22nd. This was followed by an extremely successful attack on the morning of the 23rd. The German forces took Fleury, and were eventually lapping around Souville, the last obstacle to the advance on Verdun itself, for from there onwards it was a downwards slope, difficult to defend.

It was at this point that Pétain made a telephone call to Castelnau, at 3 p.m. Though outwardly calm for the benefit of his troops, he was pessimistic about the turn that things had taken. He warned Castelnau that if the Germans reached the slope, he might have to withdraw to the left bank. A third of the French guns were on the right bank, and withdrawal of them would have to start.

Joffre, writing long afterwards, contrasts Pétain's pessimism with the comparative optimism of Nivelle, who was still sending reassuring news; Nivelle was preparing a counter-attack on Fleury, and had men ready for further action, if that was necessary. He had never envisaged the possibility of a retreat to the left bank.

Joffre's account makes Nivelle the more sensible of the two; but, given the gravity of the military situation, it was surely unwise not even to envisage having to withdraw, which is all that Pétain is accused of. As Horne points out, it would have taken three days to withdraw all the French guns; whereas a successful continuation of the German attack could have flung the French soldiers back across the Meuse far more quickly. The eventual German failure makes hindsight possible; but Nivelle himself was not as confident as was later claimed, and nor was Joffre.

Pétain's attitude, in fact, was one of realism, of catering for the possible eventualities. If the German attack had continued to succeed (and it was only faults and lacks on the German side which prevented it from doing so), it would have been Pétain whose foresight would have salvaged as much as possible from the wreck. Despite his belief that Verdun was of utmost importance to French morale, he was not prepared to throw away needlessly men and guns in a way which would only slow down the ultimate capture of the city, which would be inevitable once those guns and men were taken. So, carefully, he envisaged what to do if the worst happened. Joffre accuses him of being too 'impressed' by the enemy; but Horne's account shows that he had cause to be impressed by them.

While there is a certain amount on which Pétain can be criticised later in the war, from the point of view of pessimism or defeatism, his action on 23 June 1916 appears completely justified.

Unfortunately, both enemies and friends have clouded this issue. The enemies, Joffre and the G.Q.G., are quite clearly biased, as even Poincaré saw: 'According to Pénelon, that is to say, in this matter, according to the G.Q.G., General Pétain was very depressed the day before yesterday by the taking of Fleury; he even thought of abandoning the left bank; General de Castelnau had to cheer him up. I have no idea whether this news is trustworthy. Pétain doesn't always have the liking of the G.Q.G.'[20]

Joffre's memoirs may similarly be taken to express a biased view, making of Pétain's foresight (and pessimism) a crass defeatism. Pétain's friends, however, do not exactly help him. Serrigny, determined to defend him at all costs, said that he rang Joffre at his (Serrigny's) instigation, to blackmail him into sending more troops: ' "The situation is grave at Verdun: if I am not sent some fresh troops, I will be obliged to retreat to the left bank." It was simply a manoeuvre of intimidation.'[21] Admittedly, new divisions were sent on that day, but the force and danger of the attack had made that inevitable. Pétain's action had been tactical and reasonable, if pessimistic, and had no need to be defended by easily-detected fabrications like those of Serrigny.

On the German side, unknown to the French at this stage, tactical errors and lacks of equipment (including an appalling shortage of water) were contributing to making the attack far less successful than it seemed. By evening it was clear that no further progress was going to be made, and that Souville was safe. Pétain was able to telephone again, more hopefully than in the afternoon. Joffre, of course, interprets this as follows: 'In the evening,

General Pétain telephoned again; this time he saw the situation more calmly: his telephone call contrasted strangely with the previous one.'[22]

'That evening', says Horne, 'Knobelsdorf knew that his supreme bid to take Verdun had failed.'[23] Fighting continued furiously for some days, however, with brilliant counter-attacks by Mangin.

While Pétain's actions on the 23rd appear to have been justified, there is no denying the gloom and pessimism which were already becoming a large part of his reports on the general situation at Verdun. Realistic they may have been, in their insistence that only the provision of more men, and an immediate attack elsewhere by the British, could save the situation; and Pétain was no doubt justified in his gloomy assessment of the state of morale among the troops; but there is no denying that from early 1916 to the end of the war, a reading of Pétain's statements would make one far more gloomy than those of any other general. Realistic, no doubt; but even realism can sometimes cease to be a virtue, particularly when it fails to take into account the possible drawbacks of a situation to the enemy as well.

On 24 June Briand, the Prime Minister, visited Haig, who described his visit thus: 'The real object of M. Briand's visit was to urge me to attack without fail in order to withdraw pressure from Verdun. He wished our attack to be hastened because General Pétain (at Verdun) at a recent Council meeting had stated that "the game was up". "The French Army could not go on", etc. unless the British attacked at once. I had already been told of the bad condition of French troops.'[24]

On 25 June the Minister of War, General Roques, visited the Verdun front. Obviously political circles were aware of the danger that had just passed.

Pétain was not the only one to be demanding troops and artillery. Nivelle, too, was extravagant in his demands. Joffre, still hoping to save these supplies for the Somme, had been continually forced to send some of them to Verdun.

On 1 July the Somme offensive finally began. Despite its disastrous losses, it drew German troops away from Verdun, and apart from one violent German attack on Souville in early July, the defensive battle of Verdun had finally finished. The battle was to continue for the rest of the year, but from now on the boot was to be on the other foot.

Nothing startling was to happen straight away, however. After a fairly disastrous attack by Mangin on 11 July, Pétain was determined to keep Nivelle and Mangin in check until a proper counter-offensive could be prepared. The fighting spirit of Mangin was to be used for once in a constructive way; troops were to be spared, not squandered, and it was going to be the enemy who made most losses. In September the preparations began. 'Appropriately enough', says Horne, 'Mangin, ever straining at the leash, was to execute the attacks; Nivelle, to be responsible for the detailed planning; Pétain, for the overall planning, for the scale and timing of the attacks.'[25]

The first objective was to be Douaumont. Overwhelming artillery support was provided, and organised by Nivelle (an artilleryman in origin); it started with a massive artillery preparation, and continued with a creeping barrage behind which the infantry would advance. (The gunfire moved forward, ahead of the troops, so that both were advancing at the same time.) Close liaison between artillery and infantry contributed to the success of the attack, as well as the careful preparation, which included battle-courses over an exact replica of the battleground.

The attack, which finally took place on the 24th, was an overwhelming success. Through its careful organisation, it was irresistible. In a few hours Douaumont was taken.

Later in the year, a second counterstroke took place, with equal success, on 15 December. A properly organised attack, for limited objectives, had proved to be feasible, and Nivelle and Mangin, whose earlier offensive tactics had proved so costly, had managed to discipline themselves to the new tactics.

The laurels for these successes were to go to Nivelle, in what to us seems a certain amount of injustice. Pétain, the 'hero of Verdun', had been out-shone by an even greater star, as it seemed, who, with the greater clamour of the offensive, made people forget the achievement of the main part of the Battle of Verdun, the stubborn defence with which it had started.

With Verdun certain characteristics of Pétain became clear, and others formed themselves for the first time. His natural cautiousness, his mistrust of the facile optimism of so many of his colleagues, had led him to a certain pessimism, in which a gloomy assessment of any situation seemed the more natural; this tendency was no doubt strengthened by the efforts he had to make to obtain reinforcements whether of men or artillery. This 'pessimism' could, however, become dangerous as a habit, as the events of 1918 were later to show.

As far as his men were concerned, he had shown himself, as before, to be sparing of their lives, and concerned about their morale. But above all, he had shown himself to be one of the few commanders who had any concern with the feelings of his men, a concern which at times amounted to empathy. Pétain's emotional involvement with the fate of the men at Verdun is illustrated by one famous passage from his own book on Verdun:

My heart contracted when I saw our young men of twenty going into the firing-line at Verdun, thinking that with the changeability of their age they would pass too quickly from the enthusiasm of the first engagement with the enemy to the lassitude brought by sufferings, and perhaps even to discourage-ment in face of the enormous task to be accomplished. From the steps of the Mairie of Souilly—my command post, which was so well placed at the crossroads of the roads leading to the front line—I gave them my most affectionate attention as they went into the line with their units: thrown around in uncomfortable lorries or bowed beneath the weight of their combat equipment when marching on foot, they encouraged each other to appear indifferent by songs or jokes, and I liked the confident look they gave me as a form of salute. But what discourage-ment there was when they returned, whether individually as wounded, or in the impoverished ranks of their companies! Their gaze, impenetrable, seemed to be fixed on a vision of terror; their walk and their attitudes betrayed the most complete exhaustion; they were weighed down by terrifying memories; they scarcely replied when I cross-examined them, and in their troubled minds the joking voices of the old soldiers awoke no echoes.[26]

Other of Pétain's attitudes became clear. He disliked the G.Q.G., the G.Q.G. disliked and mistrusted him. But above all, he had a contempt for politicians which was to remain throughout his life. Poincaré, President of the Republic, had, in March, incurred this contempt when, told by Pétain that he might well, if events necessitated it, still retire to the left bank of the Meuse, he replied: 'You cannot think of it, it would be a parliamentary catastrophe!'[27] A parliamentary catastrophe, not a national one! On the same day Poincaré, after listening to the reports of Pétain's officers, found nothing to say to them, despite Pétain's request to do so. From now on, Pétain's attitude to Poincaré was a cold and ironic one. As with his superiors before the war, he was not prepared to ingratiate himself with those he despised. And this was not to stand him in good stead. Later, in 1917, Abel Ferry was to note: '[Painlevé] told me the difficulties he had in getting Pétain appointed as Chief of Staff. Pétain was foolish enough to say one day to Poincaré: "We are neither commanded nor governed." Poincaré, in a cold rage, set to work Maginot, Malvy and the spectre of military dictatorship.'[28]

Strangely enough, Pétain the hater of politicians and politics had, like many such 'non-political' men, been known to express political opinions of a certain type. After a dinner with Poincaré in April 1916, in which the disorganisation of the war effort had been discussed, Pétain told Poincaré that a proper co-ordination of the wheels of government was only possible if there was a dictatorship of the Head of State. 'But General,' replied Poincaré, 'what about the Constitution?' 'The Constitution', replied Pétain, 'I don't give a damn for it!'*

Serrigny sees in this a mere straight-faced joke such as Pétain often made, though Poincaré certainly didn't see it as such. Neither should we. It was mere fantasy on Pétain's part, but it is all of a piece with that contempt of parliamentary government felt by many military men in the war. This contempt was expressed by Pétain in a private letter to Mme Hardon (his future wife), written on 20 January 1917. 'There is more narrowness of mind in those who rule our country than it is possible to believe unless one has seen them at close quarters. Whatever the interests at stake, all their actions are inspired by this one point of view: to be sure of a parliamentary majority. These people make me sick.'[29]

Pétain may have had contempt for politicians, but he was prepared at times to use them; prepared, above all, to complain about G.Q.C. or the Verdun situation to those who were prepared to listen. Haig notes, on 3 May 1916: 'Briand ... compared Pétain to a motor engine in that he went tap tap tapping out all kinds of opinions to parliamentarians who went to Verdun

* Serrigny, op. cit., p. 82. Serrigny tells of the superficiality he and Pétain saw in all the politicians who came to their headquarters 'Superficiality is inherent in the profession.' Serrigny, op. cit., p. 68

32

expressly to get facts with which to fight the Government. "The generals", he said, "must be united!" '[30]

In his ability to criticise his superiors behind their backs Pétain was not untypical of French generals of the First World War; we shall see further examples of this tendency at the time of the Nivelle offensive.

Nivelle and his offensive

Throughout 1916 dissatisfaction with Joffre had continued, and various attempts had been made by the politicians to find a successor to him. The main problem was that the most obvious man was General de Castelnau, whose appointment as chief of staff had not given him as much power over Joffre and the G.Q.G. as had been hoped, and who was now certainly the next in line for the post of commander-in-chief, as well as deserving it on his merits. Unfortunately, Castelnau was not only a Catholic, but was known to be extremely clerical (as opposed to Foch and Pétain, both Catholics, but less markedly so; Foch was *pratiquant*, but Pétain was not even that); the forces of anti-clericalism in the Chamber of Deputies would never countenance Castelnau at the head of the army.

So the year 1916 witnessed a series of attempts to find someone to replace Joffre. In May Terrier writes: 'It is impossible for the present situation to continue. The High Command must be modified and the *camarilla* of Chantilly liquidated. They are going to ask once more for a Secret Committee . . . The aim is to ask the Government to end the present regime. The Right will take part because it wants General de Castelnau, but it is hoped that the plan will end up with General Foch. It is on him that everyone is counting. The Germans are talking a great deal of General Sarrail and General Lyautey. But nobody is thinking of taking them from their present posts. So it is on Foch that everyone is putting their money to change traditions.'[31]

A few weeks later, on 1 June, Terrier writes a new letter. The campaign against Joffre continues, but a new name has emerged, that of the hero of Verdun, Pétain: 'The campaign against General Joffre has started up again even more strongly. And I believe that it will get stronger still. André Tardieu and Maginot are in the thick of it. It appears that it is now to the advantage of General Pétain.'[32]

So, at the beginning of June, Pétain's fame was at its height. And Joffre's was at its lowest, as during the year the Secret Committees revealed the bungling that had gone on before Verdun, and as the parliamentarians became more and more aware of the dissatisfaction of the soldiers with the conduct of the war, and with the idea of yet another winter campaign. One of Pétain's great supporters in the Government at this time was Paul Painlevé, later to be Minister of War in the Ribot Government.[33]

Briand succeeded in out-manoeuvring those who wished to use events to overthrow the Government, however; and in the process Joffre managed somehow to remain at the head of the army, though in an even weaker position. 'In short, the Government has triumphed. Has the High Command triumphed as well? It appears that General Joffre entirely believes so. That is not, however, exactly the impression we have here. The High Command comes out of the debate diminished.'[34]

Joffre thus gained some time. But a further *Comité Secret*, whose results were to come out in December, looked like being an opportunity to get rid of him. 'Rumours of changes in the command have quietened down a little, awaiting the end of the *Comité Secret*. The main rumour was about General Joffre, that he would be placed at the head of the Allied Defence Committee, which would let the command be given to General Roques, according to some, or to Generals Castelnau and Nivelle (very much in the public eye), according to others. . . .'[35]

In these rumours, Pétain does not even seem to have been mentioned, despite the fact that the army itself was in favour of his appointment.*

The stubborn defence of Verdun, which had made him the great hero of the first part of June, appeared to have been overshadowed by the more exciting and morale-boosting offensive of October, for which Nivelle, at the head of the 2nd Army, had got all the credit. Gradually it became clear that Nivelle was to be the choice: 'The name that is in every mouth is that of General Nivelle. He himself has put forward some objections to the formidable role which people want to entrust to him, a successful soldier who, only a colonel at the beginning of the war, already has responsibility for an army . . .'[36]

Nivelle not only had the popular appeal of the moment; he also appeared, to many, to have found the secret of a successful offensive. Pétain, on the other hand, though he had the support of Painlevé, 'the coming man in the Cabinet',[37] had gained many enemies, not the least being Poincaré, the President of the Republic.† And he was disliked by the G.Q.G., who saw his carefulness as lack of fire, his defensive tactics as unworthy of a commander, and his perpetual demands for reinforcements as an incapability of seeing the large-scale military situation. Joffre was later to say:

If history gives me the right to judge the generals who operated under my orders, I want to affirm that the true saviour of Verdun was Nivelle, well seconded by Mangin. General Pétain arrived at Verdun at the moment of the disorganisation he inherited from General Herr, restored order with the help of a well-chosen staff and by means of the influx of fresh troops. That was his merit, and I do not dispute the greatness of it. But in the conduct of the battle, and particularly in the June crisis, the most important role was played by Nivelle, who had the rare merit of raising himself above his battlefield, of seeing what I expected of him over the whole range of my commitments, and of keeping his sang-froid and his

---

* Ferry, 12 July 1917. Fayolle also mentions the apparent eclipse of Pétain at this time: 'Paris rumours. According to them, Foch will be replaced by Nivelle, and Joffre by X. . . I have seen Doumer, who declares that the French Army is not being commanded. He has no confidence in Joffre. Others say the same. Pétain's shares have fallen in value.' Fayolle op. cit. p. 191, 4 December 1916

† Pétain seems to have realised the fears he aroused in Poincaré and in other politicians. Fayolle notes in his diary on 5 January 1917: 'Pétain believes himself to be a great man. He seriously declares that the Republic fears him.' Fayolle, op. cit. p. 197

will to fight when his commander was addressing to the Minister of War the anguished accounts of which I have several times spoken.[38]

Though Joffre's account must, as always, be taken with a pinch of salt, there is no doubt that his views on this matter were typical of the G.Q.G., and of some influence.

So, when Joffre was finally 'kicked upstairs' to be 'technical counsellor to the Government', it was Nivelle who was made commander-in-chief of the armies in the north and north-east, on 12 December 1916. Haig, who received the news the next day, was informed by the French colonel who brought it, that the clerical issue had been the main one: 'General Nivelle (who recently did well at Verdun) will command in France. Foch was objected to as the successor to Joffre because he has a Jesuit brother and is a churchgoer. Also his handling of the French in the Somme battle was much criticised. Pétain, because he was brought up by Dominicans and is also a churchgoer. Castelnau is still more objected to because he goes to Mass and is very Catholic.'[39]

This reasoning on the part of the French colonel is over-simplified, however. Castelnau was clearly unacceptable for religious reasons; Foch, and Pétain (who was *not* a churchgoer) were clearly more acceptable. But Foch was in semi-disgrace for the Somme, and Pétain had momentarily been outshone by Nivelle. However, this is a clear example of how, to contemporaries, the anti-clerical issue could seem even stronger than it was, so that everything could be laid at its door, until positions on each side became even more extreme.

Nivelle's name will always be connected with the ill-fated offensive which he commanded in April 1917. Despite his original diffidence with regard to his command, as noted by Terrier, he was as convinced as his subordinate Mangin that the victorious attacks at Verdun had shown the success of a new method. As Mangin said to his troops on 18 December: 'We have the method and we have the leader. It gives us the certainty of success.'[40] Nivelle himself said: 'The experience is conclusive. Our method has proved itself. Victory is certain, I give you my assurance. The enemy will learn it at his own cost.'[41]

The plans for the Spring offensive were at once begun. It was to be unlike the Somme and the other wasteful battles of the war; a decisive blow which would force its way through to the enemy third and fourth lines. The methods were to be those of the Verdun offensives—saturation bombardment on a large scale, to destroy the enemy position, followed by a swift, brutal assault by infantry behind a creeping barrage, leading eventually to a breakthrough, and the open warfare for which the armies had longed since the original stalemate of the war.

The mistake of Nivelle was, firstly, to translate into massive terms the techniques which had been successful on a small scale. Here he showed that, contrary to Joffre's opinion of him, he remained a man unused to high command and the methods of large-scale strategy. His experience (like that of Pétain) had been that of a line colonel, at the outbreak of war; and he seemed unable to see that the elements which had caused the success of the Verdun offensives—restricted objectives, surprise, and overwhelming superiority of artillery, were lacking in this massive offensive. The myth of the 'breakthrough' had recurred, and all was to be wagered on this one vast onslaught.

An onslaught which the enemy could see, and thus ward off. The 1917 offensive was the most widely-publicised of all French actions of the war, which is saying something. The Germans knew where it was to happen, they knew the date, and, just to help them further, they had even been able to capture a copy of the plan. Since Verdun, the Germans had formed a new system of defence in depth, which should be proof against the methods which were used there. And on the front to be threatened by part of the offensive, the Germans were already withdrawing to an ultra-strong fortified line, the Hindenburg Line.

So Nivelle's attack was bound to be futile. The French army would be battering its head against a brick wall. The French artillery was not yet strong enough to destroy the German defences as Nivelle hoped. Ammunition was still short. The German defences, in their new state, would easily be proof against the French infantry, with or without creeping barrage. And the Germans were ready and waiting. All was set for a disaster of the first order.

Nivelle remained unfailingly optimistic. By a mixture of charm and confidence he had succeeded in winning over most of the French and British politicians, including Lloyd George, that normally violent opponent of offensives. Lloyd George and the British had originally had grave doubts about the prospects of a great offensive on the Western Front. As Hankey says: 'It was not until it was clear that the hearts of the military men were not in the alternative that they [Lloyd George and Milner] consented to the Nivelle plan. And when they did consent, it was to a plan which they were assured was not open to the objections which they all, or nearly all, felt towards attacks of the Somme type. Nivelle promised a smashing blow or nothing.'[42]

Nivelle unfortunately led the French soldiers to believe that this was to be the final blow of the war; this assurance was to have dire consequences later.

Soon, in February and March, doubts began to spread about the feasibility of the plan, both among Nivelle's subordinate generals and in Government circles. Lyautey, who had come from Morocco to become Minister of War in December, was particularly disturbed; but he hesitated to act, feeling that his long stay in Morocco might have made him out of touch with European strategy. The British, too, were worried. But, as Hankey says: 'The position of the British Government in the matter was peculiarly delicate. They had been persuaded to agree to the offensive not without difficulty. They had, so to speak, put their money on Nivelle. It was difficult for them to stop him so long as he wished to go ahead. Moreover, their military advisers were in favour of going ahead—even Robertson, whose point of view at this stage did not differ widely from their own. They had no ground for intervening.'[43]

So nothing seemed able to stop the offensive. Nivelle's confidence was unshaken; he even saw the German withdrawal as being favourable to his plan. But suddenly a ray of hope came: Lyautey, after a scene in the Chamber, resigned in mid-March; and his resignation brought about the fall of the Briand Government. In the new Government, formed by Alexandre Ribot, the Minister of War was Painlevé, a man much more in favour of the Pétain manner of waging war, who had, in the previous year, even put forward the name of Pétain for commander-in-chief. Ribot gives the impression of a conscientious nobody, easily led by his energetic Minister of War; and Painlevé, whom Hankey described as 'a definite sceptic about both Nivelle and his plan',[44] determined to do something about investigating the widespread doubts about the offensive.

The offensive, put back because of bad weather, was eventually planned for 16 April. Painlevé, having had one long talk with Pétain on 1 April, invited Pétain and General Franchet d'Esperey to dinner with him on 2 April (without the knowledge of Nivelle). Ribot, the Prime Minister, was invited as well: '[Painlevé] told me that Nivelle had been told of it; I accepted the invitation to this *diner intime*, in order to meet Pétain, whom I had not yet seen. After dinner Lacaze [Minister of Marine] and Thomas [Minister of Munitions] came without my having been warned: it began to look like a conference.'[45]

Poor Ribot! This was not the only embarrassment to come of that evening. The next day, Pétain wrote to Nivelle to tell him about it, and, as Ribot says, 'Nivelle rightly complained.'[46]

Pétain's correctness in later telling Nivelle did not prevent him, however, from making full use of the occasion to express his doubts about the offensive, and to state the tactics he himself would use:

> Franchet d'Esperey said nothing of interest . . . Pétain explained that he did not believe in the success of an all-out offensive. For him, there was only one form of tactics: to wear out, to test the enemy, by punches which would gradually daze and weaken him. He is very intelligent, more intelligent than Nivelle, but he has above all a critical mind, making *boutades* but never inspiring full confidence. One does not have, when talking with him, a feeling of security. He is very probably right in the criticisms he makes of Nivelle's plan. But is this the time to change the plan, when the Germans have brought up all their reserves opposite us, and when, if we do not attack, they will certainly attack us and will probably take Reims, which is almost touched by their front lines?[47]

Ribot here states the dilemma which faced all critics of the scheme; the attack plans had gone so far that it was almost impossible to withdraw. He also states what will be one of the main criticisms levelled at Pétain throughout his military career: that his was essentially a negative, critical mind. Nivelle, too, was to describe him as a 'negative' man.[48] That this was true of his attitude to his superiors at various points in the war is no doubt true:

but he was capable of creative thought with regard to tactics, as was shown on several occasions.

At any rate, Pétain loyally informed Nivelle that the dinner had taken place. And Poincaré, disturbed by reports of what had happened, called a War Council meeting for the 6th, at which the Commander-in-Chief and the Army Group Commanders concerned would attend. Meanwhile, on the 3rd, Ribot had received written criticisms of the offensive, ostensibly from General Micheler*; but Micheler then denied them, saying that he had merely lunched with the go-between, Messimy, and had not told him to bring anything to Ribot. 'How can one know the true opinions of the generals?' sighs Ribot. 'They speak in different languages in front of their commanders from when they are away from them.'[49]

At the War Council on 6 April, this view of Ribot's was borne out. Poincaré (President), Ribot (Prime Minister), Painlevé, Thomas and Lacaze were there from the Government, together with Generals Nivelle, Castelnau, Franchet d'Esperey, Pétain and Micheler. Nivelle first gave a résumé of his plan, and the other generals were then asked for their opinions. 'Castelnau merely says some vague things, apologising for not knowing the directives. Franchet d'Esperey does not believe that we will be able to advance more than thirty kilometres, because of the state of the ground. Micheler believes that the offensive must take place without delay, or we will be attacked in bad conditions. He thinks that the breaking of the third and fourth lines will demand rather costly sacrifices: he does not know how far we can go; he thinks that we must rely on the judgement of the Commander-in-Chief. Pétain, embarrassed, briefly makes reservations.'[50]

So Micheler and Pétain, the two main critics of the plan, remained comparatively silent. Pétain has been praised for this by his faithful biographer, Laure, who says that Pétain, 'as a disciplined soldier, would have preferred not to be consulted, and not to attack, by the opinion he was asked to give, the authority of the commander responsible. Pétain, during these weeks preceding his elevation to the top of the hierarchy, only gave up his customary reserve on 6 April, on the orders of the Government, and later carried out strictly his commander's orders for the attack on the Monts-de-Champagne which was entrusted to Army Group Centre.'[51]

This is, of course, nonsense, aimed at the picture of Pétain the man of discipline, loyal to his commander. Pétain did, as a good soldier, carry out all orders given to him. But, as we have already seen, he did not necessarily keep a bridle on his tongue, and criticisms of his superiors, and the G.Q.G., and their plans, were certainly to be found in his mouth on occasions. Pétain's reticence on the 6th was because he was in the presence of his superior officer; but he had certainly spilled the beans when not with him.

What the politicians should have realised was that military discipline was such that no general would openly criticise Nivelle. The whole idea of the meeting had been a farce. As Herbillon says: 'It was a strange idea,

---

* Micheler was certainly an opponent of the plan as it stood. See Serrigny, op. cit. p. 118

which proves a great lack of knowledge of the military mind, for how can an officer, interrogated in front of third parties, discuss one of his commander's exposés in the latter's presence?'[52]

Despite the reticence of his generals, Nivelle saw that they were critical of his plan. He also knew that Pétain had seen the politicians (all except Poincaré) four days earlier. As Loucheur wrote in his diary the same day, when he heard about the meeting: '[Painlevé] has certainly been put up to it by Pétain, who is opposed to a grand offensive.'[53]

The whole meeting must have been seen by Nivelle as a put-up job which had rather misfired. In the circumstances, he did the dignified thing and offered his resignation. But the politicians made him take it back. As Ribot said, 'Our hand has been forced: it is too late to go back.'[54]

On 16 April the attack took place, on the Chemin des Dames ridge, on the Aisne line between Laffaux and Fort Brimont, with another attack taking place in Champagne. The results were disastrous, despite certain initial gains. For Nivelle had promised a breakthrough, and this was clearly not to take place. Ludendorff, the German commander, describes the initial French successes, and then adds laconically, 'On the 17th and 18th the enemy renewed the attack, but could not achieve any results. . . The climax of the April battle had been overcome.' Not only this, but the French tactics had led to huge and unnecessary losses: 'In the battles the French infantry had attacked closely bunched together, and had suffered unusually large losses.'[55]

Crown Prince Wilhelm, in his memoirs, tells of the wonderment of the German troops at these futile but heroic attacks: 'The commander of a machine-gun company . . . described to me the overwhelming view of the battleground, on which France's best regiments were being destroyed in continually renewed, hopeless attacks.'[56]

In the first day of the attack there had been 120,000 casualties; Nivelle had said that there would be about 10,000. Hospital services were as ill-prepared as the attack had been ill-conceived. Nivelle had promised the Government that the attack would either be a success, or be stopped. But obviously he did not have the same interpretation of 'success' as them; he ordered the attacks to continue. On the 19th, Painlevé came to see him to get the offensive stopped; but Nivelle was convinced that the attacks must continue. Gradually the whole thing had developed into the Somme-like action that all had feared.

The Government was faced with a dilemma. Politically, it feared a crisis; interruption of the offensive might publicise the failure of it, and set off the crisis. It let Nivelle continue. But Painlevé was already campaigning for Pétain to become commander-in-chief; and the newspapers of the Right were supporting the same candidature (a fact which might well reinforce the fears of Poincaré, and arouse those of ministers such as Malvy). Ribot, in his usual manner, places the pros and cons before us, and shows the reasons for a weak decision:

Painlevé is wondering with anguish whether it is possible to let Nivelle continue his offensives; he wants us to take the advice of Pétain, who advises against any further forward movement, and wants us to confine ourselves to the defensive. Should we replace Nivelle by Pétain? The question has been asked; there is a campaign in favour of Pétain, particularly in the papers of the Right. We hold several meetings in the President's Cabinet, with the Minister of War, the Minister of Marine, and M. Maginot. I feel all that there is to be said against Nivelle and the G.Q.G.: but it would be a mistake to sacrifice Nivelle, above all just after a battle. What would our allies think, and what shouts of joy would our enemies give?[57]

Maginot, who had spread the rumour at the time of Painlevé's appointment as Minister of War that, being Pétain's protector, he would soon cause a crisis of army leadership,[58] was originally against any change, as was Poincaré, for whom Pétain's nomination would be a defeat.[59] And Haig, who wanted the offensives to continue, showed opposition to Pétain's appointment.[60]

On the 26th Painlevé made another attempt, saying that he could not accept the responsibility of leaving Nivelle in command, and insisting that a decision should be taken before the new attacks planned for the beginning of May. But at the War Council he was in a minority of one: 'Maginot accepts the criticisms, and would be happy for the question to be discussed after the coming offensives. Bourgeois does not even want the question to be asked. Malvy is opposed to the appointment of Pétain, whom he regards as dangerous.'[61] Soon after this, Ribot saw Haig, who continued to defend Nivelle, saying that he would regret a change of commander in the course of operations.[62]

By the 28th, however, the Cabinet had come round to an idea given by Painlevé after the previous meeting, that Pétain could be made second-in-command to Nivelle, with the title of Chief of General Staff. This seems to have been a revival of the kind of tactics tried in relation to Joffre and Castelnau. Pétain was rightly dubious of it if it meant being in close contact with Nivelle, seeing it as capable of producing conflict, or a kind of sub-ordination 'which would lower him in the eyes of the army.'[63] So the War Council unanimously decided, on the 29th, that Nivelle would not be removed, and that Pétain would be Chief of General Staff at the Ministry, a Paris post, as principal military adviser to the Government.

At the beginning of May, the new attacks began, only to be repulsed even more bloodily by the Germans from their strengthened positions. As Ludendorff was to say: 'On the Aisne and in Champagne General Nivelle tried once again to wrest victory at the beginning of May. Our front had been ordered and strictly organised once more, so that on both battlegrounds of this powerful double battle the new attack was destroyed with the heaviest of losses. On 7 May fierce fighting broke out again on the whole front, and then the attack on the Aisne, and from the 9th onwards in Champagne, died down. . . . The French offensive had failed in a particularly bloody way.'[64]

Meanwhile, at the Paris Conference on 4 May, a joint statement by Nivelle, Pétain, Haig and Robertson, while unanimous in saying that offensive operations should continue on the western front, had also shown the Pétain influence in that it countermanded the original Nivelle plan, saying that 'it was no longer a question of breaking through; it was now a matter of wearing down the enemy's strength, and the generals were unanimous that this object could be achieved by relentlessly attacking *with limited objectives*, while making the fullest possible use of our artillery.'[65] Lloyd George strongly supported this, and the French ministers accepted it.

The question of the Command was raising its head again. Even Maginot was now convinced that something had to be done soon. On 10 May the decision was taken to make Pétain Commander-in-Chief, despite the doubts of Malvy, and Foch Chief of General Staff. Nivelle at first seemed willing to go; but Ribot wisely warned Painlevé that he should have demanded a letter, as by the morrow all would be different. Sure enough, on the 11th Nivelle, who had seen the politicians Briand and Malvy, had changed his mind, and refused to go. Poincaré, as a true politician, wanted to 'get everyone together.' Maginot, now completely converted, wanted quick action in the interests of the army. Meetings took place, with Nivelle taking, as Ribot puts it, a '*triste attitude*', even denying facts. For days this went on. On the 14th Ribot saw Briand. On the 15th he saw Nivelle, telling him that as he was not supported by the Minister of War, the only worthy attitude was to resign. But Nivelle continued to resist, even writing Ribot a letter during the meeting of the Council. The same day, however, Pétain was appointed.

The comings and goings of these few days show how right many military men were to despise the politicians, and their reasons for action. Certainly they show that political factions often decided military decisions. And Ribot, a weak nonentity, was clearly unable to take decisions in face of such divisions. Pétain may have been justified in his statements to Poincaré about the need for a dictator in war; at all events, Clemenceau was later to show that personal power was an efficient substitute for war by committee.

Pétain's appointment was received with relief by many. Colonel Herbillon, liaison officer between G.Q.G. and the Government, notes, 'The appointment of General Pétain has had a good effect in all circles, people justly have confidence in him.'[66] At last Pétain was in complete command, able to carry out his own policies. But first he had to deal with a new danger that had arisen: mutiny.

Chapter Three

Pétain in command

To anyone with acute powers of observation, the state of morale in the French army for the last year and more would have been a grave matter for concern. Even in December 1915 Terrier, returning to France after an absence of a few months, had noticed a change that had taken place both in military and in public attitudes: 'An officer told me yesterday that when his men are going now to the trenches, they leave their camps marching slowly but regularly, like pilgrims, going to their duty without weakness, but with a certain lassitude in their marching. It's a bit like French opinion concerning the war. It is true that this attitude has struck me all the more because when I left France at the end of September it was amid the enthusiasm of the first news of the Champagne offensive.'[1]

So resignation reigned at the front, and among the civilians whom the soldiers saw on their leave. By May, Terrier is noting that the morale of the troops needs raising, and that they are fed up by the idea of a third winter campaign;[2] he notes, too, the irritation of the troops against the High Command, which keeps so far from the firing line.[3] He speaks of the need to prepare public opinion for a new winter campaign, and of the foolishness of recommencing offensives like those of Artois and Champagne, with their great losses (the Somme was about to start); a 'new spirit' for the army is indispensable.[4] In June he reports that 'Many rumours are arriving from the army about the discontent of the men at the idea of another winter campaign.[5]'

On 1 September 1916, Terrier wrote an important letter summarising some of the causes for complaint: 'I must tell you about the discontent in the army. There is still a strong resentment on account of the methods of the present war, the distance of the Command from the troops, and the insufficiency of artillery' . . . Even after two years of war, he says, commanders are prodigally wasting their troops: 'That infantry, so rare and so precious today, should be wasted in insufficiently prepared attacks, this is something which one could not believe after two years of war unless so many testimonies came forward to cry it out to us. This state of mind on the part of the men's officers is truly appalling for those who observe it. Even if it is not justified—which the gods alone can judge—there is cause for concern. What will all this produce, in any case, after the war? What terrible settling of accounts, true or false, and bitterness and vengeance? It is at a moment such as this that we need at the head of the army a strong man who has had no part in all this drama.'[6]

This man was, of course, to be Pétain, whose reputation at Verdun and elsewhere had been that of a man careful of the lives of his troops, and never prepared to undertake an offensive until everything had been organised down to the last detail. But Pétain was not to become commander-in-chief till May 1917, when it was almost too late.

In December 1916, civil and military dissatisfaction had reached a new height. In Paris, shortages and the difficulty of material life had led to great depression. At the front, 'the state of mind of the troops, who read the newspapers . . . is not good at the moment, according to several witnesses.'[7]

In this winter of 1916, it was clear that dissatisfaction at the front was being matched by a pacifist campaign behind the lines, to which the Government appeared to be turning a blind eye. The Press, meanwhile, had been doing much to criticise the conduct of operations. All in all, the soldier found his grievances reflected in what he read, and his hopes of peace raised by the tracts and newspapers of international pacifism (some of them, in fact, subsidised by the Germans).

Soon after Nivelle's appointment he had to write to the Minister of the Interior complaining about the number of anti-militaristic tracts being sent to the army. But Malvy (later to be tried, under Clemenceau, for his activities as Minister of the Interior), does not appear to have done much about it. On 25 January 1917, Nivelle wrote to the Minister of War, warning him that news of strikes and go-slows in vital munitions factories was demoralising the men. On 28 February, the G.Q.G. sent a letter both to the Minister of War and the Minister of the Interior, again complaining about the tracts, which were now a veritable flood.[8]

But it was Nivelle's offensive, above all, that had brought things to a head. The heavy losses of 1916, of Verdun and the Somme, had contributed to making the men weary of offensives; but their morale, before this offensive, was in fact better than it had been for some time. For Nivelle had promised that this was to be the last of the offensives, and that success was in their grasp. The men had gone into battle confident that the method to beat the Germans had at last been found.

Small wonder that the effects of those first days of the offensive should be disastrous. The losses were high; and, while this was not necessarily the most unsuccessful offensive of the war, the contrast between the high hopes that had been placed on it and the actual results it had achieved was demoralising in the extreme. Even if it had been left at that, however, no mutiny need have occurred. It was the futile continuation of the murderous fighting into the month of May, coupled with the other elements we have been discussing, which set if off. The example of the Russian Revolution, too, was a strong incentive.

These mutinies were extremely serious—far more serious than anyone knew in the public at the time. Isolated outbreaks had started at the beginning of May, and had been summarily dealt with. But within a few days of Pétain's taking over command, the situation grew widespread. From 19 May onwards there were several outbreaks reported each day. The form the mutiny took was usually that of a 'strike' on the industrial model; refusal to go into the firing-line, refusal to obey discipline, etc. In many cases, the mutineers organised themselves in the Russian manner, electing 'delegates'. Some groups were violent, but most were quite well organised. Some attempted to organise a march on Paris. The types of mutiny varied greatly, but by June fifty-four divisions were affected, that is to say half of the French army.

General Pellé, commanding the 5th Army Corps, which was one of those affected, wrote a secret report on the events at this time. The report was never sent, but it is of interest for the causes it ascribes to the events:[9]

> ... It is evident that the initial cause of this discontent is tiredness of the war, heightened by the disappointments of the last offensive. The soldiers wonder how and when the war will end: — 'We're fed up with it.'
>
> This lassitude and discontent have been exploited by *agents provocateurs*, whom we have not caught ...[10]

A main cause of the discontent was that the Army Corps had been in the same sector since December, where it had prepared the April offensive, and taken a brilliant part in it. The men had hoped after this to be taken out of the front line; some imprudent promises might even have been made: 'By a very understandable feeling, the soldiers of the 5th Corps have taken a strong dislike to the sector where they have striven and suffered, where they have seen crash so many hopes that had been raised by the April offensive, and where so many of their comrades have fallen. . . '

Pellé concluded that they should be replaced. If they were, they would soon be in shape again. If they were not, the discontent would grow.

Further causes, he noted, for the events were: (1) The lack of junior officers, and their poor quality; gaps made by the offensive had been difficult to fill. In the 4th Regiment there were 'almost no company commanders worthy of that name.' (2) Many of the men came from Paris, and many had just returned from leave. Certain officers had noted disorder at the Gare de l'Est, and an irreverent manner on the train on the part of the soldiers. It seemed that workers' militant action, with its pacifist and revolutionary tendencies, had had a great effect on those on leave in Paris. And in general, the pessimism among the civilians, the complaints about the price of food, etc., had demoralised these men. (3) The soldiers avidly read the newspapers every day. In them they found: accounts of strikes; complaints about food restrictions; news of the Russian revolution with its proclamation of soldiers' rights, manifestos of committees of revolutionary soldiers, suppression of the salute to an officer, fraternisation between Russian and German soldiers in the front line; accounts of the Congress of the French Socialist Party, deciding unanimously, with many parliamentarians there, to enter into relations with the German Socialists at Stockholm (at the International Socialist Congress). 'Cannot', asked Pellé, 'the censors do something about this?'

Pétain's analysis of the situation, as set out in a report to Painlevé on 29

Joffre, Poincaré, George V, Foch, and Haig at Beaquesne. August 1918

Presentation to Marshal Pétain of his baton at Metz, December 1918

May, was similar to Pellé's in certain respects, especially in the blame it laid on Nivelle's offensive: further demoralisation, he thought, had been caused by the indecisions after the failure of it. Men had had their announced attacks put off from day to day, and had become progressively demoralised by the uncertainty. (The essential difference between Pétain and Pellé was that Pétain, though further from the troops, was better able to gauge their feelings, to put himself in their place; another aspect of the 'empathy' we have already discussed.) Men had not been sent far enough from the line between fighting; they could not recover physically or morally in an area which was under bombardment; they should be sent, for rest, to the rear. They must not, however, expect as a right a long rest after a period of fighting.

Pétain, like Pellé, blamed the Press too, though for him their greatest crime was their criticism of the ideas and methods of the High Command, and their reprinting of all the questions asked in the Chamber of Deputies.

Like Pellé, he saw danger in reports on the situation in Russia; the soldiers' committees, the abolition of salutes for officers, etc. And the Socialist Party's agitation for the Stockholm conference was equally abhorrent to him. And there was the publicity given to strikes, and to the economic and material conditions faced by the soldiers' wives and children.

All this was added to by the soldiers' own conditions—the question of the irregularity of leave, the weariness, the awareness of the faults committed by the High Command. Weakness in punishment of military offences had led to slackness, the ever-present supply of *pinard* had occasioned a great deal of drunkenness and insubordination.

A surprising criticism, from one who had been described as himself 'tap tap tapping out all kind of opinions to parliamentarians who went to Verdun expressly to get facts with which to fight the Government,'[11] was Pétain's attack on the deputies who had visited the front on parliamentary missions. He described them as asking general officers for all kinds of information, and encouraging criticisms of the High Command. They also went to the lower ranks, and collected all the current complaints. They even promised to look after the soldiers' interests, and assured the granting of leave as a right. The Government ought to stop these visits.

Are we to assume that Pétain, seeing the mutinies, had realised the dangers of his own previous custom of complaining to deputies? His first criticism of them, is obliquely, a criticism of himself. But perhaps Pétain, always prepared to speak out on matters where he believed his superiors to be wrong, had not realised that his criticisms at the time of Verdun would be used by the deputies to whom he talked.

Another strong judgement which he was to make in the account he gave, years afterwards, of the mutinies, was again in a sense a criticism of himself. Having planned an offensive, he said, which was 'the product of hysterically high hopes and of fantastic strategic over-confidence', the planners set out to undermine the confidence essential to any success: 'The War Council held at Compiègne on 6th April, 1917, was a real blunder, and it would have been wiser not to voice the doubts concerning the plan's success which emerged at the Conference. A ban should at least have been imposed on Press comment, to protect the prestige of those entrusted with the nation's fate. This was not done and the whole Press of every political shade of opinion reported the doubts that had been raised and the agonising questions that had been posed.'[12]

Pétain, it is true, had said little at the War Council; but this was almost certainly, as we have seen, because of the presence of his superior officer. He had certainly poured out criticisms at the private dinner a few days earlier, criticisms of which he presumably hoped that notice would be taken. What is Pétain doing? Has he realised the faults in his own behaviour? Or is he merely conveniently forgetting it? (Even at the time of the writing of this later account of the mutinies, no details were known to the public of the dinner of 2 April.) At all events, he blames the politicians for asking questions, even though he himself had provided complaints and criticism in answer.

Given all the causes for dissatisfaction among the soldiers, Pétain saw the relaxation of military justice as pure foolishness. Yet the measures which had been taken at the beginning of the war (including the summary Courts Martial in which three judges could take immediate action, and in which the judgement could be by two to one, without revision or appeal) had been revoked. In 1916 the Courts Martial were suppressed, and there was re-establishment of the admissibility of evidence of extenuating circumstances, and the right to give suspended sentences. In the same year, the right of appeal against the death sentence was reintroduced. All this despite the protests of Joffre, who, as Pétain said, 'might as well have saved his breath to cool his porridge.'[13] On 20 April 1917, the Minister of War forbade the General Officer who had convened a military court which gave the death sentence to have the sentence carried out without the express authority of the Head of State. All this, in Pétain's eyes, had been a mistake. Military crimes of discipline had multiplied alarmingly even before the mutinies, and such humanitarian mitigation of the harsh provisions of military justice was unjustified in periods of national crisis such as this.

This last criticism shows better than anything else how much Pétain was the man for the job which was now set for him. A deep understanding of the mind of the common soldier, an 'empathy' with his feelings, was essential for any reorganisation of the situation which had produced the dissidence; but it would not have been enough by itself. To quell the dissidence, a strong feeling for military discipline was necessary, and the hardness with which to carry out its imperatives. The combination of these qualities in Pétain was to prove the answer to the problem.

The immediate action to be taken was the re-establishment of discipline: 'In the grave circumstances of the moment, the most urgent necessity was that the activity of the principal troublemakers should be broken on the spot. Mutineers, drunk with slogans and alcohol, must be forced back to their obedience, and every means must be used to reduce to impotence the criminals who had exploited the distress of the fighting troops.'[14]

Officers were punished for weakness. Some had claimed that they had been unable to act because of the collective character of the outbreaks of mutiny: Pétain's directive of 8 June read: 'This argument is unacceptable. It is, in fact, always possible to turn collective disobedience into disobedience by individuals. All that is necessary is to tell certain men, starting with the most disaffected, to carry out some order. If they refuse, such men are at once arrested and handed over to the law, which should take its course as swiftly as possible.'[15]

On the basis of weakness, two generals, nine lieutenant-colonels, fourteen battalion commanders and eighteen lieutenants or second lieutenants were deprived of their commands.

On 1 June, Courts Martial were reintroduced. In a capital case, those in charge should telegraph the Commander-in-Chief, and as soon as he had telegraphed the agreement of the Head of State, the sentence should be carried out. On 11 June, even this last was removed, and the Commander-in-Chief could himself give permission. On 8 June, 'Traitors convicted of inciting or aiding troops to go over to the enemy or join an armed rebellion', and 'instigators or leaders of mutinies who had committed acts of violence during armed disturbances, refused to disperse or persisted in their in-discipline' were deprived of the right of appeal. (These measures were temporary, and were revoked in July.)

In fact, the actual death sentences which were carried out were com-paratively few. The figure that Pétain gives, out of 413 condemned to death, is 55. The number has been questioned, but it is probably about right. The others were, however, taken away from their regiments, and often the impression given to their fellow-soldiers was that they, too, had been executed. All this had a deterrent effect. Pétain showed himself inflexible, even when the Minister of War pleaded in favour of certain moving cases. Discipline was indispensable.

Another important thing was to protect the men from the contamination of pacifist propaganda; Pétain called on the Government to control dissident organisations, expel suspected neutrals, imprison agitators and foreign spies, censor the Press, forbid Press criticism of the High Command, and ensure discretion in the reporting of the Russian Revolution and home strikes. He also succeeded in getting the passports of those Socialists wishing to attend the Stockholm congress revoked. Tracts and leaflets were banned as far as was possible; though the attitude of Malvy, the Minister of the Interior, was still fairly unco-operative.*

To supplement these measures of discipline, however, Pétain saw the positive need to revive morale. A new attitude was needed among the officers. In a note of 19 May, Pétain advised commanding officers to welcome advice from their subordinate officers, many of whom, by hesitating to speak out, had allowed plans to continue which their information could have modified

---

* Hankey, in May, described the situation in Paris thus: 'The general impression of Paris struck me as very bad—a weak Government, a tiresome Chamber, intrigue everywhere, and a troubled and rather dejected people.' Hankey, op. cit. vol. 2, p. 629.

or stopped.* He encouraged them to be approachable and friendly, though firm when a decision had been taken: 'An attitude of kindness and goodwill on the part of commanders is in the noblest tradition of the French Army and in no way excludes firmness. It is when such an attitude is lacking in a unit that an unfortunate and blameworthy spirit tends to arise.'[16]

Good conduct awards were reintroduced for the troops, and fair arrangements with regard to leave were organised. On their way to leave, the troops would now travel in comparative comfort, and quickly (as opposed to being pretty well shovelled into cattle-trucks which often remained stationary for hours). Reception centres were provided, and comfortable leave camps. 'This humane cushioning process was much appreciated by the men, who had never resigned themselves to being treated as mere cyphers.'[17]

Rations were improved, and their distribution made more efficient. Wine supplies were, however, restricted in order to combat the widespread drunkenness. Rest periods, too, were organised, so that units could take turns in the front line and in the rear in a regular manner, though after two or three days' relaxation those 'at rest' would have a course of retraining. Sport and entertainments were encouraged, including army theatricals (just as Pétain had done on the Artois front in 1915).

Pétain himself raised morale by going round to the various units in the front line, visiting a different one each day. He talked with officers and men, telling them to talk freely, after which he gave them his views on the general situation. To the men he distributed not only souvenirs and gifts of tobacco, but also medals; he inspected field kitchens, took the food with the men, gave ideas for improvements. All this with that simple friendliness tempered with aloofness which he had shown on the Artois front, and which had been noted by Mordacq. Pétain, while among his men, nevertheless remained apart from them; but in this he was far more effective than any man showing spurious bonhomie would have been.

Even before he became Commander-in-Chief, the men had known him by reputation as a commander sparing of lives, who had no mind for futile and costly adventures. Now, he laid before them his new strategy, one of defensive care matched by limited offensives in which things were less costly to French troops, and more costly to the Germans. Above all, he stressed to them that the Americans, who had now entered the war, would soon be arriving in large numbers, and that the best strategy was to stand on the defensive and await their arrival.

By all these means, Pétain succeeded in silencing the mutinies. By the end of June, the danger was past; though it was to remain present in Pétain's mind for a long time to come. The re-establishment of the situation seems almost a miracle; in May, it had looked as though the French army was out of the war. Luckily the Germans had had no real inkling of it until later; and even the English were unaware of its full extent.

* Serrigny had already written of Pétain, in Autumn 1914, that under him 'everyone can express an opinion, he listens, and then decides.' Serrigny, op. cit. p. 3, entry for 26 October 1914

Pétain had been the man for the job; the mutinies of 1917 were his second claim to fame, and the one of which he was most proud in his later years.

The new strategy

To most of those involved, the significance of Pétain's succession to Nivelle was clear; though their reactions were suitably different. Crown Prince Wilhelm notes that, 'with the appointment of Pétain as Commander-in-Chief a strategy based on limited objectives and safe results gained control of the French Command.'[18]

Haig, on the other hand, had been against Pétain's appointment. Still a partisan of the offensive, 'he fears', as Ribot tells us, 'that General Pétain, if appointed, would abandon all offensive plans. Having pressed the English to make every effort, we might abandon them *en route*.'[19]

Haig had already met Pétain on 3 May, shortly after the latter was appointed Chief of General Staff: he had found him 'most clear-headed and easy to discuss things with', but had nevertheless experienced 'the difficulty . . . (which one has always had in agreements with the French) to know to what extent we can depend on the French to carry out their attacks.'[20]

Within a couple of days of his appointment as Commander-in-Chief, Pétain, with Serrigny, again visited Haig, on 18 May. Haig was again impressed by him personally, finding him 'business-like, knowledgeable, and brief of speech. The latter is, I find, a rare quality in Frenchmen!'[21] At this meeting Pétain promised Haig one French army for the coming Flanders offensive, and promised three limited offensive battles to distract the enemy: one on the Chemin des Dames ridge, one at Reims and one at Verdun. (The mutinies had not, of course, yet appeared in their full strength.) Pétain and Serrigny were nevertheless aware of Haig's mistrust with regard to their plans.

The offer of three 'limited' offensives was in no way contrary to Pétain's new theories, of course. On 19 May he put forward the first statement of the new French strategy in his secret 'Directive No. 1', addressed to army and army group commanders. For many of them, this directive was to be a tremendous shock, containing as it did the categorical statement: 'The balance of the opposing forces on the northern and north-eastern fronts does not allow us for the moment to envisage a breakthrough followed by strategic exploitation.'[22]

The thing to do was to 'wear out the enemy with the minimum of losses.' For this, there should be 'attacks on limited objectives, suddenly unleashed on a front as wide as will be permitted by the number and properties of the various types of artillery at our disposal.'[23] The attacks should be 'applied successively to different parts of the front', and 'follow each other as quickly as possible in time, in order to hold the enemy down and deprive him of freedom of action.'[24] For this strategy, there must be an 'appropriate organisation of the front', which would enable swift movement of troops from one place to another.

The difference between this concept and that which had reigned up till now is very clear; but it is doubtful whether Haig, in his acceptance of Pétain's offer on the 18th of three 'limited offensives', had been quite clear about what this meant in Pétain's eyes. To help his Flanders offensive, he would have expected wasting offensives such as had happened on the Somme to take pressure off Verdun, or on the Chemin des Dames, not these surprise attacks which, while successfully striking a blow at the enemy from strength to weakness, would nevertheless be over almost before they began. However the next day Haig was to receive a letter from Sir Henry Wilson stating that Pétain had told him that any attacks of his would be for strictly limited objectives, and that when they were gained the offensive would cease. 'He did not believe in another Somme.'[25] From now on, Haig must have been clear as to Pétain's policy.

Pétain's policy, as stated in this directive, was thus formulated and disseminated before the mutinies began; but it was to be of immense service in restoring the confidence of the soldiery. 'Waiting for the Americans' was not only sense, given the state of the French army, and the Western Front situation; it was also extremely acceptable to the soldiers, worn out by futile attacks. At the same time, a few well-organised and successful attacks on limited objectives restored their faith in themselves and in the war effort.

The mutinies now came to take Pétain's attention, and it was not until 20 June that his Directive No. 2 appeared. This directive, on training for the men, succeeded in combining the popular measure of regular rotation of units for rest periods with the practical use of retraining the army in the new methods, on the principles of careful saving of the infantry combined with extensive use of the artillery. As Pétain had often said, 'the artillery fights, the infantry occupies.' Close liaison was organised between the various arms.

Directive No. 3, on the general deployment of the army, and on the new weapons now available, came out on 4 July. In it Pétain stated the policy of 'defence in depth', another policy which, in its details, was to be a bone of contention in the months before the German 1918 offensive. The sections on artillery stressed the need for massive artillery support. Apart from these Directives, the army was also set to close examination of German techniques.

The British Passchendaele offensive started at the end of July 1917. True to his promise, Pétain sent General Anthoine and the 1st Army to take part. With it he sent very large artillery support. Anthoine was, however, obliged to continue his attack for longer than the Pétain doctrine would have allowed; nevertheless, his achievements were comparable to any in the first days of that campaign.

Despite the mutinies, Pétain was still able to perform two of the limited offensives that he had promised Haig; though they had to come a little later in the year. And they were 'limited offensives' in the sense of his Directive No. 1, rather than the wholesale and lengthy offensives which Haig would have wished to take the pressure off the Passchendaele offensive.

Not only were these attacks in full accordance with Pétain's considered theories; they were also good therapy for the French army, giving it confidence in itself and in its commander.

For they were both complete successes. The first was at Verdun, on the left bank of the Meuse. Its objective was for the 2nd Army to retake the valuable positions of the Mort 'Homme and ridge 304, and at the same time to inflict great losses on the Germans. More artillery was to be used here, in proportion to the troops employed, than ever before in the French army. After eight days of preliminary bombardment, the infantry advanced on 20 August, and took their objectives without any trouble, taking 10,000 prisoners as well, with minimal losses to themselves. The limit of advance had been set at 3,000—4,000 yards, and no further attempt at advance was made.

The success of this action not only did a great deal to restore the morale of the army; it also gave new hope to the country as a whole. For the whole summer the people had been depressed not only by the failure of the April offensive, but also by the proofs which nationalist newspapers like *L'Action Française* had been producing of the nefarious activities of traitors behind the lines, such as Vigo, alias Almereyda, the editor of the *Bonnet Rouge*, and also the pacifists and international socialists (such as those who wished to go to Stockholm), whom *L'Action Française* also accused of treachery. In a letter of 25 August, Terrier notes a change in public attitudes: 'The splendid news from the front, and above all from ridge 304, is driving away the spectres of Vigo and Stockholm. It was time, too. All evidence goes to show that the army is getting better. The nation, as well.'[26]

On 29 August Pétain received the Grand Cross of the Légion d'Honneur.

The second limited offensive, which was to take place around Fort Malmaison at the western end of the Chemin des Dames ridge, was extensively put back in time, to await full preparation. It eventually took place on 23 October. The army involved was the 6th Army, under General Maistre, supported by the overwhelming artillery support of almost a thousand heavy guns, and 624 field guns. The target was again an advance of a few thousand yards. There were six days of preliminary bombardment, and again success was complete, with thousands of prisoners taken. Not only this, but the attack had turned the German flank, and they were obliged to evacuate their positions on the crest of the invaluable Chemin des Dames ridge. For the Allies, this was the one ray of light at the worst stage of Passchendaele. Hankey describes meeting Pétain at the Ritz with Painlevé on 1 November: 'I congratulated Pétain on his recent victory, describing it as the cleanest bit of work done this year. No, he said, Verdun was just as clean. He seemed very pleased with himself. At the moment of the Caporetto disaster it was particularly encouraging to find that the French were getting their tails up.'[27] This was a sad time for the Allies, nevertheless. In Flanders, all was not well. In Italy, the sweeping victory of the Germans and Austrians at Caporetto on 24 October not only drastically weakened the Allies; it should also have shown them that the Germans appeared finally to have resolved the problem of the breakthrough (as they were to show again in March 1918). In Russia, Kerensky was falling, and a peace attempt seemed fairly certain between the Russians and the Germans.

Meanwhile, Pétain's theories, successful as they had been proved, were already coming under attack. His 'Instruction for the offensive action of large formations in battle', issued a few days after Malmaison, and confirming the tactics which had been used there, was unpopular among many of his officers, who ridiculed it as 'the red book'; it was too 'methodical' for them, it did not show enough of the offensive spirit. Clearly the 'offensive at all costs' school was reviving again, if it had indeed ever declined.

Later in the year Pétain was to shock his opponents even more by his Directive No. 4, which was devoted to the defensive. It stated that, with the effects of the Russian defection (now a fact), 'The Entente will not recover superiority in fighting forces until the American army is capable of sending a certain number of large formations into the line; until then we must, under the threat of inevitable wastage of our forces, keep up a waiting attitude, with the definite idea of taking up again, as soon as we can, the offensive which alone can give us the final victory.'[28] Following this, Pétain made clear, both here and in the 'Instruction for the defensive action of large formations in battle' (20 December) that for a proper defensive to be conducted, the main battle must always be fought in the second positions. The first positions must be lightened; they will be needed only to 'break or at least slow down the enemy's first onslaught.' Though these were, in fact, the tactics that had been adopted by the Germans, and were now being adopted by Haig (in fact, even Joffre had seen the danger of packing the forward positions), Pétain's proposals shocked many, with their implicit assumption that one could give up positions that had often been won at great cost. For many Frenchmen, for whom the offensive was still the only morally justified military action, hanging on to all that one had gained was the next best thing, and similarly sacred. Flexible defence such as Pétain proposed was anathema. We shall see Pétain's difficulties both with his subordinates and with the Government at the time of the German 1918 offensive, on this matter.

To return to the question of a French offensive, however. Pétain's attitude of waiting was reasonable, given (1) the still convalescent state of the French army, (2) the prospect of eventual American reinforcements, (3) the prospect of the large German forces now freed from the Russian front, and available in the West.

This did not prevent, however, extensive criticism of these waiting tactics, both in military and in parliamentary circles, in late 1917. The criticism of the October instruction was merely one sign of this. Among the politicians, Paul Doumer (whom we have seen in 1915 and 1916 criticising Joffre for the same reasons) called for a grand offensive; but luckily Painlevé, who had become Prime Minister in September, was to remain in power till mid-November, and Pétain still had his protection. Clemenceau, the new Prime Minister, was to be a different matter. Meanwhile, the hostility of his own generals towards Pétain was enough for Ferry to note that he worried them more than the Boche did.

Lloyd George, of course, was a supporter of Pétain's strategy. In a long talk with Hankey on 15 October (on which Hankey took extensive notes), three alternative solutions were discussed: '(1) To continue Haig's plan of remorselessly hammering the enemy. (2) To adopt Pétain's tactics of striking here and striking there, always carrying out the first and successful stage of an attack, but never carrying it through to a prolonged offensive. (3) To carry out (2) in conjunction with a great offensive elsewhere, for example in Turkey.'

Hankey plumped for the first. Neither (2) nor (3), he said, would suffice to keep the Germans on our front. He also urged 'that if an offensive was to be carried out at all it might as well have some strategical aim. Pétain's tactics had no strategical aim. On the previous day he had asked Franklin Bouillon and Foch what was the underlying strategical idea, and Franklin Bouillon had frankly admitted that there was not one, and that the plan was based on the theory that big operations with strategical objectives were a mistake in existing conditions.'[29]

Lloyd George, however, opposed this. Haig's offensive, which Hankey had described as 'hammering, as it were, on a serious bruise', with every blow telling 'with redoubled force on Germany's strength' was for Lloyd George merely another of those attacks which 'at once drew in the reserves and multiplied the strength of the defending force, so that any advance must be very slow and costly.'[30]

What he wished to avoid in 1918, he said, was the terrific losses inevitably bound up in an attack of this nature. 'He admitted that a continuance of Haig's attacks might conceivably result in bringing Germany to terms in 1919. But in that case it would be the U.S. who would deal the blow and not we ourselves. If our Army was spent in a series of shattering attacks during 1918, it would, indeed, be in exactly the condition the French Army was in at this moment, with its numbers reduced and its morale weakened.'[31] For the enemy completely to be defeated was impossible in 1918; the Americans would not yet be here in enough strength. The Allies should reserve their main strength and make a terrific effort in 1919: 'He believed that by means of Pétain's tactics the Germans could be sufficiently occupied on the Western Front to prevent them dealing decisive blows against Russia, and that this result could be achieved without the great sacrifice in life involved in a continuance of Haig's operations.'[32]

Meanwhile Haig, though opposed to a change in strategy, had nevertheless found both Pétain and his staff agreeable to work with. In September Pétain had saved Haig from some double-dealing by Foch:

'[Foch's] experiences in London should have done him good. He had gone there behind the back of Pétain and myself to get the British War Cabinet to sanction 100 French guns being withdrawn from my command. The War Cabinet then handed the question to me to arrange with Pétain. This we have done satisfactorily for all. I found Pétain today straightforward and clear in his views, and most business-like. And, as he said himself today, "the Marshal and I never argue and haggle about such matters." '[33]

The mutual esteem between the two men was reinforced by the difficulties both of them were having (admittedly, on the whole for different reasons) with politicians. They were more than once to find themselves, before the 1918 offensive, in agreement in opposing proposals from these sources. We shall find this, eventually, in relation to such things as the question of a unified command and unified reserves; while even on matters on which they disagreed Pétain and Haig were to remain on cordial terms, up till the start of the March offensive.

Criticisms of Pétain's defensive attitude were continuing in France. Painlevé's Government fell on 13 November 1917, and Clemenceau became premier. It was becoming clear to most thinking men that the Russian defection was going to bring an all-out German offensive in the West, and that the Allies' only possible plan for the moment could be the defensive, in face of such heavy odds. The military representatives on the new 'Inter-Allied Military Committee' which had been set up at the Rapallo Conference in November—Weygand (France), Cadorna (Italy), Wilson (Great Britain) and Bliss (U.S.A.), agreed with Pétain's views, and said, in 'collective notes' to their Governments, that it was necessary to keep up a defensive attitude in early 1918. But the French army was not convinced, and nor was the Government. At a meeting of the War Council on 13 December, Pétain was strongly criticised for his defensive tactics; Pétain offered to resign if it was wished, but was persuaded not to.

Clemenceau, won over in large part by Foch's enthusiasm, found Pétain far too cautious. On 19 December he suggested, for example, to Poincaré that Pétain's chief of general staff, Debeney, was temperamentally too much like his superior, and should be replaced; which he was. Several other matters brought Pétain and Clemenceau into conflict.

The army view of Pétain, in November and December 1917, is well exemplified by a series of letters written from General Pellé to the politician Albert Thomas, in those two months.

'You know that I am an optimist,' he writes to Thomas. 'I believe that you are another, and I will speak to you as such. I would be forced to speak another language if I was writing to the Old Gentleman or to the Head of State.'[34]

In a later note to the same recipient, he declared that the whole experience of the war had shown that in this war the attacker made less losses, and used less forces than the defender. This had been shown at Champagne in 1915, at Verdun, on the Somme, in Flanders, and even probably at the Nivelle offensive. The only way to stop the German offensive was by an offensive of their own.[35]

In the same month of December, Pellé prepared for Thomas a note, 'On the Breakthrough', which showed that for him at least tactics had not advanced since 1915. He criticised strongly Pétain's technique of limited objectives, and said that 'prolonged offensives . . . of the type of the Battle of the Somme, the Battle of Flanders, the last Battle of the Aisne—have shown themselves by experience to be the most powerful means of gradually destroying the organised forces of the enemy.'[36]

Finally, in a letter marked 'strictly personal' written on 30 December, Pellé told Thomas:

I am very much afraid that Parliamentary Control, the Secret Committees, the letters from the Socialist Party, and the indignation of M. Renaudel and others against the offensive of 16 April [the Nivelle offensive] may be in the process of producing the unfortunate consequences for the conduct of the war that might have been expected.

And you may perhaps be able to do something to combat this attitude.

I fear that the Government and the High Command may be limiting their objects at the moment to *awaiting* the German attack. Not counting the risks run by this attitude, it is certain that the attack, on the day it happens, will obtain successes which will be at least temporary and local.

Then those who cried out most against 16 April will cry out even more strongly. But the harm will have been done and the danger will perhaps be great. It will be easy to blame the Generals whose divisions will have been struck down —but the true responsibility will lie nevertheless with the Commander-in-Chief, the Government, and beyond them the Parliament, and in particular the Socialist Party.[37]

A far greater figure, however, was taking much the same attitudes: Foch, who was having great influence on Clemenceau. On 1 January 1918 Foch wrote to Weygand in letter which eventually reached Clemenceau, that the armies must have: 'the resolution to seize every opportunity of imposing their will on the enemy by taking up again, as soon as possible, the offensive, the only way of gaining victory.'[38]

Among other matters in this letter, Foch also takes up the question of enemy attacks, which must be stopped, and counter-attacks made, on the very ground that is attacked.

Pétain wrote a reply to this, addressed to Clemenceau, on 8 January: 'Whatever desire we may have once more to take the initiative of operations, we must face facts and base our forecasts not on speculation but on reality... In reality, the 1918 battle will be defensive on the Franco-British side, not from the absolute wishes of the Command, but from the necessity of the situation. The lack of materials forces this on us. It is better to realise it now and organise ourselves accordingly. My Directive No. 4 and my instructions with regard both to offensive and defensive organisations of the ground, and to the distribution of our forces, are the answers to these needs.'[39]

Haig, whose attitude up till now had been entirely offensive, now however came round wholly to Pétain's point of view. On 24 January the two commanders put forward their plans at a military meeting at Compiègne, on the 30th they did the same at the Supreme War Council, much impressing their audience. Both of them made it clear that only a passive strategy was possible until the Americans arrived in force, which would not be soon.[40]

Meanwhile Clemenceau was not merely confining himself to criticism of

Pétain's main strategy; he was also undermining his tactical instructions with regard to the defensive. Foch and Roques had convinced him that Pétain's views on the withdrawal of the main forces to the second line were contrary to the proper procedure, and dangerous to morale. He wrote to Pétain on 8 February, trying to get the procedure changed. Pétain managed to defend his opinions, and maintain his Directive No. 4 and his Instructions in force. But the divergence of views, known to the army commanders, many of whom disapproved of Pétain's ideas, meant that they were in fact encouraged to oppose and to disobey these directives.

Haig and Pétain

Much of the period just before the German offensive is marked by the strange alliance which took place between the two Commanders-in-Chief. Their agreement on strategy, in opposition to Foch and others, is but one mark of this. Equally important was the joint front they put up in face of projects for a unified command, and for a unified reserve—though here their collusion was to lead to unfortunate results.

Gradually, many people among the Allies had been coming to the conclusion that some form of unified command was needed. At the same time, Lloyd George, seeking any way to curb the power of his *bête noire* Haig, had been attempting with the other Allies the formation of some sort of Inter-Allied War Council. This was finally formed at the Rapallo Conference on 5 November 1917. There would be a *Conseil Supérieur de la Guerre*, with a *Conseil Militaire Interallié* at Versailles, which would be the executive organ. One military representative would be on the latter from each country.

Foch (later followed by Weygand) and Wilson were the French and British representatives, neither of them likely to please Haig or Pétain; the two commanders were thus against any powers for the committee.

As for the question of a unified Command, Pétain's views were expressed in a note which he showed to Haig on 1 November, and which Haig approved: 'Pétain showed me a short note which he had written on the question of an Allied Commander-in-Chief (à la Hindenburg). It was possible among allies only when one Army was really the dominant one as in the case of the Central Powers. Our case was different. The British and French Armies were now in his view on an equality. Therefore, he and I must exercise command, and if we disagree, our Governments alone can settle the point in dispute.' [41]

No doubt Pétain's view was affected by the fact that it would probably not be him that would be this Allied Commander; he was at this time in disagreement both with Haig (who did not come round till a couple of months later) *and* much of the French Government and army. This is not necessarily to suggest that personal ambition was involved; it was likely that his *strategy* would be overborne, and it could have been as much for the French army as for himself that he took this attitude.

At the French War Council, on 18 November, Pétain spoke up, however, in favour of a unique command, while severely restricting the powers any such command would have.

The return of Foch from Italy at the beginning of December, however, with the danger that he might become Supreme Commander, put Pétain back in opposition to the measure. Haig and Pétain would clearly not accept any such delegation of their command.

Meanwhile, more trouble was brewing in the form of the Executive War Board (*Le Comité Exécutif*), set up by the Supreme War Council on 1 February to supervise the creation of a general reserve for the whole of the armies on the Western, Italian and Balkan fronts. Foch was its chairman; the other members were Wilson, Cadorna and Bliss.

Haig, of course, in his *persona* of the bluff soldier, despised all such 'committees', especially ones with Wilson (a buddy of Lloyd George) on them; and Pétain, when faced by the decisions of the committees, was in agreement with him.

On 6 February Foch sent to Haig, Pétain and Diaz (Italy) his plan for an Inter-Allied general reserve. This reserve would be 30 divisions: behind the western front, 10 French and 7 English; behind the Italian front, 3 English, 3 French, 7 Italian. All reserves would be supervised and distributed by the Executive War Board.

Haig and Pétain were, of course, appalled. Pétain wrote back, sending copies of his letters to Haig: 'General Clive arrived from Compiègne with copies of General Pétain's letters sent in reply to Versailles' request for certain Divisions to be placed in "General Reserve". Briefly, he says that he has no Divisions available for the purpose. Pétain sent these letters to me *personally* so that we can work in the closest touch in the matter of Versailles.'[42] Pétain's other arguments were: (1) that a committee could not run a battle, and (2) that he could not upset in this way all the plans he had already made with Haig.

Haig's letter, written much later on 11 March, hardly surprisingly 'was of an inspiration in all ways similar to that of Pétain.'[43] Haig's opposition was even stronger than Pétain's, and he was more clever in the way he went about it. On 24 February, Clemenceau visited Haig. He talked in a worried way about the friction between Foch and Pétain on the question of reserves. Haig now said that he could not earmark any Divisions for Inter-Allied reserves, either, without upsetting his plans for defence, 'and that rather than change my plans at a time when at any time the enemy might attack in force, I would prefer to resign my Command. M. Clemenceau at once said that my statement indicated his line of action. He would arrange to "*écarter*" (set aside) Foch gradually. He personally looked upon a close agreement between Pétain and myself as the surest guarantee of success.'[44]

In this way Haig influenced Clemenceau (who approved of him) in a way that Pétain could never have done; for between Foch and Pétain Clemenceau's tendency would have been to choose the former. Clemenceau's influence soon made itself felt. On 2 March Haig noted: 'After the Conference I had a talk with General Clive who had come from Compiègne. He stated that at a War Council in Paris last Thursday (Feb. 28th) at which President Poincaré presided, General Foch was distinctly told that he (Poincaré) as President of the French Republic had his responsibility also in the matter of the French Army, and that it would be impossible for him (Foch) to control the Reserves in the manner contemplated by the Versailles Council. In fact, Foch was set aside, and Pétain's position upheld and strengthened. This was the result of my meeting here with Clemenceau.'[45]*

So the game seemed won on the French side; what of the British? Haig's opposition was strong, and Hankey notes, on 13 March, that Henry Wilson 'was bothered because Haig won't give up his quota to the Allied General Reserve. In the circumstances he advocates a suspension of the whole scheme, which is tantamount to allowing Haig to flout the Supreme War Council.'[46]

On the 14th, at the Supreme War Council, Lloyd George took the Haig-Pétain line, followed by Clemenceau. The French and English Governments had decided to approve the plan which the two commanders had themselves worked out for mutual support. An Allied reserve would only be set up after the arrival of the Americans in force.

'Altogether', Hankey says, 'the Executive War Board had already become rather "fly-blown".'[47] Foch reacted violently to the attitude of Lloyd George and Clemenceau, and started a violent altercation with the latter, until Clemenceau shut him up by shouting 'Silence'!

On this almost comic note the last chance for any kind of Allied reserve ended, and the two armies were left to rely on an agreement between their commanders. This was, in the end, to turn out to be completely insufficient.

The measure of agreement between Pétain and Haig by 1918 is shown by their reactions to a matter in which their two nations might well be presumed to disagree violently. This was the question of the extent of the front which was to be covered by each army.

For some time the French had been requesting the British to extend their share of the line. The French army was holding over three times as much of the line as the British; and moreover, its losses of 1916 and 1917, and its weakening by the mutinies, had meant that it could only with difficulty continue to do so. The British, on the other hand, were very dubious about any extension. Haig's army was, in 1917, deeply involved in the Flanders campaign; and, if the French army, as seemed likely, was too worn out to participate in the final offensive, the British army needed even more clearly to be reserved for that purpose.

The Boulogne Conference in September 1917 was the place where this question was discussed on the political level. A couple of days before it, on 22 September, Pétain, who had been asked for his views by the French Government, replied that the British army should from 1 November

---

* Poincaré gives us a hint of what went on behind the scenes: 'Pétain, who saw Clemenceau this morning [28 February], says he is very satisfied with their conversation . . . His own reserves are left at his disposal. He confirms what Clemenceau told me, that Haig would have preferred to resign than to accept a reserve army under the orders of Versailles. Clemenceau, says Pétain, gave in with good grace to his objections.' Poincaré, *Au Service de la France,* vol. 10, *Victoire et Armistice 1918,* Paris 1933 p. 63.

extend its line as far as Berry-au-Bac. Lloyd George's representative at the conference on 25 September, General Robertson, was unable to promise anything specific, but announced to Painlevé and Foch 'that the British Government admitted the principle of some extension.' This was impossible at the moment, he added, because of the continuing Flanders offensive, but he suggested that the question might be reconsidered in connection with the plans for 1918. The following resolution was adopted: 'The British Government having accepted in principle the extension of the line held by the British Army on the Western Front, the two Governments are agreed that the question of the extension and the time at which it should take place should be left for arrangement between the two Commanders-in-Chief.'[48]

So the whole thing was to be left to Haig and Pétain. Unfortunately, however, the French Government, extremely keen that the extension should start as soon as possible, continued to pursue the question on the political front. Painlevé and Foch visited London on 9–10 October, and made the proposal that the British should take over sixty miles of the French line.

'Perhaps', says Hankey, 'the French Government's pressure was overdone. Whether for this reason, or owing to the determined opposition of Haig, now supported by Robertson, to any extension while the battle of Flanders continued, or because the Boulogne Conference had remitted all details to the two Commanders-in-Chief, the War Cabinet rather resented the attempt of French Ministers to forestall their meeting. . . . They were not in the mood to be rushed.'[49]

On 13–14 October, at Chequers, Franklin Bouillon and Foch formally demanded an extension before 1 November. But the position remained the same. The whole thing was, as before, to be taken up through military channels.

To appreciate the extent to which Haig and Pétain fell over backwards to be agreeable to one another, we should consider for a moment or two the strong feelings which were extant on either side over this question. For the French, it was clear that the nations were almost equal in population, and that the British appeared to be taking on far less than themselves; and, always in the back of certain French minds, there was that mistrust of ultimate British objectives which, particularly in military circles, has poisoned relations in two world wars. Was Britain, by harbouring her resources, going to gain the greatest advantage out of the war, they wondered? Fayolle, as far back as 1916, had posed this question: 'The whole of Europe will wear itself out in this war, both in men and wealth. To whose profit? The Anglo-Saxon race. . . . It is England who will gain the greatest advantage from this war. Once more she will have led the Continental nations to cut each others throats for her greater profit.'[50]

On the British side, the same capacity for mistrust and dislike existed. And on this particular question details, such as the longer leave given to French soldiers, made British feelings quite strong, even in Government circles: 'Why, it was asked, should British soldiers be expected to take over more of the line in order to give the *poilus* longer spells of leave than they received themselves? They had borne the brunt of the fighting all the summer and autumn and were still bearing it. They were not even fighting in their own country as were the French.'[51]

It is a tribute to both Haig and Pétain that, though they both felt strongly about this question, they were prepared to negotiate and come a little way towards the other's position. At their meeting at Amiens on 18 October, Pétain made it clear that if Russia dropped out of the war, the French army (which was losing forty thousand men a month) would have to shorten the line in order to create the necessary reserves for the subsequent German offensive. He asked whether the British would take over another six divisions-worth of line, up to Barisis. Haig modified this, and said he would do his best to transfer four divisions from the coast. The British War Cabinet, however, would not commit itself to this. The news of the Caporetto disaster in Italy on 26 October led to the two Governments agreeing to shelve the problem.

By 2 November, however, Haig had agreed to extend his troops to the Oise, and just beyond. Haig and Pétain (according to the instructions of the Boulogne Conference) had come to agreement on their own. Military events stood in the way of this, however; Caporetto had necessitated the sending of reserves to Italy, and German counter-attacks near Cambrai had diverted some of the troops involved. French protests were made, but Haig made the position clear in reply.

For Pétain the position appeared to be becoming desperate. He told his Government in December that he could no longer take responsibility for holding the French front unless the British made a great extension of their line, and unless he got 200,000 more civilians to prepare fresh lines of defence. He wrote to Haig on 14 December, and Clemenceau wrote to the British Government, asking them to take over the French line as far as Berry-au-Bac, Clemenceau threatening to resign if they did not. (Berry-au-Bac was about fifty-nine kilometres beyond Barisis, the furthest point Haig had been willing to consider).

On the 17th, Haig and Pétain met. Haig described their meeting thus:

> Pétain spoke about the great front to be held by the French Army, and the possibility of the Germans attacking him about Châlons and through Switzerland.
> I told him exactly how tired the British troops were, and the shortage of drafts. I told him I could relieve two Divisions on January 10th and extend to the Oise by the end of January, but the latter date must be subject to a settlement later according to the situation. He accepted this.[52]

Despite the basic disagreement on this matter, the atmosphere was obviously cordial: 'I was much struck with the different bearing and attitude of the present Officers at G.Q.G. The present ones seem much more simple, more natural and practical than their predecessors, and are more frank in their dealings with the British. In fact, the relations between G.Q.G. and G.H.Q. are better than I have ever known them.'[53]

Haig fulfilled his promise, and took over the line as far as Barisis by 30

January. By this time, however, Pétain was feeling the need for an even greater takeover. At the Supreme War Council on 2 February he asked for about forty-eight kilometres' extension beyond Barisis. Haig said that an extension of any kind was out of the question. (As Hankey says, the case was strong on both sides.)[54] A possible compromise was an extension of nineteen kilometres to the Ailette. This compromise was agreed in principle: 'Eventually', says Haig, 'it was agreed to accept the proposed extension *in principle*, but it was left to Pétain and myself to decide when to carry it out.'[55]

Pétain himself showed Haig, however, that he did not wish to press the point. 'After this Pétain came along to me and said that he had no intention to "taquiner" (worry) me over this.'[56] The proposed extension never took place. This was to have some importance at the time of the German offensive.

On this question, as on that of the General Reserve, relations between Haig and Pétain had been far more cordial than might have been expected. Haig admired Pétain more than any of his predecessors, and the admiration was mutual. This is what makes the eventual attitudes of the two men at the time of the German offensive so striking in their difference.

Meanwhile, Pétain's relationship with his own compatriots was far from happy. The tremendous opposition to his Directive No. 4 from so many of his generals had led to him being regarded purely as a man of the defensive; a man, moreover, who was prepared, for tactical reasons, to give up some of the hard-won ground in the front line. We have already seen some of this opposition, which had reached into political circles, with even Clemenceau taking part. (Between Foch and Pétain, it was clear which Clemenceau would approve; and it was only the weight of Haig which had made him tip the balance of his approval on the matter of reserves.) Above all, there was Foch, the man of the offensive, the complete opposite of Pétain in almost every way. If one had combined the *good* qualities of these two men, as Fayolle noted, one could have created a leader complete in every way.[57]

Foch had had a somewhat chequered war career, but was now very powerful once more. After brave if foolhardy action in the Battle of the Frontiers in 1914, he had been put in charge of co-ordinating Allied action during the 'rush to the sea'. Then, at the head of an Army Group, he organised first the Artois battles, and then the Somme. After this he was *limogé* (removed from his command), in semi-disgrace. The beginning of his return came in 1917, when, after Nivelle's removal, he was made Chief of Staff to Pétain, at Pétain's own request (the alternative being Fayolle, somewhat more of a lightweight, whose appointment would, Pétain feared, be taken to mean that he wanted no counterweight to his authority near him).[58] This post, which Pétain had held under Nivelle for just over a fortnight, was attached to the Government rather than to the Command, as a kind of technical adviser.

In late 1917, however, Foch's position became more active. The defeat at Caporetto in October necessitated the sending of a French general to observe and to advise. Pétain and Foch each saw this mission as being part of their job. After an argument, however, Pétain gave in, and Foch went to Italy, with full powers. The brilliance of his fulfilment of his task made him, *de facto*, the commander of the French army in Italy, and even of that in the east. Pétain, in a sense, remained merely the commander of the western front.

On Foch's return to France, he naturally seemed more than merely 'Chief of Staff'. And with Clemenceau now Prime Minister he had strong political support; the two men were alike in temperament and in war aims. From this comes the fact that Foch became so important in the Inter-Allied Councils that we have seen.

Meanwhile, Foch was continually scheming for Pétain's removal as Commander-in-Chief. Pétain's unpopularity had made rumours of his removal rife;[59] but Foch, as Fayolle's diary shows, was actively plotting:

Foch was very pleasant. The outcome of all our conversations is that he would like to replace Pétain, at any rate to be the director of the war. At the moment, he is the military representative of Clemenceau, the true Minister of War....[60]

This in January; in February the situation was even clearer:

Dinner with Foch. I still feel his hostility towards Pétain. He is aiming at his removal, and in his view I ought to succeed him. At Rome he had already made this understood....[61]

So Foch saw Pétain, now, as merely the western front Commander, but wanted him removed even from this.

Foch is taking over more and more the direction of the war. He will have the power without its responsibilities. I will be his man on the French front, as he wanted me before to be his man in Italy....[62]

Two days after this, Fayolle was dining with Pétain:

Compiègne.... Pétain does not know what to do with me. He shares my opinion on Foch, and is as embarrassed as I was in Italy by his intervention.[63]

A week later, on 26 February, Fayolle was informed once again of Foch's intentions:

At lunch, Duval confirmed to me that Foch wishes to topple Pétain in order to put me in his place. It is being talked of. I don't wish to. This evening, dinner with Pétain.[64]

One gets the impression that Fayolle was being chosen by Foch for the same reasons that Pétain had rejected him, i.e., that he was too much of a yes-man. Be that as it may, Foch's plots had not come to fruition by the time the German offensive started. Indeed, on 14 March his Inter-Allied plans for a general reserve had been flouted in public at the Supreme War Council, by both Lloyd George and Clemenceau (put up to it, as we have seen, by Haig and Pétain).

So the Haig-Pétain alliance was Pétain's great strength at this time. Behind the scenes, on the French side, hatreds lurked. And above all the enmity of Foch. This was hardly the most favourable atmosphere in which to await the expected German attack.

The March offensive

For some time, since the Russian collapse, it had been clear that a German offensive was going to take place on the western front.* In face of this obvious threat, and of the state of the Allied forces, even the normally belligerent Haig had been forced to come round to the idea that, for the time at least, the Allied role would have to be that of the defensive.[65] Only in French military circles had there been disgust at this policy. But Pétain was still Commander-in-Chief, and the defensive remained the policy of the French army.

Where was the attack going to take place? Rumours abounded. In December, it was thought that it would be around Cambrai and in Alsace. In January, that it would be in Champagne. And so on. But when it did occur, its point of departure came as a surprise to the Allied forces.

The decision had been a difficult one for Ludendorff, the German commander. Many alternative schemes had been formed and discussed, involving the whole line of the front. Finally, on 21 January 1918, the decision was taken; the plan entitled 'St Michael' would be put into effect. This involved an attack on the southern part of the British army, between Arras and La Fère (just north of Barisis).

The reasons for this decision are interesting. On the negative side Ludendorff abandoned his favourite scheme of attacking the British in the fifty miles south of the coast (the St George plan) because of the danger from the weather, which had been shown so clearly in the muddy destruction of the British attacks at Passchendaele; and the section from Béthune to Arras was held in strength, particularly Vimy ridge. Ludendorff's aim, to destroy the Allies, depended in his eyes very much on the destruction of the British, so the sector between Arras and La Fère remained to him.

There were more positive, and more important, reasons for the choice however. Firstly, Ludendorff had learned that Haig had agreed to lengthen his line as far as Barisis, about forty miles, while still protesting of his shortage of men; the German attack, if slightly extended, was therefore striking the join between the British and French armies. Secondly, the attack would mean that reserves would have to be transferred from the coast area, where the St George attack could then take place. And this was even more certain because Franco-British attitudes were such that it was unlikely that the French would do much to help the British out. As one of the German Staff Officers, General von Sauberzweig, wrote:

The Eighteenth Army will . . . have only British opposite it. This will make the situation more favourable to us.

* As early as 13 December 1917, we find Terrier writing to Lyautey: 'And amid all this . . . our troops are awaiting the great German offensive, the result of the Russian defection.' B. Inst., MS 5903

The offensive is principally intended to strike against the British. They now stand opposite to us on the whole front of the Army Group which is to make the offensive. It need not be anticipated that the French will run themselves off their legs and hurry at once to the help of their Entente comrades. They will first wait and see if their own front is not attacked also, and decide to support their ally only when the situation has been quite cleared up. That will not be immediately, as demonstrations to deceive the French will be made by the German Crown Prince's Group.[66]

So we see the dangers of the policies pursued by the Allies in late 1917 and early 1918, mainly through the efforts of Haig and Pétain. There was no unified command; there was no general reserve; the defence of the line rested on private agreements between the two Commanders-in-Chief. This situation was to be deliberately exploited by the enemy, which was for a time to have considerable success in doing so.

Reports were varied, up till the last, as to where the attack would happen. An effort had been made, for example, by the Germans to make the French think it was going to take place on the Champagne front; and Pétain's belief that this might still be so, with St Michael as a feint, explains some of his reactions. Haig felt it was likely to fall more to the north; and he, too, suspected that the preparations which finally became obvious on the St Michael front in the week before the attack were nothing but a feint. So the two British armies most concerned (the 3rd under Byng, and the 5th under Gough) were not greatly reinforced; and Gough's army, in the south, was numerically incapable of resisting the vast onslaught which eventually descended on it.

The Germans, as well as possessing superior power in the sector where they attacked, had also perfected new offensive methods of infiltration, and of fluid penetration of the line, whereby any strongly defended positions which held out were by-passed, and left for others to mop up. Groups of storm troops formed the first wave, followed by battle units in larger entities. An important innovation was the fact that reserves were to be used to support those parts of the line that were advancing, and not those which were held up.

On 21 March, the attack took place, with uneven success. The greatest advance was that of the German 18th Army, under von Hutier, in the south opposite Gough. But at this stage, though the situation was serious, there was no cause for alarm on the Allied side. Haig remained calm. Herbillon, the French Liaison Officer between Paris and the High Command, described French reactions thus: 'The President of the Republic and Clemenceau are calm, General Pétain as well; but all are grave, for they feel the seriousness of the hour.'[67]

That evening, Pétain, in accordance with the agreement with Haig which had replaced the proposed general reserve, started sending three divisions to reinforce Gough behind his right flank. These would take until the 23rd to get into place.

The second day of the onslaught, the 22nd, followed in much the same manner as the first. The northern part of the German front advanced slowly; the southern very quickly. In accordance with its general tactical policy (though changing its original strategy, which was merely for the southern section of the line to guard the flank of the rest), the German High Command poured in reserves behind von Hutier, opposite Gough's army.

The Allies began to be more conscious of the great danger of the situation. Pétain, however, was reassuring in his report to Paris: 'General Pétain has told Challe to say in Paris that there is no need to be very anxious, for he has made his arrangements: all that is necessary is for the British to hold on the Somme—and that river seems easy to hold—and, with the forces he is getting together, he will get to work on the enemy flank. It will be a battle which we will take up in the best of conditions. The essential thing is for the British to hold on that front. Douglas Haig has promised him that they will. . . .)' [68]

However, as the day wore on Pétain's doubts about the British capability of holding on began to grow: 'General Pétain has repeated to me what Challe had told me, but, towards evening, he has become more anxious, seeing that the British are continually looking backwards; and he wonders whether they will really be able to hold on the Somme.' [69]

From this time on, the situation really began to deteriorate, though the main crisis came on the 24th. While the actual military situation was serious, however, the breakdown of the understanding between Pétain and Haig made it even more so. Many have been the criticisms of Pétain's behaviour at this time; his contemporaries, in their memoirs and diaries, have all found something to blame. Did he have a failure of nerve? Did he propose a defeatist policy? To what extent did his conversations with Haig rest on a misunderstanding? Let us examine the facts, and then try to make up our minds.

Saturday, 23 March: 'The situation is becoming serious. The British retreat is continuing.' [70] Poincaré tells us that Herbillon was sent by Pétain to see him, to warn him and Clemenceau that the situation was grave. 'The English were retreating too quickly and General Gough seemed to have lost his head. If the enemy advance is not stopped soon, the road to Paris could be threatened. Pétain is to go to see Haig this afternoon, to ask him to hold his army and bring reserves from the north.' [71]

At 4 p.m., Pétain went to see Haig. Their interview shows the first cause of their misunderstanding. Haig feared a German breakthrough to the north far more than the break-up of his right wing, which he felt that the French ought to relieve, for him to take troops north to Arras. Pétain, on the other hand, was worried that there were many German reserves still unused, and that they might attack the French elsewhere (the feints which the Germans had planned had had their effect). Nevertheless, both believed in the necessity for the two armies to stay in contact, and not be separated.

The two points of view are expressed quite clearly in two documents; Haig's diary, and Herbillon's memoirs (Herbillon, close to Pétain, seems to be expressing the views of the General here). Haig describes the meetings as follows:

> General Pétain arrived about 4 p.m. He has arranged to put two Armies under General Fayolle on my right to operate in the Somme Valley and keep our two Armies in touch with one another. Pétain seems most anxious to do all he can to support me and agrees that the only principle which should guide us in our movements is to keep the two Armies in touch. In reply to my request to concentrate a large French force (20 divisions) about Amiens, Pétain said he was most anxious to do all he can to support me, but he expected that the enemy is about to attack him in Champagne. Still, he will do his utmost to keep the two Armies in touch. If this is lost and the enemy comes in between us, then probably the British will be rounded up and driven into the sea! This must be prevented even at the cost of drawing back the North flank on the sea coast.[72]

Haig shows here, by the very form of words he uses, his uncertainty about Pétain. 'Pétain seems most anxious to do all he can to support me, *and agrees that the only principle . . . is to keep the two Armies in touch*', is followed by 'Pétain said he was most anxious to do all he can to support me, *but* he expected that the enemy is about to attack him in Champagne. *Still, he will do his utmost to keep the two Armies in touch.*' As Ludendorff had foreseen, national worries were bound to affect overall strategy in a divided command. This was true on the English side too, as Herbillon's memoirs show: 'Douglas Haig, asking help from General Pétain, is not trying to help him, in that he is continually thinking of moving northwards to cover his bases and not of trying to join up with us; it is we who have to stretch out our hand to him, and we are stretching too wide . . . we are stretching too wide. It is dangerous. Douglas Haig is fleeing from Pétain, one might say, and the unity of action which had been hinted at does not exist.'[73]

That this was essentially Pétain's view is shown by the similarity of phraseology in his speech on this subject, in 1931: 'I insisted on the irremediable character of any break between our armies, if he refused the hand I was holding out to him.'[74]

So, while both Commanders stressed the need for no break of the line, both were concerned with their national interests. This is not to deny the fact that Pétain was pouring in quite a large number of troops to support Gough. But the attitudes were there, and were to become more pronounced in the next couple of days.

The 24th was the great day of crisis. The evacuation of the Flesquières Salient by the 3rd Army meant that the lynch-pin of the Allied defence had gone. At 10 a.m., Pétain called Herbillon to him, and told him to head for Paris to see the Government:

> The situation is becoming even more serious, for the Germans have crossed the Somme and a possible break with the British army must be envisaged. He will do all he can to avoid this, and is bringing in divisions in all haste; it will be all the easier in that he had foreseen the situation, and the transport plan is fixed; it is

being carried out with the greatest rapidity, but the persistence of the British retreat, and Douglas Haig's obstinacy in continually leaning to the north, make him fear that he will be unable to hold the link; at any rate, he will cover Paris at all costs. . . . He urgently requests the Government to press the British to come towards him and not force him to stretch out indefinitely to reach them; without which they will be separated, and, in that case, Douglas Haig will find himself in a situation where he will be unable to hold out.[75]

Four things are important in this report: (1) The continued insistence on the need for the armies to remain united. (2) The stressing of Haig's obstinacy and unco-operativeness. (3) The importance of the defence of Paris, above all else (a national reaction). (4) The suggestion of the dire effects on the British army of a break in the line. All these things will have bearing on Pétain's line of action in the dramatic events later in the day, and in the next few days.

Herbillon's other message was to ask Clemenceau to go to see Pétain that evening. Before Herbillon's departure for Paris, three-quarters of an hour later, Pétain called him back to tell him that the situation was even worse, and that he might have to take grave decisions. Herbillon then departed for Paris.

The same morning, Loucheur, one of the French Ministers, went to see Pétain, who gave him a long résumé of the situation. It is Loucheur who gives us the first hint that Pétain was not as calm as he usually was: 'I have often seen him during the war, in the most difficult hours, always in control of himself, with a calmness which was impressive and at the same time reassuring. On that day, he was more worked up than usual.'[76]

Pétain explained that he had always feared a break with the British army. For this reason he had put several reserve divisions behind his left wing. But he could never have conceived such a destruction of the British line. The British 3rd and 5th Armies were retreating to the north. He envisaged the possibility that the left wing of the French army, separated from the British, might easily be turned and outflanked. He would then have to stretch out his front in order to rest that left wing on the sea. The only way to do this was to retreat and abandon Amiens, which was impossible, because of the importance of Amiens as a rail-centre. To sacrifice it would be to put Paris itself in danger. Everything must be done to avoid this danger. He had only a small number of reserve divisions, and would have to strip the front from Reims to the east. But there were certainly German preparations going on there for an imminent attack.

He was going to go, that evening, to see Haig to discuss the means of re-establishing the junction of the British and French troops.

Meanwhile, in Paris, Clemenceau, according to Poincaré, was full of pessimism:

Clemenceau believes the situation to be very grave. He expects our divisions between Guiscard and Chauny to be cut off from the British army, which is drawing back too quickly and too far to the north, without keeping contact.

Clemenceau can already see our mining area being invaded, our army turned, Paris threatened. . . .

Herbillon has brought me the news he gave to Clemenceau. It does not yet appear to me to justify the latter's pessimism. The break between the British and us has not yet happened; we are merely hard pressed. . . .

I fear greatly the contact that will take place between Clemenceau and Pétain this evening. Oh for the magnificent sang-froid of Joffre! Clemenceau, the romantic, the neurotic: France defending itself as far as the Pyrenees. Pétain, the critical mind. May not all this lead us to disaster?[77]*

Clemenceau visited Pétain that evening, setting off from Paris about eight o'clock. During the day, the events had moved quickly, and Pétain's pessimism had grown. This had, however, the opposite effect on Clemenceau than Poincaré had expected, as his remarks on seeing Clemenceau again show: 'Clemenceau . . . went to see Pétain yesterday at Compiègne. He blames him for speaking in an exaggeratedly pessimistic manner. "Can you believe it", the Prime Minister told me, "he said to me that if we were beaten, it would be the fault of the British" . . . Clemenceau has changed; he is now of the same opinion as myself. We must make a supreme effort to "close the gap", and not leave Paris at present. He blames Pétain for not doing quickly enough or willingly enough what was necessary, under the pretext that he might be attacked in Champagne. . . .'[78]

All was now set for Pétain's confrontation with Haig, which took place at Dury at 11 p.m. In this interview, Haig's first impression, like Loucheur's, was one of Pétain's mental state. This had become more aggravated since the morning, however: 'Pétain struck me as very much upset, almost unbalanced and most anxious.'[79]

Pétain's attitude in relation to a possible Champagne attack remained the same: 'I . . . asked him to concentrate as large a force as possible about Amiens astride the Somme to co-operate on my right. He said he expected every moment to be attacked in Champagne and he did not believe that the main German blow had yet been delivered.'[80]

But now came the shock for Haig. The realisation that for Pétain, and for the French, the defence of Paris was in fact more important than the liaison between the two armies, and that in that case the British army might be left to its own devices. As Pétain continued to speak, Haig became aware of the awful possibilities: 'He said he would give Fayolle all his available troops. He also told me that he had seen the latter today at Montdidier where the French Reserves are now collecting and had directed him (Fayolle) to fall back south-westwards towards Beauvais in order to cover Paris. It was at once clear to me that the effect of this order must be to separate the French from the British right flank and so allow the enemy to penetrate between the two armies. I at once asked Pétain if he meant to abandon my right

---

* Pétain's orders for the day to Fayolle have often been criticised. They were (a) to keep the French army as much together as possible, and not let the reserves be cut off. Then, (b) if possible, to keep in liaison with the British forces.

flank. He nodded assent, and added "it is the only thing possible, if the enemy compelled the Allies to fall back still further." '81

Any pretence of the Allies doing anything other than protect their own separate national interests was thus discarded. Pétain, worried by Haig's reactions, laid part of the blame on his Government: 'From my talk with Pétain I gathered that he had recently attended a Cabinet Meeting in Paris and that his orders from his Government are to "cover Paris at all costs." '82

No trace of any such meeting exists; indeed, the only statement we have about 'covering Paris at all costs' at this time is in the message Pétain sent to Paris via Herbillon that morning. Later, after the war, Haig asked Poincaré about this meeting, and was surprised to receive blank incomprehension in reply: 'From what he said, the President was evidently quite unaware that at the most critical moment of the German Offensive in March, 1918, Pétain had given orders to dispose his army so as to cover Paris from the German advance, instead of continuing to have as its main strategical objective the maintenance, at all costs, of close touch with the British Army ... Pétain said that he fully realised the consequences of the divergent retreat of his Army, but he "had his orders from his Government." '83

Pétain's use of his Government as scapegoat appears to have been false. The decision was his own. And it was a decision which, together with his obvious agitation, finally broke Haig's already waning confidence in him. In Haig's opinion, the very existence of the British army in France depended on keeping the British and French armies united. He rushed back to his headquarters, and telegraphed England to report the serious change in French strategy, and to ask for Lord Milner and the C.I.G.S., Sir Henry Wilson, to come to France 'in order to arrange that General Foch or some other determined General who would fight, would be given supreme control of the operations in France.'84

So Haig, in his reaction against Pétain, had finally become aware of the necessity for a united command, and was even prepared to serve under a Frenchman to achieve it. Only the events of the last couple of days could have forced him into this attitude. He had realised the dangers of a divided command, but he had also realised that he could not rely on Pétain; and, unable to make the French dismiss their own commander, he was to use the new post as a way of keeping Pétain down. As he was to put it much later: 'What was urgently needed at that moment was *a French Commander-in-Chief who would fight*, because Pétain had resigned himself to a policy of defence, and was ordering his troops to fall back, before there was good reason or they had been driven back by the enemy. I was prepared to subordinate myself to any French General who would keep the two Armies united, and contest every foot of ground with the enemy in his efforts to separate the British Army from the French.'85

The next morning in Paris, no idea of Pétain's decision appears to have got through. Clemenceau, recapping for Loucheur's benefit what Pétain had said to him last evening, merely said that the situation could rapidly get worse, and that if enough reserves could not get soon enough to 'close the gap', the British army would be forced to retreat northwards, whereupon the French army, to save itself, would have to retreat as well, resting its left wing on the coast. This is seen as a possible dire result of failure, rather than a policy in itself: 'We were all three (Clemenceau, Poincaré, Loucheur) agreed. What was important above all was to close the breach between the French and British armies. It was in this direction that General Pétain was already working. It was necessary for us to find out what he had prepared for this object.'[86]* Loucheur was therefore sent to Compiègne to see Pétain; while there, he was to fix up a conference for 5 p.m., in which Lord Milner would take part.

At lunch with Pétain, Loucheur was informed of the mounting losses of the British army. He also noted that Pétain was withdrawing many troops from the eastern frontier. Apart from this, not much in the way of strategy appears to have been discussed.

The conference, at 5 p.m., consisted of Poincaré, Clemenceau, Loucheur, Pétain, Foch and Lord Milner. Pétain explained that he was pouring in reserves, and Foch approved in general, stressing the urgency of as many reserves as possible. Milner, no doubt at something of a loss as the only British representative, said that he could not really speak without his own military men. A new conference was therefore arranged for the morrow, at Doullens at 11 a.m.

On Pétain's bearing on this day, the 25th, differing views exist. Fayolle describes him as 'calm'.[87] Pershing, the American Commander-in-Chief, who met him at 10 p.m., described him however as having lost his usual air of confidence and serenity. A great anxiety, he says, could be seen on his face.[88]

On the next morning the delegates began to arrive for the conference at Doullens. They were Poincaré, Clemenceau and Loucheur from the French Government, Milner from the British, and Generals Pétain, Foch, Haig, Wilson and Lawrence. Of these, most have produced diaries or memoirs. As is often the case in relation to this study of Pétain, and particularly with regard to the events of 1918, these witnesses are often biased. *Post facto* memoirs can be presumed to be more carefully organised than diaries, but even these latter reflect the preconceptions 'on the spot' of their authors. Nevertheless, from the tangle of evidence on the Doullens conference certain things are clear.

Before the conference, Clemenceau appears to have told Poincaré that he had discovered Pétain's true attitude. (This would seem likely, given the fact, as we have seen, that the French were ignorant of it, and that the British knew it; Haig or one of the other British may have told Clemenceau.)

'Clemenceau sadly informs me that General Pétain is envisaging a withdrawal of the French army to the south while the British army would be withdrawing to the north. Pétain had, added Clemenceau, given orders in

---

* Cf. Poincaré, op. cit. p. 86. 'Clemenceau . . . is of the same opinion as myself. We must make a supreme effort to "close the gap", and not leave Paris at present. He blames Pétain for not doing quickly enough or willingly enough what was necessary. . .'

consequence. Foch confirms to me this last bit of information and communicates to me the order for retreat signed by Pétain.'[89]

Foch declared himself to be completely opposed to this. A short time later Clemenceau took Poincaré aside and said: 'Pétain is infuriating with his pessimism. Can you imagine something he said to me which I would confide in no-one else but you. It is this phrase: "The Germans will beat the English *en rase campagne*; after which they will beat us as well." Should a General talk or even think thus?'*

The conference opened with Clemenceau asking whether Haig meant to defend Amiens, or to continue falling back. Haig assured him that he would hold on north of the Somme, though there was nothing he could now do south of it—besides, he had now put under Pétain's command all that remained of the 5th Army. Immediately Pétain drily intervened: 'Very little of it remains, and one can really say that that Army no longer exists.'[90] Haig continued his report.

Then came Pétain's turn. 'He set forth the situation as he saw it and as it was in reality, that is to say pretty bleak, and brought out all the difficulties which had faced him since 21 March.'[91] He announced, however, that having thinned out his eastern front he now had twenty-four reserve divisions that were being sent into the battle area. Of course, they were far from being fresh, and some had just fought. And the realities must be faced. A considerable time would be needed to get them into action. Nevertheless, he had sent all available troops into the Amiens sector, not hesitating to strip the French front in the centre and the east. He asked Field-Marshal Haig to do the same.

Haig replied that there was nothing he would more like to do, but that he unfortunately had no reserves. A lengthy silence followed this statement.

According to certain accounts Foch, during Pétain's slow analysis of the situation, had burst out 'We must fight in front of Amiens! We must fight where we are now! We must not give up an inch of ground!' After which Haig said: 'If General Foch will consent to give me his advice, I will gladly follow it.'

Milner and Clemenceau now withdrew to a corner to discuss things. They returned with a proposal. The draft of it read: 'General Foch is appointed by the British and French Governments to co-ordinate the action of the British and French Armies around Amiens. To this end, he will come to an understanding with the two Generals-in-Chief, who are requested to furnish him with all necessary information.'[92]

Pétain agreed to accept this. But Haig did not think it went far enough.

---

* This statement appears in Clemenceau's memoirs in the following form: '. . . The exclamation of a French general who, pointing at Sir Douglas Haig nearby, said to me quietly: —There is a man who will be obliged to capitulate *en rase campagne* within 15 days, and we will be lucky if we are not obliged to do the same.' Clemenceau *Grandeurs et misères d'une victoire* Paris 1930, p. 22. That the phrase is authentically Pétain's is shown by its use (*'capitulation en rase campagne'*) in an account by Herbillon of a statement made by Pétain the day before. Herbillon, op. cit. entry for 25 March 1918

He suggested that Foch should be put in charge of all Allied armies from the Alps to the North Sea.

'It was decided that AMIENS MUST BE COVERED AT ALL COSTS,' he writes. 'It was proposed by Clemenceau that Foch should be appointed to co-ordinate the operations of an Allied force to cover Amiens and ensure that the French and British flanks remained united. This proposal seemed to me quite worthless as Foch would be in a subordinate position to Pétain and myself. In my opinion, it was essential to success that Foch should control Pétain; so I at once recommended that Foch should *co-ordinate the action of all the Allied Armies on the Western Front.* Both Governments agreed to this . . . Foch seemed sound and sensible, but Pétain had a terrible look. He had the appearance of a Commander who was in a funk and had lost his nerve.'[93]

In this way the supreme command came to Foch. New orders were despatched on the 27th to Fayolle, commanding the troops which had replaced Gough's 5th Army. They contradicted those he had received a few days before, and insisted on maintenance of the liaison between the two armies, and the protection of Amiens. Even now, however, Foch and Pétain did not give exactly the same orders; the difficulties of a commander-in-chief of the French army having over him a supreme generalissimo were already showing themselves: 'So, since yesterday, Foch has intervened. We must cover Amiens. Important order: (1) Amiens, (2) Noyon. Pétain, this morning, telephones me and says: (1) Noyon, (2) Amiens. The day before yesterday, "Withdraw to the Oise." Moreover, he has no plan. . . .'[94]

Fayolle, who knows little of the dramatic events at Doullens, though he realises that the Government must have intervened, cannot understand Pétain's change of mind: 'All in all, Pétain has no plan, and has given two different directives. The first, to support ourselves on the Oise and give up Amiens; the second, to cover at the same time both Paris and Amiens, which is impossible. Foch gives a different directive, but a bad one, which is to re-establish the front in the gap of sixty kilometres between Noyon and Amiens. . . .'[95]

By the 28th it is clear to Fayolle, however, that 'Pétain is floating in the wake of Foch, who still displays the same audacious, iron temperament.'

The decision to close the gap between the two armies, and to fight, was taken at Doullens. Foch's co-ordination of the Allied forces meant that the outwards movement (the British to the coast, the French to Paris) was checked, and that the armies presented a united front. By the end of March the first danger was past; though, as Barrie Pitt has shown, the halting of the German advance was as much due to faults in the German fighting forces as to anything else.

How does one explain Pétain's part in all that happened? The problem rests on three points: (1) Was Pétain tactically and strategically incorrect? (2) Did he show pessimism in relation to the events concerned? (3) Did he show panic or any emotional weakness? And if these things are true, how does one explain them?

(1) On the question of his tactical decisions. It is clear that the divided

command lent itself to the pursuit of individual interests rather than the good of the whole. The arrangements made between Haig and Pétain with regard to reserves were inadequate for such a vast German onslaught. To his credit, Pétain far exceeded the amount of reserves he might originally have been expected to give. But the two Generals were unable to agree as to general tactics. Haig feared an attack in the north, and wanted to send his troops there, while the French replaced his right wing. Pétain feared an attack in Champagne, and merely wished to send troops to support the British right. Thus there appeared the possibility of a gap between the armies. By the 24th, however, both Generals were aware of this danger; and, while Haig felt that the contact between the two armies was the most important thing, Pétain did not do so. For him the defence of Paris came first, even if it meant abandoning the British army.

That he gave this order is clear. Certain biographers have attempted to deny it. Others have muddled the various meetings of these two days (e.g., Blond). Others have attempted to say that the order of the day given to Fayolle on the morning of the 24th ['(a) To keep the French army as much together as possible, and not let the reserves be cut off, (b) then, if possible, to keep in liaison with the British forces'] was the order referred to, despite the fact that the situation, and Pétain's own mind, were clearly different by the evening. Others have attempted to palliate it in other ways; Bourget, for example, intercalates the italicised phrase into the following quotation from Haig's diary: ' . . . had directed him, *if the enemy continued his advance*, to fall back south-westwards towards Beauvais in order to cover Paris.'[96] Pétain's order was, however, definite. Fayolle's remarks in his diary on the 27th have made that clear. Further evidence is given by Poincaré's memoirs, in which Clemenceau informs him of the order, and Foch shows it to him, on the 26th. Pétain's defenders have often accused Poincaré of being a hostile witness to the events of 1918; but he can have had no knowledge of Fayolle's diary (published in 1964) or of Haig's diary (published in 1952). The way in which the evidence fits together shows that it must be true.

Pétain's decision was unknown to his Government; yet he used his Government's name to support it. It was a measure which he clearly felt was in the interests of his country; yet he must have realised that it was a purely short-term interest. With the British driven to the Channel ports and defeated, France could not have lasted long.

This foreshadows 1940 in more senses than one. Haig's initial insistence on 'withdrawing his hand while the French held out theirs to him' instilled in Pétain a mistrust of the British and of their egocentric approach to the war. On the other hand, Pétain's own insistence on his national interest, his disregarding of the safety of his ally, his shortsighted view that France came first, was repeated in the Second World War as well.

(2) Was Pétain pessimistic? The answer appears to be yes. The tactics we have just seen are hardly those of an optimistic man. This could, however, be described as realism. The might of the Germans was such that it was better to look things in the face, perhaps.

The fact remains that a General should not instil in others the unease that he himself feels. Yet Pétain clearly made a whole series of remarks that could hardly be aimed at anything else. Again, while it might be argued that one or two observers might be biased, the weight of evidence is such that it is clear that he did speak thus.

He had, of course, a reputation for irony and for *humour noir*. He also had a reputation for speaking his mind. Bourget suggests that his main aim may have been to shock his hearers. But, if he was being ironical, the most that one can say is that his irony was misplaced. Certain well-meaning biographers have suggested that it was better to be realistic and to speak one's mind, than to live on false hopes; yet realism does not have to go so far as suggesting that all is lost.

At any rate, this was not realism. The outcome of the March campaign made it clear that a firm line would save the danger. Yet if Pétain had been allowed to continue with his line all *might* have been lost.

There are two forms of 'pessimism' in Pétain. One, which was a rational belief in the importance of the defensive and the difficulty of the offensive, and which was qualified as 'pessimism' by his colleagues, was purely a tactical sense supported by strong arguments as to the dangers of the alternatives. The other, with which we are dealing here, is true pessimism in the face of a threat from the enemy; a belief that all is going as badly as it possibly can.

We have already seen hints of this pessimism in earlier events of the war, particularly at Verdun. There is little doubt that the experiences of the war, and particularly of Verdun and the mutinies, had accentuated in Pétain a natural tendency to look on the black side of things. This, too, will be of importance in relation to 1940.

(3) Did Pétain show panic, or any emotional weakness? This is hard to answer. Pessimism does not necessarily imply panic. Pétain was certainly worked up during these few days. Such different men as Loucheur, Haig and Pershing all noticed it. His normal calm had deserted him. Other reports describe him as calm;[97] but some of these were written after the event (Mordacq) and some are obviously unreliable. Loucheur, for example, describes Pétain on the 26th as 'having his usual calm, tranquil confidence',[98] but this is in one of three large set descriptions, outside the diary format, which cover the days of the 24th, the 25th and the 26th; and some months later, discussing the writing of the set piece on the 25th, Loucheur writes that he has taken it to Clemenceau who 'asks for two little suppressions so as not to attack Pétain. They do not change the sense, so I accept. . . .'[99]* This makes Loucheur's account of the 24–26th rather suspect, as being written after the event. Milner's account is, however, more convincing. He saw Pétain as 'cold and circumspect', a man 'playing for safety'.

So Pétain may or may not have been worked up. But does it necessarily

---

* Poincaré writes, in his entry for 27 March, 'Loucheur is not happy with Pétain, whom he finds completely defeatist, and who said to him a few days ago: "We must start negotiations for peace".' Poincaré, op. cit. p. 93

mean, in Haig's words, that he had 'the appearance of a Commander who was in a funk and has lost his nerve'? Haig was never the best judge of character. Pétain may merely have been angry with the British attitudes of the last few days, and angry at the appointment of his enemy Foch (despite Herbillon's later statement that Pétain had welcomed it). Certainly it was clear from now on that Pétain and Foch would be at loggerheads. Clemenceau mentioned these fears to Haig on the 30th: 'Clemenceau spoke most freely about Foch's position. He had no fears about me loyally doing my best to co-operate. It was Pétain and Foch who he feared would squabble. "Pétain", he said, "is a very nervous man and sometimes may not carry out all he has promised." Personally, I have found Pétain anxious to help and straightforward, but in the present operations he has been slow to decide and slower still in acting. At times his nerve seems to have gone, and he imagines that he is to be attacked in force. Hence the troubled position of affairs round Amiens.'[100]

The question of whether Pétain had 'folded up' or not is doubtful. His natural pessimism, without panic of any kind, may have been the cause for his actions. But these actions, and the reasons for them, had caused him to be in a poor position in relation to his rival Foch. Clemenceau and Poincaré were now even more clearly than before on Foch's side. This was to have important results in relation to the May campaign in Champagne.

Chapter Four

Foch and the armistice

EARLY in April Foch's hand was strengthened still more by the Allied Governments. At a conference at Beauvais on 3 April, the following agreement was made:

> General Foch is charged by the British, French and American Governments with the co-ordination of the action of the Allied Armies on the Western Front. To this end all powers necessary to secure effective realisation are conferred on him. The British, French and American Governments for this purpose entrust to General Foch the strategic direction of military operations. The Commanders-in-Chief of the British, French and American Armies have full control of the tactical employment of their forces. Each Commander-in-Chief will have the right of appeal to his Government if in his opinion the safety of his Army is compromised by any order received from General Foch.[1]

So Foch was responsible for strategy, Pétain merely for tactics. And, while Haig might be heard if at any time he complained to his Government, Poincaré and Clemenceau, faced by a complaint from Pétain, would be more likely to agree with Foch. This situation was to bedevil the French cause for the rest of the war, for whereas Foch had been the right man at the right time in a crisis, Pétain was clearly the man most capable of assessing a military situation in normal circumstances. In the conditions of 1918, Pétain's calm rejection of the heroic for its own sake, his assessment of the requirements of a reasoned defence, were what was needed. As we shall see, in the May campaign his was the more useful role, when he was allowed to play it.

Meanwhile, in April, the main German attack had shifted to the British line north of Béthune (a modified form of the St George plan, minus the Ypres part). The pressure was off the French for a while. Fayolle, describing Pétain during this period, finds him in varying moods. On one occasion he finds him '. . . Very gay. I think it is because Foch has taken charge of operations.'[2] But most of the time he finds him 'pessimistic.'[3] By this Fayolle clearly means that Pétain does not believe in the offensive for the moment. It is for this reason that one must closely examine the accusations of 'pessimism' and 'defeatism' flung at Pétain during this war. Only too often they mean that Pétain is not in agreement with the opinions of the writer, and that he is avoiding a useless offensive. This is a far cry from the more real pessimism to which we have seen Pétain a prey at Verdun and at the

March Offensive. Fayolle's remarks run as follows on one occasion: 'Lunch at Beauvais with Pétain (Hôtel Continental) ... He says some deplorable things, showing that he does not believe in the possibility of an attack... This man does not believe in the offensive. A little more, and he would be defeatist! He does himself harm and it is doubtful whether he will finish the war as Commander of the French forces...'[4]

It was becoming clear to many, in Paris as well as at headquarters, that Pétain was no longer the main figure on the French side. Terrier writes to Lyautey on 4 May: 'I have learned that the star of General Pétain is rather low in the firmament. He is said to be blamed for being discouraging and for having remained in stagnation, awaiting the German offensive. As for General Foch, he is highly in favour [*sa côté est absolue*].'[5]

It is easy to see that Foch's views on the offensive, which Pétain and Haig had both discounted, were coming back into favour now that he was in power. And on another matter, even more vital, Foch now expressed himself, contradicting Pétain's policy.

We have seen how, in early 1918, both Foch and Clemenceau had criticised and contradicted Pétain's views on the defensive, whereby defence in depth, with the main force in the second line, would prevent useless losses. Now, on 5 May, Foch sent a note to the Commanders-in-Chief, and to the army and army group commanders, which entirely contradicted Pétain's Directive No. 4:

> ... On those parts of the battle front where we must keep on the defensive, the main aim is to dispute the ground with the enemy foot by foot, and in all events to prevent a rapid penetration of our positions.
> ... Consequently, there can be no question of lines of advance posts or observation posts, and of lines of resistance.
> ... On all the battle front, there is close contact with the enemy, and he is aiming at close and important objectives. Any withdrawal, even on the most limited scale, would thus be playing the enemy's game.
> ... Hence the imperious obligation, on the whole front, for no unit to retreat of its own accord.
> ... Every unit, whatever its position, must defend at all costs the position that has been entrusted to it.
> ... There can be no question, for any reason, of a voluntary withdrawal.
> ... There must be organised, without delay, behind the first line position, a series of lines of defence. ... On the day of an enemy attack, these lines should be filled with some light units, coming from the reserves or from the rear.[6]

This was, of course, the opposite of Petain's orders, in that it placed the main defensive force in the front line, and forbade any form of fluidity or tactical withdrawal. Fayolle, bewildered once more by the contradictory orders he was receiving, had a row about this with Pétain on the 7th: 'I had a row with him, because of the divergences between the orders or indications that he gives, and those of Foch. Basically, the latter has taken over the whole command and I find myself right between them. Pétain is not at all happy. His situation is a good deal diminished, that is certain. But I can do nothing about it. . . '[7]

By the 19th, the discord between Pétain and Foch was even clearer: 'There is still discord between Pétain and Foch. The latter would like to attack, the former does not want to. Pétain exaggerates the strength of the Boche, Foch does not appreciate it at its true value. They are both right and they are both wrong. They ought to be combined to make one single man, a truly complete leader.'[8]

Meanwhile, it was becoming clear that a new German offensive was imminent. Haig and Foch were convinced that it would come north of the Somme, near Arras. Pétain objected early in May to the weakening of his own sector, and was sent some British troops, who had fought in the April campaign, and who were thus being sent to a 'rest sector'. As the month went on, however, signs came that the attack might well be coming in the Chemin-des-Dames area, though these were on the whole ignored until a day or two before the German attack, which took place on 27 May.

The German breakthrough was immediate and complete. Within one day the German assault troops advanced twelve miles, an unheard-of distance. What had happened?

The main trouble was that Duchesne, the general whose 6th Army held most of the threatened front, had insisted on putting most of his men in the front line. Though Pétain was still putting forward his own views on defence, and though many generals were following them, a man such as Duchesne, fixed in his ways (and a former Chief-of-Staff to Foch), was able to disobey them with impunity, because of Foch's directives, and known opinions. Duchesne's attitude had been much discussed, but Pétain had not felt himself capable of insisting on his authority, and had finally allowed him to do as he liked.

Most of the men were destroyed in the two and a half hour bombardment that preceded the German advance. By midday the Germans had advanced five miles and had crossed the Aisne, where Duchesne had been too late in destroying the bridges.

The true causes of this collapse were not made known at the time. Abel Ferry, however, the clear-minded parliamentary representative who was sent to report on it, expresses his opinion in his diary thus:

> I was asked to make a report on this retreat, which was so incomprehensible to all at first. I pressed my enquiries and finally found where the smell came from. Pétain had not been obeyed. But Foch and Clemenceau were accomplices of the disobedience.
>
> Ah! If I only had to deal with a Government which I did not wish to support! But Foch is untouchable since he has come to represent the little military authority we may have over our Allies. And Clemenceau is at the moment the depositary of the moral patrimony of France.
>
> I say enough in my report for them to understand. I say enough to cover and support Pétain. I don't say enough to create . . . a weapon of opposition.[9]

Pétain now found himself in a bad position. His reserves, as he complained to Mordacq on the 28th, had been sent to the north by Foch. (No doubt Pétain had 'cried wolf' so often about an attack on this Champagne front that nobody had taken it seriously, not even himself.) As the German forces advanced, nothing seemed to stand between them and Paris. Pétain flung some reserve divisions before the onslaught, giving him time to dig a stronger defensive position. Finally, what with American reinforcements and the deterioration of the German troops, the German attack was halted, on 1 June.

Meanwhile, in Paris, unaware of the rights and wrongs of the case, people were demanding that heads should roll; Duchesne, Franchet d'Esperey, Pétain, Foch, all were mentioned. But on 4 June, Clemenceau declared his faith both in Foch and Pétain, and gained a rousing majority in the Chamber. Nevertheless, throughout the month criticisms of Pétain mounted (Ferry's report had not yet been made). On 26 June, Loucheur noted: 'Clemenceau is talking of the enquiry that will have to be made about the Aisne battle. One feels that it will perhaps be necessary to come to the point of replacing Pétain.'[10] A few days later Clemenceau, coming from the front, told Loucheur that he had seen Pétain, who had offered to sacrifice himself, asking only for the command of an army corps. Clemenceau had replied that there was no question of that at the moment.[11] The same scene is described by Clemenceau in his memoirs.[12]

The Germans had left the French very little respite. On 9–10 June they attacked again, in the region of Noyon. Here again, but to a lesser extent, Pétain had been hindered by Generals Humbert and Debeney's adherence to Foch's principles of defence. But enough had been done to ward off the German attacks, and on the 11th, Ludendorff called off this offensive as well. The area was commanded by Fayolle, and both he and Mangin (who had now returned to active service) were infuriated by Pétain's refusal to countenance the counter-attacks which seemed to them so opportune. Fayolle's diary on the 10th, 11th and 12th reflects this annoyance, culminating with the following remarks: 'Pétain is infuriating with his lack of confidence. In fact, we are living from day to day, putting up with the enemy's will. When one spends one's time parrying without being able to riposte, the danger merely grows with time, because we are worn out as time passes.'[13]

Fayolle is here unjust. The Noyon defence was the best so far, and it was the Germans who were getting worn out, not the French.

There now occurred a rest for the Allied forces. For over a month the line was to remain fairly static. Any drama was provided by the relations between the Generals. After the Battle of Noyon, Pétain was told by Foch to send units north to the British. Foch felt that the next attack would take place around Arras; it was also clear that the British had sent many troops to the Noyon front. Pétain, however, was convinced that the Germans were going to attack in Champagne. Invoking the Beauvais agreement, he made use of his right of appeal to his Government on 16 June.

Clemenceau was embarrassed. After consulting Poincaré, he upheld Foch, while managing to make the demands a little less excessive. Nevertheless, he decided to withdraw from Pétain this right of appeal.

Relations between Foch and Pétain had not been helped by the former's removal of the latter's Chief of Staff, General Anthoine, and his replacement by a more 'positive' character, General Buat, and by the fact that these things had been done without prior consultation with Pétain.

The Foch-Pétain situation was to be further aggravated during the final German offensive, which fell in Champagne on 15 July.* Before this attack, when it became clear that it was to threaten mainly the Eastern sector of this front, Pétain and Foch did admittedly come to agreement about the general strategy to be followed; but events were to destroy this fragile agreement.

This strategy was one of elastic defence east and south of Reims. (The two Generals were now in agreement on this principle of elastic defence.) This was to be followed by counter-attacks on the sides of the German advance; and then a large attack was to be launched on the whole west flank of the Marne bulge, by the 10th Army under Mangin, the fiery colonial officer who had once more, with Foch's ascension to the command, returned from disgrace, with his reckless courage and offensive spirit undamped.

In contrast with his June attitudes, Foch had also agreed to a strong reinforcement of this front, and had sent reserves from the Amiens area; for on this occasion it was clear where the attack was coming.

On the question of methods of defence, Pétain was slightly more successful than he had previously been in persuading the Generals on the spot to obey his directives. Admittedly Degoutte (on the south bank of the Marne, covering Paris), and Berthelot (between the Marne and Reims) did not obey them; the first, probably because of the danger to Paris and because of the mythical importance of the site of the first Battle of the Marne, the second, probably because of his own crass stupidity. But Gouraud, east of Reims, fulfilled Pétain's wishes as to elastic defence.

Gouraud had not always been as willing to accept this idea; indeed, at first he had been angered by it. But either he was won over by Pétain's arguments, or else, if he tried to appeal over Pétain's head, he received no encouragement. For Clemenceau, as Ferry informs us,[14] had by now become aware of the reasons for the initial disasters of May, and 'no longer dared attack Pétain's directives'; and Foch also had come to accept Pétain's tactics.

The German attack took place on 15 July. It laboured under two disadvantages before it started; the lack of secrecy in its preparation, and the fact that it had been announced to the German troops as the 'Peace Offensive' (a fact which would tend to discouragement if the attack did not immediately succeed). In fact, the Germans had here put themselves into a position almost identical, in these two disadvantages, with that of the French at the time of the Nivelle offensive in 1917.

---

* Accounts, after the event, of Pétain's goodwill towards Foch (such as those of Serrigny, and of Pétain himself) are rather suspect.

On Gouraud's front east of Reims, the German advance was at first seemingly easy; but eventually they reached the main line of the French defences, which were almost unharmed by the artillery bombardment. The French machine-gunners, safely ensconced in their prepared positions, shot them down before they had any chance to get to grips. Few of the Germans ever reached the main French defences.

West of Reims, the Germans had easily broken through Berthelot's front; and further west still, they had succeeded in crossing the Marne, which Degoutte had thought that they would find most difficult. All was well, however. Pétain, realising the weakness of Berthelot's defensive measures, had concentrated his reserves on the slopes of the Mont des Reims, five miles behind his front, and these reserves halted the German attack; while the German troops which had crossed the Marne, through Ludendorff's awareness of the dangers of their pressing on by themselves, had to halt of their own accord.

By noon on 16 July, it was clear that the attack had not only come to a standstill, but had also failed. The architect of this French defensive victory was certainly Pétain. As Ferry was to say in his diary, Pétain's method had been applied, and 'it was this method by which Gouraud was able to hold on, and to serve as a pivot for Foch's counter-offensive. It was this method which saved Paris. But the Government arranged things so that nobody talked in the Press either about the method, or about the true victor, Pétain.'[15]

Pétain's defence may have succeeded; but in the meantime a disastrous rift had taken place between himself and Foch. The original plan had been for Mangin's counter-attack to take place on the west of the Marne bulge; but on the morning of the 15th, at the height of the German attack, Pétain, finding himself short of troops because of the deployment of his reserves behind Berthelot's line, rang Fayolle at 10 a.m. and told him to suspend the preparations for Mangin's counter-attack. It was too early for Pétain to tell whether his defensive measures were completely succeeding, though it was clear the Gouraud's line was holding; and he was dangerously short of reserves.

Meanwhile Foch, going to Mouchy to meet Haig, happened to call in at Fayolle's headquarters. He was much annoyed when he heard of Pétain's order. He had promised the British that Mangin's attack would take place; he was, at any rate, convinced above all of the value of offensive warfare; and he did not see the situation around Reims in as dangerous a light as did Pétain. Even if it were dangerous, Foch saw the remedy to it in a counter-attack of this type, which would threaten to strangle the German forces. So he countermanded Pétain's order on the spot, told Mangin to continue his preparations, and had a telephone call made to Pétain, telling him to change nothing in his plans.

Tactically, Foch was no doubt right. As in other circumstances, Pétain was too inclined to 'play safe'. He was unable to take a calculated risk, or, indeed, to view a whole situation strategically. The defence of the Gouraud and Berthelot lines showed his virtues; the postponement of the Mangin counter-attack suggests one of his faults, while Foch's refusal of this postponement shows one of *his* few virtues. As Fayolle had said, some combination of the two men would have made the perfect commander. Certainly, from this stage of the war onwards, Foch's offensive spirit came into its own, and was indispensable.

But Foch's method of countermanding the order, without consultation with Pétain, was insulting beyond belief. Fayolle's statement of what happened shows the bluntness of it all:

> Our counter-offensive looks good. It will take place the day after tomorrow. Yesterday, at 10 a.m., Pétain suspended it. At noon, here, Foch re-ordered it. That's a good thing. . . .[16]
>
> Pétain wanted to give up the counter-offensive to close the Marne pocket. Foch reverted to the counter-offensive. The success is due to him. It all took place in my office at Noailles. We were delighted, after having been consternated by Pétain's decision. At heart, the latter is very timorous. It was evident that the counter-offensive should be allowed to go forward, since on the right Gouraud's line had held.[17]

The counter-attack, which took place on the 18th as planned, was a great success. Ludendorff's army lost many men, and much material. From now on the war was to be a question of Allied advances.

Within the French army, the dispute of July 1918 led to bitter recriminations. Mangin, above all, was highly critical of Pétain. His letters, published later,[18] show this, as did his conversations at the time. Ferry, writing on 30 July, deplores the attitude of the generals:

> I have just come back from the front. What mediocrity of character there is in our great leaders! They are even more backbiting than parliamentary deputies. They are devouring each other in victory, as they did in defeat.
>
> Mangin . . . clearly, from his conversation, has only one preoccupation: to win over his interlocutor. He aspires to becoming Generalissimo, and he already has people on his side.
>
> I am forced to admire the feline suppleness of his attacks against Pétain. They have in them something that is strange, indefinable and savage. It is not conversation, it is a poisonous palaver from Central Africa.
>
> Pétain did not want the July 18th offensive . . . The proposition came from him, Mangin; the Americans understood that the only thing was the offensive; Pershing gave the order to burn Pétain's instructions.
>
> And I sense a grim effort on the part of the generals, as they struggle against each other for the favour of the Allies.[19]

Fayolle's diaries reflect the same kind of dissatisfaction, but in a minor key. He appears to disapprove of both Foch and Pétain, both of whom he believes to be seeking the limelight while it is he, Fayolle, who is doing the work and earning the victory.[20]

But it was clearly Mangin who was the most vociferous of such critics;

Fayolle's criticisms, for example, were mostly confided to his diaries. Mangin organised his own publicity:

> There is a complete publicity campaign organised round Mangin. There is a complete campaign of silence around Pétain. Besides the differences in character of the two men, there are two principles in opposition to each other: Pétain is a *Cunctator*, Mangin a man of the offensive. Pétain spares the blood of his men, and is a kind of Turenne: he is popular. Mangin, among the troops, is called *the Executioner*. I have just seen his unpopularity in the tank units. He is however a brave man, who risks his own skin as much as that of others. He is what the eighteenth century would have called an *homme de main*. Pétain is a brain.
>
> Poincaré and Clemenceau are for the offensive method. They don't like Pétain, whose pessimism annoys and disconcerts them. Pétain exaggerates difficulties, and those who govern us like illusions.[21]

So Pétain's part in the achievement of July was played down, and never reached the Press, while both Foch and Mangin received great publicity for the more spectacular achievements of the offensive. There was even a campaign to whitewash the Nivelle offensive of 1917. This had started in June, as Terrier tells us in one of his letters: 'General Nivelle is returning to court, and it would not be surprising if M. Clemenceau brought him back one day.'[22] By August, Ferry makes it clear that the campaign was gathering momentum. The claim was that Nivelle's offensive would have succeeded, and had only been stopped by the politicians. Mangin and Foch supported it, because of their rivalry with Pétain (and because of Mangin's own part in the offensive). Poincaré, Briand and Viviani were among the politicians who took the same line. And, finally, there was Clemenceau 'not unhappy to see Painlevé destroyed and Pétain taken down a peg or two.'[23] Ferry, however, published the facts about the Nivelle offensive in *L'Oeuvre*, and the campaign fell to the ground.

Mangin's self-advertisement was felt by some, however, to be more than an attack on his enemies, and a desire for military advancement. Ferry, on 6 September (two days before his death), went to warn Clemenceau about the political dangers of Mangin:

> I went to see him about the publicity given to Mangin in the papers. Great ladies are going round the newspaper offices on his behalf. It's like the beginning of a Boulangist dawn. . . .
> —Ah, I am very glad you've spoken to me about it, said Clemenceau, who then spoke of his tribulations with all these generals who spend their time quarrelling and playing tricks on each other. Annoyed by Mangin's publicity, he had got Foch to write to him. Mangin believed that it was Pétain who had set Foch against him and complained to Clemenceau, who undeceived him.[24]

Amid all these squabbles, however, the Allied campaign continued well. Admittedly, from now on the French were to play less part than the Americans and the British. A memorandum sent by Pétain to Foch on 31 July, had shown how few reserves the French had, and how exhausted their forces were.

A series of offensives, in which the French forces ably seconded the British and Americans, took place in August and early September, and drove the Germans back at various points of the line. It was on 26 September that the final, major Allied assault began. By early October, Pétain was ordering his troops to attack with unlimited objectives, and to allow the enemy no respite. The time for carefulness was past, the enemy was in disorder, the war was almost over.

In these last weeks of the war, discussions naturally took place as to the terms on which an armistice with the enemy could be reached. On 25 October, Pétain, Foch, Haig and Pershing met at Senlis. All were agreed that an armistice should aim at preventing the Germans starting to fight again if there was a breakdown in the peace negotiations. Pétain and Foch insisted on the necessity for the occupation immediately of the left bank of the Rhine: 'Pétain followed and urged the same terms as Foch,' writes Haig, 'viz. the left bank of the Rhine with bridgeheads. . . . Pétain spoke of taking a huge indemnity from Germany, so large that she will never be able to pay it. Meantime, French troops will hold the left bank of the Rhine as a pledge!'[25]

Pétain was here clearly looking beyond the armistice to the eventual peace terms. In looking for a French occupation of the left bank of the Rhine, he was in line with the majority of French military thought, which saw the natural barrier of the Rhine as the only real defence against a German resurgence. These military considerations were, for many Frenchmen, matched by political ones—the detachment of the Rhineland from an only recently united Germany, France's historic (and Napoleonic) claims to the left bank, and so on. A campaign had for years been waged by the *Ligue des Patriotes* on this subject; from 1917 to 1919 the campaign reached a climax, with Maurice Barrès producing fulgurating articles in *L'Écho de Paris*, closely followed by Maurras, Daudet, Pujo and Bainville in *L'Action Française*. The *Petite Bibliothèque de la Ligue des Patriotes* produced a series of volumes on the subject in these years. Though this appeared mainly a movement of the Right, Barrès was proud to proclaim in 1917 that men of all parties belonged to his 'Committee of the left bank of the Rhine.'[26]

The aim of this committee, stated in 1917, was 'No more German soldiers on the left bank of the Rhine'. With great foresight, Barrès declared: 'Our studies and our propaganda are inspired by the idea that no "scrap of paper" is worth anything to Germany, and that we must take precautions, "guarantees", against her.'

Many of the studies were, however, based on claims other than those of fear, and the justification for France's 'rightful' claims was made much stronger.

It is not clear that Pétain shared any of these further convictions; but it is certain that, like most other French commanders, he feared a German resurgence, and saw the left bank as the only guarantee, together with crippling reparations.

After the war, it became obvious that France's allies did not share her fears, and that they would not support the permanent taking of the left bank. Partly this was because of a belief in French 'imperialism', which some of the pamphlets of the *Ligue des Patriotes* can have done little to discourage. But it was also because of an incomprehension of the more reasonable French fears. At the Treaty of Versailles, the military (in the person of Foch) were to be, in their opinion, betrayed.

For the moment, in Pétain's eyes, the important thing was thoroughly to defeat the enemy. In the severity of some of his suggestions for armistice provisions lay the hope that the Germans would refuse them. The Germans must definitely be shown that they were beaten, and not allowed to find excuses of betrayal.

Pétain had planned a grand offensive, with the Americans, through Lorraine. The German left-wing facing them was falling apart, and they could strike right into Germany. But the armistice negotiations prevented this happening. In Pétain's repeated lamentations at this event we see not only the frustration of a military leader, but also a fear for France's position. On 9 November he spoke to Foch: 'I explained to him the immense differ-ence there would be between an agreement at our present positions and a brilliant, clearly French, victory over Germany . . . "I can well understand that Lloyd George and Wilson do not want too brilliant a victory, but what does Clemenceau really think." '[27]

Foch was not in agreement. He felt that the armistice could give as much as a victory, and said that he could not continue letting French soldiers be killed; Pétain felt that one should not think of the soldiers who would fall in the last offensive, but of the 1,500,000 who had already died, and who deserved a victory worthy of their sacrifice. Foch declared he felt he was doing his duty. Pétain, in despair, wept for the first time in his military career, on his own admission.

Throughout the inter-war period Pétain was to express his regret at the 'premature' armistice. In his speech on Marshal Foch to the French Academy in 1931, for example, he was to say: 'The armistice that he signed on 11 November, on French territory, spared the proud German army from a humiliating disaster, and allowed it to recross the Rhine without any worries.'[28]

Pétain's mistrust of the Anglo-Saxons was shown in his mention of Lloyd George and Wilson. As the years went by, he was more and more to feel that Britain had purposely betrayed the French so that they could not have the left bank of the Rhine. (The Americans were for some reason exempt from this criticism.) Pershing, the American, had wished to continue the advance with him, but the British had stopped them. In 1938 he was to say to Mrs Pardee, the wife of an American: 'Neither Pershing nor I wanted the Armistice. The complete left wing of the German army was in rout, and we could have gone as far as Berlin. But the English had been betraying us since August 1918, so that we should not have the left bank of the Rhine. It is easy to prove to the German people that they have not been beaten. I only hope that that does not lead us to a second World War even more terrible than the first! On the evening of the armistice, I wept.'[29]

On this note Pétain received the armistice, which took place on 11 November 1918.

Pétain in 1918

On 8 December 1918 Pétain became a Marshal of France. Within four years he had come from almost complete obscurity to the fame of a public figure; and in the years to come he was to be perpetually in the public eye. What impression do we get, from his 1914–18 career, of the kind of man he was, and of the kinds of attitudes he was likely to take?

Militarily, he was clearly an intelligent general, whose concepts of the nature of the war were modified as he came into contact with hard facts. His pre-war theories on the nature of fire-power had been proved to be in essence correct. But, faced by the new phenomenon of trench warfare, he had been one of the first to realise its significance. Seeing the techniques needed as being those of siege warfare, he had nevertheless at first believed in the possibility, and necessity, of a breakthrough; but the experience of the 1915 Artois campaign made him realise, one of the first to do so, its impossibility. Thereafter he moved to the concept of attrition; of attacks upon limited objectives, with overwhelming fire-power, in which enemy losses would be far greater than those of the attacker; of a gradual eating-up of the enemy reserves, which would prepare the situation for the final all-out attack. In the end his theory was proved correct, but not because the French had managed to save their own men while battering the enemy; rather because of the influx of new and fresh men from the United States and the Commonwealth. In defence, he developed new methods of elastic defence in depth, which took full advantage of the new conditions.

One would have expected such a man, in the inter-war years, to have appreciated the inevitably changing methods of war. Unfortunately this was not to be the case. He remained fixed in the attitudes of the 1914–18 war, as the colleagues he criticised had remained in the attitudes of the war of 1870.

The 1914–18 war made of him essentially a man of the defensive. When the enemies were equal, he could see that there was nothing to do but sit tight. Offensives were possible, but only when you had a superiority of three to one, and overwhelming artillery support. Even then they had to be limited, as enemy reserves would rush up to close any gap formed, and one must break off before casualties began to become equal.

In most of the 1914–18 conditions these attitudes were to be sensible. Artillery, machine-guns and barbed wire weighted all on the side of the defence. Gas was an uncertain weapon. Tanks (especially the light Renaults which the French used) had not really proved themselves. The use of air power had not really developed. In the inter-war period, however, tanks and aeroplanes were to right the balance, without Pétain's fully realising it.

The same attitudes were not even reasonable in late 1918. Pétain's care, once open warfare had asserted itself once more, was out of place, and for once men such as Foch and Mangin were right. It was only when the German armies were in rout that Pétain's offensive spirit broke our once more, and he wished to pursue the Germans to Berlin.

Pétain's care for his men is legendary, and certainly he was one of the few first-war generals to bother about 'morale'. His arrangements for the men on taking over the Artois front, his insistence on the 'noria' system of replacements at Verdun, show this care for the fighting man. The mixture of firmness and humanity that he showed at the time of the mutinies witnesses to the same concern for morale.

But it is possible to exaggerate this into an emotional concern to save the life of each man, surely a weakness in a general. Pétain was a general, and a good general. To get men to fight well, it is important to keep up their morale. To win the war (especially a war of attrition) it is essential to save the lives of your own men, and kill as many of the enemy as possible. This is proper military strategy, and not weak humanitarianism. Pétain's conversation with Foch in November 1918, about the possible continuation of the war, shows that he was prepared for more deaths in order to get a complete victory.

Pétain's concern with the defensive was matched by a growing pessimism, as the war went on, with regard to military events. The shattering effect of the defence of Verdun in 1916, and of the army mutinies in 1917, had led him to view most subsequent events in their gloomiest light. When faced by an unexpected crisis, as in March 1918, he tended to fear the worst.

This is not necessarily to say, as some people have claimed, that he ever panicked; for this the case is obscure and not proven. But he not only foresaw what the worst possibility might be; in this case he acted on the presumption that it was going to happen.

And in the process he showed that for him, in the alliance, France came first (just as, to a great extent, for Haig up till this point, Britain had come first). When it seemed to have come to a choice between protecting Paris, or breaking the line and cutting the British off to the Channel ports, Pétain chose the former, even though this would eventually have meant defeat anyway; and he clearly saw the possibility of needing to sue for an armistice.

Haig's attitude in the two or three days before the crisis of 24 March, when he appeared selfishly to be moving his own troops northward, (and when both Pétain and Haig seemed to be at cross-purposes) had installed in Pétain a mistrust for British selfishness, which allied to the usual mistrust of the French military for 'perfide Albion', led him to believe in British treachery in the matter of the armistice, and their determination to do down the French. This mistrust of Great Britain was to colour many of Pétain's later views.

He developed other dislikes which were to be of importance, too. The mutinies of 1917 had shown him the dangers of international Bolshevism, and, like many other military men, he was never to lose his fear of this force. In his more political career from the 'thirties onwards, this was to be of great importance. So, too, was his contempt for politicians. Like many professional soldiers, he saw the wartime Government as having been weak and self-seeking. Criticisms of politicians abound in accounts of his conversations during the war, whether with Henry Bordeaux, with Serrigny, or with politicians themselves.

Not only politicians receive his criticism, however; at times, the form of Republican government too is criticised, as unable to deal with a war effort. His comments were at times made to the politicians' faces.

For he had retained that bluntness of speech which had characterised his pre-war utterances to his superiors, and which had been partly responsible for his lack of advancement. This, and a cold irony, were often supplemented by a straight-faced humour which disconcerted those it was aimed at, while disarming other observers.

Pétain's private personality had remained much as it was pre-war. He loved light conversation, questionable jokes (some of his colleagues were shocked at his apparent superficiality), reminiscences of past amorous adventures. Above all, this old bachelor still continued his own series of love-affairs. Indeed, at one time it appeared that the Germans might have planted one attractive woman on him as a spy. (French Intelligence managed to get hold of a telegram from the German Ambassador in Madrid referring to the matter.)[30] Despite the fact that Pétain had re-encountered a former love, Eugénie Hardon, in 1916, and that he was to marry her after the war, the bachelor existence appears for the moment to have remained unchanged.

So Pétain emerged from the war. As we have seen, his career seems to have fluctuated in 1918; but the public was little aware of this. Created a Marshal of France on 8 December 1918, Pétain marched into the inter-war period with the eyes of France on him. The hero of Verdun stood, above all, for the summit of French heroism in the war; that heroism which was to be commemorated on so many War Memorials and in so many Old Soldiers' Associations. He was to be a symbol more than a man, and as the other Marshals gradually died off, he was to remain alone as a kind of father-figure of France, the man to whom she could turn in an hour of trial.

Of this he became more and more aware. The self-satisfaction which Fayolle noted at his meetings with Pétain during the war was to remain a constant part of his character—hidden under the appearances of modesty. In a quiet, decided way Pétain was certain that he was superior to other men; the aura of the Marshalship did little to dissipate this impression.

PART II

Chapter One

Private life, 1918–39

THE various public activities which occupied Pétain in the inter-war period would seem to leave hardly any time for a private life. Nevertheless, in the first couple of years after the war it looked as though he was preparing for that retirement which had already been on the cards before the war. On 14 September 1920, he got married, at the age of sixty-four. He and his future wife had already been house-hunting, and had found a country house in the South of France, 'L'Ermitage' at Villeneuve-Loubet in the department of Alpes-Maritimes.

Like many men in military life at that time, Pétain had remained a bachelor throughout his active military career. His bachelor existence had, as we have seen, been filled with amorous adventures. He was a handsome and striking man, whose amazing clear blue eyes seem to have exerted a fatal fascination on women; and he himself was strongly and physically attracted to the opposite sex. Even by the time of the 1914–18 war, when he was at the sixty mark, these adventures do not seem to have lessened in number. Pétain was always aware of the presence of attractive women; in his short-lived military diary of 1914, some of the best-documented facts had been the physical descriptions of the women in the houses at which he had stayed. His attitude to women was, on the whole, that of any other garrison man: he was prepared to talk about past affairs, and to laugh and joke about the women with whom he and others had been intimate. There appears to have been little other than the physical in these relationships. At the end of his life, senile and in captivity, he was to recapture some of these attitudes in his conversations with his jailer, Joseph Simon: '*Le con et la gueule, il n'y a que ça de vrai!* . . . I have had some mistresses for whom, afterwards, I kept my friendship.'[1] Senile as he may have been at this time, the statement rings true.

Many men who enjoy such fleeting affairs, nevertheless have at the same time one or more lasting relationships. This is true of Pétain. He had known Eugénie Hardon since her childhood; she was over twenty years younger than him. In 1901, when she was twenty-one and he was forty-five, he had asked her parents for her hand in marriage, but had been refused owing to the discrepancy in their ages. In 1903 she married a young painter, Pierre de Hérain, with whom she was to have some happy years of marriage; they separated, however, just before the war. It was in 1913 that Pétain was to get in touch with her once more.

The passionate letters which M. Amouroux has printed in his book *Pétain avant Vichy—la guerre et l'amour*, show us a Pétain at first ignored by the woman he loves, and in despair. In 1914 Mme de Hérain was finally divorced, and returned to her maiden name of Hardon. Soon, the letters became more intimate, but Mme Hardon still found Pétain too 'impregnated with physical love' to return to her; Pétain replied by saying that the physical side was essential to love. On his departure for war, Pétain was still filled with 'moral tortures' caused by the harshness of his loved one. It is in 1916 that the breakthrough seems to have occurred; indeed, we now know that it was with Mme Hardon that Pétain was spending the night at the Hotel Terminus-Nord when Serrigny came to call him to Verdun.[2]

From Verdun, Pétain wrote to her almost every day. This seems to have been the time of the height of his love. As the Verdun campaign went on, he began to refer to settling down in some quiet spot after the war with her; the South of France was the specific spot he mentioned. In 1919, though worried as to whether they would be happy together if he lost his independence, he finally decided that happiness would lie in this marriage, and the ceremony took place in September 1920.

Did his love for Eugénie Hardon mean that he gave up his old habits? Many of his wartime letters seem to have been devoted to quietening his future wife's jealousy and suspicion: 'Be assured that you have nothing to fear from A, or from anybody.'[3] 'Modification to my letter of June 26: in place of "I have little time to devote to your enemies, women, read 'I have not the slightest time to devote to your enemies, women"';[4] 'I cannot deny that people are greatly occupying themselves with me, and in particular women. If I had not found you again, I would doubtless have continued to glean here and there, without becoming permanently attached to anyone, for there is one fact that you cannot contest; since you have come back to me, all my old flames have disappeared as of no interest.'[5]

Are we to take such letters at their face value? There is no knowing. Amouroux takes every word as having been sincere, and indeed they may have been. Pétain's love may have been so strong that he had no other affairs on the side. On the other hand, if he had, his letters to Mme Hardon would have been much the same. Pétain was obviously strongly susceptible to the physical delights of love, and may well, when away from his loved one, have assuaged his desires in the way he always had done. The story of the 'beautiful spy' dates from 1917. On the other hand, he was also very fond merely of the company of women, and the many women who were around him at this time may not have been more than company. It is almost impossible to tell, and it is of no real importance, except that Amouroux's hagiographical picture of the perfect lover may not be as true as he would like to think.

Certainly Pétain does not seem to have been an absolutely perfect husband. Though he appears to have continued loving his wife, he also, despite his age, had mistresses as well. Whether, in every case, the relationship was physical (given his age) it is hard to say; but his contemporaries believed them to be so. He also, of course, enjoyed flirtatious conversations with perfectly respectable women such as Mrs Pardee; but with other women the relationship was more serious. One lady who knew him in the 'thirties replied to me, when I innocently asked what he was like as a person: '*C'était un jouisseur, voilà tout . . .*' ('He was a man devoted to the enjoyment of women, that is all.') And she went on to say '. . . *Et derrière ces beaux yeux bleus . . . il n'y avait rien*' ('And behind those beautiful blue eyes . . . there was nothing.')

In his senile ramblings to Joseph Simon, Pétain mentioned that he had often deceived his wife with other women. He also boasted that he had last made love in 1942, when he was eighty-six: 'You have to be healthy for that!' While we know that Pétain was physically remarkably preserved, with surprising strength for an old man, one cannot really trust the last statement, though we know that he did deceive his wife continually in the 'twenties and 'thirties.

Pétain's private love-life has little bearing on his public life (except in so far as the cult of purity under his rule at the time of Vichy, and his worship of the cult of the family, seem rather out of place). Other aspects of his private life do, however, find echoes in his publicly-expressed ideas; and some of the contacts he made in the semi-public life of Paris were to be of influence on him.

Firstly, 'L'Ermitage'. The time he spent in this retreat was certainly not as much as he originally intended. While there, however, he was able to play the part of the simple peasant, attached to the land. These were sincere emotions; not only was he proud of his peasant origin, but he took delight in the simple pleasures of country life. It was also part of his traditional view of the life of the nation, supported by the simple peasant virtues, which was to be so important in his political thought. 'I love the simple pleasures,' he wrote to Mrs Pardee, 'and making my own wine, even though it is not of superior quality, gives me great joy and a certain pride.'[6] His letters, to his wife and others, were full of details with regard to crops and wine-making. Photographs showed him at work; one delightful one showed him with a basket on his head, surrounded by grape-pickers. 'It is very hot,' he wrote in a 1924 letter, 'the grapes have ripened well, and the picking will begin tomorrow, with the help of the young girls and young women of the neighbourhood. There are arguments about places . . . there are about fifteen of us; we enjoy ourselves, and laugh very much.'[7]

These rustic pleasures were but a small part of Pétain's life, however. His new eminence meant that he was received in the highest circles in Paris. Not only military and governmental circles, either. He frequented the *salons*, and became part of the *vie mondaine* in the capital. Even during the war, when he was Commander-in-Chief in 1917, he had been a centre of attraction for society women; Serrigny, his aide-de-camp, had written: 'These women seized every pretext: charity, propaganda, politics, the needs of the sick, etc. Today it was Baronesse Henri de Rothschild, tomorrow Mme Harjès, wife of the American banker, Miss Morgan, actresses, women of letters, women in love. Many of these women received, I think, unequivocal evidence of the chief's admiration. At any rate, he delighted in inviting them to his table. . .'[8]

Now Pétain was *persona grata* in the Paris salons. Here he met many people of importance, in the fields of politics, the arts, and high society. One of the politicians who was to be of great importance to him, Henri Lémery, describes how he met him: 'I had fought under Marshal Pétain's orders at Verdun without knowing him, and without coming near him. After the war, the chance of mutual acquaintances had led us to meet at Her Majesty Queen Amélie of Portugal's, at Count de Leusse's, and at other *mondain* lunches.'[9]

As well as *mondain* life, Pétain became part of certain smart intellectual circles. Two exclusive literary clubs to which he belonged were the Déjeuner Paul Hervieu, and the Dîner Bixio. At the first of these he met the politician Louis Barthou, whose political opinions were so different from his own, but for whom he had trust and affection. They were to be colleagues in the Doumergue Government. Other important figures who were members of this same lunch-club included Léon Bérard, who was to negotiate with the Spanish nationalists, and draw up the agreements which Pétain, as ambassador, defended in 1939; Maurice Paléologue, the diplomat; Maurice Donnay, Pol Neveux and Paul Valéry. The last-named was one of the Marshal's greatest admirers, and produced the great speech in his praise, for his reception in the French Academy, which is still quoted in all works in honour of Pétain.

Valéry became quite a friend, as did one or two other literary and artistic figures. Some might be expected: Henry Bordeaux for example, who had spent quite a bit of the war at the front and with Pétain, as official historian. Others were less expected: Abel Hermant, the author of *Cavalier Miserey*, for example, and the artist Forain. The last-named was a brilliant caricaturist, who had produced some violent and vicious work in the magazine *Psst!* at the time of the Dreyfus Affair. A close friend of Huysmans, he had been converted to Catholicism at the beginning of the century. He remained, however, a man of brilliant, if usually superficial, ironic wit. His irony was more on the surface than Pétain's; nevertheless the two men found a certain amount in common, and took pleasure in each other's company.

The Marshal not only had literary friends; he also had literary aspirations. Most of his speeches and articles were written by subordinates, yet he spent as much time correcting their style as their content. Two or three witnesses declare his purist care for the French language. He cut down their prose to the bare minimum, and produced a sparse, clear and classical style. His favourite reading, like de Gaulle's, appears to have lain in the French seventeenth century. One of his greatest delights, when an academician, was to go to the regular sessions on the Dictionary, whereby it was decided which words should be included.

It is a custom in France for military men to become members of the French Academy, and, indeed, to become members of the other academies comprising the *Institut de France*. Pétain became a member of one of these other academies, the *Académie des Sciences Morales et Politiques*, on 5 July 1919. The speech in his honour, with which he was received, was made by M. Morizot-Thibault, President of the Academy. It was an eulogy of Pétain's military skills and valour. Pétain, however, chose to point out, in his reply, the close links between the nation and the army, and the educative role of the academicians. He started with an example of his famous irony; his first sentence must have come as a shock to the serious academicians: 'The ladies are certainly interested in the choices made by the Institute.'[10] He went on to explain that a young woman he knew, surprised by his being chosen, had written to him, suggesting that as he obviously did not know very much at the moment, she would lend him some books so that he might educate himself.

He went on to describe the army as being not only vitally connected to the nation, but also a sociological reflection of it. 'It is, inevitably, the seat of those complex social phenomena to which you all—philosophers, historians, moralists, statisticians, jurists, financiers, economists—devote your lives of work and reflection.' Their works went out to the whole world, and, in France, contributed to the formation of the soul of the country, and of the army. On their side, the military leaders had contributed new fields for study. Army and scholars were thus collaborators.

In view of Pétain's political fear of the effects of Republican education, and of intellectualism, which we shall see later, such views are surprising. We must not forget, however, that this speech was made on a public occasion.

Pétain did not reach the great honour of becoming one of the 'forty immortals' of the French Academy until 1931, when he was unaminously elected to the chair vacated by Marshal Foch. The reception took place on 22 January. The speech of welcome was made by Valéry (Barthou had tried to get it, but had been refused). This is a glorious piece of French prose, and one of the greatest passages of praise of Pétain ever to be written. Pétain's own task was to make a speech on his predecessor Foch. When he had given his subordinates the material to make up the speech, they had been surprised by the lack of praise; all it had been was a series of criticisms. The final speech, written by Major Montjean on the basis of a plan by Major Audet, contained a certain amount of praise, but a great deal of criticism. Pétain had not forgotten his disagreements with Foch, nor had he forgotten the mistakes he believed to have been made in the strategy of the war.

Pétain's sponsors were Paul Bourget and Maurice Paléologue. Most people had not expected Marshal Lyautey—at enmity with Pétain since the Riff War—to turn up, but he arrived with one minute to spare, bounding agilely across a table (at the age of seventy-three!) to reach the door before it closed. Lyautey had been a member of the Academy since 1920.

The Academy soon made Pétain *conservateur* of the Château de Chantilly, an honorary post which nevertheless gave him a flat in the lodge at the entrance to the château. Here he spent some very happy times. There is a splendid photograph in existence of him and his wife on horseback in the park before the château.

Pétain's public life in the 'thirties consisted of official missions to Italy, Poland, the United States, Great Britain, Yugoslavia; of a military campaign in Morocco, and an ambassadorship in Spain; of the highest military post from 1920 to 1931, followed by an important position on all top military committees; of a governmental post in 1934, followed by a certain amount of political involvement. Yet despite this he managed to have a full and varied private life, ranging from the peasant pleasures of 'l'Ermitage' to the society world of Paris, and from the domain of Chantilly to the company of literary men. Everywhere he went he was accepted, and gatherings of people were dominated by his calm and impressive figure.

Chapter Two

Military career, 1918–39

THE Third Republic had, until the First World War, neglected to continue the custom of creating Marshals of France. The title, though glorious, was filled with monarchical and imperial overtones; and among the last holders of it had been Bazaine and MacMahon, both of them politically anti-Republican.

At the height of the war, however, the title was revived. Not for any glorious reason, but to give a sop to Joffre's pride, as well as to disarm public opinion, at the time of Joffre's removal from the command of the French Armies at the end of 1916. Soon other Marshals followed. On 6 August 1918, Foch was made a Marshal of France; Pétain, on this occasion, was given the Military Medal. On 20 November, just after the armistice, Pétain was given the title. He was to be followed by others: Lyautey, Franchet d'Esperey, Fayolle.

The ceremony of Pétain's elevation to the rank of Marshal took place at Metz on 8 December 1918, the day of the triumphal entry of the French army into that town. It took place in front of Joffre, Foch, Haig, Pershing, and representatives of the Italian, Portuguese and Polish armies. The Marshal's baton was presented by Poincaré, who said in his speech: 'You have obtained from the French soldier all that you asked of him. You have understood him, you have loved him, and he gave back to you in obedience and devotion all that you gave him in solicitude and affection.' The legend of Pétain the leader who cared for his men was to continue throughout the years to come.

The presence of Joffre at this ceremony was in part due to Pétain's own solicitude for his colleague. The Government had said that if Joffre wished to take part in the triumphal entries into Strasbourg and Metz, he must get there under his own steam. Pétain had sent him his private train.

Pétain's elevation to the rank of Marshal heightened his already strong impression on the people of France. For whole sections of the people, forgetful now of all the criticism they had showered on the generals at critical points of the war, the victorious generals were a race apart, the saviours of France. Not knowing the events of 1918, the furious feuds between the generals (who were now publicly assumed to have 'been on perfect terms'), they tended to see them as all worthy of praise; but especially Pétain, whose name was indissolubly connected with the defence of Verdun, the symbol of French valour in the war. Pétain was seen, too, as the general who had closest to his heart the welfare of his men. The Old Soldiers' Associations, formed to keep all these memories alive, naturally looked to him as the symbol of all they stood for. Most of the French army had, at one stage or another, passed through Verdun; Pétain stood for their sacrifice.

Being a Marshal added to this. It is hard for British people to understand the almost religious fervour which was aroused by this office. We tend to see generals, and even field-marshals, as being like other men. They may be good at war, but they are not necessarily good at peace. They do not necessarily stand for 'all that is best' in a country; their views are not necessarily more valuable than those of others. The amusement with which many of the post-war views and attitudes of Field-Marshal Lord Montgomery of Alamein are received clearly makes this point. In France, however, there was at this time an almost mystical fervour with which many people received the holders of this office.

Pétain was eventually the last of these Marshals to remain alive. After Lyautey's death in 1934, only he and Franchet d'Esperey remained. Unlike Marshal Juin, who in the 'sixties was the last remaining Marshal of France after the Second World War, Pétain was not in a position where the worth of the Marshalship had been once more devalued by a recent holder of it; nor was he governed by a two-star general who, refusing promotion, had made of his present rank something more glorious than being merely a Marshal. Pétain, as Marshal of France, was the holder of the nation's honour.

All this must be understood if the amount of trust put in him in the inter-war and Second World War period is to be comprehended. He was the well-loved leader of men, and at the same time the charismatic symbol of French victory. Politically, his views were not really known; like many other military men, he declared himself not to be interested in politics. But in comparison with the others (Lyautey, Weygand, etc.) his reticence made him seem really non-political; and so, without effort on his part, and without real justification, he became known as 'the Republican Marshal'. One more reason for the Government, despite his advanced age, to entrust him with important posts of various kinds in the years to come.

Pétain rather than Foch?

From the armistice to February 1920, Pétain remained Commander-in-Chief of the French armies. This was, of course, the period of the troubles over the peace treaty. Foch, still Generalissimo of all the Allied forces, took a strong line over the question of the Rhine frontier. Like Pétain, he saw it as the only safeguard for France in the future. The army, and the French Right, considered that the Rhineland should either be annexed (an extreme measure) or should become autonomous. There was a lot to support the second measure: historically, there was a Rhineland mistrust of Prussia, which had been strengthened by Rhineland Catholic apprehensions about Prussian religious policy. The Allies, however, saw French fears as 'imperialism', and French interference in German internal affairs as power politics of an unreasonable kind.

Foch's concern was above all military. He had spoken in a note on 27 November 1918, of the necessity for a 'barrier of common security' on the Rhine. On 25 February 1919, Clemenceau, taking the same view, suggested an independent, neutral left bank of the Rhine, under League of Nations guarantee. This was strongly opposed by the British and Americans, who saw the prospect of another Alsace-Lorraine situation, and further troubles. On 14 March Lloyd George, President Wilson and Clemenceau met, and argued the matter out. Lloyd George proposed an alternative: a guarantee of immediate aid to France, if she were attacked by Germany. The French can be pardoned if they thought such an offer inadequate compared with the territorial guarantees they were asking for. On 17 March Clemenceau, while moving towards the Anglo-American proposition, asked for further guarantees: demilitarisation of the left bank, and of a strip fifty kilometres in width on the right bank.

Foch, when he heard of this, was furious and felt that Clemenceau had betrayed France by stepping from the original position. Clemenceau, of course, claimed he was being realistic, because the Anglo-Saxons would never have agreed to the original claims. From now on, Foch's activities became an active annoyance to the Government, who began to see Pétain as the reasonable man among the military men. Pétain, as we have seen, felt strongly about the left bank of the Rhine; but not once in this period do we hear of his making a public statement on this subject. Where Foch and Mangin were to get themselves thoroughly politically embroiled, Pétain remained aloof, and thus gained the Government's confidence.

Foch certainly did not remain aloof. He did all he could to oppose Clemenceau. By 28 March he had got Poincaré, President of the Republic, to write to Clemenceau opposing the proposed agreement; Poincaré refused, however, to intervene more fully, for legally and constitutionally it was Clemenceau who had the real executive power. On 31 March Foch, by his own request, set forward his ideas to the Council of Four: Clemenceau, Lloyd George, Wilson and Orlando. He was received coldly, and barely politely, and no notice was taken of his views. On 6 April Clemenceau made it clear to Foch that, though not all negotiations had been completed, Foch's left bank requirements would not be fulfilled.

From now on, even the bounds of politeness had been crossed. To Foch's request for all the delegates to be called together once more, Clemenceau replied that he no longer considered him to be a member of the French delegation. On 17 April Clemenceau asked Foch to arrange for the German plenipotentiaries to meet them on the 25th, to be informed of the treaty conditions. Foch was shocked that all should have been decided without a final consultation with him.

Things had reached breaking point. Clemenceau felt that Foch was being insubordinate; Foch felt that he was being snubbed. Each now acted in his own way. Foch arranged for an article to be published in *Le Matin* on 18 April which put forward his view on the question. He also gave an interview to the *Daily Mail* (published on the 19th) containing his criticism of the way things were going. Clemenceau, even before seeing this, had sent for Pétain on 18 April, to sound him out as to how he would feel about taking over from Foch.

On 28 April, unaware of this, Foch, who had learned the final treaty conditions, threatened to resign if they were not modified. Clemenceau, having already consulted Pétain, was able to take Foch at his word. Lloyd George and Wilson agreed to Pétain as Generalissimo, and Clemenceau got in touch with Pétain. Foch, out-manoeuvred, withdrew his resignation. He nevertheless, on 6 May, spoke out at the Peace Conference against the clauses in question, throwing everyone into some confusion. The British and American delegates were amazed at what amounted to insubordination on the part of the military. Bonar Law, who was present, felt that no British general would have been maintained in his command if he had behaved in this way to his Government.[1]

Meanwhile, in the Rhineland itself, Foch's subordinate Mangin had been encouraging local separatist elements, and, above all, had decided to back a certain Dr Dorten as opposed to such men as Konrad Adenauer. On 1 June Dorten published a manifesto declaring the foundation of a Rhenish Republic. This was an almost immediate failure. The important thing, for our purposes, is that though much of Mangin's activity was undertaken off his own bat, he clearly had blanket approval from Foch, as did General Gérard, in a similar operation in the Palatinate. The Allies, and particularly Lloyd George, condemned the actions of the French generals.

Pétain appears to have kept clear from such ventures as much as possible. He made no public pronouncements, and avoided any political commitment. It did not merely need the fact that his old enemies Foch and Mangin were involved to make him take this attitude. He clearly, though feeling strongly about the Rhine situation, felt it was a matter for the Government. Indeed, when in 1923 the question of Rhineland separatism again raised its head, and Mangin brought Dorten to Paris to meet various important people, military, political, and journalistic, Pétain was the only major military leader not to be visited; it was clear that he had given the impression that he did not wish to be involved.

Clemenceau said of Mangin and Gérard, on 2 June, 'At the moment, I have to struggle every day against generals who leave their own domain and commit faults that I regret.'[2] It has been suggested that, if they had succeeded, Clemenceau might not have had this opinion of them. Be that as it may, the intrusion of French military men into politics (Foch, Mangin and Gérard) was by now causing Clemenceau much embarrassment with his allies.

Foch showed further concern with politics when, the Germans having demurred at the peace conditions, he was asked to put forward an Allied plan of attack on Germany. The strategy he put forward, based on the fact that they now had only thirty-nine divisions, was not a direct march on Berlin, but an advance along the valley of the Main, while encouraging a separatist policy for south Germany. He suggested that the Allies should be prepared to treat with the individual States, Bavaria, Würtemberg, Baden, the Palatinate, etc.*

Clemenceau, when this was put forward to the Council of Four on 16 June, rightly declared that this was political, rather than military strategy. Some while ago, Foch had presented a perfectly reasonable military plan to attack Berlin; now he was asking for political action, and saying that any other was impossible. Lloyd George made the same comments, suggesting that Foch was letting politics cloud his judgement on military matters. Weygand, Foch's adjutant, angrily attacked Clemenceau. Tempers were high, and Weygand's actions were not to be forgotten.

After the meeting, the politicians agreed that this had been a mere continuation, on a larger scale, of a Mangin-type separatist policy. It was Foch's new way of trying to get his own way. As for Wilson, he was convinced, as he put it, that the greatest danger was to leave Europe in the hands of General Weygand. Here, in the council room, he had seen a threat of that militarism which it was his aim to stamp out. Prussian militarism was not for him the only dangerous form of this attitude.

On 23 June, twenty-five minutes before the expiry of the Allied ultimatum, the Germans agreed to sign the treaty; there was no more need for a plan to invade Germany. On 29 June in the Hall of Mirrors at Versailles, the treaty was signed. Foch was conspicuously absent, as was Pétain. (Joffre, too, was absent, getting an honorary degree at Oxford.)

The events of these six months do much to explain the almost immediate disappearance of Foch from the public scene, and the choice of Pétain to rule military affairs in France. Foch was dangerous and political. Pétain, despite his remarks during the war, had remained aloof from any kind of political action in these hectic months, and therefore seemed comparatively safe. His military tactics had done much to win the war for France, and he would clearly take all the care possible about the military side of things; he did not have (or at least he did not show) political ideas about strategy, nor did he, like some other military men, appear a danger to the Republic; he was a 'Republican Marshal' who would never be suspected of fomenting a *coup d'état*; he was still active, despite his age. The highest posts were now open to him.

Pétain's inter-war military career

The war being over, the post of Commander-in-Chief of the French Armies was due to disappear, as soon as demobilisation had been satisfactorily achieved. So it was that in January 1920 Pétain gave up his command. Now, if any, would have been the time to replace him by Foch (whose command had also ceased), if the feelings of summer 1918 had still been extant. But, as we have seen, Foch had blotted his copy-book by his political actions of 1919. Pétain, therefore, was the Marshal chosen to head

* Right-wing writers, such as Bainville in *L'Action Française,* had for a long time been stating that the only answer to the German danger was for Germany to be divided up once more.

the army, with powers which eventually exceeded those he had held until now.

On 23 January 1920, Pétain was appointed Vice-President of the *Conseil Supérieur de la Guerre* (Army Council). The presidency of this body was held by the Minister of War. The Vice-President was in fact the military head of the body. He it was who would command the French Armies in time of war. The peacetime organisation of army matters consisted of a division between 'the authority which prepared for war and the authority which commanded in war'.[3] The former was headed by the *Chef d'état-major général* (Chief of General Staff), who was, for the first few years of Pétain's appointment, General Buat. The second was headed, as we have seen, by Pétain, who was also appointed Technical Adviser to the Minister. The General Staff, and therefore the Chief of General Staff, were in fact under his authority.

The Conseil Supérieur de la Guerre, as set up, was an unwieldy body, in which age had a preponderant influence. All Marshals of France were to be life members (Joffre, Foch, Pétain, Fayolle, Franchet d'Esperey, Lyautey). To these were added certain generals who would be retained beyond the age limit, and ten divisional generals (including the Chief of General Staff). They all had equal voting powers. The power of the aged in French military matters was marked right up to the Second World War, with disastrous results for French policy.

Pétain's authority was further strengthened when, on 18 February 1922, he was appointed Inspector General of the army. This confirmed his authority over the General Staff, and it was stipulated that the Chief of General Staff should submit for his approval anything to do with the structure or mobilisation of the army, before sending it for the Minister's signature.

Pétain's powers were thus very great. It has even been suggested by some writers that he had more power than the Minister himself. Certainly in the years 1920–31, when he held this post, Pétain ran French army policy. Around him he had former subordinates, who knew him of old and were on the whole prepared to fall in with his ideas: The Chiefs of General Staff were Buat (1920–3) and Debeney (1923–30), though Weygand came in for the last year (1930–1).

As Inspector General, Pétain also had a seat (in an advisory capacity) on the *Conseil Supérieur de la Défense Nationale* (Supreme Council for National Defence), the political body concerned with military matters of all arms, which contained both politicians and military men.

Throughout the 'twenties Pétain, from this position of great influence, put forward a policy based on what he took to be the lessons of the First World War. It was a policy based on defence, and on the use of strong fortified positions. Out of it grew the Maginot Line. We shall see in a later chapter the details of this policy, and the mistaken direction in which it took the French military effort. We shall see, also, the various other policies which Pétain pursued at this time. For the moment, the important thing is to stress the powers which he held, which enabled him to put forward such doctrines and see them obeyed.

It must not be forgotten, however, that his power to put these measures through was enhanced by the trust that army men, and the country as a whole, had in him. At this period his expressed views on strategy and tactics were hailed by almost all as being the valid voice of experience. It was only in the 'thirties that voices began to be raised in disagreement, and even then they did not have the power to break the grip of Pétain's policy.

During Pétain's period as Inspector General and Vice-President of the *Conseil Supérieur de la Guerre*, certain military events took place which naturally involved him: the occupation of the Ruhr (1923–5), when the French, to enforce payment of reparations, marched into the German industrial area; the Riff War, in which Pétain himself took a leading part; and the crisis caused by the influenza epidemic among the Rhine troops in 1928–9.

By 1930 both Pétain and Debeney were thinking of retirement; to succeed them, the choice basically restricted itself to two men, Weygand and Gamelin. In 1930, Weygand succeeded Debeney as Chief of General Staff. A year later, on Pétain's retirement at the age of seventy-five, Weygand became Vice-President of the Army Council, while Gamelin became Chief of General Staff.

Pétain was not to go into full retirement, however. On 9 February 1931 he became Inspector General of Aerial Defence of the Territory. Many people were shocked at his taking this minor post, and thought that it would have been more dignified for him to go straight into retirement; but Pétain happily set about his new job.

Much of his effort in it was concerned with attempting to persuade others to form methods of co-ordination of the various services, particularly with regard to air-power. In September 1931 he was himself given the task, by Premier Laval, of co-ordinating the measures against the nation's vulnerability to air attack; but he soon found that, with regard to the three departments concerned, Army, Navy and Air, he had no real powers. In December he wrote to the Premier suggesting the founding of a 'Ministry of National Defence'.

In the Tardieu Government, in February 1932, such a Ministry was created, with Piétri as Minister. It had no strength, however, because there was no military figure connected with it, as Chief of General Staff of National Defence. Pétain, speaking to one of the under-secretaries, pointed out this fault, and clearly hinted that he, who had been put into such a post by Laval, would be a suitable incumbent. Nothing came of this, however, and when Piétri created a new *Haut-Comité Militaire* (High Military Committee), Pétain was not on it. In a later letter to the Minister, on 18 April 1932, Pétain again stressed the need for a Chief of General Staff of National Defence (though in a letter to Weygand he suggested that he [Weygand] should be the man for the job). As he was not on the *Haut-Comité Militaire*, he tried to get Weygand (who was) to put forward his views.

The advent of the Herriot Government in June 1932, seemed to change the situation, however. Painlevé, Pétain's old friend and protector, became Air Minister, and took up the question of co-ordination of National Defence. In the *Haut-Comité* which the Government set up for this purpose, the Inspector General of Aerial Defence of the Territory (Pétain) was to take his place beside the delegates from Army, Navy and Air Force. Unfortunately, this committee never met; and meanwhile the military members of the old *Haut-Comité Militaire* (which did not contain Pétain) continued to meet. In October, Pétain sent a note on his views on the organisation of the High Command to all the relevant ministers and service chiefs. He got no reply from anyone except the navy, who opposed his plan (the details of which will be discussed in a later chapter); the rest appear to have ignored him. It is not even certain that they read his project at all thoroughly; he appears to have been regarded as aiming at something impossible. Altogether, his exercise of power seemed to be coming to an end.

This might have seemed to be borne out by the fact that a new *Haut-Comité*, which was to be set up to discuss the various problems and the diverse views upon aerial warfare, and at which Marshal Pétain was meant to preside, never met, 'for reasons of finance and of opportuneness.'

It took the Daladier Government, in 1933, to bring Pétain back into the limelight. Pierre Cot, the new Air Minister, and Denain, the Chief of General Air Staff, informed Pétain of their projects for the reorganisation of the Air Ministry, and particularly the admittance to the Air Council of people from the other war departments. Pétain, on the other hand, suggested that the best thing would be to submit all this to the *Haut-Comité*. In this Pétain was being crafty. Painlevé's *Haut-Comité* (which included Pétain) had, as we have seen, never met; and the new Minister, who had not heard of it, was not to know this. Pierre Cot read the details about it, thought it a good thing, and got Daladier to preside over it. It met twice, and the final result was that Pétain's own ideas, as opposed to those of Pierre Cot, were in principle accepted.

The fact remains, however, that the years 1931 to 1934 were those in which Pétain had the least actual power, and when his ideas seemed to attract the least attention. Suddenly, in 1934, all was changed, and for a political reason. Following on the riots of February 1934, and the fall of the Daladier Government, Doumergue, the new Premier, set about creating a Government which would restore national confidence. Who was more suitable to serve in such a Government than the Marshal of Verdun? Once more Pétain was called on to restore morale, this time civil morale. He entered the Doumergue Government as War Minister. The Government lasted until November, and during this time Pétain once more held the military reins; where, when he was Vice-President of the War Council, he had seemed almost more powerful than the Minister, he now, as Minister, exerted a great deal of power over his successor, Weygand. Indeed, being now a politician, he often took decisions which would have been amazing in him before; ministerial collective responsibility came before military needs, and he at times overbore or even ignored Weygand's views. He ruled alone, too, ignoring the views of the *Conseil Supérieur de la Guerre*, and neglecting to call together the *Haut-Comité de la Défense Nationale*.

This short spell in Government was important to Pétain's military career for other reasons, however. It restored him to a position of power on military matters, and he was to retain some of that power in a different form after the fall of the Government. In November 1934, he refused to serve in the Flandin Government, but his old friend and collaborator General Maurin was made Minister in his place. Maurin set up again the *Haut-Comité*, giving it wider powers as a *Haut-Comité Militaire*, and not merely a co-ordinating committee. On this committee Pétain was to sit by personal right (the only person not there because of his function, whether as minister or commander). At the same time Pétain was made, in his own right, a member of the *Conseil Supérieur de la Défense Nationale*, the body which, uniting politicians and army men, was at the head of the nation's armed forces. And this was not merely in an advisory capacity, as it had been in the 'twenties; Pétain had a *voix délibérative*, and had thus almost the powers of a minister.

So, in a finally co-ordinated system, Pétain held *in his own right* two ex-tremely important positions. And while others, members through their functions, might change, he remained. He also, as a Marshal of France, automatically held a place on the *Conseil Supérieur de la Guerre*.

On one more occasion he looked as though he might take up the political reins again; when, on 1 June 1935 Bouisson stated his new Cabinet (after the fall of Flandin), Pétain's name figured as Minister of State, alongside Caillaux, Marin and Herriot. But by 5 June the new Government had fallen. Until 1940, Pétain was not again to hold a Government post.

In 1939, however, a new career opened to him; that of ambassador to Franco's Spain. In early March he headed for Spain, from which he was to return at the time of the crisis of the fall of France.

This has been a short summary of Pétain's military career in the inter-war years, which will serve as framework to the more detailed studies of his military policy which will follow, as well as a parallel to his other activities as a public figure. The important thing to be understood is that, apart from a short period of three years, Pétain stood at the centre of France's military policy: from 1918 to 1920 as Commander-in-Chief; from 1920 to 1931 as Vice-President of the *Conseil Supérieur de la Guerre* and Inspector-General of the army; in 1934 as War Minister; and from November 1934 to 1940 as a permanent member, in his own right, of the *Conseil Supérieur de la Défense Nationale* and the *Haut-Comité Militaire*, as well as being, in his capacity as a Marshal, a permanent member of the *Conseil Supérieur de la Guerre*.

Chapter Three

The Riff War, 1925–6.
A military event

IN 1925, Pétain was called on once more to take over a military command, this time in a colonial war. The event is interesting not only because it shows us Pétain in a completely new type of military situation, but also because of the strained relations into which it placed him with another Marshal of France, and the insight it gives us into another facet of Pétain's personality. And, incidentally, certain political actions in Paris during the course of this war confirmed Pétain in some of his already negative political attitudes.

Some explanation of the background to the Riff War is needed, if we are to understand these matters.

In 1912, when France had established a Protectorate over Morocco, a Spanish zone had been created, covering much the same area as the Spanish 'sphere of influence' which had been agreed by a secret convention in 1904. The Spanish zone was the very northern part of the territory, opposite Gibraltar. With the exception of Tangier, which was an international zone, it stretched from the Ceuta peninsula to Melilla in the east, and inland to an imaginary line near the Wergha river. It contained the Riff, an area of high inaccessible mountains, with to the east a plain stretching as far as Melilla and to the west the Ceuta peninsula. The inhabitants, the Rifi, are mainly of Berber stock.

The Spanish protectorate had never been a happy one. Before the 1914–18 war it had been marked by heavy-handed tactlessness on the part of the Spaniards, and rioting and violence on the part of the inhabitants. The Spanish rule had not extended far beyond the coastal ports, though in 1913 Tetuan, the chief town of northern Morocco, had been captured, and was made into the Spanish capital. The mountains of the Riff remained on the whole independent.

In the French zone, on the other hand, things had been in the hands of one of France's greatest colonial administrators, General Lyautey, who had the political and military post of Resident General. This 'monarchist who provided an empire for the Republic' was fired by an aristocratic ideal which saw the best in the civilisations of others. His aim was to enable the Moroccan élite to rule for themselves under French tutelage. He saw the military's role as a social one, both in his own country and in conquered territory. Indirect rule, in the form of control rather than administration, was the ideal. His was a paternalistic view, which would find little favour nowadays, but in pre-war and immediately post-war Morocco it proved to be one of the most successful of colonialist ventures. So much so, that during the First World War Lyautey was able to control that part of Morocco which was already under French rule, with the minimum of troops, and despite the subversive activities of the German manufacturers based in the Spanish zone.

In the gradual conquest of the French zone (which was not to be completed until shortly before the Second World War), Lyautey relied on a technique of slow penetration, with each step being preceded by thorough preparation. He developed the technique of the *tache d'huile* (the 'oil-slick' method, as the Americans were to name it in Vietnam, where they pursued it with much less success). The gradual winning-over of the small areas, one after another, was however done by a mingling of military and political means. Lyautey was convinced that the *permanent* winning-over of dissidents could only be done by friendship; moreover, they were to be won over to the rule of the Sultan, not of the French. For Lyautey, the Protectorate was what its name claimed it to be, and the French, by supporting the power of the Sultan, and by extending it to the furthermost territories of Morocco, were unifying a nation, and enabling it to obtain all the advantages of modern nationhood. The French were the directors and organisers of this process.

To the murmurs of nationalists in Paris, who required quicker victories and a proper subjugation in the accredited colonial manner, Lyautey could say, as he did in a letter to Albert de Mun: 'This country should not be treated with force alone. The rational method, the only good method, the one for which, moreover, I myself was sent here rather than anyone else, is the continual, combined use of politics and force. . . . If impatient public opinion (oh, how impatient it is, particularly on the part of colonials and nationalists!) prefers premature lightning blows to this slow, but so sure method, all they had to do was not send me here, but nothing will make me give up this method, which, for me, is that of my conscience.'[1]

By slow preparations, tenacious methods, and diplomatic attitudes, Lyautey had succeeded, by the mid-twenties, in extending the Sultan's power to all except a few small centres of dissidence.

In the Spanish zone, things were not as happy. But in 1918 General Berenguer, recently appointed High Commissioner and Generalissimo of the Spanish forces in Morocco, went to Rabat to see Lyautey and take his advice. Berenguer, convinced by this advice and by what he had seen, returned proclaiming that there was no more need for unnecessary bloodshed. However, the reactions of the natives, used to former Spanish methods, were predictable, and war broke out once more. By 1920 the Spanish were at the edge of the Riff proper.

It was now, however, that the force of two personalities began to work towards eventual Spanish discomfiture. The first of these men was Abd-el-Krim, the son of a judge, and a judge himself. He had been educated at Fez, and was a man of intelligence and judgement. Though he and his father had originally been in favour of the Spanish influence, hoping for advantages to the Rifi from the contact with a more civilised nation, and though Abd-el-Krim himself became Cadi in Melilla, he became convinced not only that the Spanish aim was exploitation, but that they would never treat the natives as their equals. It was this man who, aware of Spanish designs on the Riff itself, set about organising the various tribes, and succeeded not only in silencing the warring factions, but also in preparing them for warfare against a modern army.

The other man was General Silvestre, an impetuous Spanish soldier to whom King Alfonso XIII, impatient with Berenguer's slow progress, and fearful for the fate of his own régime if a brilliant victory was not to be made in Morocco, gave *carte blanche* over the head of Berenguer, and even of the Minister of War. In 1921 Silvestre advanced into the mountains; by the end of that summer his modern army of 20,000 Spanish troops and 4,000 native auxiliaries had been surrounded, and defeated, by the superior tactics of the Rifi under Abd-el-Krim. The disaster took place at Anual. 18,000 men (almost the whole army) were lost. 19,000 odd precious rifles, about 400 machine-guns and 129 cannon were captured, and about 1,100 Spaniards taken prisoner. (Many historians have traced the fall of the Spanish monarchy to this defeat.) The repatriation of the prisoners, for the sum of £150,000 (four million pesetas), enabled Abd-el-Krim to obtain even more armaments for his men, and to establish his position.

With the Spaniards returned to their comparatively safe bases, the ports, Abd-el-Krim set about the organisation of the Riff state, which should be able to defend itself against the eventual Spanish desire for revenge. In July 1921 he proclaimed the independent Republic of the Riff. A fuller declaration in January 1923 notified those powers who had taken part in the Algeciras agreement of 1906 that they had made the mistake of thinking that the Riff formed part of Morocco. It was different both in race and language: 'We Rifians are no more Moroccans than the English would consider themselves Dutch. Probably it is this racial mixture that makes us very like the English in our absolute will of independence and in our desire to be in touch with all the nations of the world. By this declaration we invite all people from any part of the world to come and explore our unknown regions with scientists, geologists, chemists and engineers—commercially and not with warlike intent.'[2]

He stressed the independence of the Sultan of Morocco, and the integrity of his territory, while affirming the Riff's independence from him.

This was a revolt of a new kind in colonial history. It was not a localised rebellion, nor was it a 'holy war'. It was far more in the nature of a war of national independence on the modern model. The Republic of the Riff sent representatives to plead their cause in Paris and London; they received the support of international Communism; they were sympathetically reported in the British and American newspapers; Abd-el-Krim himself wrote, in 1924, a dignified letter for help to the British Prime Minister, Ramsay Macdonald; and in 1926, just before his final campaign, he wrote a letter to *The Times*, speaking of the Rifi desire for an honourable peace. This was no illiterate rebel leader; he was a man on an international scale, a man, moreover, who

Marshal Lyautey from a painting by de Laszlo

Abd-el-Krim

had succeeded for the first time in welding together the warring Rifi factions into a coherent whole.

Meanwhile, from 1921 to 1924, the situation remained relatively calm, with little in the way of Spanish offensive action. Primo de Rivera, who took power in Spain after a *coup d'état* in September 1923, took charge of the Moroccan campaign, and had decided by 1924 that the best policy was to concentrate the Spanish troops in the coastal towns, and give up any idea of territorial subjugation of the interior.

This retirement to the ports left the French in a somewhat exposed position. At the beginning of 1924 Lyautey (now a Marshal of France) had informed the Sultan and the French Government of the dangers of the independent Riff state. During the year, fearing a spread of Riff power into the French zone, he sent troops north of the Wergha to establish a line of outposts facing the Riff, in response to requests for help from some of the local tribes.

On 20 December 1924, Lyautey, even more aware of the danger, wrote urgently to Paris, requesting reinforcements to bring his forces up to the 1923 strength, as it had been before men had been removed because of the French domestic financial situation, and because of the occupation of the Ruhr. He had been told that only ten battalions would be available; so he asked for ten, pointing out that 'if I have forced myself only to ask for this minimum, it is because I am profoundly convinced of the difficulties there would be for France to give me more.'[3]

The question of reinforcements was to be a controversial one later, when Lyautey had resigned and the Lyautey-Pétain question was at its height. Lyautey and his supporters contrasted the military aid given to Lyautey and that supplied to Pétain. Pétain's supporters (e.g. Laure), stressed the fact that Lyautey got the reinforcements he asked for. The truth lies between the two, and is to Lyautey's credit. Though in such vital need of reinforcements, in face of a well-armed force which outnumbered the troops at his disposal, he nevertheless took into account the needs of France as a whole, and not merely his own front. (This attitude contrasts strangely with that of most generals, including Pétain, in the First World War.) A letter from Lyautey to Terrier, written on 4 November 1925, puts his point of view:

Why did I only ask for this minimum? Because at the end of my October visit to Paris, the Chief of General Staff... told me with anxiety of the situation of the French army, the necessity of covering the Rhine, the necessity of National Defence, and the impossibilities resulting from the shortening of national service and the liberation of the call-up classes, and made it a *cas de conscience* for me not to ask for more than it was materially possible to give me, that is to say, by scraping the bottom of the barrel, ten battalions.

So I acted in good faith, regarding it as my duty as a Marshal of France and a member of the *Conseil Supérieur de la Guerre* to put on the same level my local and my general responsibilities, and that is why I asked *as a minimum* for what I was being offered *as a maximum*.

Almost immediately, my deputy Chief of Staff received official advice of the existence of reinforcement M, which would offer me a little more at my disposition, and it was on this that I concentrated when making my supplementary requests at the beginning of the crisis.

But it was clearly established that, beyond this, *there was nothing to be hoped for*; that is why I never for a moment thought of asking for massive units, seeing that it was impossible to envisage them in the least without compromising the security of France.[4]

The reasons for the parsimony with regard to reinforcements may, indeed, have been those given to Lyautey; but it is also clear that Parliament, with a majority of the Left since the victory of the *Cartel des Gauches*, in 1924, was unlikely to encourage reinforcements for 'colonial ventures'; and that the nation as a whole, weary of war, was unlikely to welcome such involvement until it was proved to be absolutely necessary.

Meanwhile, Lyautey's policy was one of containment; of making sure of the loyalty of the northern tribes, particularly the Beni-Zeroual, and of protecting them. Certainly not of setting foot in the Riff itself, or of provoking Abd-el-Krim. It has been suggested by an impartial observer, however, Walter Harris, *The Times* correspondent, that the eventual war was a tragedy of misunderstanding; that each side believed in the hostile intentions of the other, and that in face of French precautions against attack the Rifi took steps to protect their own country from invasion. Each lot of reinforcements on one side led to reinforcements on the other, until it was only a question of when war was to break out.

It is difficult, now, to assess the intentions of Abd-el-Krim. Some writers have seen him as desiring an immediate attack on Fez (easily within reach of a determined army) to become sultan; others have seen him as attempting a *tache d'huile* technique in the manner of Lyautey, gradually winning neighbouring tribes over to his side. Others, including Furneaux, have believed him to have had no basically offensive aims (his statement on the difference between the Rifis and the Moroccans would seem to support this), but to have been bound by honour to support dependent tribes, such as the Beni-Zeroual, who called for his help, and to have been alarmed by the French advance north of the Wergha, into territory which, by the partition, was French, but which was by nature part of the Riff.

Be that as it may, the important thing is that most of the French believed his intentions to be offensive; and that his eventual attack, in April, was in fact clearly aimed at Fez.

Hostilities broke out on 12 April. Supporters of each side have different accounts of what sparked them off, but the immediate result was clear. The French outposts on the Wergha were surrounded, and, one by one, overrun. Immense bravery on the part of the outnumbered small French garrisons meant that the Rifi were held up more than they had expected. But the local tribes came over to them, the Wergha was crossed, and the important centre of Taza appeared in grave danger, as did Fez.

On 5–6 June, two telegrams were sent from Rabat to Paris, expressing the grave dangers of the situation. Painlevé, the Premier and Minister of War, decided immediately to go to Morocco himself. On the 9th he arrived in Rabat, where he remained until the 15th.

The faithful Laure, determined to put all in the best light for Pétain, and in the worst light for Lyautey, tells of Painlevé's realisation of the large numbers of reinforcements which had already arrived; '36 battalions, 5 squadrons, 15 gun batteries . . . not counting 3 Madagascan battalions which the Minister sent as soon as he returned to Paris. . . .'[5] This does not, however, ring true. Laure is the only person to give this account; Lyautey's own account of the matter, given to Terrier, seems more in accord with the facts: 'This conception [that he could have no more reinforcements] was confirmed at M. Painlevé's visit in June, since, at the most gravely critical moment of the crisis, when I was begging him to send me the Moroccan division from the Rhine, he replied that it was completely impossible, even if it were merely a regiment – which General Jacquemot confirmed even more formally – and he told me, basing himself on a note General Debeney had given him, that all I could count on *à la rigueur* was three Madagascan battalions.

And so it was that fifteen days afterwards, at the most tragic moment, when it was a question of evacuating Taza, I could only be certain of the fact that I could not materially be given any more help, and all my decisions, all the measures I took, were based at that time on the fact that I could only count on my present forces.'[6]

The attack on Taza, to which Lyautey refers, was one of the turning points of the war. Lyautey, agreeing to the evacuation of women and children, decided nevertheless to hold on in the town, despite the lack of reinforcements to relieve it if it got into trouble. The gamble paid off, and the main Rifi force struck once more to the west.

The immediate crisis in Taza was over, and Marshal Lyautey was able, on 6 July, to send a rather more optimistic telegram to Paris. The general situation remained extremely serious, however. During the Taza crisis Lyautey had sent telegrams to Paris of which he later said:

People may have found them too tragic, but they nevertheless had the advantage of opening people's eyes on the situation, and persuading them finally to send powerful reinforcements which, I had up till then been assured, were impossible.

Only, at the same time, it was not at my disposition that these on the whole sufficient reinforcements were to be put, after I had had all the effort and all the merit of holding on under the strongest blow with the most reduced forces.[7]

By this last remark Lyautey is referring, after the event, to Pétain.

Lyautey's reports had, in fact, shaken the Government into action. They set about hastening the evacuation of the Ruhr, and decided to send the whole of the Moroccan division. *The Times* correspondent ascribed the sending of reinforcements to 'the fact that the French Parliament is now adjourned and the Government is relieved of one form of immediate criticism.'[8] Be that as it may, at the end of June Pétain went to the Ruhr to negotiate the final withdrawal of the French troops. *The Times* of 27 June reported: 'The *Kölnische Zeitung* reports that Marshal Pétain has arrived in Düsseldorf in connexion with the evacuation of the Ruhr, and that it is believed that certain of the occupying troops may be withdrawn within the next few days.'[9]

From the beginning of the year onwards, Lyautey, now seventy-one years old, had been making it clear that he wished to divide his duties of Resident General and military commander, and that he would like an adjutant to take over the latter. Among the generals he suggested were Weygand, Guillaumat and Serrigny. Weygand, above all, seemed to him a suitable man. But Parliament, who mistrusted Lyautey for his right-wing views and for the dangers which they felt they represented for the Republic (a mistrust which had added to the reasons for not sending reinforcements in the first half of the year), disliked and mistrusted Weygand for the same reasons. The presence of two such men in Morocco was unacceptable to them. So it was that eventually, in July, General Naulin, a rather obscure figure, was sent to fill the post, as *commandant supérieur des troupes du Maroc*. Marshal Lyautey was to have the general direction of the war, while Naulin actually commanded the troops on the ground.

Naulin arrived with very 'European' ideas on the type of battle, and the type of victory, that was required. His ideas reflected those of Paris and the parliamentarians; the necessity for a quick and crushing victory. Lyautey, with his experience of colonial warfare, saw the necessity of building for the future, of containing the enemy and making sure that he realised the futility of further action. He expressed himself to Naulin's subordinates Mast and Loustaunau-Lacau as follows: 'Forget all that you know, and exercise your judgement on men and on facts as they present themselves to you. Be new in a country that is new to you. Above all, have no planetary conceptions. It's a question of defeating rebels, and rebels only. When we have enough battalions, the dissidence will weaken, and then disappear. Every military school memory, here, is superfluous. Kill as few people as possible, send reinforcements where they need to be, and all will be well.'[10]

In other words, if you show the rebels that all is in vain, you will defeat them without needing to destroy them. Naulin, a man prepared to admit his ignorance of Morocco and to take the Marshal's advice, soon changed his original 'planetary conceptions' and fitted in with him on the essential point, which was 'to defeat the Beni-Zeroual, the most powerful and most threatening tribe, at the gates of Fez.' This plan, agreed between Lyautey and Naulin, was soon to be 'criticised with virulence' by Marshal Pétain, a man less prepared to confess his ignorance.[11]

Meanwhile the Government was impatient with the apparent lack of desire for an all-out victory. From a reluctance to send reinforcements, or to get embroiled in a colonial war, they now, having sent reinforcements, and having realised that the first danger was past, clamoured for the destruction of the rebels. In World War terms, this was reasonable, in the way that victories were demanded on the western front, and counted by the number of casualties. And, unaware of the differences of colonial warfare, the parliamentarians wanted immediate results.

Two decisions were taken: to start discussions with the Spanish about a possible joint action (for which purpose M. Malvy was sent to Madrid), and to send Marshal Pétain himself to Morocco, to examine and comment on the situation. He arrived there on 17 July, a few days before Naulin's official takeover.

In a sense, it was reasonable that Pétain, who as Vice-President of the *Conseil Supérieur de la Guerre* was ultimately responsible for all that happened of a military nature, should come on a fact-finding mission, particularly if the situation was serious. As the press hand-outs put it, he was 'to make a general survey of the situation which General Naulin will have to deal with on taking over chief command of the troops in Morocco.'[12]

Lyautey certainly welcomed Pétain's arrival in this spirit. He sent a telegram to the Government on 16 July welcoming the decision to send the Marshal, stating the difficulty of the military situation, the uselessness of peace talks with Abd-el-Krim until the French had a clear superiority of forces, and the necessity of strengthening these forces, 'to stop the dissidence of the tribes, which is now a more immediate peril than the Riff aggression, which is nevertheless the cause of it.' The French had to show their superior power, or else the slow work of persuasion of the Moroccan tribes, which Lyautey had been pursuing since before the World War, would be brought to nothing, and they would all become dissident once more.

'Nobody is better qualified', added Lyautey, 'to appreciate the situation and the measures to be taken than Marshal Pétain, in whom I have full confidence, and whose mere arrival will immediately produce here both on the troops and the natives the most salutary impression.'[13]

He asked for this telegram of his to be shown to Pétain before his departure. It shows that Lyautey not only saw that Pétain might help him get more troops; he also felt that the victor of Verdun would provide just the sort of psychological fillip his soldiers needed, and also impress the inhabitants. He clearly did not fear at this time any interference with his own policies.

Pétain arrived in Rabat on the 17th, and spent the morning of the 18th talking with Lyautey and his staff, and then having a long interview with the Sultan. He then went on to Fez. 'The first impression is not too bad,' he wrote to his wife on the 19th. 'With a little skill it should sort itself out, but there is not a minute to lose.'[14] One already senses a criticism of the methods so far used, and a conviction that he must do something to put them right. He had already had this impression when still in Paris, when, long before he knew he was being sent to Morocco, he had written to his wife that 'the direction of operations down there leaves a lot to be desired.'[15]

Lyautey, unaware of all this, sent on 20 July a message to Pétain, who had gone from Fez to Taza to visit the northern front, which praised him for the moral effect his presence had given (while still stressing that this had meant that France would support the cause to the full, i.e., send as many reinforcements as possible):

'I want you to know, according to all the information I have received in the last few days, the great impression of confidence produced by your presence, in all circles, military, European and Muslim, above all with the Sultan. Everyone sees in it a decisive proof of the resolution of France to make every possible effort to safeguard the protection and security of the sherifian empire, and I myself personally feel all the benefit it has done to my authority in the task I have to accomplish. The Sultan has just requested me to express to you his gratitude. To this I add my own.'[16]

Pétain's role was not necessarily, however, in his own eyes that of support-ing Lyautey's authority. His report to Paris, written on 22 July, predictably stressed the need for more reinforcements, but also the necessity of con-quering the whole dissident region. And, to achieve this, he immediately set about those conversations with the Spaniards which, even before his departure from Paris, he had considered as the best plan, and had en-couraged the Government accordingly to send Malvy to Madrid. On 27 July, Pétain headed by sea from Casablanca to Ceuta, and went from there to Tetuan, where he had discussions with Primo de Rivera on what *The Times* described as 'the joint operations of French and Spanish forces, to begin shortly.'[17]

Those who suggest that Lyautey was kept in the dark about such discus-sions at this stage, must presume that he read no newspapers. However, it is obvious that whenever he got to know these things, he would have been troubled. For this was the prelude to the head-on collision of two doctrines. Lyautey's doctrine, which Naulin came to share, was that the main action should take place against the Beni-Zeroual, the main dissident tribe in the Wergha area, and that the force of the French should be so shown in this area that the other dissident tribes would return to French domination, and that Abd-el-Krim should withdraw into the Spanish zone; there he should not be followed, but should rather be attracted to peace terms, and possibly to nominal subjection to the Sultan. Pétain's doctrine was to destroy Abd-el-Krim and the Rifi once and for all, with Spanish help, attacking them from all sides.

The clear disadvantages of the latter policy, from the point of view of Lyautey and his supporters, were as follows: (1) This was not a colonial policy, at least not as Lyautey understood such things. The aim seemed to be to destroy rather than to win over; yet if one did not 'win over' people, one laid up resentments which would eventually cause trouble once more. This was a 'Spanish' policy. (2) There was no need for all-out war of this kind, as far as the French were concerned. All that was needed was a show of force, a scapegoat or two, and a gradual regaining of ground. (3) Tactically, the techniques of European warfare were wasteful, and not very useful against guerrillas. (4) From the point of view of native esteem, the worst thing one could do was to go in with the Spanish who, as General Durosoy, then one of Lyautey's subordinates, has said to me, 'were regarded by the natives as being even worse than the Jews'.[18] (5) The action would clearly be on behalf of French and Spanish colonialism, rather than on behalf of the Sultan.

For Lyautey and his officers, all that was needed were massive reinforcements, for their plan to be capable of being carried out. But it was Pétain who was eventually to get such reinforcements, for his plan; Lyautey was to be seen as a man who by incompetence and inability to realise how many reinforcements were needed, had jeopardised the fate of French Morocco. Such are the misconceptions that can be fostered. Certainly Lyautey had many enemies in Paris, who might foster any rumours against him, and few people realised the truth about the reinforcements question; but over and above this, his methods were completely misunderstood by the Government and by Pétain, who could not conceive of any victory which was not complete.

On 28 July, Pétain returned to France. Press reports declared that his chief task had been the reorganisation of the French command. *The Times* reported: 'It is no secret that one of the obstacles to French success hitherto has been the division of responsibility between the Resident General, Marshal Lyautey, and the commanders at the front. The appointment of General Naulin to take command of the troops in the field with independent authority was designed to improve matters, but it needed the great prestige of Marshal Pétain, who is in effect Commander-in-Chief of the French Army, to co-ordinate powers as they should be.'[19]

The report sent from Fez, but unconfirmed, was that 'the main conclusion which the Marshal had come to was that two more divisions of European troops were required to finish the campaign successfully before the autumn.'[20]

Nothing more was made public about Pétain's conclusions at this time. When on 10 August, Pétain's report was published, though it had remained secret hitherto, it contained, as *The Times* said, nothing that was not common knowledge. It praised the bravery of the outnumbered troops in the early days, and the priceless task of holding up the enemy; it praised 'the great chief . . . who in spite of his age* and all the weight of his trying colonial career, has been the soul of this defence and has been able to preserve from the inrush of these barbarians his work of civilisation that is the admiration of the whole world'; it stressed the brighter prospect now faced, thanks to further reinforcements. As a public relations exercise, it was excellent; but it did not really tell anyone anything. As *The Times* remarked, it was 'probably . . . really intended to counteract the depression caused by the news from Syria and the bitter campaign which is being waged by the Catholics and the Nationalists against General Sarrail.'[21] On the same day, Lyautey had written Pétain another enthusiastic letter, describing him as 'the great leader I admire, and the friend whose fidelity and sureness I know.' On the 12th, having read Pétain's report, he wrote again, saying how much he and all his soldiers, officers and men, had appreciated his account of events.

* Pétain was only two years younger than Lyautey

Pétain was indeed asking for reinforcements; but much more was happening behind the scenes. On 1 August, he saw Painlevé, and, while asking for reinforcements, spoke of the need for combining operations with the Spanish, and for moving north from Taza in the direction of Abd-el-Krim's headquarters, which would be threatened from the north coast by a Spanish landing. All troops and reinforcements must be ready by 10 September, so that the grand operation could take place before the mid-October rains. On 4 August, Pétain put the same plans before Painlevé, Briand (Foreign Minister) and Caillaux (Finance Minister), getting their approval, and getting Caillaux's promise to provide the finance. They asked Pétain personally to supervise the plan; he asked, according to Laure, merely to be put above Naulin, in charge of military affairs, with Lyautey remaining in charge of the administration. On 12 August, Pétain was officially told by Painlevé that he was being entrusted with military operations in Morocco, and that Marshal Lyautey was to be called to Paris to discuss the general political situation.

All seemed well, and there was little reason, at this stage, for Lyautey to feel any fears. The news that Pétain was to go to Morocco, announced on the 14th, did, it is true, say that he was going there *via* Madrid; the newspapers added hopes about joint operations. But this could merely mean small-scale operations in frontier areas, such as had already taken place in one area, the Wezzan. There was no hint of a full-scale campaign.

But, on the 17th and 18th, before Pétain's departure, the newspapers contained a story, obviously from official sources, which must have caused Lyautey some concern. In *The Times* it ran as follows: 'It is probable that Marshal Lyautey will shortly leave for France in order to rest and follow a course of treatment at Vichy, as he did during the summer months last year. The length of Marshal Pétain's stay in Morocco is uncertain, and will presumably depend on the progress of military events. But one of the reasons for his journey is that if Marshal Lyautey pays his visit to France it will be an advantage to have in the Protectorate a soldier who is a fitting substitute for the Resident General.' [22]

This must have been the first hint that Lyautey received of the eventual aim of the Government to displace him. Indeed, it is the first definite statement which would lead the historian to believe that the Government had made up its mind to get him out of the way. Lyautey's response was prompt, and was printed in French and foreign newspapers; one can sense the suppressed anger behind his statements, which appeared the next day: 'Marshal Lyautey has issued a denial of the report that he intends to undergo a course of treatment at Vichy this summer. Since his operation two years ago, he stated, not only had he no need to go to Vichy, but he was strictly forbidden by his doctor to do so. He had no need for treatment, and his health had never been better. As for taking a holiday, nobody would suppose that he could have such an idea so long as decisive results had not been obtained in Morocco.' [23]

Lyautey had foreseen and looked forward to another visit of Pétain's, but had imagined it would be something like his first one. The announcement that Pétain was to take over the general direction of the troops must have surprised him. And the Government's remarkably clumsy treatment of himself must have warned him what was in store.

On the 18th Pétain left for Morocco, via Spain. Painlevé declared to the Press that it was to be a long stay in Morocco, and that in collaboration with Lyautey and Naulin, Pétain was to complete a full strategical plan. 'His peculiar care will be the lines of communication, including the organisation of the difficult business of feeding and supplying the troops. He hopes to find a field of operation suitable for the employment of tanks and generally to bring into play the French superiority of mechanical equipment.' [24]

As so often between the wars, Pétain's statements, and those made about him, clearly refer back to one or other of his two great moments of the First World War, Verdun and the mutinies. Here, the reference is to his great organisation of lines of communication at Verdun. As in so many other matters, Pétain was expected to repeat what he had done before, rather than necessarily do anything new.

On the question of the use of tanks and the superiority of mechanical equipment, Pétain was determined, here as on the western front, to have overwhelming superiority before attacking. On the 14th and the 17th, Pétain had, through Painlevé, received two documents from Lyautey, setting forward the Lyautey-Naulin plans for the campaign, which were, as we have seen, to make the main effort in the direction of the Beni-Zeroual; all idea of profound penetration into the enemy territory was set aside. It was to be a limited action, until the rains, with no definite continuation the next year.

This, of course, was exactly the opposite of Pétain's plans, and, setting off from Paris on 18 August, he went first, as planned, to Spain, where he discussed, with Primo de Rivera, their agreement in principle on Franco-Spanish joint action. The interview was at Algeciras, on 21 August. The atmosphere was cordial, and the two men showed great friendship for each other. Indeed, toasting Primo de Rivera, Pétain is reported to have said: 'I toast Primo de Rivera who through his intelligence and patriotism was able to re-establish discipline and order in Spain. Perhaps circumstances may make it necessary to do in France as was done in Spain.' [25]

On 22 August, Pétain was received by Lyautey at Rabat. Lyautey knew next to nothing of Pétain's plans, and was unaware of recent events in Spain. According to some accounts, Pétain in his usual cold and distant manner said that he was now in charge of operations. Certainly from now on relations between these two men were very strained, and this visit forms a marked contrast from the previous one.*

There was much that differentiated the characters of the two men, and it was surprising that they ever got on well. Though they shared many attitudes —their love of tradition, their insistence on the social role of the army, their belief in the importance of education, their hatred of the influence

---

* Accounts of the first meal at the Residence show it to have been extremely strained, with Pétain's manner hardly doing anything to ease the tension.

of left-wing and Communist elements in the national life—these were attitudes shared by many others of their fellow officers. The differences between the two men were far more striking. Lyautey the fervent Catholic, believing in the spiritual role of French colonialism, like so many other Catholic soldiers and Arabists, yet seeing, like them, the spiritual values of Islam and the importance of Arab traditions:[26] Pétain, brought up a Catholic yet no longer practising, and completely ignorant of Arab affairs. Lyautey, who had spent most of the First World War hanging on, with very few troops, to this vast new area of the French empire, relying mainly on bravado, persuasion, and trust: Pétain, who had spent most of the war, like his other colleagues on the western front, computing how to kill as many of the enemy as possible with as little cost to his own troops. Lyautey a monarchist: Pétain nominally at least a Republican. In background and character they were equally contrasting. Lyautey, of an old military family: Pétain, of peasant stock. Lyautey, a dashing cavalry officer: Pétain an infantry officer. Lyautey's pre-war career a colonial one: Pétain's a slow advancement in France itself and a contempt for colonial ventures. Lyautey now, a feudal lord living in state in Morocco: Pétain, spending as much time as possible at his farm in Provence. Lyautey a homosexual: Pétain a womaniser. Lyautey warm and impulsive: Pétain, apparently cold and reserved. Lyautey, loved by both the natives and his own officers: Pétain, admired by his officers from afar, friendly but aloof, cultivating unapproachability, 'glacially cold'.

Each of these men was surrounded by subordinates who admired him beyond measure; and most accounts of what happened have been written from one side or other, and are not fully to be trusted. It is evident that all was not well from the start, however. Pétain's cold and unresponsive manner, his critical eye, seem to have upset officers used to warmth and encouragement. His manner, which no doubt had changed little since the last visit, was now seen in a new light. Added to this, it is clear that he may really have been wounding to Lyautey; we have seen that he thought little of the way Lyautey had been running things, and we know, from experience of the pre-war period and of the War, that he never shrank from telling people (including his own superiors) what he thought of their policies, bluntly and often with cold irony.

On 24 August, Pétain went to Fez, where, on the 25th, Colonel Catroux, explaining the psychological advantages of the Lyautey-Naulin plan, was told by him: 'You are making politics: I am making strategy.'[27] Pétain saw the whole operation as a military one, and, was going to treat it like a battle of the western front. Nevertheless, when arguing in favour of the Franco-Spanish action, with Chambrun and Naulin, he apparently pointed out the *political* advantages of such a scheme.[28]

Lyautey had been recalled to Paris, 'to discuss the operations', and departed from Morocco on 27 August. The press made many speculations on the reasons for this visit, but stressed that he had not been recalled, nor had he resigned. On 31 August, however, an account which obviously stemmed from official sources appeared in the Paris press. I quote from *The Times's* account a day later, which made free speculations as to the meaning of the official hand-out:

> The Government desires that Marshal Pétain's action shall not be hampered or criticised in any way, and the possible clash of the powers of Marshal Pétain with those of the Resident General as nominal Commander-in-Chief was doubtless the subject of today's conversation between the Prime Minister and Marshal Lyautey. The Resident General's visit to France gives an opportunity for a temporary solution of the problem which need not cause any injury either to dignity or to personal interest. If Marshal Lyautey remained in France during the remainder of the summer and early autumn campaign, the difficulties which might arise from the presence of two Marshals of France in Morocco would be avoided, and at the end of that period the situation could be reviewed.

The Times went on to discuss the criticisms which had been rife of Lyautey's handling of the situation, and then added cruelly, referring to the *contretemps* about the Marshal's proposed rest cure: 'Vichy is not the only watering-place in France.'[29]

The tactics being used by the Government against Lyautey were clearly the old-established method of expeditiously getting rid of someone: a series of pin-pricks which would eventually push him into resigning of his own accord. Lyautey was a proud man, and during previous clashes with French Governments, for whom he on the whole felt nothing but contempt, he had often thought of retirement.* But in this case, he was to hang on for a little longer.

On 3 September, it was announced that Pétain had been given sole command of the forces in Morocco, no longer subordinated to the Resident General. It was also announced that Lyautey would be returning to Morocco on the 12th, but would report back once more to Paris in October.

It was in early September that the Franco-Spanish combined operation really began to move ahead. On the 8th Spanish forces led by Colonel Francisco Franco (commander of the 'Tercio', or Foreign Legion) landed at Alcuhemas Bay, in the centre of the north coast between Melilla and

---

* See, for example, three extracts from letters from Lyautey to Terrier: 30 August 1917: 'What makes up my force and my serenity, is my resolution to give up my place with a smile on the day when my fellow citizens have enough of me here.'
15 January 1918: 'I am therefore making no projects, living from one day to the next and expecting the worst. This worst has, moreover, nothing in it that terrifies me, for its only result would be to return me to private life, i.e., to my books, my papers, my memories, and the independence for which I thirst.'
20 February 1920: 'I am less and less disposed to let my feet be trodden on. I am more and more convinced, on the one hand, of the services that I have rendered and am rendering to my country, of the recognition and good treatment it owes me, and of the force I still represent, with my physical and mental strength still intact; and, on the other hand, of the lack of recognition given to this by the country, the Parliament, and the civil power; and I am less and less inclined to continue indefinitely *ce métier de jocrisse* [this fool's errand].' B. Inst. MS 5903

Ceuta, which Franco described as 'the focal point of the rebellion, the road to Fez, the short cut to the Mediterranean.'[30] Soon more detachments joined the first. By the 14th, it was clear that the landing, under the overall command of General Sanjurjo, had met with general success; and meanwhile the French operation had started to the south, and the big attack was prepared north of Taza.

On the 18th, Lyautey returned to Morocco. Pétain found him taciturn and worried, and showing a certain amount of mistrust towards his colleague. On the 24th, Lyautey finally sent his letter of resignation to the Government. In this dignified document he said:

> From the day on which the Rifi threat developed, I had no other thought than that of holding on with the reduced forces which were at my disposal in the beginning, and of saving the situation.
>
> Today, it can sincerely be affirmed that the danger is past and that, with the strength of the forces now at work, the future can be envisaged with confidence.
>
> So it is that with a clear conscience I ask to be relieved of my duties as Resident General in Morocco.
>
> The question of the Riff opens new problems, as are exposed in the enclosed confidential letter. . . .
>
> For these new problems . . . a new man, in full possession of his powers, is needed, who will have the full confidence of the Government.
>
> I ask that my successor be appointed without delay. I will hold myself at his disposal to give him information if he should feel that my experience of the country may be useful to him.[31]

The campaign continued well. Pétain's troops, with overwhelming fire support, advanced slowly but relentlessly, while the Spaniards moved southwards under General Sanjurjo. A force under Franco captured Mount Malmusi, dominating Abd-el-Krim's capital Ajdir, at the end of September, and on 2 October Ajdir itself fell. Primo de Rivera, in his announcement of this capture, claimed that the campaign would be over in a few months.

There remained Lyautey's departure. It was decided that he would leave on the 10th. At his departure, Pétain was not present. The excuse was that he had been kept at the front by important operations. Lyautey's followers, however, saw in this one more snub for their master.

The final meeting between the two men had taken place a week earlier, on the 3rd, at Fez. It was said that on this occasion Pétain had asked whether Lyautey really felt that he (Pétain) had played a role in the eviction of Lyautey, and that Lyautey had replied that he was sure he had not done so consciously, but 'was he certain that others had not let him play that role?' To which Pétain had thoughtfully replied 'It is perhaps possible.' Whether this story is true or not, it is true that throughout the affair Pétain's position had been equivocal. It is also important to note that Lyautey nourished a hatred of Pétain for some years, using his mordant wit at his expense, and rarely calling him anything but 'Monsieur Pétain'. None of this in public, of course. As he wrote to Terrier in November, 'Above all let no one place me in opposition to Marshal Pétain. Nothing could be more unpleasant with regard to the public, or more diminishing for our moral personalities, than to give the debate the characteristics of a conflict between Marshals.'[32]

In a bitter letter, written just before his departure on 10 October, Lyautey explained to Briand, the Foreign Minister, all that had lain behind the formal terms of his resignation letter; in the process he castigated the policies of Pétain:

In the request to be replaced that I sent to you on 24 September, I purposely invoked no motives other than my need for rest, and the improvement in the military situation, which allowed me to leave my post with a clear conscience.

But if, when I was asked to await my successor's arrival, I replied that it was impossible for me to stay beyond the 10th, this was because there were other reasons for my immediate departure, reasons I did not formulate in order to avoid anything which might, while I was still in Morocco, give the impression of a divergence of views with those whom the Government had put in charge of the military operations.

Today, having given up my functions, I believe it to be my duty to the Government and myself, to explain these reasons.

The military organisation, the doctrines, the methods and the programmes which are at present installed in Morocco, were installed over my head, either without my being asked for my advice, or against my advice.

I do not wish to judge them or criticise them. But they are totally different from those which, throughout my career, and particularly in Morocco, I have always preached and applied. Rightly or wrongly, I have no confidence in their efficacity. I believe them to be heavy, slow, and unsuited to the country. . . . My conception as to the results to be reached was different, aiming at more rapid and decisive results, by the simultaneous and more intensive use of political action. . . .

I have not been in a position to give my advice, as I have not been consulted. I am perhaps wrong, and I very much hope so.

But it was impossible for me, as regards France, Morocco and myself, to keep up for a day longer, by the prolongation of my presence, any appearance of responsibility for measures against which I had no authority to intervene, and on which I differed with those who had been put in charge of them over my head. . . .

In such conditions it was really impossible for me to prolong my stay until the arrival of my successor, in relation to whom I would, moreover, have found myself in a difficult position. . . .

All this being said, because I had to say it, I have no need to assure you that as I no longer have responsibility with regard to what is happening in Morocco, I have resolved in no way to occupy myself with it, and to avoid any solicitations to give my advice on what is no longer my affair.[33]

Lyautey was as good as his word. He never spoke in public on Morocco,* though his correspondence makes it clear that he was concerned with

* He is said to have said at a dinner, to Laval, who had asked him about Morocco: 'Morocco? Don't know it.'

keeping his own reputation clear (particularly with regard to the vexed question of reinforcements), and that he got his friends, while adjuring them to keep his name out of it, to try to put the record straight.

His departure from Casablanca, on the packet *Anfa*, was a moving occasion. French and Moroccans had gathered to see the great man off, but there was little in the way of official representation. It took the British navy, off Gibraltar, to give him the honour that was his due, as the crews of two destroyers cheered him on his way. At Marseilles, only a few close friends, and El Glaoui, the Pasha of Marrakesh, were there to greet him, and there was no official reception. Lyautey headed straight for the station, and took a train to Paris.

The autumn campaign was now almost finished. On 14 October, the rains came, torrentially, and prevented any further useful operations. Primo de Rivera declared that the Spanish were moving no further, and Pétain after one more, rather costly, action, settled down to his winter lines as well, and devoted his army's time to preparations for the next year's campaign. The Riff was now surrounded, and all the ground lost in April and May had been recovered.

On the 28th the new Resident General, a civilian called Théodore Steeg, arrived at Casablanca, and was met by Pétain, who spent the next two days explaining the military situation to him. Pétain insisted on the importance of close liaison with the Spanish, and of showing the Rifi by this that they were gradually going to be squeezed to death.

On 6 November Pétain, satisfied that the situation was stabilised for the winter, left Morocco. On the 7th, at Marseilles, he declared: 'Morocco is henceforth quiet. Abd-el Krim is no longer to be feared. My military task is now finished. I hand over the affair to political action.'

The country, as even Laure points out, was not easily satisfied. They had looked for a quick victory, and the affair still seemed to be dragging on. Pétain's 'heavy, slow' methods had saved French lives, and inflicted losses on the enemy; but it was the Spanish who had had the spectacular successes. How long was it all to drag on next year? A peace movement had developed and Painlevé, the French premier, had made moves towards peace. Steeg, the new Resident-General, had even offered autonomy to the Riff, explaining that France and Spain would be prepared to let the Rifi administer themselves, under a leader chosen by themselves. These talks had, however, come to nothing, mainly owing to French military protests.

On 4 February 1926, Pétain went to Madrid to discuss the final destruction of Abd-el-Krim. Though not returning to Morocco himself, he wished, as French Commander-in-Chief, to make the plans which his subordinates were to carry out in the coming year. He was accompanied by General Georges and Colonel Laure, and, after being received by the King and Queen, had lunch at the French Embassy with Primo de Rivera, and some of his ministers, including General Jordana (Moroccan Affairs). At three o'clock discussions were held on the coming season's plan of action. In the evening, there was a gala dinner and a reception at the royal palace. On the

5th, there was a visit to Toledo, where Pétain was received by the Cardinal Primate of Spain, and where he was given the Spanish Military Medal, their highest military honour. On the 6th, Pétain gave Primo de Rivera the French Military Medal.

After all these junketings, a second discussion was held, after which both sides signed a military agreement on the plan of action for 1926. This involved a movement inwards from all sides to squeeze the Riff into submission.

On his return to Paris, Pétain was horrified to find that public opinion, fed up with the war and prepared to be satisfied with the progress already made, still wanted to make peace with Abd-el-Krim. For Pétain, this was ridiculous. Just as, in 1918, he had wished, once the situation was clearly in the French grasp, to continue with the destruction of the Germans, so in this case he saw the only solution to the Moroccan problem to be the destruction of Abd-el-Krim. He proceeded to discuss with General Boichut, who was now in charge of military affairs in Morocco, the sending of further reinforcements, and the carrying-out of the Franco-Spanish plan.

Though the Government had originally tended to follow the public wish for peace, the accession of Briand to the premiership had meant a change of direction towards war once more. On 19 February he and Painlevé agreed to Pétain's views, and on 2 March the Madrid agreement was ratified. Despite this, public opinion forced the French and Spanish Governments in early April into proposing a meeting with Abd-el-Krim's delegates at Ujda, a town in the Riff. The suggested terms were: recognition of the Sultan of Morocco, disarmament of the tribes, release of prisoners, and expatriation of Abd-el-Krim.

Many French officers saw these negotiations as leading to a 'disastrous peace'. It is clear that Pétain shared these views. Laure, his biographer, expresses views on this conference which must have been those of Pétain's circle, when he refers to it as 'the appalling Ujda conference, at which France ran the risk of compromising its prestige by accepting to have talks with a *rogui* who was in no way qualified to represent the indigenous population.'[34] While the conference was on, says Laure, Pétain lost no opportunity of using his influence on the Government, to avoid any act of weakness; and Primo de Rivera did the same with his Government in Madrid.

It was perhaps for this reason that the Franco-Spanish requirements were put so much higher; preliminary requirements included release of all prisoners, and Franco-Spanish occupation of various key positions, before the conference could even take place. These were naturally unacceptable to Abd-el-Krim. Though they were eventually withdrawn, the impression was unfortunate, as was the French and Spanish refusal to have the world press present at the proceedings, which the Rifi had requested.

By 1 May it was clear that the conference had broken down. Not all the European attitudes had been extreme, and much ground had been given; but the atmosphere of mistrust was such that the Rifi could not believe in the good faith of their enemies, and felt that once they had laid down their arms all promises would be forgotten.

So the military won, and the civil ruler of the Protectorate, Théodore Steeg, had to leave things entirely to the army. On 7 May hostilities began once more; the French and Spanish armies linked up in west and east, and by 25 May Abd-el-Krim, deserted by many of the tribes which had followed him, and surrounded on every side, decided to give in. The rebellion was over.

All that remained was for things to be tidied up by a peace conference. This took place in Paris on 14 June. The French delegates included Pétain and Philippe Berthelot, the famous French diplomat, together with various military men. The Spanish included the ambassador, Quinones de Leon, and General Jordana. It was decided to send Abd-el-Krim into exile to the island of Reunion, in the Indian Ocean (where he remained until 1947), and to restate the line of demarcation between the French and Spanish zones.

On Bastille Day, 14 July, the final scene was played out, as the élite of the two victorious nations took part in a magnificent ceremony at the Arc de Triomphe, before the tomb of the Unknown Soldier. The King and Queen of Spain, Primo de Rivera, the Sultan of Morocco, Pétain and the President of the French Republic were all there.

What does the Riff war add to our knowledge of Pétain? And what, if anything, did it add to his own opinions?

Pétain arrived at the Riff convinced of the inefficacity of the methods used up till then, and convinced that he held the answer. Whether he was right or wrong is a matter still hotly discussed by his and Lyautey's supporters. The least that can be said against him, however, was that he lacked tact, and either ignored or over-rode Lyautey, giving in the process cause for offence to several subordinate officers. This is certainly in character; Pétain had never been renowned for tact, and did not suffer what he considered to be fools gladly.

There was a great deal of arrogance in his attitude, however. Almost as soon as he had arrived in Morocco he jumped to conclusions (which coincided with his previous opinions), and ignored the views of those who had been on the spot for years, and knew the local context. And (a mistake in diplomacy) he did not discuss these matters with Lyautey, but simply reported back to Paris. When he was sent out to Morocco a second time, he did nothing to inform Lyautey that he was coming via Spain, and after his arrival he again did nothing in the way of consulting Lyautey about what he intended to do, or even discussing it with him. Lyautey was presented with a *fait accompli*.

Admittedly, the worst treatment for Lyautey came from Paris, and above all in the press reports inspired by Government sources; but Pétain appears to have done little to palliate all this. A charitable view might be that this was because of his natural coldness and reticence.

So Pétain mishandled the human situation; but how right, or how wrong, was he in his assessment of the military situation? The first thing to get clear is that he saw it as a *purely* military situation. His western front experience had led him to mistrust 'politicians', and try to keep them out of military affairs; he was not concerned with 'winning over' dissidents, or with what might result from the campaign he was conducting. The campaign was all. And it must be a military campaign in which the enemy was crushed. For Pétain, no peace treaty must prevent the French army from destroying its enemy.

The methods he tried to use were those of European warfare. Obsessed as always with the need for massive superiority of men, and armaments, he insisted on a great number of reinforcements, which he used in force. The lightning tactics of normal colonial and guerrilla warfare were not his bent; the army advanced massively and relentlessly, until it was held up by the winter rains.

Given Pétain's aim, the destruction of Abd-el-Krim, the Spanish alliance was an extremely useful move; and the Spanish proved excellent allies. The incompetence that had produced Anual had been weeded out; and dashing commanders such as Franco led the Spanish forces to resounding victories, all the more striking in that they were won in the old-style colonial manner, while Pétain's troops were toiling slowly but relentlessly forward from the south.

What ideas did Pétain himself gain from this campaign? His confidence in his own military judgement remained unimpaired; and, scorn politics as he might, one gains the impression that he felt that his victory was politically important as well. The acclamations of both the Spanish and the French served to feed his already boundless self-confidence. The 'hero of Verdun' had gained a victory in the desert, through the same military genius, and by the same tactics, that had served him so well in the World War. No, Pétain gained no new military ideas from this campaign; colonial warfare had to be influenced by his ideas, rather than vice versa.

On the political side, however, two far-reaching influences had been at work. Firstly, he had seen at close quarters the working of a military dictatorship, which had drawn a country from defeat and confusion to a new pride in itself; and the dictator himself, Primo de Rivera, had gained his admiration. Other people whom he met at this time he was to meet again in 1939, when he returned to Spain as France's first ambassador to Franco's Government.

Secondly, he had been reinforced in his opinion of the dangers of Communism, and its threat to the patriotic virtues. The actions of the members of the French Communist Party, particularly Jacques Doriot (later to be leader of the fascist *Parti Populaire Français*, and later still a leading collaborator in the Second World War), who signed articles and pamphlets in favour of Abd-el-Krim, denounced the French action, and called on French soldiers to desert, horrified large sections of the French population, but particularly shocked the military. For Pétain, with his memories of communist influence in the 1917 mutinies, Communism meant not only anti-colonialism and anti-militarism, but the destruction of civil and military order. As such, it was to be hated and feared. His later statements on Communism, though mainly based on his 1917 experience, were nevertheless further corroborated in his eyes by the communist support for Abd-el-Krim.

Chapter Four

Military policy, 1918–39

SOMETHING to be borne in mind when studying Pétain's speeches, articles, books and written statements in order to make an assessment of his opinions, is that on the whole he did not write these things himself. He relied on '*nègres*' to do the actual writing for him: we know, for example, that Louis Madelin wrote articles for him during the war, that Laure was responsible for most of the book *La Bataille de Verdun*, that Loustaunau-Lacau wrote articles for the *Revue des Deux Mondes* in the 'thirties. De Gaulle, too, was one of Pétain's writers; complications leading from this were among the causes of the break between the two men.[1]

There was nothing unusual in all this. Most of the great Marshals and Generals of this era used the same methods. Joffre and Foch, as Marshals, would have found writing a book beneath them; their subordinates wrote their memoirs for them.

This did not mean that the ideas expressed in such works were not their own. Clearly they themselves expressed the general ideas, which were then composed for them; they then corrected the final draft.

In the case of Marshal Pétain, his speeches closely reflect his thought, as do his articles and books. On the national and political level, it is not very complicated thought; on military matters, it is at times more complicated in detail. But the same general doctrines and attitudes recur time and time again, in works written by the hands of different collaborators. The main lines of his thought are faithfully expressed, and we may take it that he examined closely the detail as well.

Alone among such military men, Pétain corrected the style of his collaborators. Various writers have told us of the way in which almost every line was corrected. Adjectives, adverbs, interjections, were cut out; he wished for simplicity above all, and was a rigid purist.

Thus, though much of the content of his public works was written by collaborators, it contained his thought, and reflected his style. These written records can be trusted as reflecting his opinions; as for his private letters, they are of course another valuable source of information.

The importance of the defensive

In this inter-war period, a strange change seems to have come over Pétain's military thought. Before the war, he had been a man ahead of his time, aware of the changes that had happened to the material of warfare;

he had refused to take the set ideas of his colleagues, which were based on the memories of the last important war, and had argued logically, from his knowledge of the capabilities of modern arms, for a new approach to military tactics. During the war itself, he had shown himself one of the most adaptable of the military leaders; faced by the unprecedented phenomenon of static trench warfare, he had at first believed in a 'breakthrough' policy; after the Arras campaign of 1915, he was one of the first to realise the futility of such a policy, and had moved towards the idea of attrition; eventually he had developed a technique of small-scale well-prepared attacks with overwhelming strength, to wear down the enemy reserves while preserving his own; of artillery action taking far more part than the infantry; and of elastic defence in depth, on which the enemy would founder. In the context of the conditions of the First World War, this policy was clearly the best and the most successful. Tanks were not yet enough developed, nor the techniques of using them, and air warfare was in comparative infancy. The defensive was still the master (though some of the German techniques of 1918 spelt trouble for the future), and Pétain's techniques were perfectly adapted to this situation.

What is extraordinary, however, is that at this point Pétain's military thought appears to have congealed. It is as though the armistice, and the advent of peace, had released him from any need to think further. His pre-war views had proved right; his wartime adaptation of these views to the situation had been successful; there was no more need to adapt or change, because time now stood still. One gets the impression that Pétain 'shut off' once the war was over, and saw it as an entity in itself, with no continuation. Though, at times in the inter-war period, he pays lip-service to the new forms of armament and the subsequent need for thought, his own military policy remains firmly rooted in the First World War.

He continually, in speeches and writing, harks back to that war. Much of this reminiscence is natural, of course; as one of the great figures of that war, he continually had to make speeches to Old Soldiers' Associations, or to celebrate anniversaries and inaugurate monuments; and, though he did not write memoirs like his colleagues (giving as his reason the fact that he had nothing to hide), he did produce a volume on Verdun, and an account of the 1917 mutinies. (Originally just for the *Académie des sciences morales et politiques*, it was eventually published after the Second World War). Natural these reasons for reminiscence were, but he reminisced on many other occasions too; and even when he was not openly reminiscing, his thought remained affected by his memories. It is interesting, in his speeches on events of the First War, to see how often he draws lessons for the present from them.

Verdun and the mutinies remained central to his thought. Indeed even in 1917 Fayolle had noticed Pétain's obsession with Verdun: '... Pétain is absolutely determined for me to see Verdun with him ... Pétain is hypnotised by Verdun.'[2]

The two events recurred constantly on Pétain's tongue, as they were to do during the Second World War. They, and the concepts attached to them: heroism in defence, the morale of the army. They were not only, for Pétain, the moments of his greatest triumphs; they also carried the most important lessons of modern warfare (together with his famous saying, which was now repeated by everyone *ad nauseam*: '*Le feu tue*'.)

It is amusing to see, in Pétain's remarks about the First World War, his criticisms of the fixed attitudes of the generals who, relying on their experience of the dangers of a defensive attitude in the 1870 war, had wholeheartedly reverted to Napoleonic ideas on attack, neglecting to take notice of the efficacy of the new arms that had evolved; it is amusing, because it is an accurate parallel to Pétain's own attitude in this inter-war period, obsessed with the lessons of the First World War, and ignoring the capabilities of new weapons and tactics. In his speech (supposedly of praise) about Foch, his predecessor in his chair at the *Académie Française*, he said, at his reception at the Academy in 1931:

> The Army was enthusiastic for the simplicity and efficacy of the Napoleonic methods and, taking no account of the evolution imposed on war by modern mechanics, concluded that attack was the major instrument of strategy and tactics.
>
> Foch underwent, with his generation, the influence of this current of ideas, and shared its audacity. . . .
>
> The memory of the failures of 1870, which were in great part attributed to the passivity of the French army, accentuated even more this vigorous movement in favour of the offensive. The advantages of fire-power were contested. People refused to give it the place it deserved, despite the preponderant influence it had shown in recent campaigns. The defensive was condemned as a procedure of manoeuvre.[3]

Another speech, which nowadays would seem to us to point even more clearly at himself in self-accusation, was made on 20 August 1934, at the inauguration of a monument twenty years after the Battle of the Marne. Referring to French pre-war policy, Pétain said:

> This doctrine had its excesses. The cause must be found, for the most part, in the violent reaction which arose against the passivity of our army in 1870, passivity which was expressly made responsible for our disasters. The return to the attitude of the Napoleonic Wars, in which a violent, decisive attack seemed the supreme argument in battle, accentuated this reaction, and prevented us from attributing its true value to the progress in armaments.
>
> A long period of peace, finally, separating us from the realities of combat, let the mystique of attack impregnate our army. The failure of the Battle of the Frontiers was the cost of these errors.[4]

One again France had been through a 'long period of peace'; but Pétain seemed unaware of the parallel. For him, the only possible tactics in the first stage of a battle were to stand on the defensive. Afterwards, the moment for the offensive might come; but it was to be awaited.

Foch, at the meeting of the *Conseil Supérieur de la Guerre* (of which, as Marshal, he was automatically a member) on 17 May 1920, fought strongly against such policies. As long as the French were on the Rhine, he felt they should defend that position; once they had had to vacate the Rhineland, the only policy in a future war would be to advance immediately to the Rhine, a natural barrier which would obviate the need for defensive works. Pétain, however, supported by Buat, the Chief of General Staff, got his own way.

In 1921 the famous 'Provisional instruction on the utilisation of larger units' (*Instruction provisoire sur la conduite des grandes unités*) appeared. It was largely composed by General Debeney, but accurately reflected Pétain's ideas. Until 1936, this was to be the basic document on which the army's methods were to be based. Laure stresses that the Marshal, and Debeney, wishing to show that they remained open to possibly changing circumstances, had put in the word *provisoire*: 'Despite this title', he adds cheerfully, 'it constituted for fourteen years the bible of our army.'[5]

This document stressed the impossibility of breaking a continuous front, mainly through the strength which the new forms of fire-power had given to even improvised defences. Attack was possible only after the amassing of the most powerful forces, in the form of artillery, tanks and munitions. Tanks were, however, as we shall see, regarded as merely subordinate to infantry needs, fighting closely in liaison with them, and clearing the way for them. Aeroplanes were seen mainly as instruments for observation of the enemy. It was the artillery, supporting the infantry, which did the main fighting. The main point of the document was that such offensive tactics, meagre as they were, were seen as only possible after a prolonged defensive action, as in the 1914–18 war.

Such views were possible, and justifiable, in 1921. But, with the mounting evidence of the powers of the new machines, it was extraordinary that this *Instruction* was not replaced until 1936. An account of some manoeuvres held at Valdahon in 1934, attended by Pétain as Minister of War, shows us that even by this time the basic conceptions of the French army were still the same. The reporter, Lt. Col. Magne, contrasts French tactics with German ones, and draws a lesson from the fact that in the manoeuvres the defence lost. The article is, in some senses, rather comic, and it is worth quoting a fairly large section from it:

One of the events of these manoeuvres was the account of them given by Marshal Pétain, in the presence of the foreign military attachés, with the double authority of his past and present functions. He set forth his well-known doctrine on the importance of fire-power: 'You attack with projectiles, and it is the artillery, not the infantry, which conquers the ground.' This doctrine—as the German military attaché must have noticed—is rather different from that of the Reichswehr, which the advent of Hitler will assuredly not have modified. . . .

They (the German military authorities) have preserved more than we have, it seems, the memory of the battles of 1918, the swift advance to the Somme and Château-Thierry, followed by our counter-offensives. They believe that the progress in armaments during the last sixteen years have not diminished the possibilities of a hardy, well-instructed infantry. On the contrary, the motorised vehicle capable of going over any terrain, and the infantry cannon, have brought it an abundance of effectives, which grows from day to day. . . .

The fictional operations of the 7th Corps have done nothing to prove them wrong. The success of the attacker against a disorganised enemy with flanks has been clear. I know that there were no projectiles in the guns and that manoeuvres experiments can be criticised. But these days the umpiring system is perfectly organised; it is carried out by superior officers who have waged war, for the most part, in the infantry, and who, by this fact, are not ignorant of the importance of fire-power.

Pétain, in an attempt to explain what had happened, suggested, typically, that 'morale' had been left out of account, and that Verdun had shown that a group of men really on the defensive would have pulled out all stops; if the manoeuvres had been real, the defensive would quite probably have won.

The reporter was not convinced, however; British manoeuvres taking place in Yorkshire had had the same result.

Over there as well, the umpires gave the victory to the attackers, just as it was given to the attackers of London and Paris in the August air exercises. This is more than a series of coincidences, and is a lesson we should think about very seriously.[6]

For most of this inter-war period a struggle had gone on between a small minority who opposed the defensive policies, and a majority who followed Pétain. The minority had grown as time went on. When, at Weygand's retirement, Gamelin took over in 1935, and co-ordinated the posts of Vice-President of the *Conseil Supérieur de la Guerre* and Chief of General Staff, thus finally putting French military arrangements on a business-like basis, it looked as though changes might take place; and the *Instruction sur la conduite des grandes unités* which in 1936 replaced the 'provisional' *Instruction* of 1921 restored the importance of the offensive.

Criticisms of Pétain's strategy were rife in the informed Press in the mid-'thirties. In an article, for example, by André Pironneau in *L'Écho de Paris* of 7 August 1934, it was stressed that France could not manoeuvre except after months of passivity, caused by its defensive posture, and that this would be of little value to the small states with which she was in alliance.

The influence of the 1921 *Instruction*, however, stretched beyond 1936. Though its successor differed from it in various ways, too much had by now been done in the way of defensive preparation. The Maginot Line had engulfed most of army finance for some years: the army had been expensively trained; and the 'battle of the tanks' had been lost, for political as well as military reasons. As La Gorce puts it, 'Vain were the increasingly frequent efforts made in the last years before the outbreak of war to break through the orthodoxy that had ruled for over twenty years.'[7] The same conditions were from now on bound to prevail, even though, thanks to the scare of the Rhineland crisis, more money was now available and more armaments were now being created. By 1937 the French army was still being trained mainly for the defensive. This time, in manoeuvres which took place in Normandy, the defensive won. The remark of a German commentator is instructive: 'These manoeuvres have confirmed the impression that one must place the power of the French army very high on the scale for the defensive. Despite their double superiority, the offensive forces, methodically deployed, had no notable success.'[8]

So, despite the advantages which modern arms could now bring to the offensive, the French army was still not being trained to use them. Obsessed by their defensive dream, the French authorities saw tanks and aeroplanes as being mere appendages to the infantry.

There were, by this time, many strong opponents to defensive policy. But Pétain, in the preface written in 1938 to a book, General Chauvineau's *Une Invasion est-elle encore possible?*, which appeared in 1939, continued to hold the same ideas. In fact, he saw the new ideas as a return to old heresies, rather than an attempt to face new problems: 'One can see still certain tendencies to take up again the doctrine of a war of movement from the very beginning of operations, following the ideas in vogue before 1914. The experience of the war has been paid for too dearly for us to be able to return with impunity to the old errors. The idea of the offensive is to be preserved with care for the moment when circumstances will allow us to use it, taking great care not to try to twist the facts or to try and adapt the realities to our feelings and our passions.'[9]

He had not learned. Indeed, it is interesting to see how closely related even the expressions are which clothed his military thoughts at the various stages of the inter-war period. Other people might now be doubtful, but his influence had made the defensive French policy for over fifteen years, and he still had a respected voice on the main committees which dealt with military matters. Changes were taking place, of which he disapproved; but by now it was too late for the basic policies to be altered by anyone.

The Maginot Line

While Pétain's views upon the defensive were fully received by his colleagues and his Ministers, he had rather more trouble in putting across his specific, detailed plans for the form of permanent defences which should 'cover' France. Though everyone accepted that the logical corollary of a defensive policy was to have some kind of permanent defensive system, they did not all agree on the form it should take. Eventually, however, Pétain won through, and the Maginot Line was the result.

Pétain's first note on the subject, his *Note sur l'organisation défensive du territoire*, produced in 1921, was discussed at a meeting of the *Conseil Supérieur de la Guerre* (only the second meeting since the war!) on 22 May 1922. It received opposition from Foch, who believed the best defensive to lie in the offensive. Foch's opposition was to be expected, of course; he had already spoken against defensive policy in the first meeting of the *Conseil*, in 1920. What was more important was the opposition of others, including

General Guillaumat, to the details of Pétain's scheme. Where Pétain (and Buat) wanted a continuous line of defence, the others wanted a discontinuous system of great fortified regions, separated by spaces, which would allow more in the way of tactical deployment of forces. Pétain's plan was based on the experience of the First World War. It would be a superior, prepared front line. The usual solution to such a situation was found; it was decided to set up a committee to look into the matter. On this everyone voted unanimously. The committee met under Joffre's chairmanship, and reached an impasse, with Guillaumat and Buat supporting the two different opinions. But as, at any rate, the financial straits of France at this time seemed to rule out any action being taken on any decision, and as France was to be occupying the Rhineland for some years to come, the whole project fell into abeyance for a while.

By 1925, however, with the reduction of national service to one year seeming imminent, the thoughts of the military turned to the necessity for fortifications once more. The *Conseil Supérieur de la Guerre*, meeting on 5 December, suggested immediate action, particularly with regard to the north-eastern frontier. The *Commission de défense aux frontières* (Commisison on frontier defence), which was, in a new form, the old *Commission de défense du territoire* (Commission on territorial defence), met five times from February to September 1926, and on 6 November sent to the Minister of War, Painlevé, two reports. The first, on the defence of the north-east frontier proposed three fortified regions; the second, on the details of fortification, proposed a system of forts and lesser *ouvrages*. The first of these, which was discussed at the *Conseil Supérieur de la Guerre* on 17 December 1926 and 18 January 1927, was, though against Pétain's basic plan, agreed to by him, on the basis that a continuous line could later be arranged around these fortified regions, and that they would be a good start. The second, discussed at the *Conseil Supérieur de la Guerre* in July 1927, was strongly criticised because of its fragmentary nature. That summer Pétain went to examine the terrain and to ponder on the question.

On his return, he approved the plan for three fortified regions, but insisted that they be supported in depth by a *position de barrage*. As for the detailed organisation between the regions, he did not see it as a series of separate forts and *ouvrages*, but of groups of *ouvrages* connected by subterranean galleries.

Pétain's plans were approved by the *Conseil Supérieur de la Guerre* in October 1927. At the end of November a *Commission d'organisation des Régions Fortifiées* was set up, which proceeded to work on detailed plans. It was decided that their proceedings should be in secret; the people mainly involved were General Belhague (head of the Commission), General Debeney (Chief of General Staff) and Pétain. This decision to work in secret is typical of Pétain's views on military organisation; just as, in the war, he had disliked the way in which Parliament ran things, so now he felt that one could act more efficaciously by avoiding discussion, and by going straight ahead.

The Commission's plans were approved by the Cabinet in January 1929. By the time it came before Parliament a new War Minister, Louis Maginot, had come in. Strongly in favour of the project, he got it through the Chamber of Deputies at the end of 1929, and the Senate approved it with an overwhelming majority on 14 January 1930. One of the few people to express doubt upon the value of these defences against new forms of armament was Pierre Cot, who was to be right upon a number of other things to do with warfare, particularly when Air Minister in the 'thirties. Pierre Cot was one of the few politicians of the Left who, realising the need for knowledge about military affairs, surrounded himself with some of the best (even if apparently unorthodox) military brains available.

The construction of the Maginot Line (as it was called, after the Minister who brought it in, even though Painlevé had had far more to do with the preparation of it) now went ahead apace.

In 1930, it became clear to Pétain that the Line, which according to present plans was merely to protect the north-east frontier, should be extended along part of the northern frontier, as far as Longwy. Work was put into progress.

The decision not to take the Line further, and protect the Belgian frontier, has been much criticised after the event. If you are to have a defensive wall, why not make it complete? Before answering this, I must make it clear that Pétain was merely one among many who took this decision, which was approved by almost all; and that even when he was no longer Commander, and the question came up again, the same decision was reached by his successors.

Why did Pétain support this decision, at the *Conseil Supérieur de la Guerre* in the years 1926 to 1928, in 1930, in a letter to the same *Conseil* in 1932 after his retirement, and again when War Minister in 1934? Firstly, because a choice had to be made, with the finances available; either complete fortifications in the area where they could most easily be put or else incomplete fortifications along the whole front. Secondly, because of the *political* difficulties of the alliance with Belgium; defensive fortifications on the Belgian frontier were hardly reassuring to the Belgian allies. Thirdly, because of the difficulties of defending the industrial area of northern France by such means; it would be much easier to defend it from within the Belgian border. Fourthly, and most importantly, because Pétain still believed in the efficacy of the methods of the First World War; if the French forces advanced, immediately after the outbreak of hostilities, into their ally's territory and dug themselves in on the natural lines of the Belgian rivers and canals, they would be capable of warding off attack. The Maginot Line was not seen as the *only* method of national defence; it was a superior form, which would require less men to man it, and would thus make more men available to hold the rest of the Line. Thus would the initial manpower problems caused by reduced national service be solved. And, as always, Pétain saw things in the First World War terms of shortages of manpower at the front, the dispersal of reserves, etc. All reserves could be deployed behind the Belgian part of the Line, and come up to plug any breakthroughs. It must be stressed that there was no idea of a 'war of movement' involved and that the initial march into Belgium would merely be to create defensive positions there. As for the Ardennes, they were considered to be impenetrable. It was not an audacious offensive project, as some writers have claimed, but was right in line with French defensive policy. The Belgian declaration of neutrality in 1936 wrecked any such plan, of course; and it says something for the confusion of military policy-making under Gamelin, uncertainly swaying between defensive and offensive concepts, that part of the plan was retained, but given different objectives.

Pétain's rejection of a continuation of the Line along the Belgian frontier, if it was defective, was only defective inasmuch as his whole defensive policy was. If the one had been right, the other one would have been right too.

Even after his retirement in 1931, Pétain continued to watch over the progress of the Maginot Line. In 1932, when more money was made available for its construction, he wrote a letter to the *Conseil Supérieur de la Guerre* opposing his successor, Weygand's plan to extend the Line along the Belgian frontier. This was one of the first projects brought forward by Weygand, and its rejection shows that Pétain, though now in an inferior position, still had considerable pull.

In 1934, when Pétain was War Minister, the question of the Maginot Line came up several times. Before the *Commission de l'Armée du Senat* (Senate Army Committee) on 28 February Pétain stressed the poor state of the French army (about which he had a fortnight earlier received a pressing note from Weygand), and the need to strengthen even more the Maginot Line, which had not got the depth to it that he had originally desired. On 7 March before the same Committee, he opposed again Weygand's wish to extend the Line, saying that the Ardennes were impassable (needing only a few blockhouses to defend them), and that the tactics for the Belgian frontier were to advance into Belgium itself. Eventually he agreed, however, to some fortifications between Montmédy and the frontier of the Nord department.

On 14 June 1934, the Socialists produced a debate in the Chamber, demanding the adjournment of the military programme. It had been sparked off by the projected law, proposed on 28 February, which allowed for special credits for the army. In this debate Pétain spoke for the first time since becoming a Minister. His speech, and the tremendous reception it was given, show not only the admiration of all for the Marshal, but also the eager acceptance of his promises of safety. He was acclaimed on all sides. In this extract from his speech, justifying the extra money, he speaks of it going mostly to be used on the Maginot Line (and part of it for the extension between Montmédy and the Nord):

The money which is already at our disposal will run out before long, which would lead to a stoppage of work and the laying-off of 15,000 workers. Now, it is a question of work which must be carried out as soon as possible, between now and the winter. . . .

I insist on the immediate voting of these credits. It corresponds to the profound feeling of the population which wishes to live in peace behind solid frontiers. The fortifications are the inscription on the ground of that will.

The voting of these credits will mark once more, in the eyes of the world, the fact that France, far from nursing any thought of aggression, wants only to ensure its own security.[10]

He sat down, we are told, to 'vibrant' applause from the whole assembly. He won his vote by 472 votes to 120.

Daladier, speaking the next day, contrasted offensive and defensive strategy, and came down solidly on the side of the latter. The radicals, he said, were committed to putting their trust in concrete. In his view, the Maginot Line was inviolable.

Daladier spoke for many. To the average civilian, the Line *was* inviolable, and the country was safe. A 'Maginot Line mentality' had been created.

With the advent of Gamelin as Commander-in-Chief, however, French *military* views on this matter appear to have become sadly muddled. He was against continuation of the Line; but this may, of course, have been because he did not really believe in it. In his memoirs he says that he was more interested in tanks; many were built but, as we shall see, his tank programme was continually thwarted. The neutrality of Belgium changed all the conditions; but his new plans were merely old ones modified. One gets the impression of a man who had some ideas which were different from those of his predecessors, but who was hypnotised by the amount of money spent, the amount of training instilled, and the lack of armaments suitable for other tactics. So much so, that with such a short time available before the obviously imminent war, he ran round like a rabbit, combining two forms of tactics in a way that was detrimental to both.

The Maginot Line ate up French military finances in the ten years before the Second World War. At a time when money was short for military matters, it restricted the proper equipment of the French army in other ways, and particularly in the provision of the new weapons in sufficient quantities and their deployment in the most useful manner. As long as official policy remained firmly defensive, and as long as the new weapons were discounted, the policy was on the surface logical; but as views began to change on these matters, it became clear that the policy-making of the late 'twenties had tied everybody's hands, and that the nation was in an appalling state of unpreparedness. What is more, the opinions of the 'twenties were still strong on the *Conseil Supérieur de la Guerre*, and attempts to change policy were still difficult. Much of Gamelin's apparent irresolution may have stemmed from his being torn apart by these different forces.

One must not condemn the idea of having a 'defensive line' in itself, even though no such line could be impregnable. The worth of such a line, to impede and to direct enemy troops, was proved in the Second World War as well as the First. What was wrong with the French adoption of it was the overriding part which it took in military policy, and in military finances. This was the inevitable outcome of the French defensive policy.

Tanks

From Pétain's unchanged views on the nature of warfare, it is obvious that he was unaware of the tremendous part that was to be played in modern warfare by the mechanised weapons which first appeared in the First World War: tanks and aeroplanes. Though he on several occasions paid lip-service to the effect of these weapons, his more detailed comments on their use show that he had little idea of the far-reaching nature of their effects, nor of the way in which they could best be used. If he had, by the nature of things his whole military doctrine would have had to be modified. He was not alone in his ignorance; few French military thinkers had adjusted to the new weapons. And if he *had* realised their value, he was not a stupid man, he would have set about rethinking everything else in the light of this realisation.

In the case of tanks, much of his thought must have been affected by the experience of the First World War, in which the light Renault tanks used by the French forces had given little sign of the powerful instrument the tank was to become. He saw the tank as a useful adjunct to infantry action, which certainly added power; in the Riff, in 1925, he imported tanks to Morocco to add to the overwhelming might with which he was to crush Abd-el-Krim. He declared on many occasions that the army must exploit to the maximum the properties of the new machines; but he did not develop new tactics which could use these properties to the full. In this he was a mere example of the French military thought of his time; though, being at the head of the policy-making machine, he must bear his share of the responsibility.

There was, from the very first years after the war, an element in French military thought which had seen the possibilities of tanks. General Estienne, one of the first French officers to realise the new revolution in warfare which had been produced by the advent of the tank, publicly declared, in lectures and in pamphlets, in the early 'twenties, his conviction that completely new tactics would have to be evolved. Not only that, but a completely new strategy, and a new army organisation. He foresaw the advantages of a large force being able to cover eighty kilometres or more in a night, with all its equipment, and the overwhelming blow that it would be able to strike at the enemy. From 1921 to 1926 Estienne was Director of Tank Studies, and set about designing a tank for use; though he was followed in this (his tank was in fact used in 1939) his views on the uses of the tank were largely ignored. In the late 'twenties similar views to his were put forward by General Doumenc, who proposed armoured divisions which, with surprise attacks, would completely disorganise the enemy. He, too, was ignored on this point, though he reached some military eminence. For the traditionalist officers, Pétain included, the tank was merely another weapon to help the infantry, a weapon which was to be parcelled out among units, rather than forming a unit of its own.

Estienne and Doumenc are the main French examples of thinking that was going on in all three major European military countries. In Great Britain, Liddell Hart's studies of tank warfare were the most advanced in Europe. But Germany was the only country which had fully put these lessons into practice by the beginning of the Second World War, using Liddell Hart's writings in a way that his own country had not thought of doing.

In France the climax of the discussion over tank warfare came with the publication of Colonel de Gaulle's *Vers l'armée de métier* (Towards a professional army) in 1934. This was a restatement of the general views of Liddell Hart, Estienne and Doumenc, and drew the practical lesson from them that a special tank corps was needed, consisting of professional soldiers, not conscripts. (The one year national service was insufficient to train such specialists.) There should be 100,000 men, and 3,000 tanks, in special divisions, which should be entirely motorised, and partly armoured. The book, as one might expect, also contained references to France's mission, and to the rôle of the army in it.

In these years 1920 to 1934, Pétain showed little interest in the matter. One writer, Jacques Nobécourt, has made great play with the fact that Pétain wrote a preface of praise to Commandant Bouvard's book *Les Leçons militaires de la guerre*, which appeared in 1920. This book, says Nobécourt, 'announced the decisive action to be taken "by flotillas, by squadrons of tanks" followed by special infantry transported in lorries.' From this Nobécourt wishes us to believe that Pétain held the same views. Yet Pétain's preface, when we read it, is a short letter which praises the book only in a somewhat faint manner. It says nothing about the tank section, which was a very small part of the complete work, and suggests that some matters have not been gone into too deeply. It is merely the facsimile of a short letter from Pétain to Bouvard, and runs as follows:

My dear Bouvard,
It was a good service to render to those who have taken part in the war to explain simply to them the whys and wherefores of the subject; in this you have succeeded. Your book touches on many questions. Without going deeply into all of them it underlines their variety and complexity just enough to let the reader put his finger on the difficulties. I would be very surprised if any reader stopped before the end. Please receive my affectionate compliments.
Ph. Pétain.[11]

Pétain could hardly have realised, when writing to his friend Bouvard (even if he knew that a facsimile of his letter was going to be published), that this would be taken, in future years, to mean that he approved of specialised tank units!

Such equipment with tanks and motor vehicles as took place in the years 1920 to 1934 was not tied to any such concept. Partisans of Weygand (and Weygand himself, in his memoirs) have pointed out that he allowed Doumenc to speak before the *Centre des Hautes Études Militaires*, and that from the moment he took over as Chief of General Staff in 1930, he, realising the lack of modern tanks and of any organised policy, got Pétain and the *Conseil*

Supérieur de la Guerre to set on foot an organised programme. Nobody has ever suggested, however, that those who ignored, or who later opposed, the new ideas on tank warfare were against tanks themselves; they were aware that tanks were useful and effective additions to an army (Pétain himself had shown this in his decision to use them in the Riff campaign, as an extra bit of force to pulverise the Rifis). They merely saw them as being an *added* effective, rather than a reason to rethink tactics. Though Weygand's request was to produce a 'large mechanised unit', among other things, the description given of such a unit by the *Conseil*'s programme shows that it would contain vehicles of all sorts (armoured and unarmoured), and would be entirely unlike the 'armoured units' desired by the reformers. It is clear that the unit was to work at all times in liaison with the infantry; it was not a 'unit' of its own. The three types of purpose were to be, (1) Reconnaissance (aeroplanes, machine-gun carriers, light motorised vehicles), (2) Battle (light and heavy tanks), (3) Occupation of territory (transport vehicles). In fact, those writers who have seen in this programme a support for the reformers have misunderstood the use of the word 'unit' in this context; it clearly means the main motorised force, which could be split up for use with other arms. Such a force, and a powerful one, had been provided by 1940. It failed through being brought into contact with mechanised units formed on a new model, with a different conception of tank tactics.

Weygand's opposition, eventually, to de Gaulle's theories in 1934 and 1935 showed that an 'armoured unit' in de Gaulle's sense had never been his aim. He opposed what he considered to be the creation of two armies, and said 'we already have a mechanised, motorised, organised reserve. Nothing need be created, everything exists.'[12]

Some extreme figures, of course, denied even the use of tanks themselves. One such figure, a cavalryman called General Brecart, was even on the *Conseil Supérieur de la Guerre*. He wrote an article in the *Officier de réserve* in October 1933, claiming that the cavalry should be retained, as it was, on horseback, and that the new-fangled machines should not be trusted. France, after all, had splendid breeds of horses, and would be stupid to neglect the advantages this fact offered.[13] It would be an insult to Pétain and Weygand, however, to suggest that their views were on this level.

De Gaulle's book was taken up by the politician Paul Reynaud, who supported it in the newspapers, and in the Chamber of Deputies in March 1935. It caused quite a storm, for political as well as military reasons.

The military reasons, quite simply, rested on the belief in the defensive policy which France had until now followed. As General Maurin, War Minister, put it to the Chamber's *Commission de l'armée*, such a project was useless, undesirable, illogical and unhistorical. 'How could anyone believe', he asked, 'that we would still be thinking of the offensive, when we have expended millions to establish a fortified barrier? Are we foolish enough to go in front of that barrier, chasing all kinds of adventures?'[14] General Debeney believed that tanks were no longer as invulnerable as in 1918.

The political reasons for dislike of de Gaulle's plan were based on fear of a standing army. This fear had been constant among Republicans, and politicians of the Left, throughout the life of the Third Republic, where the army had, on the whole, stood for political reaction. At the time of this debate, nothing had proved to the Left that these fears were not justified. Men such as Weygand were not the only military men they feared, moreover. Many younger men seemed just as dangerous. And de Gaulle himself, in the ideas expressed in his book, had seemed to have a dangerously right-wing view of the army and the state. (It is fascinating, in this context, to find that Weygand regarded de Gaulle's side as 'Communist'.)

Léon Blum, in the parliamentary debate in March 1935, clearly stated the fears of the Left: 'In order to save national independence, you expose the nation to losing its internal liberty.' The debate decided the future of French tank warfare. Overwhelmingly, Reynaud was defeated.

Gamelin's new *Instruction*, in 1936, though it reintroduced the idea of the offensive, had little to say about tanks. But Gamelin himself was becoming more and more convinced of the value of them. His decision not to continue the Maginot Line, even after the declaration of Belgian neutrality in 1936, was in part due to his realisation of the need for more tanks; and in the same year, on 14 October, he spoke to the *Conseil Supérieur de la Guerre* about the German Panzer divisions, and declared the need for a French force of the same kind, but stronger (though it is not clear that he understood the organisation of the Panzer divisions). He met head-on disagreement with the *Conseil*, as he did again when he brought the matter up on 15 December 1937. The only thing he obtained was a declaration that the matter should be looked into during 1938. This examination of the question, in the event, did not take place because of the partial mobilisation for the Munich crisis. On 2 December 1938, the *Conseil* decided in principle on the formation of two armoured divisions (of only four tank battalions each), but left the details to be decided later.

Gamelin declared to Reynaud in 1937 that he was working in his direction (by which he meant that he supported more tanks),* but was being hindered by contingencies. Of these, the *Conseil Supérieur de la Guerre* was obviously the greatest, though finance was another, and the state of the French armaments industry yet another. The *Conseil* remained firmly opposed to the new-fangled ideas, and continually hindered them. Gamelin himself did not understand them. It is hardly surprising that Gamelin's pre-war military policy appears to be patchy.

What was Pétain's part in all this? He was a member of the *Conseil Supérieur de la Guerre*, of the *Conseil Supérieur de la Défense Nationale*, and the *Haut-Comité Militaire*. And, according to eye-witnesses, he took, though no longer at the head of things, a large part in discussions, and wielded quite a deal of influence, coming down occasionally on one side and helping it to succeed.

What were Pétain's views on tanks? In 1935, the year of the discussions on

* The *Instruction* of 1936 had still seen tanks as essentially to be used to support the infantry advance, which was the main element in battle.

Pétain is received at the French Embassy in Madrid, 1926. The group includes General Primo de Rivera (left on sofa) and General Jordana (standing behind Pétain on left).

Pétain between the wars

de Gaulle's book, he produced, almost certainly by a chance coincidence, a preface to General Sikorski's book *La Guerre moderne*, in which he discussed at some length the General's views, and added his own. The necessities of modern war, he said, were frontier fortifications, solid cover, defence against aeroplanes, and proper preparation for the mobilisation of the whole country. The main thing was to have sufficiently numerous and qualified forces. These should be able to rely on permanent defensive organisations.

All this seems his usual line; but he goes on to refer to the new weapons:

> In our days, modern armed forces, without giving up the benefit of numbers, which was the principal preoccupation of nations from 1870 to 1918, are moving more and more towards the search for material means characterised by force and rapidity. It is thus that the Navy is constructing light armoured vessels, that the Air Force is equipping itself with machines with an ever-growing range of action, and that the Army is enriching itself with motorised and mechanised material.
>
> The use of these new forces, combined with each other, poses new, delicate and complex questions of organisation and tactical employment. Favouring as they do swift attacks and surprise actions, these advances are of a kind to open new ways to the art of warfare.[15]

This is more than the usual trite doffing of the hat to progress. Could it be that Pétain was converted to the need for a change in French tactics and strategy? Or was he merely reflecting Sikorski's thought from the book? And, if he did believe in the need for consideration of new tactics, did this consist merely of an adaptation of present methods? After all, the preface still insists on the necessity for the defensive, and for fortifications. Did Pétain gauge the size of the problem?

The answer to this question is to be found in the 1938 preface to General Chauvineau's book *Une Invasion est-elle encore possible?* (1939), in which, as we have seen, Pétain continued to put forward the doctrine of the defensive. In the book itself, Chauvineau had declared 'As for tanks, which were supposed to be bringing us back to short wars, their failure is clear.' Pétain, in his preface, does not go as far as this; he does not condemn tanks outright; but he does make it clear that he considers their uses to be limited.

He suggests that they should be used above all for defence; and he opposes the offensive doctrines of de Gaulle's *armée de métier*, saying that any success achieved would be without a future, unless there were guarantees against possible subsequent failure. (Can he be remembering Cambrai, where in the First World War the British initial success with a tank attack was soon demolished?)

The offensive had been made difficult, he says, through the power of machine-guns and barbed wire. These can be overcome by tanks and heavy artillery; but such forces are 'expensive, small in number and relatively slow to put into action. The rarity of these materials restricts the front of attack. The time necessary to develop their useful action can be used by the defender to bring up his reserves, all the more easily as the attacked front is narrower.'

These are the lessons of the First World War all over again. Pétain is still obsessed by the 'impossibility' of a breakthrough. As for tanks: 'It seems that the technical possibilities of tanks, and the possibilities for the command of armoured divisions, have not been studied deeply enough. Above all . . . the hypothesis whereby the enemy might possess a similar army, and use it defensively, does not seem to have been envisaged. On the ground, a force exists to prevent the advance of armoured, tracked vehicles; it consists of mines, together with anti-tank fire. What would become of a tank attack, if it came upon divisions of a similar nature, carefully positioned in advance, with a pre-arranged plan of anti-tank fire over the battlefield, and natural obstacles reinforced by minefields? On the ground, up till now, every invention has in general profited the defender more than the attacker.'[16]

This last remark is as dogmatic as General Pellé's remarks in late 1917 had been on the permanent advantages of the offensive. Pétain goes on to say that tanks are 'quickly out of date and difficult to ameliorate.' They are thus best not for attacking, but in order to stop an attack, or to counter-attack against a disorganised assailant. Though the preface ends with a plea for examination of all the new weapons, it is clear that Pétain has already found tanks wanting.*

It is more than likely, therefore, that Pétain was one of those military powers who opposed, and held up, attempts to form a proper tank force. And the Minister of War, Daladier, was equally opposed in these years to the new ideas. Though pressing ahead with rearmament, he rejected a tank corps both because it would mean changing to an offensive policy, which would lead to a reorganisation of the complete military set-up, and because of the psychology of the army itself. In 1937, he declared that the Spanish Civil War had shown how useless these machines were. 'What would be the fate of our country if your specialised corps was routed?'[17] he asked in the Chamber.

Pétain's views were logical continuations of his views on the defensive; they stemmed above all from a continued 1914–18 approach to warfare. They were shared, also, by many prominent military and political figures. Against all this de Gaulle's *armée de métier* did not have a chance. By the beginning of the war, France was not deficient in tanks; but they were not organised in the proper way; unlike the German Panzer divisions, they were for the most part split among the infantry formations. Light mechanised divisions and armoured divisions were few, and badly organised.

Air force

On the question of aeroplanes Pétain's views were certainly more open than

---

* In a preface written in 1937, to a book on *L'École Militaire et L'École Supérieure de la Guerre* Paris 1937, Pétain mentions 'New machines, unsuspected yesterday', such as tanks and planes, and adds, 'Tactics and strategy have been completely changed by them.' His use of the past tense, and the fact that he is referring to the changes that have taken place already in the instruction given by the Schools, however, shows that for him the necessary changes have already been brought about.

they were upon tanks. In the Chauvineau preface, for example, he criticises Chauvineau for not mentioning air forces, and proceeds to speak of the possibilities of air-power.

In the inter-war period, however, France did not succeed in developing her air-power properly. As with tanks, the mistake was that of seeing air forces as being appendages to those forces that were already there. Attempts to rethink that whole matter, and to create a viable air force, were shot down; and Pétain was one of those responsible for obstructing these plans, despite his concern with air matters (particularly after becoming *Inspecteur Général de la Défense Aérienne*). No real attempt to modernise and properly to equip aviation was made.

The first attempt to create a modern air force was made as far back as 1923. Under the aegis of General Buat, an *Instruction sur la Constitution des Grandes Unités Aériennes du Temps de Paix*, dated 9 October 1923, was produced. This, declaring the purposes of air warfare to be divided into (a) destruction (bombers and fighters), and (b) reconnaissance, showed that no one type of aeroplane could fulfil the various functions, and proposed three main types: bombers (heavy and medium), reconnaissance (medium), and fighters (light). It proposed (and this was the revolutionary step) that the air force should reunite all the arms which had to do with the air, including anti-aircraft artillery. Stressing the need for a powerful air force, it proposed as a first measure 186 squadrons (36 of them heavy bombers) divided into five units: two fighter and reconnaissance divisions based on Metz and Paris, and three mixed brigades, based on Dijon, Tours and Lyon. Each of these large units would have a corresponding territory.[18]

Buat's death, however, in December 1923, meant that no more came of this. Debeney took over as Chief of General Staff. General Jauneaud, who was then adjutant to Buat, claims that Pétain was violently opposed to the scheme, and that Debeney supported him. Certainly it is clear that Pétain was ultimately responsible, having, as the faithful Laure puts it, 'aviation under his orders up till 1928.'

In 1928 an Air Ministry was created. Pétain was on the whole against its creation. He disliked the idea of separating air forces from ground forces. Keen as he was on the idea of unified command, he could only approve of an Air Ministry if it were part of a Ministry of National Defence, which would organise everything from the top. In one way, he was right, as he always had been in this wish for co-ordination. But in this case he clearly saw air forces as being necessarily subordinated to ground forces. As Laure innocently puts it, he preferred in the present situation 'to organise the air force as an autonomous army in the framework of the War Department,* much in the same way as had been done for the colonial army. In this way, aviation could organise itself, with its own statute and budget. But it would remain attached to the army by its subordination to the same Commander-in-Chief.'[19]

The new Air Ministry announced its intention of forming most of the

* Which did not include the naval forces.

bomber and fighter forces into an autonomous force. Pétain, as Laure says, was appalled by the suggestion that the land army, which up till now had had all air forces at its disposal, should be deprived of most of them, when it needed them for its own operations. 'He did not deny the utility, indeed the necessity, of an autonomous air force, but thought that it was the Air Ministry's task to create it *over and above* the indispensable forces for the land army—and for the navy, which was in the same situation—and not by taking planes from the quotas of these forces. . . .'[20]

Laure is perhaps naïve in his assessment of Pétain's arguments. For he has already made it clear in his book that money was extremely short for aeroplanes. Pétain knew this too, which is why his argument ended by saying that as long as the means did not exist to create this supplementary force, all air forces should remain at the disposal of the Commander-in-Chief of the army. In other words, despite his apparent openness he was opting for the *status quo*.

In the years 1929 and 1930, aided and abetted by the navy, Pétain had a prolonged argument with the Air Ministry on these matters. Laure suggests that a compromise *modus vivendi* came from this; but what in fact happened was that Pétain got his way.

Pétain's appointment as General Inspector of Aerial Defence of the Territory, on 9 February 1931, might seem somewhat ironical, particularly as the title, like so many other titles of posts and committees in this inter-war period, stressed the word 'defence'. Laure suggests that, now he had become responsible for part of air forces once more, his attitudes changed; this, however, was not so. In the three years he spent in this post, his concerns were mainly with 'co-ordination', the policy of which he had so long been in favour; he torpedoed the only real attempt to have a logical air command in this period, and his own proposals tended to make it, if anything, more fragmented than before. A co-ordinated defence organisation such as Pétain wished for was in fact essential to the proper running of the Forces; the lack of it, until too late, was to prove disastrous. But within the framework of such a co-ordinated organisation, there had to be a properly organised series of Forces. Pétain failed to see the need, within his ideal framework, for a coherent organisation of the air forces.

His first action was to fight in the interests of his new post. Air forces were under the command of the army and navy; some must be released for national defence. They would be used for defence of the territory, and for offensive reprisals. The Government, realising the difficulty of decisions or such parcelling-out of the Forces, decided that an authority must be set up Laval, the Premier, asked Pétain to be at the head of things. Pétain soon realised, however, that he had no real power, and in view of the budgetary difficulties incumbent on any decision, asked for the setting-up of a Ministry of National Defence. Such a Ministry would co-ordinate the budgetary requirements and the administration of the Services. On the military level it would have a Chief of General Staff of National Defence.

Such a Ministry was formed in February 1932 by the Tardieu Government, with François Piétri as Minister. It did not have the military link of a Chief of General Staff, however, and Pétain expressed the need for one, while pointing out that the job given to him by Laval had been this sort of post. This heavy hint was not heeded. Instead, a *Haut-Comité Militaire* was set up at the end of March, consisting of the holders of the two senior posts (Vice-President of the Council, and Chief of General Staff) from all three Services. The Inspector-General of Aerial Defence did not figure on it, however.

Much of Pétain's annoyance at this may have come from personal pique at not being 'in on things'; but he was also very keen to further the power of his own section of national defence. From now on, his main concern was to get a fair share for aerial defence. This is not, as Laure seems to think, a support for a separate air force; it is a plea for yet one more subdivision of forces, one more authority over the air forces.

His next tactic was to suggest to the Minister, in April 1932, the setting-up of a General Air Reserve, consisting of bombers and fighters. This would be under a 'Chief of General Staff of National Defence' and could be used either for the armies, or for aerial defence of the territory. He sent a copy to Weygand (now Vice-President of the *Conseil Supérieur de la Guerre*), who was not impressed.

Again Pétain returned to the attack. He put forward to Weygand a plan for four 'domains of operation'. Laure describes this ideas as 'revolutionary', but looked at dispassionately it merely appears to be a modification of the present system, to include 'aerial defence', and a further fragmentation of air forces.

The idea was, that under a supreme chief there should be four commands, army, navy, air force and aerial defence of the territory, each with its own commander-in-chief. The air forces would be divided as follows:

(1) Day fighter reserve, under Aerial Defence, to bar the way of an attacking enemy.
(2) Night fighter reserve, under Aerial Defence, to defend threatened points.
(3) General bomber reserve, under 'military chief of general staff'.
(4) Observation, reconnaissance, and other fighter and bomber forces, for land co-operation under army commander-in-chief.
(5) Seaplanes, carrier planes, observation and reconnaissance squadrons, and some fighters and bombers, under the naval commander-in-chief.

This was the furthest that Pétain's views on co-ordination were to get, as far as the air force was concerned. It perpetuates the idea of the air force as a subsidiary arm, to be used mainly for defence, and by its division of the forces prevents any idea of overall air planning. It is about as far as one can get from the Buat proposals, which were soon to come up again in a slightly different form.

In the Herriot Government, which came in on 3 June 1932, Painlevé, the new Air Minister, had a new *Haut-Comité* set up, which included Pétain and Aerial Defence; it did not, as we have seen, meet, though Pétain sent forward to Painlevé on 19 September, for a prospective meeting, the same plan for 'four domains' that he had put to Weygand. The only committee of this type to continue meeting during this Government was the old *Haut-Comité Militaire*, which did not include Pétain.

Meanwhile, the air force General Staff, under General Armengaud, the Adjutant Chief of General Staff, strongly criticised the 'four domains' theory, and made proposals which would lead to a united air force, after the Buat manner. Painlevé, the Air Minister, was, however, not entirely in favour of this. He set up a committee under the presidency of his old friend Pétain, to look into the various theories; the examination and experimentation involved never took place, by Government decision.

It was now that one of the most important figures in pre-war aviation matters came on the scene: the politician Pierre Cot, who became Air Minister in the new Daladier Government in February 1933. Cot, like all French politicians of minister level, had his own 'Cabinet' to work on the problems relating to his Ministry; and in this Cabinet he had Buat's former adjutant, Jauneaud. It swiftly became clear that Pierre Cot was going strongly to support the air force General Staff's desire for a properly organised, independent air force, capable of using aeroplanes for the tactics and strategy for which they were now suited, and of combining with other forces most efficaciously. For this, he required a combined High Command. (This should, of course, have appealed to Pétain.)

Pierre Cot, with Denain, his new Chief of General Air Staff, saw Pétain, and set forward his plan for freeing the air forces from the control of other departments, to enable them to fulfil their functions to the best of their ability. For him 'aerial battle', which had on the whole been ignored by Pétain's plan, was going to be one of the most important functions (as, in the event, it turned out in the Second World War). For the purpose of discussing this, the Supreme Air Council should be called, and should incorporate high military authorities from the other departments, to set on foot the proposed reorganisation.

Pétain now showed his capability for political manoeuvring. He suggested to Cot that the correct body for this discussion would be the Painlevé *Haut-Comité*, about which everybody had forgotten, and which had in fact never met, but on which he had a seat. Cot, convinced by Pétain, asked Daladier to set up, and preside at, this committee, which met on 20 March 1933. At this meeting the navy and the army (Weygand) strongly opposed Cot's proposals. Daladier therefore asked Pétain to try and find a compromise formula before the next meeting, a week later.

Pétain, after seeing Denain, Cot (who, says Laure, asked him to become Chief of General Staff of the Armed Forces, and supervise the reorganisation of the High Command), Gamelin, Weygand, and Durand-Viel, was able on the 25th, to produce a note as basis for the second meeting, which took place on 27 March. This note was accepted almost without discussion, writes Laure,[21] except that the army and navy succeeded in retaining the *status quo* in face of the Air Ministry's request for a co-ordinated High Command.

What was the rest of this 'compromise' paper, which was accepted? The decree published on 1 April was based on Pétain's views on the 'four domains'. It was in no way a 'compromise', but a contradiction of Pierre Cot's views. Small wonder that Cot and his staff, including Jauneaud, felt that they had been torpedoed.

In the Doumergue Government of February 1934, Pétain became Minister of War. Though his own view had always been that there ought to be a Minister of National Defence, who would govern all the Armed Forces, he thus found himself in charge of the army alone. (Doumergue did not wish to change anything in the Government, considering that the political state of the nation made stability all-important.) He therefore had little to do with the Air Force.

On the fall of this Government, however, as we have seen, he was made a permanent member of the *Conseil Supérieur de la Défense Nationale* and of the *Haut-Comité Militaire*, where he was in a position of some influence. His interests in aviation continued: in 1935, for example, he contributed a preface to a book by Colonel Vauthier, *La Doctrine de Guerre du Général Douhet*, which dealt with the air theories of the famous Italian General. Nothing leads us to believe, however, that his views on air organisation changed in any way.

With the *Front Populaire* Government, Pierre Cot again returned in 1936, and with him his 'Cabinet', including Jauneaud. It was Jauneaud who wrote, for the most part, the important *Instruction sur l'emploi tactique des Grandes Unités Aériennes* of 31 March 1937, which was signed by the Air Minister Pierre Cot, and had an introduction written by General Féquant, Chief of General Air Staff (Denain's successor). This document was a repetition, and a continuation of, Buat's 1923 *Instruction*; indeed, in his introduction Féquant summarised Buat's document, and said of it: 'This 1923 doctrine was not to emerge from the theoretical domain for several years.' He stressed the importance of an independent air force, and suggested that if the army's defensive policies (i.e., the Maginot Line) proved correct, the air force might be the only manoeuvrable force in a static battle. He quoted the decree of 1 April 1933, which stated the air force's duties as being (1) aerial operations, (2) combined operations with land and sea forces, (3) aerial defence of the territory. (He did not, however, mention the organisational chaos involved in the splitting-up of these activities under different authorities by that decree.)

A decree of 3 September 1936, had set up large aerial units, and also air infantry; and it had grouped all the formations of the Air Force into one general air reserve. This was the great achievement of the Cot administration; the whole thing was finally centrally organised. The further wishes expressed in the main *Instruction* of 1937, which had to do with the creation of an effective fighting force, were, however, to come to nothing.

The *Instruction* was a logical document. It expressed, for the first time in a state document, the forms of use for air-power, and the needs which they therefore caused in the way of aerial reinforcement for France. It hurried over reconnaissance (which to so many people had until now seemed one of the main uses of an air force), and concentrated above all on aerial battle, and on aerial participation in ground battle.

On the question of aerial battle, it made the point that unlike the army or navy, the air force had the possibility of neutralising an opposing army, navy *or* air force; it was also capable of action over all, or over an important part of, enemy territory. It could act alone, *or* in conjunction with other forces. In offensive action, its object was to destroy (1) the enemy armed forces (air, land and sea), (2) means of communication, or bases allowing the manoeuvring of these enemy forces (transport lanes, railway junctions, stations, ports, air and naval bases, etc.), (3) centres of production which supplied the Forces with all kinds of resources (industrial and economic centres, depots, arsenals, etc.). For this offensive action, heavy aeroplanes, i.e., mainly bombers, were above all important.

The defensive function was seen as consisting primarily of attacks on the prospective danger, the enemy planes, either on the ground at their own aerodrome, or in the air; it also consisted of protecting one's own planes; as a final object 'covering essential objectives' was put down. It was on the whole more offensive than Pétain's view of aerial defence.

The participation of the air force in the ground battle was also seen as extremely important; and, unlike Féquant (the writer of the Introduction), Jauneaud in the *Instruction* sees this battle as a 'battle of movement', requiring 'rapid and wide-ranging actions',[22] which can be helped by aerial transport of troops. The air force should also attack all communication centres, and places through which the enemy army must move; it must attack the enemy troops themselves, whether in camp or deployed; it must also be prepared to attack 'armoured formations'.

All this seems pretty obvious to us today, with the Second World War behind us. But in the French pre-war situation it was startlingly revolutionary, not only in its belief in the possibility of a war of movement in which armoured divisions would take part, but also in the far-reaching purposes of which it saw the air force as being capable.

For these purposes a vast amount of aircraft production was going to be needed; the present air force was not only insufficient, but was also to a large extent built up on the wrong lines. A large amount of the military budget would have to be devoted to the air force, which was in urgent need of light and heavy bombers.

But at the *Conseil Supérieur de la Défense Nationale* the whole project was shot down, and most of the military budget was directed into other services. As in so many cases, the bulk of the money went to Darlan and to the French Navy, which, thanks to Darlan's efforts, was not only the only well-prepared French Service at outbreak of war, but also one of the finest navies in the world. At the *Conseil*, according to Jauneaud, Pétain came down strongly against the air force, and strongly on Darlan's side.

The French air force was never to be properly equipped. When Guy la Chambre became Air Minister in 1938, with Vuillemin as Chief of General Staff and Bergeret as *chef de cabinet*, he succeeded in getting more money for

aviation though production was slow because of the state of French industry;*
but, despite what Feller says,[23] he did not set about *modernisation* of the
Air Force in any serious way. Buat's *Instruction* of 1923, and Cot's of 1937,
were not followed, and the French air force remained mainly an auxiliary
arm, for reconnaissance and fighter action. Above all, no idea seems to have
been entertained of the need for dive-bombers.

Pétain's part in all this was one of blocking at almost every stage. Was this
necessarily a conscious policy on his part? He had some idea of the importance of an air force, but saw it primarily as an auxiliary arm. In his Chauvineau preface of 1938, he saw the possibility of offensive action behind the
enemy lines, but stressed that the three Forces did not fight separately, but
continually reacted one upon the other. Though he paid lip-service to the
power of the air arm, he did not seem to realise its full capabilities.

In his attitudes of the 'thirties, he clearly regarded air force inadequacies
as being on the same par as other inadequacies, such as the shortage of men.
He failed to realise the overwhelming might of air-power, without which even
tank divisions were to prove to be next to useless. In this he was in good
company; de Gaulle, in his *Vers l'armée de métier*, similarly ignored the
relation between air power and tank tactics (though the post-war edition
surreptitiously put a section in about it). Pétain was one of the vast majority
of people who failed to grasp, until too late, the importance of this new
factor; and he cannot really be criticised personally for it.

Pierre Cot must, however, be praised, as must his team, for their foresight. It was they who were calumniated and criticised for their part in
French unpreparedness for the Second World War; yet, in the case of the
Air Force, as in other matters, their record is cleaner than that of their
accusers. Pétain, from statements made in the very late 'thirties, eventually
realised the inadequacy of French air-power in relation to the Germans; but
he did not realise the basic requirements and uses of air power in a modern
context.

Men, armaments and finance

Throughout the 'twenties and 'thirties, the French Government and High
Command were faced by two major problems; one the disparity between the
nation's desire to keep up a firm policy against Germany, and the natural
desire of the electorate for the shortening of national service: the other, the
impossibility of building up the nation's armaments properly in the face of a
series of financial crises. This second problem was, of course, exacerbated
from 1930 onwards by the Maginot Line policy, which ate up resources
that could have been used elsewhere.

In the case of Pétain, the interesting thing is to see the changes in his
attitude to these problems at various stages of the period.

As far as national service was concerned, there was a strong demand, once

* Pierre Cot has been much blamed for his policy of nationalisation of the aviation
  industry. This industry had, however, also been in an appalling state under private
  enterprise. It is not clear that Cot made things worse.

149

the war was over, to reduce the two-year period. Admittedly, a large section of the nation (particularly the Right, but not exclusively so) wished to 'contain' Germany; Poincaré's Ruhr venture of 1923 received much acclaim. On the other hand, a minority, but a substantial minority, of the nation took up an anti-militaristic stance. And, of course, many of those who were in the first category nevertheless, illogically, hoped that the policy could be pursued while national service was reduced. After all, it was peacetime. The 1924 left-wing election victory of the *Cartel des Gauches* was in part based on a promise to reduce national service (which had already been reduced in part).

Pétain, in the early 'twenties, was clearly against any reduction. He and Buat considered that, for the moment, two years was essential if France was to fulfil her obligations. Nevertheless, they were aware of the strong current of public opinion, and prepared for eventualities accordingly. If service was to be shortened to eighteen months, they said, three prerequisites must be fulfilled: at least 106,000 professional soldiers must be provided, and 205,000 native soldiers, plus civil employees at the rate of 30,000. None of these requirements had been fulfilled when, on 1 April 1923, the law was passed limiting military service to eighteen months, and thereby reducing the French army from fifty-two to thirty-two divisions (apart from certain colonial mobile forces and cavalry). The army now consisted of 360,000 men, each annual contingent being about 250,000. Something of a victory for the military was, however, achieved by the fact that these men remained at the disposal of the army for two years after their release.

In the same year the French had already occupied the Ruhr; manpower was extremely short. Nevertheless, the *Cartel des Gauches*, stressing the fact that France had no offensive objectives, put in their programme for the 1924 elections a reduction of national service to one year. In Pétain's view such a reduction would be fatal for the army; but, the Cartel having won, he saw it was inevitable, and (though it was not, in fact, to come in for another four years) set about trying to work out how the army could still be made into a viable force in such a situation.

Pétain was not at all happy, however. He expressed privately to Clemenceau, in 1924, how much he had suffered from 'the policy of abandonment, and of perpetual concessions, which was being carried out by those who govern us, and consequently the sabotage of the Versailles treaty. As for the army, he fully realised that it had had only Ministers of War who were either incapable or *je m'en fichistes*, and who rarely took any notice of his advice. Nevertheless, he felt it his duty not to abandon this army, in order to avoid the worst. . . .'[24]

One-year national service had many inconvenient characteristics over and above the shortage of men. For example, the period of service would be too short for the training of the specialists which modern warfare would need; and, of course, in the case of a crisis only about half the recruits (who came in two six-month batches) would be properly trained in even the basic requirements of warfare. The only real solution would be a large force of trained professional soldiers; but these were hard to get.

In 1925, just to give point to all these worries, the Riff War and the Druse revolt in Syria ate up French effectives; though the evacuation of the Ruhr helped the situation a little.

Among the stipulations made by Pétain and the High Command, if one-year national service was to come in, was that at least 106,000 professional soldiers must be available. Pétain had suggested that nobody should be allowed to be in State civil employ, unless he had served in the army over and above the compulsory limit. But the Government refused this project, and merely postulated voluntary engagement.

Discussions went on for some time, and it became clear that one-year service was inevitable. Many people have seen, in Pétain's activities in these years, a too easy acceptance of Government policy; the reality is quite different. He fought all the way, and obtained various changes which alleviated things (such as the 1923 clause about the men remaining at the army's disposal for two years after release). He realised that head-on opposition to the politicians would have been useless; and he knew that any successor of his might either be an all-out fighter of this kind, or else someone who would take anything the Government said. In 1927 he broke out against the politicians, in private talk with Clemenceau, and continued by saying that: 'Everyone was hypnotised by the obsession of peace, but of a peace, it seemed, at any price, without ever wishing to envisage properly the measures to be taken to ensure that peace. In short, the Marshal had often thought of resigning his functions. Unfortunately, as far as his successor was concerned, questions of personality were of such seriousness that, in face of certain eventualities, and of certain projects he knew of, a certain choice which would be imposed by politics, he had fully decided, in the interests of the army and consequently of the country, to stay for a while at his post. . . '[25]

On 1 April 1928, the law of one-year service was passed. It was to bring the main French army down to 20 Divisions. It stated that it would only come into force if, by 1 November 1930, 106,000 professional soldiers had been recruited, plus 15,000 military police and 15,000 *gardes mobiles*. Nevertheless, even though these 'indispensable conditions' had not been carried out, on that date the one-year service came into effect.

From now onwards, Pétain continued to stress the need for prolongation of service, even if by only a few months. At his resignation in 1931 he left a memorandum making the case once more.

So France entered the *années creuses* (hollow years) of the mid-'thirties with an army that was already inadequate and ill-trained; the *années creuses* caused by the low birth-rate of the war years would soon make it less in numbers. Despite its small size, however, it was an expensive army; and, through the financial difficulties of the 'twenties and early 'thirties, an extremely badly-equipped army. As far as armaments were concerned, the French Army was sadly lacking both in quantity and in quality.

Throughout the 'twenties and early 'thirties, defence budgets had on the whole been between 25·6 per cent and 27·3 per cent of national expenditure.[26] This was not enough, and cries of alarm were continually sent up by the

Service chiefs. In 1922 Buat signed a memorandum drawing attention to the grave danger of the situation; Pétain wrote a covering note claiming that the army would soon be incapable of performing its functions. With the financial situation getting worse, however, the Government was unable even to fulfil what it had promised.

At the beginning of 1924 Pétain produced an 'Account of the French army', in which he drew serious attention to the inferiority of French arms and material to those used by the Germans. Also, there was a bad shortage of munitions.

The financial crisis which hit France at this time, however, meant that in 1925 and 1926 the defence budgets dropped to 16 per cent of national expenditure.[27]

With the national economy back on its feet again, the armament situation began to improve in quantity from 1927 onwards; but French armaments still remained inferior in quality. To deal with this situation a *Conseil Supérieur de l'Armement* was set up, to study the question. The early 'thirties, however, saw the true reason for the failure of the French armament programme; the Maginot Line, which ate up the money provided. Added to this, of course, there was also the concentration on the old-style conventional weapons, and on light reconnaissance planes and fighters, rather than on offensive tanks and bombers. Weygand's 1930 programme was an attempt to close some of the gaps, especially with regard to tanks; but French armaments limped into the 'thirties with no real prospect of improvement on any scale. Weygand fought, year by year, but each year more cuts were made in the original modest programme.

1933 was perhaps the year of greatest alarm, as credits continued to be cut in the worstening financial situation of the country. In January, out of 4 billion francs' worth of economies over the whole national budget, 1 billion 73 million was taken from the army, and Daladier, as War Minister, decided that 5,000 out of 30,000 officers must go within five years. Weygand protested forcibly, but in vain. In late 1933 it was realised that there was a budget deficit, and again there was talk of a reduction in army credits involving a reduction in manpower. The day before the Bill containing the proposals came to the Chamber of Deputies, the *Conseil Supérieur de la Guerre* met; among those who forcibly condemned the Bill were Pétain, Lyautey and Weygand.

Pétain's appointment as War Minister in the Doumergue Government in 1934 might have seemed to open new hope on these issues. It would have been presumed that he would fight for an extension in national service, a stop to reductions in men and armaments, and a vastly enlarged armaments programme. None of this, however, came to pass. No doubt because of a feeling of the need for Ministerial collective responsibility, Pétain in this period ignored the pleas of his former military colleagues, and continued the policies of his predecessors, contenting himself with occasional minor palliations of the measures involved.

The warnings from the military were not slow in coming. On 10 February, as soon as the Doumergue Government was installed, Weygand sent Pétain a report upon the last two years. 'The army today', he wrote, 'has sunk to the lowest level that the security of France can allow, in the present state of Europe.'[28] On 23 February he sent Pétain a more detailed letter, explaining all the cuts that had taken place in the last two years. On 28 April he wrote again on the same subject.

One of the conditions on which Pétain had agreed to serve in the Government was that the army should be no further diminished; but this was not really the question now. The army had already descended so far that the only way to save it was to move positively in the other direction. Above all, the *années creuses* were almost upon France; and at some points these would mean a reduction of up to fifty per cent in the intake of recruits.

Laure, in his book, stresses the financial difficulties faced by the new Government, and the fighting power of M. Germain-Martin, the Finance Minister. Pétain, as a non-politician, must have been somewhat lost in the battles that took place for the small finances that there were. But, once decisions had been taken, he abided by them, and clung to ministerial solidarity, without open criticism of any kind. This is the explanation of his apparent change of policy.

On 28 February and 7 March Pétain appeared before the two Army Commissions (of the Chamber and the Senate). Among other things, he said that national service could not be enlarged, because the people would not stand for it.

In April a decree was passed reducing the number of civil and military employees by ten per cent. This was taken, by Pétain, to involve the reduction by 5,000 of the officer corps, which Daladier's previous decree had already provided for, and he tried to carry it out, even though Weygand and Gamelin, by obstructive tactics, managed to palliate its effects.

An interesting further act by Pétain, in early April, was his acceptance of a reduction in the pensions of former soldiers, and his persuasion of the old soldiers, by statements about duty to the country, to accept this. As *L'Écho de Paris* put it on 7 April, some of the financial steps taken by the Government to face the crisis were particularly bad for the old soldiers. Pétain had, until now, been above all the defender of such bodies; he had also, in the early 'twenties, put up a hard fight for soldiers' pay; but now Government solidarity was the thing.

On 17 April the French Government rejected a British offer, whereby French and German forces would be equalised at 300,000 men.

On 28 April, on the same day as receiving another Weygand missive, Pétain agreed to a decree reorganising troops in France, suppressing two of the twenty military regions, and thereby economising on men.

In May, Weygand, in desperation, called the *Conseil Supérieur de la Guerre* together. (Pétain was not present.) The meeting composed a note to Pétain, stressing the growing strength of the new German army, and the fact that 'in its present state, the French army would not be in a position to face up to such a threat without grave risks.' An urgent step to take was to put up military service to two years once more. 'If in the years to come Germany became even more threatening, it would be indispensible to increase the force of the French army by augmenting the permanent peace-time forces, *and by taking all measures permitting us to raise to the maximum the use of the resources of the nation.*'[29]

Pétain did not even reply to this note. Meanwhile, though he continued to obtain money for the Maginot Line, and to prepare further credits for that purpose, he did little about finance for other armaments, or for the national service question. The question of national service was, of course, a political one; but it seems strange that Pétain, above all (with all his previous talk about politicians who put their politics above the safety of the country) should have taken a political line on this.

At the debate in mid-June on military credits, Daladier and Renaudel had asked for a discussion of the question of military service, but had been told by Doumergue that it was not part of the present debate, and had not yet come under consideration. In early July Pétain, speaking before the Army Commission of the Chamber, declared that 'an augmentation of the length of service is not envisaged.'[30]

Pétain admittedly added that he reserved the right to proceed to the provision of the effectives necessitated by the external situation. This meant the incorporation of eight months' worth of recruits in six months (a measure that was a temporary palliative, rather than a long-term solution), and the encouragement of re-engagements, and of professional soldiery, particularly the recruiting of specialists. During the year he made sure, too, of full value from the one-year service, by restricting leave, and stopping premature release. To encourage volunteers, he tried to get the dole refused to those who had just come out of the army, for six months, or even refused to all those between eighteen and thirty, while giving advantages to those who served in the army (in this, of course, he received opposition from the Minister of Labour). In a harsh decree, on 8 July, he strengthened the penalties for conscientious objection.

Pétain's stress on the need for volunteers, and above all for specialists, led certain sections of the press to compare his ideas with those of de Gaulle in his new book *Vers l'armée de métier*. Pétain was, however, later to draw attention to the differences between the two concepts, in his preface to Chauvineau. He saw his own army of specialists as a *réserve de couverture*, a defensive reserve; *'l'armée de métier'*, he said, 'is an offensive instrument; the quality of its material and its recruiting make of it, for its author, an irresistible instrument. There would be some imprudence in adopting these conclusions. . . .'[31]

Pétain did, in the autumn, manage to get special credits voted through despite the fact that the Finance Minister had refused to let the expenditure through in the usual way. In his speech to the Finance Commission at the end of October, to persuade them to take this step, he stressed the Reich's military preparations, and the French need for money and men. 'While there has been no question of prolongation of service', ran the press report, 'that eventuality has not been formally set aside.'[32] But the speech was mainly financial, and one gets the impression that the oblique reference to national service was more a threat to obtain the money, than a serious proposal at this time. Pétain's scare statements produced a good deal of agitation on the *Bourse*. It must be stressed, also, that the money he obtained was more for work on the Maginot Line than for armaments.

The fact that Pétain did not really believe in the continued effectiveness of one-year service is shown by the fact that, soon after he left the Government, he wrote an important article in the *Revue des Deux Mondes* of 1 March 1935, stressing the need for two-year service. This article, entitled *La Sécurité de la France au cours des années creuses* was swiftly taken up by the national press. In *Le Jour*, for example, the editions of 3–4, 9–11 March all contained leaders on the subject. On the 11th it contained a violent attack on Blum, and claimed that for six months everyone had known that two-year service was inevitable: 'Marshal Pétain's call has caused immense repercussions, because of the great authority of its author, and also because the opportuneness of it is obvious.'[33] It declared that the law was bound to be voted.

Pétain's article had prepared public opinion; the Flandin Government, and General Maurin, the War Minister, proceeded to use it. Despite the suggestions from the press of the Right that Flandin and his Government were ruled by fear of the elector (and that Doumergue's Government had not been),[34] the opposite proved to be true. On 15 March a law of two-year service was voted through amid loud Socialist protests, particularly from Léon Blum. The 1935 influx would do eighteen months, the next three years' influx two years. Thus the danger of the *années creuses* would be overcome. (The right-wing press claimed that, by making this ruling provisional, the Flandin Government had produced a cowardly compromise, and that a future Government would be able to reverse the decision. This, however, did not happen.)

Pétain, when asked by a journalist what he thought of this vote, replied: 'I can make no declaration to you. This news, to within a few figures, has been known already for a long time, it makes official a state of things which already existed. . . . Ten Army Corps, thirty-six Divisions, what a reply to yesterday's Socialist speech!' And the journalist continues: 'And with the calm that has become legendary, the Marshal left us after making a gesture expressing the thought of a man who *knew* and whom nobody had wished to listen to in time.'[35]

So the question of national service was settled. It took the shock of the Nazi march into the Rhineland to change views on armaments, and to speed up production. From military declarations at the time it was clear that France, mainly through manpower shortage, but also through deficiency in armaments, would be incapable of standing up to a serious German challenge.

It was the Popular Front Government, which came in in May 1936, which set about the expansion of rearmament. By 1937 and 1938 military credits had risen to 32·1 per cent and 35·7 per cent of all state expenditure.[36]

And these military credits were no longer almost entirely spent on the fortification of the Maginot Line. Armaments expanded as much as dilapidated French industry could provide. During the years 1936–40, through successive Governments, Daladier was permanently Minister of Defence. And, though the plans for the armaments had clearly been made before, it was under his rule that production went forward. Some of the models were no doubt inferior, but in fact it was thanks to him and Gamelin (despite what was to be said at the Riom trial) that French armaments had reached the stage they had by 1940. There were, indeed, enough tanks, if only they had been organised in the proper way (the French and British in fact had more tanks than the Germans in the 1940 campaign); conventional arms were strongly increased, though they were still not enough, by any means; the air force, because of a blind policy in relation to its aims, lacked the planes it required.

Conclusion

Pétain's actions with regard to national service were absolutely logical, except during his 'political year', throughout this period. He opposed reductions, did his best to organise things to cope with them when they became inevitable, and eventually pressed for the essential return to two-year service. As far as armaments were concerned, he attempted to obtain adequate finance; but it was his policies which forced so much to be squandered on the Maginot Line to the detriment of other arms, and which eventually led to the lacks in the air force. Also, his views on tank warfare (shared by Daladier and many others) meant that expenditure on France's tanks was wasted.

All in all, the defensive policy which lay at the base of most of France's military problems was a hangover from the lessons of the First World War. Pétain was one among many who were responsible; but he, because of his high office and his high reputation, must bear the greatest responsibility. The French army, between the wars, was ruled by old men, whose experience of one war remained their lesson for the future. William Shirer, then an American newspaper correspondent, described in his *Berlin Diary* the difference between the German and French armies in June 1940 as follows: 'The commanding officers of the German army are, for the most part, mere youngsters compared to the French generals we have seen. The latter strike you as civilised, intellectual, frail old men who stopped thinking new thoughts twenty years ago and have taken no physical exercise in the last ten years ... The great trouble with the Allied command—especially the French—was that it was dominated by old men who made the fatal mistake of thinking that this war would be fought on the same general lines as the last war. The rigidity of their military thinking was fixed somewhere between 1914 and 1918, and the matrix of their minds was never broken.'[37]

This fits the generals in charge in 1940; apart from the reference to physical frailness, it also fits the two men who were brought in to help in

June 1940, and who had been at the centre of things in the vital years of preparation: General Weygand and Marshal Pétain.

In the years immediately preceding the war, Pétain was at times to criticise the French lack of preparation, and lack of organisation. In fact his desire to return from time to time from his Spanish ambassadorship in 1939–40 had bearing on this point. On the second count he was perhaps justified; the organisation of the command was not brilliant under Gamelin. As far as tactics were concerned, too, much of Pétain's policy had been abandoned, without anything positive taking its place. All this we shall see in our account of the 1940 battle. Pétain would, of course, dislike the abandonment of his policy, and abhor Gamelin's arrangements on this account. As far as armaments were concerned, Pétain was later to show himself illogical in his criticisms of Daladier. Daladier had, as we have seen, raised production of arms, and antiquated French industry was producing them as hard as it could. What was wrong was the initial shortages (for which Pétain was partly responsible), the lacks in certain types of arms (such as bombers, for which Pétain was again partly responsible), and the inability to use certain arms properly (such as tanks, for which Pétain was again partly responsible). Any drawbacks in tactics and armaments in 1940 stem from the Pétain era, rather than from the faults of the men left holding the baby.

Chapter Five

Political thought, 1918–39

A CLAIM to be non-political often denotes a political interest. A dislike for 'politics' and 'politicking' may just mean that one disapproves of the democratic process. It is, in fact, one of the characteristics of a certain kind of Right to make such protestations. The comments are usually sincere; nevertheless they are usually political, without those who make them fully realising it. Politics, in its narrower sense (which is the sense such people are using), is the *business* of politics, the wheeling-dealing, the deceit, the agreements, the alliances. Politics, in its wider sense, is the consideration of what is best for a community, and the means to achieve it. Most of those who disapprove of politics in the first sense do so because they have strong ideas in the second area.

Philippe Pétain was not an original thinker on anything other than military matters. His thought was mainly a reflection of the ideas, emotions and prejudices of a certain, and large, section of the French population, together with a number of ideas which were typical of military men of his time. But this is in a sense what makes him important. As a prominent public figure in the inter-war period, he was in a position to express these opinions, and to be listened to with respect; as Head of Government from 1940 onwards, he was able to set about putting them into effect, with the help of the similarly-minded men whom he grouped around him. Pétain was a kind of loud-speaker, through whom we can today pick up the evidence of a series of continuous trends in French political thought, which have remained much the same in their general outline from the first years of the Third Republic onwards. The Vichy régime was the only example of a Government based on this tradition.

In the years before the First World War, much of the support for these attitudes had been in Catholic circles;[1] but it would be a mistake to think that this was the only area where such ideas were fostered. These views, on Tradition, the Family, the Land, Work and Order, were the characteristics of a traditional Right, which in these years felt its influence to be growing less and less, and the pernicious effects of the Republic, and of the Left, to be becoming more and more widespread (one of the bones of dispute being Republican education). Much of these yearnings for traditional values was based on fear of what was happening in the present. It so happened that in these years, however, the most coherent expression of these opinions were being provided either by Catholic writers, or by writers who used Catholicism for their ends, e.g., Barrès and Maurras. The Catholic literary revival had made anti-intellectualism, and the cult of simple uncomplicated virtues, intellectually respectable, and it was thus through Catholic writers that these ideas gained their most lasting expression.

So, though much of the expression of this traditional Right had been Catholic, and though many of its supporters were Catholics, its influence was far more far-reaching; in a sense, such writers had been speaking for a vast inarticulate mass of Frenchmen. Pétain, if the events of 1914–1918 had not taken place, would have been part of this inarticulate mass; but he was now in a position to express himself. His military skills had unaccountably made of him a man whose opinions on other matters were trusted.

In the inter-war period, there were many newspapers which reflected the basic mood we have been describing. They had their variations on the theme, of course. Maurras and Daudet, in *L'Action Française*, were still followed by innumerable supporters in their conception of a return to monarchy as being a solution. Other newspapers, such as Hervé's *La Victoire*, followed a Barrèsian view of the need for an authoritarian Republic. The newspaper for which Barrès had written up to his death in 1923, *L'Écho de Paris*, generally pursued right-wing policies. As the *ligues* became more powerful, papers such as *Le Jour* and *L'Ami du Peuple* turned to support of them. The right-wing Press was powerful, and had taken over the influence exerted by the clerical Press before 1914.

It must be stressed that most of the views expressed were those of the traditional Right we have been describing, and not of the new-style fascism, destroyer of the social order. The latter found its expression in groups such as Doriot's *Parti Populaire Français*, and was another matter altogether. Though the right-wing journals we are describing found much to fascinate them in Germany and Italy, and may even at times have thought that these foreign régimes stood for some of the same opinions as themselves, an examination of the actual views which they put forward shows them to have been something else altogether.

Pétain's views, as expressed in speeches, interviews, and articles at this time, were the simple, straightforward expression of some of these traditional beliefs, which were mingled with some of the general ideas typical of military men of his time. It is not suggested that he was in any way extraordinary, but that he was typical. At the same time, however, it is clear that through his contact with various political figures, whom he met in the course of his various appointments, he built up some more detailed social ideas on this original basis; ideas which were positive suggestions, as opposed to negative fears, and which were the basis of the National Revolution of 1940.

Pétain, though of Catholic upbringing, was not *pratiquant*; his political views were those of a mass of Frenchmen, a large number of whom were Catholics, but a large number of whom were not. The measure of Catholic support for such opinions is shown, nevertheless, by the clerical nature of the Vichy Government, and the *pratiquant* pose which the Marshal had to take up at that time (including a religious marriage to the wife to whom he had been married for twenty years, and whose first marriage had been declared null since 1929).

His general political views were based, like those of so many others, on a fear of modern society, and a search for a better world. The traditional values of France had been destroyed by the Left, and the new enemy, communism, was taking things even further. Youth was being subverted by the education it was receiving.

The Vichy motto *Travail, Famille, Patrie*, which was to replace the Republic's *Liberté, Égalité, Fraternité*, sums up the basis of Pétain's doctrine. These were the bases of a healthy national life. 'They want to defend the family, guarantee the indispensable conditions for its existence', he said of the *Croix de Feu*. 'I approve of that. Everything stems from it. The French family has been expropriated, struck by exorbitant measures. One might believe that our legislators have had no aim other than to break the chain of effort and discourage the father from working for his children.'[2] The stressing of the importance of the family is a natural conservative reaction; the linking of the importance of the family with that of the state is part of a French political tradition stretching back to Bonald. In many French conservative writers this had been mingled with the idea of the importance of the land;[3] and we are hardly surprised when we find Pétain's speeches containing extensive references to 'the family and the land'. Of one of these speeches, made on the occasion of the departure of the Canadian Minister in Paris, Pétain sent a copy to Mrs Pardee: 'A red line underlined the passages relative to the family and the land, preoccupations dear to his heart.'[4]

Like so many other Frenchmen, Pétain disliked the society born of the Industrial Revolution. He regarded the salvation of France as lying with the unspoiled peasantry, who retained the primitive virtues which had made France what it was. They alone were close enough to the land. Pétain himself was of peasant stock, and was to stress this (as did Laval) in the Vichy period. In the inter-war period, an article appeared over his name in the *Revue des Deux Mondes* (15 December 1935) entitled 'Le Paysan français'. It was composed by Loustaunau-Lacau under Pétain's guidance, but it contained Pétain's own ideas. (We have already seen how so much of his writing was in fact done by others.)

These concepts were mingled, of course, with that of patriotism. Pétain's views were very much akin to those of Barrès on this subject; a patriotism based on a cult of *la terre et les morts* (the land and the dead). Referring to the moral virtues which should be inculcated in the soldier, he hoped that they would make him 'a good servant to his country', and 'contribute to maintaining intact the patrimony and the virtues of our race.'[5] As for so many Frenchmen, Jeanne d'Arc was for him the symbol of national unity against the external invader, and against internal disorder: 'Jeanne d'Arc incarnates patriotism in its most complete sense. She not only defeated the external enemy and liberated the national soil, but also calmed, internally, the discords which threatened the existence of the country. By her enthusiastic faith, she galvanised the people; by her energy and authority she rallied and led the nobles; in getting the king consecrated at Reims, she gave back to him his moral and religious prestige, and gathered around her all Frenchmen. The great lesson of unity in the service of the country, which Jeanne has left to us. . . .'[6]

It is small wonder that those newspapers which saw Pétain as a symbol of possible national unity compared him with Jeanne d'Arc, as for example *La Victoire* in its editorial *De Jeanne d'Arc à Pétain*.[7]

Just as Pétain saw the family as an essential entity, so he saw the father-land as the ideal community. In his preface to a book by General Sikorski he said: 'The only real community, in the modern world, is one's country. It is only in the framework of the fatherland that every national community, finding how to evolve according to its own tendencies, can realise itself according to its own laws.'[8]

The cult of the nation, and of the land, could be combined in the love of one's native province (cf., Barrès again). In his funeral eulogy of Marshal Lyautey, Pétain said of his retirement: 'Finding again the ferments which had inspired his youth, he abandoned himself to the power of his land of Lorraine, uniting the small and the great fatherland in the same cult.' He described Lyautey as having 'served France with passion; his entire life was illumined by an invincible confidence in the destinies of the Fatherland, by an ardent desire to greaten it and to make it loved.'[9]

In his reference to Jeanne d'Arc, Pétain mentioned the danger of civil discord. Like so many of his contemporaries, he feared the disruptive effects of modern ideologies, and felt a desire for order at almost any costs. To *Travail, Famille, Patrie* might well have been added *Ordre*. In 1937, when General Beck, Chief of the German General Staff, visited Paris, Pétain's first remark to him was one of regret that on his visit he should find a France that was not in accordance with his (Pétain's) conceptions: 'He only hoped that France's internal political difficulties would soon lift, and that peace and order would soon return to Paris.'[10]

The fate of the country, its internal order and its external safety, depended upon a sense of duty and sacrifice on the part of its inhabitants. In this they must live up to the sacrifices made on their behalf by those before them (and in particular the soldiers of the First World War). Like many others, Pétain deplored 'the material enjoyments and appetites' by which Frenchmen had been led astray in the 'twenties and 'thirties. In 1940 he was to blame these vices for France's fall, and call for expiation of them: 'the spirit of enjoy-ment' had overridden the 'spirit of sacrifice'.

The army, for Pétain, was the guardian of all these values. Its virtues should be those of the community at large: 'Military duty is more and more mingled with the duty of the citizen in general. The sentiments which inspire victorious armies—patriotic *élan*, discipline, the taste for effort, the spirit of sacrifice—these are the sentiments which also make great nations.'[11]

Morale, too, was as important in the nation as in the army. Continually reminiscing about his role in relation to the 1917 mutinies, Pétain transferred his views on military morale to civilian life. The army had a social role to perform. It was through the army that civic virtues could be learned. Army officers had a duty to educate the youth of the country in the right ways. From Lyautey's 'Du Rôle social de l'officier'[12] of 1891 onwards, many military men had felt this. Pétain was one of these men.

All these ideas were simple, straightforward ones. They were based on equally simple fears. Fears of the disruptive elements in society which were destroying its moral and spiritual bases. Fears based on a mistrust of the education being given to children by the educational system of the Republic. Fears, above all, of that intellectualism which was producing the pernicious left-wing doctrines. This explains the anti-intellectual nature of some of Pétain's remarks:

> In the modern world, which is searching anxiously for the road it is to follow, France has more need of work, of conscientiousness, of abnegation than of ideas. Ideas only too often divide, while effort unites.[13]
>
> One can make nothing of a nation which does not have a soul. It is up to our schoolmasters, our university teachers to forge a soul for the nation. We do not ask them to make our children into learned men. We ask them to make them into men, into Frenchmen.[14]

Throughout the 'thirties, Pétain and Weygand were two of the military men who devoted the most time to criticisms of the educational system of France. This sytem was destroying both the country, and the army which was the essence of that country.

The paper *L'Ami du Peuple*, in January 1936, adequately summed up the opinions of Pétain and Weygand on this question: 'General Weygand, after Marshal Pétain, has expressed his emotion at the situation our army is in, thanks to the more and more accentuated decay of our national education in the schools. An absence of physical education, an almost non-existent moral education, and patriotic education forgotten — unless it is given back to front — that is the situation.'[15]

L'Ami du Peuple blamed the prospect of a large left-wing vote at the elections on these same educational faults. And Pétain did too. His desire to take over the Ministry of Education in the Doumergue Government was allegedly expressed in the following manner: 'I'll deal with the communist schoolmasters!'

This bad education had not only turned the country to the Left, and destroyed the moral and spiritual attitudes necessary to the country, and to the army. It had also produced that internationalism and pacifism which was a canker within the nation.* Pétain, when Minister of War in 1934, pursued a very severe policy against conscientious objectors, whom his faithful biographer Laure described as 'those who were either cowards or had been led astray, who, under the shelter or under the pretext of philosophical or

---

* Most of these arguments against the educational system of the Republic were expressed by many writers from the 1880s onwards. See, for example, Jean Nesmy *Les Égarés* Paris 1906.

religious conceptions, try to get out of their military duty.'[16] Pétain was intransigent with those who had already been condemned (and who, Laure says, had tried 'by inadmissible procedures' such as hunger-strikes to get out of their punishments), and created a new law (of 8 July 1934) to prevent people getting out of military service for conscientious reasons.

A letter Pétain wrote to the Minister of Education in April of that year shows his opinions on the matter of the relation between education and the army:

There is a primordial importance in not letting the Officer Reserve Corps be contaminated (by pacifist propaganda); schoolmasters are numerous among the reserves.

It is of vital necessity for the country, both from the point of view of defence and from that of its moral regeneration, that the teaching body should employ itself in forming a youth that is resolute, virile, and fully prepared for the accomplishment of its military duty.

I have the firm conviction that by educating it in this spirit, in giving it the religion of the Fatherland, we will attract to ourselves nothing but respect from abroad, and will by that fact serve with dignity the cause of peace, to which all Frenchmen are sincerely attached.

I have no doubt that you will give me, for the accomplishment of this task, the unrestricted help which is indispensible, and I ask you therefore to call on the patriotism of the personnel of National Education.[17]

Pétain not only thought that education was of importance to the army; he also thought that the army was of importance to education. The traditional virtues must be inculcated in the youth of the country: 'Working to arm the individual morally, exalting the qualities which must at all times make good servants of their country, this is the programme which is essential for those who have a portion of authority in the national organism.'[18]

For this purpose, examples were at hand which ought to be used by the schoolmasters. The Battle of the Marne, for example: 'It is an epic story, which is in every memory. It is an immense national pride. It is what the French schoolmasters should all teach to our children to show them the virtues of the race; it is *gloire* in all that is most noble, most virile, most brilliant, most pure.'[19]

The army itself had a role to play in the re-education of the nation. Speaking to a congress of reserve officers in July 1934, Pétain told them of the effort needed to maintain peace, and added: 'It will demand of us, in the difficult times we are going through, the cult of our traditional virtues, those of which Anatole France wrote: "Get rid of the military virtues, and the whole of society crumbles." To maintain and propagate this cult with us, to collaborate in this way in the patriotic education of the nation and the power of the State, that, my dear comrades, is the nature of the great mission of the Officer Reserve Corps in time of peace.'[20]

Pointing to other countries, and envying their practice, Pétain said: 'The patriotic formation of the children, and the premilitary and paramilitary education of youth, count among the most important of their organisations. The schoolmaster and the professor are, with the parents, the prime initiators of national duty. . . . There are two aims to be achieved, and they are not thought about enough in France: (a) To give the children a moral and physical health which will stand up to anything. (b) To develop, in the youth of the country, a taste and knowledge of military matters, to prepare for the accomplishment of the most sacred of duties, the defence of the Fatherland.'

The educational policy in Vichy was to follow these patterns, particularly in the *Chantiers de jeunesse*. Moral and spiritual values, as well as physical, were cared for; intellectualism went by the board.

The army was, in Pétain's view, to be non-political. He was even instrumental in not getting the vote given to serving soldiers. On General Beck's visit in 1937, after informing him of the grave civil disorder in the nation, Pétain continued in the following vein: 'He could nevertheless assure me that the army was completely untouched by all internal political difficulties. While on this subject, he remembered the years just after the war, and his post as Chief of General Staff and Vice-President of the *Obersten Kriegsrates (Conseil Supérieur de la Guerre)*. At that time two war ministers, whose patriotism was unquestioned, Painlevé and Maginot, had required of him that the right to vote should be introduced in the army. He had on both occasions offered his resignation, and been victorious over the ministers, and he was happy to be able to confirm that his successors had remained firm as well, especially General Gamelin in the last few years. Only an unpolitical army could fulfil its duties.' [21]

By 'unpolitical' Pétain clearly meant 'untouched by propaganda of the Left', for we have already seen the political ideas that he expected education to inculcate, and the army to continue. He deplored Communist propaganda in the army, and rightly so, for its subversive intentions; yet he was happy, as we shall see, to turn a blind eye, in these years 1936–8, to the right-wing organisations within the army, *Corvignolles* and *La Cagoule*. This was, presumably, because they were designed to combat left-wing subversion; but the fact that he saw them as neither 'subversive' nor 'political' shows us the very restricted meaning that the world 'political' had for Pétain.

In one sense, it meant for him 'parliamentary'. Like Lyautey and many other military men, Pétain had a scorn for the antics of politicians. A spell in Government did nothing but confirm this. From 1934 onwards, as we shall see, he continued to despise the 'politicking' of the Third Republic; but this did not prevent him from having his own political feelings about how the country should be run, or from believing that he himself might well have a political role to play.

In another sense, 'politics' meant to him 'politics of the Left'. From this the army must be free. His experience of the 1917 mutinies, and his observation of the 1919 Black Sea fleet mutiny, had made him realise the dangers of Communism to the army; the propaganda of Doriot and others during the Riff War had shown him its dangers to the patriotic ideals of the Nation. International Socialism, too, was a pernicious influence (the question of the

1917 Stockholm Conference still rankled). But Communism was now the main enemy. His press interview for *Le Journal* in 1936[22] stressed the external danger of the Franco-Soviet Pact, and the internal danger of the Communist participation in the *Front Populaire*. After the Nazi-Soviet Pact of 1939 he was to say of Franco's Government: 'The spectre of Bolshevism frightens a Government which has not yet understood that Hitler was the *fourrier* (harbinger) of Stalin in Europe, and which obstinately insists in seeing, in the Führer, the last rampart against the Red Wave from Asia.'[23]

Amouroux has suggested, on the basis of a letter written by Pétain in 1920, that he was not as violently anti-Communist as all other evidence has shown. An examination of the text in question, however, will show that it proves nothing of the kind. I quote in full the extract which Amouroux gives:

> Affairs in Poland are going as badly as possible. The way this adventure will end is disquieting. A year ago, I asked the Government to send someone qualified to breathe some sense into Pilsudski; but no one listened to me. I tried again four months ago, with no more success.
>
> We cannot mobilise an army and send it to make war on the Russians. Poland will thus be left to her own devices, that is to say to the Soviets. She perhaps needs this Soviet treatment to re-make her unity. Time will tell.[24]

There is nothing in this to show anything like approval of the Soviets. But there is a great deal in it to show Pétain's ideas on the valuable effects of defeat, suffering and penitence. A disunited nation could be helped to regain its unity by such defeat and suffering. Such attitudes were to recur in 1940.

The counterpart to Pétain's fear of Communism, and of the forces of the Left, was his belief in the importance of the military tradition in all countries. And, opposed to the chicaneries of parliamentary government, he set the straightforward dealings of soldiers with each other. If only it were left to soldiers to run countries, and to conduct international diplomacy, all would be well with the world. The comradeship of arms was universal.

Military men were thus suited to be the heads of nations. We have already seen the remarks he made in praise of Primo de Rivera, the Spanish dictator, in 1925. They were also the most suitable ambassadors; in this many people agreed with him. His ambassadorship to General Franco in 1939, was accompanied on all sides with remarks such as: 'The Marshal is faced by military men. As men of the same profession, they understand each other more easily.'[25] 'Marshal Pétain is going among victorious soldiers. There is a solidarity of fortunes of arms against which the little *combinaisons* of interest can only break themselves.'[26] 'He was the victor of Verdun, and Franco had, I knew, a great admiration of a military order for him.'[27] Pétain's ambassadorship was, in fact, eventually very successful. Franco, his Foreign Minister, General Jordana, and Pétain, had all been involved in the Riff War together.

Pétain's feeling that comradeship in arms still existed even between former enemies is one shared by many ex-soldiers, and, indeed, it is an emotion common to many who have fought in the wars of this century. His views, as expressed to General Beck, the German Chief of General Staff, on his 1937 Paris visit, are understandable and moving:

'The Marshal once more expressed his great joy at my visit, and at having been able to shake my hand, even if this was twenty years after the end of the battle, and not two hours after it, as was customary formerly in the times of chivalry.' [28] It was perhaps the same spirit that made him shake the hand of a German officer, in Madrid, after the beginning of the war. (An act for which he has been much criticised.)

Beck was a German officer in the same mould as Pétain, and a man of honour. Part of the purpose of his visit to Paris had been to discuss with Gamelin the need for peace. As part of the German 'peace party' he had, of course, eventually little chance against the overwhelming forces of Nazi ambition. He was, nevertheless, a man worthy of Pétain's chivalrous gestures.

Göring was quite another matter. But he was a First World War hero, an air ace, and one of the most decorated men in the German forces. (It is not often realised, in relation to the cartoon jokes about Göring's medals in the Second World War, that he had on the whole earned them.) Pétain must have seen in him another military man to whom he could speak better than to politicians. It must therefore have come doubly as a shock when, at their Saint-Florentin meeting in 1941, Göring showed his true colours.

In the 'thirties Pétain and Göring saw a certain amount of each other. The first meeting appears to have been at King Alexander of Yugoslavia's funeral in Belgrade on 18 October 1934. (Göring and Pétain both seem to have been their Governments' representatives at important foreign funerals at this time.) In the funeral procession 'General Göring, in the grey-green and crimson of a Reichswehr general, was next to Marshal Pétain, in the vivid uniform of a Marshal of France.' [29]

Pétain appears to have impressed Göring. Within two months of his return to Germany, Göring was mentioning the Marshal in a speech which echoed many of Pétain's own ideas on comradeship of arms, on the shortcomings of politicians, and on the agreement which could be reached between military men. This speech, made to the Krupps workers in Essen on 4 December 1934, quoted a British politician (Boothby) who had said a few days before that an unarmed, unprotected country was in danger of war. 'Let him realise', said Göring, 'that what is true for England is also true for Germany.' Germany wanted to ensure peace; but for this they needed arms, like other countries. They needed the same rights as others:

> But we know that even for other peoples the hour will come for that true understanding which is only possible between partners of equal strength, and never possible between the strong and the weak. We see the same thing time and again: the front-line soldiers of all nations, who have taken part in that mighty struggle, speak the same language, and understand each other. Why? Because they have learned to respect each other. One cannot tell the French front-line soldier, who had to fight for four years against Germany, that the Boche are cowardly dogs. He has the experience of whether we are cowardly dogs or not.

He knows definitely that it is not true. He knows that with this people one can and must come to an understanding. But then along came the 'politicians' (*Politikaster*) and the 'pettifogging lawyers' (*Rechtsverdreher*),* and think that they can uproot this healthy, virtuous thought. Just talk with a French front-line man, with a French soldier! He will grasp the need for understanding between the great nations. A few weeks ago I had the opportunity of speaking with the old French warrior, Marshal Pétain. There is a soldier, there is a man of honour, and he understands also how to respect Germany's honour. With such people one can still come to an understanding, but not with any old party leader or *Politikaster*, men who only see their miserable activities bloom into disunity ...[30]

In May 1935 Pétain and Göring were to meet again, in Poland at the funeral of Marshal Pilsudski. *The Times* reported: 'It is considered a particularly happy thought on the part of the French Government to send Marshal Pétain to represent France. Marshal Pilsudski had great personal admiration for his French colleague, and more than once was heard to express the view that Marshal Pétain was the real hero of the War. General Graziolini will head the Italian delegation and General Göring will represent Herr Hitler and the Reich.'

On the way through Berlin, Pétain was met by Generals von Blomberg and von Reichenau, and was taken on a tour of Berlin, during which they had military discussions. After the funeral, at a reception held in Cracow by Colonel Beck, the Polish Foreign Minister (not to be confused with the German General, Ludwig Beck), on 18 May, Pétain and Laval were described by the newspapers as having talked for a time with General Göring. Later, Laval called on Göring at his hotel, and talked with him for more than two hours.

Whether Pétain realised the difference between the various German military figures he met, one does not know. Beck, in disapproval of Nazi army policy, resigned in 1938. He was to be involved in the July bomb plot in 1944, and to commit suicide soon afterwards. (Hitler was, in 1944, to describe Beck's visit to Paris as follows: 'It is interesting to read Beck's judgement of Gamelin. One would believe from it that the two great heroes of humanity had met. I can imagine a Gamelin or a Beck when faced by a good-for-nothing like Tito!') Blomberg, though a military man, was Hitler's greatest sycophant on the General Staff. Göring was a leading member of the Nazi party, responsible for much of its internal policy. Pétain may well have seen them all just as soldiers, who would understand another soldier.

His view of Germany itself had been, from the military point of view, one of containment in the years after 1918. He had believed that the greatest safeguards were needed to protect France from another invasion, and that the British had purposely pursued a policy whereby France, prevented from taking the left bank of the Rhine, would not become too powerful. He believed, too, that the decision not to defeat Germany thoroughly, but to accept the armistice, had fostered the feeling in Germany that they had not

* He uses here terms of abuse in relation to the two professions, which it is difficult to translate.

been beaten. Pétain saw the German danger, and none of his fraternisation with German officers removed this. He *did* believe in comradeship of arms, and wrongly believed that Göring would deal generously with a fallen enemy; but in the years before the war he did not underestimate the German danger. By 1939, he knew that his Spanish ambassadorship was important in that it might keep Spain neutral in the event of war with Germany; he also regarded those Germans who had remained behind in Spain after the Civil War as hindrances to the French cause. Military comradeship was still possible between enemies; but clearly they might soon become enemies again.

As far as the Nazi party in Germany, and the Fascist party in Italy, were concerned, Pétain clearly admired the faith and unity they had given to their countries, and contrasted them favourably with France, disunited under its parliamentary régime.[31] As far as Nazism was concerned, however, the Nazi-Soviet pact showed him, by the Nazi unconcern in joining hands with Pétain's bogey, Bolshevism, that it was not to be trusted.

Pétain's contacts with Italy were also mainly military and ceremonial. In March 1928 he attended the funeral of Marshal Diaz, his wartime collaborator, in Rome. On 5 March, the day after the funeral, Mussolini gave a banquet in his honour at the Military Club, and later in the afternoon Pétain was received at the Palazzo Chigi, where he had a quarter of an hour's talk with the Duce. In January 1930, he returned to Rome for the Italian Royal Wedding, arriving by the same train as the Duke of York (the future George VI). In France, certain military celebrations led Pétain to pay tribute to the fighting qualities of the Italian allies in the First World War. On 26 May 1934, he inaugurated a monument to the memory of the Garibaldians of the Argonne, and the Italian volunteers 'who died for France'. The newspapers tell us that he 'recalled the heroic hours lived on the French front by the soldiers of the Garibaldian Legion and of the Italian army.'[32] After this there was a very tendentious speech by Eugenio Coselschi, an Italian parliamentarian who was President of the Association of Italian Voluntary Combattants. It had mostly to do with the New Order in Italy, and with Mussolini; though it did stress the need for peace, and the common Latinity of France and Italy.

These were official events, and Pétain was merely performing an official function. In 1935, however, there came the abortive plan whereby Pétain should go to Rome with a party of *anciens combattants*, and present the Military Medal, the highest French military honour, to Mussolini. This, as we shall see, though approved by Laval, was scotched by the Flandin Government.

In the years before the war, Pétain came, with Laval, to see Italy as an important standby against the German threat. Some of his tie-ups with Laval were based on this concept, as we shall see.

As far as Great Britain was concerned, Pétain's basic attitudes were of mistrust and dislike. Some of this, as we have seen, may have stemmed from his experiences with Haig in 1918. Even more came from his feeling that

Great Britain had purposely let France down in 1918, indeed betrayed her
for the last three months of the war, in order that she should not have the
left bank of the Rhine.[33] British attitudes to Foch at the Peace Conference
can hardly have lessened this feeling of Pétain's. Some of Pétain's remarks
against Britain in the late 'thirties are particularly bitter: 'Of all the ills that
are falling on us, we cannot blame anyone but ourselves, or rather the various
Governments which have gone in the wake of Britain since 1919, and have
led us down into the abyss.'[34] England had done France much harm, he said,
particularly under Macdonald.[35] Chamberlain was the only person who
redeemed Britain in his eyes. Pétain had, however, visited England officially
in 1935, and spoken at Claridge's on Anglo–French relations in the Great
War.

His anti-British feeling was shown, when he was a minister, by his reception of the suggestion that France should revoke two maritime conventions
that favoured Britain (as a reprisal for the raising of the British customs
duties). Pétain is said to have remarked: 'I have been greatly impressed by
what the Minister of Commerce has said. Our policy has always been too
weak with regard to Great Britain. We cannot let her behave in this way
without vigorously reacting. I personally accept the propositions which have
been made.'[36]

As far as the United States were concerned, Pétain's attitude seems to
have been fairly benevolent, particularly in the remarks made in the presence
of his American friends, the Pardees. He obviously had a great admiration
for his war colleague Pershing, and he enjoyed his official visit to America for
the 150th anniversary of the victory over the British, in October 1931, on
which he made several moving speeches on Franco–American friendship.

Pétain's political thought, in the foreign field, was very simplified and
based mainly on emotions, which ranged from fear of Bolshevism, via mistrust of Germany, to dislike of Great Britain. On the top of all this, however,
lay a belief in a kind of international freemasonry of soldiers, who talk the
same language and understand each other, whatever their Governments
may do.

In the internal politics of his own country, Pétain looked in vain for the
military and traditional virtues. For him the family and the land must be
safeguarded, duty and sacrifice must take precedence over enjoyment, civil
order must be maintained, everyone must be educated to appreciate patriotic
values. For this, as for the maintenance of national unity, parliamentary
government was unsuited. What was needed was a strong executive, a man
at the tiller (as we shall see in the chapter on political involvement). These are
the views of a traditional Right: simple, unsophisticated.

His contacts with various right-wing thinkers (especially Alibert, whom
Lémery got to 'instruct' Pétain on social problems and who later became
head of Pétain's *cabinet civil*), may well have built up on that basic framework, even at this stage, the more detailed social ideas which bore fruit in the
Révolution Nationale, when he surrounded himself with these same men. Of

this we have no concrete proof, however, so we will deal with these questions at the moment when they became public. We must now look at Pétain's involvement in politics, and other people's support for him, in the years from 1934 onwards.

Chapter Six

Press campaigns, 1934–9

FROM the time of his participation in the Doumergue Government onwards, Pétain was the centre of a series of Press campaigns aiming at his appointment as Head of Government, in most cases with dictatorial powers. On the whole, these appeared in the newspapers of the Right; though in one case it was a campaign of the Left. Some saw Pétain as the man, above politics, who could cure the ills of parliamentary government; others saw him as a protection against civil disorder; others still, concerned about France's external position, felt him to be a bulwark against the country's enemies. It would be foolish to regard all these as small extremist follies, though some clearly were. Too many papers were involved; and it is clear that when in doubt and worry, Frenchmen saw the Marshal as a rock of safety. Pétain himself never came out in support of any of the campaigns; but on the other hand he never openly dissociated himself from them, a fact which some took as tacit approval. He was certainly flattered by the attention he was given, as extracts from his letters show.

It was Pétain's participation in the Doumergue Government which first drew Press attention to his value as a political symbol. Doumergue himself, the old and safe man who was called on to reassure the country after 6 February 1934 and the fall of the Daladier, was one of the old men, the 'Fathers of the Country', to whom Henri de Kérillis referred in a famous article written in 1943, when he said that it was a French rite to call on such men to save the country.[1] (Clemenceau, the 1940 Pétain, and the 1958 de Gaulle are merely a few examples of this trend.) Doumergue, in continuance of this policy, chose Pétain as his war minister; and from the start, Pétain's symbolic value was stressed above all. André Pironneau, for example, in *L'Écho de Paris*, referred to the 'presence at the War Ministry of Marshal Pétain, the venerated symbol of our victory.' He went on to speak of the 'great prestige and good judgement of the Marshal', and regretted that he was not being placed above the political struggle.[2]

The same writer, criticising later in the year the state of France's military organisation, called on the Marshal to change things. He was a symbol, but also a man in an important post; he thus had double power to change things:

'The extent of the prestige and the power of Marshal Pétain is the very measure of his responsibility. The Marshal, in the post he occupies, is no longer merely the symbol of a glorious past, but the man whose actions influence the future. France is counting on him to give her, without delay, the army she needs.'[3]

Pironneau, while showing some exasperation here, was nevertheless still expressing the power of the Marshal's figure as a symbol. We have already seen how much of the Marshal's public esteem rested on this symbolic nature of his public figure. And, indeed, Press reports of his public appearances in this period show an almost religious reverence for his presence. A description of him as he made his first speech in the Chamber is typical of this devotion: 'Perhaps, at this moment, the glorious soldier is astonished at being in a position that he has certainly never desired. One is astonished, nevertheless, to see him there, and one admires him for being there. What a handsome face! The wide brow, the thick eyebrows model the upper part of his face in vigorous relief. The white moustache falls beside an energetic mouth, with a severe line to it. The tall figure has not bowed an inch beneath the weight of years and the two hands are placed energetically on the desk, in a natural attitude of command. The Marshal speaks without a gesture, in a slow and clear voice.'[4]

Pétain's every public appearance gave rise to such descriptions, and to evocations of his glorious past, and his symbolisation of French greatness.

After the fall of the Doumergue Government on 8 November 1934, Pétain refused an offer to continue as War Minister in the Flandin Government. However, the newspapers did not forget him; from now on he was to be the father figure for most anti-democratic projects.

The first occasion of this was of rather an unusual kind. The popular newspaper, *Le Petit Journal*, began in that very November to speculate about the possibility of a dictatorship putting things to rights in France. The Doumergue 'national' Government had merely succeeded in temporarily stemming the chaos of the Third Republic; the experience of other nations had shown the efficacy, in their case, of this alternative type of régime. On 16 November a leading article asked the question 'Is dictatorship the order of the day?' On the 18th, another leading article was entitled 'Republic or Dictatorship?'

Then, on 20 November this newspaper announced its great idea. It was going to organise a referendum of its readers, to choose the French dictator. It was a gimmick in a paper the equivalent of one of our popular Sunday papers; but it can also be taken seriously, in that it did enable a view of one section of public opinion on this question, and in that it did influence other writers. The paper provided, on the 21st, under the title 'A Dictator? But Who?' a list of forty names from which their readers could choose. It was a wide-ranging list, containing names from Left and Right, from Parliament, from journalism, from the *ligues*, from the army. It is an interesting list, including: Bergey, Bergery, Blum, Bouisson, Cachin, Chéron, Chiappe, Citroën, Daladier, Daudet, Dautry, Déat, Denain, Doriot, Doumergue, Flandin, Franchet d'Esperey, Herriot, Jeanneney, Jouhaux, La Rocque, Laval, Lebecq, Lebrun, Mandel, Marin, Marquet, Maurras, Nicolle, Pétain,

Pichot, Jean-Renaud, Louis Renault, Paul Reynaud, Tardieu, Henry Torrès, Taittinger, Weygand.

Every day, through November and December 1934, *Le Petit Journal* took three of these candidates and, fairly impartially (including even men of the Left like Cachin and Blum) discussed the pros and cons of their candidature. When, on 2 December, Pétain was discussed, the pros were: (1) He was the most popular of the war leaders (Verdun was mentioned, of course), (2) As a leader, he always remained human (evocation of his closeness to the *poilus*). (3) His experience at the War Ministry, and the good speeches he had made. The cons were: (1) A war leader is not necessarily a good leader in times of peace. (2) His age (78). (3) His political inexperience.

The nature of the newspaper involved can be gauged by the fact that, from 5–9 December, even the horoscopes of the candidates were consulted!

On 11–12 December, four more candidates were introduced: 'Marianne' (the symbol of the Republic), the Duc de Guise (the royalist pretender), 'L'Inconnu' (the unknown one), and Prince Napoleon.

It was on 11 January 1935, that the results of the referendum were announced. 194,785 readers had voted. First, with 38,561 votes, came Pétain. Second with 31,403, Laval. Third, with 23,864, Doumergue. Fourth with 20,102, 'Marianne'.

The emergence of Laval as second is somewhat surprising to those who would think of him as the essence of the Third Republic politician, tarred with every parliamentary brush. But one must realise that the first three were all members of the Doumergue Government, which had brought some stability to the country, and that the choice of 'Marianne' for fourth shows that, far from being a vote for dictatorship on the German or Italian model, this was a vote for stable government in a democratic context.

Le Petit Journal itself made this point. Far from trying to force dictatorship on France, it said, it had tried to 'establish the diagnosis for our anxiety and above all draw up the balance-sheet of our hopes.' No superman had emerged, and there had been a wide range of voting. None of the three men concerned, it said, wanted power; indeed, they protested their fidelity to the present form of government. Why had these three men come first in the referendum?

It is because they symbolise perfectly the present aspirations of the country: Pétain: victory and humanity. Laval; external peace. Doumergue: internal peace. In this trinity is harmoniously expressed the nation's desire to preserve in tranquillity in the present the array of virtues which are transmitted to it by its great dead.

In Pétain, our readers have honoured the great captain who, having saved the fatherland at Verdun, finally brought it triumph and gave to the tricolour flag a new brilliance in the world; the man who, having manifested his compassion for the suffering soldier, for the anonymous hero of the trenches, showed his will to spare the nation, from then onwards, from such terrible experiences and tried to turn away from her the most awful of nightmares, that of imminent carnage.

In Laval, our readers consecrated the skilful diplomat who, three times in one month, was able to dissipate anguish, reject pressing anxiety, and make conciliation triumph... In Laval, the man is acclaimed who made the spectre of war vanish, and who, on each of his journeys, brought us a little more security.

In Doumergue, our public applauded the wise man who, giving up his own personal tranquillity, saved the country in those atrociously murky days of last February, from intestine discord, and saved France from the shame of civil war. What the vote for his name signified above all was the horror of factions and the scorn of factious people, the desire for concord and the need for a breathing-space... [5]

Le Petit Journal could not have expressed more clearly the negative attitudes of the France of the 'thirties; the fear of war, which must be avoided at all costs, and the need for a symbol of past glories. The shadow of 1940 was already on the country. But an important other point is the poor showing which the various extremist factions made in this vote. The French might be in despair at the apparent failure of the Third Republic, but rather than look for dominant extremists, they looked for safe father-figures.

The same picture comes from the rest of the voting. 5th and 6th came Flandin and Herriot, politicians of differing colours, with 14,612 and 13,004 votes respectively. Only then did the first of the *ligueurs* come, Taittinger of the *Jeunesses Patriotes*, with 11,163. After another politician, Tardieu (10,083) came La Rocque, the head of the *Croix de Feu*, with only 6,402. Then came Bergery (5,094), General Weygand (3,789), and Chiappe, the former chief of police (3,685). The royalist candidates, the Duc de Guise and the Comte de Paris, got only 1,041 votes between them, and Maurras and Daudet of the *Action Française*, having got below 1,000 votes, did not even appear on the list.

The victorious candidates were interviewed by the newspaper. Pétain's reactions at being told the news were described by the interviewer, Philippe Boegner, thus:

There was not a gesture, not a movement of that impassive face. Another man would have protested, smiled, expressed in one way or other a perfectly legitimate emotion... No, nothing happened, absolutely nothing.

Standing, having shaken my hand, the Marshal replied:

Thank you for having taken the trouble to communicate this news to me. I am very flattered by the confidence the French people places in me. I insist however on saying that I will not make use of it.[6]

Laval made similar noises, assuring the reporter that France and the Republic were indissolubly united.

A gimmicky referendum in a popular newspaper is not in any way a serious campaign; but it does show the extent of the popularity in a restricted section of the public of certain figures. Perhaps it was mere coincidence that the first serious campaign launched in Pétain's name started up in the very next month; or perhaps the author of that campaign had already seen the popularity of Pétain's name in *Le Petit Journal*. Certainly other, later writers commented on the referendum vote, to prove Pétain's popularity, when putting forward his name.

This was the famous '*C'est Pétain qu'il nous faut*' campaign, started by Gustave Hervé in his paper *La Victoire*. Hervé is one of the more extraordinary figures in French politics. A left-wing pacifist before the 1914–18 war, he had been one of the figures whom Péguy had most strongly criticised in the *Cahiers de la Quinzaine*. At the outbreak of war, he had suddenly become one of the most vociferous of patriots, distinguished from such groups as the *Action Française* only by the remnants of left-wing policy which he retained with his new patriotism. After the war, in *La Victoire*, he had continued to produce nationalist doctrines, while criticising more and more the debilitated parliamentary machinery of the Third Republic. Gradually he came to believe in the need for an 'authoritarian republic on a corporative basis', with one leader, nominated by plebiscite, which would give him the necessary authority to break all forms of individual and corporative egotism. The resultant state would still be a republic; public approval would be safeguarded by referendums.

This idea of an authoritarian republic is a constant one in France. It was the ideal put forward by Maurice Barrès;[7] it became reality with General de Gaulle. Hervé may have been as much influenced by this tradition (including Barrès's 'national socialism') as by foreign models, though the success of Hitlerian dictatorship no doubt encouraged him in his ideas. What must be stressed is that for Hervé and his followers this was not a right-wing policy of the *Action Française* type, but a desire to put forward correct (i.e., left-wing) social measures in an authoritarian context.*

Hervé's influence, while not negligible, was, however, not great. He was, and had always been, something of an isolated figure. His campaign aroused few echoes at first. On 6 February 1935, the anniversary of the events of 1934, Hervé's editorial read as follows: 'A year ago patriots fell in the Place de la Concorde "for France to live in honour and cleanliness". But alas! after a great hope of liberation, the country is in agony, in the clutches of freemasonry and the foul parliamentary régime.'[8]

Other numbers of the paper, around this date, asked when the 'clean sweep' was to come, and on 11 February a full statement of the need for an 'authoritarian republic', which would save the country from civil war, was put forward, with an appeal to the 'militants of the national and nationalistic organisations, who are the only yeast capable of lifting the soft paste of the moderates and peaceful people of order in our country, France.'[9] Hervé declared that he had two names to propose, either of which in itself would be a guarantee of victory: Pétain and Weygand.

The next day, under the headline 'A Leader? Pétain or Weygand,' the paper described the two men in glowing terms. Pétain, as usual, was described physically: 'When Pétain entered the Ministry of Public Safety of

---

* Though of course the social measures were less 'left-wing' than Hervé claimed, being more in the line of a Le Play—like paternalism.

175

good old President Doumergue, when we saw once more that great soldier's head, resplendent with intelligence, will, and gravity, we said to ourselves: "A leader? there's one!"

And when Weygand, the other day, was cast off because he gave umbrage to those gentlemen of the "Republic of pals",* we thought: "A national leader, a president for an authoritarian Republic, there's another!"[10]

What was needed was to go forward at the 1936 elections as revisionists of the Constitution. They would get about six or seven million revisionist votes, out of ten million voters, and could then hold a plebiscite a few weeks afterwards, with eight or nine million '*oui*' votes for Pétain or Weygand. These men were both old, but so was Hindenburg when he was made President of Germany. Neither of the two men would lead France to war. (Here again we see the French inter-war obsession with peace at any price.)

Within two days, however, Weygand's name had been dropped. On 14 February the article with the famous title '*C'est Pétain qu'il nous faut!*' appeared.

The reasons for rejecting Weygand were only to be given six weeks later, when, in a leader entitled '*Non, pas Weygand! Pétain!*' Hervé criticised those *anciens combattants* who preferred Weygand to Pétain (because of Pétain's treatment of Lyautey in Morocco), and said that Weygand would frighten the Left, because he was too reactionary, as opposed to Pétain.[11]

In the opening salvo on 14 February Hervé stressed that Pétain had not been consulted about the use of his name; but the paper was justified in using it, at any rate:

> If Marshal Pétain did not have the same patriotic anxieties as us, he would not have agreed to join the national ministry of good old President Doumergue. There is no need, moreover, of his acceptance at this moment; his military situation and the high conception he has of his duty and of his honour as a disciplined soldier might make him refuse it. It is enough for the national and patriotic organisations to be able to say to the anguished nation: 'You want to know whether we have at hand a great servant of the country, a man who has given proof of intelligence, organisation, decision, patriotism in high public office, and who has not been deformed by politics, to whom you can confidently give the direction of the country... Yes! We have such a man. We are all agreed on his name! He is called Pétain!'[12]

Once again Pétain's 'non-political' nature was pointed out; he was 'outside, and above' the parties. Hervé showed, too, his confidence that Pétain would fall in with these plans: 'When the nation acts, Pétain will too. Does he look like the sort of man to hide himself away?' The dangers of a victory of the Left, supported by the Communists, at the 1936 elections were pointed out, and Hervé likened Pétain to Hindenburg, as a 'name' around which national forces can gather. 'In 1935, Pétain is the lifebuoy for France in its terrible mess, just as Hindenburg was for Germany in 1925.'[13]

---

* Weygand had retired at the beginning of 1935. Many newspapers had protested at this.

The campaign that started with this flourish of trumpets was to continue in *La Victoire* almost every day until the elections of May 1936. It was then to recur in 1937 with the second, up-dated edition of some of the arguments in book form. Some of the most interesting statements were, however, made in the first month or so. On 15 February Pétain was favourably contrasted with the Bonaparte pretender, who was too young. Pétain was experienced, and moreover 'his illustrious name does not come up against the republican fibre which is so deeply ingrained in the hearts of the French people, despite their disgust with the parliamentary régime. France is fed up with the parliamentary Republic. But she is not fed up with the Republic. And Pétain, for the mass of French workers and peasants, is still the Republic'. As a Republican military man, he was described by Hervé as being like General Boulanger, though Boulanger was false, while Pétain was the pure and genuine article.[14]

So Pétain was the choice because of his apparent republicanism, because he did not appear to be a man of the Right, and because workers and peasants would fall in behind him. On 21 February Hervé addressed the left-wing paper *L'Oeuvre*, and called on it to help by bringing in much of France of the Left behind Pétain, so that the new régime should not lean too much towards the Right, and become monarchistic or imperialistic.

'*Mais voudra-t-il marcher?*', the title of a leader on 26 February shows the main concern of some of those who would like to support Pétain. Hervé rounds on such people, saying that of course Pétain would not, if it was only *La Victoire* which was calling on him to do so. But all Frenchmen must have confidence, and call on him. 'Pétain', he said, 'in his glory as a great soldier, who has never made politics or agitation of any kind, stands above all the parties as the incarnation of the country itself.' Again, as so often, Pétain's value seems to be that of a symbol rather than a man.

Despite Hervé's campaign, the massive support he was hoping for did not seem to be forthcoming. And what there was came only from the Right. At the beginning of March *La Voix du Combattant* (Journal of the National Union of Combattants) and *Le National* (one of the organs of the *Jeunesses Patriotes*) declared their support.

Meanwhile, however, another newspaper, right-wing and impatient with parliamentary government, began to take up the name of Pétain. This time, however, it was for reasons of external dangers to France. In *Le Jour*, the paper run by Léon Bailby, a leader appeared on 21 February written by André Suarès. The headline ran as follows: 'Those who govern us have not the energy to think. In face of the threat, it is up to the leader to arise and impose his will.' In the article Suarès told of the danger of a German invasion, and of the terrible state of parliamentary democracy, which was unable to cope with the situation. 'One cannot expect', he said, 'electors and elected to think greatly and nobly of the country, which was the greatest and noblest under the heavens, and which must become so again or disappear.'[15] To what must one have recourse? To a strong and courageous mind. But this is rare; thousands are capable of giving up their lives, and facing up to the greatest danger, and yet are incapable of thinking with force. 'Let the Marshal finally speak.'[16] Suarès suggested that Pétain and the generals should rule the country, and take the necessary measures for its safety (including two-year military service, which was being held up by electoral considerations).

Pétain's article on military service in the *Revue des Deux Mondes* only a week later was received enthusiastically by *Le Jour*, whose editor Léon Bailby devoted a leader to it, and continued to quote it in subsequent numbers. On 4–5 March Bailby attacked the Flandin Government for its pusillanimity, and declared the need for energy and union. The editorial on the 8th was entitled 'The Country, or the Parties?' Parliamentary government, it said, was ruining France's defence, and preventing such necessary measures as two-year military service. By 11 March, however, it was clear that the measure might get through. Bailby, violently attacking Blum, said that Pétain's call had aroused vast repercussions 'because of the great authority of its author.'[17]

When the vote was passed on the 15th, Bailby, at first enthusiastic, was by the 20th furious at the compromise whereby Flandin had made the measure provisional. This had been done 'for reasons of political strategy.'[18] Hervé had come to the same realisation on the very day of the vote; the headline of *La Victoire* of 16 March read as follows: 'Despite Marshal Pétain and the General Staff, M. P. -E. Flandin sacrifices national defence, in a cowardly manner, to the electoral interests of the radical-socialist politicians. He avoids voting in the re-establishment of the two years' law, and contents himself with an oblique, equivocal solution.'[19]

It was on 22 March that Bailby, in *Le Jour*, clearly came out in favour of dictatorship. In an editorial entitled 'Will the Leader's hour come?' he spoke of the need to defend the country by reviving both national education and national defence. 'To execute this, we need a leader without title and without party, in other words a leader pure and simple, who has decided to take up his responsibilities.'[20]

To this Hervé replied next day in *La Victoire*, in a front-page article entitled 'The Leader's hour has come.' 'Will he act?' he asked. 'You well know, Léon Bailby, that he will only act if constrained and forced to do so, if he is carried along by the vast wave of the nation, if he is called by the great voice of the people. Come, Bailby! Come, Henri de Kérillis! Throw his name to the crowd, and you will see if it will act.'[21] Bailby, however, never mentioned Pétain's name specifically, as his writer Suarès had done, but contented himself (particularly in April) with juxtaposing articles in praise of Pétain with articles on the need for a dictator.

Meanwhile, Hervé was depressed by the lack of left-wing support for Pétain. 'It is not Pétain that they need, it is a Lenin or a Stalin!'[22] he cried out in one editorial.

In early April another great national paper, this time the royalist *L'Action Française*, took up Pétain's name. Like André Suarès, Léon Daudet was appalled by the German danger, and saw Pétain's name as being the only solution. 'Everything is happening', he said, 'as though Germany is holding itself ready for next summer. The true Prime Minister, for the present moment, should be Marshal Pétain, *with full powers*. My conviction is that the spectre of war would immediately the removed.'[23] Like so many people, Daudet saw Pétain's worth as residing in the effect of his name and his past glory.

It was in April and May that *Le Jour's* campaign got really under way. In mid-April it published a report suggesting that Pétain was going to accompany a group of *anciens combattants* to Rome, and that he was going to present the French Military Medal to Mussolini while he was there.* Five days later, on 17 April, another report made it clear that Pétain had not been able to go. On the 18th, an account was given of what had happened. All had been arranged, and Laval had been in favour. Seats had even been booked. But the mission had received no official approval. Flandin had promised to see to the matter at a Cabinet meeting in the afternoon, but there was nothing about it in the Cabinet report: 'Let us not insist on the matter. It would be too cruel. Did they fear the popularity of the old Marshal? That would be to be ignorant of the fact that it cannot be affected, neither more nor less. It is equal to his glory itself.'[24] Two days later Suarès wrote in the same paper: 'May he come! Oh may he finally come! The man with the powerful heart, who will raise up all that is falling!'[25] On the 22nd there was an editorial by Bailby against the Flandin Cabinet, citing their behaviour in the Pétain case. The different matters all came together in time, with a natural connection between them.

In May the same syndrome appeared. This time it was sparked off by the visit of Pétain and Laval to Marshal Pilsudski's funeral in Warsaw. On 22 May Suarès wrote an article of praise for the dead man, entitled 'He was a leader: and his example remains.' After dealing with Pilsudski, it went on to draw other more general conclusions: 'A country is on the slopes to disaster, it is condemning itself, when it governs itself in such a way that not only does it have no leader, but also it makes it impossible for the leader to reveal himself, at the very time when, from every side, everyone is calling out for him. There are certain peoples in which there are always great figures. But it is terrible that the régime should be opposed to their being known, and even more to their being given power, the power of which they alone are worthy: nature created them to exercise it, and the baseness of men or the miserable nature of the times exiles them from it.'[26] In the same number, Bailby's editorial 'The Franc is solid. But is politics?' criticised the fact that the nation's finances were not to be discussed until after Whitsun, and added: 'This is not the thing to give, both inside and outside the country, the impression that the country is being kept in hand and run by a leader.'[27] From the 23rd to 25th Flandin's request for 'full powers' was criticised, and Flandin himself categorised as hopeless; on the 27th Flandin's plans were described as 'the dictatorship of a man in whom the country and the *anciens combattants* have no confidence . . .'[28] It is clear, from earlier numbers

* It was not stated that there was a delegation of *Jeunesses Patriotes* involved as well.

of the same paper, in whom the *anciens combattants* would have confidence!
Once again, Pétain's name is not mentioned; but, from Suarès's article of
21 February onwards, it had been clear whom *Le Jour* had in mind.

The fall of the Flandin Government led to the formation, on 1 June, of a
new Ministry under Bouisson. In this Ministry Pétain accepted a post,
and this news was greeted with delight by the newspapers of the Right.
Bailby, in his editorial of 2 June, typically praised Pétain for 'giving his
name and his counsels to the Government.'[29] His name again! 'He has
always fled from honours, and has no attraction towards politics', he went
on, 'but he was found to save Verdun, to heal the mutinies of 1917, to
quieten down the agitation stirred up by extremists in the reservist camps in
1928, to give his help to M. Doumergue in February 1934.'[30]

The Bouisson Government fell, of course, on 4 June. For many, this
seemed the final failure of parliamentary democracy. Civil war was feared.
The *ligues* had become more and more powerful, as had the Communists
and left-wing agitators. On 6 June Hervé wrote: 'If providence accords
France a respite of a few months, the patriots of Right and Left must,
without losing an hour more, prepare the great peaceful wave of universal
suffrage to sweep out political factions and give the great soldier of Verdun
full powers to prevent France from ending up in blood and shit.'

After three days of parliamentary chaos the Laval Government was
formed, which was to remain in power until the next January. Hervé,
welcoming it, said 'Everyone in France already knows that a Pétain dictatorship is in the air. Soon nobody will be able to make a Ministry without
taking Pétain into it as a lightning conductor.'[31] In this, of course, he was
entirely wrong. Pétain was never again to be a part of a peacetime Government.

Throughout the second half of 1935, the power of the right-wing *ligues*
became ever greater, with above all the *Croix de Feu* growing immeasurably
larger in numbers and in force. As Rémond points out in *La Droite en
France*, this movement really began to grow (though it had been in existence
since 1928) after the events of 6 February 1934, and had become by 1935 a
powerful mass movement. It was in this situation that support for a Pétain
dictatorship came from a most surprising quarter.

When the Bouisson Government had been formed, Bailby in *Le Jour* had
hailed Pétain's taking part in it, because it was obvious to him that 'the
dissolution of the *ligues*, of which the rumour had been spread by the
adversaries of the Cabinet and denied by M. Bouisson, would never be
accepted by the Marshal.'[32] In November, however, an edition of the
left-wing journal *Vu* appeared, in which Pétain was acclaimed as the man
who could take away the power of the *ligues*.

This was a special number of *Vu*, devoted to the forces at work in France.
On the cover was the sentence 'If the French fought, National Front against
Popular Front, who would win?' After an introduction by Henry Bidou on
the danger of the *ligues*, there was a series of chapters on the various *ligues*
comprising the 'National Front': the *Croix de Feu* under La Rocque, the

Action Française under Maurras and Daudet, the *Jeunesses Patriotes* under Pierre Taittinger, the *Solidarité Française*, which had at first been under Jean Renaud with the support of the millionaire Francois Coty, and the *Francistes*, under Marcel Bucard. The forces of the *Front Populaire* were then discussed, followed by the Government forces; the police, the army, the *garde mobile*.

It was the article on the army which stated the case for a Pétain take-over; and the case was argued so well that the editor of the journal, Lucien Vogel, on a later page, gave a full-page picture of Pétain, with the words 'Will he have to be called again? Pétain, the republican Marshal.' A short paragraph stressed the veneration in which he was held, his prestige with the officers, his popularity with the public (as shown by *Le Petit Journal*'s referendum), his perfect loyalty, and his absolute political independence.[33]

The article on the army was, surprisingly, written by Pierre Cot, the left-wing politician. In it he declared that the army would not take part in any revolutionary action. He then went on, however, beyond his brief, and considered what action the Government should take if a crisis occurred. The President of the Republic, he said, had the right to entrust to a man, taken from outside the political struggle, the task of ensuring order for the duration of the crisis. Everyone would approve. If the President felt public opinion to be nervous about this, he could let it be known that the country would be allowed once more to decide its own destiny as soon as possible. France had to judge whether she wanted to retain a democratic régime, or adopt a fascist regime.

Does such a man exist?, he went on. The choice is delicate. His courage, his intellectual probity, his uprightness must be indisputable and undiscussed. No one must be able to suspect him of wishing to carry out a personal operation. One of the dominant traits of his character must be loyalty. Such a man exists: it is Marshal Pétain. *He* is the true moral leader of the army. There is not one *ancien combattant* who does not have a profound gratitude to him—less, perhaps, because he was the greatest leader in the war, than because he was the most human, and the nearest to our misery. With him, there would be no trouble to fear! A word to the *anciens combattants*, an energetic gesture, and order is assured and calm is born once more. Would it be too much to ask of him? I do not think so. It is not a question of definitively handing over to him the Government, or France; it is a question of letting order reign for a few hours, and of allowing a Government to form itself freely, to rule a people of free men. Some people will find my idea strange or dangerous; I think I will have the approval of all those who have seen that astonishing thing: the gaze of Marshal Pétain.[34]

So the legend of Pétain the republican Marshal could lead to his being considered a bulwark against the *ligues*. And, far from seeing him, as *Le Jour* and *La Victoire* had done, as an alternative to democracy, Pierre Cot and Lucien Vogel saw him as a safeguard of that very democracy, who by a short temporary use of dictatorial powers could silence once and for all the supporters of autocracy. Again, Pétain said nothing, and so people of all kinds could continue to think of him as being their kind of man. (It is interesting, too, that Pierre Cot was another one who had been affected by the Marshal's appearance). Not until the 1936 elections did Pétain make any public statement about the *ligues*; and what he said then would have shocked Pierre Cot.

In late 1935 the Pétain campaign had relentlessly continued in *La Victoire*, with only the Abyssinian crisis in early October cutting it out temporarily. Always there was the prospect of the 1936 elections in view, with the terrible possibility, now that Daladier had taken the radicals into the Left camp, of a resounding victory for a *Front Populaire* Government which would include Communists. All the Right was looking for a leader. Laval's name had been suggested, but Hervé dismissed it as standing for a warmed-up version of the chaos of parliamentary government. Pétain was 'something new, a psychological shock, the highest incarnation at the present time of the Republic of the *tricolore*, and ... despite his title of Marshal of France Pétain, in the eyes of the masses, is still the Republic.'[35] Pétain's continued silence was explained by Hervé by the fact that 'Pétain, as Marshal of France, is bound to remain silent—for marshals, in our country, remain on active service for the whole of their lives.'[36] Few French marshals, it must be admitted, ever seem to have felt that they should keep quiet on political matters!

In view of Pierre Cot's idea of Pétain, it is fascinating to see *La Victoire*, around the turn of the year, alternating its Pétain articles with enthusiastic eulogies of the *Croix de Feu*, the force which could save France from the Communists. Indeed, in mid-January Hervé even suggested that if La Rocque's men were to march behind Pétain, under the aegis of *La Victoire*, France would be saved.[37]

On 8 March 1936, the newspapers carried shocking news for France. Hitler had marched into the Rhineland. In this hour, when it seemed that all the fears of German regeneration were justified, and when the military guarantee of a disarmed Rhineland had disappeared overnight, more faces turned to Pétain. In *L'Ami du Peuple*, the important right-wing newspaper founded by the millionaire François Coty, and the organ for Jean Renaud's *Solidarité Française* movement, an article by Pierre Taittinger, head of the *Jeunesses Patriotes*, called for Pétain to head a national Government. The *ligues*, against whom Cot had presumed that Pétain would act, were now looking to Pétain for leadership!

Taittinger's article was directed at Sarraut, the Prime Minister. It deplored the weakness of his statements: 'To speak strongly to Germany, to speak French to it, a Government must be strong, and French. It must not be a slave to Bolshevism* and ready to make of Paris a satellite of Moscow, which gives Hitler's speeches a weighty argument.' Taittinger called on Sarraut to form a 'Government of National Union' and to reject

---

* The Franco-Soviet pact, which was just taking place, was strongly opposed by this newspaper. In particular, an article by Robert Valléry-Radot on 25 February had stressed the dangers of any alliance with Bolshevism.

his friendships, and his governmental tendencies towards the 'bolshevising extreme-left' of his majority. 'If it is not done electorally, it doesn't matter. France will do without elections.' Such a Government would save France from two nightmares; foreign war, and civil war. It would break down the parliamentary and electoral formulas which created divisions and hatred among Frenchmen. The man to whom such a Government should be entrusted was 'Pétain, the man of Verdun', who would have the perilous but magnificent honour of presiding over the reconciliation of Frenchmen. 'Twenty years after the battle, this name would be a symbol and a solemn affirmation of our will.'[38] Once more the word 'symbol' is used of Pétain's value as a leader.

Another paper which turned to Pétain in this hour of danger was *Le Figaro*. In it Wladimir d'Ormesson called on the French to stop their intestine quarrels, and to put off till later the 'fatal elections around which the whole life of the nation seemed to be suspended', while Germany was able to take over the Rhineland. He adjured Frenchmen to group themselves around the only man capable of achieving the union of all the healthy forces in the nation, Marshal Pétain.[39]

Hervé, of course, took up what these two papers had written with delight. On 17 March he wrote of the 'awakening of the sacred union' (a name of some emotional content to many Frenchmen, as it symbolised the 'sacred union', above parties, with which the 1914–18 war had started). 'After a year's conspiracy of silence about our campaign for rallying behind Pétain', he wrote, 'people are beginning to look towards him.'[40] Taittinger and d'Ormesson (and also Bailby and Daudet), would no doubt have been horrified to be connected with Hervé, however.

Finally, at the end of April, came the elections. Right-wing journals had approached them with much foreboding; much of their space had been devoted to violent attacks on Léon Blum the socialist leader, and on the Communists. People were exhorted to 'vote national', for the nationalist parties, to avoid the dangers of a Popular Front Government. The example of Spain was produced to show how dangerous such a Government could be.

The first round of voting, on 26 April, showed how much their fears of defeat were justified. All seemed set for a Popular Front victory. The second round was to take place a week later, on 3 March.

It was at this moment, between the two rounds, that Marshal Pétain took the unexpected decision to allow some of his views on politics to be published, in an interview for the paper *Le Journal*. Given the complete public silence he had always kept on matters political, the decision is somewhat surprising. But it is clear, from the interview, that his fear of Communism and of *Front Populaire* government had made him do this. The interview is an exhortation to the voters to 'vote national'. Indeed, the headline runs: 'Marshal Pétain's watchword: *Rassemblement National.*'

The interview with a journalist called Jean Martet, was, of course, dressed up in the usual protestations of being non-political. Indeed, it started with the Marshal's unreceptive greeting to the journalist: 'Sir, I don't see very clearly what you expect of me, and indeed I am astonished that doors have opened for you. I have made it an absolute rule never to give an interview and never to make politics.'

Martet replied that it was not a question of politics, but rather of an article by Pétain on military organisation, which was about to be published by the *Revue des Deux Mondes*. Pétain thereupon spoke for a short while on that subject, and national defence, ending with the phrase: 'France, sir, is seriously threatened.'

Immediately Martet picked up this statement. 'Do you not think, Marshal' he said, 'that the Franco-Soviet pact has done a grave disservice to us, by giving the official recognition to communism that our Governments had until then refused?'

'You are very indiscreet, sir,' replied the Marshal, but then went on to give his opinions: 'Indeed, I believe so. In holding out our hand to Moscow, we have held it out to Communism, and brought to it a number of good people from our country who, until then, kept away from it. We have allowed communism to enter the circle of confessable doctrines. We will probably have reason to regret it.'

Nothing could have been a clearer attack on the *Front Populaire* win which was about to take place. It was a clear warning to the voters not to vote for a *bloc* which included Communists.

The reporter, by adroit questioning, got Pétain to clarify this: 'Marshal, am I to conclude that your feelings on the present situation. . .'

'I am anxious, sir,' replied the Marshal. 'Anxious for the safety of France, and for the liberty of Frenchmen. For it is not merely the collectivity which is involved. It is each of us, in respect of his rights. It is the bourgeois. It is the worker. It is the peasant.'

From this, the reporter naturally moved to the *ligues*, which set themselves up as protectors of these very 'rights'. He asked the Marshal what he thought of the *Croix de Feu* (and we must remember that the *Croix de Feu* was, at this stage, still a movement directed to extra-parliamentary action). Pétain's answer is important:

In my opinion, everything that is international is dangerous. Everything that is national is useful and productive. The *Croix de Feu* represent one of the healthiest elements in this country.

They want to defend the family, guarantee the indispensable conditions for its existence. I approve of that. Everything stems from it. The French family has been expropriated, struck by exorbitant measures. One might believe that our legislators have had no aim other than to break the chain of effort and discourage the father from working for his children. I see also that the *Croix de Feu* occupy themselves with the moral and spiritual improvement of youth. You know that this is an idea I have held for a long time. One can make nothing of a nation which has no soul. It is up to our schoolmasters, our university teachers to forge a soul for the nation. We do not ask them to make our children into learned men. We ask them to make them into men, into Frenchmen.

In its assembly of some of Pétain's favourite themes, the family, moral education, anti-intellectualism (which are all favourite themes of a certain Right), and the placing of them in relation to a single movement, the *Croix de Feu*, Pétain's speech here showed that these themes are in themselves political, whatever protestations he might make. They are themes which were, in his mind, opposed to the doctrines of the Left, which were therefore extremely dangerous. (One can imagine Pierre Cot's dismay at Pétain's support for one of the *ligues*.)

So far in the interview, the Marshal had merely been expressing general opinions, even though they were obviously aimed at specific political application. Now, the reporter brought up explicitly the question of the elections: 'Marshal, the French people went to vote last Sunday and are going back to vote next Sunday. I would like to pass on your watchword to them.'

'No,' replied Pétain firmly, 'that would be politics.' One wonders what he thought the rest of the interview had been.

Martet returned to the attack, bringing out all the clichés about Pétain's value as a symbol: 'Marshal, you represent the French victory, and the most noble fusion there has ever been between the *poilus* and their leaders. There is in France no personality more symbolic than yours, to transmit to the men of today the sense of the sacrifice made by the men of yesterday.'

And then, despite his protestations of never making politics, Pétain gave his views to the nation, views which stressed the inferiority of France to Germany and Italy (in spite of the material inferiority of those countries), because the latter had faith, leaders, and no doubt in themselves: 'Say this, then. Say that France is less unhappy than Germany, less unhappy than Italy. The question of bread is less important with us than elsewhere. Yet neither Germany nor Italy have doubts. *We* have doubts. Our crisis is not a material crisis. We have lost faith in our destiny, that is all. We are like mariners without a pilot, without a tiller. That is the thing we must struggle against. That is what we must find once more: a mystique. Call it what you will: mystique of the fatherland or, more simply, mystique of remembrance: without this, there is no hope. We come after millions of beings who have struggled and suffered for us to become what we are. They have the right to demand of us that we should at least continue their task.'

'If you were asked to sum up your thoughts', asked Martet, 'what would they be in a word.'

'National Unity', replied Pétain. This was the watchword of those of the *Front National*, and the message to the voter was obvious.[41]

This 1936 text is important not merely because it shows Pétain attempting to take a positive part in politics. It also shows, in French internal politics, an admiration for the *Croix de Feu*, and a hatred of the forces of the Left; and, externally, an admiration for the achievements of the German and Italian dictatorships, which are contrasted with the pilotless, tillerless waverings and doubts of parliamentary democracy. These were much the views of those papers which had supported Pétain's candidature, *Le Jour*, *L'Ami du Peuple*, *La Victoire*.

The second vote, however, merely consolidated the victory of the *Front Populaire*. Amid the wailings of Hervé that his advice to rally behind Pétain had not been heeded, the parties of the Left triumphed. Hervé's campaign, and those of the other papers which had taken Pétain's name up, ceased for a while.

Though Pétain's name was to recur on various occasions in this and other contexts in the national Press in the next three years, much more pressure was being put on behind the scenes, as we shall see in the next chapter. However, let us look briefly first at the Press comments of these years.

Hervé, during his campaign, had produced in book form a series of the articles concerned, under the title *C'est Pétain qu'il nous faut*. A year after the elections, in 1937, he produced a new edition of this, completely revised and with a new preface. In it he stressed the fact that his predictions of the effects of a *Front Populaire* Government had come true: France was now in a revolutionary situation. The occupation of the factories by the workers, etc., had however merely produced, among conservatives and moderates, the aim of detaching the radicals from the *Front Populaire*, in order to form a new Government of the centre. This would be appalling, he said; they were still too attached to the parliamentary regime. The game of 'ministries of national unity', as played in 1926 and 1934, was dangerous: each time a 'revolutionary wave', like those of 1924, 1932 and 1936 would beat down on France. Each time the wave had been worse, thanks to the 'new generations who, thanks to the continuous and underhand workings of irreligious education with anarchistic tendencies, are more and more abandoning the radicals and moving to the extremist revolutionary parties.'[42] If they went on like this, France would finish up like Spain, or Russia. What was needed was a great figure like Pétain. He, Hervé, was starting up his campaign again.

The revised texts had the following evocative titles: (1) 'The Red Wave.' (2) 'The Dam: The Authoritarian Republic with a professional basis.' (3) 'The Providential Man: Pétain.' (4) 'The Pétain Front.' (5) 'What Pétain would be like in power.'

Though M. Pierre Bourget suggests in his book[43] that Hervé's aims changed between the editions of *C'est Pétain qu'il nous faut*, the texts he uses do not substantiate this. Hervé had always said that Pétain's dictatorship should be achieved by universal suffrage, that it should be classless, that it should be based on a corporative system similar to the ideas of Le Play, that it should bring about national conciliation, order, and liberty, and that it should be neither of Right nor Left (though of course, Hervé's use of these terms is idiosyncratic).

Little came of Hervé's new campaign. Pétain still remained silent, and public opinion did not follow it. It was behind the scenes that the most important moves to further Pétain's political career were to take place.

In 1938, after the fall of the Chautemps Government on 10 March,

Henri Lémery wrote an article on Pétain in *L'Indépendant*, suggesting that his presence at the head of a Government of concord and revival would signify that 'the hour of discipline' had struck, caused by peril and the spirit of sacrifice.[44] As we shall see, Lémery was on several occasions to attempt privately to get Pétain to accept office, in the years 1938-40.

The nomination of Pétain as ambassador to Franco in 1939, aroused tremendous enthusiasm in the Press of the Right, as we shall see. And the Press of the Left, smarting at France's recognition of the new Spanish Government, was furious at the ambassadorship, not because Pétain seemed to them a dangerous man, but because, in Blum's words, 'Such an ambassador all the same raises too high the apprentice-dictator to whom he is accredited. The most noble, the most humane of our military commanders is not in his rightful place next to General Franco.'[45] He was even praised by *L'Humanité*, which spoke of the humiliation inflicted on France by seeing 'her most honoured soldier await the goodwill of the traitor Franco.'[46] The right-wing Press, on the other hand, described Pétain as 'trailing clouds of glory, and going among victorious military men.'[47]

A month later, there were the presidential elections. As we shall see, much behind-the-scenes pressure was put on Pétain to stand. But there was also public pressure, of the type of the articles in *France Vivante* (organ of the 'Living France Movement') which drew attention to the dangers of war, and the crisis of authority and responsibility in the country, following the example at the head, which led to bad organisation of work and demoralisation: 'There is only one remedy, an authority . . ., a universally recognised arbitrator, capable of choosing and inspiring the team of men of character who will demand from every Frenchman the full responsibility of his acts. Only then will Parliament be able to fulfil its mission of control, renouncing a confusion of powers which is fatal to the nation. To save France and its liberties, the universally recognised arbitrator can have only one name: Pétain. Let him be President of the Republic!'[48] Another paper strongly to support Pétain in 1939 was *Le Grand Occident*, run by Paul Ferdonnet, which called for Pétain as dictator, to protect France from the Jew-Mason, the true enemy of France. Ferdonnet was later an announcer on the German radio, which led to strong accusations with regard to Pétain, in the anonymous volume *Pétain et la Cinquième Colonne* (published clandestinely during the occupation). As with the other campaigns, however, there is no proof of Pétain either having inspired or accepted this campaign, which was at any rate far more extremist than any other.

What was Pétain's attitude to these various campaigns? As we have seen, he kept silent about them. He gave them no public approval and no public disapproval. It is clear, from various remarks that he privately made, (e.g. to Lémery in January 1940), that he knew of some of them. But, while he might approve of the general sentiments expressed (and his view of the French situation, as stated in April 1936, can be taken to mean that he would), and while events show that he had boundless self-confidence in his own abilities to help France when in need, the campaigns themselves were not of a kind that ever looked like succeeding, and any public statement might well have rebounded on him. So he was wise not to speak in favour; but his failure to dissociate himself from such things was perhaps unwise. He did, in fact, refuse several important positions in these years, even resisting requests to stand as President of the Republic. But none of these posts would have dissociated him from the Governments concerned, who might have sullied his reputation; and the Presidency of the Republic held few powers in relation to the Government itself. So these refusals prove little. Pétain's attitude to 'personal power' at this time remains an enigma.

It is evident, however, that the perpetual praise showered on him in these campaigns, and in other newspaper articles, was not disagreeable to him. He was obviously happy about the praise he was getting. In September 1939 he wrote to Mrs Pardee: 'Keep the cutting from Bailby's paper, it is a good thing that you should have before your eyes a list of the services I have already rendered to my country, and that I will perhaps render to it again if I keep my health.'[49] Other remarks made in these years show that he felt that if France really got into trouble, he was the man to be called on to get her out of it. Some of these remarks were, of course, to cause him trouble at his trial.

So although nothing can really be known of Pétain's attitudes to campaigns in favour of *himself* as dictator, we know that he felt that France needed leadership, and that he considered Germany and Italy to have an advantage over France because they had that leadership. We know, too, that he considered himself to be a man on whom France might at some time have to call (but whether this means militarily or politically one cannot be certain). What *is* clear is that years of praise for him, in the papers, led to a belief in himself both as symbol, continuator of a heroic tradition, and moral influence. Often, during these inter-war years, he had spoken of his desire for retirement; but always he had continued to work, taking on new posts, retaining power on military matters. Would he, despite his reiterated desires for peace and rest, be prepared to take on political responsibility? The answer lies not so much in his non-existent public reactions to newspaper campaigns, as in his private reactions to more serious and private requests; and the final answer came when he assumed power in the summer of 1940.

Chapter Seven

Political involvement 1934–40

SINCE the last war, there have been many suggestions as to Pétain's political involvement in the immediately pre-war years. This chapter is an attempt to define his political contacts in that period; we have already seen what his general political views were. One extreme has been to cast him as a perpetual political plotter; the other to cast him as a man with no political involvement whatsoever. The truth, as we shall see, lies between the two.

The Doumergue Government

Before 1934, Pétain had taken no direct part in politics. He had privately held views on the matter, of course, and had expressed them in conversation and in letters; these views reflected, in large part, those of many other army officers of the day. But despite his strong views upon such matters as the occupation of the left bank of the Rhine, the dangers of Communism, or the shortcomings of the parliamentary system, he kept silence in public on them, and gained a reputation for being a Marshal 'outside politics'. His public statements were restricted to exhortations of a general nature, on education, honour, patriotism, etc.; he appeared to have no political ambitions.

It was the events of 6 February 1934, which started off his political career. These have often been described as a fascist putsch. René Rémond however, in his book *La Droite en France*, has conclusively shown that this was not so: the main movements involved (the *Croix de Feu*, the *Jeunesses Patriotes*, the *Union Nationale des Combattants*) were of a far more traditional Right, and consisted in large part of disgruntled ex-servicemen appalled by parliamentary incompetence and dishonesty. This had, of course, been brought to a head by the disclosures about the Stavisky scandals, the succession of financial crises since the 1932 elections, and the impressions of muddled parliamentarism and horsetrading that had been brought about by Daladier's attempts at reshuffling and compromise to form a new Government to replace that of Chautemps, which had fallen on 27 January. The programmes of these movements had little in common with Fascism. And it was hardly a putsch; as Rémond points out, it was merely a 'street manifestation'. A 'fascist putsch' would hardly be satisfied with the return from retirement of a 'safe old man' to head a Government on national unity! No, it was an anti-parliamentary riot which turned out badly, with bloodshed, and therefore seemed more important than it in fact was; it gives little impression of coherent organisation, for though the date was fixed in common, each group pursued its own demonstration.[1]

Be that as it may, it brought about the fall of the Daladier Government which had allowed it to be fired on. The President of the Republic, under strong pressure from such men as Laval, sent for the former President, Gaston Doumergue, to form a Government as premier. This old man, coming out of his retirement, formed a Government by 9 February, which leaned to the Right, despite the fact that there had been a large left-wing majority in the 1932 elections. This was made possible by support from the Radicals, who after their recent experiences were only too happy to support a Government of national unity. The presence of Doumergue, and the shift to the Right, reassured much of the population, including those *ligues* who had taken part in the riots. Further reassurance was provided by the presence of Marshal Pétain as war minister.

We have already seen the praise that was showered on him at this time, as a symbol of France's greatness. The acclaim he was given justified Doumergue's decision. We have also seen his attitudes to military policy in his period in office—the ministerial solidarity, which made him agree to cuts in men and armaments which he knew to be dangerous (though it must be admitted that he got special credits voted later in the year for military purposes, i.e., the Maginot Line) and his acceptance of continuation of one-year service (which he was going to condemn as soon as he was out of power). What, if any, was his *political* action in this year?

Firstly, what was his attitude to the riots? He certainly had no part in them. Nor, despite persistent rumours, had any other major military figure except Lyautey, and even he did not actually take part on the 6th. Lyautey had been involved, since his retirement, in right-wing politics; and he had always had contempt for parliamentary government. But he dined, on the evening of the 6th, with his old friend Wladimir d'Ormesson (some say, in order to avoid implication). The next day, he saw many political figures of the Right, however, particularly the leaders of the *ligues*, and then told the Government that he himself would march at the head of the protesters that afternoon unless Daladier's Government resigned. The next day, the 8th, after the Government had resigned, Henri de Kérillis stated in *L'Écho de Paris* that if it had not, anything might have happened. General indignation at the bloodshed of the day before had swelled the ranks of the protesters: the *anciens combattants*, the *Jeunesses Patriotes*, and the *Action Française* would have stormed the public buildings. 'And', he said, 'Paris will not learn without poignant emotion that Marshal Lyautey had decided to march at the head of the *anciens combattants*, saying simply "If men must fall, it is better that it should be old men like me, rather than young men of twenty."[2] Lyautey, seeing the public effect of 6 February, had tried to turn it to account by uniting the *ligues* around his great figure as Marshal of France. Only La Rocque, leader of the *Croix de Feu*, apparently refused to follow him.

Pétain certainly took no part in these events. But he could hardly have failed to be sympathetic to the kind of men who took part in them. While he believed in loyalty to the civil power, he nevertheless shared these men's distaste for the workings of parliamentary democracy under the Third Republic. And after all, many of them were his *anciens combattants*. This explains why he visited not only the police wounded, but also those of the other side. On 13 February he visited the bedside of Georges Lebecq, the president of the *Union Nationale des Combattants*, who had been wounded in the riots. This was highly praised by the *Voix du Combattant* of 22 February: 'The old and respected leader has brought to our President proof of his sympathy ... the *anciens combattants* thank you profoundly, Marshal, for your fraternal gesture. They well know that your heart is beating in unison with theirs.'[3] This was going a bit far. Pétain naturally identified himself with *anciens combattants*; he even shared some of their views on Governments; but he did not necessarily approve of their policies or their doctrines. The Doumergue Government had in part been formed to try to calm the worries of the *ligues*. Doumergue himself was to put on the uniform of the *Croix de Feu* and take part in their march-pasts. As Rémond points out, this last fact shows not so much that Doumergue got involved with fascism, as that the fascism did not exist.[4] The groups of 6 February were not fascist mobs hungry to overthrow society, but groups of exasperated right-wingers and traditionalists, bent merely on the forcible expression of their disapproval of the Government of the day. As such, they were just rather more forcible, and anti-social, expressions of opinions shared to a certain extent by some members of the new, more traditional and right-wing Government.*

Pétain, when joining that Government, had publicly expressed his own non-political nature: 'The President has told me that the country has need of me. I have not avoided this duty, but I have never made politics and I do not wish to do so now.'[5]

We have already seen that, in one sense, to claim to be non-political is in fact to be political. But while Pétain held strong political views he did, for most of the period of this Government, not take part in political man-oeuvring. In this sense he did not 'make politics'. He devoted himself to military matters, and his infrequent appearances in the Chamber and before the Army Commissions were unmarked by controversy. In the Cabinet, he argued for the army, but remained loyal to ministerial respon-sibility when the decision went against him.

Among those in the Government with him were an old friend, Barthou, and a man who was later to be of importance to him, Laval. Laval, with whom Pétain had come into contact at the time of the former's premiership in 1931–2, had started out in the Doumergue Government as Minister of Colonies, but took over as Foreign Minister on 13 October, after Barthou's assassination. Doumergue apparently one day said to Pétain 'The Republic is rotten; they have no one left', but then pointed to Laval, saying 'but there's still that man'. Pétain used often to repeat this remark in the later

---

* Lyautey, at his death at the end of July, was given full honours, including a magnificent funeral oration by Pétain.

'thirties according to Loustaunau-Lacau, who was on Pétain's staff at the time.[6]

Among others in the Government were the Radical Herriot who became minister without portfolio, as did Tardieu; Albert Sarraut, who became Minister of the Interior, and Chéron, Minister of Justice. (The Government was to have representatives of all parties except the Socialists and Communists.)

Pétain rarely took an active part in political matters in the Cabinet. When he did, according to contemporary witnesses, he sometimes made fairly decisive intrusions into quarrels. One can imagine his dry comments suddenly breaking through the excitable discussion. He despised politicians and felt himself apart from them; these were just the sort of people for whom his irony was made.

A decisive comment he made, in October, has been recorded for us. It happened on the 13th, four days after the assassination of King Alexander I of Yugoslavia and Louis Barthou, the French Foreign Minister, at Marseille. Albert Sarraut, the Minister of the Interior, had resigned because he felt his department to bear some responsibility. Paul Marchandeau had taken his place, and Laval had become Foreign Minister. Chéron, the Minister of Justice, was talking about the Stavisky Affair. Pétain suddenly spoke: 'There is still a dead weight in our team', and made it clear that he meant Chéron. Chéron immediately resigned. His resignation was accepted, he left the room, and the meeting continued without anything more being said on the subject.

What was Pétain's reason for acting in this way? Laure, and Amouroux, suggest that it was because of the way in which Chéron had been handling the Stavisky affair. The hearings had gone on and on. Chéron had enthusiastically given promises of results, but results had not been reached. The murder, or suicide, on 21 February of Albert Prince, a lawyer who was presumed to have inside knowledge of the case, was not solved, and Chéron's department again gave an impression of incompetence. Worse still, Prince's death had given rise to violent rumours about freemason plots,[7] and eventually about the implication of the former premier, Camille Chautemps. Judicial procedures had even allowed Tardieu, who was accused of being involved in the case, to make a violent public attack on Chautemps, and other Radicals; this in turn had caused a crisis in the Doumergue Government, with Herriot demanding Tardieu's resignation. Though consideration of this matter had been postponed, it was still hanging over them. Pétain may have seen Chéron as being ultimately responsible for this danger to the Government, by his mishandling and enthusiastic prolongation of judicial proceedings. He may, also, have had in mind the fact that Chéron would now be having to deal with another fragile case, that of the recent assassinations. He may just have felt that Chéron was unsuitable for government. Chéron was a slightly comic figure, a plump, good-humoured man who loved the limelight the Stavisky affair had given him. It has been suggested that Chéron thought that Pétain referred to him as a 'heavyweight' rather than a 'dead weight', and took this personally. Be that as it may, his immediate resignation was dignified; but he does not seem to have been missed.

Herriot had, by this time, firmly decided to down the Government, and his opportunity occurred in November. Doumergue, convinced as much by recent events as by the history of the Republic since the war of the need of greater power for the Prime Minister and for the executive, had been proposing certain measures, from September onwards, which might produce this result. The system up till now had made it too easy for Governments to be frivolously overthrown, because this did not mean a dissolution of the Chamber and a new general election, but merely a reshuffle of those already there. Doumergue suggested that the President of the Republic, on the Premier's recommendation, should be able to dissolve Parliament, and send everyone before the electors once more. This should make for more stability in the Chamber. Another suggested measure, tending towards efficiency, was that no private member could propose specific expenditures for the budget.

Herriot, looking for an excuse to finish off the Government, feigned to see, in these measures designed to strengthen the Republic, designs to finish off the régime entirely. Doumergue dug his heels in, despite hints from Laval that concessions might have to be made. On 8 November, Herriot and the other Radical ministers resigned. The Government fell.

Pétain was furious. He had seen the Doumergue reforms as being the only way out of the 'politicking' of the little men who made up the successive Governments. His hatred of Herriot, the man who had destroyed these plans, dated from this time.

In typical manner, at the time of the crisis, he had suggested that they could carry on without the Radical ministers. The others could double up their Ministries. He, for example, was prepared to take Education as well as War. (This is yet one more example of his interest in, and belief in the importance of, education). According to Lémery, he stated this bluntly as follows: 'We can do without them. I will willingly take National Education as well as War. I would deal with the Communist schoolmasters!'[8]

Pétain was not quickly going to forget the fall of the Doumergue Government, or to forgive those who had brought it about. In a letter written to Doumergue three years later, on 28 April 1937, he expressed his feelings on the matter:

Your 1934 ministry could have led the country into a road which would have assured its safety, if your project with regard to the constitution had been adopted. All my life, I will remember the Cabinet meeting which finished with the resignation of the Ministry. I have not forgiven the President of the Republic for remaining impassive, and, one might say, inert, when presented with the news you brought him. In my view, he ought not to have accepted this resignation, and should, on the contrary, have helped you to replace the departing ministers, an action which would at least have allowed us to present your project to the Chambers, and make them responsible for its non-acceptance.

Be that as it may, the definitive abandonment of the project has been disastrous for the country. We see the consequences of it today. What has the future got in store for us. Can order be re-established without bloodshed?

I am sorry to end my letter on such black forebodings.[9]

A few days before the fall of the Doumergue Government, Pierre-Étienne Flandin had made it clear to the Radicals that he was prepared to form a Government with them. By the evening of the same day as the fall, it had been formed. Laval remained at Foreign Affairs, Germain-Martin at Finance. Pétain was asked to remain at the Ministry of War, but refused.

Pétain had joined the Doumergue Government on the basis that he had been entering a 'ministry of truce', in which he would be able to accomplish his task while remaining outside 'politics'. Now some of his colleagues, 'on the instances of their party'[10] had broken that truce, and had obliged the Prime Minister to resign. He had followed suit, and was leaving the politics of parties.

When he later accepted a post in the next ministry after Flandin's, one newspaper at least explained his refusal to join Flandin's as follows: 'If he refused to collaborate with M. Flandin, it was because he disapproved of the latter's treachery with regard to their common leader.'[11] The reappearance of 'the parties' and the fall of the 'ministry of truce' left their mark upon Pétain.

Parliamentary involvement

Pétain had shown, in his resignation from the Doumergue Government and his refusal of a place in that of Flandin, his fundamental dislike for the 'parliamentary game'. His taste of parliamentary power, however, had left him with a feeling that he might have a political role to fill, and that his views on Government were the only way that France might be saved. What were these views? They went beyond the 'special powers' of Doumergue. What he wanted was a strong leader. This has been stressed by his intimates, by his letters, and by his own sparse public statements on the matter. Hints of this were given by his speech on Primo de Rivera, and the parallels he drew with France, in 1925;* it came out clearly in his public statement, in April 1936, when he referred to the French as being like 'mariners without a pilot, without a tiller', and compared them unfavourably with the Germans and the Italians.† Friends and colleagues give evidence of his indifference as to the régime, so long as there was unity of command, and stability, 'and above all no ministers thirsty for popularity.'[12] To his friend Mrs Pardee, in 1940, he wrote that 'the best form of government would be the Republic, if all men were wise, but they are not!' He went on to say that the best thing was to live in a country where too many laws did not get in the way of individual liberty.[13] To Lémery he described government as a command, with a leader at the head, and capable

* See page 117
† See page 185

ministers. When things did not work, the ministers should be replaced. But the one leader should remain and the powers of the Head of State and the Head of Government should be mingled.[14]

Pétain wanted, not dictatorship, but a strong Republic under a President who would at the same time be head of the executive. As in military commands, he reasoned, decision could only come from strong leadership. Under the Third Republic, the President was a cipher, usually chosen because he was harmless. The Premier held most of the power, but was liable to be upset by combinations of the parties. This was the situation that had caused the chronic parliamentary disability of the Third Republic (and was to do the same to the Fourth Republic, until de Gaulle stepped in).

In June of 1935, Pétain did agree to serve in another ministry, that of Bouisson, as Minister of State. The Ministry asked for emergency powers to deal with the financial crisis, but it fell on the day it presented itself to the Chamber. The fall of this Government showed Pétain even more clearly the follies of parliamentary government under the Third Republic. His statements about the fate of France, in his letters, became more and more foreboding.

Meanwhile, Hervé's Press campaign was at its height, and Suarès, Bailby and Daudet had also, in their different ways, taken up Pétain's name. Though Pétain made no public reaction to these campaigns, their untrammelled praise for him can hardly have left him unmoved. He is reported to have jokingly said, at a meeting that June where everyone was saying that he was the only man who could save the country, 'Yes, the last cartridge, eh!'[15] Just as he had been prepared to be drafted, in the Doumergue Government, because the country 'had need' of him, so he was prepared to hold himself ready again; indeed, in 1940 his speeches were to show this very attitude.

Pétain did not become a member of the Laval Government, nor of the succeeding Sarraut Government, which took France down to the elections of May 1936.

In 1935 and 1936 the powers of the *ligues* grew, and facing them was the ever-increasing threat of the *Front Populaire*. We have already seen Pétain's attitudes to these matters, as stated in a newspaper interview given at the strategic moment between the two election counts.* In it he showed his fear of Communism, and his approval of the ideals of the *Croix de Feu*, as well as his willingness to interfere in 'politics'.

When the *Front Populaire* resoundingly won the 1936 elections, many Frenchmen felt the end of the world had come. The Marshal once more became the rock of tradition to which people turned. But his contempt for the office of president, under the present form of the Third Republic, is shown by a remark he is reported to have made at this time, when it was suggested he should stand for President: 'The presidence of the Republic is only good for defeated marshals!'[16] The immediate reference was to

* See pages 183–5

195

MacMahon, first President of the Third Republic; but the remark showed scorn for this post, which was truly the place for failed politicians.

Some suggestions as to Pétain's future were more serious, however. From the beginning of 1937 onwards, Laval was on and off to be thinking of the prospect of a Pétain Government. Pétain and Laval had known each other for some time. The first known contact had been in 1931 on military matters, when Pétain was Inspector General of Aerial Defence, and Laval Prime Minister. They had since been colleagues in the Doumergue Government, where Pétain had been impressed by Doumergue's opinion of Laval. And in June 1935 they had been colleagues on the ill-fated Bouisson Government (in one of the official pictures, they were clearly in conversation, standing next to each other).[17]

What had Laval's career been, up to this time? He had started as Socialist deputy for the working-class district of Aubervilliers, which he had been throughout the First World War. After electoral defeat in 1919, he had left the Socialist party, and, as Independent, had become mayor of Aubervilliers, which would normally have been a left-wing stronghold, and which he ably held against the Communists till 1944. On this basis, he became a deputy in the 1924 Chamber as part of the *Cartel des Gauches*. Gradually he shifted to the Right (a parliamentary Right, far different from the archetypal French Right to which Pétain and the military belonged). He had immense personal charm, and a great deal of persuasiveness, and succeeded in keeping former supporters, and gaining new adherents. From 17 January 1931, to 16 February 1932, he was Prime Minister. After the left-wing victories of 1932, he was in the wilderness for a while, but returned as Foreign Minister in the more Right-Wing Doumergue Government of national unity. He remained Foreign Minister under Flandin and Bouisson, and then took over as Prime Minister and Foreign Minister from 7 June 1935 to 22 January 1936. In foreign policy he was a partisan of understanding with Germany and Italy. That many of the French people saw him as a champion of stability is shown by the results of the *Petit Journal* referendum in January 1935; but, more than this, he was one of the wiliest politicians of the Third Republic, a horsetrader and wheeler-dealer in the best French tradition.

To be taken up by such a man was indeed a serious matter; and Pétain and Laval were to remain much in contact with each other during these years.

The first hint we have of Laval's interest comes in a conversation between him and one of General Franco's agents, in which Laval expressed his fears of Communism, and, having said he was in touch with Doriot, La Rocque and Pétain, declared the salvation of France to lie in a Pétain Government. The Marshal, he said, was determined to assume this responsibility.[18] Warner, quoting this, doubts whether this was necessarily accurate, and suggests that Laval may not even have got Pétain's support.

About this time, Pétain was writing to friends about the joys of retirement.[19] Now while he did this at various times of his life, and yet never really retired (his military journeys alone, in 1938 and 1939 led Mrs Pardee to exclaim with amazement that so much could be done by a young man, let alone a man of over eighty) it is quite possible that he saw himself as some kind of Coriolanus, who would only come back when needed.

Meanwhile, France's troubles continued. Blum's Government fell on 21 June 1937, amid financial crisis, and the workers' discouragement. Its successor, the Chautemps Government, was still a Popular Front Government, in that Chautemps was a Radical, and Blum was serving in it. But, as Brogan says, 'that the Front was cracked was denied by everybody, but cracked it was.'[20] The franc was devalued, but the finances were still in a mess. As Pétain wrote to his wife, though the 'great penitence' was on, the State was still spending as much, and everything had to come from the taxpayer's pocket. And the strikes were continuing.[21]

In January 1938, Chautemps drove the Socialists out of his Government. He himself handed his Government's resignation in on 10 March. Pétain wrote from Paris to Mrs Pardee: 'A new political crisis is beginning, and it worries me because it may become grave.'[22] It certainly did become grave: it lasted three days, and during that period the Germans annexed Austria, on the 12th. In *L'Indépendant*, Lémery's article appeared suggesting that Pétain should be prime minister. Behind the scenes, Lémery was putting forward the same candidate. He went to see President Lebrun, asking him to call for the Marshal to form a Government. But Lebrun was amazed at the idea of taking a non-parliamentarian, and nothing came of it. On 13 March, Léon Blum formed a new Government.

The fate of this new Government was sealed from the start. Blum had tried to form a kind of 'National Government', but the right-wing parties refused to join in. The Government therefore consisted of Radicals and Socialists. Hamstrung by strikes and dissension, the days of the Popular Front were numbered.

In this atmosphere, eyes were once more on Pétain. In the first days of the Blum Government, Henri Pichot, President of the *Union Fédérale des Anciens Combattants*, went to see President Lebrun to ask him to make Pétain Head of Government, and got little change out of him. Jacques Bardoux, of the Institute, also wrote a letter to Lebrun demanding a Government of Public Safety under Daladier or Pétain.[23]

More serious support for Pétain was available, however. Parliamentary support, and that of one of the most wily parliamentarians, who, knowing that the Blum Government was short-lived, was planning ahead. It was Pierre Laval once more. On 17 March, he told Landini, the Italian press attaché (in utmost confidence) that he was forming a National Government, 'of which he would be the driving force and which would be headed by Marshal Pétain, who had decided to accept from patriotic motives.'[24] President Lebrun, terrified, was opposed to this. But Laval and his supporters were sending politicians of all parties to discuss it with him, and give him the impression that it had wide support.

This *may* explain the actions of Lémery and Pichot, though neither of them mention Laval in this context, and his project may have been separate from each of theirs.

A letter written by Pétain to Mrs Pardee on 24 March, however, showed him in a somewhat different mood. He described himself as being 'besieged by a number of people inciting me to accept functions which I do not desire, and which would be a crushing load for me', and went on to evoke his 'desire for independence and liberty, which does not go with the projects people have for me.'[25]

A second conversation which Laval had with the Italian press attaché on 4 April also shows the situation as having changed. Laval said that his Pétain plan was beginning to develop, 'but that I was not to believe that the offer was going so smoothly. The Marshal had a will and prejudices of his own and it required considerable tact to make him see reason.'[26]

There are several possible interpretations of Pétain's attitudes at this time. The two most extreme ones would be to say, either that his letter to Mrs Pardee told the truth about his attitudes, and he had refused to have anything to do with these things, or that it was untruthful, and hid a secret agreement with Laval. Both these interpretations are unsatisfactory, for various reasons. In the first case, his continued meetings with Laval, and his later actions, show that he *was* interested in such political questions; in the second, Laval's second conversation shows that there was *not* full agreement.

Warner's hypothesis is a good one. It is that Laval presented his proposal to Pétain, who at first 'seemed disposed to accept the responsibility of power', but that Pétain, refusing to be made use of and eventually realising that Laval intended to use him merely as a figurehead, created difficulties which held up the project.[27] The letter to Mrs Pardee, if Warner's hypothesis is correct, may have been written in these later stages of the discussions, when Pétain may have been getting disillusioned about the idea; it may have referred to the initiatives of Lémery and others; it may have expressed reluctance at something which, through 'duty' and 'France's need' he might have to accept; (This rings true: his statements, both when entering Doumergue's Government in 1934, and when taking over the Government in 1940, shows the same sense of reluctant duty, and Laval said, in his first conversation, that Pétain had decided to accept 'from patriotic motives'); and it certainly reflected Pétain's well-cultivated *persona* of the man who was keen to avoid public duties. (In fact, in these years when he had no official post, he took on so many public duties that Mrs Pardee was amazed at his energy.)

Laval, at Pétain's trial, was to admit his plan to put Pétain in power. He had felt that the Marshal's authority and prestige might help to rectify the French position abroad, which had been jeopardised by the Popular Front. He said that at the time he had made no secret of this, but had discussed it with many colleagues. He had infrequent conversations with the Marshal, who 'seemed disposed to accept the responsibility of power if the opportunity was presented to him.'[28]

The last sentence is an important one. Pétain was not the Marshal for a *coup d'état*. He would take over, if asked to, from a sense of duty, though one senses from many of his remarks in these years that he gained a certain satisfaction from the fact that he might be needed. Above all, we must remember that he believed in 'one man at the head', and that he disliked the politicking of the Third Republic. Any feeling that he was being used would have frightened him off, and this is no doubt why his negotiations with Laval at one point bogged down.

We shall probably never know whether, given a little more time, the proposed Pétain-Laval combination would have come off, because it was rendered useless by the premature fall of the Blum Government on 8 April, after which Daladier formed a far more stable 'Government of National Defence', under Radical lead. Pétain and Laval were to remain in contact, however, upon political matters.

As 1938 passed by, the international situation got worse and worse. Then, in September, came the Munich Agreement. Pétain's reaction to this was that of many Frenchmen; why should they go out of their way just because of the Czechs? Letters to his wife, on 10 and 14 September, expressed his confidence that there was no danger, and that the Czechs would give in; if the French were dragged into this *bagarre*, their rulers must have lost their mind.[29] On the 16th, he wrote to Mrs Pardee, who had written to him about the crisis, and said:

From what you say in your letter, it appears that the papers you read are rather out of touch with what most French people are thinking.

I am sending you a letter I received this morning. It is from the widow of an officer who was killed in the war. She naturally has a great horror of war, and devoutly wishes that it will not take place, but the arguments she uses are truly touching, and a woman like you, endowed with sensibility, should be able to understand them.

England did us much harm under the MacDonald régime, but since Mr Chamberlain's arrival in power she has clearly been trying to make up for her faults. Mr Chamberlain has shown much courage and disinterest in making his *démarche* to Hitler. I cannot explain to you all the reasons for this in a letter, it would be much too long. I ask you to have confidence in me, otherwise, it will definitely be the concentration camp for you. . . .*

As in England, the Czechoslovak situation divided people across parties, and across normal political divisions. It is interesting in France, however, to notice how closely the division between Vichy and the Gaullists was to reflect this other division, in the first month or two after the 1940 defeat.

As 1938 drew to a close, people began to look ahead to the presidential elections which would take place in the spring, on 5 April 1939. Again eyes turned to Pétain. But, as we already know, Pétain had little regard for the Presidency in Third Republic conditions, seeing it as virtually powerless in relation to Parliament, and 'suitable only for defeated marshals.' In October he had written: 'Enlightened people are beginning to realise that our internal

---

* Pardee, op. cit. pp. 24–5, 16 September 1938. The last remark is a reference to a private joke, whereby he had threatened on one occasion to put her in a concentration camp if she misbehaved.

politics must change, on pain of death, but the politicians remain divided and the people have not yet understood. They talk now of dissolving the Chamber and having new elections. Will this be better than the old? It is doubtful, because the electors have not yet suffered enough, they would still let themselves be caught by the ploys of those tub-thumpers who are soliciting their votes.'[30] It is hardly surprising, therefore, that the overtures made to him received rebuffs.

Some of the overtures were made as early as December 1938. Mrs Pardee describes a conversation she had with him, in Cannes, on 6 December. He had received, at his 'Hermitage', many letters that morning, and he was rather pensive. She asked him what had happened. Showing her the letters, he replied 'I am being incited to take power, as if they did not know that I do not desire it at any price, and that I desire my independence.' (The close similarity in wording between this reported conversation and the letter of 24 March, makes Mrs Pardee's evidence here rather unreliable, but the rest of the conversation does perhaps reflect attitudes which Pétain habitually expressed, in their general terms). 'Could you not', she asked, 'save the situation and perhaps avoid war?'—'No,' he replied, 'I know nothing of politics. I don't know what they have done with our finances, and also, as far as the French are concerned, one must succeed quickly. I cannot and will not do so.' He then added 'The politicians detest me. I don't know why, I have never made politics.' Then, after a moment of silence: 'In fact I do know the reason, and I will tell you it, I annoy them, I live too long. But when they have put France on the edge of an abyss, and we are on the verge of a catastrophe, it is always me whom they come to seek.'[31]

This is, as reported conversation, unreliable. But it does express certain typical Pétain traits: the dislike of politics and politicians; the desire to believe that they also hate him (which, as we have seen, was not true, even of Blum and the Socialists), in order to show how 'non-political' he was; the dislike of public opinion, and of the need for 'politicians' to take account of it, which he could not and would not do; the feeling that the politicians had ruined France's finances, and led her to the edge of the abyss; the confidence that, when France was in such a situation, they all called on him. All these were arguments against associating himself with Third Republic government, but not against him answering the call of duty in a different situation.

His dislike of the prospect of being involved in the presidential election was declared to his wife, in a letter of 21 March, where he said he was going to do his best not to be involved in the affair, of which the mere prospect horrified him.

Pétain was already in Spain, where he had been made French Ambassador on 2 March. He had arrived there on 16 March.

Meanwhile, several politicians were looking to Pétain for the presidency. Among the leading ones were Henry-Haye, Lémery and Adrien Marquet. Among their supporters were men of very different parties, including some Socialists. Henry-Haye has given some of the reasons for their choice: 'Basically, we thought that it was necessary for the Congress to elect to the highest office the victor of Verdun, if only to give a warning to Hitler. It would perhaps make the dictator think: the election of a soldier, and the most glorious among them, would have the value of a symbol; it would be a sign of recovery. Within the country, the Marshal's name would perhaps crystallise our failing energies.'[32]

Henry-Haye was later to say that he had collected about a hundred sure votes for Pétain.

Another politician, Henri Lémery, who had already acted on Pétain's behalf at the time of the Chautemps-Blum crisis, in relation to the prime ministership, was now one of those who strongly tried to persuade the Marshal to stand for the presidency.

Pétain appears, at one stage, to have become interested in these projects. But he soon told his supporters that he was not standing. On 25 March he wrote to Henry-Haye, who had asked to come and see him in Spain: 'My dear friend, I can only too easily guess the object of your *démarche*. The tone of the Press for several days let me foresee it. The reflections it led me to have only confirmed me in my determination to refuse the offer which might eventually be made to me. I am convinced that your arguments, however persuasive they may be, will not shake my decision. This state of mind makes it a duty on my part to ask you to abandon your project, to save yourself a tiring, boring journey. Your insistence is for me a high token of esteem, but your friendship shows a faith in me which is well above my capacity to fill the office you envisage for me.'[33] He wrote a letter of a similar kind to Lémery.

Some people, including Colonel Fabry, head of the Army Commission, had, however, seen it as impossible for the Marshal to put forward his candidature, but had nevertheless felt that he should be drafted as President In a conversation recorded by Loustaunau-Lacau, Fabry stated that the election should be a manifestation of French unity in face of danger. Only the Marshal's personality could create this unity, not only at the election, but in the months to come. If there was no decisive result on the first round of voting, the Marshal would be unable to refuse their requests, and would have to go back on his decision. The only way in which this situation would be avoided would be if President Lebrun agreed to continue for another term of office, in which case there would be a decisive result on the first vote.[34]

Fabry was perhaps right in thinking that Pétain might change his mind, and respond to a call for help. Many have been the cases where men have declared themselves to be non-runners in a competition, only to become reluctant, or apparently reluctant, winners.

Pétain had, in fact, been forced to make public his refusal. The public statements of General Brécard (whom some believed to be the unconscious instrument of Bouisson, or of the other candidates) had declared Pétain to be a candidate. Pétain was forced by this to send a note, to be made public, which ran: 'I maintain my decision: I am not a candidate for the Presidency of the Republic'. With it he sent a letter to Brécard, saying that he felt he could serve France better in Spain.

On 5 April, Lebrun, who had finally agreed to stand again, was re-soundingly re-elected to the Presidency, on the first round. So there is no chance of knowing whether Colonel Fabry's prognostications would have been true.

In this election, Laval abandoned Pétain. He even argued against Pétain's supporters. This is surprising, in view of certain opinions he was to express within the next twelve months. Laval's own candidate was Bouisson.

It is possible, of course, that Laval was still smarting at Pétain's rejection of his plans in March and April 1938. And, as was clear from another conversation with Landini, he supported Bouisson in the hope of becoming prime minister when the opportunity occurred.[35] Warner mentions, however, a far more wide-ranging possibility, based on the evidence of a certain Mlle Petit at the Pétain trial.[36] Mlle Petit had been the secretary, from 1935 to 1941, of the Italian director of the journal *L'Italie Nouvelle* in Paris, Mirko Giobbe. This man, she asserted, had been an Italian secret agent, the 'Italian Abetz'. In January 1939 Laval asked to see Giobbe, to discuss a policy 'which was the one in which the Axis would like to see France engaged. This policy involved, in internal politics a dictatorship, and in foreign policy, a reversal of alliances. . . .' Laval claimed that he was 'supported in this enterprise by a high-ranking military figure, by nine-tenths of the General Staff, and by an important section of the Chamber and Senate.'

'His plan was as follows', she went on. 'To prevent the possible re-election of M. Albert Lebrun, or an election of M. Daladier, which was not entirely out of the question, since people were beginning to talk about it in the Press. His candidate was Fernand Bouisson, who had been won over completely to his policy, and who would, to hide what was going on, confirm Daladier in power as Prime Minister when he came to give in the traditional Cabinet resignation. At that moment, Pierre Laval would take care to slip a banana skin beneath the Prime Minister's feet, and bring down the Government in a way which would seem perfectly normal to public opinion.'

Warner stresses, however, that Mlle Petit may well have been producing a highly embroidered account of certain projects of Laval's; certainly the atmosphere of Pétain's trial, and the events of the war, may have led her imagination along. It is unlikely, for example, that if so many important people supported the project, no other evidence of this has come down to us (though, of course, Laval may merely have been referring to the fact that he knew these people to approve of the idea of dictatorship in general). Warner does point to other evidence of Laval's plans of the moment, which certainly included the possibility of some form of dictatorship. So he may have hoped for Bouisson as President for this purpose, though the rest of the story may well be imaginary.

No proof exists of any Pétain involvement in such a plot. While he is known to have approved of much of Laval's foreign policy, and had also had previous discussions, and was to have subsequent discussions, with Laval; and while he shared Laval's dislike of the present form of parliamentary democracy, there is nothing to suggest that he was the 'high ranking military figure' of Laval's account, or of Mlle Petit's imagination (unless, as suggested, Laval merely meant that he knew him to be in favour of strong government of a dictatorial kind).

Pétain's refusal to stand may have been because he did not want power at all; it may have been because he felt the post of President to be an unsatisfactory one, and Third Republic politics to be unsavoury; it may have been because, as Fabry suggests, he could not present himself, but must wait for the nation to call him. Be that as it may, on 2 April he had written to his wife that he had been put in touch with various attempts at *combinaisons* with regard to the election, in which he had refused to participate; and he felt that his distance from Paris had been of real service from this point of view.[37] This is very much in character. *Combinaisons* were for him the mark of the Third Republic. He did not like plots either (and this is one reason for discounting Mlle Petit's evidence). He was interested in power, insofar as he could serve the State; but the State must call on him of its own accord, when it was in a mess which only he could get it out of. He was not a man to want power for its own sake, or to plot for it. He was merely convinced of his own worth, and of the fact that he would at some time be needed.

On 10 April Pétain paid a brief visit to Paris, in relation to his ambassadorship, and in July and early August he spent three weeks in France. In late August, as the war-clouds grew, he asked Loustaunau-Lacau, who was at San Sebastian and was going to Paris, to go and see Laval and ask him what he thought of the political situation.[38]

When war broke out in September, Daladier attempted to form a National Government, in which he offered Pétain a post. Pétain, though he was to remark to his friends 'I do not intend to remain here *ad infinitum*', at which they declared themselves relieved,[39] refused a post in the Government, making it clear in his letter to Daladier that he did not wish to be part of a Government 'established on almost exclusively political bases', which by this very fact seemed to him to be 'little qualified to ensure the proper direction of the war.'[40] He objected therefore, to the fact that this was still a Third Republic Government, containing 'interests', and 'parties'. He objected, above all, to the presence of certain politicians, who would be 'an obstacle to proper relations with Spain and Italy, and who will therefore produce a deplorable effect upon the morale of the country, and of the army.' Pétain's attitudes when in the Reynaud Government in 1940 were to show that Daladier himself was one of the 'politicians' of whom he disapproved, and whom he persuaded Reynaud to get rid of. His main target at the moment, however, was Herriot, whom Daladier intended to make Foreign Minister[41] (though on the 13th he took over the post himself). Herriot was for Pétain the essence of the 'party' man; the minister who had destroyed Doumergue's Government of national unity. Daladier was hardly better in his book; the man 'who had created the *Front Populaire*' by taking in the Radicals with the Socialists and Communists.

Daladier claimed later that Pétain tried to persuade him to make Laval Minister of Foreign Affairs, because he would bring Italy into a more favourable attitude towards France. Pétain's and Laval's views on the need for agreement with Italy were, as we have seen, very similar; and Herriot was being strongly criticised at the time by Laval. Élie Bois has said that Laval persuaded Pétain not to join the Daladier Government;[42] if he did so in order to discredit Daladier's Government, he succeeded, as he was later in the month to tell Pétain how discredited the Government had become by this refusal. The views of many people were expressed by General Anthoine in a letter to Pétain in which he said he hoped to see Pétain enter the Government, 'but not any old Government', because that would be to become a crook without achieving anything.[43]

Loustaunau-Lacau (who may have passed on this first bit of advice) now wrote a letter to Pétain, on 22 September, containing a résumé of a conversation he had had with Laval, 'who is on very good form.'[44] Laval had described the bad reception of Daladier's new Government, as a result of Pétain's refusal. Daladier had for four years been Minister of Defence, and was responsible for the lack of material, particularly heavy artillery. His Government was being strongly criticised, and Daladier had suggested that this was Pétain's fault for refusing to join the Government. But the parliamentarians had deduced that Pétain had refused to join the Government in order not to support by his authority a hopeless *combinaison*.[45]

There was therefore no other real alternative but a Pétain Cabinet, Laval went on. Pétain was the only person who had a greater influence in Italy than his own, and he and Laval could form an agreement with Mussolini. Pétain would be popular, too, in France; he had shown in the First World War that his main aim was to spare French blood as much as possible. There should be a small war Cabinet, with Pétain himself doubling up as Prime Minister and Foreign Minister. 'Having saved such a difficult situation in Spain, he had shown that he was the greatest of ambassadors.'[46] By his side as ambassador, he would have a great diplomat, like Noël, who could help out. He himself, Laval, would take over the Ministry of the Interior.

Pétain appears to have raised no objection to all this. Laval, once more, was hoping to use Pétain, as a conversation of his with Élie Bois in October showed. When Élie Bois suggested that Pétain was too old, and senile, Laval replied that it did not matter. All that Pétain needed to be was a figurehead, a name.[47] One would have thought that Laval would have learned from his earlier experience, in 1938, that Pétain was unlikely to take easily to such a role.

In October, Pétain asked permission to return to France from time to time for meetings of the *Conseil Supérieur de la Guerre*. This request was refused by Daladier, who said that Pétain was more useful as ambassador in Spain than in France. Some have suggested that Pétain was, by this request, trying to bring himself more onto the political scene, for the collapse of the Daladier Government. But it is more than likely that the reason he gave was the real one. He had been much in attendance at the *Conseil* when in France, as we have seen; and his presence had not merely been decorative. He was 'worried about the bad state of preparation he had noticed at the time of his

Admiral Darlan

Bonnet, Daladier and Gamelin in London, 1938 (left to right in front)

departure',[48] and the war was now on. What more natural than that he, with his natural confidence in his military ability, should have wished to help to direct operations?

At this time he was, however, clearly interested in politics as well. Laval's comments appear to have aroused his interest. Gazel, Pétain's counsellor at Madrid, later said: 'One day, on two occasions, he showed me lists of ministerial Cabinets which he was envisaging.'[49] Laval's and Lémery's names were on both. In October, Pétain had a visit from Lémery and Alibert, a right-wing politician who, on Lémery's recommendation, had acted as Pétain's 'mentor' on matters to do with worker-employer relations. These two men discussed the make-up of a possible ministry with Pétain, in which various names were juggled around, including always that of Laval.[50] (It is interesting that in 1940, when called on to form a Government, Pétain produced a ready-made list from his pocket.)

The Daladier Government, surprisingly, continued in power, and Pétain remained in Spain. On 15 January he wrote a letter to General Vauthier which explains his attitude at that time. Because of the state of his physical strength, he was 'giving up the idea' of taking office (this shows that he had considered it). He had been asking himself how he could best serve his country, and had decided that after leaving 'his present job' he would place himself at the disposition of the army. Perhaps failure in morale would happen 'either at the front, or in the rear, as in 1917', which would lead him to play the same role as then.[51] As always, his memories either of Verdun or of the 1917 mutinies recurred, and he saw his role as being in some way tied to them. Indeed, his view of his potential political role was much the same; and in 1940 the 'morale' of the nation was to be his first main interest when he became Head of Government.

After the war, much was made at his trial of 'a secret visit' he paid to France at this time. It was suggested that it was made for political purposes as part of a plot with Laval. Noguères has successfully demolished this hypothesis. The visit was not incognito (though Pétain had described it as such to General Georges in a letter). The agenda of Captain Bonhomme, Pétain's aide-de-camp, shows the visit was semi-public. Pétain left Madrid on 22 January, stopped at St Jean-de-Luz on the 23rd, where he received the *sous-préfet* and attended a reception by the British colony, and reached Paris on the 24th. On the 25th he openly went to his office in the Boulevard des Invalides. There he received about twenty people, most of them military men; though they also included Dr Ménétrel (his personal doctor, who was to be of some importance at Vichy), Léon Bailby and Henri Lémery. To the latter he repeated much of what he had said to Vauthier, but added that Daladier did not want him to return to France, because he saw him as a rival. He asked him to stop his campaign in Pétain's favour.[52]

Pétain's interests, as expressed in the letter to General Georges, were military. He was appalled by the disorganisation of the High Command: 'My dear Georges, I have come to spend three days in Paris incognito. I have seen some mutual friends and also some military men who have put me *au courant* with the bad organisation of the army command. The army knows about the lack of agreement between the great commanders, and its causes. . . . Whether it is liked or not, the organisation of the command must be modified. No one is in the right place, and the responsibilities *overlap*. It is anarchy. Hold on, and have confidence in the future. . . .'[53]

Pétain had, the previous October, asked to be allowed to return to Paris because 'he was worried by the bad state of preparation of which he had been aware at the time of his departure.' He was clearly scornful of Gamelin's arrangements, and felt that he could help. There is no evidence to show that Pétain's visit had any political motive behind it. And he does not appear to have met Laval on this occasion.

Another charge levelled at Pétain after the war, based on evidence by M. de Monzie, was that he had foreseen, months in advance, that by the second half of May the country would need to call on him. Such foresight of the date of the German onslaught must have shown that he was conniving with the Germans, it was said. Noguères has conclusively proved, however, that M. de Monzie's story is extremely unlikely to have been factually true, particularly with regard to dates. The most likely date for Pétain to have seen Monzie, and to have said this, if at all, was early May, on his Paris visit, when Reynaud was already asking him to join the Government.

In March, Laval violently attacked the Daladier Government on its conduct of the war. On 20 March Daladier resigned. He was succeeded by Paul Reynaud, the Finance Minister, who retained Daladier at the Ministry of Defence, and took over foreign affairs himself.

In early April Pétain, in a letter to Mrs Pardee, referred to the French newspapers he was receiving, which were 'going over and over the same old stories; that I should take over the direction of the country, the war, and perhaps also of their personal interests?'[54] He shows some scorn of this.

Yet on 1 May when asked by Reynaud whether he would be prepared to take a ministerial portfolio in his Cabinet, Pétain immediately accepted. Reynaud was planning to get rid of Daladier, who as Minister of National Defence had been preventing him from getting rid of Gamelin as Commander-in-Chief, and so was preparing a Cabinet reshuffle. Pétain, meanwhile, was to return to Madrid to clear up certain matters.

On the 9th, Reynaud brought up the question of Gamelin once more. Daladier rebuffed him. Thereupon Reynaud announced the resignation of the Government (which would, after he had been to see President Lebrun, have enabled him to constitute a new Cabinet, without Daladier). Reynaud had discussions with Lebrun at the Elysée. But on the 10th the German attack began, and the Government had to continue as though nothing had happened.

Pétain had been in Paris until the 9th, when he returned to Madrid as arranged. It was almost certainly during this visit to Paris, with the German attack looming, and the knowledge that the Government was probably going to call on him, that Pétain made his much-criticised remark to M. de Monzie.

Meanwhile, Daladier too, may have been thinking of Pétain. There are accounts of a discussion in which Daladier approached Laval with the idea of overthrowing the Reynaud Government. Laval's own account of this goes into further detail: he told Admiral Darlan, shortly after the fall of France, that he and Daladier had agreed at this time to work for a Pétain Government (in which they would both, of course, have important posts) which would set peace negotiations on foot.[55]

Warner states that he believes that this story is very unlikely to have been true. All the stories stemmed from Laval.[56] But given the hostility to Reynaud which Bonhomme noted, and the reputation that Laval had as an overthrower of Governments and a prime political intriguer, such a combination seems quite possible, indeed probable. Whether a Pétain Government, or peace overtures, were involved is another matter. They probably were (particularly the peace overtures) on Laval's part; but he may not have told Daladier this explicitly.

At any rate, unknown to them, Pétain had already been secretly snaffled by Reynaud.

On 10 May the German offensive began in the Low Countries. On the 15th, the panzer divisions broke through at Sédan. The next day, Pétain received a coded telegram, asking him to return to Paris. Bonhomme noted: 'The war can be considered as lost.'[57]

In the crisis, Reynaud's reshuffle took place, but without the removal of Daladier. On the 18th, the changes were announced. Pétain was appointed Deputy Prime Minister, Georges Mandel became Minister of the Interior, Daladier was moved to Foreign Affairs, Reynaud himself took over Defence, and Yves Bouthillier became Finance Minister. Gamelin was sacked as Commander-in-Chief, and was replaced by Weygand. The papers welcomed the return of the victorious trio of 1918: Pétain, Foch (in the person of his greatest disciple, Weygand), and Clemenceau (in the person of his right-hand man, Mandel). Once again, France was looking for reassurance to its glorious past. A new chapter was about to begin.

Extra-parliamentary movements

In the years 1934 to 1936, the political paramilitary movements popularly called the *ligues*, some of which had existed for some time before, came into a great deal of prominence. Some, like the *Croix de Feu* (numerically the strongest) under Colonel la Rocque, and the *Jeunesses Patriotes*, under Pierre Taittinger, combined patriotism, anti-Communism and military anti-parliamentarianism in a fairly traditional mixture; to this group must also be attached the *Union Nationale des Combattants*, and the oldest of French right-wing extra-parliamentary forces (which now fought parliamentarily as well), the royalist *Action Française*, under Charles Maurras and Léon Daudet. Then there were those groups, small in numbers and fairly ineffective, which seemed to base themselves on foreign-style authoritarianism: Bucard's *Francisme*, Jean Renaud's *Solidarité Française*. These were of little importance. The only serious attempt at fascism on pre-war French soil was eventually Doriot's *Parti Populaire Français*, founded in 1936.

Now while Pétain, like many other military men, found himself attracted to the first of these groups, whose political views were so close to his own, he certainly did not associate himself publicly with their policies or tactics. Where Lyautey, at a *Jeunesses Patriotes* rally, cried out 'I also am now a *J.P.*,'[58] Pétain steered clear of any political commitment of that sort. He did, at one stage, express publicly his approval of the principles of the *Croix de Feu*,[59] and he did, like other members of the Doumergue Government, attend church services and other events connected with that movement. But this tacit approval did not mean that he involved himself with them, or that he ever relied upon them to further his own political ends, as Lyautey had tried to do just after the political events of 6 February 1934. The *Action Française*, which was to be such a support to him in the years 1940–4, does not even seem to figure in his life before that time. For Pétain, though his views coincided so closely with those of the *ligues*, was not a man to act unconstitutionally.

Soon after the *Front Populaire* came to power in 1936, it abolished the *ligues*. The *Croix de Feu* successfully converted itself into a political party, the *Parti Social Français*, which by 1938 claimed to have three million adherents; though as it had been formed after the 1936 elections, it had no chance to prove its voting power in practice, as the war intervened.

Meanwhile, within the army, two new right-wing forces were forming, both of them secret. Much has been written about them, and I will confine myself to the salient facts. The first of these, *Corvignolles*, was founded by Major Loustaunau-Lacau, who was on Pétain's staff at the Ministry of War in 1934, and again on his staff from March 1935 onwards. In 1936 Loustaunau-Lacau set about creating an organisation whose purpose was to oppose 'subversion, indiscipline and anti-militarism' within the army. 'The Germans are there', he said, 'and the main thing is to be ready to reply to them.'[60] He believed, from what he had seen at the War Ministry, that the Communist party had formed an enterprise of systematic demoralisation, aimed at the morale of the army, 'which had a precise aim: to ruin the confidence of the soldiers in their commanders.' To deal with this, and to purge the army of Communist cells, he set up a network of both active and reserve officers. Every military district, every military unit, every air base and every armaments factory was to have at least one officer gathering information. When he set about sounding out his brothers-in-arms, he claims that he got not one refusal. The organisation, within eighteen months, was a great success.

Among important military men, Marshal Franchet d'Esperey, who at this time was beginning to fish in troubled waters, gave a large amount of money to this movement. Pétain was not ignorant of it, and was one of the people to whom regular reports of the activities of the network were sent; but he was not a part of it, nor did he help it on the scale of Franchet d'Esperey. Admittedly, at the beginning of 1937 he handed Loustaunau-Lacau a document on the 'Communist putsch' (sic) in Spain, and the methods it had used, 'which would be the same if there was a Communist putsch in France', which Loustaunau-Lacau thereupon sent around to the commanders of all the military regions, through the official channels, via General Gérodias, head of the 2nd Bureau.* A violent outcry happened, and Gérodias was removed from his post. It was declared that Pétain had handed the document to Loustaunau-Lacau merely to have it sent to the 2nd Bureau, and that Loustaunau-Lacau had made a mistake. But, given what we now know about *Corvignolles*, one wonders whether this was necessarily the case. Among Pétain's immediate entourage, both Loustaunau-Lacau and Captain Bonhomme belonged to it.

As *Corvignolles* was being set up, Loustaunau-Lacau became aware that there was another network already in existence. This was what was to be called '*La Cagoule*' (The Hood), but which was properly called the M.S.A.R. (*Mouvement Social d'Action Révolutionnaire*) which was ruled by a committee, the C.S.A.R. At the head of it was a former naval engineer, Eugène Deloncle. *La Cagoule* was a far more violent body than *Corvignolles*. Far from being merely concerned with the collecting of information, and the prevention of subversion, it was also prepared to take subversive action itself, to provoke the Communist reactions it feared. It eventually attempted a 'putsch' in November 1937.

In the autumn of 1936, Marshal Franchet d'Esperey got Colonel Groussard to give him a detailed report on *La Cagoule*—its methods, its members, its objectives. In December of the same year, Pétain, who had also heard of it through Loustaunau-Lacau, sent the latter to General Duseigneur, one of its main figures, to find out more about it: 'Towards the end of December', writes Loustaunau-Lacau, '. . . Marshal Pétain, whom subversive agitation did not leave indifferent, sent me to visit General Duseigneur, recently retired. Duseigneur received me with the inimitable pleasantness of a former cavalry man, and did not hide from me the fact that he was organising armed groups against Communism. I spoke to him of the external situation, and explained to him that a civil war in France would be playing into the hands of the Germans.—We will never start it! he replied.' [61] When he got back to Pétain, Loustaunau-Lacau exclaimed: 'Marshal, there are arms!' 'It is regrettable', replied Pétain. 'The man who has arms has the temptation to use them.' [62]

At the end of December 1936, Loustaunau-Lacau met Groussard, who suggested that he should go and see Franchet d'Esperey.

In March 1937 Loustaunau-Lacau finally met the leader of *La Cagoule*, Eugène Deloncle. It was Marshal Franchet d'Esperey who had brought them together. The two men disagreed as to basic aims. Deloncle was not only violently anti-communist; he also thought that the only way to save France was to 'renew the State', i.e., do away with parliamentary government. Loustaunau-Lacau, by his own account, was more obsessed by the German problem and, seeing that Deloncle's plans could favour Germany, refused to take part in them. Deloncle understood this, but then suggested that they might at least exchange their information on Communism. To this Loustaunau-Lacau agreed.

* Military Intelligence

Pétain appears to have known about *La Cagoule*. Shortly after this, Colonel la Rocque (an enemy of the M.S.A.R.) brought Pétain a list of the officers at the Nice garrison who were members of it. To get to Pétain, it had to pass via Loustaunau-Lacau, who said (by his own account): 'If the Marshal accepts this paper, he will be obliged to report on it to the Minister. We are not sneaks. I refuse it,'[63] and threw it into the waste-paper basket. La Rocque complained to Pétain (who thus knew about it); at first the Marshal was angry with Loustaunau-Lacau, but when the latter had explained his reasons in the same way as to La Rocque, calmed down. The Minister never heard of it. This story, which might seem unbelievable, is confirmed in broad outline by La Rocque's own testimony.

Though Pétain knew about *La Cagoule*, and did nothing, he does not seem to have taken an active part in encouraging it or *Corvignolles*, as Marshal Franchet d'Esperey did. Perhaps he merely had a military sense of comradeship which prevented him from 'squeaking'. Probably the fact that both these networks were aimed against Communism made him approve of them in principle; and even the anti-parliamentarism of *La Cagoule* was not made to displease him. But he remained aloof from it all, receiving information and 'keeping himself informed', but doing little else.

His reason for remaining aloof may be contained in the remark he is reported to have made to General Duseigneur's daughter in 1938, after the failure of the *Cagoule*'s attempt at a putsch on 15–16 November 1937, when she asked him to intervene on her father's behalf. Pétain replied: 'It is possible that I may have a role to play. I cannot compromise myself in this affair.'[64]

The High Command was generally suspected of having been involved, and particularly the two Marshals, Pétain and Franchet d'Esperey. Gamelin, asked by Daladier to look into it, said that the only possible thing was to ask each member of the *Conseil Supérieur de la Guerre* separately whether they had had anything to do with the people involved, or had known anything about it. 'It seemed to me that I could trust their word,'[65] he said. Naturally he would not ask the Marshals, even though he suspected that they were the most seriously involved. So he asked only the generals, all of whom categorically denied any contact with the group.

In 1938, too, *Corvignolles* was discovered. The police were informed about Loustaunau-Lacau by one of his agents, a reserve officer at Nancy, and he was put on the non-active list, thus leaving Pétain's staff.

Pétain, when interrogated after the war in the presence of his lawyers, claimed that he had only known one *cagoulard* in his entourage, and that was Loustaunau-Lacau. (This in itself is false; Loustaunau-Lacau was never a member of *La Cagoule*). The moment he had discovered he was a *cagoulard* he had asked him to leave his staff. As we have seen, this is not true. Pétain had known about *Corvignolles* and even about *La Cagoule*, even though he had not been actively involved in either of them, and had known about Loustaunau-Lacau's activities.

And, after Loustaunau-Lacau had departed from his staff, Pétain still remained in close contact with him. We have seen how Pétain used him as a go-between with Laval in August and September 1939. Loustaunau-Lacau is also known to have been received by Pétain in Spain on 29 October, 2, 6, 8, 12 November and 21, 25 December 1939.[66] These are merely the meetings of which we have proof; they show that others may have existed.

So Pétain, much as he may have denied it later, kept in contact with Loustaunau-Lacau; he also knew of the networks, and, while not taking part in them, did not give them away.

Conclusion

In his political activities, Pétain had shown that from 1934 onwards he had had much more interest in these matters than before. His time in the Doumergue Government had strengthened his dislike for the parliamentary methods of the Third Republic, for the 'régime of the parties', but had shown him that possibilities of reform existed, which could create a more powerful executive, and remove a great deal of the chaos and incompetence. The ill-fated Bouisson Government in 1935 had however shown him the impossibility of Third Republic politicians even allowing such trammelling of their independence. He was left with an ill-defined desire for a Government with a strong head, a 'hand on the tiller'.

To what extent he ever thought of himself as that man is uncertain. The newspaper campaigns in his favour seem to have bolstered his never inconspicuous ego. And, as he saw France descending into what seemed to him to be ever-increasing chaos, he appears to have begun to see himself as the man who might eventually be called on to put things right, both through his 'name' and symbolic value, and also through his inherent superiority.

As far as acceptance of posts is concerned, he obviously felt he must be 'called on', rather than engineer his own return. But he was clearly flattered by the offers made to him by men such as Lémery and Laval, and also trusted Laval's judgement of political matters. He refused the presidency, possibly because of his scorn for that post; he refused a place in the Daladier Government, because of his dislike of the 'régime of the parties', and of Daladier and Herriot; but he accepted a place in the Reynaud Government, when it was clear that he was needed. He may well, in Laval's words, have been 'disposed to accept power if the opportunity was presented to him', or even, at Laval's promptings, have 'decided to accept' the premiership 'from patriotic motives', or have 'been determined to assume this responsibility' if it was pointed out to him that 'the salvation of France lay in a Pétain Government', in 1937 and 1938. This does not necessarily mean involvement in a plot. The fact is that in both years events prevented the necessary constitutional moves (as did Pétain's stubbornness with regard to his own role in any eventual Government).

In 1939, when prompted again when it looked as though the Daladier Government was going to fall, Pétain showed interest, and even began to plan ahead for his administration. The Daladier Government's continuing power and his growing concern with the military situation, however, made him eventually decide to devote his time to military matters.

Despite a number of his usual remarks about age and desire for independence in the early months of 1940, he immediately accepted the post of Vice-Premier in the Reynaud Government when it was offered to him in May, before the German offensive, when things were still nominally the same as in the previous eight months, and when there was no sign that France was to fall.

As far as extra-parliamentary activities were concerned, Pétain, though he sympathised with such bodies as the *Croix de Feu*, never got involved with them. He was not involved, as far as one knows, with *Corvignolles* or *La Cagoule* either; but he knew of their existence, and his silence about them, even if it was prompted by feelings of military honour and brotherhood, nevertheless amounts to connivance.

The general impression one gets of Pétain in this period is that of a man who, convinced by the adulation of others, felt that he had a role to play in the future of his country, when it was in need. He was not a plotter, or a man to work illegally; he merely held himself ready, and was prepared to let politicians work on his behalf at times of crisis, when it looked as though he might be of use. One thing above all must be made clear; there is no evidence whatsoever of a 'plot' such as some of his accusers later imputed to him, which involved working with the Germans for a French defeat. Pétain's greatest virtue was his patriotism; everything he did was done, he believed, to further the cause of his country.

Chapter Eight

Ambassadorship, 1939–40

AT the beginning of 1939, as the Spanish Civil War drew to a close, and it became clear that the Nationalists were in sight of victory, a strong current of opinion made itself felt in France, which demanded how soon there was going to be French diplomatic representation at Burgos, the Nationalist headquarters. In the early days of the French *Front Populaire*, Government sympathy had on the whole been on the side of the Spanish Republicans, despite the original adherence to the joint Anglo-French policy of non-intervention. Many French 'volunteers' had taken part on the Republican side, and eventually arms and munitions had been sent. But since the advent of Daladier's Government in April 1938, the *Front Populaire* as such had ceased to exist. Daladier's Government was a realistic one, which saw the dangers which were mounting against France in Europe, and which did not wish to add to them by having an implacable enemy on her southern frontier. While the cries of Léon Blum and other Socialists became more and more insistent for France to intervene on the Republican side, the French Government remained silent. Throughout January, as the Republican defeat became a rout, the French newspapers were full of this other battle, with the newspapers of the Right demanding whether France wished to have Spain as an ally or not; Taittinger, for example, said that France, by not sending a representative to Burgos, was putting herself in the danger of finding herself in the same situation there as in Rome.[1] (Laval's policy of agreement with Rome having been abandoned by the Governments from 1936 to 1938.)

At the beginning of February, M. Léon Bérard was sent to Burgos, to have talks with General Jordana. This was the same general as had been Chief of General Staff in Madrid at the time of the Riff War, and who had had discussions with Pétain at that time; in fact, they had worked out the joint plan of campaign together, and Jordana had also taken part in the Paris peace conference in 1926. He was now Franco's 'right-hand man', and Foreign Minister. The talks took place from 4–7 February, when Bérard came back to report to the French Cabinet, suggesting that an official representative should be sent, i.e., that the Burgos Government should be recognised. In the Cabinet, there was some opposition to this in certain quarters, but on 14 February it was decided to send Léon Bérard once more to Spain, to arrange matters for recognition of Franco's Government. Bérard had some more meetings with Jordana, between 18 and 23 February. Meanwhile, in France, the Chamber of Deputies voted to recognise the

Spanish Government by 323 to 261 votes, on 14 February. On Saturday, 26 February, Bérard and Jordana signed at Burgos an agreement of 'good neighbourliness'.* On the next day, Paris and London simultaneously recognised the Franco Government.

The immediate concern of the newspapers was the question of who would be nominated as ambassador. It was known that Bérard had refused to take it on. Names suggested included Peyrouton, Léon Noël, and Giraud. On 1 March the papers gave the first hint that Pétain might be chosen. On the 2nd, it was a fact; the Cabinet unanimously voted to nominate him to the post.

Reactions from all sides were immediately favourable to Pétain, as we have seen. The difference was that the right wing were delighted that France's greatest soldier should be sent to Franco, while the left wing were appalled that Franco should be honoured in this way.

It has been suggested that Daladier sent Pétain to Spain in order to get him out of the way, because he considered him to be a political danger. This was not so, however, according to Georges Bonnet, the Foreign Minister, who claimed that it was he who chose Pétain. With the Second World War clearly on its way, it was essential to bring about a reconciliation between France and Spain. He had at first thought of Bérard, who had brought about the important Bérard-Jordana agreements. When Bérard refused, he immediately thought of Pétain. His reasons were that Pétain had been in contact with Jordana at the time of the Riff War† (Bonnet had been the man sent by Painlevé to see Pétain at that time), and that Pétain, the victor of Verdun, was the object of Franco's military admiration. When Bonnet mentioned Pétain's name to the former Spanish ambassador in Paris, Quinones de Leon (who had been Franco's unofficial ambassador during the Civil War, and who had also taken part, with Jordana and Pétain, in the Paris peace conference in 1926), the latter had said that this was the best possible choice.[2]

When the matter was put to Pétain, he immediately accepted. The first reaction of the Spanish was encouraging: 'This nomination does us honour, for Marshal Pétain is not only a great military figure, but a man with firm conservative convictions, whose life is nothing but *pondération* and upright-ness from every point of view.'[3] The admiration was not confined to the Spanish; even the German newspapers took the opportunity to extol the victor of Verdun. The *Deutsche Allgemeine Zeitung*, for example, wrote as follows: 'Anyone who has met with the ever-youthful, strong appearance of the Marshal, whose high broad forehead embodies wisdom, whose eyes denote clarity and goodness, whose strong chin shows power and decision, would scarcely believe that he is in the presence of an eighty-three-year-old man. Four years of war, which Pétain began like so many others as an infantry

---

* By this agreement, Franco was to make the German and Italian volunteers leave Spain within two months. He agreed to a peace policy with France at the Pyrenees and in Morocco, and to remain neutral in the event of war.

† We must not forget that Franco had played an important part in that war.

colonel, and which he also spent as army commander at Verdun, more with the troops than in his headquarters, have left hardly a line on his fine visage, and only his mouth, overshadowed by a heavy French moustache, has perhaps become more silent—silent, as is the good custom of those officers, whom death has so often passed by.'[4] It went on to praise him immensely.

The suitability of sending a soldier to a military Government was pointed out by newspapers of all nations. French newspapers, above all, referred to the 'comradeship of arms'. *Le Jour-L'Écho de Paris* expressed feelings which Pétain himself may well have felt: 'Trailing clouds of glory, Marshal Pétain is going among victorious soldiers. There is a solidarity of the fortunes of arms against which the little *combinaisons* of interests can only break themselves.'[5]

On 16 March Pétain arrived in Spain. His first letter to his wife, from his house in San Sebastian, described his 'triumphal arrival at Hendaye and Irun' and the 'good impression' he had.[6] A letter written on the same day to Mrs Pardee showed that he was not unaware of the difficulties that awaited him. Having commented on the house he was to live in, which, having been uninhabited for three years, needed certain things to be done, he continued: 'What is more difficult is to regain the confidence of the Spanish.'[7]

This was, indeed, the difficulty. The new Spanish Government, remembering France's partisanship in the war, was ill-disposed towards her now. There was even a series of boycott measures against French goods. In a letter to his wife, written on 21 March, Pétain said: 'People are very severe in relation to France; in certain circles feelings are being manifested that are near to hatred. We are paying for the faults of our Governments in the course of these last few years.'[8] Pétain's views on the *Front Populaire* were thus being reinforced by his observation of the results of their foreign policy. He saw his own role as being to 'expiate the sins of the *Front Populaire*'.[9] (Note the religious terminology.)

Franco's reception of Pétain at Burgos on 24 March was correct but cold. He hardly spoke a word. It was almost a monologue on Pétain's part.

Both men were hampered by the opinions of a large number of their compatriots. Many of Franco's victorious companions were violently anti-French; several members of the French Government were violently anti-Franco, and did their best to hamstring Pétain in his negotiations. On 1 April Pétain wrote to Mrs Pardee: 'I have much to do here, and the situation is difficult. The Spanish reproach us greatly for not having helped them in the first years. The reconstruction of Spain is a fearful problem. If France does not come to Spain's help we will make an enemy of her.'[10] On the 5th he wrote again: 'My mission here is full of difficulties. Armed warfare is over, the warfare of papers, of interminable discussions, has begun. If only I could at least succeed in getting the Spanish refugees back home, that would be a first victory! But I cannot hope to get that result for a long time.'[11]

On 10 April Pétain departed for Paris, 'to get people interested in my fate, because my situation here is very difficult.'[12] He had discussions with Daladier and Bonnet, and returned on the 13th. The French newspapers were puzzled. Why, they asked, had there been so little Franco-Spanish *détente*, and so little result from Pétain's ambassadorship? Pétain himself noted, on his return, that the situation was just as bad as ever.

Pétain's main object was to assure Spain's neutrality in the event of war, and to get the Bérard-Jordana agreements fulfilled. He was not aided by the anti-French feelings of so many Spaniards, nor by the continued presence of large numbers of Germans and Italians. Up till June, nothing seemed to happen. Gradually, however, as the year went by, his situation got better and better, by a mixture of correctness, politeness and severity on his part. August was the turning point. Gazel, Pétain's Counsellor in the embassy, was able to write to Bonnet that things now seemed on the right road in the *politique de détente* with Spain: 'The Marshal's personal credit is considerable. He has certain projects which we have spoken about and which he will tell you of. We must go slowly and not be too ambitious. We are beginning to neutralise a current which was very hostile. Time can and will work for us, if we are able to act with intelligence and prudence . . . and disinterest.' He then went on to stress what he thought to be the aspect of Pétain which had most helped to ease things: 'The Marshal is faced by military men. Between men of the same profession, they understand each other more easily. . .'[13]

On 3 August Franco had received Pétain properly for the first time, at Burgos. Franco had apparently told his entourage that he had long hoped for this meeting. Pétain had declared that he would not visit the palace until the execution of one of the essential clauses of the Bérard-Jordana agreements. This, far from upsetting the Spanish, had raised their opinion of the French Ambassador. Pétain and Franco both, on this occasion, complimented each other effusively. Franco informed Pétain of his satisfaction at having France represented by the most illustrious of her sons. He thanked him warmly, according to the newspapers, for his patient and firm actions in his post, and assured him of his collaboration in the future. In this spirit the question of the security of the Pyrenean frontier, and the question of refugees, would be discussed. (The Spanish had been building fortifications on the frontier; Pétain had firmly protested about this.)

If Pétain was patient and firm with the Spaniards, he also had to be so with his own Government and Foreign Office, where there were many people who disliked Spain, and who would have liked to see the Bérard-Jordana agreements lapse. As Léon Bailby (an enthusiastic admirer of Pétain, but nevertheless right on this specific point) wrote:

Pétain, that astonishing man . . . the most tenacious of diplomats, saw the thread he was trying to weave between our former friends and us gradually being undone before his eyes. But he did not give in to despair.

Twice or three times, he came to France to explain, with his firm, lucid mind, the situation as it is. He had been sent down there in order that he should succeed in his mission. He must therefore be given the means. And he was not the man to be contented with half-measures. As the Jordana-Bérard agreement had been signed, there could be no question of revoking it. And France's representative would not lend himself to such a revocation. In short, the Marshal finished by obtaining, despite Léger and his followers, all that he judged necessary for the success of his plan.[14]

On 19 August the Spanish Government decided to free all French prisoners of war held in Spanish concentration camps.

From now on, Franco-Spanish relationships were fairly affable. Pétain continued to have pleasant contacts with the Spanish officials (in particular with the new Spanish Foreign Minister, Colonel Beigbeder), and to attend Spanish military functions. On 31 October he attended the funeral of his colleague General Sanjurjo, who had commanded the Spanish forces in the Riff (with Franco under his command), and who had gone on to become a hero of the Civil War.

On 20 November Pétain moved to Madrid, as all foreign embassies were now to be installed in the capital.

Pétain's main task was to ensure Spanish neutrality. Firmly, he had protested against the erection of Spanish fortifications on the common frontier. In supple manner, he discussed all the important questions with the Spanish foreign ministry. Despite a number of voices which claim that in this period the Marshal was ageing badly (a judgement which was not entirely accurate), most judgements of Pétain's ambassadorship have been highly favourable. Noguères attributes Spanish neutrality in the Second World War to Pétain's efforts. This is, however, going too far; Spain's neutrality was more a product of uncertainty about the outcome of the war than of anything else.

Pétain's return to Spain, after Reynaud's offer in early May 1940, was ostensibly to settle up his affairs. But it has been suggested that he also went to confirm Franco in his agreements. Be that as it may, this was the end of a successful ambassadorship. Franco has claimed that he tried to persuade Pétain not to return to France; and that Pétain had replied 'My country is calling, and I owe myself to her. It is perhaps the last service I can render her.'

Whether this pious story is true or not, a new chapter was about to open in Pétain's career. Some observers claimed, during his ambassadorship, that the signs of age were upon him. This was only true to the extent that he tired easily, and could only work at full pitch a few hours a day. But there was no lessening in his mental powers. The legend that has made the Pétain of 1940 an old man no longer responsible for his actions is false. As we shall see, his actions were not only clear and logical; they are also explicable by his character and actions over the period in which we have already seen him. At any time during the period 1918–39, Pétain could have been expected to behave in the way he eventually did in 1940.

PART III

Chapter One

The fall of France and the collapse of the Third Republic

FRENCH military policy in the period immediately preceding the German invasion had been strangely indecisive. We have seen how that product of French defensive policy, the Maginot Line, had not originally been extended to cover the Belgian border, for various reasons, including the impossibility of building a defensive line behind the ally you were meant to be protecting. The declaration of Belgian neutrality in 1936, however, had not led to any change in this policy; no extension of the Maginot Line was planned.

Admittedly, by this time the deficiencies in France's armaments seemed far more serious than anything else, and the money that had been spent on the Maginot Line, and had thus not been available for these other things, was present in everybody's mind. Coupled with this was the growing questioning of the defensive policy which lay at the basis of the Line. Gamelin's new Directive had reinstated the concept of the offensive; but all France's money had been spent on armaments and material which were aimed at a defensive policy. On these facts the indecision of 1939–40 rested.

The plan which Pétain had put forward for the Belgian front was, though it involved an advance, a primarily defensive plan. Too many writers have seen it as offensive, because of that initial advance. The idea was, in conjunction with the Belgian army, to advance to easily defensible positions on the Belgian rivers and canals, from which the Germans could be warded off in the First-World-War manner, once the Allies had dug themselves in. The Maginot Line would thus merely be the permanent part of a continuous defensive line.

Once the Belgian alliance had gone, however, the quick creation of such a line became far more difficult. The French could not enter Belgium until the Germans attacked it; the result would be a race to the right positions. As it became more and more clear that Holland and Belgium were the line through which the Germans were bound to advance, still nothing was done to resolve the basic problems.

In fact, Gamelin seems to have done his best to get the worst of both worlds. The natural plan, to follow a defensive policy, would be to advance as far as the Scheldt; this was near, easily reachable in plenty of time, and formed a strong defensive line. Gamelin, however, eventually opted for a line from Louvain to Namur, part of which would be on the River Dyle. This line was sixty miles from the French frontier; the Dyle, moreover, was very narrow, and the part of the line between Wavre and Namur had no natural defensive characteristics. To be fair to Gamelin, however, it must be said that this line, stretching from Antwerp to Dinant, on the Meuse, defended much more of Belgium, and in fact protected Brussels.

The final acceptance of the Dyle Line by the French was on 15 November 1939. But by the New Year Gamelin had thought up a new variant on this plan, which was eventually embodied in a Directive issued on 20 March 1940. This plan, (which was approved by the British as well), involved the use of far more French troops, and consisted of sending a whole army of seven divisions (the 7th Army, under General Giraud) at top speed up through Belgium to Holland, in order to link up with the Dutch army. Thus the major part of the Allied Forces were to be committed in the Low Countries, most of them far too far north. There was to be next to no strategic reserve of any importance, and this was to be disastrous. Here again, a possible excuse for Gamelin was that, if the Dutch were attacked, the Allies would by this plan be able to help them.

Tactically, though, both of these plans were nonsense. If the French army had been properly organised and fitted out for action in open country, there might have been some sense in them. If the defensive policy typical of most of France's inter-war period were to be followed, however, the Scheldt Line was the only real possibility. Gamelin seems almost to have believed that, because he had restored the concept of the offensive, he had created the means to carry it out. Yet France had only between 150 and 175 bombers, to Germany's 1,400; 54 dive-bombers, to Germany's 342; 700 fighters, to Germany's 1,000.[1] Though she had tanks (the French and British combined in fact had more than the Germans), they were organised as appendages to the rest of the army, rather than as a powerful fighting force in their own right. There was a grievous shortage of anti-tank and anti-aircraft guns. All the money had been sunk in concrete. Owing to the immense force of the German Luftwaffe, much of the advance to the Dyle would have to take place by night.

So Gamelin fell between stools on this matter, and placed the Allied armies in great danger. This danger was disastrously heightened by his other great mistake: the neglect of the Ardennes front.

Since the war, great blame has been laid on Pétain for his 1934 statement that the Ardennes were impenetrable. It is not often noticed, however, that he had claimed that certain preparations were necessary for this state to be achieved. The kind of force which Gamelin placed on the Ardennes front was ridiculously small and ill-prepared. Pétain's statement had been made as part of the reason for not continuing the Maginot Line; he did not necessarily mean that ordinary defences should not be provided. And even if he had, that was no reason for the opinion to be perpetuated by his successors. Gamelin and the High Command of this time were fully responsible for their neglect of this sector, through which the German Panzer Divisions were to make their lightning advance. What is amazing, in all the Allied plans, was the little that had been learned from the Polish experience.

Pétain's worry about the French army, stated on several occasions in 1939–40, was no doubt in large part based on its incoherent tactical policy. (His policy, if wrong, had at least been logically unified). It was also based on the incoherence of organisation. The command was not only complicated by Gamelin's delegation of the western front to General Georges, but also by the chaos involved in Gamelin's movement of one of the headquarters to Montry, between Paris and La Ferté. He placed the 4th Bureau (transport and supply) at Montry, the 3rd Bureau (Operations) at La Ferté with General Georges, and the 2nd Bureau (Intelligence) at the headquarters at Vincennes with himself. Even in peacetime, this caused tremendous chaos and delays. Once the invasion had begun, the situation was soon to get out of hand. Pétain criticised, in January 1940, the disagreements between the High Command, and the reasons for them (i.e., tactical); and he also criticised the disorganisation of the High Command, where no one was in the right place, and where responsibilities overlapped.[2]

Gamelin had many critics and enemies in the army; but he also had strong critics in the Government, the most prominent among them being Paul Reynaud, who became Prime Minister on 21 March 1940. From the first, Reynaud wanted to get rid of Gamelin; but he had had for political reasons to keep Daladier, a strong supporter of Gamelin's, as Minister of National Defence, and at first had to keep Gamelin too. Then, in April, after the Norway campaign, in which Gamelin had not shown up well, he tried to get rid of him, but Daladier, at a meeting on 12 April prevented this. On 9 May, baulked at another attempt, Reynaud announced that the Government could be considered as having resigned, though until a new Government was formed this was to be considered as confidential;[3] but the German invasion on the 10th prevented a new Government being formed, and the Government continued as before, with Gamelin also remaining Commander-in-Chief.

The German Attack

The campaign of May and June 1940 has been excellently described in three recent works;[4] there is no need, therefore, to give a detailed account of the fighting except insofar as it affected Pétain and the French Cabinet.

The Dyle plan was put into effect from the start, including the variant whereby Giraud's army was sent north to Holland. This Holland army was soon forced to withdraw, while the rest of the Allied Forces began to set themselves up along the Dyle Line. The main attack, however, came in a surprise punch through the Ardennes, by the German mechanised divisions, leading to a victory at Sédan at which the overwhelming effect of air power in such a battle was shown. The French were, finally, being given the military lesson which they had ignored for so many years.

After Sédan, the Panzer Divisions wheeled to the west on 14 May, heading to the coast in order to cut off the Allied Forces in Belgium. That day, at 5.45 p.m., Reynaud sent an urgent telegram to Churchill, saying that the enemy was striking in the direction of Paris (a mistaken belief), and asking Britain to send ten more squadrons of fighters, because if the enemy were to break through the fortified line at Sédan, it would be owing to the French inability to resist the combined attack of heavy tanks and bombers.[5] The faults in pre-war preparation were now showing to the full. (Reynaud was not yet aware that the German tanks had already broken through.)

Churchill's reply was that the matter was being considered. On the morning of the 15th, Churchill was awoken at 7.30 a.m. by a telephone call from Reynaud: 'He spoke in English, and evidently under stress. "We have been defeated." As I did not immediately respond he said again: "We are beaten; we have lost the battle." I said "Surely it can't have happened so soon?" But he replied: "The front is broken near Sédan; they are pouring through in great numbers with tanks and armoured cars"—or words to that effect.'[6]

Churchill believed, wrongly, that this anxiety was exaggerated; a break in the line seemed to him, from his First World War experience, to be less dangerous than it was now to turn out to be. By the morning of the 16th, however, it became clear that the enemy had penetrated over sixty miles, and that the crisis was grave, though there was no clear picture of what was going on. He decided to go to Paris that afternoon.

Meanwhile, in Paris, even Reynaud found difficulty in getting news. In order not to tread on Daladier's toes, so Baudouin tells us, Reynaud did not telephone to Gamelin direct on the 15th, but asked Daladier to do so. When asked what Gamelin's reaction were, Daladier glumly replied: 'He has no reaction.'[7] Reynaud confided to Baudouin that he wished Pétain were there, because his wisdom and serenity would be of great help in influencing Gamelin. A little later on, Reynaud's military secretary Colonel de Villelume, when ringing up Vincennes for information, was sharply informed by Gamelin's *chef de cabinet*, Colonel Petitbon, that he had had enough of all this interference, and that if it went on, he would give no information at all. Clearly nerves at Vincennes were not of the best; though the mad system of communications which Gamelin had devised may have meant that he, too, was at times in the dark. Reynaud's reaction to Petitbon's statement was that things had gone far enough; he informed Baudouin that he had decided that he himself must take over from Daladier as Minister of National Defence, and that Daladier must either resign or go to Foreign Affairs.[8] It was on this day too, 15 May, that a message was sent to Pétain in Madrid, asking him to return.

Churchill arrived at Le Bourget just after 4 p.m., on the 16th, and found the situation 'incomparably worse than we had imagined.'[9] By 5.30 p.m. he was at the Quai d'Orsay, with Reynaud, Daladier and Gamelin. 'Utter dejection was written on every face', he comments. Gamelin gave a run-over of the situation: the Germans had broken through on a front of fifty or sixty miles, and the French army in front of them was destroyed or scattered. 'A heavy onrush of armoured vehicles was advancing with unheard-of speed towards Amiens or Arras, with the intention, apparently, of reaching the coast at Abbeville or thereabouts. Alternatively they might make for Paris. Behind the armour, he said, eight or ten German divisions, all motorised, were driving onwards, making flanks for themselves as they advanced against the two disconnected French armies on either side,'[10]

When Gamelin had finished, after a silence Churchill asked, ' "Where is the strategic reserve?" and, breaking into French, which I use indifferently (in every sense): "Où est la masse de manoeuvre?" General Gamelin turned to me and, with a shake of the head and a shrug, said "Aucune".'

Churchill was flabbergasted, and rightly so. How could any army in the field not have had a strategic reserve? What had the Maginot Line been for, if not to economise troops? We have seen, however, that Gamelin, by committing the 7th Army to the Dutch venture, had milked his reserves; and he had far too many men on the Maginot Line. The lackadaisical nature of his military policy had at last come home. Daladier, whom Baudouin describes as being 'red in the face . . . like a schoolboy in disgrace', clearly realised this, for he said to Baudouin *sotto voce:* 'The mistake, the unpardonable mistake, was to send so many men into Belgium.'[11]

Towards the end of the meeting, Churchill turned to Gamelin and asked when and where he was going to attack the flanks of the Bulge. 'His reply was: "Inferiority of numbers, inferiority of equipment, inferiority of method"—and then a hopeless shrug of the shoulders. . . That was the last I saw of General Gamelin. He was a patriotic, well-meaning man and skilled in his profession, and no doubt he has his tale to tell.'[12]

The High Command were all insistent in their request for more fighters. These Churchill was able to provide on this occasion, after a telegram to London. But this reduced the squadrons in Britain to twenty-five, which he considered the absolute minimum, and from now on Britain's attitude, amid incessant requests by the French authorities, was to be adamant. This has been a bone of contention between the two countries ever since; and during the war it was one element in French anti-British feeling.

17 May was an inconclusive day. The Panzers halted, under Hitler's orders. Clearly, too, their objective had not been Paris, but the sea. In Paris, Reynaud was preparing to take over the Ministry of National Defence from Daladier; he had recalled General Weygand from Syria the night before, and Marshal Pétain should soon be returning too. By evening, the Panzer movement to the sea had resumed.

The great reshuffle took place on the 18th. Pétain was appointed Deputy Prime Minister, Reynaud became Minister of Defence. Daladier moved to the Foreign Office. Georges Mandel, who had once been Clemenceau's right-hand man, became Minister of the Interior.

Pétain in the Reynaud Government in Paris, 18 May—10 June

Immediately after the Cabinet meeting at which Pétain was appointed, Reynaud and Pétain set off to visit the armies. It is significant that instead of going directly to Gamelin (where Daladier, too, was awaiting them), they went first to see Pétain's old friend, General Georges. Finally, over three hours late, Reynaud and Pétain reached Gamelin. Both Georges and Gamelin gave them a highly pessimistic view of the situation.

In Paris, however, the return of Pétain had brought a surge of optimism. Not only the Senate, but the population at large, were relieved by the return of this venerable figure. The headlines, on the 19th, read: 'The Victor of Verdun in the Government.'[13] As in the inter-war period, he was believed capable of anything. Not only that, but his prestige in itself was seen to be of immense effect. Papers referred to 'the incomparable prestige of his name, the counsels of his limitless experience, the flame of his extraordinarily lucid mind.'[14] On 19 May Reynaud replaced Gamelin by Weygand, and once this was known the papers became delirious with enthusiasm about this other great soldier, of whom Foch had said on his deathbed: 'If France is in danger, send for Weygand.' With these two great men, it was felt, France could not be lost. The great popular trust in Pétain and Weygand was initially to be of great help to Reynaud; but eventually it was to make these men in reality more powerful than the Prime Minister himself, as the fall of France became clearer, and as their desire for peace moves clashed with the Premier's determination to fight to the last.

Weygand was a good soldier. By his implication in France's defeat he has since been underrated; but to take over an ill-prepared army when it was already on the verge of defeat was not an easy job. Some of the tactics which Weygand evolved in the next few days would have been reasonable if his armies had been better equipped. As it was, nothing seemed to be able to stop the German thrust. And relationships between the British and the French were becoming strained, with the blunt General Ironside, convinced of the defeatism of some of the French generals, making his feelings abundantly clear.

Weygand's first action had been to fly north to see the situation. Churchill criticises this decision for, he says, it was not the time to leave the main controls. Reynaud, too, had been worried by the dangers of this flight. Pétain, however, had supported Weygand's venture; thinking no doubt of his 1914–18 experiences, and of the importance of morale, he declared that 'nothing was equal to the presence of the Commander-in-Chief.'[15]

On 22 May Churchill had come once more to Paris. The situation was appalling, and required the British army either to try to cut its way southwards with the French and the Belgians, or to fall back on Dunkirk and attempt a sea evacuation under almost impossible conditions. Churchill was greatly impressed by Weygand, and accepted his plan for an attack southwards in the direction of Bapaume and Cambrai.

By the 23rd, however, either the British Commander, Lord Gort, or his Commander-in-Chief, General Ironside, had come to the conclusion that the Weygand plan had no chance of success. The only way to save the B.E.F. to fight another day, it appeared, was to withdraw to Dunkirk. This decision was to cause great recriminations throughout the years between the British and French; and Pétain was to see in it, as with Haig in 1918, an example of British selfishness and lack of concern for their allies. Weygand reported what was happening, to Reynaud and Pétain, in the presence of Baudouin, on the morning of 24 May. 'The situation is very grave,' he said, 'the British are turning back to the ports instead of attacking southwards.'[16] He had not been entirely surprised by this, because of General Ironside's tone on the telephone the night before. He now had little hope in his order of battle, which must however continue. Pétain, Weygand and Reynaud began to consider the possible lines of defence, to defend Paris, if the northern armies had to surrender. Reynaud declared that he was determined to fight to the end, for the honour of the French army.

Reynaud sent two 'reproachful telegrams' to Churchill that day, saying that the British army had retreated twenty-five miles (the correct figure is in fact about fifteen). Churchill was clearly unaware of the British military decisions that had been taken, as his replies (quoted in *Their Finest Hour*) show. He confirmed the British army's support. Late that night General Ironside resigned as Chief of Imperial General Staff, to be replaced by Sir John Dill.

By the night of the 24th, Weygand had already realised that there was now no hope of carrying out his plan. All he could now do was order the Allied armies in the north to form an arc covering the ports. What was left of the French army in the south would be powerless to defend Paris; there would be only 50 divisions to resist 150 German divisions and 10 armoured divisions. That day Pétain and Weygand told Reynaud, according to the latter, that if the Battle of France was lost, they must seek an armistice.*

Hope revived on the morning of the 25th, with receipt of a telegram from Churchill saying that Gort would continue in the joint plan. By evening, however, another telegram arrived, confirming the retreat of two British divisions near Arras, which again imperilled the plan.

At a War Committee meeting that evening, the question was raised of what the Government should do if peace were offered to it. Such a peace would be more advantageous before the destruction of the French armies, said President Lebrun, who, while stating that France had signed agreements not to conclude a separate peace, nevertheless thought that offers should be looked at closely and objectively. Weygand felt there was no harm in discussing things with England, before committing oneself to fighting to the end. Reynaud said that if an offer of peace were made to them, the French should ask England what she thought of it. Weygand said it was advisable, in view of the situation, to take up the matter with England as soon as possible.

Pétain now spoke up. And in his contribution to the discussion we can see all the bitterness, in relation to Britain as an ally, which the experience of these two wars had brought to him. There is an echo, too, of the feeling that 'Britain fights with French soldiers'. His attitude explains much that was to happen in the coming month.

* This Reynaud said before the parliamentary Commission of Enquiry in December 1950.

As Baudouin quotes him, Pétain 'wondered if there was a complete reciprocity of obligation between France and England. Each nation has a duty towards the other in direct proportion to the aid the other has given it. Now in the present situation England had only thrown ten divisions into the battle, whereas eighty French divisions were fighting. A comparison ought to be made not only between the military effort of the two countries, but also between the sufferings awaiting them.'[17]

Reynaud agreed, however, to go to London the next day. Meanwhile Weygand told him to ask for more material help: divisions, tanks, and anti-tank guns. General Vuillemin, the Air Minister, made further anti-British statements when he said that, though the British said they had sent 100 fighters a day over the Continent, he had not been able to verify this. The English fighters had hardly been engaged. They were all in England.

Weygand's final speech was again ominous for the future. If the army fought to the end, he said, it would mean the complete destruction of all French armed forces. Order must be kept in the country, however. If the army were destroyed, no one could say what troubles might result.[18] The argument from order was one which was much to be used in the next few weeks.

On Reynaud's visit to London, Churchill tells us, he 'dwelt not obscurely upon the possible French withdrawal from the war. He himself would fight on, but there was always the possibility that he might soon be replaced by others of a different temper.'[19] On his return, Reynaud told Baudouin that he had not even mentioned the matter of peace moves.

In the next few days Pétain's views and attitudes were to become even clearer. The man who has told us most about this, Paul Baudouin, in his book based on notes taken at the time, is, while perhaps not always to be trusted in his account of his own part in affairs, probably fairly honest in these descriptions, which ring very true. The Marshal was violently against Daladier, whom he held responsible for the *Front Populaire*, and determined to get him out of the Government; he was also determined that the army should be saved, to make the peace and to start the work of reconstruction.

Weygand, too, was in favour of saving the army. On the 26th he told Baudouin that 'he wished to avoid internal troubles, and above all anarchy.' He was furious at the speed of the British retreat. The same day Pétain came to see Baudouin, and stated his annoyance at the *limogeage* of fifteen generals. 'I cannot allow', he said, 'the errors of the politicians to be blamed on the army. The real culprit is Daladier. It was he who created the *Front Populaire*.* It is unsuitable that he should be at the Quai d'Orsay. If negotiations have to be undertaken with Germany or Italy, how could such a discredited man take on such responsibilities?'[20] He went on to some reminiscences, describing how, when Léon Blum was Prime Minister for the second time (in 1938), he, Pétain, had opposed sending three divisions to Catalonia, at the *Conseil Supérieur de la Défense Nationale*.† If he had not been there, he

---

* Note how the same prejudices recur time and again on Pétain's tongue.

† This, if it is true, shows how active a part he still played on that committee.

said, Gamelin would have agreed. 'I truly prevented a catastrophe which the *Front Populaire* was about to unleash on France.'

In the same conversation, the Marshal declared that he did not believe in fighting to the last. 'It is easy, and stupid, to say that one will fight to the last man. It is also criminal, in view of our losses from the last war, and our low birth-rate. . . We must save part of the army, because without an army grouped about some leaders in order to maintain order, a true peace will not be possible, and the reconstruction of France will have no starting-point.'[21] He went on to say that he had not slept all night; with tears in his eyes, he said that all this was a terrible trial for a man in his eighty-fifth year, who had only had one desire, to serve his country to the end, and who now had to do so in such appalling circumstances.

People were already beginning to think about Pétain as Head of Government, however, feeling that no civilian would have the same authority to negotiate (and shying off Weygand, who was still to many a political devil incarnate). They might have been surprised, however, at the amount of time which Pétain, with an old man's persistence, was devoting to his personal vendetta against Daladier in this hour of crisis.

The next day, 27 May, Pétain made similar remarks to Baudouin about the dismissed generals, and about Daladier. Baudouin told Pétain that he had informed Reynaud about it, but that Reynaud had been suspicious of Pétain's intentions. And from what we already know about the relationship between Pétain and Laval, these suspicions may well have been well-founded. Reynaud suspected that Pétain was working to get Laval into the Government, as Foreign Minister in place of Daladier. Pétain protested that such was not the case. When he met Reynaud later that day, however, he did not mention Daladier's dismissal.

That evening the King of Belgium announced the capitulation of the Belgian army. Military affairs were now disastrous. The Dunkirk evacuation had begun, bringing with it further anti-British recriminations; by 2 June accusations were being flung around that the British were evacuating all their troops, and leaving the French to defend the place. Added to this, it was claimed, no further fighter squadrons or divisions had been sent to France. Britain was not behaving as an ally should.[22] Weygand, on the 3rd, spoke very violently about the actions of the British, saying that Gort's army had stopped its offensive plans on the 23rd on orders from London, and that Churchill had been playing a double game, and had abandoned France to herself. 'The manoeuvre of a junction between the army of the north and the French forces on the Somme would have been effected, affirmed General Weygand, if the British had not continually been looking backward at the ports. "They cannot resist the call of the ports", declared the General. "Once before, in March 1918, they wished to embark." '[23] This was to remain part of French military opinion for years, and Pétain's attitudes were to be strengthened by these memories of 1918.

Meanwhile, Weygand and Pétain, who had met to discuss matters during Reynaud's absence in London on the 26th, presented a note to Reynaud on the 28th,* which said that the British must realise that a time would come when the French might find themselves unable to continue the struggle. Nevertheless, on the next day the question of a defensive redoubt in Brittany was broached, and a study of the matter approved by Pétain. Pétain and Weygand appeared once more to be considering further resistance, though by the 31st Weygand was already expressing doubts about the possibility of creating such a redoubt.

The alliance of Weygand and Pétain at this time was in one sense surprising. Weygand, the loyal follower of Foch, had always shared his master's dislike of Pétain. Yet he now declared, to Baudouin, his preparedness, in the interests of the country, to forget all that separated them.[24]

On the 5th Dunkirk fell, and the main battle to the south began. During the last few days, in one of France's darkest hours, one would be forgiven if one thought that one of Pétain's greatest interests had been the removal of Daladier (and now Sarraut as well) from the Government. Forgetful of his own 1914–18 dislike of Government intrigues in time of national danger (or perhaps confident in the belief that he himself was not acting politically, but was merely acting against politicians), he doggedly kept up his pressure on Reynaud.

So it happened that, on the very day when the new German offensive started, a Government reshuffle took place, which got rid of Daladier and Sarraut. Other people who were removed were Lamoureux and Monzie.

In the morning, Reynaud had offered Pétain the Foreign Ministry. This Pétain refused, and was later supported in this by Weygand, who felt that this office would have removed him from the conduct of military affairs. 'The great prestige of the Marshal', he said, 'must remain one of the essential bases of the army's morale.'[25]

The relevant meeting of the Cabinet took place at 11.30 p.m. Daladier had already been informed by Reynaud that he must go, and had violently protested. At the meeting Reynaud called for a collective letter of resignation from all, after which the new Ministry would be constituted. According to Chautemps, Daladier then said that there was no need for this, as he knew he was the man who must go, and was prepared to give in his personal resignation.†[26] Reynaud, however, aware of the political advantage of a collective resignation, insisted on it.

Pétain, capable as always of cold irony even in the gravest of situations, remarked as he signed the resignation that 'his political career had been very brief'. He was the only person to speak.[27]

As arranged between Lebrun and Reynaud, the former refused the resignation of all the ministers except those for whom a successor had been

---

* Weygand later stated that this happened on the 29th. Baudouin's contemporary notes, however, show that it must have been the evening before.

† The reactions of certain sections of the public were, however, very favourable to the removal of Daladier. Paul Claudel, in his private diary, noted the changes, and Reynaud's wireless speech, adding: 'The new France will have nothing more in common with the France we have seen for the last twenty years. Amen to that!' Claudel *Journal Intime* 6 June 1940, unpublished.

designated. Reynaud himself took over Foreign Affairs, with Baudouin as Under-Secretary of State. Yves Bouthillier replaced Lamoureux as Finance Minister, Yvon Delbos replaced Albert Sarraut as Minister of Education, Frossard replaced Monzie as Minister of Public Works, and Prouvost replaced Frossard as Minister of Information. Not an inspiring Cabinet change; the whole exercise deserved Chautemps's criticism that it revealed 'mediocre preoccupations at so grave a moment.'[28] The only significant move was the appointment of General de Gaulle as Under-Secretary of State for War.

Meanwhile, military matters had taken a turn for the worse. Britain was sending neither planes nor divisions, and was strongly criticised by Reynaud and Weygand that morning. Weygand no longer held out any hope of using the Breton redoubt; all the army could do was try to hold on as long as possible. Pétain strongly expressed his agreement with Weygand.

The next day, 6 June, the situation continued to worsen, and the arguments with the British (in this case Spears) went on as usual. Baudouin noted: 'Paul Reynaud is condemned to fighting every morning for an hour or even more to try and obtain British help which, despite his efforts, fails to materialise. It is certain that if these facts were not carefully hidden from public opinion, a violent wave of anglophobia would immediately arise.'[29]

Weygand stressed the unlikelihood of use of the Breton redoubt, to which Reynaud replied that if France was refused a peace commensurate with honour and with her vital interests, she must continue the war in North Africa. Weygand, however, stressed the weakness of the forces in North Africa, and again dismissed the Breton redoubt as fantasy. Pétain declared that if the present battle was lost, there would be nothing to do but to treat with the enemy.

The Cabinet reshuffle had not pleased Pétain as much as it might, for Reynaud had included the soldier with whom he had had strong links in the inter-war years, General de Gaulle. Pétain had his own reasons for disliking de Gaulle, who had once been his protégé.* On the 7th, despite the urgency of the general situation, he complained to Baudouin about de Gaulle's appointment, and asked him to use his influence with the Prime Minister to prevent de Gaulle attending the morning meetings. He described de Gaulle as 'proud, ungrateful and embittered.'[30] Baudouin suggested that he should see Reynaud himself.

The German Panzers had now broken through the French Line, and it was decided on 8 June to retreat to the lower Seine. Weygand spoke of the bad spirits of the troops, who had been encouraged for months into over-optimism. Pétain declared his horror of the evidence he was finding every day of the army's unpreparedness. 'Nothing has been done for months, or rather for years,' he said. 'Everything in this country must be started afresh.'[31] Defeatism was growing among the Cabinet. Dining with Baudouin, Chautemps declared that the war must be ended, and that it was Pétain who saw the position clearest.

* See Appendix

The departure of the Government from Paris began to be prepared, not without some confusion. Meanwhile, Pétain was continuing to press his point. At the morning meeting on the 9th, he read a memorandum which stressed the inconveniences of a Government departure from Paris, particularly from the point of view of morale. As far as the military position was concerned, the main thing to do was to seek an armistice with a view to cessation of hostilities, if the conditions of such an armistice, though hard, were acceptable.

In the resultant discussion, Reynaud stressed that no honourable armistice was to be expected from Hitler, and moreover that it would be imprudent for France to cut herself off from her allies. Pétain's answer, as reported by Baudouin, was the one that might have been expected: the interests of France came before those of England. 'England has got us into this position. Let us not restrict ourselves to putting up with it, let us try to get out of it.'[32]

When Baudouin was asked for his opinion, he said that Reynaud ought to have sounded out the British, on his visit to London on 26 May. (It is clear that Reynaud had let no one know that he had warned the British of the danger of an armistice demand.)

Weygand then came in and gave an account of the worsening military situation. If the last effort, on the Seine and on the Marne, were lost, all was finished. The armies would be separated and destroyed.

On 10 June the Government left Paris for Tours. Weygand had earlier in the day handed a note to Reynaud which declared that the final enemy breakthrough was imminent, and that though the armies would go on fighting until exhausted, there was a danger that all cohesion would be lost.[33] Later he said to Baudouin that he thought an armistice was essential, because the fighting had become meaningless. Baudouin clearly agreed.

So the Government left Paris with more than one member determined on an armistice, and with the Commander-in-Chief of the same opinion. In these early June days, the British had kept up continual pressure on the French to avoid such a course of action, cajoling and occasionally threatening. Churchill describes a scene on 31 May in which Spears threatened Pétain with not only a blockade, but bombardment of the French ports in such an eventuality.[34]

Spears, Churchill's man in Paris, saw a certain amount of Pétain during this period, and his descriptions are acute and convincing. On 25 May he had seen Pétain for the first time for many years:

... Now here was Pétain himself, walking towards me, still erect but so very much older, and in plain clothes which emphasised the break with the past. His face had never been other than white and expressionless. I had always known him bald; the long fair moustache, though whiter, was the same, but he seemed dead, in the sense that a figure that gives no impression of being alive can be said to be dead. .. He looked very sad even for him, who seldom struck one as gay, but his words of greeting were kind "You are very welcome—*vous êtes le bienvenu*". There was warmth in his voice as in his words. Then he seemed to disappear from the scene, almost from sight, for not another word did he utter, and when I occasionally looked towards him he seemed not to have heard what was being said. After all, he was in his eighty-fifth year.[35]

Pétain indeed remained silent throughout most Cabinet or military meetings; he was indeed deaf (though Spears on a later occasion was forced to admit 'This deafness ... had disappeared');[36] events were, however, to show that he was in no way 'switched off'. His interventions were often to be decisive, especially in the last couple of days of Reynaud's Government. His views were fixed, as were his attitudes; age meant that he reserved his strength; but when they were needed, he had the clarity of mind and the decisiveness of purpose which were to make him a force to be reckoned with.

He was pessimistic, as he had been in 1918; but there was no sign of panic or emotion in his pessimism. Some have described an element almost of self-satisfaction in his attitude to the defeat brought, he thought, by the inefficiency of others. Spears describes the distance Pétain seemed from the struggle: 'He did not disguise the fact that he considered the situation catastrophic, and stated in so many words that he could see no way out. I could not detect any sign in him of broken morale, of that mental wringing of hands and incipient hysteria noticeable in others. He had none of Weygand's ups and downs, no alternations of "We will manage somehow" with "All is lost." He was perfectly calm, as if the whole responsibility were that of others and he was observing the development of a rather tiresome, very sordid and almost boring drama taking place in a distant branch of the family, from which his attention could not be entirely withheld.'[37]

Pétain, Spears shows us, was emotional about only one thing; the faults of politicians and schoolmasters, who were responsible for the state of the country: 'The country has been rotted by politics. The people can no longer discern the face of France through the veil politicians have thrown over it. As you know, a matricide is led to the guillotine with a veil over his face. It is that sort of veil, but it is over the face of the mother. The murderer has thrown the veil over his mother's face.'[38]

The Reynaud Government in Touraine, 10—13 June

The next six days were to be filled with the question of an armistice. In Touraine, the question was above all one for the Cabinet. In Bordeaux, which the Government was to reach on the 14th, the powers at work were far larger, and the field far more open to intrigue. In both fields, all was working for Pétain and against Reynaud.

On 11 June Churchill came over to France once more, at Reynaud's request. The meeting took place at the Château du Muguet, at Briare, near Orleans. Churchill 'displayed the smiling countenance and confident air which are thought suitable when things are very bad', but found the French colonel who had been sent to meet him dull and unresponsive.[39] The French Government was distributed through various châteaux, and communications were poor. Churchill found that the Château du Muguet 'possessed but one telephone, in the lavatory. It was kept very busy, with long delays and endless shouted repetitions.'

The various accounts of the meeting which took place at seven in the evening differ, especially in relation to the remarks made by Pétain. Weygand stresses Churchill's advocacy of the Breton redoubt, and his own rejection of it. He then says that Churchill suggested guerrilla warfare to gain some months in the hope of American intervention. Pétain retorted to this that it would mean the destruction of the country.[40] Pétain was evidently already fearful of the 'Polonisation' of France, i.e., that the Germans would treat France as they had treated Poland.

Churchill claims that 'there were no reproaches or recriminations' at this meeting, and that he urged the French to defend Paris. He mentions recalling to Pétain the situation in March 1918, 'and how he, as I put it, not mentioning Marshal Foch, had restored the situation. I also reminded him how Clemenceau had said "I will fight in front of Paris, in Paris, and behind Paris".' To this, he says, Pétain replied quietly and with dignity that he had in those days a strategic reserve of up to sixty divisions; now there was none. 'He mentioned that there were then sixty British divisions in the line. Making Paris into a ruin would not affect the final event.'[41]

General de Gaulle's version of this episode is more convincing, given the attitudes we have already seen Pétain taking. According to de Gaulle, who was present, when Churchill had made his reminiscence Pétain replied, harshly: '—Yes, the front was re-established. You, the English, were routed. But I sent forty divisions to get you out of trouble. Today, it is we who are being broken to bits. Where are your forty divisions?'[42]

If we can take this as the correct version, Pétain's attitude on the 11th seems to have been in line with what we have seen before: defeatism, fear for France under a German invasion, and a certain anti-British feeling. The meeting discussed once more the question of the British air force, with no new result.

At dinner, Reynaud told Churchill that Marshal Pétain had told him that France would have to seek an armistice, and had written a paper about it which he wanted Reynaud to read. 'He has not', he said, 'handed it to me yet. He is still ashamed to do it.'[43] Churchill makes the point that, if Pétain was convinced that France must give in, he ought to have been ashamed to support Weygand's demand for Britain's last twenty-five squadrons of fighters.

The next day, discussions resumed. After Churchill's departure, there was a Cabinet meeting in the evening, at the Château de Cangé, at which Weygand expressed his strong opinion that France should seek an armistice. He referred to the danger not only of military disorder, but of public disorder. Once again, the spectre of civil disorder was, for Weygand, one of the greatest threats. Reynaud, answering Weygand, made a point of great importance, particularly in relation to the view of military honour among enemies which we have seen Pétain holding in the inter-war years. 'You take Hitler for Wilhelm I,' he said, 'an old gentleman who took Alsace-Lorraine from us and left it at that. But Hitler is Genghis Khan!'[44] For him, it was essential for the French to go on fighting, even if they were driven out of France.

Pétain, with Prouvost, was one of the only two people to support Weygand in his request for an armistice. He ranged himself on the side of the military commander, who, he said, was the only one really to know what was happening. The Cabinet meeting, however, went on in some confusion, until Chautemps suggested that Churchill should be invited to come back to discuss the situation.

The paper composed by Pétain, to which Reynaud had referred to Churchill, was still being held in readiness. During the course of the day, Pétain had it read out to Bouthillier, who that evening was to be very zealous, behind the scenes, for the cause of the armistice, going to see, among others, Marin and Dautry.

On Churchill's return to France on the 13th, one of the first people to see him was Paul Baudouin, who, 'in his soft, silky manner',[45] spoke to him of the hopelessness of French resistance. Mandel, on the other hand, impressed Churchill by his energy and defiance; he was determined to fight on to the end in France, so as to cover the greatest possible movement of people across to North Africa. Reynaud came next, and put the question to Churchill about an armistice which the Cabinet had asked him to. The British declared that they could not agree to a separate peace. 'Whatever happened, we would level no reproaches against France; but that was a different matter from consenting to release her from her pledge.'[46] Churchill urged Reynaud to send a new appeal to President Roosevelt.

Before his departure, Churchill saw Herriot and Jeanneney, who were determined on a fight to the death. Others, however, and in particular Baudouin and Bouthillier, continued their surreptitious work in favour of an armistice.

The Cabinet meeting, on the evening of the 13th, was to be the most important of the Reynaud Government. It started at Cangé about an hour late, because Reynaud, Baudouin and Mandel had been at Tours meeting Churchill. In that hour, much lobbying went on, with people moving from group to group in front of the château.

Reynaud had not invited Churchill to the Cabinet meeting, as he had promised to. This caused some acrimony, as did his statement that he had told Churchill that, the day before, the Cabinet had not accepted the armistice project.

Now the Marshal finally read the note that he had kept in reserve for the last few days. In it he stated the themes which were to be central to his defence of the armistice: the need to stay in France, to prepare a national revival, and to share the sufferings of the people. Having rejected the idea of a 'redoubt', he continued:

It is impossible for the Government to abandon French soil without emigrating, without deserting. The duty of the Government is, come what may, to remain in the country, or it could no longer be regarded as the Government. To deprive France of her natural defenders in a period of general confusion is to deliver her up to the enemy. It is to kill France's soul, and to make any renascence impossible.

We must wait for the French revival by remaining on the spot, rather than reconquering our territory with allied guns, in conditions, and after a period of time, which it is impossible to foresee.

I am thus determined not to leave French soil, and to accept the suffering which will be imposed on *la Patrie* and her sons. The French renascence will be the fruit of this suffering. . . .

I declare, so far as I am concerned, that, if need be outside the Government, I will refuse to leave the home soil. I will remain amid the French people, to share its afflictions and its miseries.

The armistice is, in my eyes, the necessary condition for the continued existence of eternal France.[47]

Ybarnégaray, an extreme right-wing member of the *Croix de Feu* who had been brought into the Government on 10 May (as Aron puts it, as a 'parliamentary ex-voto on the altar of battle'[48]), now, in true military manner (he had been one of the soldier-deputies of the First World War) rallied behind the military leaders, who had told everyone their duty.

So the pro-armistice group was growing. But several ministers, of varied political colours, continued to argue against it. Weygand lashed out against them, blaming them for even leaving Paris. Like Pétain, he said he would never leave France. (He also warned of the possibility of a Communist uprising in Paris.)

A strong division thus existed in the Cabinet in the hour of crisis, and nothing further in the meeting was done to remove it. A decision was made to move to Bordeaux, because of the rapid German advance; but it was a divided Government that set off on its new move, whose only action had been to send the appeal to Roosevelt.

The Reynaud Government in Bordeaux, 14–16 June*

Bordeaux is the city to which the French Governments have fled in face of a German invasion, in 1870, 1914 and 1940. On this occasion, however, the city was to surpass all that had happened in it before in the way of parliamentary intrigue. A divided Government arrived, and with it the rest of Parliament, who could now take a part in affairs. Prominent among the new figures on the scene was Pierre Laval, who, though he had been out of Government since 1936, wielded an enormous influence behind the scenes.

It had not needed Laval and the other parliamentarians to appear on the scene, however, for plotting to have begun. Already, without Reynaud knowing it, plots were forming within the Cabinet itself. Weygand received,

---

* From this point onwards the sources are many, and specific sources will be given only in the case of quotations, or where they are otherwise needed. The main sources for the general narrative are listed in the bibliography.

Pierre Laval

Paul Reynaud arrives at Downing Street for a meeting of the Supreme War Council, March 1940

at 5 p.m., a message from Pétain and Baudouin, sent before the departure for Bordeaux, which said that his presence at Bordeaux was essential. A Cabinet meeting would be held late the following morning. Weygand was to turn up at Baudouin's place before 10.30 a.m. Pétain believed, the message said, that the latest moment to make a decision was Sunday, the 16th.

In Bordeaux on the 14th, the groups began to form. Herriot, Jeanneney and Mandel, together with Campinchi and Monnet, formed an anti-armistice group; they were joined by Léon Blum. Laval, who had left his home for Bordeaux convinced that Pétain should take over the Government, went to stay with his friend Adrien Marquet, the mayor of Bordeaux (who had been one of those to support the idea of a Pétain Government in the late 'thirties). The incoming parliamentarians went to the *mairie* to search for both lodgings and news, and Laval and Marquet seem to have taken advantage of this situation to do a great deal of persuasion. Gradually they created what came to be known as the Bordeaux *Commune* which, in the absence of the Presidents of both Senate and Chamber, grouped the leaderless deputies and senators into a fairly coherent, if unconstitutional, body.

Weygand did not manage to arrive in Bordeaux till after lunch. In secret, he met Admiral Darlan, Pétain, Baudouin and Bouthillier. Darlan, who only the day before had said that if an armistice was signed he would depart with the fleet, was now well in the armistice camp.

The Cabinet met at four o'clock, and Reynaud produced a new alternative to an armistice. This was that the Government should, like the Dutch, order its army to lay down its arms, after which it would leave the country, and continue resistance from abroad. This proposal of capitulation, when suggested to Weygand earlier in the afternoon, had been violently rejected by him as a manoeuvre to put the responsibility for the cessation of hostilities on the army rather than on the Government. At the Cabinet meeting, however, Pétain appears to have agreed with Reynaud, who, feeling that Pétain would perhaps be the one man to bring Weygand round, delegated him to go and see him (Weygand was in an adjoining room). The opposite happened from what Reynaud had hoped: Pétain returned a quarter of an hour later, convinced by Weygand that capitulation would be dishonourable.

In the typical parliamentary manner, compromise solutions were now sought to break the deadlock. Ten ministers wanted an armistice, the Premier and fourteen ministers wanted to leave for Africa. How was unity to be achieved? Frossard suggested that the only way to unify them would be if Hitler's armistice conditions were so dishonourable that nobody could accept them. This appears to have given Chautemps the idea for the famous, or infamous, Chautemps proposal. He suggested that they should get a neutral authority to enquire what the terms would be. If they turned out to be honourable, they could agree (and perhaps the British would agree) to study them. If they were not, they could all agree to fight on. The Government would thus remain undivided.

The armistice group rallied to this, and it was voted through by 13 to 6. The danger was that both sides felt that it would prove them right; it was not a real unity which emerged. Also, the principle of an armistice had now been accepted, and the power of Pétain and Weygand (who was not even in the Government) had reversed the majority opinion in the Cabinet.

Reynaud offered his resignation, but it was refused by President Lebrun. He therefore stayed on, and agreed to further the Chautemps proposal, though he got the Cabinet to agree to wait until Roosevelt replied to their appeal.

The next morning Roosevelt's reply came; apart from vague promises, it was impossible for the President to do anything. Only Congress could make military commitments.

At the morning Cabinet meeting Pétain read out a letter of resignation from the Government, saying that the only way to save the country was an immediate cessation of hostilities, and that the daily meetings of the Government contained discussions which were merely manoeuvres to waste time, which would lead to the abdication of French sovereignty.[49] He therefore wished to resign. As so often during these critical days, he read what he had to say from a prepared paper; this leads one to believe that some at least of these statements were drafted for him by other people. In the case of this particular document, Pétain himself said at his trial that he believed someone had drafted it for him, and asked him to read it to the Cabinet; but he could not remember who it had been. Suggestions have included Laval, Marquet, Baudouin, Bouthillier, Alibert, and Dr Ménétrel (Pétain's doctor, who was to have great influence over him at Vichy). Pétain had always had his speeches drafted for him, however, as we have seen, and because this one was drafted by someone else it does not mean that it did not accurately reflect his thought. In this case, his main thought seems to have been to force the Government's hand by his threat of resignation.

President Lebrun persuaded him to hang on until the British reply to the Chautemps proposal came. Two telegrams eventually arrived from Britain, one before lunch and one in the early afternoon. They made it clear that the British Government would only agree to an armistice if the French fleet was immediately sent to British ports. The question of the fleet was, of course, to be one of the most prickly problems in this whole business. The British rightly feared its falling into German hands. The French saw it as one of their principal bargaining counters in the negotiations with Germany. So long as Germany had a chance of the French navy being merely neutralised, the terms she offered would probably be more generous.

Neither of these telegrams reached the Cabinet meeting held later that afternoon, however, because in the meantime de Gaulle had telephoned from London to Reynaud, to give the British Government's offer of joint nationality for Frenchmen and Englishmen, in a Franco-British union.

The delight of Reynaud at this offer was unrealistic. He should have realised the strong mistrust of Great Britain that existed among the members of his Cabinet, and in particular with Marshal Pétain. Though at that afternoon's Cabinet meeting, Reynaud was supported by four or five of his ministers (Mandel, Monnet, Marin, Rio and Dautry), most of the others were persuaded against him by the arguments of Chautemps, Ybarnégaray, and Pétain. Chautemps and Ybarnégaray saw the offer as a device to make France subservient to Great Britain, as a kind of extra Dominion. Pétain thought it was an attempt once more to delay the armistice. Both constructions were caused by the archetypal French concern that 'perfidious Albion' would never do something for nothing.

The session was stormy, with Mandel flinging accusations of cowardice, and Chautemps and others replying in kind. But clearly Reynaud had lost. The Chautemps proposal was once more put forward, and the Cabinet adjourned. Some accounts say that Reynaud resigned at this meeting, and that his resignation was refused by President Lebrun. At any rate, in later private discussions it became clear that Reynaud would not accept the Chautemps proposal, and though one or two members (including Herriot and Jeanneney) tried to get Lebrun to ask Reynaud to form a new Government, Reynaud himself advised Lebrun to call for Pétain.

The Pétain Government up to the armistice, 16–24 June 1940

Pétain had been preparing for his Government for some days, and others had seen it as inevitable. Darlan, indeed, had made suggestions to Pétain on the 15th as to the make-up of his future Government;[50] and when Lebrun sent for him, Pétain produced from his pocket a list of ministers. Pétain had, in some senses, accelerated the departure of Reynaud; his own threatened resignation of that morning had been one more push down the slope, for the resignation of Pétain would have destroyed any Government in this crisis.

Among the new figures brought into the Government were Weygand as Minister of National Defence, and Raphaël Alibert as Under-Secretary of State to the Prime Minister. Alibert, who had been of much influence on Pétain's political ideas since he had been introduced to the Marshal by Lémery, had been until now director of Pétain's *cabinet civil*. A staunch right-winger, a monarchist and a supporter of the *Action Française*, a dogmatic theorist, he held certain views upon the social organisation of the country which were to be at the base of the *Révolution Nationale*.

Other figures of importance were Chautemps as Deputy Prime Minister, Darlan as Minister of Marine, and Ybarnégaray as 'Minister for *Anciens Combattants* and the French Family' (a title which speaks for itself).

What of Laval? Here Pétain miscalculated. Pressure had been brought on him by Darlan (who, like most of the military and naval men, mistrusted Laval) not to make Laval Foreign Minister, but to put Baudouin in that post. This Pétain did, and nominated Laval as Minister of Justice. What he had not anticipated was Laval's annoyance at not being Foreign Minister. What Laval said to Pétain is not certain, but he may well have threatened to resign; and Pétain, who clearly wanted Laval in the Government, backed down and gave Laval the Foreign Ministry. Strong pressure from Charles-Roux (permanent head of the Foreign Office) and Weygand, did not at first change Pétain's resolve; but when Charles-Roux threatened to resign if Laval was Foreign Minister, Pétain was forced to back down once more.

This time Laval refused the Ministry of Justice and did resign. This led to his friend Adrien Marquet, the proposed Minister of the Interior, resigning as well, to be replaced by Charles Pomaret.

The new Government took over immediately; by midnight Baudouin was asking the Spanish Ambassador to submit to Germany a request to cease hostilities at once, and for Germany to make known its peace terms. At 12.30 a.m. Pétain, without consulting his ministers, issued his first call to the French people. On this unconstitutional note the new Government made its first departure from democratic procedure. The speech, which was broadcast on the wireless, shows the extent to which Pétain had become the character which the French people had imagined him to be in the inter-war years: proud, honourable, full of compassion. It shows confidence in the concept of military honour. It also breathes self-satisfaction. The phrase *Je fais à la France le don de ma personne* is almost untranslateable into English, with the idea of voluntary oblation, yet of the conviction of the value of the oblation, which it involves. That it was accepted seriously by so many Frenchmen is a proof of the almost religious fervour that the marshalship by now involved. Here is the text of the speech:

> Frenchmen! At the call of the President of the Republic I am assuming from today the direction of the Government of France. Sure of the affection of our admirable army, which is fighting with a heroism worthy of its long military traditions against an enemy superior in numbers and arms, sure that by its magnificent resistance it has fulfilled our obligations towards our allies, sure of the support of the *anciens combattants* whom I had the honour to command, sure of the confidence of the whole people, I make to France the gift of my person, to attenuate her suffering.
>
> In these unhappy hours, I think of the unfortunate refugees who, in a state of extreme deprivation, are lining our roads. I express to them my compassion and my solicitude.
>
> It is with a heavy heart that I say to you today that the combat must cease. I have, this night, addressed myself to the adversary to ask him if he is prepared to seek with us, between soldiers, after the battle and with Honour, the means to put an end to hostilities.
>
> Let all Frenchmen group themselves around the Government over which I preside during these harsh trials, and let them silence their anguish and listen only to their faith in the destiny of *la Patrie*.[51]

The Marshal should perhaps have shown this to his ministers before pronouncing it. The phrase 'the combat must cease' (*il faut cesser le combat*) led many soldiers, indeed whole regiments, to believe that they must immediately lay down their arms. Weygand had to send an order to the army saying that fighting must go on until an armistice was signed; meanwhile, the official printed version was changed, to become 'we must try to end the combat' (*il faut tenter de cesser le combat*).[52]

The enthusiasm of the country for the Marshal was tremendous. He was welcomed by people as diverse as Claudel, Gide and Mauriac, and also by the vast mass of untutored Frenchmen who saw him as their saviour.

Meanwhile another sign of the future had happened. Georges Mandel was arrested by order of Alibert. Though President Lebrun succeeded in getting him released, some of those who knew of it felt that the Marshal's entourage was showing itself to be a dangerous and rather questionable one.

The Germans hastened to improve their military position still more before agreeing to the armistice, so that they would be able to conduct negotiations on the best possible terms. While things thus remained uncertain, the Cabinet and Parliament proceeded to divide themselves on the question of whether to head for North Africa or not. On the 18th, faced by Herriot and Jeanneney (the Presidents of the two Chambers), who were determined to go, and President Lebrun, who was favourable to their view, Pétain reiterated his determination not to depart. He agreed, however, to delegate his powers to Chautemps, who would set off with President Lebrun and all the other parliamentarians to North Africa. He himself would remain to protect his compatriots. Baudouin, Bouthillier and Weygand would remain with him. The departure was arranged for the 19th. On the morning of that day the Germans agreed to open negotiations for an armistice.

The men who took the most part in breaking up this African operation were Alibert and Laval. The story of the abortive venture whereby the *Massilia* would transport the Government, on the 20th, to Africa, is a complicated one and has been told many times. Suffice it to say that certain events caused the indecision; the slowness of the German acceptance of the suggested French plenipotentiaries, followed by its receipt at 11.15 a.m. on the 20th; Weygand's subsequent persuasion of President Lebrun to remain until 6 p.m.; a lie by Alibert in mid-afternoon, in which, in order to prevent Chautemps and Lebrun heading for Africa, he said it was untrue that the Germans had crossed the Loire, and that there was therefore time to postpone the decision to the next day; and, finally, the influence of Laval, Marquet and the 'Bordeaux Commune'. A delegation from that body came to Pétain on the 20th to protest at Lebrun's departure, and was told that this departure had been postponed. The next day they called on Lebrun, and with Laval as their main spokesman, put pressure on him not to go. Though Lebrun remained undecided, Pétain by now realised the strength of his own support, and, according to Baudouin, would even have been prepared to arrest Lebrun if he had tried to depart.[53] The occasion did not arise however. Thirty deputies and one senator eventually headed for Africa on the *Massilia*, not having realised that plans had now changed.

On the 20th, Pétain had made another call to the nation, telling them that plenipotentiaries had been chosen for an armistice. He had described the decision as 'hard for a soldier's heart', but the military events had forced it on them. The request for an armistice had been inevitable since 13 June. He explained the shortage of troops, of arms, of planes, of allies. 'Too few children, too few arms, too few allies, these are the causes of our defeat.' He then turned to the lessons which the French must learn from the defeat: 'All peoples have experienced, in turn, successes and reverses. It is by the manner in which they react that they show whether they are weak or great. We will learn the lesson of our lost battles. Since the victory (of 1918) the spirit of enjoyment has been stronger than the spirit of sacrifice. People have demanded things, rather than serving. People have wished to spare their efforts; and today we encounter misfortune.'

The message, thus, was one of a need for expiation of these former sins, and for the rebuilding of a new France. 'I have been with you in the glorious days. As Head of Government, I am and will remain with you in these darker days. Stay at my side. The combat remains the same one. It is a question of France, her soil, her sons.' [54]

On the evening of the 21st, the German armistice terms arrived. They were harsh, but not completely unacceptable. The German aim was to persuade France not to bring her empire and her fleet against them, nor continue the fight from abroad. If these two important strengths could be neutralised, they would be satisfied. It has also been suggested that memories of 1870–1 (those same memories which had made Weygand fear civil disorder), of the continued resistance of a divided France, and of revolution, had made them think it was better to keep a constitutional Government in charge of France. Be that as it may, the demands were made more modest than they might have been. It is now known that Hitler was terrified of the French fleet being used by the British.

The main articles were as follows: (1) Hostilities must cease. (2 and 3) Two-thirds of France, including Paris, and the whole Atlantic coast, were to be occupied by the Germans. (4) All except 100,000 men of the French forces were to be demobilised and disarmed. (5, 6 and 7) All arms, aeroplanes and fortifications were to be handed over to the Germans. (8) All the fleet, except a small part needed to safeguard French colonial interests, was to be demobilised and disarmed in its home ports. (9) The French Government bound itself not to undertake any hostile action against the Reich; it was to prevent members of its armed forces from leaving the country or fighting against Germany.

On the credit side, France retained her empire, and Germany solemnly undertook not to lay claim to the French fleet.

Various suggested changes having been refused by the Germans, the armistice was signed on 22 June. The Italian armistice terms, which were extremely moderate, were accepted on 24 June.

Between these two events, a surprising change was made in Pétain's Cabinet, by the inclusion of Laval, as Deputy Premier, and Marquet, as Minister of State, becoming on 27 June Minister of the Interior. These two dangerous men were now in two of the most important positions in the Government. Laval had apparently repented of his resignation, and Pétain, persuaded by Lémery and Alibert, had agreed to take him and Marquet back once more. With Laval, Marquet, Alibert and Baudouin in the Government, and Lémery and Dr Ménétrel in his personal *entourage*, Pétain was in strange company indeed, and the Third Republic was in great danger. Laval had avoided being a member of the Government that had signed the

German armistice; he was now a member of the Government which was to destroy the Republic.

Views on the armistice have always been divided, and it is not my intention here to go into the rights and wrongs of the subject. What I have been trying to give are the arguments and attitudes that led up to it. At the time, if the war as was expected finished within a few more weeks or even months with a German victory, many felt that France had done the only possible thing. Pétain was supported by a large majority of the country, and the call to resistance made by General de Gaulle from London on the 18th was heeded by comparatively few. As time went on, and German victory became less certain, and German demands more harsh, the initial agreement became less and less defensible, and many opinions changed. But that is another story, to be dealt with later.

The fall of the Third Republic[55]

Both Pétain and Laval had long blamed parliamentary government, and the methods of the Third Republic, and it is hardly surprising that their new Government should have tried to set these methods aside.

On 29 June the Government moved to Clermont-Ferrand (Bordeaux being in the Occupied Zone). It was here that the question of a change in the régime was first discussed, on the next day, by a small group consisting of Pétain, Laval, Alibert, Baudouin and Bouthillier. At first, only Alibert and Laval seem to have been in favour of such a change. The others demurred. Laval then broke out, claiming that such a move was not only possible, but necessary, in order to be able to negotiate properly with the Germans. In face of the strong division in the group, Pétain brought up the obstacle of President Lebrun. Laval immediately claimed that he could persuade Lebrun, and rushed off to see him, returning with the news that he had agreed. (Lebrun himself claims that he merely noted what Laval said.) Pétain was seen to be full of admiration of Laval for the swiftness and certainty of his actions, and gave in with the words 'Then give it a try.'[56]*

On 1 July the Government moved to Vichy, where it was to spend the next four years. This spa town was, in one sense, an understandable choice, in that the large empty hotels were very suitable for Government departments; though Lebrun, according to Pomaret (who was for a short time Minister of the Interior, until replaced by Adrien Marquet on 27 June), saw the disadvantages of that town: 'Pomaret, try to avoid Vichy, if we go to Vichy they will say, in France and abroad, that we are a Casino Government.'[57] Pomaret states that he considered various towns, but that Toulouse was no good, because 'the choice of the fief of the Sarraut brothers and the *Dépêche de Toulouse* was bound to be opposed by Laval.'[58] Lyon was suggested, but was opposed by Laval and Marquet, because it was Herriot's town. Finally, Clermont-Ferrand was chosen. Laval was pleased, because he was Senator of the Department, had his property at Châteldon, and owned

---

* Baudouin and Bouthillier both agree on the general points of the scene as here described.

newspapers in Clermont. Only two days in Clermont, however, and its unsuitability was realised. Everything was much too cramped. Again a move had to be considered, and this time it was Pétain who objected to Lyon. Baudouin suggested Vichy, and it was accepted.

Soon after the Government was installed, another small meeting was held on 2 June, this time with Weygand present. Weygand and Baudouin opposed Laval's plan, Baudouin fearing that it would fail. But Laval once more forcefully made his point, and the meeting agreed to let him continue.

Before the next Cabinet meeting, on the 4th, Mers-el-Kebir had occurred, and much of the meeting was occupied with the new situation with regard to Great Britain. Nevertheless, Laval put forward to his colleagues the text that he proposed to get ratified by the Assembly, which ran as follows: 'The National Assembly gives up all powers to the Government of the Republic, under the signature and authority of Marshal Pétain, Prime Minister, in order to promulgate by one or several acts the new constitution of the French State. This constitution must guarantee the rights of labour, the family and the fatherland. It will be ratified by the Assemblies it creates.'[59]

Alibert is said to have collaborated in the composition of this, and certainly the phrase 'Work, Family and the Fatherland' (*Travail, Famille, Patrie*), which was to become the motto of the Vichy State, is more in accordance with Alibert's social ideas than those of Laval. Alibert now set about composing a fuller document for Laval to put forward eventually to the Assembly, which contained most of the themes on which the National Revolution was to be set up. Over the next few days, he was also to be of great help to Laval in his persuasion of the deputies and senators.

The Cabinet, though almost entirely in favour of ruling without the Chambers, had, as we have seen, worried mainly about whether Laval's scheme was not a viable one, and whether it might not rebound on them and on the Marshal. They also, on the whole, mistrusted Laval, one of the great examples of the old system. However, the Cabinet had now agreed to let him get on with it. Over the next few days, by a mixture of bullying and wheedling, he worked on the mass of deputies and senators to try to win them over. By the 10th, he had created the remarkable achievement whereby the National Assembly voted itself out of existence.

Pétain's part in all this was an equivocal one. It was in his name that Laval was speaking, and most of the parliamentarians had admiration and trust for him. On the other hand, those who were afraid of Laval looked to Pétain as almost the only way to save themselves from him. On 5 July the first attempt to get the Marshal's help came; one of the senators, Jean Taurines, got together twenty-five of his colleagues who were also *anciens combattants*, and as a group they decided to get the Marshal to defend the Republic. The 'order of the day' which they voted was as follows:

The ex-service senators, gathered at Vichy on Friday, 5 July under the chairmanship of M. Jean Taurines, . . . salute with emotion and pride their venerated leader, Marshal Pétain, who, in these tragic and miserable hours, has made a gift of his person to the country.

They put their confidence in him, that he will, within the bounds of Republican legality, reorganise the national force, galvanise energies and prepare the moral ground which will remake a France worthy of their sacrifices.[60]

Unfortunately, the delegation which was meant to present this text to the Marshal found it difficult to get to him. Telephoning to arrange an appointment, they got through to Alibert, who promised to get in touch, and was then out when, six hours later, they telephoned again.

The next day, however, having tried in vain to reach Pétain through the proper channels, they tried again through Captain Bonhomme, of Pétain's military staff, whom one of them knew personally, and their delegation was received by the Marshal at 6.15 p.m. on 6 July. As Aron puts it, 'It had taken twenty-six hours for a group of ex-service parliamentarians, whose only fault was to be hostile to Laval's policy, to end up by being granted an interview with their Verdun commander.'[61]

Pétain immediately set their minds at rest. He declared that he had no real ambitions for power, and that once peace was agreed he would retire to his house in the south. In the meanwhile, he wished to be spared the difficulties Lebrun had faced, the outmoded groups and parties, the intrigues that had bedevilled the Governments of the Third Republic. He had no desire to be an absolute dictator, or to misuse his absolute powers. On hearing this, Paul-Boncour declared that they would be prepared to confer on him, as had been done in ancient Rome on various occasions, a dictatorship. Pétain replied that he was not a Caesar, and did not wish to be one.

He continued that he had no desire to get rid of Parliament, and wished to act openly, submitting the new constitutional texts to parliamentary commissions as they were worked out. The delegates were clearly delighted by this, and Paul-Boncour said they would be happy to suspend the constitution till peace was signed, and that Pétain should have full powers to govern by decree, and work out, in collaboration with Parliament, the bases for a new constitution. 'That is a proposal', said Pétain. 'Let me see a text.'

This looks like an agreement opposed to Laval's wishes. Aron suggests that Pétain was playing a clever double game: if Laval won, it was absolute power; if the senators won, he could still govern without Parliament. He may indeed have been playing such a double game, though he may just have been agreeing because all these distinctions did not interest him.

Both these projects involved constitutional reform, though that of the senators insisted on ratification of such reform by Parliament. A more radical opposition to Laval's ventures was, however, produced by Pierre-Étienne Flandin on his arrival in Vichy on the 7th. He spoke to the deputies, and was strongly approved by them, when he said that constitutional reform was a useless exercise, and that there were far more important things to be done. He continued by saying that everyone wanted Pétain at the head of the country: his name and his prestige would be of value not only in negotiating with the Germans, but also in guaranteeing the reorganisation of France. What they must do was ask the President of the Republic, Lebrun, to resign, and elect Pétain in his place. In this way they would get Pétain as head of state, and maintain the constitution.

It is important to notice that all three of these proposals, so opposed to each other, put forward Pétain as head of state. Nobody questioned the fact that he was the most suitable man to lead the nation at this time. France had fallen back once more on a father-figure, as she had done in 1917 and 1934, and as she was to do yet again in 1958.

When Flandin saw Pétain on the 7th, the Marshal agreed with him in the way he had with the senators, saying that all he wanted was full powers, and freedom from accountability to Parliament, till peace was signed.

Meanwhile the senators had drafted their proposal, which made it clear that Pétain would rule by *décrets-lois*, and that he would prepare, *in collaboration with the competent commissions*, the new constitution.

Was Pétain playing, as Aron suggests, a double (or even triple) game? Or was he, as others have suggested, in agreement with these people when he saw them, and later persuaded over by Laval? It is clear that from the start he had not been violently enthusiastic for Laval's plan, so the second suggestion may be true. By the evening of the 7th, however, he had clearly decided to come down on Laval's side, though he was still indifferent as to whether Laval won or not. The impression he gives throughout these episodes is of not really being concerned with this, to him, unimportant problem, so long as he could rule with full powers.

When the senators brought their text that evening, they were dumbfounded to hear Pétain explain that they must now convince Laval, who was the Government's representative in this matter. Laval, when they arrived to see him, said 'Here come the conspirators!', which was hardly likely to encourage confidence. He refused their text, and said that he would be making a statement in the National Assembly, in Pétain's name, which should satisfy them. The senators retorted that they were tabling their amendment to a *projet de loi* that had already been tabled, and had no need of any statement in the Assembly. Laval furiously replied that if their amendment was accepted, he would resign, and Weygand would then become dictator. In a dignified manner, their spokesman replied that Laval had already threatened them with the spectre of the Germans; now it was the spectre of Weygand. What would it be next? They refused to back down.

Laval, to beat these men and Flandin, had to have the unequivocal support of Pétain, whom all these men respected, and without whom no project would be successful. When receiving Flandin, after Pétain had approved the latter's plan, Laval had dashed his hopes by saying that Pétain agreed with everyone, when they saw him. (He had tied Flandin up by showing that, for his plan, Lebrun's agreement to resign was essential; an agreement that was not forthcoming.) Laval now went to Pétain to get a written document giving him Pétain's support; without this, he said, he would not go before the Assembly. Pétain signed for him a letter of support.

On 8 July the text of Laval's project, together with Alibert's *exposé des motifs* (the basis for the future *Révolution Nationale*), was placed by Laval before the deputies. He stressed the need for a new régime, while reassuring those who feared a military dictatorship, saying that civil liberties would be assured. He then put the same texts to the Senate. Later, at a Cabinet meeting that evening, he tricked Rivière, who supported the senators' amendment, by saying that he had come to full agreement with them (which was, of course, untrue).

The 9th was devoted to the official meetings of Chamber and Senate, both of which were to join for the National Assembly on the 10th. The two chambers had merely to pass motions expressing the need for constitutional reform, which would then be discussed the next day. Both meetings were almost formalities, the first marked only by the excitability of some of the extremists on Laval's side, such as Tixier-Vignancour, Montigny, and Xavier Vallat. The interesting thing is that the Presidents of both Chambers prefaced their remarks with praise of Pétain: Herriot, President of the Chamber of Deputies, spoke of the veneration inspired by his name, and the accord which had been established under his authority, before going on to say that reform was necessary, but that Republican principles retained all their virtue. Jeanneney, President of the Senate, expressed his veneration for the Marshal, and the gratitude that was due to him for 'the renewed gift of his person'.

Léon Blum later described, at the Pétain trial, the atmosphere of fear that corrupted the parliamentarians during these two days: fear of Doriot's street-gangs, fear of Weygand's soldiers at Clermont-Ferrand, fear of the Germans at Moulins. Laval knew how to play on these fears, or, where this failed, how to play on people's ambition or self-interest. He has been described by onlookers as imperturbably moving from person to person, dominating the scene, influencing people by his mere presence.

Laval had suggested that on the 10th a secret and informal joint session should be held before the main assembly. At it, in order to try to win over the ex-service Senators, he modified his text to say that the constitution would be ratified, not by the Assemblies it had created, but by the nation as a whole. They were still not satisfied. In reply to them, Laval read out the letter Pétain had given him, which ran: 'The constitutional project tabled by the Government over which I preside will come up for discussion on Tuesday and Wednesday, 9–10 July before the Assemblies. As it is difficult for me to to take part in the debates, I ask you to represent me there. The passing of the measure submitted by the Government to the National Assembly seems to me to be essential to ensure the safety of our country.'[62] As we have seen, Pétain was essential to all schemes; this letter brought many people over to Laval.

Laval continued by stressing the foolishness of the Governments which had brought disaster on France. He attacked England; he attacked the *Front Populaire* for sabotaging his Italian policy; he quoted a remark of Daladier's which showed the Third Republic sacrifice of principles to votes; he evoked the picture of Göring saluting Pétain at Marshal Pilsudski's funeral. Discipline and patriotism were needed, he said, and under Pétain France's soil would be made safe.

At the public meeting that afternoon and evening, by a clever ruse it was decided to take the Government's motion first, and the two main amendments, one by Vincent Badie and the other by the ex-service senators, after it. Despite an unseemly physical struggle between Badie and three of Laval's supporters (one of them being Bouisson) at one point, this order was followed. The Assembly accepted the bill by 569 votes to 80. Laval thanked them, in the name of the Marshal and on behalf of France.

The new régime was about to begin. Paul Claudel, who was by no means in favour of Pétain or Laval on other counts, spoke for a whole section of the French nation when he welcomed the news in his diary on 10 July: 'Vote of the National Assembly and end of the parliamentary régime and of the domination by freemasons and schoolmasters. At least let's hope so. Nothing will really have been done until the French University and classical education have been thrown down.' [63]

The destruction of the Third Republic and its institutions had been the dream of the French Right since the 1870s; to many the unexpected victory must have seemed like a miracle, even though it had been brought about by national defeat.

A miracle, indeed, in that the Republic had voted itself out of existence; but a man-made miracle, created by the guile of Laval and the prestige of the Marshal.

Chapter Two

Vichy 1940

THE day after the National Assembly had voted itself out of existence, Pétain's first constitutional Act appeared in the *Journal Officiel*:

We, Philippe Pétain, Marshal of France, according to the constitutional law of 10 July 1940, declare that we are assuming the functions of Head of State.[1]

The 'royal we' was to be a feature of Pétain's pronouncements from now on. What is interesting is the speed with which the transformation from Prime Minister to Head of State (*Chef de l'État*) took place. The new constitution might have to wait some time to be elaborated; but the personal power of Pétain himself must be immediately consecrated, not only by the Assembly's vote on the 10th, but also by a new title dissociating him from the Republican régime. As Du Moulin de Labarthète says, 'Did he not in fact have the feeling that, of his two tasks, governing and preparing a constitution, the first was by far the most urgent, and the most hard?'[2] The first three constitutional Acts of the new Head of State confirmed his own powers (promulgation of laws, assurance of their execution, nomination to civil and military posts, command of the armies, right of pardon and amnesty, negotiation and ratification of treaties, etc.). All this until new Assemblies were formed. Small wonder that the formation of the new constitution, and the new Assemblies, was not rushed. An important point, however, was that the only right which Pétain did not possess was that of declaring war, without recourse to the Assemblies.

One can now see a possible reason for Pétain's lack of firmness in the matter of Laval's proposed measure and the amendments of the ex-service senators and Flandin. Some have suggested that he was just easily malleable (as Laval was soon to suggest on other occasions); but an equally possible solution is that the Marshal was not even interested in the matter. Whoever won, he was clearly going to get full powers; the way in which an eventual constitution was going to be ratified must have seemed a rather academic matter. He may not even have bothered to try to understand the differences between the various cases; they may have seemed so similar that his agreement to one did not cut out approval of another.

All this in no way denotes senility. Too many people have claimed that in 1940 Pétain was already finished mentally. What we have seen of his actions and words in May, June and July does not, however, seem to denote this.

In some accounts, he appears deaf and cut off; some of these accounts, however (especially that of Spears), show that this deafness varied according to the subject of discussion, and could be a good gambit to avoid an unwelcome subject. He was silent for a great deal of the time; yet the remarks he made appear to have had a devastating effect, and to have been well-timed. He read, rather than improvised his speeches, which were sometimes written by other people; but he had always done so, and the way in which his various utterances hang together logically, and the way in which they reflect his perennial concerns, show that, as always, his writers were reflecting his own thought. He came under the strong influence of certain people, admittedly (e.g., Alibert and Laval); but he was always freer of them than they thought, playing one against the other, and occasionally decisively showing his claws (as in the removal of Laval in December). He was physically old; he was mentally old only in the sense that his old preconceptions had become even more firmly entrenched than before, and that his simple ideas on political, social and national problems were not affected by the realities of power. He was old, also, in that he tired easily. But by conserving his strength, his formidable will was still able to get its own way, as others were to learn to their cost. Laval had in a fourth constitutional Act been named as his dauphin; but as long as Pétain remained alive all Government action had to come through him. Laval, and others, did not fully realise for a while how much power they had given up to him.

In the country as a whole, enthusiasm for him was immense, and the régime rested on his personality. This was known by those around him, and therefore, however much they might wish to direct him, he had the ultimate power. The armed forces, too, were not only in great part enthusiastic about him; they were also bound by their loyalty to a military leader, and their training made them unquestionably follow his orders. Many military and naval men must have been like that admiral to whom Claudel had timidly said, on 30 June: 'Do you think that . . .', only to receive the swift reply 'I do not think, sir, I obey!'[3] At this stage in the war, few officers followed de Gaulle's call, and very few indeed of those were high-ranking. De Gaulle was a dissident, who refused to obey the orders of his superiors, and who endangered France's future by his flouting of the armistice agreements, which had been negotiated by the legal Government of France. Contempt for him and his forces was such that at the time of the Syrian campaign in 1941, very few of the defeated French forces opted to come over to the Allies, the majority preferring to be shipped back to France. And it took the decision of Darlan, as Pétain's dauphin at the time and as the Commander-in-Chief on the spot, to bring the French North African, and West African, forces over to the Allies in November 1942. Until that date, the bulk of the armed forces remained loyal to Pétain. Enthusiasm among the officer class for Pétain stemmed partly from his rank, but also from his political ideas, and from the measures he introduced. Within a year, the 100,000 strong armistice army was provided with the first peacetime chaplains since 1870. Military men felt that the Marshal was pursuing 'the first really Christian government policy in 150 years.'[4] Many of the political ideas to be put forward in the *Révolution Nationale* were dear to the officers' hearts. De Gaulle might well be of the same political tinge; but he did not have rank, authority, or legality, nor did he have the power to put these policies into effect within France. Pétain was providing the opportunity to put right all the things the officer corps thought to be wrong in the French State. As Paxton puts it: 'Under the Marshal, French officers were serving the first really sympathetic administration since the good days of Thiers and Marshal MacMahon. Not only had Marshal Pétain won the threatened army the right to survive as an institution; he set it free at last to reassert its proper place in French society, properly honoured and properly consulted on matters of national policy. The Armistice Army basked in the warmth of a friendly government, as no generation of French officers had done for sixty years.'[5]

Among the people, support for the Marshal was fairly widespread at the time of the armistice, and was not confined to circles of the Right. These, however, were among the most enthusiastic, and grew even more so as the policies of the new Government became clear. Maurras and the *Action Française* group, for example, had originally believed in a fight to the end, carried if necessary abroad to the empire. When the news of the armistice reached them, however, Maurras immediately accepted the judgement of the military pundits, Pétain and Weygand, and declared that all must now work for national revival, under the aegis of Pétain. When Pétain's Government overthrew the Third Republic, the *Action Française* saw this as its dreams come true. One of its strongest members, Paul Courcoural, said in *La Nouvelle Guyenne*: 'A great good fortune has come to us in our immense misery. God had prepared for us a great leader. Marshal Pétain has gathered up France in the very day of her distress. . . . What is taking place, as a result of the decisions taken at Vichy. . . . is the Counter-Revolution. With Charles Maurras and all his friends, we salute the first acts of this Counter-Revolution with an emotion, a pride, and a hope which are explained by our life, which has for fifty years been devoted to these same principles. . . .'[6]

The *Action Française* was, as we shall see, to have a great deal of influence at Vichy. In one sense, Pétain was to become the king for which this royalist movement had always worked.

Catholics, too, after all the years in which they had seen themselves as a minority in an actively anti-clerical country, now found with delight a Government which was religious in its policy. As early as 6 July Paul Claudel, drawing up the pros and the cons of the present state of France (one of the cons being governed by men like Laval), put at the head of the pros: 'France has been delivered after sixty years from the yoke of the anti-Catholic Radical party (teachers, lawyers, Jews, freemasons). The new Government invokes God and gives back La Grande Chartreuse to the monks. There is hope of being delivered from universal suffrage and parliamentarism, and also from the evil and stupid domination of the teachers, who in the last war covered themselves with shame. Restoration of authority.'[7]

The Church was to be one of the mainstays of the new régime, for which Pétain, whom we have seen as a non-practising Catholic, took up the appearances of faith

Pétain, in these early days, was surrounded by men who, even if they were not card-carrying members of the *Action Française*, were among its strongest supporters, or found their political ideas strongly in sympathy with it. Alibert, who had such a great influence on the Marshal's political ideas, was a strong sympathiser. Paul Baudouin, Yves Bouthillier, Du Moulin de Labarthète, General Brécard, Henri Massis, Gillouin, and many others, were strongly marked by this movement, which even if it did not have a vast member of card-carrying members, spoke for a great part of the French traditional nationalist Right.

The Government formed on 13 July was taken from a very narrow political spectrum. There were more military men, says Paxton, in it than in any ministry since Marshal Soult's in 1832. They were: General Weygand at National Defence, General Colson at the War Ministry, Admiral Darlan as Navy Minister, and General Pujo as Air Minister. Then there was Laval as Vice-Premier (Pétain was officially, until 1942, both Head of State and Premier), and Marquet as Minister of the Interior. Baudouin remained as Foreign Minister, and Bouthillier as Finance Minister. Alibert became Minister of Justice, while Lémery became Minister for Colonies; this brought two old friends of Pétain's actually into the Government. A new Ministry, with the significant title 'Youth and the Family', was entrusted to Ybarné-garay, while Pierre Caziot had Agriculture, and Belin (the only left-winger among them), Industrial Production and Labour. François Piétri was Minister of Communications, and Émile Mireaux Minister of Public Instruction and Fine Arts.

There was an inner circle (Laval, Alibert, Baudouin, Bouthillier, Darlan, Weygand) which met every day. The rest joined them for proper Cabinet meetings about twice or three times a week.

The Marshal also had very much a personal entourage, of whom he saw more than he did his ministers. The only minister to belong to it, and to see Pétain regularly outside meetings, was Alibert, who took his meals with the Marshal. Many of the others were introduced to Pétain by Alibert, and were of the extreme Right: René Gillouin, a writer who wrote a number of his speeches, Admiral Fernet, General Brécard, and so on. Others were companions of Pétain's from Madrid: Henri Du Moulin de Labarthète, who now became head of his *cabinet civil* in place of Alibert, and had been the financial attaché in Madrid, and Major Gorostarzu, who was now in Pétain's *cabinet militaire*. Others were old friends and helpers of the Marshal: General Laure, Major Bonhomme, and Dr Ménétrel, Pétain's young doctor, who was to have over him an influence which many people saw as extremely unfortunate.

Most of his ministers, and most of his companions, were either political men of the extreme Right, or military men. In this first stage of the Vichy State, particularly, Alibert was to have enormous influence. Laval and

Marquet were disliked by the military men, and mistrusted by many of the civilians, in that neither their ideas on internal politics, nor their personalities, fitted into this group. They had both been brought into the Pétain Government late, and had almost immediately stepped into positions of great power: Laval as Deputy Premier and Marquet as Minister of the Interior. Laval was now not only Deputy Premier, but also Pétain's dauphin. How did it come that Pétain gave such power to a man who was in so many ways alien to his ideas? There was, of course, the close connexion they had had in the pre-war years, and their shared hatred of the parliamentary system of the Third Republic; yet Laval still had many characteristics of that system, and as Paxton points out, 'Laval's parliamentary past, the unmistakable odours of anti-clericalism and anti-militarism that still lingered from his "socialist" days, his *roublardise*'[8] were all calculated to arouse the dislike of the military men at Vichy. Yet even before Laval was chosen by Pétain, Reynaud had thought that Pétain's attitudes towards Daladier were intended to bring Laval into the Government. There is no doubt at all that Laval, at this stage, enjoyed Pétain's favour to a high degree; how else could this man, who had not been in any Government since 1936, have risen so high so quickly?

The answer seems to be that, as in 1939, Pétain saw Laval as the man most capable, by his experience, of treating with the Italians and Germans. His pre-war leanings towards peace and understanding with these nations might well now stand France in good stead. Pétain had chosen most of his ministers for their views on internal affairs (though Baudouin of course, as Foreign Minister, was vitally concerned with foreign policy). Laval devoted himself almost entirely to Foreign Affairs in this year 1940, and had little concern with the internal *Révolution Nationale* (indeed he openly showed his scorn for what he considered a useless exercise).

The removal of Marquet from the Government in the reshuffle on 6 September should have warned Laval of danger to himself, yet his own removal in December (with which we shall be dealing later) took him completely by surprise.

Pétain, meanwhile, became the centre of a cult which was nationwide. Everywhere he went, bells rang out joyously, and crowds waited to cheer him. Presents were ceremonially brought to him, religious images incorporating him abounded. Like a later successor of his as Head of State, he used to plunge into the crowds, shaking hands, kissing children, making a spiritual contact with his people.

For these people the National Revolution was a hope of regeneration, a rebuilding of a French State that had collapsed, and must now be built up again by suffering and effort. Let us now consider the principles of the National Revolution, before moving on to the foreign policy of the Vichy Government in 1940.

When reading Pétain's words in the war years, as before, we must not forget that most of his speeches were written for him by others; Bouthillier, Gillouin, Bergery, Massis, Caziot, Du Moulin de Labarthète, etc. But, as before, it is clear that they reflected the main lines of his own thought, and that, on the other hand, he was more than ever the mouthpiece of a traditional Right in which he had his place.

The National Revolution

Much of the atmosphere around Pétain was Maurrasian; but we must realise, when dealing with the National Revolution, that the *Action Française* was merely one aspect of a traditional Right which has run through French life under five Republics. The integral nationalism of the *Action Française* hit a chord in the men of Vichy which gained an immediate response; but one must not think that, for example, the movement's monarchism gained a similar response (except to the extent that it devolved on the figure of the Marshal). Pétain himself had never been a member of the movement, or even loosely attached to it. It was one among many of the French movements of the Right. But, over the years, it had shown a resilience matched by no other, and now, in the war years, it came to stand for the ideas of that eternal Right which now emerged into the full light of day.

This Right, as we have seen in our pre-war study of Pétain's political ideas, was far wider in scope than any one movement could be; indeed, some of its strongest adherents firmly believed themselves to be entirely non-political. It rested on certain strong hatreds and fears, and certain simple principles: the family, the land, duty, order, patriotism. On this simple basis, however, other more complicated ideas grew up in certain areas of this trend, regionalism, corporatism, and so on. Among the intellectual forebears of the National Revolution must be placed de Maistre, Bonald, Blanc de Saint-Bonnet, Donoso-Cortès, and Le Play, together with the more recent influence of Barrès, Maurras and Péguy.[9]

Alibert had been Pétain's political mentor, and it was he who was the moving force behind the National Revolution. In the ideas he put forward on the social organisation of the State there was much influence of Le Play's corporatism. The term 'National Revolution' was first used in this context in the *Exposé des motifs du projet de loi constitutionnelle* which Laval read out to the deputies on 8 July (though there was a work written by Georges Valois in the 'twenties, entitled *La Révolution Nationale*, which contained some of the features of eventual Vichy policy). This *exposé des motifs* was written by Alibert, and contains the broad lines of the new policy. (It must, however, be noted that a note written to Pétain by Weygand as early as 28 June had pointed out the main lines of the reforms that should be brought about—education, support of the family, work, and even worker-employer collaboration.)[10]

It started by saying that the lessons of the last battles must be learned, and the guilty punished. (The search for scapegoats, which was to culminate in the Riom trials, was already being demanded, and on the 9th, Tixier-Vignancour was to press for a vote on a motion demanding that those responsible for the defeat should be sought out and punished.) But the country should not confine itself to useless regrets. France must be reborn. 'It is in military defeat and internal disorder that other countries have gained the force to live once more, and to transform themselves. At the most cruel moment in her history, France must understand and accept the necessity for a national revolution. She must see in it the condition for her immediate safety, and a pledge for the future.'[11]

Everyone must give themselves up entirely, with an ardent faith, to this venture, the exposé went on. It was for this reason that the parliamentarians, who must all be aware of the faults in the system, were being asked to change it. What was needed now was a Government with power to decide, undertake and negotiate, to save what needed to be saved, destroy what needed to be destroyed, construct all that needed to be constructed. It was for this that they were being asked to put their confidence in the Marshal.

The main lines of reform were to be:

GOVERNMENT: sovereignty of the State, and independence of the Executive, to be restored. Legitimate authority was to be freed from the pressures of oligarchies. Continuity of Government, assisted by a 'national representation' in the form of assemblies. (No indication is given of the methods of choice of representatives, or of their powers.) A policy of firmness combined with a respect of the 'necessary liberties'.

ADMINISTRATION: a modern, simple basis for the administrative and judiciary institutions of the country. An impartial arbitration of the interests of all Frenchmen. Strict economy of public expense.

EDUCATION: 'National education and the formation of the young will be among the greatest of our cares. Conscious of the mortal dangers which the intellectual and moral perversions of certain people made the country run in a decisive hour, the state will favour with all its power institutions which will develop the birth-rate and protect the family.'[12]

SOCIAL GROUPS: 'The Government well knows, moreover, that the social groups: family, profession, communes, regions, exist before the State, which is merely the political organ of national *rassemblement* and unity. The State must therefore not interfere with the legitimate activities of these groups, but it will subordinate them to the general interest and the common good; it will control them, and arbitrate between them.'[13]

ECONOMY: A completely new orientation. 'Integrated into the continental system of production and exchange, France will become once more above all an agricultural and peasant country, and its industry will have to find once more its traditions of quality.'[14] The present economic disorder must be replaced by a rational organisation of production, and of corporative institutions.

THE SOCIAL ORDER: A new social order must be produced. Employers and employees have an equal right to find, in the enterprise they both belong to, the means to ensure a worthy life for themselves and their family. The social organisation will ensure a juster sharing of the profits, by getting rid of the dictatorship of money and plutocracy, and misery and unemployment.

THE HIERARCHY OF VALUES: This must be restored. Everyone must be put where he will serve the country the best. 'One sole aristocracy will be recognised: intelligence; one sole merit: work.'

On this basis most of the National Revolution's doctrine was to be built. The exposé aroused immediate enthusiasm in many who heard it. Claudel wrote in his diary on the 9th: 'In the *exposé des motifs* one recognises the evil that has been done by education without God. It is the entire University, the work of Napoleon, which must be f . . . . d to the ground.'[15]

The mood in which this call to reconstruction came was one of sacrifice, of the necessity to expiate past sins. Before the war, in 1938, Pétain had already drawn attention to France's descent since 1918, and had found the cause to be as follows: 'The French, forgetting that the greatness of a country is made of the sum of personal efforts, let themselves be dragged away towards enjoyments and material appetites. The unity which had been created in the face of danger evaporated in well-being, and everyone took on again his egoistical habits of peacetime.'[16]

This lesson was repeated by Pétain in the moment of France's defeat, in his speech of 17 June: 'We will learn the lesson of our lost battles. Since the victory, the spirit of enjoyment has been stronger than the spirit of sacrifice. People have demanded things, rather than serving. People have wished to be sparing in their efforts; and today we encounter misfortune.'[17]

This call to a communal *mea culpa* comes again and again in his speeches at this time, becoming linked with the need for a moral and spiritual renaissance. France would revive through suffering and effort. Pétain had said of Poland in 1920 that a defeat and occupation by the Russians might help them to set their own affairs to rights.* He obviously felt the same thing about France and the defeat of 1940.

The policies of the National Revolution were based upon a reaction against all that had been wrong with society. The new education stemmed from hatred of the old; the return to the land, the new social order, and the corporative policy stemmed from a hatred of bourgeois capitalism, of the class struggles inherent in it, of socialism and of egalitarianism.

The falseness of the education given to the young under the Third Republic had been criticised strongly before the war by Pétain, Weygand and others. Pétain now returned to the attack: 'There was, at the basis of our educational system, a profound illusion: that of believing that all that is needed is to instruct minds in order to form hearts and make characters. There is nothing more false or more dangerous than this idea.'[18] What was needed, he said, was discipline and family influence. Individualism, too, was dangerous (how many echoes there are in all this of the teachings of Maurras, and of other right-wingers of the 1870–1914 period!). The individual only exists through the family, society, the fatherland. It was individualism that had caused the French defeat. What should be taught in French schools was respect for the human person, for the family, for society, for one's country. Neutrality was

* See page 165.

out of the question. One could not be neutral about 'truth and falsehood, good and evil, health and sickness, order and disorder, France and anti-France.'[19] The French school should be national above all, to 'rebuild the House of France on the unshakeable rock of French unity.'

On the details of the new education, Pétain was convinced that it should give up its 'purely bookish' character, and have a reality linked with the work going on around it. There should be co-operation between scholars and industry. At the primary level, work should be less theoretical, and more space should be given to manual work, both for its educative and social value. Élites of all kinds should be formed. Everything should be aimed at making Frenchmen who had a taste for work and a love of effort. There should be an encouragement of initiative and leadership. Part of the way to do this was to encourage sports and physical culture, but also to encourage workmanship.

The organisation of youth under the Vichy régime very much followed this pattern. The outdoor life was encouraged, sportsmen and musicians (e.g., Borotra and Cortot) wrote articles encouraging physical exercise, or the educative nature of singing (as a form of work in common, encouraging young people to give up individualism). For a time, the organiser of youth movements was the writer Henri Massis, who had for years been a follower of Maurras.

We have seen how closely Pétain had, before the war, connected the military life and education. His theories were now to be put into effect by a new experiment, the *Chantiers de la Jeunesse*, which was formed to give young people a semi-military training for eight months at the age of twenty. Feeling that the military virtues should be inculcated to those outside the army, especially now that there was no military service, and now that the army had been so drastically reduced in numbers, the Government set up in July 1940 these work camps for the youth of the country, under the direction of General de la Porte du Theil. They were to remain entirely in military hands throughout their existence, and had military discipline, ranks, and ceremonial.

General Niessel, in the *Revue des Deux Mondes* on 15 December 1941, described the *Chantiers de la Jeunesse* as fulfilling the need 'to fight against the selfishness of individualism, and to revive the spirit of duty.'[20] General de la Porte du Theil himself, in his manual for the movement, described its aim as being an educational mission, on the national level: 'The aim is to give to the young men of France, with all classes mixed together, a complement of moral, virile and professional training, which will make leaders out of the best qualified, and will make healthy, honest men out of all, in communion in the fervour of the same national faith.'[21]

This combination of physical and moral education was to be found, too, in the leadership schools formed by General de Lattre de Tassigny, in which national pride and social responsibility were taught, with an emphasis on team-spirit.

Work, the Family, the Fatherland (*Travail, Famille, Patrie*), these were the principles upon which the new State must exist. But what were the details by which these principles were to be put into effect?

To the extreme Right as well as to the extreme Left, the bourgeois capitalist society created by the nineteenth century had been anathema, and each had reacted against it in a different way. The traditional Right's reaction had been a spiritual return to a perfect society which must have existed before this time; a society where everyone knew their place in the social hierarchy, where employer and employee worked together in perfect harmony without a hint of a class struggle, and where the traditional values of a fixed social order were observed. They believed that they found traces of that perfect society in the peasantry, who had not been corrupted by the life of the cities. In the new Vichy State, a 'back to the land' policy was inevitable. For the land, the soil, was also the living embodiment, the 'real presence', of *la Patrie*. Pétain's decision to stay in France had had a great deal to do with a belief in the close relationship between *la Patrie* and its own soil, a relationship which would be broken by a Government which fled abroad.

Alibert's *exposé des motifs* had expressed this need to get back to the land, but had placed it in the context of a 'continental system of production and exchange' formed by Hitler's New Europe, in which France would do what she was best at, i.e., agriculture. The exposé gave away the emotional content of this concept, however, when it referred to France once more becoming a 'peasant' country.

Typical of Vichy's concern with the land was the new publication of such works as Olivier de Serres's sixteenth-century *Le Théâtre d'agriculture et mesnage des champs*, which appeared in a filleted form in 1941, with a preface by Pétain himself. In this preface Pétain praised the peasant, thanks to whom France might be revived: 'Does not France find herself at this moment in one of those difficult periods, of which she has already known so many, and from which she has always succeeded in emerging, thanks to the qualities of her people, and above all of her peasantry?' Agriculture was one of the most important facets of French life, he went on: 'As in the time of Olivier de Serres, a healthy understanding of present necessities encourages us to replace agriculture in the first rank of the diverse branches of national activity.'

Bound up with all this was the necessity for work, he continued: 'You will find gathered together in this book all the great principles which must guide the good cultivator, without forgetting the notion of "Diligence": "Our farmer should not think of becoming rich by speeches, or of making his fortune with his arms folded." The French peasant has always been inspired by this precept, which ought to be pondered on by all those who wish to return to the land, or who have left it for less hard tasks. . .' This book, says Pétain, ought to be on the shelves of all the 'rural libraries' he hoped to form in every village school. 'Every rural schoolmaster will frequently be able to choose in it a subject for reading which will be of great profit to the young peasants.'[22]

Pétain's admiration for the French peasant had been expressed before the war in articles and speeches, and continued to take a large part in his utterances now. He took pride in his own peasant origin (just as Laval stressed his own Auvergnat peasant character). In the course of lectures, 'The Fresco of French Pride', given by de Lattre de Tassigny at this time (and written by Robert Garric), there was only one lecture which contained anything about events since the French Revolution. It was entitled 'The Great Peasants of France', and contained the following figures: Jeanne d'Arc, St Vincent de Paul, Mgr Affre, Joffre, Clemenceau and Pétain.[23]

Intimately bound up with this question of the land was that of regionalism. It was a tradition of right-wing nationalism (Barrès, Maurras) that was closely connected with the desire for decentralisation. The French Republic had always been immensely centralised, based on Paris. Now, with the Vichy Government at any rate barred from Paris, the move towards the re-creation of the old provinces of France began. In his speech on 11 July Pétain said: 'Governors will be placed at the head of the great French provinces. Thus, the administration will be concentrated and at the same time decentralised.'[24] On 13 November he declared his plan to be to divide France into 20 regions, each grouping 3, 4 or 5 departments. There would be a governor over each.

The reaction against the industrial society did not only contain a return to the land. It also involved a return to the principles of good, skilled work as opposed to mass production. The *exposé des motifs* had spoken of a return to 'traditions of quality' in industry. The idea of the 'artisan' of the old type, who did a good piece of work and was proud of it, and for whom a strike would have been a *contre-sens*, had always been an important figure in right-wing mythology, and now once more he came to the fore.

The social organisation of workers and employers, in the Vichy ideal State, owed much to such theorists as Le Play. It was based on a mistrust of those two products of the industrial age: international capitalism, and socialism. In his speech of 11 July Pétain said:

'The Work of Frenchmen is the supreme resource of the Fatherland. It must be sacred. International capitalism, and international socialism, which exploited and degraded it, are part of the pre-war years. They were all the more fatal in that, while opposing each other on the surface, they looked after each other in secret. We will not put up with their murky alliance. We will suppress the dissensions in the city. We will not let them into the factories and farms.'[25]

The *régime des partis* at Government level, the parties being merely 'political trade unions', had encouraged the discord in the relationships between management and workers.[26] Everyone had been at fault, demanding things for themselves rather than for the community as a whole. Workers, technicians, employers, all were to blame. Their egotism had produced, among other things, the misery of the industrial worker.

The other great fault with the economy was caused by free enterprise. Pre-war experience had shown that the liberal economy had failed; on the one hand, stocks of necessities which had to be destroyed; on the other, millions of people lacking these very necessities. The Vichy policy must try to set these problems right.[27]

The economic situation must be solved by organisation and control. 'The State's co-ordination of private activities must break the power of trusts, and their power of corruption. Far from destroying individual initiative, the economy must liberate it from its present bonds by subordinating it to the national interest.'[28] The currency must be at the service of society.

There must therefore be strong control of the currency: on the international plane, control of exports and imports. 'On the internal plane, a vigilant control of consumption and prices, in order to maintain the currency's buying power, to prevent excessive spending, and to bring more justice into the sharing of products. This system makes no attack on the liberties of the individual, except to the liberty of those who speculate, whether for personal interest, or for political interest. It is a system conceived entirely from the national interest.'[29] The system must be put into effect with rigour. The working class and the bourgeoisie must together make a great effort to throw off the routines of laziness, and become conscious of their common interest as citizens of a henceforth united country. Among other policies, the Frenchman must be guaranteed work by provision of public works to avoid unemployment.

The speech in which this system was put forward was in fact written by Gaston Bergery, who had decided to leave Vichy that October, and had produced the text as an example of what he thought Vichy should be doing. Pétain, according to Du Moulin de Labarthète, was very impressed by it, and said that it contained what he had always felt, and that he must read it on the wireless. Bergery and a small group worked on the text together, making it sound more like the Marshal (the passages on foreign policy, which we will discuss later, did not please Laval, who demanded that the speech should not be made; nevertheless, Pétain made it). In the detail of these economic theories, as with much of National Revolution doctrine, one can see that they were the work of an expert rather than of the Marshal himself; but the aims to which these details added up were clearly in accordance with his thought. The policy of economic control was favoured by the *dirigistes* at Vichy, who were for the most part former members of the X-Crise group, founded in 1930. Their doctrine of State intervention in the national economy was to reach its greatest hopes at the time of Darlan's deputy premiership, from February 1941 onwards, when men like Pucheu came into prominence in the national life.

This then was the economic solution which Vichy favoured (though, as external affairs took on more and more importance, it was, like other National Revolution desires, never fully put into effect). What, however, of the important social problem of the relations between employers and workers?

Here the proposed solution was one which went right back to the grass-roots of the French Right: an idea which is central to Le Play's social doctrine, and which had since been taken up by such thinkers as La Tour du Pin, Barrès, and Péguy. This was the paternalist concept whereby the class war could be prevented by the creation of corporations, or trade unions, which would contain both employer and employed, working in conditions of harmony for the common good. (France seems today to have returned to this paternalist conception with its new policy of 'participation'.)

This policy was put forward at its fullest in a speech Pétain made at Saint-Étienne on 1 March 1941. (It was at this time, under the Corporatists in the new Darlan Government, that this policy was properly attempted.) In it he suggested that the only way to improve the lot of the worker, and bring social justice and peace, was to reform society. This the State could not do by laws; it had to restrict itself to sanctioning the social order after men had created it. But it *could* help men towards a proper solution, by indicating to them principles and a direction for action, and by stimulating initiatives. 'In reality', he said, 'the causes of the class war can only be suppressed if the proletariat, which today lives bowed down in its solitude, finds in a community of work the conditions for a worthy, free life, and reasons to live and hope. This community is the enterprise itself. Only its transformation can form a basis for the organised profession which is itself a community of communities.' There was an élite of men, among both the employers, the skilled and the unskilled workers, who might be able to bring about this change, and it was to them that Pétain was appealing.

The main thing he asked for was for them 'to be filled with the doctrine of the common good over and above personal interest. To instruct themselves in the methods of organisation of work capable of permitting better production and at the same time, more justice, by giving everyone his chance in the enterprise and in the profession.' What was important was to create the organisms whereby everyone could get together to discuss the problems, 'to defend their legitimate interests, and to express their needs and aspirations.' The separation of employers and trade unions, which had created the class struggle, would thus be overcome. 'This will be the object of our first law on professional organisation. It in fact limits itself to creating simple organisations which will not be class organisations, but social committees in which employers, skilled and unskilled workers will together seek the solutions to the present problems in a common desire for justice, and in the constant care of lessening, by mutual aid, the miseries and the anguish of the hour.'[30]

It must not be thought that such a system in any way rested on the idea of equality among men. In the true tradition of the French Right (Rivarol, Bonald, Blanc de Saint-Bonnet, Bourget, Péguy, etc.), the Vichy Government abhorred 'the false idea of a natural equality among men.'[31] The new régime, said Pétain, was to be a 'social hierarchy'. It would not rely on 'natural equality', but on equality of opportunity to show that one could serve the State. (As the reader will notice, this is different from 'liberty of opportunity' as we know it.) 'Only work and talent', he went on, 'will become once more the foundation of the French hierarchy. No unfavourable prejudice will touch a Frenchman because of his social origin, so long as he integrates himself in the new France, and brings it support without reserves. . . Thus the true élites will be reborn, which the last régime spent years in destroying, and which will form the ranks necessary to the development of the well-being and dignity of all.'[32]

To the idea of hierarchy is joined that other idea dear to the French Right, order. As with so many thinkers, Catholic and non-Catholic, this implied liberty within order, which was so much more satisfying than the constrictions of independence. (See writers from Rivarol to Claudel.) The new régime was to be 'hierarchical and authoritarian', but, said Pétain, let no one fear that they were losing their hard-won liberty. 'Authority is essential to safeguard the liberty of the State, the guarantee of individual liberty in face of coalitions of particular interests. A people is no longer free, despite its voting papers, as soon as a Government which it has freely brought into power becomes the prisoner of such coalitions. What, moreover, would liberty—abstract liberty—mean in 1940 to an unemployed worker or a ruined small employer, except the liberty to suffer helplessly amid a vanquished nation. We will only be losing some of the deceiving appearances of liberty, in order to save its substance. History is made up of alternate periods of authority degenerating into tyranny, and of liberty leading to licentiousness. The hour has come for France to substitute for these dreadful alternatives a harmonious conjunction of authority and liberty.'[33]

The social and political ideas of the National Revolution, as set out in Pétain's speeches and articles, are part of a continuing tradition of the Right, containing as they do the concepts of work, the family, the land, the peasant, hierarchy, and order, together with the idealist concept of a State in which all people might work together for the common good. The detailed social ideas are close to much that has been put forward in recent years in France: regionalism, participation, and the control of prices and incomes. In the 1940 context the main lines of this policy were doomed to failure, particularly as the Germans, as we shall see later, did all in their power to stop it; and immediately after the war, some of the more acceptable parts of the policies, by the mere fact of having been part of the National Revolution were rendered unacceptable. Now that some of the detailed measures are going forward, we will be able to see what measure of success they are likely to have, and whether, because of the conservative and paternalist nature of such an idea as 'participation', such ideas will ever be acceptable to the French public as a whole, relying as they do on an ideal picture of men's relation to each other in society.

While so much of this social policy rested on an ideal, albeit an ideal of the Right, the nature of the society at Vichy meant that certain other, less palatable attitudes of the Right took root there as well. These included the unreasoning hatreds of freemasons, foreigners and Jews, which were such a feature of right-wing thought in the Third Republic.

M. René Gillouin has described to me the strongly anti-semitic atmosphere at Vichy in this year. To the strong anti-semitism of those affected by the *Action Française* was added the ingrained anti-semitism of the military. Pétain himself does not seem to have felt strongly about this matter; but as M. Gillouin put it to me: 'He was not anti-semitic; but, like most French military men, he was not anti-anti-semitic.'[34] And he was surrounded with people like Dr Ménétrel, who had strong feelings in this direction.

Pétain appears to have had little concern for the Jews as such, but to have had a lot of concern for Jewish ex-service men, alongside whom he had fought in the First World War. His distinction between French and non-French Jews, and between ordinary Jews and ex-service Jews, seem to show that for him patriotism and comradeship of arms made them worth fighting for, even if the others had to go in the process.

The Jewish laws passed in Free Zone were, it is true, less drastic than those made in the Occupied Zone by the Germans; and there was never any question at this stage of French laws of deportation or extermination, which would have been repugnant to all but the most fanatical of French anti-semites. But the laws put forward in late 1940 showed that French anti-semitic, anti-freemason, and anti-foreigner attitudes were now coming into their own. On 12 July and 17 July anyone not of French parenthood was barred from being a public functionary. (Exceptions were made for *anciens combattants*.) On 22 July a law ordered the revision of all naturalisations since 1927. On 13 August all secret societies were forbidden, particularly freemasonry. On 27 August the law forbidding anti-semitism in the Press was abrogated. On 3 October the *Statut des Juifs* kept the Jews out of most public employment, including the army, and a great deal of private employment. On 4 October a special police organisation was set up to deal with foreign Jews, Algerian Jews lost their citizenship, and the question of internment camps was raised.

As Léon Poliakov points out in a document he produced for the Eichmann trial,[35] in the Free Zone the authorities set about disorganisation of the Jews at this time, but not about wilful destruction such as the Germans were already setting on foot in the Occupied Zone. There, after the *Erste Verordnung* of 27 September, in which all Jews were registered (160,000 of which 140,000 were in the Paris area), a *Zweite Verordnung* on 18 October declared 'Economic aryanisation', i.e., the dispossession and ruin of the Jews, with their enterprises being taken over by provisional administrators. This was, Poliakov points out, easier said than done, in that French opinion made it difficult; progress was slow.

At the beginning of 1941, the Vichy Government agreed to the German suggestion of a *Commissariat Général aux Questions Juives*. The Germans needed a French organisation to help through the unpopular anti-semitic measures; the French needed to keep an eye on, and keep some control over, the German 'aryanisations'. 'In this way', says Poliakov, 'agreement was reached'. We shall see more of these questions later.

Let it be said now, however, that during the more serious Jewish measures taken later in the war by the Germans, the attitude of Vichy (and particularly

Laval) meant, not that the measures were stopped (which would have been impossible), but that they were modified and slowed down to such an extent that France's percentage of Jewish deaths is lower than that of any other occupied country.

The difference between the National Revolution and National Socialism

Nothing could have been further from fascism, whether of the Italian or German variety, than the National Revolution. And this Abetz, the German Ambassador in Paris, saw clearly. He was a Nazi who still believed the social ideas on which the movement had been founded, and who deplored the reactionary, hierarchical principles of Vichy. He also saw, in them, a nationalism which was dangerous to the European concept of the New Order, and which was, indeed, dangerous to the German cause in the war as well.

On 8 October 1940 he wrote to Ribbentrop: 'From talks with members of the Cabinet, and information received from informers, it emerges that at the present moment the French Government have adopted, by a strong majority, an anti-parliamentary, anti-British, and anti-Semitic attitude. Some ministers, such as Alibert, Baudouin and Bouthillier, are hoping for an eventual restoration of the Bourbons.'

After giving some examples of their anti-communist and anti-semitic actions, he went on: 'In this internal political action, the French Government has the greatest support with the army and the clergy, of whom the majority are however opposed to the policy of Franco-German collaboration, towards which the Government is tending, and are advising it to adopt a simple attitude of *attentisme*.'*

On the other hand, certain elements in the opposition, such as Déat, Flandin, Doriot, Marquet and Faure, are only adversaries of the Government on internal politics, and approve its programme for external politics.

Abetz then touched on the National Revolution. 'The plan concerning the return to the land of the town workers', he wrote, 'a plan elaborated by the Government of Marshal Pétain, is very theoretical and would need years to obtain a practical success. From the German point of view, it is obviously undesirable that France should suddenly become a solely agricultural nation, because, by all traditions, the natural counterweight to the chauvinist tendencies in France lies in the proletariat, and a return to the land by all the French people, without exception, might have as its results a strengthening of our Western neighbour from the biological point of view.'[36]

In December another of Abetz's reports to Ribbentrop warned him that Vichy was dominated above all by rich bourgeois and generals, without roots in the mass of the people (as was true also of the few intellectuals in the Government). They were, he said, trying to set up a military dictatorship, helped by the prestige of the victor of Verdun, and with the willing aid of the Church.[37] He felt that only Laval and Darlan were capable of combining the traditional French anti-clerical liberalism with a modern social policy, in such a way as to keep Communism from monopolising all

* 'Waiting and seeing', until the opportunity came to oppose Germany once more.

the popular opposition to the old-fashioned Vichy reactionaries. In other words, Abetz felt that the 'new order' of Fascism had a popular appeal which could vie with Communism, while the 'old order' of Vichy did not.

Abetz strongly encouraged the French fascists of Paris—Doriot, Déat, Brinon, Luchaire, etc.—in their opposition to Vichy, particularly after Pétain's dismissal of Laval, whom Abetz saw as an ally, in December 1940. In a telegram to Ribbentrop in February 1941, Abetz declared that French public opinion was 'against the reactionary activities of the Vichy Government', and told Ribbentrop of the creation of a new *Rassemblement National Populaire*: 'This movement, directed against the reactionary tendencies of Vichy, announces as the principal points of its programme collaboration with Germany and the setting-up of a social and national revolution.'[38]

Some of the reasons for the failure of the policies of Vichy's National Revolution were caused by positive sabotage on the part of Abetz. In a report written on 23 June 1941, he categorically stated to Ribbentrop that 'the German embassy is supporting all forms of internal politics which bar the road to a lasting instalment of the Vichy military dictatorship.'[39] He went on to declare that it was thanks to this policy that it was possible to prevent the setting-up, which had been attempted by the French Government, of 'single national fronts in the unions, the rural and artisan professions, the *anciens combattants* organisations, the youth movements and political groups', so that now, in each of these domains, there were several tendencies which were fighting amongst themselves.

Abetz's policy was based partly on a dislike of reactionary political doctrines, but partly also on a fear of the nationalist tendencies inherent in such doctrines, which would serve Germany ill in its control of France and in its conduct of the war, and would also hinder the creation of the 'new order' Europe which he so heartily desired. It must not be forgotten that Abetz was, and for years had been, a Francophile, and that his vision of Europe contained a lasting Franco-German friendship. This vision was not necessarily shared by the majority of his compatriots. But Abetz was, at this time, in a particularly privileged position.

In furtherance of his designs Abetz saw Laval as one of his greatest counters; and this fact was to be of great importance in the crisis which took place at the time of Laval's dismissal by Pétain in December.

Foreign policy

Laval was not particularly interested in the National Revolution. If he thought of it at all, it was with contempt. In a Government which, after the ministerial shuffle of 6 September, consisted almost entirely of non-parliamentarians, most of whom had been chosen for their adherence to principles more or less in accordance with those of Pétain's internal policy, Laval stands out like a sore thumb (as, to a lesser extent, does Admiral Darlan, whose political complexion, and political contacts before the War, when he had been known as an 'admiral of the ante-chambers', had been quite different from what those of Vichy now turned out to be).

Darlan's continued presence in the Government was understandable; as commander of the nation's strongest (and only undefeated) force, he was of major importance, especially as the navy was now one of France's strongest trump cards with the Germans. But how did Laval, who was hated by most of the rest of the Government, and had so little in common with them, remain in the strong position as Deputy Premier, and as Pétain's dauphin?

The answer is that Pétain kept him there. Not because of any attitude Laval might have towards internal politics, but because of Pétain's trust in him as a diplomatist, and particularly as a man with experience of negotiating with the Germans and Italians. Laval's great reputation, in the 'thirties, had been made as Foreign Minister. We have seen his popularity in the 1934–5 referendum in *Le Petit Journal*, on this basis; we have seen, too, Pétain trying to persuade Daladier to make Laval Foreign Minister in his 1939 Government, and the feeling which both Laval and Pétain had had at that time, that with a Government in which they both had a place, relations with Italy would be restored, and a reversal of alliances perhaps occur.

Now, in the French defeat, Pétain appears to have seen Laval as the one man capable of negotiating with Germany and Italy on favourable terms. Laval's dismissal in December has been interpreted by some as meaning that Pétain disapproved of his basic policy; but the real reasons appear to have been different; a realisation that Laval's negotiations were not leading to any significant relaxation on the part of the Germans, together with a fear that Laval might attempt to take the Marshal's power from him.

The atmosphere at Vichy in June and July was decidely anti-British. Emmanuel Berl, in *La Fin de la IIIe République*,[40] has described the strength of these feelings even before the armistice. After the armistice, the British attack on the French navy at Mers-el-Kebir on 2 July added strongly to these feelings. Darlan, in particular, saw this as a personal insult, as his word had been doubted. He had assured the British that his fleet would never fall into the hands of the Germans (and the scuttling of the French fleet when the Germans marched into the Unoccupied Zone in November 1942 shows that he had been speaking the truth); and yet here were France's former allies committing aggression on her. To the natural Anglophobia of any French naval man was now added this strong grievance; and for any understanding of Darlan's future actions, and of the attitudes of the Germans in relation to him, this must be taken into account.

Anglophobia did not, however, for most of the French Government mean Germanophilia. Abetz's reports have shown us how much he feared the nationalism of the Vichy régime, and the fact that it might eventually turn on Germany.

At the moment, however, *attentisme* was not the main feature of Vichy, as it was to become. In 1940 it looked as though Germany had won, or was about to win, the war. The attitude of Pétain and Laval appears to have been that it was important to get as many concessions out of Germany as possible.

For this purpose Laval, with Pétain's approval, took over most of the powers of the actual Foreign Minister, Paul Baudouin. Laval's main German contact was Otto Abetz, who had been in France before the war, and had known many prominent Frenchmen, before being expelled from the country for spying. Abetz was at this point a representative of Ribbentrop's in France, but was soon promoted to ambassadorial rank.

Laval's negotiations in the months of July and August were, however, of little avail. The French might well offer co-operation, or collaboration, with the Germans in return for various concessions; Hitler mistrusted French intentions, and also had various plans for French territories, in relation among other things to Italian claims. The pattern of attempted negotiations was already forming, whereby Germany was eventually to lose any French co-operation by its refusal of concessions, as Abetz was later wearily to point out.

On 6 September, important Cabinet changes took place, in which Pétain removed all former parliamentarians, except Laval. Weygand, too, was removed, and sent to North Africa as Pétain's representative.

What were the reasons for these changes? Suggestions have been made that they were intended to cut out pro-German influences; but Weygand's removal ill accords with this. The most probable causes have little to do with pro- or anti-German feeling. One is that Pétain, concerned with internal politics rather than German relations, wished to get rid of parliamentarians (of whom he had such a strong dislike), and especially of people like Marquet, whose opinions might be regarded as inimical to the National Revolution. The other probable cause was a growing impatience with Laval whose only virtue in his eyes had been as a negotiator with the Germans, and who had been making so little progress in that task; besides which, Pétain was already regretting having given Laval so much power, and fearing that he might wish to get more. The removals from the Cabinet, and particularly the removal of Marquet, had left Laval without allies. Laval had failed in an attempt to get the Ministry of the Interior put under himself, now that his friend, Marquet, was no longer to hold it. And the new Minister, Peyrouton, who took over from Marquet, was one of those instrumental eventually in getting rid of Laval. Without a friend at the Ministry of the Interior, Laval was in a precarious situation. Only three days after the changes, Pétain was suggesting that the Act whereby Laval had been made dauphin should be repealed, and the choice of his successor thrown before the Cabinet.[40] This was opposed by Laval, of course. At this stage Pétain did not insist.

Pétain may well have kept Laval in the Government because he hoped Laval might still have a hope of getting something out of the Germans; but he had safeguarded himself within the Cabinet against any attempt by Laval to usurp further powers, and had made it possible for himself to remove Laval if it came to the crunch. This, and the desire to have around him men who actively supported the National Revolution, seem the most probable reasons for the changes.

Pétain now set about his own attempt to negotiate with the Germans. He got one of his staff, an air ace of the First World War called Colonel Fonck, to get in touch with Göring for him, to try to arrange a meeting between himself and Hitler. (It is interesting to see how Pétain believed in a military contact, between brother-officers in the international spirit of the comradeship of arms, while Laval did most of his negotiations through civilians.) This attempt he tried to keep secret from Laval. It had, at first, as little result as Laval's attempts to negotiate.

Why did Pétain start this attempt? Certainly not to contradict Laval's views, whatever pro-Pétain writers may have claimed. The eventual Montoire interview shows that Pétain was essentially following the same line as Laval, as do his statements to the Germans after Laval's dismissal. Pétain seems merely to have been applying another, more direct approach, through military channels, to try to get through to the Germans.

Though none of these approaches at first seemed to have much effect, gradually the Germans were coming to realise that they had further need of France than what they had already gained from the armistice. The armistice had, originally, put out of action the French fleet and the French empire; as such, it had fulfilled all German requirements of the time. But as the Free French forces run by de Gaulle in London became more powerful, and as some of the French African territories (Equatorial Africa, Tchad, Cameroun) began to split off, it became clear that the second of these two requirements was not being fulfilled. The French must be encouraged to be prepared to defend their colonial territories.

Preliminary minor breakthroughs on the diplomatic front appear to have been made by General Huntziger, at the Armistice Commission, and Laval, with Abetz. Then, on 11 October, Pétain made the important major speech about Vichy affairs which we have already discussed in relation to internal matters. Written by Bergery, it nevertheless seems to have reflected the Marshal's own thought (and that of his closest collaborators) on the matter of Franco-German relations.

This speech apparently annoyed Laval. Why, it is hard to see. Laval was not interested in the National Revolution, so the internal part can hardly have moved him. As for the part on foreign affairs, it appears in many respects to have reflected Laval's own thought. One is left with the impression that Laval was annoyed that the Marshal spoke on foreign affairs without consulting him, and that he resented a personal intervention of the Marshal in these matters.

In this speech, Pétain spoke of France's preparedness to seek collaboration in all fields with her neighbours. He referred to the criminal neglect of Franco-German relations in the past, and the importance of these relations in the future. Germany could decide between 'a traditional peace of oppression and a new peace of collaboration.' In the second case, this would depend as much on the defeated as on the victor.[41]

It may well have been this speech that decided Hitler to negotiate directly with Pétain. Later in the month, on the way to have talks with Franco, he arranged personal meetings with Laval, on the 22nd, and Pétain on the 24th. Both these meetings took place in the little village of Montoire.

Much ink has flowed about the Montoire meetings, and much of what it has recorded has been contradictory. Those who have wished to defend Pétain have shown him spurning, in a dignified manner, the Führer's most extreme demands. Those who have wished to condemn him have shown him cravenly giving in to all that was asked of him. The truth lies between the two, as far as we can gather it from the closest contemporary accounts.

At the Laval-Hitler meeting, the Führer made it clear that Germany was going to win the war, and that France must see where her best interests lay. He mingled threats and promises in a general kind of way. Among other things, however, he stated that if all went well, France need not lose any of her possessions in Africa, even though Italy, Germany and Spain had claims which must also be settled there. That is, England's defeat and the redistribution of her colonies would solve this particular problem.

Hitler then went on to see Franco, having arranged to meet Pétain on his return. At Hendaye he had little joy. Franco hedged in an expert manner when asked to commit himself to the Axis cause. He had offered to join the Nazis in June, when he thought the war was won and that he would get French territory; and then the Germans had not shown much interest. Now the situation was quite different, and Franco was concerned not to involve himself.

While Hitler was away, Laval returned to Vichy, and told Pétain of the proposed meeting. Pétain, despite his secret attempts via Fonck and others to achieve this very result,* pretended to be worried at having to meet Hitler. At a Cabinet discussion on the matter, Laval tried to get all the ministers to agree to Hitler's offers. These offers had been so vague, however, that it was impossible to know whether they involved actual entry into the war on Germany's side, or merely collaboration of other kinds, including continued defence of the colonies. Baudouin shows us a Pétain determined not to give in on the first of these points.[42] France would not enter the war on the German side.

At the Hitler-Pétain meeting on the 24th (at which Laval was also present), it was made clear that France wanted co-operation with Germany, but that Pétain and Laval were unprepared to define this co-operation. Everything would be done to defend the French colonial territories against any invader; but any further commitment at this time would have to take account of public opinion, and a definite series of conditions might even damage the Franco-German relationship. Laval then pointed out that Pétain was constitutionally unable to declare war without referring the matter to the Assemblies, but suggested that France could collaborate effectively without taking this step, by offering resistance in the colonies.

The talks, therefore, merely ended with a general statement on the

---

* Abetz, in a report to Ribbentrop of 8 October 1940, mentions that Pétain had got in touch with him again to try and arrange an interview.

mutual desire for collaboration, with details to be settled as the cases occurred. Both sides appear to have been satisfied with this: Hitler may not have got France's entry into the war (which it is not at all certain that he even hoped for), but he had been assured that she would defend her colonies. This cleared up one important issue, and might neutralise the French empire once more, as had been decided by the armistice. Pétain and Laval got general assurances of German goodwill, which looked as though they might lead to positive concessions and advantages.

Much has been made of certain negotiations which were being carried on in London in this same month of October. Professor Louis Rougier, who was at London, certainly had interviews with Churchill; on this basis many writers, including Robert Aron in his *Histoire de Vichy*, have built a theory whereby Pétain, in secret agreement with Churchill on the future of the war, was playing for time with Hitler at Montoire. Added to this theory, there comes the picture of Pétain and Laval completely at odds on foreign policy, which was to lead to Laval's dismissal in December. The second of these theories we shall see to be on the whole untrue when we come to Laval's dismissal; the first has been dismissed by several writers, including Warner. Dismissed, that is, as to its importance in relation to Montoire; Rougier never made any agreement with the British. He does, however, appear to have spoken to Churchill as a man of Vichy; and Churchill in *Their Finest Hour*, describes him as 'a certain M. Rougier, who represented himself as acting on the personal instructions of Marshal Pétain', and goes on to speak of British policy towards Vichy. 'Our consistent policy was to make the Vichy Government and its members feel that, so far as we were concerned, it was never too late to mend.'[43] Neither Pétain nor Churchill seem to have placed much importance on Rougier's negotiations, though Pétain, by every source possible, was making it clear to the British that, while France would defend her colonies, she would not in any other way take up arms against her former allies.

Montoire was obviously Pétain's main effort in foreign affairs. Any slight dallying with the British, if in fact it took place, was, if double-dealing, double-dealing to the British. The main line of Vichy foreign policy was clear, and was stated publicly by Pétain to the French on 30 October:

... Such an interview was only possible, four months after our defeat, thanks to the dignity of the French in their trials, thanks to the immense effort of regeneration in which they had engaged themselves, thanks also to the heroism of our sailors, the energy of our colonial leaders, the loyalty of our native populations.* France has pulled itself together. This first meeting between the victor and the vanquished marks the first recovery of our country.

It is freely that I accepted the Führer's invitation. I did not have to put up with any '*Diktat*' or pressure from him. A collaboration has been envisaged between our two countries. I have accepted the principle of it. The details will be discussed later. To all those who are today awaiting the salvation of France, I say that salvation is above all in our hands. To all those who have noble

* i.e., the fleet, and the defence of the colonies as at Dakar, helped negotiations.

scruples which keep them opposed to our thought, I say that the first duty of all Frenchmen is to have confidence. To those who doubt, as to those who remain obstinate, I will recall the fact that by excessive stiffness the most fine attitudes of reserve and pride risk losing their force. He who has taken into his hands the destiny of France has the duty to create the atmosphere which is most favourable to safeguarding the interests of the country.

It is with honour, and in order to maintain French unity—which has lasted ten centuries—that in the framework of an activity which will create the European new order I today enter the road of collaboration.

Thus, in the near future, the weight of our country's sufferings may be lightened, the lot of our prisoners bettered, the charges of occupation lowered. Thus the line of demarcation may be made more supple, the administration and victualling of the territory facilitated. This collaboration must be sincere. It must exclude all idea of aggression. It must carry with it a patient and confident effort. The armistice, meanwhile, is not peace. France is bound by numerous obligations to the victor. At least she remains sovereign. This sovereignty imposes on her the duty to defend her soil, to extinguish divergences of opinion, to put down the dissidence in her colonies. This policy is mine. The ministers are solely responsible to me. It is I alone who will be judged by history.[44]

The wording of this speech shows that Pétain felt that many would object to his actions at Montoire, but that he was determined to persuade them that it was France's only way out. He spoke not in pride but in resignation. This speech, with its acceptance of responsibility, is paradoxically one of Pétain's most moving utterances. The self-satisfaction is gone, and a chastened man emerges, concerned above all for his country, and prepared to take the most unpopular decisions.

Montoire did not live up to the hopes that had been placed on it. The Germans did not make the concessions that Pétain had expected; indeed, one of the first things to happen after the meeting was the expulsion of many inhabitants from Lorraine (now part of Germany again) into France. Ribbentrop, who was meant to be coming to France to discuss details, was distracted from doing so by the Greek campaign. No positive advantages to France were seen, except for a minor concession on prisoners of war.

On the other hand, British propaganda was playing up the treachery of the Montoire meetings, and French public opinion was having its first real revision of its view of Pétain. Many of those who had welcomed him with open arms in July, now began to see just what policies France had let herself in for. A man such as Paul Claudel, referring to Cardinal Baudrillart's call to collaboration 'with great and powerful Germany', was to confide in his diary that '*bien pensant* Catholics are showing themselves to be disgusting through stupidity and cowardice.'[45] While many flocked to the policy of collaboration, many now turned against the Vichy Government.

13 December, 1940

Laval was disliked by most of the Cabinet, and was by now mistrusted by Pétain. In the group of reactionary ministers, bent on the revival of the country by the National Revolution, he stuck out like a sore thumb.

Pétain had supported him in office, because of his supposed ability to negotiate with the Germans; but Pétain had now shown, at Montoire, that he himself was capable of success in negotiation—and he had perhaps not been unaware of Hitler's conflicting impressions of himself and Laval. (Hitler was impressed by Pétain, but contemptuous of Laval, as he showed by later comments on the interview.) Laval, too, was taking too much on himself, acting too much as a free agent, and not keeping Pétain sufficiently informed. Pétain, and his colleagues, were angered by Laval's attitudes.

Laval had lost his main use; and this alone, with the pressures which the rest of the Cabinet continually exerted to get him removed, might have been enough to move Pétain to action. Added to this, however, was fear of Laval's intentions. Laval clearly regretted the great powers which had been given to Pétain, and wished to usurp them; the Marshal had not been the mere figurehead which Laval had hoped he would be. In early December Laval, impatient with his lack of powers, made it clear to several people that he wanted to take over. Rumours of this definitely reached Pétain, and he began to worry about what Laval might do. He had isolated Laval in the Cabinet by the September reshuffle; but the Germans were another force which might help Laval.

The myth which has grown up since the war is that Pétain dismissed Laval because of disagreement with the policy of collaboration. There is little evidence, either before or after the dismissal, that this is true. It is nevertheless possible that Pétain had a fear that Laval might go beyond collaboration, to active involvement in the German cause.*

Cabinet pressures on Pétain were becoming stronger. Bouthillier, annoyed by Laval's concessions to the Germans in the economic sphere, pressed very strongly in mid-November for his removal. Baudouin and Peyrouton joined him in this pressure.

By early December Pétain seems to have been deciding on Laval's removal, and Darlan had joined those putting strong pressure on him to take action. Flandin had been invited to Vichy for discussions about succeeding Laval. On the 9th Pétain wrote a letter to the Führer telling him he was dismissing Laval, and wished to appoint Flandin as his successor. The letter was never delivered, possibly because Pétain changed his mind.

Laval might well have continued in power, but for an event which aroused all Pétain's latent fears of his Deputy Premier. Hitler decided, as a friendly gesture to France, to send the ashes of Napoleon's son, the Duke of Reichstadt, to Paris from Vienna, the city where he had died in exile, the young 'eaglet' of French popular romantic sentimental myth. A ceremony was to take place in Paris on 15 December, and Pétain was invited to it.

Pétain's eventual refusal to go had nothing to do with a desire not to be

---

* Warner goes too far, I feel, in laying all the cause for Laval's dismissal on things that had nothing directly to do with the Franco-German situation. Documents show (as we shall see later) that rightly or wrongly Pétain thought that Laval wished to enter the war on the German side.

seen acting in a friendly manner with the Germans, as has sometimes been suggested; he had, after all, at Montoire and in his subsequent speeches, shown that collaboration was his policy. The handshake of Montoire was a far more serious gesture that the acceptance of a national gift could ever be. No, Pétain's refusal was based on fear. He saw the invitation as an excuse to get him into the Occupied Zone, and to bring pressure on him to give up all his powers to Laval, who would then form a new Government of an entirely different type.

These fears were almost certainly unjustified. Hitler's later reactions were more those of a spurned benefactor than of a disturbed plotter. Laval had certainly discussed overthrowing the Government in the previous weeks, but his overwhelming desire for Pétain to go to Paris was probably simply what it claimed to be, a desire not to offend the Germans. (Justifiable in view of Hitler's violent reactions to the 'insult'.) British agents appear to have played some part in spreading the impression that such a plot was on foot; but it would have required little to set off the apprehensions of Pétain and his entourage on that score.

Laval, furious at Pétain's original refusal to come to Paris, went down to Vichy himself on 13 December. Under pressure, Pétain finally gave in, and agreed to go. It was then that the 'plotters'—Peyrouton, Bouthillier, Baudouin, Alibert, Darlan and Huntziger—decided to act. They went to the Marshal, Peyrouton producing all the 'evidence' he had gathered about Laval's intentions. It was decided that Laval was to be dismissed, and arrested.

At the Cabinet meeting at 8 p.m., Pétain asked (in Third Republic style) for a collective letter of resignation from all the ministers. The way he handled this meeting shows that his ironic sense of humour was still strongly alive. Laval had no idea that his resignation was going to be accepted and thought that the whole manoeuvre had been organised to get rid of someone else. He signed happily. Pétain then calmly announced that his resignation had been accepted. After some recriminations, Laval departed. By 11 p.m., he had been arrested (on orders of Peyrouton, Minister of the Interior, whose appointment in place of Marquet had been such a blow to Laval's power), and sent to custody at his estate at Châteldon. The next day Pétain announced his dismissal to the nation, and the appointment of Flandin in his place.

German reactions to Laval's dismissal were mixed. The German military had never liked Laval; as a German officer, von Neubronn, was to say later in the war: 'Just as Pétain was the typical chivalrous soldier, Laval was the typical non-soldier, an intriguing party politician tarred with every brush. Pétain was a strict Catholic, Laval a convinced atheist. Pétain was a man of the simplest and most measured way of life, Laval was given over to pleasure, always concerned with enlarging his possessions. . .'[46] This over-simplified view of the two men was based on German admiration for Pétain the soldier. The comradeship of arms was still one of the strongest of ties, and contempt for parliamentarians a military virtue.

Abetz, however, was appalled by what had happened. On the 14th, he got his representative on the armistice commission to tell the French that no change must be made in the Government until he had talked to Pétain. On the 15th, when Darlan and Laure came as Pétain's representatives to the Reichstadt ceremony in Paris, he told them that the French could have what Government they liked, but that without Laval there could be no collaboration.

On the 16th Darlan visited Abetz, to warn him that any re-establishment of Laval would mean the resignation of Pétain, and to advise him not to go to Vichy. Abetz nevertheless went there later that day, with an escort of ten S.S. men. On 17 December he had an interview with Pétain and Darlan (Flandin was ill in bed), and threatened them once again that the policy of collaboration would not be continued. He demanded, among other things, Laval's reinstatement as Minister of the Interior, the setting-up of a directorate consisting of Laval, Darlan, Huntziger and Flandin, and the dismissal of Peyrouton and Alibert. Pétain declared that the dismissal of Laval was irrevocable, but each time Abetz got up as if to go, he asked to go on discussing the matter. Laval was brought from Châteldon, and caused a terrible scene, accusing Pétain publicly of shiftiness and mismanagement. That afternoon Pétain composed a letter to Hitler, saying that he would look into all that had led up to Laval's dismissal, and particularly Abetz's charges against Peyrouton and others.

This may even have been a step towards Pétain giving in. But Flandin now put his weight in the balance, and got the Cabinet to approve the decision not to reinstate Laval. The statement they sent nevertheless stressed Pétain's desire to continue the policy of collaboration as agreed at Montoire.

Meanwhile, Abetz had on 18 December sent to the German Foreign Minister a telegram outlining all that had happened so far. In it he admitted that internal politics had no doubt played a role in Laval's dismissal, and that the lying rumour about Laval's intentions in Paris had been the direct cause of it. He nevertheless claimed that the statement that the reshuffle denoted no change of policy was a lie. Pétain had been heard to say that Laval was not looked on with a favourable eye by foreign Governments (i.e., Anglo-Saxon). Vichy was prepared to engage in talks with the British, and had disapproved of Laval's wish to intervene directly in Africa against de Gaulle and the British, Abetz added. In much of this he may have been playing up the differences in the French camp, in order to get support in attempting to reinstate Laval. He was certainly far more keen on reinstating Laval than anyone else on the German side seems to have been.

Abetz went on to blame the closed society of Vichy, and the senility of the Marshal, for what happened. The *Action Française*, too, had far too much influence there:

A secret report of the *Action Française*, which has fallen into our hands, proves that this movement is the moving force behind the scenes and that it regards the great majority of the ministers, and all the Marshal's entourage, as being their men. The *Action Française* displays anti-semitic, anti-masonic, and to a certain extent anglophobic tendencies. However, its traditional hatred of the Germans is stronger than all these motivations, and it is only interested in filling all the key posts in the Government, the administration, and education, with men who wish to make France ready, as soon as possible, for military resistance to Germany. The external adhesion to the policy of collaboration is only to deceive us, and to make us believe that it is a question of a movement of national renovation like fascism or national socialism.[47]

Once again Abetz was pointing to the need to get rid of the reactionary régime at Vichy. What was needed, he said, was former parliamentarians open to new ideas. Laval was such a man: 'Consequently, the *Action Française* acted logically when it had Laval arrested and tried at all costs to prevent his going to the Occupied Zone, for the presence of Laval in Paris would have placed in our hands, over and above means of military pressure, means of very efficacious pressure on internal politics.'[47]

This last statement gives us perhaps the reasons for Abetz's final acceptance of the situation. At Vichy meanwhile, the directorate had been set up, with three rather than four people in it, and Darlan at the head, with Flandin in charge of Foreign Affairs. Abetz was pleased by Darlan's appointment, because Darlan was violently anti-British, and was also one of the few people in the French Government who was on reasonably good terms with Laval.

Communications were strained. Pétain, however, wrote a further letter to Hitler, which was handed over to Hitler personally by Admiral Darlan on 25 December. In this letter, Pétain stated that Laval's behaviour at their meeting, which was public knowledge, now made it impossible for him to take Laval back into Government. Darlan made it clear to Hitler that the dismissal of Laval meant no modification of the French Montoire attitudes, and that the French wanted collaboration to continue. Hitler, while expressing no strong opinions about Laval, declared how revolted he had been at the interpretation that had been put on his gesture about the Duke of Reichstadt's ashes.

This theme was to recur again and again in Hitler's thought. His sentimental gesture had been rebuffed; Pétain had insulted him. Above all, Pétain, by including his announcement of Laval's dismissal in the same letter as his refusal of the invitation to Paris, had cast a slur on the Führer's intentions; later explanations had showed what double-dealing the French had thought him capable of. For a man of Hitler's temperament, Pétain's snub was far worse than any purely political matter. As late as April 1941 Ribbentrop, when explaining the French situation to the Japanese Foreign Minister Matsuoka, stressed the importance of this one act:

The German Foreign Minister . . . depicted the Führer's efforts to bring a real co-operation with France into being. He touched on the Montoire meeting and the gesture the Führer had made to France, by sending the ashes of the Duke of

Reichstadt. In the letter in which Marshal Pétain thanked the Führer for this gesture, he had at the same time announced the dismissal of Laval. This naturally made a very bad impression in Germany, as Laval had placed himself with Pétain in favour of the Montoire policy, i.e., France's collaboration with Germany.

Moreover it was known to Germany that Pétain, when he received an invitation to come to the reception of the Duke of Reichstadt's ashes at Les Invalides in Paris, had uttered the view that he should not go, because he did not wish to be imprisoned by the Germans. The opinion which this expressed had caused the Führer to regard the chapter of collaboration with France as closed, because a trustful relationship with Marshal Pétain, who had such an opinion of the Führer, that he thought he wanted to inveigle him to Paris so shortly after the Montoire meeting in order to imprison him there, was naturally no longer possible.

Matsuoka was visibly impressed by these remarks. He said several times that he could not imagine such behaviour on the part of Pétain.

The Reich Foreign Minister repeated that the whole event was all the more unfortunate, in that on the German side a very positive impression had been received from Pétain at the Montoire meeting. Petain was, though physically healthy, not completely on top mentally, and surrounded by bad advisers. Moreover, he was perhaps a good example of the fact that a good general usually makes a bad politician.[48]

For Hitler, therefore, the events of 13 December were more than an insult; they were a sign that proper negotiations from trust were impossible with the French leadership. Those who claim that 13 December was of importance only to Abetz fail to realise that, for others including Hitler, it was not Laval's dismissal that mattered, so much as the atmosphere of mistrust that had set it off. It is quite possible that Ribbentrop's view was correct: that full collaboration had been on the cards, and that 13 December had destroyed that chance. On the other hand, it may have been that Hitler had decided against concessions at any rate, and was using this as an excuse. From now on Abetz, still an ardent devotee of collaboration, was to find that his Government failed to produce any of the concessions which might have made such a policy workable.

Meanwhile, the French Government, unaware of the profound effect of these events, and seeing them as having relevance mainly to Laval, were attempting by every means to assure the German Government that the dismissal of Laval had not meant that they wished to give up the policy of collaboration. At Darlan's meeting with Hitler on 25 December he stressed this point. Throughout January other approaches were made; it became ever clearer that the Führer's susceptibilities had been damaged by the French action, and protestations of lack of intention abounded.* None of this got anywhere.

The situation was of course bedevilled by Abetz's concern with Laval's dismissal, which made this seem to the French perhaps the most important

---

* e.g., Darlan's note, brought to Abetz by Benoist-Méchin in January, mentioned in telegram from Abetz to Ribbentrop, 12 January 1941.

aspect of the affair. In early January, Abetz sent Benoist-Méchin to Vichy to inform Pétain and the Vichy Government of the necessity to reinstate Laval, and the dangers of not doing so. The French asked two questions: (1) Could collaboration only continue if Laval returned? (2) Was Berlin in fact backing Abetz's statements? The answer to both, we now know, was 'No'. Laval does not seem to have been regarded as of great importance by either Hitler or Ribbentrop. Hitler seems already to have decided that proper collaboration was impossible.

A personal message which Huntziger sent to Ribbentrop on 16 January shows how much the French Government was desirous of continuing collaboration, and the difficulties they were finding from the German side. This was a personal message, and was sent by a rather roundabout route, via one of the French delegates at the Armistice Commission, who gave it to Richard Hemmen, the German economic representative, who then passed it on in a telegram to Ribbentrop. Huntziger, said Hemmen, felt that it was important to give Ribbentrop a personal account of the situation at Vichy: 'He, Huntziger, does not believe that the difficulties between the Marshal and Laval can ever be overcome. Pétain has lost all trust in Laval and cannot bring himself to trust him once more. On this account Huntziger does not believe that it would be in the German and French interest to push the matter.'

This, of course, would have been of no great interest to Ribbentrop or Hitler, who were not 'pushing the matter'. Mention of the Marshal's mistrust of Laval, however, was hardly likely to please the Germans, with its reminder of the mistrust of 13 December.

'He, Huntziger', continued Hemmen, 'asks for our confidence in him, when he assures us that he will continue collaboration exactly as before. For Darlan and Flandin this is equally true. The present Government is on this account not against further co-operation. . . .'

Huntziger continued with a plea that the situation was still the same. Let talks continue, he urged. Let the Armistice Commission's negotiations go forward: ' . . . Despite the present political difficulties in Vichy, especially the dismissal of Laval, for which he could authoritatively say that there had been exclusively internal political reasons, no change in the desire for co-operation in the work of the Armistice Commission should arise.'

The man who had given this message to Hemmen, de Boisanger, then added a few comments of his own, including the important one that 'the coincidence, in the same letter, of Laval's dismissal and the return of the mortal remains of the Duke of Reichstadt was to be ascribed to clumsiness on the French side [he discreetly hinted, adds Hemmen, that it was the Marshal's own clumsiness], but that actually the two actions did not stand together in any kind of causal connection.'[49]

This last statement shows that the French, while being aware of the Führer's annoyance at the joining of these two matters in the same letter, were perhaps unaware of how much he knew of Pétain's fear and mistrust before the event, and thought that they could still persuade him that there was no connexion between the two events. We know, however, from the Ribbentrop conversation already quoted, and from Abetz's telegram of 18 December, that the Germans were perfectly aware of what had happened.

Laval's dismissal had made no difference to the French desire for collaboration. Pétain, Darlan, Huntziger, Flandin, were all keen to continue this policy, and to get concessions. Pétain may, perhaps, have feared that Laval wished to head for all-out alliance with Germany on a war footing; but, as Laval had pointed out at Montoire, nobody, by the new Vichy constitution, could declare war without the agreement of the assemblies. Laval's dismissal, then, was caused by (1) Dislike of his parliamentary background and ideas, on the part of the most of the 'National Revolution' men in the Government, (2) Anger on Pétain's part at the amount Laval took upon himself, and his tendency to keep the Marshal in the dark, (3) A realisation on Pétain's part that Laval was not indispensable in foreign affairs, (4) Fear of Laval's possible intention to take over as Head of State (with Abetz's approval) and form a new Government opposed to the National Revolution.

On the German side, the events of 13 December appeared to show the lack of trust on France's part, and the impossibility of real collaboration. It may, of course, have been a mere excuse not to collaborate, as Hitler from now on showed no real interest in French understanding. Be that as it may, the policy of collaboration as it had been outlined at Montoire was now dead. From now on it would be only the French who were asked for concessions, which they would have to give for fear of losing still more.

Pétain, who had started with immense popularity as the saviour of the nation, had lost a good deal of it with the handshake of Montoire. If collaboration had worked, he might have regained some of it. As it was, from now on he was the captain of a sinking ship, who, despite all efforts to save it, was to go down with it.

Chapter Three

The Directorate and
the Darlan Government, 1941

THE beginning of 1941 was devoted to the question of Laval and his possible reinstatement. Laval was now in Paris, where he had been taken by Abetz. Vichy was under a directorate consisting of Darlan, Flandin and Huntziger, under Pétain as Head of State. Though Pétain agreed to see Laval on 18 January, he was clearly unwilling ever to have Laval back again; in addition to the reasons he had had against Laval before 13 December, there were now the insults that Laval had flung in Pétain's face, in the presence of his ministers and of Abetz. It is also not certain that Laval was keen to return; he seems to have been keen to clear his name of the accusations that had been flung at him, but not much more. Abetz kept on optimistically, however, at his work.

Despite the fact that Hitler was now beginning to believe that Darlan should now be the French dauphin, with Laval staying in Paris as a potential alternative if Vichy threw in its hand with the British, Abetz continued to try to give the impression that Laval had to be reinstated.

Convinced by Abetz's statements that collaboration could only be resumed if Laval returned, Pétain and his Cabinet were in a dilemma, and at a meeting at the end of January the military succeeded in beating the civilians (Peyrouton, Bouthillier, Flandin, each of whom had in his way to fear the return of Laval), and agreeing to his return. Pétain wrote to Abetz, saying that he had decided to give Laval a Ministry in the Government, and that Darlan would be Vice-Premier. A telegram sent by Abetz to Ribbentrop on 1 February requested permission for Darlan to come to Paris,[1] and Ribbentrop's reply agreed, but insisted that Laval must not be allowed to go into the Unoccupied Zone.[2]

When Darlan saw Laval, Laval refused the offer he had been made, and (almost certainly with Abetz's connivance) demanded the following conditions for his return, according to Abetz: '(1) That the Marshal should restrict himself to the functions of Head of State, and Laval should be appointed by an official decree as Pétain's official substitute and successor. (2) That Laval should become Prime Minister, the post which Pétain had held until now, and Minister of the Interior and Foreign Minister. (3) That the other Cabinet ministers should be appointed by Laval, and responsible to him.'[3]

These conditions would, of course, be equivalent to the measures which Pétain had feared in December. Pétain would lose all his powers, and in effect be a figurehead, with Laval as real Head of State. Can Laval really have believed that these conditions had any hope of being accepted? Did he, perhaps, even wish not to be reinstated? Or did he feel that German pressure might achieve even this?

Darlan's description of their meeting says that Laval was prepared to see Darlan as Pétain's dauphin; though what that would have been worth, with the Marshal's reduced powers, it is hard to see. Laval wanted to get rid of all present members of the Government except Admiral Darlan and General Huntziger.[4]

Abetz had, in all these negotiations, been acting off his own bat. Ribbentrop now brought him back to order, with a sharp message sent on 5 February, in which he told Abetz that Laval must be kept in the Occupied Zone, and that no *entente* should for the moment be brought about between Laval and Vichy.[5] Abetz had already been told this by his authorities, but had taken no notice.

So Abetz had to give up his ideas, and declare that the Germans would be quite happy if Laval was not reinstated. Darlan was clearly the new German favourite, and he was also well thought of by the Marshal and others of the Vichy Cabinet. On 9 February he took over as Deputy Premier, Foreign Minister and Minister of Defence. Huntziger remained as Minister of War, Bouthillier as Finance Minister. Alibert and Flandin were dismissed from the Government, probably as a sop to the Germans, and Peyrouton followed them on 17 February, the Ministry of the Interior being taken over by Darlan himself.

Pétain retained his powers as Head of State, but the events of the last couple of months appear to have aged him a great deal. Laval, when he saw him on 18 January, reported to Abetz that he had found the Marshal much older.[6] All accounts make of him a man whose moments of 'absence' were far more frequent, and who could be led more easily. The gradual realisation of the failure of his policies of collaboration and of internal regeneration by the National Revolution may have led in part to this. The ever-increasing pressures laid on the French by the Germans may have accentuated his feelings of helplessness on a slippery slope. But, as we shall see, he was still capable of decisive action on his own account, often at the most important moments.

The appointment of Darlan can hardly have displeased the Germans. Of all the French leaders, Darlan was probably the man with the strongest Anglophobia. To the natural hatred of England felt by most French naval men had been added the violent emotions caused by the attack on his fleet at Mers-el-Kebir. His fleet, indeed; he had spent much of the 'thirties building up the French navy until it was one of the finest in the world, and the only part of the French forces which was properly prepared for the World War. The fleet, which was now one of France's trump cards in her negotiations with the Germans, was, after France itself, Darlan's principal concern. As with Pétain, and as with Laval, one must not forget, despite his other actions, that France came at the top of his list of priorities.

Internal policy

In internal matters, Darlan must have disappointed Abetz, who at one time had seen him and Laval as the only two men at Vichy really capable of producing a new social policy, as opposed to the reactionary principles of the National Revolution. For under Darlan the National Revolution, though it had for many reasons been brought to failure, continued in principle if not in fact. And, despite the introduction of many new figures into the Government, its character as a military dictatorship was not really changed. In politics, Darlan might well be a figure far from the ideas and prejudices of the average military man; he was, however, concerned with efficiency, and some of the men to whom he now turned were technocrats of a new kind, who nevertheless shared many of the principles of the National Revolution.

The type of such a man was Pierre Pucheu, who became Minister of Industrial Production, and later, on 11 August 1941, Minister of the Interior. He, and men such as Barnaud (at Franco-German Economic Relations) and Lehideux (at the Ministry of *Équipement*) were essentially *dirigistes*, or planners, who saw the proper running of the State as being a matter for the State itself. Pétain's speech of 11 October 1940 had shown the main lines upon which economic policy should run. These men were now able to try to put it into effect. Corporatists who saw the solution to the class struggle in corporations which comprised both employers and workers, they were the prime movers behind the *Charte du Travail*. This document was promulgated on 4 October 1941, and in the next month a *Conseil Supérieur de la Charte du Travail* was formed. Aron suggests, in his *Histoire de Vichy*, that the *Charte du Travail* was a hybrid document which was created from the diverse forces of syndicalism and corporatism. In reality, the document was essentially corporatist. The workers could, it is true, choose between three possible systems, some more transitional than others. But all three systems were corporatist in outlook: all workers and employers must join together in joint unions, and any political or religious activity was forbidden to such groups; strikes were forbidden, as were lock-outs; the trades union system was abolished; State intervention was the basis for arbitration and for economic control.

Many of the corporatist theorists had seen the system as being essentially a free one, based on the goodwill of men when released from the class struggle. Pucheu and his companions, however, were realists and at the same time technocrats; State coercion was the only possible way, for them, of making things work.

Unlike the idealists of the National Revolution, first phase, these men were cold and business-like experts, for whom little mattered but efficiency. Pucheu, when Minister of the Interior, was to transfer these attitudes to more human problems, and to make those mistakes which were to make of him the first Vichy man to be condemned to death after the war. As with many efficiency experts, human understanding was lacking.

One theory must be discounted. Many people have seen evidence of some kind of plot in the sudden prominence of these men. Some had been members of the X-Crise (which we have already discussed): at least two, including Pucheu, had been extremely successful members of the Banque Worms. A whole mythology was built up, on this basis, of a *synarchie*, a kind of secret society based on X-Crise, and of a plot based on the Banque Worms, both of which were aimed at taking over the nation. There is no proof of such plots. Many of these men held common views, many of them had met at various times to discuss them. But their position at Vichy was a natural one both in view of their corporatist opinions, their support of State intervention, and their own successes as economic experts in their previous existences.

These men were successful in putting forward corporatist measures. Whether these measures would have succeeded is another matter, for in normal circumstances the workers would hardly have given up their trades union freedom for such paternalist policies, and in the Vichy situation no one really had time to devote themselves to such policies. At Laval's return in April 1942 most of the men concerned were dismissed.

The oath of fidelity and other measures

On 27 January 1941, under the Directorate, there had been a constitutional Act which had obliged Secretaries of State, high civil servants and dignitaries to swear an oath of allegiance to the Head of State. On 14 April, under Darlan, this obligation was extended to the army, and to the magistrature. On 4 October this was extended to all public servants. The Marshal's powers were now vast, particularly in relation to the army, for whom an oath was an oath, as we shall see at the time of the Allied landings in North Africa in November, 1942. His powers over the magistrature were also a dangerous sign, but the Riom trials were to show how useless they were.

A turning-point had taken place on 12 August 1941, when Pétain, at Vichy, gave a message in which he declared that things were not well in France: a 'bad wind' was present, anxiety or doubt were in many minds, the authority of his Government was being questioned. Even his orders were often badly carried out. It was essential to take action. Several dictatorial measures were announced, including suppression of political parties, and of parliamentary privilege. Trials were to be set up to judge those responsible for the defeat. All state functionaries were to swear allegiance to the Marshal.

All these measures show the distance that had been travelled from the joyous acceptance of Pétain in July 1940. The mere fact that such measures were necessary shows the extent of dissidence even within the framework of the Vichy State. A secret report from the head of the *Sicherheitspolizei* in France, written in this same August, gives us the picture: 'The reputation of the Head of State, which was formerly a bond between all Frenchmen, is much attacked. Even though the last speech of the Marshal's was on the whole received with respect, people do not seem to be in agreement with it. Without giving too much importance to the damage to pictures of the Marshal, which agents may well have carried out on orders, it can be stated that belief in the Marshal is not what it was. The Admiral of the Fleet is also strongly criticised, and this is repeated by the British radio.'[7]

Pétain and the Vichy Government had lost most of their popularity. On the one side of them was the Resistance in its various forms, including those owing allegiance to de Gaulle. On the other were the Paris collaborators, who felt that the Vichy form of collaboration did not go far enough, and was too anti-German. These included Doriot, Déat and Luchaire. Amid mounting dissidence, Pétain was forced into various measures, including the oath of loyalty.

The extension of this oath to the magistrature was the prelude to the Riom trials, in which 'those responsible for the defeat' were to be tried. We have already seen how, at the time of the defeat itself, some people were already crying out for the guilty to be punished. This demand was still strong: Abetz noted, in a report on 23 June 1941, that everyone was searching for those responsible: the military were accusing the parliamentarians, and *vice versa*. 'The internal political life of France', he wrote, 'has been dominated up to the present by the fear of being made responsible one day by the "opposite side". On this question, the military men have the Church, the *Action Française* and the old right-wing groups on their side.'[8]

The Riom trials were intended to settle the issue. The *Front Populaire* leaders were to be found responsible. Yet even on this point there was disagreement. The Germans wanted them to be found guilty of declaring war; the Vichy Government wanted them to be found guilty of losing the war, through lack of proper preparation.

Pétain had not only made the magistrature swear loyalty to him. He also took it on himself to tell them, before the trial, what their verdict should be. On 29 September 1941, he formed a *Conseil de Justice Politique*, of which the members were nominated by himself; on 15 October, in a public message, he declared their verdict on how the guilty should be tried:

Made up of *anciens combattants* and the best servants of the public good, the *Conseil de Justice* has unanimously been of the opinion that detention in a fortified precinct — the strongest punishment allowed by Constitutional Act No. 7 — should be enforced in the cases of M. Édouard Daladier, M. Léon Blum, and General Gamelin.

In consequence I order the detention of these three persons in the *Fort du Pourtalet*. . .

But the *Conseil de Justice Politique* has asked me to preserve the power of the judiciary from the encroachment of political power. This respect for the separation of the powers is already part of common law. So it is that I have willingly complied with this respect, which corresponds with own private feelings.

Consequently, the matter is referred to the Riom court . . . The hearing is about to begin.[9]

This message is contradictory in itself. The decision has been made, the hearing will follow it. But the magistrature, and even the Vichy ministers, were not prepared to see such flouting of justice. The presiding judge declared to the accused, on the first day, that the Court would act as though the preliminary verdict had never existed; the Vichy Minister of Justice, Joseph Barthélémy, published an article in *Le Temps* which showed that the decisions of the *Conseil de Justice Politique* could not affect the independence of the trials.

These trials were a farce. In them, the accused succeeded in turning the tables, and laying a great deal of blame on Pétain himself. As the months went by, it became clear that the only people who were losing anything by this exercise were the Vichy Government, and in particular Pétain. The Germans, too, were furious at the way things were going, and in particular at the fact that the trials were not about the guilt of declaring war, but the guilt of losing it. In March 1942 Hitler ordered the trial to be suspended. The accused were sent to captivity in Germany.

The Jewish question

At the beginning of 1941, the Germans persuaded the Vichy Government to set up a *Judenamt*, a *Commissariat Général aux Questions Juives*. For the Germans, it was important to have a French organisation which could be responsible for the unpopular Jewish measures both in the Occupied and Unoccupied Zones. For Vichy, knowing that whatever happened such actions would be taken, it was important not to let things slip entirely out of their sovereignty. Darlan expressed himself willing to form such a body.

One of the difficulties in attempting to form it, however, was the attitude of Marshal Pétain, who, while he had no strong fellow-feeling for Jews as such, felt that certain exceptions ought to be made for those who had lived in France for a long time, and particularly for his *anciens combattants*. Abetz explained the situation in a telegram on 6 March 1941:

> On the question of the founding of a central *Judenamt* for France Darlan has shown himself ready to let the French Government bear the responsibility of such an arrangement, but he pointed out that Marshal Pétain's attitude to the Jewish question showed a certain amount of vacillation. The Marshal would like not to give the same treatment to old-established residents, and to French Jews who have distinguished themselves in war service for France, as to the Jews who have immigrated from abroad. Despite this attitude of Pétain's which hardly leads one to expect any very active functioning on the part of a central *Judenamt* founded by the French Government, it is recommendable to let the French Government undertake such a foundation. The central *Judenamt* will thereby gain a legal basis, and it can be so activated by German influence in the Occupied Zone that the Unoccupied Zone will be forced not to exclude itself from the measures in question . . .[10]

By their acceptance of this, the French were once more falling into the German hands. German influence over the French handling of the Jewish question from now on became more and more marked.

By early April, a Commissioner for Jewish Affairs had been appointed in the person of Xavier Vallat, a right-wing former deputy who had been seriously wounded in the First World War. On 3 April he called on Abetz at the German Embassy in Paris. Abetz, in his report on this interview, described Vallat as having, 'as a member of the Chamber of Deputies, for many years shown himself as being anti-semitic, particularly in polemics against Léon Blum.'

Abetz described Vallat's duties as being of a threefold nature: '(1) to supervise the carrying out of the Jewish laws already passed by the French Government. (2) To co-ordinate the Jewish laws laid down by the French Government for the whole of France with the Jewish ordinances issued by the Military Commander in France on the recommendation of the Embassy, which applied to the Occupied Zone. (3) To work out further French Jewish laws.'

This third duty was a difficult one, in view of Pétain's attitude. As Abetz put it: 'As Darlan only succeeded in having a Commissioner for Jewish Matters appointed after strong opposition on the part of Pétain, and as the resistance against the activities of the Commissioner will certainly continue, as a result of American pressure, it is advisable for Vallat to carry out the third duty in stages, in order not openly to place himself in conflict with Pétain's views.'

Though Vallat must work carefully, he must do what he could to get Jews (who were already excluded from Government, army, the Press, the radio, and the theatre and film industries) out of all the remaining professions, and out of economics and commerce, and 'prepare the ground for their emigration'. Because of Vichy's tendency to distinguish between 'old-established' and recently naturalised or foreign Jews, at the moment any laws which concerned them all would be full of loopholes, whereas laws dealing merely with the recently naturalised and foreign Jews could be much more definite. Vallat was therefore, for the moment, to content himself with the latter course.

Abetz, however, was looking to the future, for means to cast the net wider: 'However, so that at a later stage the "old-established" Jews may be included in the same measures as the foreign and newly naturalised Jews, a law is now necessary, which will empower the French Jewish Commissioner to declare as "foreign" all "old-established" Jews who have offended against the social and national interests of the French nation. With the help of such a law the "old-established" Jewry, which makes up about a fifth of the total number of Jews now living in France, will gradually be completely brought to emigration.' [11] He suggested to Vallat that he should bring the project for such a law forward at Vichy.

Vallat's first laws were aimed at alignment with the German laws in the Occupied Zone. In June and July, 'aryanisation' laws on the basis of the German *Zweite Verordnung* of 18 October 1940, allowed dispossession of Jewish proprietors, and the taking over of their businesses by provisional administrators (despite a promise made in October 1940, that Jewish goods would not be touched). *Anciens combattants* were not excluded from this law. Jews were on the whole kept out of the liberal professions. By December

1941, it was made possible to put any foreign Jews who had entered France since 1 January 1936 into concentration camps or into labour gangs.

Still, however, the Germans pressed for more; and Vallat was not prepared to go further. He refused to order the wearing of the yellow star and to order a Jewish curfew. He made it clear, too, that he did not wish the French position to be the same as the German one on these matters. The Germans withdrew his pass into the Occupied Zone, and he was thus forced to resign in February 1942.

Pétain's attitude on the Jewish question appears to have slowed up the Germans and the French anti-semites. It was not taken, as we have seen, from a point of principle about the Jews themselves, but from a point of principle about Frenchmen and about *anciens combattants*. For whatever reason the attitude was taken up, however, it succeeded in saving many Jews from the measures concerned, and was to save many more from death in the future.

Foreign affairs—Syria

Collaboration as it had been envisaged at Montoire was now out of the question as far as the Germans were concerned. It was important to them, however, to have a man like Darlan at the helm in Vichy France. His Anglophobia, they felt, would keep him from any *rapprochement* with the British. It was as good as having Laval as Deputy Premier.

And, at first, Darlan lived up to their expectations. Convinced still that the Germans were going to win the war (and at this date this still seemed to many the most likely outcome) he set about attempts at collaboration with them. Meanwhile, too, the Germans began to put ever-heavier pressures on the French. Armaments were demanded from French industry, as were raw materials such as aluminium and copper. Over France's head was held the threat of 'polonisation' (i.e., being treated as Poland had been) if she did not make the various concessions which were demanded.

Pétain and Darlan both, by different channels, complained of France's treatment, Pétain pointing out that no concessions of any kind had been made by the Germans, and that the whole country was being pillaged of food and material. No reply of any consequence came to these messages. The Germans had decided on the futility of collaboration.

In May, however, events made the Germans realise the need of some help from the French. Rachid Ali, the nationalist leader, had begun an insurrection against the British in Iraq. This had been in fact in part set off by German agents, and the Germans wished to help the insurgents in order to further their own plans in the Middle East. But in order to get there, the Germans had to go through Syria. On 3 May Abetz sent for Darlan, and offered him collaboration, but this time on new terms.

This time the French Government was expected to give active assistance to the German cause, by giving arms from Syria to the Iraqui rebels, and by letting German planes land in Syria on their way through to Iraq, and be refuelled and repaired. In return for this, important concessions would be made by the Germans.

This was a step beyond anything yet conceived by the French negotiators. Only a month previously, Pétain had declared in a radio speech that honour would never allow the French to undertake anything against their former allies.[12] Darlan, however, agreed to the proposition on 6 May (without apparently at this stage referring back to Pétain). In return he gained the promise of various concessions: the demarcation line was to be made less of a barrier, the occupation costs the French had to pay were to be reduced, those prisoners of war who were 1914–18 *anciens combattants* were to be released, and the French were to be allowed to rearm certain ships.

One must not think, however, that Darlan gave in purely for concessions. Fear of what might happen if he did not was one of the moving forces in his action. The empire was one of the trump cards which was saving France from being totally occupied, and from being 'Polonised'; the trump card now had to be used in a new way. Darlan did not yet realise that German demands were a slippery slope down which France must now slide, continually faced by newer and greater requests.

On the same day Darlan sent a telegram to General Dentz, the Commander in Syria, which read: 'Conversations of a general nature are in progress between the French and German Governments. It is of the greatest importance for their success that if German aeroplanes heading for Iraq land on an airfield in our mandated territories, all facilities should be given to them to continue their route.'[13] So, before any agreement was signed, one of the main decisions was taken.

On 11 May Darlan met Hitler at Berchtesgaden. Hitler's attitude was a threatening one: collaboration was no longer possible in its original form, German interests must come first; if France was awkward, dreadful consequences would ensue, including extensive loss of territory; if, on the other hand, France co-operated, things would not be too bad for her. Germany was bound to win the war, and not only was France unlikely to have any influence on the conflict, but Germany had no need of her to win. On the other hand, her attitude could either prolong or shorten hostilities. If the former, she must take the consequences; if the latter, concessions might be possible.

Darlan showed himself willing to follow the German line. And on 14 May he reported to the Marshal and his ministers in the following terms:

It is our last chance to have a *rapprochement* with Germany. If we favour the British policy, France will be crushed, dismembered, and will cease to be a nation. If we try to have a seesaw policy between the two adversaries, Germany will make a thousand difficulties for us in the exercise of our sovereignty, and will foment disorder. At all events, the eventual peace terms will be disastrous. If we collaborate with Germany, without thereby lining up with her to make war deliberately on England, that is to say by working for her in our factories, and giving her certain facilities, we can save the French nation, reduce to a minimum our territorial losses, both in France and in the colonies, and play an honourable, even important role in the Europe of the future. My choice is made,

I will not let myself be dissuaded by the conditional offer of a boatload of wheat or a boatload of petrol.[14]

The last reference is almost certainly to agreements made in February between Weygand and the Americans, whereby the Americans agreed to supply various products (including petrol) to French North Africa, in return for an assurance that any attack on North Africa, from whatever quarter, would be opposed by the French troops.

Darlan's statement shows that, though prepared to help the Germans (who, he was sure, were going to win the war), he still kept to the line that no declaration of war on England was either possible or desirable. In other words, he was disguising war aid as essentially 'economic' aid. By collaborating in this way, the French assured themselves an 'honourable place' in the new Europe and avoided being crushed. This seems to have met with the agreement of those present, and Pétain declared the new policy in a speech on the radio on 15 May:

Frenchmen—You have learned that Admiral Darlan recently had a meeting in Germany with Chancellor Hitler. I had approved the principle of this meeting.

This new conversation allows us to light up the road ahead, and to continue the conversations which have been engaged with the German Government.

It is today no longer a question, for a public opinion which is often anxious because it is ill-informed, of calculating our chances, measuring our risks, judging our gestures. For you, Frenchmen, it is a question of following me without question on the road of honour and of national interest.

If, within the narrow discipline of our public mind, we can bring to a successful issue the negotiations in progress, France will be able to rise above her defeat and maintain in the world her rank as a European and colonial power.[15]

Further negotiations took place in Paris on 21 May. Three agreements, called the 'Paris protocols' were signed by Darlan on behalf of the French Government, though much of the detailed discussion had been undertaken by General Huntziger. The agreements were not only to let the Germans through Syria, and to supply them with munitions, petrol, etc. (which was already happening owing to the order given by Darlan on 6 May); they also proposed to let the Germans use Bizerta and Tunisia to help the Rommel army, to sell guns and lorries from French Africa to the Germans, and also to let the Germans use Dakar in French West Africa as a submarine base.

These agreements, however, were never to come into effect. Before Pétain could ratify them (and, as Head of State, he alone could ratify such agreements) Weygand, alerted no doubt by Pétain's and Darlan's wireless speeches, had come up to Vichy from North Africa. He had been down there since the previous September, training the French army for future use, building up French resources, waiting in an *attentiste* pose for the war to take its course. Now he saw France on the verge of offering herself up to the Germans, and losing that freedom of action which he saw as hers. He alone seems to have fully seen the dangers; and beyond that, he was violently

Germanophobe. He saw that action such as the Government wished to take would endanger rather than insure the empire, for internal dissidence and external attack were thereby made far more likely.

Weygand reached Vichy on 2 June, and spoke strongly to the Marshal about the matter. On 3 June, he was present at a Cabinet meeting at which Darlan presented the case for the Protocols, stating that it was a case of collaboration or destruction, and that the previous see-saw policy would mean the loss of important territory.

In reply, Weygand read a note which he had prepared in Algiers:

It is not only important to refuse a military collaboration, we must no longer at any price let ourselves be dragged down the slippery slope of a military collaboration which has not explicitly been agreed to, but which risks being made almost inevitable by acts of provocation which must be stopped.

For my part, I can see no other means of succeeding in this than by a new public affirmation by the Government of the principles which are the foundation of French Africa's trust, and which I have enounced in the course of this letter: no base in Africa can be put at the disposal of the Germans or the Italians. French Africa will defend itself against whoever attacks it, with forces which are purely French. France will not deliberately go to war against her former ally.[16]

He thereupon gave his resignation and left. Pétain, declaring that the policy being pursued by himself and Darlan had been strongly criticised, asked the ministers for their opinions. Most said little, but the military declared the weakness of their forces, in the face of an attack by the British, and Jacques Chevalier (Minister for Family and Health) qualified Weygand's departure as catastrophic.

That afternoon Pétain, General Huntziger, General Laure and Admiral Platon all tried to put pressure on Weygand to withdraw his resignation. Weygand, in reply, suggested that the way to get out of the Protocols was to demand 'concessions' (allowed for in the agreements) which were bound to be refused by the Germans.

By 6 June Darlan, too, had come round to this view, especially as even the concessions agreed on 6 May were not being carried out properly. In Syria he had given, and had not received. The German agreements did not seem to be of much value. He suggested that the Germans should now be asked for the following: French sovereignty over the whole of France, including the Italian zone and those parts which had been counted in with Belgium; while the military were still there, the line of demarcation would mark the limit of military occupation, but there should be complete freedom of movement across it; a special régime for Alsace-Lorraine until peace was signed; a cessation of the payment of occupation costs; the return home of all non-Jewish Frenchmen, and liberation of all prisoners; a guarantee for the French colonies; and other concessions of the same kind.

Some writers have ascribed Darlan's and Pétain's change of heart to Weygand's intervention; others, including Du Moulin de Labarthète and Robert Aron, believe that Darlan and Pétain had already changed their minds, and that they were using Weygand as a cover against German displeasure. Be that as it may, the policy had now been reversed. The Germans, when they received Darlan's note on 14 June, broke off all negotiations with France.

Meanwhile, under pressure from the Gaullists, the British began an invasion of Syria on 8 June. The Vichy troops valiantly defended themselves, but within six weeks Syria had been taken. During the course of the fighting, despite the terrible situation their troops were in, the French Government had strongly refused the help of the German air force, on 17 June. The idea of military collaboration was now dead, it seemed, once and for all.

The loss of Syria showed the way in which Vichy was always going to fall between two stools. For fear of German reprisals, and in order to maintain the French empire, the French fleet, and a semblance of free government in the Unoccupied Zone, Darlan had given in to all German demands with regard to Syria; but in return he had lost Syria, because of the concessions he had made, which laid him open to attack. And, to stave off the attack, he would not take the further step of receiving help in the form of military collaboration. The French stood on their own, and lost both ways. They had also lost any hope of negotiations with the Germans.

The Syrian campaign had showed, however, the loyalty of the Vichy troops. The oath of loyalty to the Head of State had only recently been demanded of them, and was no doubt fresh in their minds. But even without it, their duty was clear. Pétain must be right in what he did; what he had done with regard to the German planes must have been in the French interest; to break the armistice, and not to defend the empire, would mean the invasion of the Unoccupied Zone, and the taking of the fleet. They fought well against the British troops (and a small contingent of Gaullists), and, after the battle, when offered the choice between joining the Free French and returning to France, only about ten per cent chose the former. General Dentz, their Commander, was a violently anti-German Alsatian; but he remained loyal to Pétain.

The question of hostages

The German attack on Russia in June 1941 had greatly added to the number of dissident movements in France, by the addition of the French Communists. Many other Resistance networks were already coming into existence, though with nothing like the extensive organisation they were to have by 1943. Throughout France, dissatisfaction with Vichy was being felt. Many of those who had acclaimed the Marshal most rapturously in June and July 1940 were by now violently opposed to him. The policy of collaboration appeared to many a policy of cowardice; to others, it was merely a policy that was not working. The perpetual concessions made to the Nazis did not seem to bring anything in return. The handshake of Montoire, the new Jewish laws, the Syrian help to Germany all had their enemies. Added to which Syria was now lost, and the National Revolution which had raised such high hopes had clearly failed. France was no longer a united nation.

On the other hand, the extreme collaborators, most of whom were in Paris, viewed Vichy's vacillating policies with contempt and hatred; they, too, were dangerous forces.

The Marshal's loss of prestige, and Vichy's lack of popularity, were accentuated by such ways of communication as the British radio, and by British agents. A wave of dissidence was filling the country. Pétain's violent speech of 12 August, which we have already discussed, shows his anxiety at the state of affairs.

In the Occupied Zone violence was mounting. On 27 August, at a cere-monial parade of the L.V.F. (*Légion des Volontaires Français contre le Bolchévisme*), a body founded to fight on the Russian front, Laval, Déat, and one or two others were wounded by the bullets of a young French ex-sailor called Paul Collette. Fearful of public opinion if Collette were executed, Laval and Déat petitioned Pétain for the man's reprieve, which was granted.

Six days before the Laval assassination attempt, on 21 August, a German soldier called Moser was shot down on a metro station. The Germans deman-ded 100 hostages, of whom 50 were to be shot. They soon relented, however, saying that this would not happen if the French set up a special tribunal to judge 'communist and anarchist' activities, and if this tribunal condemned to death six Communists who were already in jail (and had been before the murder). A warning was given that any further such happenings would lead to hostages being shot.

So French justice was to condemn innocent men, in order to save other hostages! These men were, however, Communists. Pétain sent his thanks to the Germans on the 23rd, via Brinon, 'that in the seriousness of the event the occupation troops had refrained from general measures against the whole population.'[17] The tribunal in fact condemned only three of the men. Their lawyers appealed. Dayras, Secretary General of the Ministry of Justice, telephoned to Pucheu, pointing out that the men were in prison before the assassination; but Pucheu replied that they must die. Under German pres-sure, the other three were retried, and condemned to death as well.

In October, German pressures became even stronger. After the assassina-tion of the Commandant of Nantes, Colonel Holz, on 20 October, it was decided to shoot fifty hostages. Pucheu, as Minister of the Interior, was presented with the list. Appalled at finding a large number of *anciens combattants* of 1914–18 on it, he showed his horror. The Germans presented another list, consisting almost entirely of Communists, which he accepted. Forty-eight hostages were shot in the next couple of days. Fifty more were threatened with death, if the murderers were not found.

So it was that once more Vichy played with justice. Communists were, for many Vichy men, less Frenchmen than others. They were classed with the Jews and the freemasons in this. On 25 October Abetz, writing to Ribbentrop, described the Vichy attitude thus: 'The shock of the French Government at the execution of the hostages seems more display than real. This can be explained by the fact that the great majority of the hostages are Communists, and with them elements unwelcome to the Government disappear.'[18]

One man at Vichy was, however, horrified at what was going on: Marshal Pétain. On the 24th, according to Du Moulin de Labarthète, Pétain declared to him his deep emotion at what had happened, and his conviction that Vichy was now dishonoured. What must he do? Protesting was not enough. He must go to Paris and offer himself up as a hostage.

Before the departure, he planned to make a speech on the wireless. The text of this speech, which was never delivered, was later sent to Abetz by Pucheu. It runs as follows:

Herr Führer and Chancellor of the Reich, I turn to you in the most direct way, to beg you in the name of the holy principles of humanity to put a stop to bloody reprisals. Because German officers are being murdered in a cowardly manner by unknown people, of whom there is no proof that they are Frenchmen, 100 Frenchmen have already been executed in two days, and others are threatened.

We are determined to discover and to punish the guilty, and with all our might to fight against the foreign influences which have put the weapons in their hands, but I cannot allow the blood to be shed of those who have no part in these murders. I would be betraying my people if I did not address a solemn protest to you. If you decline to listen to my voice, and if you need further hostages and victims, take me.

I will arrive at the demarcation line at Moulins at 2 p.m. today, where, while awaiting for your decision, I will consider myself your captive.[19]

The message was never delivered on the radio, and the Marshal did not go to the demarcation line. After his decision, he had been approached by quite a number of his ministers, who were against his going. Finally he gave in to them. The 'great gesture' was never performed.

Why did the ministers dissuade Pétain? After all, the gesture was one which might well rally popular opinion round the Marshal once more. As it was, Pétain said nothing on this matter, except to condemn the assassinations of German soldiers in a broadcast on 27 October. There was not even a public protest against the killing of hostages, on the part of the Vichy; and, though the Germans reprieved the fifty extra hostages, public opinion knew nothing of Pétain's initial reactions. The unpopularity of Vichy continued to deepen.

The main thing of which one can be certain is that Pétain did attempt this gesture. On this matter Du Moulin de Labarthète, often so unreliable, is backed up by the evidence from Abetz's telegram. On all other details, however, the two sources differ. Du Moulin describes the gesture as Pétain's own idea, and says how shocked and surprised he himself was by it, only to be won over to it. Abetz, on the other hand (who appears to have got his information from Pucheu), saw it as a plot by some of those in Pétain's entourage: 'This plan which has been communicated to me may be a bluff, to blackmail us into quashing the intended 100 extra shootings. According to information now available to the Embassy, however, it may equally well be a question of a plot by the same elements in the Marshal's entourage who were responsible for 13 December, thought out by the Marshal's *chef de cabinet civil* Du Moulin de Labarthète.'

The reasons for the opposition to this plan by ministers such as Darlan, Pucheu and Romier have been seen by several writers as being based on fear of Pétain being replaced by a Gauleiter, and the whole of France being 'polonised', while no more prisoners were released. According to this account, they persuaded him that he would be deserting the very people he had made it his duty to protect.

Abetz's view at the time, however, was that Pétain's action would have (and was intended to have) disastrous effects both for the Germans and for Vichy:

> If the Führer had accepted such a proposition on the part of Pétain, then, in the opinion of this circle (Du Moulin and Pétain's entourage) the prerequisites would be created for the outbreak of disturbances in France and in North Africa, because France would then have no Head of State. If, on the other hand, Pétain's proposition had been refused by the Führer, then the Marshal would have found himself in an impossible situation, so that a crisis of State authority would have been unavoidable. Marshal Pétain himself did not see through the motives of his plotting advisers, and immediately accepted the proposal, which he saw as something chivalrous. He was eventually dissuaded from it by the energetic protests of Darlan and Pucheu.[20]

Whether Pétain thought up the plan himself, or whether, as Abetz suggests, it was a plot by his entourage, it is clear that Pétain himself was appalled by the executions, and that his actions were undertaken in good faith. It is equally clear that his actions might have led to unpleasant results for Vichy in one form or other. He was perhaps right, in one sense, to be won over not to offer himself up as a hostage; but in the process he lost a great deal of possible public support.

The extra hostages were reprieved. Not, as has sometimes been believed, because of Pétain's intervention, but because of advice from Abetz, who declared the danger of completely estranging French public opinion.[21] This was not to prevent, however, the same kind of measure from being introduced later on.

Foreign affairs—Weygand's recall and the Pétain-Göring interview

After the French attitude to the Paris protocols, Franco-German relations had been extremely strained. Diplomatic relations had been broken off, and Abetz was sent away from Paris for a while. Military government, under General von Stülpnagel, became sterner in the Occupied Zone. Pressure was put on Vichy from all angles.

Determined not to lose the empire, the fleet, or the French North African army, Darlan and Pétain tried desperately, by a series of minor concessions, to bend the German Government's attitude. They allowed, among other things, the buying of lorries by the Germans in North Africa, and the setting up of a larger German Commission there. Against this Weygand objected bitterly, pointing out the danger of a Syria-like situation, and the creeping towards military co-operation.

Weygand himself was to be one of the sacrifices made to the Germans. As early as December 1940 he had been the object of much distrust from the German side: what was he doing in North Africa? Was it safe to leave him there? It was because of uncertainty on these questions that the Germans had drafted in December 1940 a plan for invading the Unoccupied Zone — the 'Attila' plan which was to be used in December 1942. After Laval's dismissal on 13 December, Hitler had made it clear to Darlan on the 25th that he believed that Weygand might have been blackmailing Pétain, by a threat of a North African breakaway, into this action. At the time of the discussions about Laval's return, in January, fear of Weygand's possible intention to go over to the British was expressed. This mistrust, in this form, was on the whole unjustified. Weygand was unlikely to go over to de Gaulle, as was most of the French North African army at this time. They, like the Syrian army, saw de Gaulle as a dissident. Weygand was violently anti-German, and his policy was one of straightforward *attentisme*: building up the French army, in preparation for when it might be used once more. Abetz claims that later in 1941, 'Though the information we had about Weygand did not indicate the intention of betraying us and rallying to the enemy, we had however a sufficiency of proofs that Weygand had remained, in his senility and obstinacy, an irreconcilable enemy of Germany.'[22]

Weygand opposed with all his might the various concessions which Pétain and Darlan attempted to make to the Germans, concessions which he saw as leading them down the slippery slope to military co-operation. It is unknown whether he changed their minds over the Paris Protocols, or whether he was merely used as a scapegoat; but to the Germans he was the wrecker of that agreement. The Germans began to demand his removal from the dangerous post he held. Darlan, too, began to work to that end, whether because he believed it to be a good concession to make to the Germans, or because he hated and feared Weygand, one cannot be sure.

In July, Darlan wrote a couple of letters to Pétain, trying to get himself made Commander-in-Chief of all armed forces, and complaining about Weygand's attitudes. He believed Weygand to be opposed to the Darlan Government, even though he was loyal to Pétain. 'A smell of Gaullism floats in the wake of General Weygand', he wrote. 'I will add that a desire for independence is to be seen in the acts of the Delegate General. . . . You have designated me as your eventual successor. I am not sure that, should the occasion arise, he would respect my authority. If he opposed it, there would be separatism on the part of French Africa. . . .'[23] Shortly after this came Weygand's opposition to the lorry deal in North Africa.

On 8 August Weygand, called by Pétain, arrived at Vichy. Huntziger had already warned him that Darlan wanted fuller powers. At first, all seemed normal. Pétain invited him to dinner in the country with the writer Paul Valéry, and the three men, who were all members of the French Academy, appear to have spent the meal talking about matters to do with that institution.

The next day, however, the meeting took place between Pétain, Darlan, Huntziger and Weygand. Weygand opposed Darlan's desire for extended powers, and pulled his arguments to bits, finally suggesting that there should be a combined Ministry of National Defence. He also, before his departure, reaffirmed his statement that there should be no concessions to Germany in Africa.

Meanwhile, German demands for the removal of Weygand were becoming pressing. In August, Göring had told Brinon that collaboration was impossible with Weygand still there. On 25 September, Abetz transmitted a message from Hitler to Pétain, which described Weygand's presence in North Africa as being an insurmountable obstacle to any constructive Franco-German policy. At the beginning of October, Abetz and Stülpnagel continued to put on the pressure. Darlan, in early October, warned Pétain of the possible results of not giving in to the German pressure. If the French did not give in, fifteen months of Franco-German negotiations would be lost, and no further propositions would come from Germany. It was better to break with the Americans, even if that meant the loss of American supplies in North Africa, and danger to the French West Indies.[24]

Weygand, called to Vichy on 16 October, arrived there on the morning of the 17th. Pétain offered him, in exchange for giving up his North African post, a post as Minister of State, entrusted with the preparation of a 'constitution for the empire'. Weygand violently refused, saying that if the Government wished to sack him, he did not wish any bargain in exchange. After a couple of days of somewhat embarrassed discussions, the fiery little general departed once more for Algiers, to continue his job. Some days after this departure Pétain, who had written to Hitler to say that he found it impossible to separate completely from his most sure collaborator, received a letter from Hitler which contained the most violent recriminations. Franco-German relations had never been at a lower ebb.

Darlan continued his work against Weygand. The Germans were returning to the attack too. At the funeral of General Huntziger (who had died in an air-crash when returning from Africa), Abetz handed Pétain a letter from Hitler, saying that collaboration, which was necessary, was impossible with Weygand still there. (It also deplored French attitudes, which were causing stern measures on the part of the Germans.) Pétain replied that Germany had never really had a collaboration policy with France; she just took what she wanted.

These brave words, however, hid secret fears. And when Abetz made it clear that no German negotiator would speak to Pétain if Weygand was not removed, Weygand was sent for to come to Vichy once more.

He arrived on 16 November; with him he brought a note he had written, in which he pointed out the importance, once it was clear that the German air bombardment of Great Britain had failed, of French North Africa, a counter in the international game whose loss would be disastrous. This the French Government was running the risk of, through letting the Germans in.

Weygand was informed of the German demands. Offered a change of post, he refused, leaving Pétain and Darlan with the choice of defending him against the Germans, or sacking him. On 18 November, they chose the latter. Weygand left in a dignified manner, warning them that 'the way to negotiate with the Germans was not always to give in.'[25]

World opinion, especially American, was appalled by Weygand's removal. In the Vichy Government, Barthélémy came out strongly against the decision, and Carcopino threatened to resign, as did, in the Marshal's entourage, Du Moulin de Labarthète and General Bergeret. None of these resignations were accepted however. And Pétain had, by this dismissal, received what to him seemed a very important concession: he was to be allowed to talk 'soldier to soldier' with his old acquaintance Göring, in the hope of further negotiations.

Pétain placed great hopes on this meeting. His old belief in the 'comradeship of arms' was still strong, and he believed Göring to have shared it when they met in the 'thirties. Surely, now, he and Göring would be able to talk on a plane higher than that of mere civilians like Abetz. He was, unfortunately, to be bitterly disillusioned.

Göring, in the train on the way to meet Pétain at Saint-Florentin, is reported to have said to General Galland, who was accompanying him: 'In twenty minutes I shall have finished with the old gentleman.'[26] He too, was to be disappointed, and to emerge from the meeting an angry man.

Göring had been determined to get, from Pétain, military collaboration and the use of North African bases. Pétain, on the other hand, was determined to get concessions from Göring, and to that end had prepared with Darlan a paper giving France's requirements. After the preliminary discussion, he read this paper out, stressing the liberation of prisoners, the removal of the demarcation line, and the rearming of the French army. He finished, according to Abetz's report, with a reproof to Germany, who had broken her Montoire promises:

> I understood that collaboration implied treating between equals. If instead there is a victor above and a vanquished below, there is no more collaboration, there is what you call a *Diktat*, and what we call *la loi du plus fort*.
>
> France committed, in 1919, the error of not making a peace of collaboration. She had won the war, she had lost the peace. You can win the war alone, you cannot make the peace alone. You cannot make the peace without France. By not making a peace of collaboration, you lay yourself open to losing the peace. Remember what I say.[27]

Göring was furious, and shouted out 'Who are the victors, you or us?' Pétain replied that 'he had never felt more profoundly than in the course of this interview to what extent France had lost the war.' He continued with the words, said simply and with dignity: 'I have confidence in the destiny of France, and in her recovery. As for me, personally, you must realise that for a man of my age there is an escape that it is easy to take, the step from life into death.'

Pétain was determined that Göring should take away his paper, containing France's requests. Göring furiously and childishly refused it on two occasions. Finally, angry himself, Pétain thrust it into Göring's pocket, where it remained. Göring emerged from the conference looking extremely angry. Schmidt, the interpreter, could see no reason for the meeting having taken place at all.

Why did Pétain take such a firm stand? He was, of course, above all interested in possible concessions from the Germans, and Göring was not. Pétain was, as always, determinedly against full military co-operation. And Göring's lack of interest, and overbearing manner, must have made him realise the hopelessness of negotiation. All the hopes he had based on Göring's military comradeship must have collapsed at the sight of his blustering, arrogant conqueror. So he behaved with dignity, even in the face of his crushed hopes. Darlan later made it known that he felt that Pétain had been 'too intransigent' at the interview, and that he, Darlan, would have preferred it 'if less had been asked for, and more given.'[28]

Be that as it may, the Saint-Florentin interview, and the entry of America into the war on 7 December, mark a new phase in the drama of Vichy. The one event had shown the impossibility of proper collaboration. The other had shown that Germany was not necessarily going to win. From now on Darlan and Pétain, while attempting to save France from 'polonisation', and from the results of German threats, were to be less co-operative with the Germans. This attitude was gradually to lead to German pressure for the return of Laval.

Chapter Four

Events of 1942

ON 20 December Göring demanded (1) whether France would agree to camouflaged supplies being sent to Rommel's army via Bizerta, and (2) whether they would in principal agree to fight on Rommel's side if he was flung back by the enemy into south Tunisia. The French Government replied by demanding exorbitant returns for any such agreement: complete military, naval and air freedom in Africa and the west Mediterranean, remilitarisation of south Tunisia, supplies of all kinds of petrols and oils in large quantities, etc. Nothing came of the proposed agreement.

Instead, Vichy's attitude to the Germans became gradually less and less friendly, for the reasons discussed at the end of the last chapter. Their many protests and refusals of co-operation showed that the French were now prepared to be awkward. Most important of all, military collaboration was rejected.

By the end of January, it became clear that the Germans wanted to get rid of Darlan; and on 24 February Pétain was informed that if Laval was not brought back into the Government, a Gauleiter would be appointed. Once again, the threat of 'Polonisation'. In March the same threats were repeated.

In Vichy itself, many people were against Darlan. Others in Pétain's entourage had even been won over to the idea of Laval's return. All these people were worried by the breakdown of Franco-German relations, which they blamed on Darlan. They blamed him, too, for the failure of the National Revolution, and the chaos into which the Riom trials had degenerated. Nothing had gone right for him. Under their influence, the Marshal began to move towards the idea of Laval's return.

In Paris Laval, as well as trying to glean support from the main collaborationist groups, was also in touch with the Germans. In March, through Marquet's good offices, he met Helmut Knochen, one of the main S.S. men in Paris, and declared that he was extremely worried by the deterioration in Franco-German relations, and would like to discuss this with somebody of importance on the German side. Göring was coming to Paris two days later, so Knochen arranged an interview for Laval with him.

In the interview, according to Laval, he could hardly get a word in edgeways. Göring made a long tirade attacking the French, whose real feelings of hostility to Germany were now clear. Germany would treat France in accordance with these feelings. The threat was clear; France would get its Gauleiter.

Laval's son-in-law, René de Chambrun, brought the news of Göring's threats to Pétain at Vichy on 25 March. The next day, Pétain met Laval in the Forest of Randan. Laval stressed the danger of Darlan's policies and the weakness of the Government. The situation was grave, he declared. Pétain said he would speak to Darlan.

Pétain appeared to be in a cleft stick. He still could not stand Laval, but if it was a choice between Laval and 'polonisation',—well, he would have to give in as he had done over Weygand. Anything to save the French people from terrible suffering. And Laval might well be the man of the moment, to keep Germany at bay. When Pétain saw Darlan, he persuaded the furious Admiral to offer Laval a post in the Government. This Laval refused, probably because he wanted Darlan's place or nothing.

All was now in a state of indecision. And it was at this moment that an outside power took action which was, in fact, to have the opposite effect from that intended. The United States, appalled by the idea of a return of Laval, threatened to break off diplomatic relations if he were included in the Vichy Government. Though Pétain's immediate reaction seems to have been to follow the American wishes, the ultimate effect of the American intervention, when it was made known to the Germans, was for even greater pressure to be put on from the German side for Laval's return. Sources disagree as to the extent to which Hitler himself presented an ultimatum on this matter; but clearly, by the time the German Government's statements reached Vichy, via Laval's friend Abetz, the French Government were faced with the choice between Laval's return and Hitler's displeasure.

Pétain was thus caught between two fires. Which was the worse, to displease Hitler or to displease the Americans? Eventually he chose the latter course; once more the dangers to France of a far more stern German attitude were clear to him, and he had to give in. He had to scrap the Government changes he had planned at the beginning of April, and consider how to bring Laval into the Government. All this not without some to-ing and fro-ing, however. On 10 April it was decided to offer Laval the post of Foreign Minister, with Darlan remaining Vice-Premier. It was expected that Laval would refuse this, and that all would be thus settled. When Darlan saw Laval on the 11th, however, Laval added to his refusal a demand to be made head of the Government. This Darlan, appalled by the dangers to France, was at first prepared to get accepted by Pétain. Further waverings on both Darlan's and Pétain's part were resolved on the 13th by the arrival of Dr Ménétrel, Pétain's confidant, at Vichy with the news that Abetz had renewed the threat of a choice between Laval and the appointment of a Gauleiter. That afternoon Brinon arrived by 'plane from Paris, to urge a quick decision.

Darlan had suggested to Pétain, as one of the solutions to the situation, that Laval should become Deputy Premier, while he himself became Commander-in-Chief of all the armed forces. This proposal Pétain now accepted, and it was put forward by Darlan and Brinon to Laval on the same day.

Within the Government there was great opposition in certain quarters to Laval's return; and it was those very quarters for whom Laval himself held the greatest rancour. The 'men of 13 December' had not been forgotten by him—Darlan appears to have been the only one to escape his vengeance—and they knew what awaited them if he returned. Their efforts to stop this return were unavailing, however. Talks between Pétain and Laval took place on 14 and 16 April, and on 18 April the new Government was announced.

The return of Laval

Laval's position was a new one, very much in accordance with the powers he had demanded in February 1941. He was now *chef du gouvernement* or Prime Minister, as opposed to Deputy Premier. He was responsible only to the Head of State, Pétain, many of whose powers he had now taken over. He was also Foreign Minister, Minister of the Interior, and Minister of Information. Darlan, who was now Commander-in-Chief, did however remain Pétain's dauphin.

Pétain had not only lost a great deal of power on paper; he was also, over the next six months, gradually dominated more and more by the personality of Laval. Laval was now the chief executive. It was he who initiated the policies of Vichy. As Constitutional Act No. 9 put it:

'The effective direction of France's internal and external policy is assumed by the Head of Government, appointed by the Head of State and responsible only to him. The Head of Government presents the ministry for approval by the Head of State; he renders to him an account of his initiatives and his actions.'

Pétain had thus become merely a figurehead. Laval saw him every day to get his policies approved, but this was a mere formality. And the old Marshal, less and less in command of the situation because of his age, was also by now dominated by Laval's personality. Above all, though Pétain had the constitutional right to sack Laval, he now knew that he could never do it without the Germans invading the Unoccupied Zone. He was in an impossible situation. From now on, in the general running of the nation's business, he played next to no part. He remained a symbol for the people of France, of whom few realised how much his power had been curtailed. It was he who retained so many people's loyalty to the Vichy Government, and it was to him that the army still owed its loyalty. In times of stress, therefore, such as November 1942 and December 1943, he still had a part to play. But for the rest of the time it was Laval's decisions which were paramount.

Laval's ministers, too, were no longer ministers in the generally accepted sense of the word. It was he who made the decisions, and it was they who carried them out. In the circumstances, their names are not of as great importance as those of previous Governments had been. It is interesting nevertheless to note that not only the 'men of 13 December' departed, but also most of Darlan's other ministers, including the technocrats. In their place

Pétain making a broadcast

Pétain and Hitler. The handshake at Montoire, October 1940

came certain old cronies of Laval's, and particularly Pierre Cathala at the Finance Ministry (though Adrien Marquet refused to join). The only men of importance from Darlan's Government who remained were Lucien Romier, Joseph Barthélémy (Minister of Justice), Admiral Platon and Jacques Benoist-Méchin. Among the more sinister additions were Paul Marion and Ferdinand de Brinon.

Sinister as these two may have been, however, they were nothing in comparison to the Paris collaborators whom Laval had used in his attempt to return to power. It is all the more surprising, therefore, that Laval put neither Doriot nor Déat into his Government. He used them, and then relinquished them. By playing the two off against each other, he managed to give nothing to either. This gives credibility to Warner's view that his opinions were far from those of these extremists.[1] This view will be born out, also, by a study of Laval's policies at this time.

Seven months of government

The return of Laval marked the end of any pretence that the National Revolution had succeeded. That it had had small chance of success had been clear to those in power for some time. Not only had German interference hindered the basic workings of the proposed system; the ever-present problem of France's relationship with Germany had also caused these internal policies to recede into the background as unimportant. Where, in 1940, most of the Government had been far more concerned with internal reform than with Franco-German relations, the realities of the situation had gradually forced themselves upon Vichy, until what would, even in normal conditions, have seemed an enormous task of national reorganisation, was seen to be impossible in a situation of national crisis. One might, if one were a cynic, add that any corporatist system based on the goodness of mankind, such as the proposed Vichy system of corporations run by both employers and employed, was doomed to failure through the conflicting interests of unregenerate mankind.

Laval had never been interested in the National Revolution. He was not so much opposed to it as scornful of it. He saw it as an unrealistic pastime which diverted the French Government from more important matters. His dismissal in 1940 had in part been caused by his isolation within a 'National Revolution' Government. His return meant that the failure of the policy, already apparent to many, was publicly consecrated. We hear little more of the matter.

Laval's views on internal politics remained very much as they had been before the war—a belief in an authoritarian republic. If, in his speeches in these months, he at times paid lip-service to a fascist ideal of a 'new order', it was in order to assuage some of the pressures upon him, both from the Germans and from French fascists such as Doriot, rather than because he believed in these ideas. A speech he made on the wireless on 20 October 1942 contains, for those reasons, an almost classic statement of fascist theory (the destruction of the capitalist system, the setting-up of a

L   301

new order, the maintenance of that order by force—the last of these propositions, with its pessimistic view of human nature, being the main point
which differentiates Fascism from Communism, whose 'new order' should in
theory eventually work of its own accord, with every man free to decide
for himself to join in the work for the communal good). Describing the
threat of Soviet victory, Laval said: 'It would ... mean the end of the
human, generous policy ... of real socialism which, built on the ruins of a
capitalism which has abused its power, will impose itself on Europe tomorrow, while at the same time respecting the individual genius of each nation.'[2]

The statement might have been made by Doriot; and it shows the extent
to which Laval was prepared to bend to pressures, though it does not tell
us anything about his actual political opinions.

The pressures on Laval at this time were many. Most important, of
course, were the Germans; but the Americans, too, were among his worries.
At home, he had the strong opposition of the Paris collaborators, especially
Doriot, and the growing power of the Resistance. It is typical of Laval's
fate that, trying to steer amid all these shoals, he succeeded in pleasing
nobody except perhaps possibly himself. Though who is to say how much
he may have saved for France through his incessant bargaining?

For Laval, Germany still had a great chance to win the war. But, whether
she won or lost, it was in France's best interest to stay at the moment on
the German side. Unlike Darlan, for whom doubts about German victory
had meant doubts about collaboration, Laval saw the importance, at the
moment, of safeguarding French interests, and, in the future, of resisting
Bolshevik domination of Europe.

The Germans, however, were less interested by now in agreement with
France than in what they could get out of her. German attitudes were com-
pounded of suspicion of French motives (which they saw as basically
attentiste or even secretly hostile) and greed for French resources, including
now French workers. Laval, far from being the important figure to the
Germans that recent ultimatums had made him seem, was in fact regarded
with either scorn or mistrust by most Nazi leaders. Laval's work, then,
was immeasurably harder than he at first realised.

Nevertheless, Laval managed by hard bargaining to produce various
results. By sanctioning the departure to Germany of French workers to
replace those on the Russian front, he managed to make a bargain with
the hard-pressed Germans whereby for every three skilled workers one
French prisoner of war was paroled (though this was far less than he had
hoped for). His speeches exhorting French workers to go, on behalf of the
Europe for which Germany was making so many sacrifices, were, however,
little heeded. The numbers never reached the figure that the Germans had
wanted. In fact, they were merely a fraction of it. In the circumstances,
the Germans made a decree making everyone in German-administered
territories liable to labour services. Laval reacted violently, saying that
France was not German-administered. Typically, however, he created a
French law making compulsory labour service; the principle was carried

through, but French sovereignty was saved. It was Vichy that would do the compulsion. This is typical of many steps, including those in relation to the Jews, in which the safe-guarding of French sovereignty meant doing the Germans' dirty work for them. By November, however, the numbers still remained very low in comparison with German demands, and one is left with the impression that Laval, by his usual procrastinating methods, had cheated the Germans of their aims while pretending to help them. Nevertheless, he had in public supported the German aims, and passed the law permitting compulsion; this was to stand him in bad stead both at the time, in the matter of popularity, and after the war, at his trial.

The same is true of Laval's attitude to the Jewish question at this time. Convinced that the Germans had the power and the will to put into effect the deportations which in this year became part of their policy for France, Laval, instead of opposing the policy in its entirety, devoted himself to what he considered to be the 'politics of the possible'. On 11 June 1942, the Germans demanded 100,000 Jews. By the 23rd of the same month, the order came that all Jews were to be deported from France.

The anti-semitic laws in both zones of France had been as nothing in comparison to this. And, whether or not the authorities knew the eventual fate awaiting the deported, it was clear to all that the intention was not a favourable one to the Jews. In the circumstances, one might have expected even the Vichy Government to resist the whole policy with all its might.

This was not Laval's strategy, however. Convinced that the Germans could not be stopped entirely, he endeavoured, in his usual market-place manner, to try to save French Jews by giving up the foreign ones. And, in order once more to assert 'French sovereignty', he got the French authorities to assist in the rounding-up of these foreign and stateless Jews. The *grande rafle* of July 1942 was one of the results, in which 13,000 foreign Jews were interned in appalling conditions in the Vel d'Hiv (a sports ground) in Paris. Other such Jews were brought by train from the internment camps in the Unoccupied Zone to the Occupied Zone in August. By the end of August about 27,000 Jews had been deported.

Laval's position in this, as on so many other things, is a difficult one to grasp. He had nothing against the Jews; indeed, he did much to reduce the numbers taken from France in the next two years, as we shall see. Léon Poliakov, a Jewish historian, wrote of Laval in the evidence he gave to the Eichmann trial: 'We shall see that the ruses and manoeuvres of this disconcerting character were not always unfavourable to Jewish interests. (Did he not go as far as to exclaim at his trial after the war: "I would have wished to be judged by a jury of French Jews!") The symbol of French "collaboration", Laval was a politician completely without principles, but also completely without fanaticism. He willingly expressed his sympathy for the Jews, even under the occupation, in the presence of functionaries of the Third Reich.'[3]

Laval's attempt to make the best of a bad job, and to save the French Jews, put him, however, in the position of one of the persecutors of the foreign Jews, a role which he pursued with some vigour. He appears to have had none of the feelings for them that he possessed for the French Jews. Once again, his policy of bargaining may have had some good results in the saving of lives; but the lack of principles at its base made the French Government once more the instrument of a barbarous policy. The Jewish persecutions drove even more Frenchmen against the Vichy Government. Contemporary documents show, however, how much Laval's attitude, and his skilful use of Pétain's figure, did to save French Jews. A document sent to Berlin by S.S. Standartenführer Knochen in September shows how the Germans had to give in on this matter:

Subject: Deportation of Jews from France.
After the arrest of Jews of foreign nationality in the occupied and unoccupied territories was completed, an attempt was made to arrest also Jews of French nationality. The political situation and President Laval's views on the matter do not permit action without considering the consequences.

I had a discussion with the French Police Chief Bousquet. Based on the results of this discussion and in view of Laval's opinion and the present situation, the Higher S.S. Police Chief sent a teletype letter to the Reichsführer S.S., pointing out that in view of Pétain's attitude such an action would have severe consequences.

The Reichsführer S.S. concurred in this opinion and ordered that no Jews of French nationality are to be arrested for the time being. Large scale Jewish deportations are therefore impossible.[4]

Laval's views may well have reflected Pétain's. We have seen, earlier in the war, Pétain's attitude to French Jews, and above all to ex-service Jews, as opposed to foreign Jews. But whether Pétain really took the same attitudes as Laval, or whether Laval was using his name and prestige, as on other occasions, we will never know.

Laval had by now, as we have seen, fully taken over the reins of government. One of the external signs of this was the importance now laid on Laval's public speeches, and the dearth of public utterances by Pétain. For the public, however, Pétain still remained ultimately responsible for French policy; as, in a sense, he was, for he still had to be consulted by Laval, officially. Claudel's views at this period, expressed in his private diary, show how public blame was laid on Pétain. He refers to the 'terrible persecutions against the Jews', and then goes on: 'The war of Christ has been declared against the people of Vichy. On Laval's part all this is natural, but what can one think of the Marshal! One more step down into shame! This is the same infamous individual who wrote to Hitler to congratulate him on liberating France from British aggression and *cleaning* the territory of aggressors. Will there ever be enough spittle for that traitor's face!'[5] Claudel's last sentences refer to Pétain's reaction to the Dieppe raid, which we will come to later.

Faced by Germany on one side, Laval continued to attempt collaboration. He also tried to palliate certain measures by his bargaining. On the other hand, he was also faced with adverse attitudes from the United States. Here, too, by bargaining and concessions, Laval succeeded in getting concessions in return. Yet this, again, put him in the bad books of the Germans. In this situation Laval, with pressure from both sides, could hardly win.

It was the same in internal French affairs. On the one side there was the Resistance, daily growing stronger. On the other, there were the Paris collaborators, especially Doriot, who was furious at having been left out of Laval's Government, and now, to many, seemed to be threatening Laval's position as Premier, and possibly to be intending to take his place. It was possibly for fear of a German-aided Doriot threat that Laval's public pronouncements took on a decidedly more 'European' tinge, with 'national-socialist' overtones.

Pétain, as we have seen, was by now taking a back seat. But there are a few moments in these months when his public attitudes (though this was later denied) seem to have shown him as being in harmony with the Government's policy. And despite the later denials, there is little evidence that this was not so, at any rate on foreign policy.

The first case in which his attitudes are in doubt is the question of the speech made by Laval on 22 June, in which he not only put forward an exhortation for workers to go to Germany, but also added: 'I desire the victory of Germany, because without it bolshevism would tomorrow install itself everywhere.' This statement, an accurate account of Laval's stance at this time, was to be one of the major indictments against both Laval and Pétain after the war. Pétain claimed later that he had protested against it; but there is no contemporary evidence to support this claim, and, indeed, Laval insisted that he had shown the text to Pétain before the broadcast. At the time, said Laval, Pétain had merely objected to the phrase 'I believe in the victory of Germany' (claiming that Laval, not being a soldier, could not believe in it), and that he had not demurred when Laval had replaced it with 'I desire the victory of Germany.' This rings true; Pétain's finicky corrections to the speeches written for him by his *nègres* contained just such points. At the trial, Pétain objected to Laval's account, but the prosecution produced a written statement by an eye-witness to the scene, Charles Rochat of the Foreign Ministry, which corroborated Laval's evidence. Pétain, in fact, appears to have raised no objection to the content of the speech. As in so many cases, his post-war evidence is an attempt to white-wash himself.

Other interventions of Pétain at this time had to do with military col-laboration with the Reich, of which he had now, with growing danger to France from the Allies, become partly in favour, if it was used for France's own defence. At the end of May he had two interviews with Rahn, of the German Embassy. Abetz, in a telegram on 1 June, described the content of these interviews: 'He [Pétain] stated, with extraordinary care, that he considered Anglo-American attacks against France or North Africa as inevitable. As far as North and West Africa are concerned, Marshal Pétain asked for Franco-German preventive measures to be envisaged following talks between the German and French general staffs ... Marshal Pétain declared that in the case of an Anglo-American attack against Metropolitan France, he would consider it a duty for the French Government to offer to the German command the co-operation of the French army, and should the occasion arise to assign it a small sector of the Atlantic coast.'[6]

This shows Pétain's willingness, if French territory was threatened, to join in the defence of it. It is also connected with a wish to reinforce the French army.

In August, after the abortive raid by British and Canadian troops on Dieppe, Pétain sent a letter to Hitler, again stressing the need for Franco-German collaboration on defence. (The authenticity of this letter was questioned at the Pétain trial, and in later years by such writers as Noguères. Warner, however, has produced new evidence which makes its authenticity far more likely.[7]) This letter ran as follows:

> After a conversation I have just had with President Laval, and following the recent British attack which, this time, took place on our soil, I propose to envisage France's participation in her own defence. If you approve the principle of this, I am prepared to examine in detail the forms of this participation. I ask you, M. le Chancelier du Reich, to consider this initiative as the sincere expression of my desire to allow France to make a contribution to the protection of Europe.[8]

Pétain regarded British attacks, whether on France or her empire, as acts of aggression; and he clearly wanted France to help in her own defence. These facts must be borne in mind when we view his attitudes at the time of the American landings in November.

It is not clear, however, whether Pétain sent to the German Commander-in-Chief the letter of congratulation on the repulsing of the Dieppe raid which was made public, and which aroused much revulsion, including that of Claudel in his diary in the passage already quoted. Pétain, and others, may have been glad of the German success; or they may, privately, have wished to show their solidarity with the Germans; but they must have realised that a public statement of this kind would cause them immense unpopularity. As Warner has pointed out, however, it is when we find that the message was handed over by Brinon that we realise that Pétain's later disclaimers may well have been true, and that Brinon, the arch-collaborator and believer in a German Europe may well have made up the message himself.

So the year drew on, with the threat of Allied landings making Pétain draw nearer to military collaboration. In the background however, Darlan, was already in contact with the Americans, offering them his support should a landing occur (though the Allies never really trusted him in this). France's position with the Germans had been bedevilled earlier in the year by the escape of General Giraud from German captivity. He was now living in Vichy France, as yet another important military figure. Though he had given his word of honour as an officer to do nothing which could in any way harm France's relations with the German Government, Giraud, too, was in touch with the Americans as early as June, and was preparing with them and the various North African residents the preliminaries to the November landings. It was these landings which were once more to put everything into the balance in Vichy France.

The North African landings, November 1942

Pétain's reactions to the North African landings have been much discussed, and many different interpretations have been given of them. The existence, or non-existence, of certain secret documents which no longer exist has been one of the factors contributing to the confusion. When we look closely at the evidence, however, we can at least see that many of Pétain's actions are explicable by his previous attitudes, even though certain areas of the events of this week remain obscure.

The American landings took place on the night of 7–8 November 1942. They had in part been prepared for by various conspirators in North Africa itself, especially the now famous 'Five', working on behalf of General Giraud. The Americans did not receive the welcome they had expected, however. This was partly because, not fully trusting the French, they had launched the attack earlier than stated, and Giraud was not yet on the spot. It was partly, also, because by chance Admiral Darlan was in North Africa, owing to the illness of his son Alain. It was, above all, based on a misunderstanding, both on the part of the Americans and the conspirators, of the nature of the loyalty of the North African army to the Marshal and his appointed representatives. Giraud had been chosen because, quite rightly, it was seen that the army would not come over to de Gaulle at this stage; but the question of loyalty and military discipline had been neglected, and it was not realised that Giraud, too, was inadequate for the task.

Some of the army was in with the conspirators. Indeed, on the night of the landings General Béthouart, the commander of the Casablanca division, placed under arrest General Noguès, the Resident General of Morocco, who had ordered resistance to the Americans. By the time the landings took place, however, loyal troops had freed Noguès and arrested Béthouart. In Morocco and Algeria resistance was the order of the day. General Destrée at Casablanca, General Boisson at Oran, remained loyal, while in Algiers an attempted revolt by the conspirators only succeeded in holding on to various public buildings for a short while, not long enough for the Americans to reach them.

So it was that Darlan, the Marshal's representative, became of prime importance. He was furious with the Americans (with whom he himself had been in contact) for keeping him in the dark about their plans; there was a certain amount of personal pique involved. But he was also aware that the fact that landings had taken place in North Africa, and not in France itself, could make things extremely serious for France. His view had always been that such landings must be simultaneous; otherwise the 'polonisation' with which France had so often been threatened might well take place. Many of the actions taken by both Darlan and Pétain over the next few days can be explained by this fear.

Above all, Darlan was loyal to Pétain. He, and all the armed forces, had taken a personal oath to the Marshal. The strength of such ties, within such a traditional body as the French army and the French navy, must not be underestimated.

Meanwhile, what was Pétain himself doing? The news of the landings reached Vichy at 3 a.m. Vichy time. An hour later, a message was received from President Roosevelt explaining the American act, and stressing that it had been done to help liberate France from the Axis yoke. Roosevelt affirmed that the United States was not ambitious for territory, and that North Africa would remain French.

It says a great deal about the organisation of Vichy when one realises that Pétain was not awoken to receive the news or this message. He did not surface until 7 a.m. Meanwhile Laval, who had arrived from Châteldon at 4.15 a.m., was drafting the reply which the Marshal should send to Roosevelt. He was also considering the question of German air support, which had already been mooted. Admiral Auphan, the Minister of Marine, was told to send a telegram to Darlan asking what kind of Axis air support he would like.[9]

Pétain awoke at about 7 a.m., and was informed of what had happened. Dr Ménétrel handed him Laval's draft reply to Roosevelt, which he willingly signed:

> It is with stupor and grief that I learn this night of the aggression of your troops against North Africa. I have read your message. You invoke pretexts which nothing justifies. You ascribe to your enemies intentions which have never been translated into acts. . . . I have always declared that we would defend our Empire if it were attacked, and you knew that we would defend it against any aggressor, whoever he might be. You knew that I would keep my word. . . . We are being attacked, we shall defend ourselves. That is the order that I am giving.[10]

Shortly after this message had been sent off, Pétain sent a telegram to Darlan, telling him to act on his behalf in North Africa, and assuring him that he had his full confidence. This has been taken by some historians, e.g. Aron, to mean that Pétain was playing a double game, and leaving Darlan free to negotiate with the Americans; nothing in the telegram itself, or in the situation at the time, however, seems to support this contention. Pétain was merely confirming Darlan's position as his representative, and plenipotentiary. 'You can act, and then inform me.' the telegram ran. 'You have my full confidence.'

Pétain's attitude at this stage seems to have been the logical one described in the telegram to Roosevelt. France had declared her neutrality, and her intention to defend herself and her colonies against all attackers. She must thus oppose the American landings. Pétain's first duty was to the people of metropolitan France, who were being endangered by these landings. That he was not alone in these attitudes is shown by the unanimous approval given by the Cabinet that morning to his orders for resistance.

Meanwhile, Laval had been in touch with the Germans. To a German request for France to break off diplomatic relations with the United States, he had responded with a request for a German guarantee of the French empire and territories such as had been given by the Americans. Continually trying to displease neither the Germans nor the Americans, Laval was also trying to find compromise solutions on such problems as German air assistance. Darlan, similarly trying not to put France in too categorical a position, and aware of the probable German reaction if no help was accepted, had asked merely for Axis air help against Allied shipping, and not against the land forces, and had insisted that the planes used their usual aerodromes in Sardinia and Sicily. Laval accepted this compromise plan, which was militarily fairly useless.

In the afternoon, a German demand for France to declare war on the United States and Great Britain was received. Laval did not agree to this, though, despite his later claims, it is not clear that he gave a downright refusal at this point.

Meanwhile, Pétain had sent for Weygand, for advice. Weygand's reaction, as might have been expected, went to the opposite extreme: to declare war on Germany, and to join the Americans. This advice was ignored by Pétain.

That evening, the Vichy Government, while deciding not to break off relations with the Americans as a positive thing, decided in order to avoid German retaliation, to declare that the Americans had, by their action, broken off relations.

By the end of this day, then, resistance to the Americans had been decided, but a general declaration of war had been avoided. Vichy, determined to protect those in France, was doing all it could to placate the Germans, short of such a declaration. They were between two stools. The policy was, of course, doomed to failure. By the end of the day the Americans were clearly winning in North Africa, and the dreaded German invasion of the Unoccupied Zone seemed near.

By 7 p.m. on 8 November, General Juin had, with Darlan's agreement, started negotiations for a cease-fire in Algiers itself. Just after midnight Hitler, mistrustful of French motives, demanded German and Italian use of air bases in Algeria and Tunisia, a demand to which the French had to give in.

The 9th was to be a day of negotiations. Laval headed for Berchtesgaden to see Hitler and Mussolini. Juin had meanwhile signed an armistice with the Americans in Algiers, and Darlan, approached by the Americans about a cease-fire agreement throughout North Africa, had not rejected the proposals, but had asked for the details of them. Laval, before his departure for Germany, had however persuaded Pétain to order Darlan not to continue any negotiations until his (Laval's) return. So during this day things remained in suspended animation, with Laval on the way to Germany, Darlan in Algiers, and Pétain at Vichy. Darlan, obeying orders, received the

American proposals for a cease-fire that evening without replying to them; he merely sent them on to Pétain, assuring him that any order he gave would be carried out.

The hour for Pétain's decision was approaching. The day of the 10th was the fatal moment. Torn between the Germans and Americans, but above all attached to his native France, he had to decide which of many evils was the least. It was now clear that the Allies were not going to land in metropolitan France. Should he fly, therefore, to North Africa? This would be to leave the French in France to the fate from which he had tried to save them in 1940, or to an even worse fate, the 'polonisation' with which they had been so often threatened. To anyone who knew him, the Marshal's answer to this proposition would be obvious. Another possibility was to allow negotiations with the Allies in North Africa, while himself remaining in France; but this, too, would not save the Unoccupied Zone from invasion, nor the French from punishment. Resistance to the Germans, in the Unoccupied Zone, would be heroic, but futile without Allied support. Among other possibilities was that of retiring, and opting out altogether; but of this Pétain would have been incapable. He had truly given France the '*don de sa personne*' in 1940. The other main line of action which would be possible would be to stick with the Germans, and to continue resistance in North Africa.

Pétain's actual actions at this time will always remain a matter of controversy, for reasons which we shall see. One thing is sure, however; in the absence of Laval, and with the armed forces still owing their loyalty to him personally, Pétain had once more taken the centre of the stage. And he retained a will of his own. Many were those around him who tried to persuade him to fly to Africa; he steadfastly refused. This solution, at least, he counted out, for, as he said, he could never leave the tiller of France in this dark hour.

At 1.30 p.m. on the 10th, news reached Vichy that, despite Pétain's order of the previous day, Darlan, under heavy American pressure, had surrendered, with all North African troops. Laval, when he heard of this, telephoned from Germany to protest that any negotiations he might have with the Germans would be wrecked by a premature surrender. Whether under the influence of this telephone call or not, Pétain sent a telegram to Darlan telling him to continue the struggle: 'I gave the order to defend Africa. I maintain that order.'

This reaction would seem to be in accord with the line of action which would do most, at this time, to save the French population from German vengeance; i.e. continued resistance. It must therefore not be discounted as not being Pétain's own decision, even if Laval's telephone call may have had some effect, too.

On receipt of Pétain's message, Darlan said he would annul his order, and give himself up as a prisoner. Much has been made, however, of secret telegrams which were sent from Pétain to Darlan on this day, using a secret naval code unknown to the Germans, which encouraged Darlan to continue acting as he had been doing, with the Marshal's full confidence. We have, unfortunately, little proof on either side on this question. Opinions are divided. On the one hand, it is pointed out that the story is one created after the event, and containing added details, on the other, that there is little to contradict it, even if there is no direct evidence.

The most that can be said is that even without the secret telegrams, Pétain's actions on this day and the next were coherent and explicable; and that Darlan's eventual actions can be, as we shall see, perfectly well explained by other facts.

Pétain, while ordering the continuance of the struggle in North Africa (which might keep the Germans out of the Unoccupied Zone,) nevertheless took precautions against the eventuality of a German invasion. He took over the command, in Darlan's absence, of the armed forces in France, and gave orders for action in the case of a German invasion across the demarcation line.

Meanwhile, at Berchtesgaden, the Germans had been demanding that their troops should be allowed to land in Tunisia. Laval had said that the best way for this to be brought about was for an ultimatum to be sent to Vichy about it. When this came, Pétain, though strongly criticising Laval, in conversation, for having given in too easily, nevertheless allowed the order to be sent telling the French forces not to resist the German and Italian forces.

Despite all the efforts made by Pétain to avoid such an event, on the morning of the 11th the German invasion of the Unoccupied Zone took place. Laval learned, in Germany at 4 a.m., that the order had been given. A letter from Hitler to Pétain, announcing it, reached Vichy at 5.30 a.m. By 7 o'clock, the German troops were already pouring across the frontier. There was no French opposition; Pétain had been asleep when Hitler's message was received, and, without consulting him, his ministers gave the order not to oppose the enemy, a heroic gesture which would have had little effect.

Pétain, when he awoke, declared that the breaking of the armistice agreements meant that France was now in a state of war with Germany (or so, at any rate, he was reported to have spoken, according to German sources).[11] But this was too late.

What was the French Government now to do? Weygand, and Admiral Auphan, suggested that the order should be sent to Darlan to cease fire in North Africa. Platon and Rochat, however, argued against this, particularly because Laval had warned the latter that the Germans might exact terrible reprisals if Vichy seemed to go in with the Allies. So it was decided to take no decision until Laval's return, except to make General Noguès, the Resident General of Morocco, Darlan's successor as the man in command in North Africa.

Pétain nevertheless took a decision that was to influence the situation immensely. Egged on by Weygand, he decided to deliver a strongly-worded public protest to the Germans. He received Field-Marshal von Rundstedt at 10.40 a.m. and read him the protest, which had in part been drafted by Weygand. The text was then read out on the wireless. It ran: 'I have during this night received a letter from the Führer, in which he informs me that military necessities force him to take measures which have the effect of destroying the content and basis of the armistice agreement. I solemnly protest against decisions which are incompatible with the armistice conventions.'[12]

This statement, and the indication it gave of the Marshal's attitude to the German invasion, was to be of enormous effect. In North Africa, it influenced Darlan to the extent of convincing him that he could take up once more his freedom of action;[13] indeed, this is what appears to have directed his actions, rather than any secret telegrams which may have existed. He ordered resistance to the German landings. In France and North Africa, it made many change sides. And it made the Germans, aware of these effects, even more mistrustful of Pétain's aims than before.

An official German telegram sent that evening ran as follows: 'In circles friendly to Germany people are pointing out that Pétain's protest is the final scene in a comedy which has been being played for a long time, and which has been in preparation for open betrayal of Germany. They continually point out that only energetic measures can save the situation. The falling away of so-called collaborators is growing from hour to hour, as many people have been strongly affected by the attitude Marshal Pétain has taken up. People are turning away from the Germans, in order not to compromise themselves.'[14]

So the effect of Pétain's attitude was tremendous, even though in Paris itself many people, through German interference, had been unable to hear the protest itself on the wireless.[15] This must be remembered whenever we wish to assess Pétain's attitude at this time. His waking anger (attested by even German sources) and his dignified and courageous protest are some of the last examples we shall have of what was best in his attitudes. From now on fear of German reprisals against the people of France was, on the return of Laval at 2 p.m. on the 11th, to take the upper hand in his thoughts.

For Laval's return was the turning-point in these events. At a Cabinet meeting at 5.30 p.m., at which Admiral Auphan spoke in favour of a cease-fire in North Africa, Laval clearly stated that a cease-fire in Africa would mean war in France itself. The Cabinet accepted Laval's proposal that Pétain should announce his reliance on the French North African army continuing its struggle.

To this Pétain agreed. Once more he had been persuaded by Laval that the fate of those in France depended on giving in to the German demands. His moment of heroism had passed; but it had enabled many to see that their duty lay in opposition to the Germans.

That evening orders were sent to Admiral Derrien, in Bizerta, to continue opposition to the Anglo-Saxons, and to allow the German forces through. This was but one more in a series of orders and counter-orders which Derrien had received. The chaos in Bizerta had been immense, as orders came from Darlan, Noguès and Pétain, each contradicting the other. In the course of one day, the French troops there had been ordered (1) to maintain neutrality, (2) to attack the Germans and Italians, (3) to maintain neutrality again, (4) to fight the Allies.

On this same day, 11 November, General Noguès signed an armistice in Morocco with the Americans. By the next day, the 12th, it was clear to all, including the Americans, that the French forces were not resisting the Axis troops in Tunisia. Noguès had an unpleasant interview with the fiery American General Clark, who told him that he did not recognise either Pétain or Noguès, and insisted on Giraud being brought into any agreement.

It was this threat that must have moved Noguès to send an urgent telegram to Vichy at 3.30 a.m. on the 13th, requesting that Darlan be reappointed Pétain's representative, in order to negotiate a general armistice and to keep the traitor Giraud out of power. The rest of the telegram seems to imply that Darlan would then take a neutral role, as opposed to the anti-Axis combatant role which Giraud might take up. To this telegram no reply was sent for at least twelve hours, by which time the situation had considerably changed.

By three o'clock that afternoon a Franco-American agreement in North Africa had been reached. Darlan was to be Head of Government of French North Africa; Giraud was to head the armed forces (though for the time being this latter fact was to be kept quiet, as the French forces would follow Darlan, Pétain's representative, rather than a man they must presume to be a traitor). Noguès announced that he had handed over all his powers to Darlan; Darlan said that he had taken over responsibility on behalf of the Government, and with the agreement of the Americans.

Laval's reply to Noguès's telegram thus came too late. Admiral Auphan claims that the Marshal agreed to Darlan's reinstatement, but that Laval refused to send a telegram till he had consulted the Germans. A delaying telegram was sent just after 4 p.m. (when nothing was yet known about the Franco-American agreements) saying: 'Marshal has received telegram, will send answer soon.' This was signed both by Laval and Auphan. Laval explained the addition of Auphan's name as being 'because people know that we do not hold the same position.' Knochen, in a telegram to Germany reporting this, added that 'Auphan is regarded as an Americano- and Anglophile.'[16]

The addition of Auphan's name on this official telegram might be a sign that the story of 'secret telegrams' was true; it might have been a warning to Darlan to expect another of these missives. Auphan claims to have sent such a message, similarly telling Darlan to wait for a reply, but stressing that Pétain and Laval were in private agreement with Darlan's reinstatement, but were waiting for consultation with the Germans. As in other cases, whatever the truth of the 'secret telegram' theory, it had little effect on events, which were already decided in a way which went far beyond the mere reinstatement of Darlan.

The news of Darlan's public statement on taking over power reached

Vichy later that evening, and received an immediate reply from Laval saying that it was entirely against the Government's instructions. When the full text was received the next day, the 14th, Pétain, after much discussion, sent a reply disavowing Darlan and ordering the army not to take any action against the Axis forces. As Knochen reported to Germany, Pétain had withdrawn all powers from Darlan.[17]

On the next day, the 15th, Vichy received two conflicting telegrams on the North African situation. One, from Noguès, stressed the fact that Darlan was in charge and that Giraud had put himself under his orders. The Americans definitely held the whip hand, but they had promised to respect the territory of the French empire. Everyone was against de Gaulle. The important thing had been to keep North Africa united behind the name of the Marshal, and not given over to other factions. He stressed the fact that military co-operation with the Americans would merely extend to defence of the Algerian and Moroccan frontiers.

The other telegram, however, was the report of a speech by Giraud, in which he said that his aim was to clear both North Africa and France of Axis forces; this he would do in the name of the Marshal. This was a different matter.

So when the Vichy Cabinet met that afternoon, they were aware that the North African forces might well be soon fighting on the side of the Allies. They also had before them a demand, from the Germans, for a French declaration of war on the United States, or at least a recognition that a state of war was in existence. The Cabinet was divided; and when Laval stated that France should seek to be treated by the Germans not as a vanquished nation, but as an ally, there was what Aron describes as a 'cascade of resignations'.[18] Those who most disapproved of Laval's pro-German policy resigned; Admiral Auphan, Gibrat, and Barnaud. For them, there was no place for a French Government when France was completely occupied. Only Laval's plea that all would collapse if there were more resignations kept Barthélémy, Minister of Justice, in the Government.

It was a good thing that Barthélémy remained. The next day, when Laval suggested admitting that a state of war was in existence, Barthélémy, with legal weight, pointed out that only with the agreement of the National Assembly could war be declared. German ultimatums continued to flourish; Laval ended up merely by announcing the formation of a legion of volunteers to defend the empire, the *Phalange Africaine*.

Pétain relinquishes most of his remaining powers

France was now a completely occupied country. For Laval, however, the only way in which he felt he could deal properly with the Axis was to have full powers, and not have to refer either to the Marshal or to the Cabinet when making decisions (particularly in view of the difficulties he had just had with the Cabinet). He set about getting Pétain to give him these full powers, justifying his aim by saying that he would thus be taking over all responsibilities too.

The proposed Constitutional Act No. 12 ran: 'Apart from constitutional acts, the Head of Government may, by his signature, promulgate both laws and decrees.' Laval would therefore have no need of either Marshal or Cabinet, except on constitutional matters. He would be a dictator in all but name.

Why did Pétain give in on this? Lassitude, perhaps. The reaction after a week of stress. Or perhaps the feeling that, now that France was under complete German domination, his role was reduced to that of a figurehead at any rate. He may even have been influenced by the realisation that from now on the German demands would be increasingly harsh, and the opportunities for opposing them far less; for France had lost two of her trump cards, the empire and the nominal independence of the Unoccupied Zone, and the third trump card, the fleet, was to be lost within two weeks. Whatever the reason, Pétain gave in, but only after he had got a written pledge from Laval that he would not use his powers to declare war, that he would guarantee the Alsatians and Lorrainers, and that he would respect the spiritual traditions of France, protecting religious and philosophical convictions, religious rights, the rights of the family and of the human being, and so on, as well as not arrogating to himself the right to promulgate constitutional acts. No member of Government could be appointed without Pétain's consent.

Thus Pétain gave up most of the powers with which he had been entrusted in 1940. In the day-to-day running of the country he could take little part. On certain important matters—constitutional acts, and the appointment of ministers—he insisted, however, on retaining some influence. It is only on such matters that, in 1943–4, we shall find him doing anything of any importance. In all else he was a figurehead, to whom people could turn, and whose personality Laval could sometimes use to effect in his discussions with the Germans.

Shortly after Pétain lost his powers, France lost her remaining trump cards. On 23 November French West Africa went over to Darlan and the Allies. On the 26th the French fleet at Toulon, attacked by the Germans, was scuttled by its officers according to the orders given to them by Darlan as long ago as 1940.

Chapter Five

The beleaguered State, 1943

THE destruction of the fleet truly marked the end of Vichy autonomy. As the Resistance writer Vercors was later to write: 'Now, without Algeria, without a fleet, without an army, Laval no longer has anything, not an iota more to exchange in his horse-dealing. We are in the same plight as Poland, Greece, Norway. All that remain are the Germans and us.'[1]

The assassination of Darlan in North Africa on Christmas Eve meant that the succession lay between Giraud and de Gaulle. Ultimately, as we know, de Gaulle won through. The event had, however, reinforced many in their view of the arbitrary nature of events in the chaotic political situation left in the wake of Vichy. As Vercors wrote of the assassin: '*Cui prodest*? Giraud? De Gaulle? Pétain? Only one thing is certain: we are *en plein Shakespeare*, where power is not delegated, but is *taken*, according to interests, intrigue and violence.'[1]

In France, similar chaos was now the rule. Laval held most of the little power that was going. For the coming year, he became the Government. The Government had become more and more isolated from the people. Where, in 1940, it might have been taken that a vast majority of the country supported Vichy, it was now very much a discredited régime. The North African landings had been Pétain's last hope to recapture the heart of the country. If he had gone to Algeria, the Vichy and Gaullist and Giraudist French might all equally have flocked to him. His concern for the people, which had been his main reason for staying in France, did not serve him well with them. Disaffection flourished.

The Resistance now became more powerful than ever before; in addition, it became better organised, with the main movements combining into one united body. Assassinations abounded; secret courts sentenced collaborators to death, and often the sentence was passed on to the condemned man before it was carried out. In town and country, industry and transport were disorganised by numerous acts of sabotage. Militarily, much useful information was passed on to the Allies. The clearer it became that ultimately the Allies were likely to win the war, the more people joined the Resistance cause. Others, in Government circles, tried to keep certain ways open to justify themselves when the time came.

In this situation, with hundreds of killings and thousands of acts of sabotage recorded between the North African landings and September 1943, the reactions of the people being attacked were varied. The Germans, particularly the Gestapo, multiplied their activities to discourage the Resistance; torture and every kind of repressive measure were the order of the day. Laval, who still managed to maintain the appearance that France retained some sovereignty, formed, under German pressure, a *Milice* (militia) which could serve as a supplementary police force, and which was made up of members of the former *Légion des Combattants*, under the command of Joseph Darnand. This force, the formation of which was opposed by certain members of the Government, was to be in many ways as bad as the Gestapo in its actions—worse, in fact, because it was dealing with its own countrymen. Pétain was later to express his horror at many of its actions; the fact that he appeared to approve it in 1943 shows the extent to which his own personal power was in this year by-passed by Laval.

Other reactions to the situation included that of the Paris collaborators who, under perpetual threat of attacks by the Resistance, saw the only solution as being the formation of a stronger Vichy Government, which would of course include themselves. Throughout the later part of the year their demands became more insistent. These demands were on the whole well countered by Laval, who knew of the strong unpopularity of such collaborators not only in the nation as a whole, but also in the Government, the administration and the police.

Pétain, on the other hand, saw one possible solution of the problem as lying in another dismissal of Laval. This view led to the crisis at the end of the year, which led to the opposite of what he had intended, with the Paris collaborators entering the Government. Before we move on to that crisis, we should perhaps examine one or two other facets of the French Government in this year, and Pétain's part in it. This part was small, in that it was effectively Laval who was running the Government.

During this year the French, though they were not officially allied with the Germans, formed several volunteer forces to fight alongside the Axis troops.*

The other main pressures put on the French in this year by the Germans related to the obligatory labour forces for Germany, and further measures against the Jews. In the first case, Pétain was little involved; Laval, while giving in on certain points, succeeded by various methods in undermining the Germans' efforts to bleed the French labour force. In the second case, however, Pétain had some part to play, as we shall see.

The Jewish Question 1943

In many of his negotiations of this year Laval had used Pétain's name and prestige as a counter, or as an excuse, when faced by German demands. This had been the extent of Pétain's involvement. In the case of certain demands made in relation to the Jews in August 1943, however, it is clear that Pétain took a part, though by no means so trenchant a role as that of

---

* The most notable of these forces were the *Légion Tricolore* and the *Phalange Africaine*. Others had already been in existence for some time. The most famous of them being *Légion des Volontaires Français contre le Bolchévisme*.

Laval. Many of Laval's best tactics, throughout the Jewish problem in France, had been delaying ones. These tactics were now to be used to even greater effect.

The problem in this new case, from the German side, was the stand that the French Government had already taken in relation to Jews of French nationality. It will be remembered that, at the time of that discussion, the Germans had decided that it would be useless to pursue that matter, particularly as the French were prepared not to make a fuss about foreign Jews. By 1943, however, the S.S. was faced with a remaining Jewish population which was almost entirely French. So the Germans tried to persuade the French Government to denaturalise Jews of foreign origin who had been naturalised of recent years. The proposed date of division was 1 January 1927; about 70,000 Jews were involved.

It is not certain whether at any time Laval had approved any part of this project; what is certain is that by August, when it was officially presented to him, he was determined to stop it to the best of his ability.

As early as 7 August, Laval told Knochen, an S.S. representative, that the obvious German intention was immediately to deport all Jews who were thus denaturalised, an intention which would make it clear that this had been the sole reason for the law.[2] This view of Laval's was quoted by Brinon as one of the main reasons for Laval's actions: 'Another reason for not having signed the law is the declaration by Laval that he could not take as his responsibility the fact that Frenchmen would simply be denaturalised in order to be thereupon deported by the Germans. On the one hand, he could not as President sign this law, and on the other, his conscience would not allow him to take this responsibility.'[3]

At an important meeting on the 14th with two S.S. officials, Roethke and Geissler, Laval pulled out all his extensive parliamentary tactics. First of all, as so often, he used Pétain's name: 'Pétain has been acquainted with the proposed law. He is very worked up over the fact that the wives and children of the Jews in question are going to be denaturalised as well. Pétain wishes to see both original drafts.'[4]

The two drafts had been drawn up, one by Bousquet the police chief, and one by Darquier de Pellepoix, the Commissioner for Jewish Affairs. Laval now went through a comedy of searching for one of them, which was described in his report by the obviously irritated Roethke.

'The one draft, that of Bousquet, had been brought by the latter's *chef de cabinet*. Laval had allegedly had Darquier's draft searched for for three days already, in Paris and Vichy. This draft was finally "found" by one of Laval's secretaries during the discussion, after Laval had ordered the secretary more than three times to search diligently.'[5]

After this preliminary delaying skirmish, Laval moved on to sterner stuff. The S.S. men stated that they were there to ensure the swiftest carrying-out of the Bousquet proposals. To this, Laval replied with a series of objections.

The first of these was that, when he signed the Bousquet proposals, he had had no idea that the Jews in question would be immediately arrested by the Germans. He had only just been explicitly told this by the German authorities.

The fascinating thing about Roethke's account of this meeting is the way in which the S.S. men on the spot tried earnestly to answer every objection of Laval's. In this case, they pointed out that it had been known for over a year that this was the intention. In the margins of Roethke's report, however, there are far more impatient remarks, in the handwriting of S.S. General Oberg, which show his anger not only with Laval, but also with his own men on the spot, who were unimaginatively allowing themselves to be taken in. Exclamation marks abound. At this point in the discussion, Oberg's remarks are: 'Typical . . . the old fox has known for a long time.'[6]

Laval's next objection was that he had fully to discuss the proposals at the Cabinet meeting which would take place on 17 August. He would assuredly be asked by several colleagues what the aim of promulgating such a law was, to which he would only be able to reply that the Jews in question would be interned and deported.

Next, Laval turned to the figure of the Marshal. He himself, he said, was unable on his own responsibility to sign a document of such importance. (This, of course, we know to have been untrue in the 1943 situation.) Only the Marshal, he said, could sign such a document, for naturalisations and denaturalisations were, like amnesties, only to be ordered by the Head of State. Besides, the Marshal had been very interested in the law, and he, Laval, must discuss it again with the Marshal as soon as possible.

The S.S. men were a little taken aback by this. Geissler pointed out that Laval had already signed both drafts, and had already had the Bousquet draft officially recorded. To this Laval replied that every day he had to sign great piles of documents, and that he had not specially thought anything of signing the Darquier draft, in the belief that all was in order.

From organisational delaying tactics, Laval now turned to other reasons for not acting. The first of these was the attitude of the Italians. After the war, Knochen was to declare that one of Laval's greatest weapons for hindering Jewish measures had been the way in which he played off the Germans against the Italians, because of their very different attitudes to the Jewish question. 'He made of it a problem of foreign policy for the Axis,' said Knochen, 'and, with his great experience of foreign affairs . . . used the possibility of weakening Axis policies by the use of the Jewish question, taking advantage from the different views of the Germans and Italians on this subject.'[7] Realising that they would never agree, and that German-Italian negotiations would be necessary, Laval saw this as a way of gaining time.

This policy he now pursued in his Roethke interview. He pointed out that the Germans had up till now been unable to shake the Italian view. He asked them to understand that, as Head of Government, he found himself in a delicate situation. In France at the moment there were four different sets of regulations for the Jews. (In the former Occupied Zone, in the former

Unoccupied Zone, in the Italian sphere of influence, and in those northern departments which were under the German military rule for Belgium.)

The S.S. men replied that the solution of the Jewish problem was not merely a French matter. He must reckon on a change in Italian attitudes. The solution of the Jewish problem in France must on no account be allowed to come to a halt. (Mussolini had by now fallen, and Oberg's marginal comment 'Since Mussolini!' shows that the Germans hoped for more Italian co-operation against the Jews.)

Laval now turned to another argument. 'Laval then said, that the law could only be used in a form whereby the Jews concerned must be given a period of time of three months (cf. Article 3), during which time the proposals for arrangements with regard to exceptions could be advanced to be included in the text of the law. Police measures against the Jews falling under the law could thus be undertaken at the earliest three months after the law was decreed. In the Zone of southern France he could at all events not permit any other course of action. If we wished to proceed against the Jews before this time in the former Occupied Zone, he must as Head of Government formally protest against it. He knew, of course, what we did with his interventions ... (Laval was clearly, and rightly, thinking of the waste-paper basket).'8

At this point, Oberg makes another of his violent marginal comments: '*Frechheit wird Methode!*' (Insolence is becoming a method of procedure).

Even in the former Occupied Zone, Laval went on, he could not place French police at the Germans' disposal; if they went ahead with their own forces, he could not hinder them.

Roethke saw the dangers of this delay, and declared it to be unacceptable. Within the three months, the Jews would make so many proposals for exceptions that a further delaying period would have to be decided on. (This Laval had obviously realised.)

The irritating discussions went on. Roethke finally expresses, in his report, his whole impression of what the meeting had shown: 'To sum up, one thing must be established: the French Government will no longer co-operate in the Jewish question.'9 The Bousquet draft, he went on, would clearly run aground at the next Cabinet meeting. Further, he had a clear impression that Pétain wished to obstruct the realisation of the law. 'There is a further impression, that Laval would find an intervention by Pétain not unwelcome. It is now very comfortable for him to take cover behind Pétain, although he once more stated, at this discussion, that he was definitely not anti-Semitic, but was fundamentally not a *Judenfreund* (Jew-lover).'10

Roethke also noted that the need to take the proposals before the Cabinet was a new one. It had never been heard of before. 'The impression remains that Laval is seeking, by all means, the possibility of obstructing the appearance of the law, or at any rate of delaying it.' (At this point Oberg wrote in the margin '*Der alte Parlamentarier*' [the old parliamentarian].)

Roethke's views appear to have been right. And by the 24th, after the Cabinet meeting, Pétain declared to Brinon that he would not agree to the setting-up of the law. Obstructions from the French prevented the denaturalisation programme from ever getting off the ground, as Roethke ruefully admitted almost a year later.[11]

What part did Pétain play in all this? In other cases, he had probably been merely used as an excuse by Laval, to further his own designs. But here he seems to have played a far more prominent part. Laval, as the tactician, did all the delaying of the Germans; but in this he was backed up by Pétain, as the Germans knew.

Brinon gave one of the reasons for this participation by Pétain: 'The Marshal had declared that two days before, Monseigneur Chapoulie, representing the Cardinals of France, came to see him and declared that the Pope was very anxious at hearing that the Marshal was tolerating new anti-Semitic measures in France. The Pope was personally worried about the Marshal's salvation. The Marshal was manifestly very impressed by the visit of this high dignitary of the Church.'[12]

It must be admitted, however, that Pétain's concern, as always, was partial. 'The Marshal', continued Brinon, 'would be disposed to hand over to the Germans, as stateless people, the Jews who had been denaturalised. But he cannot allow a global action, that is to say against all the Jews in question, and for his peace of mind he wishes to examine each case individually. . . . He has given instructions to effect as soon as possible the individual verification of the naturalisations given since 1927.'[13] Pétain was worried that men who had rendered services to France[14] (i.e., *anciens combattants*) might be included. Once more, his concern was with Frenchmen rather than with foreign Jews. It must be admitted, however, that whatever Pétain's reasons, his too were delaying tactics which were extremely effective. Indeed, in the state of French administration at the time, the commission he set up to verify the facts was bound to do much to sabotage any action. Thus the German scheme failed, with both Laval and Pétain doing much to achieve this result.

Moves towards removing Laval

Though the Marshal had little actual power, he still had prestige. And he could still, behind the scenes, command obedience from many. In the state into which France had fallen in 1943, he gradually began to see that the only way out was to get rid of Laval once more. An abortive attempt in April, by which he told the Germans that the Laval Government did not meet the needs of the situation, and that, not wishing to retain responsibility for the Government, he was prepared to resign from his post as Head of State if the Germans did not help him get rid of Laval, was quickly snubbed by Hitler, who sent a letter to Pétain telling him that the German Government would not tolerate a repetition of the events of 13 December 1940.[15]

Warner suggests that the fall of Mussolini in July was what made Pétain start considering trying again.[16] Within a day of Mussolini's downfall, Pétain appears to have been making remarks that might be construed as attacks on Laval. Pétain's attitude can partly be explained by a growing realisation that the Germans were going to lose the war, a realisation which Laval either did not share or chose to ignore. Another explanation, however, was the growing chaos within France, and Pétain's feeling that as long as Laval remained Head of Government it was bound to continue.

Pétain's actions at this time show him, despite the tiredness and lassitude he had shown in late 1942, to have been still capable of decisive action. He was supported, too, by the news that a secret meeting of the Radical party at Lyon had shown that the majority of those present were still prepared to follow the Marshal if he took the right line. Many of these, and of other former parliamentarians, were terrified of the prospect of de Gaulle taking power after the liberation. Others were terrified of the spectre of Communism. All went to show that Pétain, if he now got rid of Laval and returned to parliamentarism, would have a great deal of support, and would get rid of the odium of collaboration by placing it all on Laval. So it is that, at the end of this year, we find the surprising picture of Pétain, the anti-parliamentarian, changing his spots and attempting to return to that parliamentary government which he had so despised.

Attempting to play safe, nevertheless, he also sent a secret messenger to Algiers at the end of August, to contact de Gaulle and Giraud, and declare that if they, under the French army's oath of allegiance, remained loyal to him, he would hand over to them and retire after the liberation of France.[17] In this way legitimacy of succession would be maintained.

Meanwhile, plans within France proceeded. On 13 September Admiral Auphan, whom Pétain had asked to form a plan for France in the new situation of 1943 (Sicily landings, fall of Mussolini, etc.), produced a document, called the *Plan de redressement de la politique française*, which stated as one of its most important items the dismissal of Laval, and the Marshal's resumption of full powers, over a Government 'so limited in its political liberty that it can only be a Government of functionaries, assuring order and the administration of the country in neutrality, and preserving the national patrimony with the aim of uniting one day all Frenchmen.'[18] Other measures were to include the suspension of the scheme for sending workers to Germany, the dissolution of the *Milice*, and, though the Communist Party should remain forbidden, the acceptance of former Communists. Also the L.V.F. should be disbanded. The Ministry of Information should be suppressed, and the Jewish policy should be re-examined on more Christian lines.

As far as relations with the Germans were concerned, Auphan saw that either the Germans would soon force on France a Government consisting of violent collaborators, or else the Marshal should first take the initiative. This initiative should take place as soon as possible, and definitely within the next few months. A draft letter to Hitler was appended to Auphan's report, which pointed out that Pétain in dismissing Laval was doing so mainly because of the internal situation of France, which was aggravated by Laval's presence.[19]

The possible German reactions, according to Auphan, would either be an annoyed toleration of the new Government, or else the arrest of everyone concerned, and the appointment of a Gauleiter. Either solution would be good for France, particularly if Pétain appointed a regency council in the case of his being unable to exercise his powers.

'If the Government is tolerated by the Germans', Auphan went on, 'it risks not being so by the population, which would take away much of the benefit of the operation. It must therefore maintain itself, with dignity, on the verge of breaking with the Germans, without losing contact with opinion, frankly pointing out to the occupying power that this is the only means of maintaining a minimum of order and administration in the country, which the Germans would be incapable of ensuring alone against Frenchmen in their unanimity.'[20]

As far as the Anglo-Saxons were concerned, Auphan pointed out that though they were to be mistrusted, they could also be negotiated with. 'The worst enemies negotiate even when fighting, and our ex-allies, even if they call for some mistrust on our part, are all the same not our worst enemies.'[21]

As for the Resistance, all efforts should be made for the new Government to get in contact with them; no measures should be taken against them, while in return the Anglo-Saxon propaganda against the Marshal should stop.

Auphan's plan, as described here, was to have enormous effect. The events of November and December 1943 were in large part to be based on Pétain's acceptance of it.

The crisis builds up

The first of Auphan's suggestions to be put into effect was the appointment of a regency council to serve in the event of Pétain being deprived of the power to carry out his functions. On 27 September Pétain approved a revised draft of Constitutional Act No. 4, which had up till now appointed Laval (in succession to Darlan) as Pétain's dauphin. In this new draft Pétain explained that, seeing that five different acts had had to be made in three years in order to ensure the succession, he had decided to entrust it instead to a college of non-political public servants. This *Directoire* was to consist of Admiral Auphan, Yves Bouthillier (formerly Finance Minister), M. Caous (a legal dignitary), M. Gidel (rector of the Sorbonne), M. Porché (Vice-President of the *Conseil d'État*), and two others, neither of whom knew until after the war of their nomination: Léon Noël, the former ambassador, and General Weygand, now a prisoner in Germany. The abrogation of the act relating to Laval, and its replacement by this new act, was for the moment kept secret.

In September and October, feelers were put out as to possible German reactions to the proposed *coup*. Pétain, trusting in the German military as opposed to the Embassy or the S.S., contacted General von Neubronn, the German military representative at Vichy. This decent old soldier would have liked to help, but it was soon clear that his superior, General von Rundstedt, refused to do so. 'Unfortunately', wrote von Neubronn, 'Rundstedt held himself apart from any exertion of political influence. Through this the administrative task of the military commander General Heinrich von Stülpnagel was likewise made more difficult. I have heard many a complaint from this passionate opponent of Hitler's policies, about the passive behaviour of the Commander-in-Chief. The executive power in France was moving over more and more to the Embassy, the S.S., the Gestapo and the Party organisations.' [22]

Rundstedt suggested that Pétain himself should write a letter from Head of State to Head of State. But it was clear that this could only go through the embassy. Pétain feared that it might not be sent on, and asked Neubronn whether it could be handed on personally by the Adjutant-General. Neubronn, however, had to reply that even the Adjutant-General had to go through the embassy: 'When I told him that the General too had to go through the embassy, the Marshal resigned himself with a bitter smile. He must have seen that his plan to set Laval aside was not to be achieved with the collaboration of German military circles. It was shaming for me to have so openly to admit the powerlessness of the highest military authority in France.' [23]

Pétain made feelers in other directions, too. On 12 October his representative General Brécard saw Knochen in Paris, to ask him whether Hitler still felt as strongly against the replacement of Laval. Knochen's reply we do not know.

It was in late October that the crisis began openly to break. On the 26th, Pétain confronted Laval, saying that France was in a terrible state of anarchy and potential revolution, and that some of Laval's most important ministers should be replaced. The meeting was a stormy one. After it, Laval appears to have made plans for his own kind of reshuffle, including getting rid of certain people from the Marshal's entourage. A few days later, on 1 November, Laval, though aware of plots against him, was described by an eyewitness, Pierre Nicolle, as being calm, seeing the plots merely as annoyances hindering his task as Head of Government. [24]

Meanwhile Pétain was not losing time. On 8 November Laval received a note from him confirming what had been said at their interview. But it was on the 12th that the most serious actions took place.

On that day Pétain showed Laval two texts. The first was yet another revision of Constitutional Act No. 4. The secret version of this had been seen to be too dangerous, in that the Germans would immediately arrest all those named in it. So in this new version it was declared that the Marshal, in the case where he might die before a new constitution for the French State could be ratified, should be succeeded by the National Assembly. The other document which Pétain showed Laval was a speech he proposed to broadcast the following day, in which he declared that the draft of the new constitution was ready, but that he was worried by what might happen if he died before the task was completed. He spoke of himself as incarnating French legitimacy, which he wished to transfer at his death to the National Assembly, if the new constitution was not yet ratified. Above all, disorder must be avoided. [25]

Laval, surprisingly enough, showed no immediate opposition. He even claimed that as an old parliamentarian he would not feel out of place at the National Assembly. (He did, however, point out to Pétain the strange position in which this formerly anti-parliamentarian Marshal now found himself.) He asked, however, that they ought to wait a little, to get German approval. This move may explain his apparent friendliness; as with the Jewish question, he may have been trying to stop the action by more subtle means than frontal opposition.

Pétain agreed to tell the Germans, though not to ask their permission. The German Minister Krug von Nidda was informed. German reactions were confused, but by 6 p.m., on 13 November an order came though, an hour and a half before the broadcast was due, forbidding it and threatening force to stop it. German troops indeed began to occupy the radio installations.

In this situation, Pétain's pride moved him to one of his courageous acts of the war. He received Krug von Nidda and read him the following declaration:

A communication from the German Government asks for the postponement of the message which I was to pronounce this evening, and M. de Brinon has just let me know that military measures will be taken by the German authorities to prevent the broadcast.

I note the fact and I yield.

But I declare to you that until the moment when I am in a position to broadcast my message, I will consider myself as having been rendered unable to exercise my functions.[26]

The Marshal, as Ménétrel said at the time, was now on strike.

Collapse

Three weeks went by, in which the Germans did next to nothing publicly, while the Vichy Government was at a standstill. The Germans were not lacking in activity behind the scenes, however. On the one hand, they were preparing an ultimatum for Vichy, and had brought Abetz back to France in order to hand it over. On the other, they were bringing up security forces round Vichy, in order to make sure that the ultimatum was delivered from force. The fact that the one action could not proceed without the other is shown by a report written for the Führer's own eyes on 3 December, which showed that the ultimatum had to await the setting-up of the security forces:

Notice for the Führer, with information on the state of affairs at Vichy:
(1) As the Führer has already been told, the letter to Marshal Pétain was not handed over by Ambassador Abetz immediately on his return to Paris. It was clearly necessary to undertake this delivery only after an adequate police protection had been provided at Vichy. This protection will be in place by Sunday, 4 December, so that Abetz will hand over the letter on 4 December at 11 o'clock.

By this protection it will be, as far as is possible to human judgement, assured that neither Pétain nor his circle will be able to leave the Vichy district against our will.

(2) After the delivery of the letter the reaction of the Marshal must be awaited, so that after this reaction decisions can be taken.

(3) In the event of the Marshal resigning, there is, according to Ambassador Abetz, an easily supervisable château near Paris at his disposal as a place of residence. . . .

(4) If on the other hand the Marshal does not resign, our further action against his circle is planned in such a way that a day when, as he often tends to do, he goes to a château in the neighbourhood of Vichy, shall be used to arrest all the inmates of the floor of the Hotel in Vichy which is inhabited by Pétain and his circle. If the Marshal was present, he could in the event of resistance be injured, which is to be avoided. The captured inmates should then, in so far as they are unsuspected, be released, while the dangerous elements are kept in custody. . . .[27]

The report went on to say that all the French archives, whether the Marshal resigned or not, must be examined, and that all this must be explained to the Marshal, if he had not resigned, by the fact that his immediate circle had been planning to take him to North Africa, and that he had had to be protected against this.

By the morning of 4 December, the security forces, under the command of Otto Skorzeny, were all around Vichy. At 11 a.m. Abetz handed over Ribbentrop's letter, dated 29 November. This letter began by an attack on Pétain's attitudes, which were not in accord with the spirit of collaboration. It then forbade any remittal of power to the National Assembly. Finally, it put forward a three-pronged ultimatum: (1) All modifications to laws must be submitted to the German Government for approval. (2) Laval must be without delay entrusted with remodelling the French Cabinet in a way acceptable to the German Government, and which would guarantee collaboration. (3) The supreme leadership of the French nation were responsible for taking measures to eliminate immediately from the administration all elements hindering the serious task of reconstruction, and for appointing people to these posts who were worthy of confidence.

The letter ended with threats of force, and with a declaration that the Marshal was free to resign if he wished.

Faced by these threats of force, Pétain was eventually forced to give in. Not, however, before he had struggled a little. On the 5th he gave Abetz a written note saying that he would resume his functions again, and would speak on the other matters in a later note. This was far too vague for Ribbentrop, who saw it as an attempt to by-pass the ultimatum, and who wrote to Abetz on the 6th as follows: 'Your telegram states that the Marshal will remain in office and that he thus relinquishes his former attitude. The declaration of the Marshal, however, does not contain the acceptance of three of our demands. It appears that instead he wants to reply to them and my letter in writing. I consider this an attempt to delay matters and to get around the demands, which is something we must not tolerate under any circumstances.'

Ribbentrop therefore asked Abetz to go and see the Marshal, and tell him as follows:

The Reich Government has taken notice of the declaration of the Marshal to the effect that he is resuming his functions as Head of State, within the limits that he exercised them before 30 November. The Reich Government, however, finds that this written declaration does not contain the acceptance of the three demands stated in the letter of the Reich Foreign Minister to the Marshal of 29 November, the acceptance of which—as stated explicitly in the letter—are the prerequisites for further collaboration with the French Government. Therefore the Reich Government expects the Marshal to forward an immediate and unrestricted acceptance—without any reservations—of the three demands in question.[28]

Ribbentrop insisted that every Frenchman who might appear not to be in full agreement with the Germans should be removed from the Government. He told Abetz to prepare a list of people in important administrative positions who could not be considered as politically dependable, and who must therefore be eliminated.

All was now paving the way for a Government which would include the Paris collaborators, and which would exclude all who were not pro-German. Pétain continued to struggle. In a letter of 11 December he retained the vagueness of his former missive. By the 18th, however, he had under German pressure been forced to agree to the first ultimatum, about all modifications of laws having to be submitted for approval to the Germans. He still held out, however, against the German pressures for Government reorganisation, which probably meant including such collaborators as Doriot, Déat, Darnand and Henriot in the Government. By the end of the year, however, amid numerous German arrests of those close to him, the old Marshal had to give in. Though, for the moment, Doriot and Déat remained outside the Government (Doriot because he was on the eastern front, Déat because he was dissatisfied with the jobs offered him by Laval), Darnand became Secretary-General for the Maintenance of Order, and Henriot Secretary of State for Information and Propaganda. The French Government had taken one more step on the downward path. Pétain's heroic gesture had come to nothing.

Chapter Six

Decline and fall

THE rest of Pétain's public life makes sad reading. Reduced more than ever to the role of figurehead, he took no active part in governmental decisions, and remained an onlooker as France gradually disintegrated into civil war, and as the Vichy Government became more and more German-dominated, particularly with the advent of Déat as Minister of Labour in March.

Reports differ upon the Marshal's personal attitudes during this period. His attitudes, for example, to the *Milice* appear to have been particularly contradictory. There is enough evidence, however, of his desire not entirely to wipe out the *maquisards* of Glières at a time when Darnand was all set to do so, and of other such episodes, for us to realise that he was not entirely subjugated by the new policies, nor too old and senile to react against them, with whatever little hope of success.

On one occasion, before the Allied landings, he took a decision of his own. This was a visit he made to Paris in April. Of recent weeks Allied bombing raids had been raining destruction down on French cities, and one of the worst of these raids took place over Paris on the night of 20 April 1944. In it, there were 651 dead and 461 wounded. At Vichy, Pétain and his entourage were horrified. In Paris, a special religious ceremony was arranged in honour of the victims, and General Brécard, its organiser, privately suggested that Pétain himself should come to Paris to attend the ceremony. This Pétain decided to do. Despite German demands that this should be an entirely private visit, and that the Press should contain no mention of it, the papers were full of obvious hints as to the Marshal's arrival. So, on 26 April, Pétain visited Paris for the first time since 1940. In Notre-Dame, the service for the dead took its solemn course; then, as Pétain stepped forth from the cathedral, a vast crowd gathered outside joined those within the cathedral in a fervent shout of '*Vive le Maréchal!*' Later, at the Hôtel de Ville, an even greater crowd welcomed him, and, amid the singing of the Marseillaise, he made his way into the City Hall. Outside, the crowd grew larger and larger; eventually, the Marshal appeared and made a short speech, which included a phrase which was to cause immense trouble with the Germans: 'Today, it is a first visit I am making to you. I hope I will soon be able to return to Paris, without being obliged to forewarn my jailers; I will be without them and we will all be at ease.'

The German wish for a quiet visit had not only been unfulfilled; Pétain had also, in front of a vast crowd, shown what he thought of his captors, and how much he saw the eventual liberation of France as being a logical development from his policies. And the public had shown, by their delirious enthusiasm, how much they still saw him as the symbol of French unity.

Meanwhile, however, German pressures were all the time forcing the Vichy Government to split the French nation still further, above all by action against the Resistance forces. And Pétain was forced, only two days after his trip to Paris, to make a broadcast condemning the 'so-called liberation' as the 'most deceiving of mirages', and calling for total fidelity until, thanks to Germany's defence of the continent, European civilisation would be made safe from the Bolshevik danger. This he did under the threat of a vicious destruction of France by the Germans.

From the beginning of May onwards, Pétain, whose disappearance the Germans feared, was moved around like a brown-paper package from place to place. First, to the Château of Voisins. Then, for further safety in the event of an Allied landing, it was decided to move him nearer the centre of France. Pétain only agreed to move, on this occasion, if he was allowed to make a tour of the towns of eastern France on the way. This he did, passing through Nancy, Épinal, Dijon and Lyon. Again, he received tremendous ovations. On 6 June, while this tour was still in progress, news came of the Allied landings in Normandy.

The end of the Vichy Government

During the Allied advance across France, Laval hastily tried various ways to bridge the gap as a kind of peacemaker, and to ensure some kind of continuity of government which would exclude de Gaulle. In this he appears to have been encouraged by the Americans, who were worried by the prospect of de Gaulle taking over; messages passed on to Vichy by way of Spain show this American preoccupation.[1] Laval even set on foot a plan to bring Herriot out of retirement, and place him at the head of a reconvened National Assembly. This would prevent Gaullism, and civil war. To all of this Pétain appears to have agreed, or at least not to have objected. On 12 August Laval had Herriot released from the asylum in which he was being kept near Nancy, and on the 13th Herriot arrived in Paris.

Pétain, in the meantime, had been preparing his own relations with the Allies and with de Gaulle. On 11 August, he had signed a letter entrusting Admiral Auphan with the task of negotiation. The letter ran as follows:

> I give power to Admiral Auphan to act as my representative to the Anglo-Saxon High Command in France and, eventually, to make contact on my behalf with General de Gaulle or his qualified representatives, in order to find a solution to the French political situation at the moment of the liberation of the territory, a solution of a kind that will prevent civil war and reconcile all Frenchmen of good faith.
>
> If circumstances permit it, Admiral Auphan will refer to me before any decision of a governmental order.
>
> If this is impossible, I trust him to act in the best interests of the Fatherland, provided that the principle of legitimacy that I incarnate is safeguarded.

If I am no longer free, Auphan will open the note which was given by myself to the Vice-President of the *Conseil d'État* and the *Procureur-Général* of the *Cour de Cassation* in 1943.[2]

This note to which he referred was, of course, the revised version of Constitutional Act No. 4, which he had produced on 27 September, 1943, and which set up a Regency Council in the event of Pétain being deprived of the power to carry out his functions.

At this stage, Pétain was also considering trying to escape from the Germans, and join up with the American forces. This venture was, of course, eventually overtaken by events, when the Germans deployed their forces around Vichy to constrain Pétain to depart in their company.

From Laval's point of view (and he appears to have known nothing of Pétain's latest moves), Pétain was urgently needed in Paris, to confer legitimacy on the Herriot operation. Urgent telephone calls abounded. Pétain, however, demurred. Some historians have suggested that this was because he required guarantees for his personal safety, if he was to go to Paris. This seems hardly likely, however, if the future of France was at stake. A rather more plausible explanation would be that he covered, with his many excuses for not going, the fact that he himself had his own plans at this time, which might be ruined by his going to Paris, which was far more solidly in German power. Also, it may have been that he was still moved by the strong antipathy he had always felt for Herriot. If all Pétain's 'sacrifices' had been made merely to reintroduce a Herriot Government, one can see his horror at such an outcome. Like many old men, he retained the prejudices of earlier days in an even more fixed form.

Be that as it may, on 16 August the Germans reacted in Paris. Herriot was rearrested. The orders had come from Himmler direct, and not from Ambassador Abetz; those concerned were left with the impression that it was Brinon and Déat, furious at what was happening, who had spurred the Germans to action.

On the very next day, the 17th, a German order was received which said that, in view of the danger both to Paris and to Vichy, the French Government must move to Belfort, in the east of France. It added an assurance that they would never 'be asked to leave the national territory'. In Paris, Laval, who had already threatened to resign unless Herriot were set free, held a small Cabinet meeting, which approved a letter of refusal to the German demand. In reply, a note was received from Abetz which stated that the German decision was irrevocable, and that in the case of refusal force would have to be used. Laval replied by his resignation:

In reply to your letter, I regret to note that the German Government would not hesitate to have recourse to measures of force to ensure the transfer of the French Government to Belfort.

I must therefore yield. But you will understand that, under these conditions, I now cease to exercise my functions as Head of Government.[3]

It was as a private citizen that Laval was driven by the Germans to Belfort that evening.

Meanwhile, at Vichy, the Marshal refused to leave the town unless it was in order to go to Paris. Two days passed. On the 19th the German Minister Renthe-Fink told him that the authorities in Berlin required an immediate departure, by force if necessary. Further exchanges of notes followed, during which the Germans pointed out that Premier Laval had set up the French Government at Belfort. They also assured Pétain that there would never be any question of his having to leave French soil. To this Pétain replied that Laval had assured Stücki, the Swiss Minister, that he would never leave Paris and Vichy so long as he was Head of Government. If, therefore, he was at Belfort, he must have resigned his post.

Von Neubronn, that decent old German, was put in the position of having to take Pétain by force if necessary. In addition, there was the threat of Vichy being bombarded from the air and by the German artillery. To save Vichy, Pétain decided finally against armed defence (which at one stage had been his intention), and dismissed his guard.

Before his forced departure, Pétain wrote two texts. The first was a formal letter of protest to Hitler:

When concluding the armistice with Germany in 1940, I expressed my irrevocable decision to bind my fate with that of my country and never to leave its territory.

I have thus been able, in honest respect of conventions, to defend France's interests.

Last 16 July, in face of persistent rumours about certain German intentions with regard to the French Government and myself, I was led to confirm my position to the diplomatic corps, in the person of its doyen, His Excellency the Apostolic Nuncio, specifying that I would oppose myself by all the means in my power against a forced departure to the east. Your representatives have produced arguments which are contrary to the truth, in order to persuade me to leave Vichy. Today, they wish to compel me by violence, in contempt of all agreements, to depart for an unknown destination.

I raise a solemn protest against this act of force, which makes it impossible for me to continue to exercise my prerogatives as Head of the French State.

Like Laval, Pétain had resigned. Far more important even than this, however, was the text which, in collaboration with Henri Massis, he had prepared as his last message to the French. This was distributed in the form of small notices on walls, etc., and eventually appeared throughout France. It ran as follows:

Frenchmen,
When this message reaches you, I will no longer be free. In the extremity to which I am reduced, I have nothing to tell you which is not the simple confirmation of all that has dictated my conduct up till now. For more than four years, determined to stay among you, I have, every day, sought what was most fitted to serve the permanent interests of France. Straightforwardly, and without

compromise, I have had only one aim: to protect you from the worst. And everything that has been done by me, everything I have accepted, admitted, put up with, whether willingly or by force, has only been so for your safe-keeping. For if I could no longer be your sword, I wished to remain your shield.

In certain circumstances, my words or acts may have surprised you. Be well assured that they gave to me even more pain than to you. I have suffered for you, with you. But I have never ceased making a stand with all my power against what was threatening you. I have warded off certain perils; there have been others, alas, which I have been unable to preserve you from. My conscience is my witness to the fact that no one, to whichever camp he belongs, can contradict me in this matter.

What our adversaries want today is to wrench me from you. I have no need to justify myself in their eyes. My sole concern is Frenchmen. For you, as for me, there is only one France, that of our ancestors. So, once again, I adjure you to unite. It is not difficult to do one's duty, even if it is sometimes difficult to recognise it. Yours is simple: to group yourself around those who will give you the guarantee that they will lead you on the path of honour, in the way of order.

Order must reign, and because I represent it legitimately, I am and remain your leader. Obey me, and obey those who bring to you words of social peace, without which no order can be established. Those who will use a language to you which is fitted to lead you towards reconciliation and the renovation of France, by reciprocal forgiveness and the love of all our people, those are French leaders. They continue my work and follow my disciplines. Be at their sides.

As for me, I am separated from you, but I do not leave you, and I hope for everything from you and from your devotion to France, whose greatness, with God's aid, you will restore. This is the moment when destiny is banishing me. I I am undergoing the greatest constraint a man could be asked to suffer. It is with joy that I accept it, if it is the condition of your salvation, if in face of the foreigner, even if he be an ally, you are able to be faithful to true patriotism, to the patriotism which thinks only of France's interests, and if my sacrifice makes you find once more the path to the sacred union for the *renaissance* of *la Patrie*.

Pétain's concern, as shown in this message, was the avoidance of civil war. He was also concerned, as in other statements, with the continuity of 'legitimate' government. Many have claimed, on the basis of this and other documents of this time, that de Gaulle was in his mind as his 'legitimate' successor. There is nothing which goes to prove this, however, apart from pious beliefs of present-day Gaullists. Pétain feared Gaullism as a divisive force, leading to civil war. For him, his true successors would be those who succeeded in uniting France, 'on the path of honour, in the way of order.' Who these men might have been, is still uncertain; but the fact that, in certain documents of this period, names were left blank,[4] does not necessarily mean (despite zealous Gaullist hopes) that de Gaulle's name was meant to fill them; it means, rather, that Pétain remained undecided as to who, while retaining the 'legitimate' succession of power, could unite (with the help of the Anglo-Saxons) the French behind him.

On the next day, 20 August, the German soldiers came early in the morning to fetch Pétain. After getting past the various members of the Marshal's household, they eventually broke into his bedroom, where—he

Pierre Cot (on right), 1944

General de Gaulle, General Spears and a friend (left) in a London restaurant (1940)

German poster distributed in France to excite anti-British feelings. Joan of Arc stands over the ruins of Rouen after bombing attacks by the British

was sitting on the side of the bed, half-dressed, doing up his shoes. 'Ah! It's you', he said. Von Neubronn declared the purpose of his visit. 'Yes, I know that from now on I am your prisoner', Pétain said, 'You might nevertheless let me get dressed.' Poor old von Neubronn is reported to have left the room pale and ashamed, and to have said 'It was not to do this kind of thing that I became an officer!'

Before leaving, Pétain saw the diplomatic corps, now reduced to the Papal Nuncio and the Swiss Minister, and handed them his formal protest to Hitler. Then, at 8.15 a.m., a convoy of cars left Vichy, and in one of the limousines was an eighty-eight-year-old man who had just ceased to be Head of the Vichy State.

Sigmaringen, and the return to France

The Allied advance was so swift that by early September it was already clear that the important French figures in Belfort would have to be moved on. The Germans decided to put them all up in the town of Sigmaringen, the old seat of the southern branch of the Hohenzollern family, on the upper Danube. Pétain, Laval, and others were to inhabit the castle. Pétain formally protested at this swift breach of the German word, given in August, that he would never be forced to leave France. But in vain. On 8 September he arrived at Sigmaringen.

The atmosphere in this small German town in the months to come must have been extraordinary. Here, gathered together, were all the debris of wartime France—but above all the most violent of the collaborators: Doriot, Déat, Darnand, Marion, Brinon, to say nothing of the large numbers of members of the *Milice* who had escaped ahead of the revengeful Allied troops. André Brissaud, in his book *Pétain à Sigmaringen*, has given a very full account of these months; Louis-Ferdinand Céline, the novelist, has captured the atmosphere even more fully in his book *D'un château l'autre*.

The life at Sigmaringen is not of importance to us, however, in our study of Pétain, except insofar as he remained aloof from it. A man such as Brinon might try to use his name in relation to the 'governmental commission' he had formed; Pétain, in a note on 29 October 1944, formally forbade him to do so. The Marshal remained completely outside any kind of governmental action.

In France, meanwhile, the *épuration* was in full progress. During the autumn tens of thousands of Frenchmen had been summarily executed. More legally, many trials had taken place, or were being prepared. Among the prominent people who were tried was the old Charles Maurras, and the young writer Robert Brasillach, who was executed on 6 February. All these trials were to fade into insignificance, however, compared with that which was being prepared for Marshal Pétain.

De Gaulle himself had privately been heard to declare that, while Pétain had to be judged like all the rest, he hoped that the old man would die before the Allied landings. Unfortunately, the Marshal had stubbornly continued to live. The fact of his being in Germany, however, seemed to enable a political trial, such as de Gaulle desired, to take place in the Marshal's absence. Arrangements were set up for the Marshal, and through him the whole of the Vichy régime, to be tried *in absentia*.

When Pétain heard of this, in early April 1945, his reaction was immediate: he must go and face the music. He wrote a note to Hitler, expressing his wish to return to France. The note, dated 5 April 1945, runs as follows:

I have just learned that the French authorities are preparing to commit me for trial, *in absentia*, before a High Court of Justice.

The hearing will start on 24 April. This information imposes on me an obligation which I consider to be imperative, and I am addressing myself to Your Excellency in order that you may put me in a position to accomplish my duty.

I received on 10 July 1940, from the National Assembly, a mandate which I have fulfilled according to the possibilities which were left to me.

As Head of Government, in June 1940 at Bordeaux, I refused to leave France.

As Head of State, when grave hours once more came to my country, I decided to stay at my post at Vichy.

The Reich Government forced me to leave my post, on 20 August 1944.

I cannot, without forfeiting my honour, let people believe, as certain tendentious propaganda has insinuated, that I sought refuge on foreign territory in order to escape my responsibilities.

It is only in France that I can answer for my acts, and I am the sole judge of the risks that this attitude may entail.

I thus have the honour of earnestly requesting Your Excellency to give me this possibility.

You will certainly understand the decision I have taken to defend my honour as leader and to protect by my presence all those who have followed me. That is my sole object. No arrangement will be able to make me give up this project.

At my age, one only fears one thing: not to have done all one's duty. And I wish to do mine.

No reply was received from Hitler. Pétain anxiously waited, but days passed by. Two weeks later, it became clear that Sigmaringen itself was threatened by Allied troops, which were within thirty miles. On the 20th Pétain was informed that the danger was such that he must be removed, the next day, further to the south-east. Pétain refused, saying that he had written to Hitler, asking to be allowed to return to France, and that this new move would put him even further away. A later telephone call from the German commander, however, insisted that this was an order which would be carried out by force. Pétain wrote another short note of protest, which again received no reply. The next day, the departure took place, amid the chaos of a retreating army; they ended up at Schloss Zeil, north of Wangen.

Finally, on the 22nd, with Germany collapsing about their ears, his captors in desperation decided to take Pétain to the Swiss border, and hand him over. The Marshal entered Switzerland on 24 April, his eighty-ninth birthday. Two days later, he crossed the French frontier, where he was received by General Kœnig on behalf of the French Government.

Trial and sentence

Pétain's trial, which took place from 23 July to 15 August 1945, has often been described. The complete text has been published; an excellent, if emotional, account by Jules Roy has done much to give us the atmosphere of this occasion. The trial itself was more remarkable for the events with which it had to deal than for the way in which they were treated. Much of our evidence for previous events has been drawn from this source.

Pétain's defence lawyers, and in particular the young Maître Jacques Isorni, did a brilliant job. Pétain himself remained silent throughout most of the trial, after an initial statement which denied the right of the High Court, as at present constituted, to try him: 'It is the French people who, by its representatives gathered in the National Assembly on 10 July 1940, entrusted me with power. It is to the French people that I have come to make my account. The High Court as constituted, does not represent the French people, and it is to them alone that the Marshal of France, Head of State, will address himself. I will make no further declaration. I will not reply to any question. My defenders have been given by me the task of replying to the accusations which are aimed at denigrating me, and which only hit those who are putting them forward.'

The rest of Pétain's opening statement was an *apologia* for his actions from 1940 onwards. It even claimed that the armistice had contributed to the Allied victory, 'by ensuring a free Mediterranean and the integrity of the empire.' This, in relation to the Vichy attitudes of 1940 and 1941, must appear as hindsight.

He was on safer ground when describing the way in which he had saved the French people from worse sufferings: 'Can you understand the difficulty of governing under such conditions? Every day, with a knife at my throat, I struggled against the enemy demands. History will tell all that I saved you from, when my adversaries only thought of reproaching me for the inevitable. . . . The occupation obliged me, against my wishes, to make statements and accomplish certain acts for which I have suffered more than you, but in face of enemy demands I abandoned nothing which was essential to the country's existence. On the contrary, for four years, by my actions, I maintained France, I assured life and bread to Frenchmen, I assured our prisoners of the nation's support.'

In a sense, Pétain may have been right in still defending his original armistice decision. But we have already seen how the high hopes born of that decision were borne down under German pressure; how Pétain himself gradually became aware, as the war went on, of the appalling situation in which France had been put, as German demands continued, and German concessions never materialised; how it became clear that Hitler was not Wilhelm II, but Genghis Khan. Added to this, Pétain now neglected to mention the calculations which had led to Montoire and the policy of collaboration; calculations which had rested, not on the maintenance of the Mediterranean for the Allies, but on the inevitability of German victory.

Pétain's statement would have been complete, and would have been truthful, if he had merely said that he had done all for France. His after-the-event glosses on this ring false when one views his earlier attitudes.

His statement, however, ended nobly, with a personal acceptance of responsibility, and a request for French unity:

> Millions of Frenchmen are thinking of me, have accorded me their trust, and keep their faith with me. . . . For them, as for many across the world, I represent a tradition which is that of French, Christian civilisation, in face of the excesses of all tyrannies. In condemning me, you will be condemning these millions of men in their hope and faith. Thus, you will aggravate or prolong discord in France, when she needs to find herself once more, and her people to love one another, to take up once more the place she used to hold among the nations.
>
> But my life matters little. I have given to France the gift of my person. It is at this supreme moment that my sacrifice must not be held in doubt. If you must condemn me, let my condemnation be the last, and let no more Frenchmen be condemned or imprisoned for having obeyed the orders of their legitimate leader.
>
> But, I tell you this before the whole world, you would be condemning an innocent man, believing that you were speaking in the name of Justice, and it would be an innocent man who would carry the weight of it, for a Marshal of France asks for mercy from no man. To your judgement those of God and of posterity will reply. They will be enough for my conscience and my memory. I rely on France! . . .

The dramatic and emotional nature of these last statements, and their evocation not only of the dignity of a Marshal of France, but also of Pétain's symbolic status, show the form which his defence was to take. The repetition of his 1940 statement '*J'ai fait à la France le don de ma personne*' points to the continuity of the Marshal's sacrifice. This is not to say that Pétain was not necessarily sincere in all he said on this score; we have certainly seen that, up to 1940, his conviction as to his incarnation of France and its virtues was complete. And while events from 1940 to 1944 may have shown him that some of his preconceptions about peace, the armistice, and the Germans were wrong, he did not necessarily relinquish the high opinion he had of himself and of his decisions.

It is clear, however, that his lawyers had decided on the importance of an emotional appeal. Added to which, the Marshal, at his age and with his deafness, might well have found it hard to play a more active part in his own defence. So it was that this trial, both in its original form and in the glosses written on it by others, has gone down as a great example of the small-minded persecution of the great and noble.

This is not to deny that the prosecution did in fact behave often in a small-minded and rather ridiculous way. And, as later in the Laval trial, they tried to amass too many forms of indictment, both from the pre-war period and from the war itself. There was a violently partisan element about the prosecution, which obscured the main issues. De Gaulle himself was later to criticise the trial as follows: 'Too often, the discussions took on the appearance of a partisan trial, sometimes even a settling of accounts, when the whole affair should only have been treated from the point of view of national defence and independence.'[5]

For de Gaulle, who had not wished Pétain to return to face trial in person, the important thing was to obtain a judicial condemnation of the policies of the armistice. Pétain's trial takes its place among the important political trials of France, more significant for the political issues at stake than for the personalities involved.

One cannot forget personalities, however. And the old man in that courtroom, deaf, possibly already going senile, and for the most part of the time silent, has emerged from the process as something of a martyr. His evidence was at times faulty, as we have seen during the course of this biography; he had lied, for example, about his relations with Loustaunau-Lacau in the inter-war years. In other respects, as we have seen, a new gloss was put upon actions which had been committed for other reasons. Yet the myth was born.

One is left with the feeling that, strangely enough, Pétain had performed more nobly in his role when, in 1940, he had produced his 'collaboration' speech on 30 October: 'This policy is mine. The ministers are solely ressible to me. It is I alone who will be judged by History.'[6] The policy of Montoire was wrong; but Pétain had freely taken it up, and, aware of his heavy responsibility and of the unpopularity and hatred it would cause him, had nevertheless shouldered these loads. The fact that, contrary to his then beliefs, Germany had lost the war, should not have let him or his supporters attempt to palliate that decision, or to make of it a 'Verdun diplomatique'.

Pétain's lawyers were brilliant. Yet the high point of the trial was the interlude in which Laval gave evidence. It gave a foretaste of Laval's trial, in which this man courageously defended his actions from start to finish, and tied up the prosecution in knots. A valiant defence by a man who knows he is already condemned is a moving thing. Another example of this was the brilliant performance of Göring at the Nüremberg trials.

Pétain was not a criminal. He was a man who, through vanity and a misunderstanding of events, had led his country into the wrong paths. He did not necessarily deserve unreasoning hatred; but no more did he deserve to become a hero. His trial failed to find him a place anywhere between these two extremes.

On 15 August he was condemned to death; though on account of his great age, the Court asked that the verdict should not be executed. For the next six years, until his death on 23 July 1951, he was kept in prison on the Île d'Yeu, deteriorating both mentally and physically. The inhumanity of the imprisonement of this old and senile man, from the age of 89 to 95, will go down in history as one of the examples of the barbarity of our age. It has also served to add to the pious hagiology which now, for many, surrounds the figure of the Marshal.

Conclusion

PÉTAIN, who had lived as a symbol for the thirty years of his public life, remained a symbol after his death. For some, he came to stand for treachery, defeatism, connivance with the enemy; for others, he became the embodiment of all that was best in the French nation, an almost religious figure whose final sufferings and imprisonment only served to enhance his sanctity. In many cases, these views were a reflexion of the writers' own attitudes during the war, and a justification for them; in others, they served as a form of indictment of the régimes since the war, and particularly since 1958; but it must also be accepted that these two extreme viewpoints are those which come most naturally to the subject, and that the latter, particularly, takes on a romantic aura, with religious overtones, which is particularly attractive even to those who did not live through this period.

The nature even of present-day French politics is such that many of the issues of the war still remain alive; and, above all, it must be admitted that the cause of the Marshal is of great service to certain political groups. For this and other reasons, an impartial study of Pétain is extremely hard to find, in French or otherwise. On a more general level, studies of the Vichy period have somewhat more chances of achieving impartiality, though even here much of the literature on this subject only too clearly shows its bias, in one direction or another. Pétain himself is an even more emotion-laden subject. For this reason he rarely seems to have been considered as a man.

What has our present study of him shown us? Neither the villain nor the saint of popular belief. Nor a man, overcome by senility and incapable of decision in 1940, as some of his apologists have made him out to be. He has turned out to be a man who behaved in 1940 as he might have been expected to behave, in a similar situation, any time in the previous twenty years; a man, moreover, on the human scale, whose apparent heroic stature came from position rather than character or intelligence.

Pétain had been, for the first fifty-eight years of his life, a soldier whose career had not been entirely successful, but who had been original in his views, outspoken in his expression of them, and remarkably clear-sighted about the paths which warfare was to take. The war was to justify him. In the 1914-18 war he proved himself to be one of the best, possibly the best of the Allied generals. His appreciation of the overwhelming force of fire-power led him to new tactics, which laid far more stress on the defensive. He was adaptable, too; his ideas on warfare were continually

339

adapted to the changing face of war. This was the time of his greatest worth, the time in which he deserved his fame.

His defence of Verdun, and his quelling of the mutinies, remain his highest achievements. Aware of the importance of morale, he became a byword as the commander who cared for his troops.

On the adverse side, however, certain of his attitudes at the time of the March offensive in 1918, and before, had shown that the experiences of the war had induced in him a form of pessimism which might even, under stress, become defeatism. A tendency always to look on the blackest side. This, and the mistrust of the British produced in him at this time, does much to explain his 1940 attitudes.

These are explained, however, even more clearly by his inter-war career. Through his First World War experiences, Pétain now became the symbol of French victory. A Marshal of France, he came eventually to 'incarnate' France for the French public, and to be regarded as the man who could put things to rights in every sphere.

At first, it was purely in the military sphere that he wielded power. Here, by some strange hardening of the arteries, he kept the preconceptions of First World War warfare through thick and thin. From being an infinitely adaptable strategist and tactician, he developed into a man incapable of seeing the changing face of warfare, a counterpart to those generals against whom he had reacted before the war. Pétain's influence on French military preparation between the wars was, for most of the time, paramount. It does much to explain French unpreparedness for modern warfare in 1940.

The explanation for Pétain's own actions in 1940 lies, however, rather more in his other inter-war experiences. This straightforward military man, admittedly a good general, had now become one of the great figures of France. As the years went by, and other great figures died, he came to stand, in many people's eyes, for the France of the First World War, the France of victory. To be a Marshal of France was already to some extent to be a symbolic figure; Pétain now took on an aura even more impressive, that of France itself.

His presence in the Doumergue Government of 1934 as Minister of War showed the extent to which he was a reassuring figure for the French public. In the succeeding years, he came to seem to many the panacea to France's ills. France needed a 'man at the tiller' who could save her from the reefs of parliamentary government, of internal dissension and of external danger. In the late 'thirties several newspaper campaigns pointed to him as the saviour. Meanwhile, behind the scenes, several politicians tried on various occasions to plan the setting-up of a Pétain Government. All this Pétain knew, and while he did not necessarily support these efforts, they did not entirely displease him.

For one of Pétain's greatest characteristics in this period was pride, and self-satisfaction. Fayolle had already noted this in 1917 and 1918. Then it had been pride in his military achievement. But by now, as some of his letters and statements show, Pétain believed himself to be the great figure he was reputed to be. He was the man who could save France, the man on whom they would be forced eventually to call. Not that he wished to force the issue; he would wait to be called, and he would be ready to do his best for France. If he were to be given power, it must be in a 'legitimate' way.

In the opinion of Pétain which was held by himself and others, there was one flaw. There was nothing to prove that the man himself possessed the virtues ascribed to him. For it was the 'symbol' which had the virtues, not the man. In most newspaper accounts at this time, much space was spent on the Marshal's value as a symbol, and on his personal appearance, which was imposing enough to match that symbol. Little was said of his personal characteristics.

A soldier becomes a Marshal; a Marshal becomes a national figure; a national figure becomes the nation's prospective saviour. The sequence does not seem inevitable to us in England; but in the France of the inter-war period it was so. Pétain, whose only experience was that of a soldier, found himself dealing with matters which, for the first sixty years of his life, had been outside his ken. But his own opinion of himself could not admit any shortcomings.

Nothing, in his inter-war words and actions, marks him out as anything but an ordinary man. He was not over-intelligent on any but military matters. His ideas were the simple, straightforward ones of many men of his type. There was nothing to show, as in the case of General de Gaulle, that the man outshone his office; rather the contrary was true. Even the strength of his character was unknown.

The events of 1940, then, put into power a man adored by the nation and by himself, who nevertheless had few of the qualities required to run a country, let alone to run it with full powers. One of his greatest virtues was, however, his love of his country, a love which sustained him throughout these terrible four years. Pétain not only loved France, he was convinced by now that he himself 'incarnated' it. This pretension was instilled in him by the adulation of others, and he can hardly be blamed for it. Louis-Ferdinand Céline, however, in a brilliant passage from his book *D'un château l'autre*, describes the intoxication brought by such a belief, and the dangers of it. (At the end of the passage, he brings in de Gaulle as another example). Here is the passage in question, in the original French; it is untranslatable into any other language, without losing its impact.

On pourra dire ce qu'on voudra, je peux en parler à mon aise puisqu'il me détestait, Pétain fût notre dernier roi de France. 'Philippe le Dernier' . . . la stature, la majesté, tout! . . . et il y croyait! . . . d'abord comme vainqueur de Verdun . . . puis à soixante-dix ans et mèche promu Souverain! qui qui résist-erait? . . . raide comme! 'Oh! que vous incarnez la France, monsieur le Maréchal!' Le coup d''incarner' est magique! . . . on me dirait 'Céline! bon Dieu de bon Dieu! ce que vous incarnez bien le Passage! le Passage c'est vous! tout vous!' je perdrais la tête! prenez n'importe quel bigorneau, dites-lui dans les yeux qu'il incarne! . . . vous le voyez fol! . . . vous l'avez à l'âme! il se sent plus! . . . Pétain qu'il incarnait la France il a godé à plus savoir si c'était du lard ou cochon, gibet, Paradis ou Haute-Cour, Douaumont, l'Enfer, ou Thorez ... il incarnait! ... le seul vrai bonheur de bonheur l'incarnement! ... vous pouviez lui couper la tête: il incarnait! ... la tête serait partie toute seule, bien contente, aux anges! Charlot fusillant Brasillach! aux anges aussi! il incarnait! aux anges tous les deux! ... ils incarnaient tous les deux! ... et Laval alors?[1]

In 1940 Pétain saw himself as the one man to get France out of its mess. His natural military pessimism had caused him to press for an armistice almost from the first; his mistrust and hatred of the British had reinforced him in this. In the face of two alternatives—continued resistance or giving in to the conqueror—he had chosen the latter. His fears for the French people were real, as was his traditional view of the need for the Government to remain attached to the land of its own country. The decision was a logical one.

His hatred of parliamentarism, and of the state into which France had got itself in the inter-war era, made him see France's defeat as a kind of punishment. His role, he believed, was to restore France to its former greatness by an internal revolution, based on the simple right-wing principles by which he had been formed. France would leave the war, through its armistice with Germany, and be able to devote itself to its own internal revival.

All very simple, in appearance. But completely misjudged. The National Revolution itself was in many ways unrealistic, the product of the pipe-dreams of successive generations of right-wing minorities. And the war was not over for France; the Germans had not won outright, as so many had believed, and as the war went on it became less and less clear that they would win. Above all, the armistice did not get rid of the German threat; their demands became more and more insistent, and the National Revolution paled into insignificance as Franco-German relations became more and more clearly the central problem of French policy.

It is as the war goes on that the figure of Pétain becomes more sympathetic to our eyes. The self-satisfied 'incarnation of France' of summer 1940 cannot have been particularly pleasant. But the successive blows to that self-satisfaction were to turn him into a figure of pathos and, at times of courage. From that summer onwards, Pétain was to be continually pushed down a slope caused by his original decision. Not that any of his decisions were definitely right, even in the circumstances that caused them. But the safety of France was still his object, and as his power grew less and less the implications of his earlier decisions must have come home to him.

Collaboration, in the Montoire mould, can now be seen to have been a mistaken policy. At the time, it can be considered to have been shameful. But, taking it at least as a policy undertaken by Pétain and Laval for the good of France, we can see how its failure affected these men. Pétain's greatest moment of truth was his confrontation with Göring, in late 1941, when he finally realised how completely France had been defeated.

As the war went on, Pétain's position deteriorated still further. In April 1942, he lost many of his powers to Laval. In November of that year, the Germans took over the Unoccupied Zone, and left Vichy in the position of a puppet Government. In that Government, almost all the power there was devolved on Laval. Added to this, Pétain was declining into old age.

These years contain, nevertheless, examples of Pétain struggling against the inevitable. He continually had to make concessions, but there were moments when the worm turned. His public reproof to von Rundstedt when the Germans invaded the Unoccupied Zone is one example; his dignified decision to 'go on strike' in December 1943 another. By formation, Pétain was unsuited to the position he had been given, and his behaviour in 1940 showed it. Within his limitations, however, he was capable of showing personal courage and dignity.

Pétain's biography, in itself, is more interesting for the historical scene which it traverses than for the man himself. It is also a great opportunity for the study of the ideas of that mass of ordinary Frenchmen whom he personified. They were what the Americans nowadays would call 'the silent majority', but who on the whole in France had been a 'silent minority': the simple, straightforward members of a traditional, conservative Right. Much has been written in this book on the nature of that Right, and there is little need to repeat much of it here, except to stress the difference between this and the new-style Right of the fascist movements of the 'thirties.

Pétain is a heaven-sent example for examination of these views. Not only did his position as a public figure in the 'thirties enable him continually to make speeches and write articles in which these ideas were put forward; the Vichy Government, and its National Revolution of 1940, became the only example in France in the last hundred years of an attempt to put these ideas into practice.

That these ideas have been a continuous undercurrent in the French political scene is clear not only from the experience of 1940, and the mass of evidence on the subject before that date, from the first days of the Third Republic onwards. They also recur in much political thought of our own day. In their most extreme form, they are to be found in those secret documents of the O.A.S., produced in 1960, which referred to their plans for the organisation of metropolitan France when it had been taken over. Here we find the old references to the 'natural communities'—the family, the local community, the national community; the necessity for provincialisation, decentralisation; reform of the army; a national State, free from Parties and from private interests; reintegration of agriculture into the national economy; a new policy for education, with the aim of producing a directing élite; and a true policy for Youth.[2]

The similarity with much of the National Revolution is startling at first; but on reflection it is hardly surprising. These, too, were military men, formed in much the same mould as those who ruled in Vichy in 1940.

This volume, then, has been two things: the study of a man, and his implication in the events of his time; and a study, through that man, of the ideas and aspirations of a whole section of the French public. In no sense has it been intended to be either a denunciation or an approbation of the man or the ideas.

Appendix
Pétain and de Gaulle

THE relationship between Marshal Pétain and General de Gaulle has been extensively studied in Tournoux's book *Pétain et de Gaulle*. For the purposes of the present volume, however, it might be worth recapitulating some of the points of contact which Tournoux found between the careers of the two men, and adding to these some more general appreciation of the similarities which existed between their ideas and attitudes.

The first contact between the two men was in 1912, when de Gaulle, just out of St Cyr, joined the 33rd Infantry Regiment of which Pétain had just taken over the command. From all accounts, de Gaulle showed great admiration for his new commander. And Pétain, in his reports, showed approval of the young officer.

During the 1914–18 war, while Pétain was making his great name, de Gaulle, wounded first at Dinant on 15 August 1914, and later, in 1915, on the Artois front, ended up at Verdun in 1916, again under Pétain's command. Here he was wounded a third time, and captured by the Germans. Pétain's citation ran as follows: 'Captain de Gaulle, a company commander noted for his great intellectual and moral value, in a situation where his battalion was undergoing a terrible bombardment, and had been decimated, and where the enemy was attacking the company on all sides, carried his men into a furious assault, a wild hand-to-hand, the only solution he judged compatible with his feelings of military honour. He fell in the melée. An officer without equal in all respects.'[1]

De Gaulle spent the rest of the war in a German prison. In the inter-war period, he soon became one of Pétain's entourage. Indeed, he became perhaps the most favoured of the young officers around Pétain, for whom his admiration was still immense. Bonds of friendship united the two men, too. De Gaulle's son, born in 1921, was called Philippe, after the Marshal (though the myth that Pétain was the godfather is untrue; he was not only a non-practising Catholic, he had also recently married a divorcee).

De Gaulle's future was not necessarily as bright as this would make it seem, however. His difficult character, his pride and stiffness, made him unacceptable to many, as did his refusal of orthodoxy in his ideas. He became, however, one of Pétain's staff as a writer from 1925 to 1927. In 1927, thanks to Pétain's influence, he gave a course of three lectures at the *École Supérieure de Guerre*. They were essentially a study of the nature of leadership. In them there was a certain amount of overt praise of Pétain.

In December 1927 de Gaulle was sent to take over the command of the 19th Battalion of Chasseurs, in the Rhineland at Trier. Here, while impressing his men, he nevertheless showed a certain *désinvolture* with regard to his superiors, caused perhaps by his reliance on Pétain's favour, but more certainly by his own proud and stubborn nature. This attitude was at first shown in such actions as a forced night march for the battalion, and a military return by night into the town of Trier, against all standing orders. There was, however, little result of all this. Soon, however, a more serious situation occurred, serious enough for him to have to have recourse to Pétain's help.

The start of it was a serious 'flu epidemic in the 1928–9 winter. Deaths had been numerous in the Rhine army, and questions had been asked in the Chamber of Deputies. In the 19th Battalion, the deaths had been even greater than elsewhere. Marshal Pétain, however, sent on a tour of inspection by the Chamber, declared himself satisfied that proper precautions had been taken; and in this he was almost certainly right.

De Gaulle's trouble came, however, as a result of the 'flu epidemic. Because of it, and because of the coldness of the Rhineland, many of the soldiers wished to be sent back to France. And, in typical Third Republic manner, they were able, through their deputies, to demand to be moved; as in other matters, the deputy's word was law, and the deputy was prepared to make any number of 'special cases'. De Gaulle, infuriated by this, declared that anyone in the battalion who made such moves to get sent elsewhere would be punished. Shortly thereafter, an official telegram came from one of the soldiers to be moved. Instead, de Gaulle put him in prison for a fortnight.

Chaos ensued. The deputy concerned complained. De Gaulle looked as though he might be deprived of his post, and punished severely. In the circumstances, there was only one thing for him to do; come to Paris and see Pétain. This he did, and Pétain managed to get him out of trouble.

From late 1929 to 1931, de Gaulle was in the Levant. On his return, he published his book *Le Fil de l'épée*. It consisted of the three lectures he had given in 1927, with two extra chapters entitled 'On Doctrine', and 'Politics and the Soldier'. The latter chapter drew a line between politics and the army, refusing the influence of one on the other. The printed dedication on the first page of the book ran as follows:

To Marshal Pétain: This essay, *Monsieur le Maréchal*, could be dedicated to nobody but you, for nothing shows, better than your fame, what virtue action can gain from the enlightenment of thought.[2]

Of the numbered editions (those special volumes produced by French publishers, with numbers inside them, as personal gifts), no. 1 was given to Pétain, with the added sentence in de Gaulle's handwriting: 'The homage of a very respectful and profound devotion.'

De Gaulle's devotion to the Marshal may still have been sincere; but the Marshal's friendship for him appears to have been beginning to cool. One of the reasons for this, which by the late 'thirties was going to lead to an open rupture, was the question of de Gaulle's status as one of Pétain's 'writers'. For some years he had been one of those officers whom Pétain used, to write his speeches, articles and books. The methods by which this was done have already been discussed. In de Gaulle's case, the main work had been on a book which, since 1922, Pétain had been planning to write; a book on the French soldier through the centuries. De Gaulle, together with such men as Colonel Bouvard and Captain Barthe, had the job of collecting and ordering the facts and ideas, and putting them down on paper. Gradually, de Gaulle became the main writer between 1925 and 1927; and Pétain was impressed and pleased with his style.

When it came to the question of the publication, however (Tournoux places this about 1930), de Gaulle asked that his name should not be left out of things. Pétain, it is believed, took this very badly; none of his other *nègres* had ever asked such a thing! It was his book, after all; de Gaulle had merely lent him his style. The growing coldness between the two men appears to have started at this time, even though the book was not published. It has been suggested, too, that Pétain was persuaded by those around him not to entrust the reception speech for the Academy (in praise of Foch) to de Gaulle, because the latter, proud of his own literary talent, would probably let everyone know that he had composed it.

Be that as it may, there were more serious causes for disagreement between the two men on the horizon. De Gaulle's book *Vers l'armée de métier*, published in 1934 and dedicated to 'the French army', contained a doctrine of warfare diametrically opposed to the Marshal's.*

The break between Pétain and de Gaulle finally came on literary grounds, however. The Catholic author Daniel-Rops, who had much admired de Gaulle's *Le fil de l'épée* and *Vers l'armée de métier*, was asked by the publishers Plon, in 1936, to edit a series of books on contemporary trends; the series was to be called *Présences*. He asked de Gaulle to write one of the books; de Gaulle signed a contract to produce a book entitled *L'Homme sous les armes* (Man under arms). However, like many authors, de Gaulle soon found that, with the pressure of his career, it was impossible to produce this new book. He suggested, instead, the publication of a book which was almost finished, a 'kind of philosophy of the history of the French Army.' Daniel-Rops tells us de Gaulle's description of how it came to be written: 'He had undertaken it, he told me, at the request and with the collaboration of Marshal Pétain, when he was on his staff. For a reason I never learned, the Marshal had given up the continuation of the work beyond the first chapters. But he had authorised Charles de Gaulle to continue and complete the work. Which was done.'[3]

Fair enough, one might think. De Gaulle had after all written the book. Not only was the style his own, but the ideas reflected his own thought. We must not forget, however, the Marshal's methods of work. He would enounce ideas, his 'writers' would clothe them in words, and he would then 'correct' the style and content. (The process must have been similar to the relationship between an American President and his speech-writers). He would not see his ideas as 'advice' to an author, but rather as 'directives' to a subordinate. The first chapters of de Gaulle's book may indeed have contained Pétain's ideas as much as de Gaulle's; as we shall see, the two men held remarkably similar opinions upon many things. As for Pétain's 'corrections' to the text, he may already have been carrying them out on the chapters in his possession.

In these circumstances, Pétain's reaction was fairly adverse when, at the beginning of August 1938, he first became aware of the proposed publication. The book was already in proof form, and this was the first he had heard of it. His first reaction was to forbid publication by de Gaulle 'of staff work which did not belong to him.'[4] Eventually, however, he allowed publication on condition that a printed dedication appeared at the beginning, in Pétain's words.

Pétain's letter to de Gaulle on this subject, written on 5 September 1938, was curt, though it was headed 'My dear de Gaulle'. It contained the draft of the dedication. Pétain declared that he had decided to spare de Gaulle's susceptibilities

* For a discussion of this, see pages 137–42

by alluding only to 'advice' for the 'preparation' of the work. He asked de Gaulle to give him his views or his acceptance. The dedication ran:

> To Marshal Pétain—who, in the course of the years 1925–1927, helped me with his advice in the preparation of Chapters 2 to 5 of this volume (*Ancien Régime, Révolution, Napoléon, D'un désastre à l'autre*)— I address the homage of my gratitude.[5]

We have no record of de Gaulle's reply. But within the next month the book appeared. True, it had a dedication to Pétain. But de Gaulle had not accepted the proposed wording. The new dedication ran:

> To Marshal Pétain, who wanted this book to be written, who directed with his advice the first five chapters, and thanks to whom the last two are the story of our Victory.

Pétain was furious, and, in a letter to the publishers, gave his reasons for so being. 'This officer', he wrote, 'has used, without asking my authorisation, a piece of staff work which he had composed according to my directives in 1925–1927, when he was under my orders. This work has been integrated just as it is into the book: it is Chapters 2 to 5 of the volume.' Pétain went on to explain that he had first heard of this when it was in proof form; that he had forbidden it, but had then relented on condition that a dedication (here he quoted it in full) was placed at the beginning. The printed dedication which had now appeared was quite different, and contained two things contrary to fact: '(1) I did not wish the book to be written, since I at first opposed it. (2) I in no way directed the writing of the first chapter. The dedication which has been printed constitutes, on the part of Colonel de Gaulle, a veritable betrayal of confidence.'[6]

Pétain therefore asked for this dedication to be suppressed, and his own draft put in its place. It had only been on this condition that he had authorised publication, and he had not changed his mind.

Pétain's demands appear to have been ignored. The dedication remained as it was. This storm over a book, however, marked the final break between the two men. Pétain was to remember it, and repeat the story to Baudouin in the first months of the war. He also, at that time, described de Gaulle as 'proud, ungrateful, and embittered.'[7]

It is interesting to note that, in the second edition of *La France et son armée*, which appeared after the war, the dedication to Pétain had been removed.

The opposition between Pétain and de Gaulle during the war needs little further commentary than has already been given to it in this book. It is important, nevertheless, to note the similarities between both men at all stages of their life, despite their difference of opinion over the running of the war.

Pétain and de Gaulle shared many ideas and attitudes. Many of these were, of course, typical of the military of their time. An innate conservatism, a mistrust of politicians and of the workings of parliamentary democracy, a belief in the military virtues, a vision of the leadership the nation required; all these they had in common. Added to this, however, there are certain other personal attitudes which link them: the personal conviction that France would call on them in its hour of need, for example. We have already seen this conviction in the Pétain of the 'twenties and 'thirties; we know it to have been true of the de Gaulle of the late 'forties and early 'fifties; what is not so well known is the fact that de Gaulle had this view even before the war. This came out in various attitudes and utterances; one statement, in particular, in a letter written in 1929 to Colonel Nachin, shows this belief: 'In a few years, people will be hanging on my coat-tails to save the Country . . . and the rabble as well.'[8]

Both Pétain and de Gaulle had a certain idea of France. And both of them, as Céline points out in his book *D'un château l'autre*, believed that they 'incarnated' it Both were proud men, both believed themselves to be men of destiny.

The two points, and important ones, which divided them were military strategy, and the attitude to be taken to the Germans in 1940. On the first question, Pétain remained attached to his experience of the First World War, convinced of the superiority of the defensive; de Gaulle, with his realisation of the new conditions brought about by the effective use of tanks, was a rebel, a man questioning the value of accepted doctrines, much as Pétain had been before the First World War.

In the Second World War itself, Pétain and de Gaulle showed the essential differences between them. Each was patriotic. But the negative attitudes of the one contrasted with the positive ones of the other. They represented the two attitudes once described by Péguy in relation to the Franco-Prussian War: those who were prepared to give up French territory in order to make a reasonable peace, and those who resolved to fight to the end.

Behind this basic difference, however, the two leaders (and, to start with, their movements), showed marked similarities. In an important document written in London in September 1942, for the benefit of Léon Blum, then in prison in France, the socialist lawyer Félix Gouin set out to describe de Gaulle's movement. When it started out, he said, its members had the following characteristics:

> Among these Frenchmen, there were some civilians, but many more military men. Most of them were men of the Right and of the extreme Right, and they brought to this movement their prejudices, their beliefs and their ideological hatreds. It is a fact that under their influence, which was, at the beginning of the movement, preponderant and without counterweight, they constituted, here, a kind of reduced copy of the Pétain Government: the same tendencies, the same excesses, the same authoritarian tendencies. The word 'democrat' was forbidden and the 1789 motto 'Liberty, Equality, Fraternity' suppressed on all official documents. The only difference was the attitude in relation to Germany: Vichy was pro-Nazi, London violently anti-German.[10]

Many of these men, Gouin went on, were still in the movement. But gradually, as it became clear that the anti-German feeling within and outside France had a much broader basis, the movement became much more democratic. De Gaulle had realised the necessity of getting everyone behind him: 'However, I cannot affirm that this corresponds to a rallying, without any reservations, to the democratic idea. It is possible that it is an evolution caused by the wish to integrate Gaullism into an action which, in France, appears more and more to be dominated by the popular masses.'[11]

Eventually, Gouin gave a description of people's impressions of de Gaulle: 'Three traits appear dominant in him: a very lively intelligence; a passion for authority; a very high opinion of himself and of the role he is playing and will be called on to play in France. These are the noble traits of this character which, in other fields, presents, it is said, certain weaknesses. He is described as extremely mistrustful; using at times oblique methods to get rid of those who are annoying him; violent and carried away on occasions and, above all, according to certain people, completely without sincerity from the political point of view.'[12]

It is a further remark by Gouin, however, which shows us the essential difference between Pétain and de Gaulle. He describes the latter as a man completely out of the ordinary. Only such a man could arouse at the same time so much criticism and praise.

Pétain, as we have seen, was essentially a soldier whose non-military greatness was brought to him by his rank and his myth rather than by his character. De Gaulle was the opposite; a man who by force of character became great.

References

Introduction

1. Laure, *Pétain* Paris 1941, p. 13
2. Letter to Paul Pomart, 29 December 1907 (Quoted in Girard, 'Les Temps Obscurs', in *Le Livre d'Or du Centenaire du Maréchal Pétain,* Casablanca 1956, p. 90)
3. Azan, *Franchet d'Esperey* Paris 1949, p. 79
4. 1911. *École Supérieure de Guerre. Cours d'Infanterie. Colonel Pétain.* (246pp.) p. 176

PART I

Chapter 1

1. Printed in *L'Aurore* 25 March 1963
2. Amouroux, *Pétain avant Vichy — la guerre et l'amour* Paris 1967, p. 35
3. Pétain, speech at Meaux for the 20th anniversary of the Marne, 9 September 1934. Reported in *l'Echo de Paris* 10 September 1934
4. Correlli Barnett, *The Swordbearers: Studies in Supreme Command in the First World War* London 1963, p. 74
5. ibid., p. 74
6. Laure, op. cit., p. 32
7. Pétain, preface to Mordacq, *Pourquoi Arras ne fut pas pris* (1914) Paris 1934
8. Quoted in Laure, op. cit. p. 33
9. A good account of this fighting is to be found in Mordacq op. cit.
10. Pétain, preface to Mordacq, op. cit.
11. Serrigny *Trente ans avec Pétain* Paris 1959, p. 1. Entry for 21 October 1914. Serrigny seems to have got the date wrong.
12. Mordacq, op. cit. p. 204
13. Fayolle, *Cahiers secrets de la grande guerre* Paris 1964, p. 60 (29 November 1914)
14. Laure, op. cit., p. 42
15. Serrigny, op. cit. p. 24
16. Laure, op. cit. p. 44
17. Quoted in Laure, op. cit. p. 45
18. Serrigny, op. cit. p. 26
19. Quoted in Laure, op. cit. p. 48
20. Quoted in Bourget *Un certain Philippe Pétain* Paris 1966, p. 60
21. Quoted in Laure, op. cit. p. 49
22. Marcellin *Politique et Politiciens pendant la guerre,* Paris s.d., vol. 1, p. 126
23. Laure, op. cit. pp. 57–9
24. Laure, op. cit. p. 59
25. Pellé, note of 29 December 1917, addressed to Albert Thomas. In Pellé papers, B. Inst. MS 4430
26. Pétain *Journal de route* 18 August 1914
27. Fayolle, p. 96. 2 April 1915
28. ibid., p. 106. 18 May 1915
29. ibid., p. 142

References

30. Letter from Terrier to Lyautey, Paris, 20 February 1915 B. Inst. MS 5903.
31. ibid. Paris, 10 June 1915
32. Marcellin, op. cit. p. 162

Chapter 2

1. Falkenhayn, *Die oberste Heerleitung 1914–1916, in ihren wichtigsten Entschliessungen* Berlin 1920, p. 183
2. ibid.
3. Macmillan 1962. Reprinted Penguin Books, 1964
4. Ferry *Carnets secrets (1914–1918)* Paris 1957. Entry for June 1916
5. ibid. Entry for June 1916.
6. Serrigny, op. cit. p. 48
7. Laure, op. cit. p. 71
8. Quoted in Horne, op. cit. p. 162
9. Horne, op. cit. p. 158
10. Laure, op. cit. p. 84
11. Terrier to Lyautey, Paris, 2 May 1916. B. Inst. MS 5903
12. Quoted in Laure, op. cit. p. 81
13. Joffre *Mémoires (1910–1917)* Paris 1932, vol. 2, p. 216
14. Terrier to Lyautey, 2 May 1916. B. Inst. MS 5903
15. Quoted in Laure, op. cit. p. 85
16. Letter from Pétain to Colonel Des Vallières, in Des Vallières *Au soleil de la cavalerie* Paris 1962, p. 151
17. Horne op. cit. p. 241
18. Quoted in Laure, op. cit. p. 91
19. Quoted in Horne, op. cit. pp. 269–70
20. Quoted in Amouroux, op. cit. p. 71
21. Serrigny, op. cit. p. 95
22. Joffre, op. cit. vol. 2, p. 226
23. Horne, op. cit. p. 289
24. Haig (Blake ed.), op. cit. Entry for 24 June 1916. This passage was inserted at a later date than the rest of the diary, and may well have been written after the war.
25. Horne, op. cit. p. 307
26. Pétain *La bataille de Verdun* Payot 1930 pp. 78–9
27. Serrigny, op. cit. p. 64
28. Ferry, op. cit. 1 May 1917
29. Letter from Pétain to Mme Hardon, 20 January 1917, Quoted in Amouroux, op. cit. p. 90
30. Haig (Blake ed.), op. cit. Entry for 31 May 1916
31. Terrier to Lyautey, Paris, 12 May 1916. B. Inst. MS 5903
32. ibid. Paris, 1 June 1916. B. Inst. MS 5903
33. Ferry, op. cit. Entry for April 1917
34. Terrier to Lyautey, Paris, 1 July 1916. B. Inst. MS 5903
35. ibid. Paris, 2 December 1916. B. Inst. MS 5903
36. ibid. Paris, 9 December 1916. B. Inst. MS 5903
37. ibid. Paris, 2 December 1916. B. Inst. MS 5903
38. Joffre, op. cit. vol. 2, p. 269
39. Haig (Blake ed.), op. cit. Entry for 13 December 1916
40. General Order of the Day to 11th Army Corps, 18 December 1916, quoted in Laure, op. cit. p. 97
41. Quoted in Amouroux, op. cit. p. 85. Horne, op. cit. 320–1
42. Hankey *The Supreme Command 1914–1918* 2 vols. London 1961. vol. 2, p. 629
43. ibid. vol. 2, p. 630
44. ibid.
45. Ribot, *Journal et correspondances inédites, 1914–1922* Paris 1936. p. 76

46. ibid. p. 77
47. ibid. p. 77
48. Fayolle, op. cit. p. 210. 10 April 1917
49. ibid. p. 77
50. ibid.
51. Laure, op. cit. p. 114
52. Herbillon *Souvenirs d'un officier de liaison auprès de Nivelle et de Pétain* Paris 1930.
53. Loucheur, *Carnets secrets, 1908–1932*, Brussels and Paris 1962, p. 40, entry for 6 April 1917
54. Ribot, op. cit. p. 77
55. Ludendorff *Meine Kriegserinnerungen* Berlin 1919, pp. 337–8.
56. Kronprinz Wilhelm *Meine Erinnerungen aus Deutschlands Heldenkampf* Berlin 1923, p. 278
57. Ribot, op. cit. p. 80
58. Ferry, op. cit. April 1917
59. ibid. 12 July 1917
60. Ribot, op. cit. Entry for 25 April 1917
61. ibid. Entry for 26 April 1917. Pétain was certainly regarded by Malvy as a dangerous political figure.
62. ibid. Entry for 27 April 1917
63. ibid. 29 April 1917
64. Ludendorff *Meine Kriegserinnerungen* Berlin 1919, p. 338
65. Hankey, op. cit. vol. 2, p. 628
66. Herbillon, op. cit. Entry for 16 May 1917.

Chapter 3

1. Terrier to Lyautey, 1 December 1915, B. Inst. MS 5903
2. ibid. 2 May 1916, B. Inst. MS 5903
3. ibid. 6 May 1916, B. Inst. MS 5903
4. ibid. 12 May 1916, B. Inst. MS 5903
5. ibid. 8 June 1916, B. Inst. MS 5903
6. ibid. 1 September 1916, B. Inst MS 5903
7. ibid. 9 December 1916, B. Inst. MS 5903
8. Laure, op. cit. p. 111
9. For an account of the mutinies by Pétain himself, see: Sir Edward Spears, *Two Men who saved France: Pétain and de Gaulle* London 1966, pp. 67–128: 'A Crisis of Morale in the French Nation at War' by General Pétain
10. Pellé—'Secret. Événements des 28–29 mai 1917 (rapport non envoyé)'. Pellé papers, B. Inst. MS 4430
11. Haig (Blake ed.), op. cit. Entry for 31 May 1916
12. Spears, op. cit. pp. 82–3. Pétain 'A Crisis of Morale in the French Nation at War, 16 April—23 October 1917'
13. ibid. p. 84
14. ibid. p. 100
15. ibid. p. 101
16. Pétain, op. cit. p. 105
17. ibid. p. 113
18. Kronprinz Wilhelm, op. cit. p. 279
19. Ribot, op. cit. entry for 15 April 1917
20. Haig (Blake ed.), op. cit. entry for 3 May 1917
21. ibid., entry for 18 May 1917
22. Laure, op. cit. p. 156
23. ibid
24. ibid. p. 157
25. Terraine *Douglas Haig, the educated soldier* London 1963

26. Terrier to Lyautey, 25 August 1917. B. Inst. 5903
27. Hankey, op. cit. p. 718
28. Laure, op. cit. p. 177
29. Hankey, op. cit. vol. 2, p. 704
30. ibid. p. 705
31. ibid. p. 705
32. ibid. p. 706
33. Haig (Blake ed.), op. cit. Entry for 7 September 1917
34. Letter from Pellé to Thomas, 3 November 1917. Pellé papers, B. Inst. MS 4430
35. Note from Pellé to Thomas, 29 December 1917. ibid.
36. Note from Pellé to Thomas, December 1917. ibid.
37. Pellé to Albert Thomas, 30 December 1917. ibid. General Micheler made approaches to President Poincaré in December as well, demanding an offensive.
38. Laure, op. cit. pp. 179–80
39. ibid. p. 181
40. General ★ ★ ★ *La Crise du Commandement Unique* Paris 1931, pp. 54–59
41. Haig (Blake ed.), op. cit. Entry for 1 November 1917
42. ibid. Entry for 12 February 1918
43. Laure, op. cit. p. 183
44. Haig (Blake ed.), op. cit. Entry for 24 February 1918
45. ibid. Entry for 2 March 1918
46. Hankey, op. cit. vol. 2, p. 782
47. ibid. p. 783
48. ibid. p. 748
49. ibid. p. 749
50. Fayolle, op. cit. p. 161. 21 May 1916
51. Hankey, op. cit. p. 749
52. Haig (Blake ed.), op. cit. Entry for 17 December 1917
53. ibid.
54. Hankey, op. cit. p. 771
55. Haig (Blake ed.), op. cit. 2 February 1918
56. ibid.
57. Fayolle, op. cit. p. 274. 19 May 1918
58. Ribot, op. cit. 15 May 1917
59. See, e.g., Terrier letter to Lyautey, Paris, 13 December 1917. B. Inst. MS 5903
60. Fayolle, op. cit. pp. 251–2. 12 January 1918
61. ibid. p. 255. 16 February 1918
62. ibid
63. ibid. p. 255. 18 February 1918
64. ibid. p. 257. 26 February 1918
65. Haig (Blake ed.), op. cit. see Haig's Instructions of 14 December 1917
66. Quoted in Pitt *1918 The Last Act* London 1962, p. 51
67. Herbillon, op. cit. Entry for 21 March 1918
68. ibid. Entry for 22 March 1918
69. ibid.
70. ibid. Entry for 23 March 1918
71. Poincaré, op. cit. p. 83
72. Haig (Blake ed.), op. cit. 23 March 1918
73. Herbillon, op. cit. Entry for 23 March 1918
74. Pétain *Discours à l'Académie Française, 22 janvier 1931*
75. Herbillon, op. cit. Sunday, 24 March 1918
76. Loucheur, op. cit. p. 51
77. Poincaré, op. cit. p. 84.
78. ibid. p. 86.
79. Haig (Blake ed.), op. cit. 24 March 1918

80. ibid.
81. ibid.
82. ibid.
83. ibid. 3 April 1919
84. ibid. 25 March 1918
85. ibid. 3 April 1919
86. Loucheur, op. cit. pp. 53–4.
87. Fayolle, op. cit. p. 262. 25 March 1918
88. Pershing *My experiences in the World War* London 1931.
89. Poincaré, op. cit. p. 87
90. Loucheur, op. cit. p. 59. Mordacq *La Vérité sur le commandement unique* Paris 1934, p. 77
91. Mordacq, op. cit. p. 78
92. Quoted in Pitt, op. cit. p. 100
93. Haig (Blake ed.), op. cit. 26 March 1918
94. Fayolle, op. cit. pp. 263–4. 27 March 1918
95. ibid.
96. Bourget, op. cit. p. 85
97. Loucheur, op. cit. p. 58
98. ibid.
99. ibid. p. 62. 9 October 1918.
100. Haig (Blake ed.), op. cit. 30 March 1918

Chapter 4

1. Quoted in Pitt, op. cit. pp. 111–12
2. Fayolle, op. cit. p. 271
3. ibid. p. 270, 10–11 April, p. 272, 30 April
4. ibid. p. 272, 30 April
5. Terrier to Lyautey, Paris, 4 May 1918. B. Inst. MS 5903
6. Quoted in Laure, op. cit. pp. 205–6
7. Fayolle, op. cit. p. 272, 7 May 1918
8. ibid. p. 274, 19 May 1918
9. Ferry, op. cit. Entry for 30 July 1918
10. Loucheur, op. cit. p. 61, 26 June 1918
11. ibid. 30 June 1918
12. Clemenceau, op. cit. p. 44
13. Fayolle, op. cit. p. 293. 12 June 1918
14. Ferry, op. cit. Entry for 30 July 1918
15. ibid. Entry for 30 July 1918
16. Fayolle, op. cit. p. 289. 16 July 1918
17. ibid. p. 292. 29 July 1918
18. Mangin *Lettres de guerre, 1914–1918* Paris 1950
19. Ferry, op. cit. Entry for 30 July 1918
20. e.g. Fayolle, op. cit. p. 299. 26 August 1918
21. Ferry, op. cit. Entry for 30 July 1918
22. Terrier to Mme Lyautey, Paris, 20 June 1918. B. Inst. MS 5904
23. Ferry, op. cit. Entry for August 1918
24. ibid. Entry for 6 September 1918
25. Haig (Blake ed.), op. cit. 25 October 1918
26. Barrès *Chronique de la Grande Guerre* vol. 10, pp. 82–5. Entry for 2 August 1917
27. Quoted in Bourget, op. cit. p. 96
28. *Discours prononcé dans la séance publique tenue par l'Académie Française pour la réception de M. le Maréchal Pétain. Jeudi, le 22 janvier 1931*
29. Pardee *Le Maréchal que j'ai connu* Paris 1952, p. 17
30. Serrigny, op. cit. p. 142

References

PART II

Chapter 1

1. Joseph Simon's private notebooks. Quoted in Bourget, op. cit. p. 104
2. Letter of 22 February 1916 Amouroux, op. cit. p. 140
3. Letter of 15 March 1916 ibid. p. 141
4. Letter of 26 June 1917 ibid. p. 146
5. Letter of 25 April 1916 ibid. p. 133
6. Letter to Mrs Pardee 5 September 1938 Pardee, op. cit. p. 11
7. Letter to Chasseloup-Laubat 21 August 1924 Bourget, op. cit. p. 157
8. Serrigny, op. cit. p. 142
9. Lémery *D'une république à l'autre* Paris 1964, p. 190
10. *Académie des Sciences Morales et Politiques, Séance du 5 juillet 1919*

Chapter 2

1. la Gorce *The French Army* London 1963, p. 159
2. Nobécourt, *Une Histoire politique de l'Armée* Paris 1967, vol.1, p. 92
3. Paxton *Parades and politics at Vichy: The French Officer Corps under Marshal Pétain* Princeton 1966,

Chapter 3

1. Quoted in Benoist-Méchin, *Lyautey l'Africain, ou le rêve immolé* Lausanne 1966, p. 150
2. Quoted in Furneaux, *Abdel Krim—Emir of the Riff* London 1967, p. 83
3. Maurois *Lyautey* Paris 1931, p. 334
4. Lyautey to Terrier, Paris, November 4, 1925. B. Inst. MS 5903
5. Laure, op. cit. p. 304
6. Lyautey to Terrier, Paris, 4 November 1925. B. Inst. MS 5903
7. ibid
8. *The Times,* 17 July 1925
9. ibid, 27 June 1925
10. Loustaunau-Lacau *Mémoires d'un français rebelle* Paris 1948, p. 63
11. ibid. p. 63
12. *The Times* 17 July 1925
13. Quoted in Laure op. cit. p. 307
14. Letter from Pétain to Mme Pétain, Fez, 19 July 1925. Quoted in Amouroux, op. cit. pp. 169–70.
15. Letter from Pétain to Mme Pétain, 11 June 1925. Quoted in Amouroux, op. cit. p. 169
16. Quoted in Laure, op. cit. p. 307
17. *The Times* 28 July 1925
18. Conversation with General Durosoy, 25 February 1969
19. *The Times* 29 July 1925
20. ibid. 3 August 1925
21. ibid. 11 August 1925
22. ibid. 18 August 1925
23. ibid. 19 August 1925
24. ibid.
25. *New York Times* 10 September 1925 (Quoted in Ryan *Pétain the Soldier* South Brunswick 1969 p. 188)
26. See Griffiths *The Reactionary Revolution* London 1966, pp. 244–54
27. Catroux *Lyautey le Marocain* Paris 1952, p. 65
28. Laure, op. cit. p. 315
29. *The Times* 1 September 1925
30. Quoted in Furneaux, op. cit. p. 205
31. Quoted in Benoist-Méchin, op. cit. pp. 262–3

References

32. Lyautey to Terrier, 4 November 1925. B. Inst. MS 5903
33. Quoted in Benoist-Méchin, op. cit. pp. 267–9
34. Laure, op. cit. p. 327

Chapter 4

1. See Appendix
2. Fayolle, op. cit. p. 197. 5 January 1917
3. *Discours prononcé dans la séance publique tenue par l'Académie Française pour la réception de M. le Maréchal Pétain. Jeudi, le 22 janvier 1931*
4. *L'Écho de Paris* 20 August 1934. Account of the inauguration of the monument of Le-Haut-du-Mont
5. Laure, op. cit. p. 268
6. *Le Petit Journal* 13 September 1934
7. La Gorce, op. cit. p. 277
8. Quoted in Nobécourt, op. cit. p. 214
9. Pétain, preface to Chauvineau *Une Invasion est-elle encore possible?* Paris 1939
10. *L'Écho de Paris* 15 June 1934
11. Pétain, preface to Bouvard *Les Leçons militaires de la guerre,* Paris 1920
12. Quoted in La Gorce, op. cit. p. 273
13. ibid. p. 272
14. Quoted in Feller *Le Dossier de L'Armée Française* Paris 1966 p. 218
15. Pétain, preface to Sikorski *La Guerre moderne, son caractère, ses problèmes,* Paris 1935
16. Pétain, preface to Chauvineau, op. cit.
17. Quoted in Feller, op. cit. p. 218
18. For the text of this *Instruction* I am grateful to General Henri Jauncaud.
19. Laure, op. cit. p. 299
20. ibid. p. 300
21. ibid. p. 354
22. *Instruction sur l'emploi tactique des Grandes Unités Aériennes*—SECRET, *1937.* Kindly communicated to me by General Jauneaud.
23. Feller, op. cit. p. 223
24. Mordacq *Clemenceau au soir de sa vie* Paris 1933, Vol. 2, p. 37
25. Mordacq, op. cit. p. 133
26. See Nobécourt, op. cit. p. 210
27. ibid. p. 210
28. Quoted in La Gorce, op. cit. p. 254
29. Quoted in Feller, op. cit. p. 202
30. *L'Écho de Paris* 4 July 1934
31. Pétain, preface to Chauvineau, op. cit.
32. *Le Petit Journal* 30 October 1934
33. *Le Jour* 11 March 1935
34. e.g., Léon Bailby in *Le Jour* 15 March 1935
35. *Le Jour* 17 March 1935
36. Nobécourt, op. cit. p. 210
37. William Shirer *Berlin Diary* London 1941, p. 344. Entry for 27 June 1940.

Chapter 5

1. See Griffiths, op. cit.
2. *Le Journal* 30 April 1936
3. See Griffiths, op. cit. pp. 261–6
4. Pardee, op. cit. p. 33
5. Speech at Verdun monument, *L'Écho de Paris* 18 June 1934
6. Open letter from Pétain on the occasion of the Festival for the fifth centenary of Jeanne d'Arc, Rouen, 23–31 May 1931
7. *La Victoire* 19 May 1934

8. Preface to Sikorski, op. cit.
9. *L'Écho de Paris* 3 August 1934
10. Ludwig Beck *Studien,* Stuttgart 1955. Anhang: Bericht über die Reise nach Paris
11. Speech at Verdun monument, *L'Écho de Paris* 18 June 1934 op. cit.
12. *Revue des Deux Mondes* 15 March 1891
13. *L'Écho de Paris* 3 August 1934
14. *Le Journal* 30 April 1936
15. *L'Ami du Peuple* 21 January 1936
16. Laure, op. cit. p. 369
17. Letter to Aimé Berthod, 5 April 1934 (Laure, p. 369).
18. *L'Écho de Paris* 18 June 1934
19. Speech at Meaux, *Le Petit Journal* 10 September 1934
20. *L'Écho de Paris* 23 July 1934
21. Ludwig Beck, op. cit.
22. *Le Journal* 30 April 1936
23. Pétain's comment on a speech by Franco, 1 January 1940 (Noguères *Le véritable procès du Maréchal Pétain* Paris 1955, p. 45)
24. Letter to Mme Hardon, his future wife, 30 July 1920 (Amouroux, op. cit. p. 197)
25. Letter from Gazel to Bonnet, August 1939 (Amouroux, op. cit. pp. 212–13)
26. *Le Jour-L'Écho de Paris* 3 March 1939
27. Georges Bonnet, on his reasons for sending Pétain to Spain, Bourget, op. cit. p. 158
28. Ludwig Beck, op. cit.
29. *The Times* 19 October 1934
30. Göring, 'Vom Segen der Volksgemeinschaft'. Rede zum Winterhilfswerk in den Krupp-Werken in Essen am 4 Dezember 1934. Göring, *Reden und Aufsätze,* hrsg. von Dr. Erich Gritzbach, Munich 1943
31. See *Le Journal* 30 April 1936
32. *L'Écho de Paris* 27 May 1934
33. Pardee, op. cit. p. 17
34. Letter to Mrs Pardee, 10 October 1938 (Pardee, op. cit. p. 26)
35. Letter to Mrs Pardee, 16 September 1938 (ibid. pp. 24–5)
36. Quoted in Amouroux, op. cit. p. 192

Chapter 6
1. *L'Écho de Paris* 9 February 1943 Quoted in Rémond, *La Droite en France, de la première Restauration à la Ve République* Paris 1968, p. 218
2. *L'Écho de Paris* 11 February 1934
3. *L'Écho de Paris* 7 August 1934
4. Report by Raymond Cartier, *L'Écho de Paris* 15 June 1934
5. *Le Petit Journal* 11 January 1935
6. ibid.
7. See Griffiths, op. cit.
8. *La Victoire* 6 February 1935
9. ibid. 11 February 1935
10. ibid. 12 February 1935
11. ibid. 30 March 1935
12. ibid 14 February 1935
13. ibid.
14. ibid. 15 February 1935
15. *Le Jour,* 21 February 1935
16. ibid. 21 February 1935
17. ibid. 11 March 1935
18. ibid. 20 March 1935
19. *La Victoire* 16 March 1935
20. *Le Jour* 22 March 1935

21. *La Victoire* 23 March 1935
22. ibid. 30 March 1935
23. *L'Action Française 3* April 1935
24. *Le Jour* 18 April 1935
25. ibid. 20 April 1935
26. ibid. 22 May 1935
27. ibid.
28. ibid. 27 May 1935
29. ibid. 2 June 1935
30. ibid. 2 June 1935
31. *La Victoire* 7 June 1935
32. *Le Jour* 2 June 1935
33. *Vu,* 30 November 1935, p. 39
34. ibid. p. 19
35. *La Victoire* 9 November 1935
36. ibid. 11 November 1935
37. ibid. 15 January 1936
38. *L'Ami du Peuple* 9 March 1936
39. *Le Figaro* 9 March 1936
40. *La Victoire* 17 March 1936
41. *Le Journal* 30 April 1936
42. Hervé *C'est Pétain qu'il nous faut* Paris 1937. Preface
43. Bourget, op. cit.
44. *L'Indépendant* 12 March 1938
45. *Le Populaire* 3 March 1939
46. *L'Humanité* 3 March 1939
47. *Le Jour: L'Écho de Paris* 3 March 1939
48. *Salut National,* quoted in Noguères, op. cit.
49. Letter, San Sebastian, 21 September 1939. Pardee, op. cit. pp. 51-2.

Chapter 7
1. Rémond, op. cit pp. 216–18
2. *L'Écho de Paris* 8 February 1934
3. *La Voix du Combattant* 22 February 1934
4. Rémond, op. cit. p. 218
5. Laure, op. cit. p. 362
6. *Le Procès du Maréchal Pétain, compte rendu sténographique* Paris 1945, vol. I, p. 355
7. See, for example, the article by François Mauriac in *L'Écho de Paris* 4 March 1934
8. Lémery *D'une république à l'autre* Paris 1964, p. 164
9. Quoted in Bourget, op. cit. p. 146
10. Draft letter of resignation, quoted in Amouroux, op. cit. p. 192
11. *Le Jour* 2 June 1935 (article by Léon Bailby)
12. General Héring, quoted by Tournoux *Pétain et de Gaulle* Paris 1964, p. 165
13. Letter, Madrid, 3 March 1940. Pardee, op. cit., pp. 39–40
14. Lémery, quoted by Tournoux, op. cit. p. 165
15. *La Victoire* 21 June 1935
16. Carcopino *Souvenirs de sept ans* Paris 1953, p. 162
17. Picture in *Le Jour* 2 June 1935
18. An enclosure in a letter from Faupel to the German Foreign Ministry, 14 April 1937 in *Documents on German Foreign Policy*, 1918–45, Series D, Vol. 3, No. 244. Quoted in Warner, *Pierre Laval and the Eclipse of France* London 1968, p. 135
19. e.g., letter to Paul Pomart, 29 April 1937. Quoted in Bourget, op. cit. p. 156
20. Brogan, *The Development of Modern France* London 1940, p. 720
21. Pétain to his wife, 11 July 1937. Quoted in Amouroux, op. cit. p. 197
22. Pétain to Mrs Pardee, 10 March 1938. Pardee, op. cit. p. 14

23. Letter quoted in *Crapouillot, Histoire de la Guerre*, vol. 3, p. 166
24. Quoted in Warner, op. cit. p. 136. Landini to Luciano 18 March 1938, Italian Documents (St Anthony's College), 148/043539–44
25. Paris, 24 March 1918 (Pardee, op. cit. p. 15)
26. Quoted in Warner, op. cit. p. 136. Landini to Luciano, 6 April 1938. Italian Documents (St Anthony's College) 148/04345–54
27. Warner, op. cit. 137–8
28. *Le Procès du Maréchal Pétain* vol. 1, p. 509
29. Amouroux, op. cit. pp. 202–3
30. Letter to Mrs Pardee, 10 October 1938 (ibid. p. 26)
31. Pardee, op. cit. p. 30
32. Conversation quoted by Bourget, op. cit. pp. 155–6. (Though Bourget applies it to the wrong event, i.e., the crisis after Chautemps' fall, later mentions of Laval and Bouisson clearly make this refer to the presidential election, as do references to the 'highest office', and similarities with Henry-Haye's remarks on the same subject in *La Vie de la France*.)
33. Quoted in Bourget, op. cit. p. 157
34. Noguères, op. cit. pp. 14–15
35. Quoted in Warner, op. cit. p. 139. Landini to Luciano 8 March 1939. Italian Documents (St Anthony's College), 148/043630–34
36. *Le Procès du Maréchal Pétain* vol. 1, pp. 317–22
37. Amouroux, op. cit. p. 209
38. Noguères, op. cit. p. 53
39. Letter from General Anthoine to Pétain, 2 October 1939. Noguères, op. cit. pp. 13–14
40. *Le Procès du Maréchal Pétain* vol. 2, p. 902
41. Gamelin *Servir* vol. 3, p. 106
42. Bois *Le Malheur de la France* London 1941, p. 64
43. Letter from General Anthoine to Pétain, 2 October 1939. Noguères, op. cit. pp. 13–14
44. ibid. p. 56
45. ibid. p. 361
46. ibid. p. 56
47. Bois, op. cit. p. 112
48. 'Note de Sigmaringen' (justificatory note written by Pétain). Noguères, op. cit. p. 18
49. *Le Procès du Maréchal Pétain* vol. 1, p. 230
50. Lémery, op. cit. p. 233. Lémery makes his visit into an innocent one, and the making of the list into a kind of game. But this was written after the war.
51. Letter to General Vauthier, 15 January 1940. Noguères, op. cit. p. 38
52. Lémery, op. cit. p. 227
53. Letter to General Georges, 28 January 1940. Noguères, op. cit. p. 37
54. Madrid, 9 April 1940. Pardee, op. cit. p. 62
55. Darlan *L'Amiral Darlan parle* Paris 1952, pp. 102, 135
56. Warner, op. cit. pp. 158–9
57. Noguères, op. cit. p. 33
58. *L'Écho de Paris* 19 March 1934
59. *Le Journal* 30 April 1934
60. Loustaunau-Lacau, op. cit. p. 112
61. ibid.
62. ibid.
63. ibid, p. 116
64. Tournoux, op. cit. p. 166
65. Gamelin, op. cit.
66. Noguères, op. cit. p. 53

Chapter 8
1. *Le Jour-L'Écho de Paris* 18 January 1939

References

2. Bonnet, in conversation, quoted by Bourget, op. cit. p. 158. A conversation similar in all its important details is quoted by Amouroux, op. cit. pp. 209–10.
3. Reported in *Le Jour: L'Écho de Paris* 4 March 1939
4. *Deutsche Allgemeine Zeitung* 2 March 1939
5. *Le Jour: L'Écho de Paris* 3 March 1939
6. Letter to his wife, 17 March 1939. Amouroux, op. cit. p. 211
7. Letter to Mrs Pardee, 17 March 1939. Pardee, op. cit. p. 40
8. Letter to his wife, 21 March 1939. Amouroux, op. cit. p. 212
9. Laure, op. cit. p. 421
10. Letter to Mrs Pardee, 1 April 1939, Pardee, op. cit. p. 41
11. ibid. 5 April 1939, ibid. p. 42
12. ibid. 10 April 1939, ibid. p. 42
13. Letter from Gazel to Bonnet, Amouroux, op. cit. p. 212–13
14. *Le Jour: L'Écho de Paris* 8 August 1939

PART III

Chapter 1

1. Horne *To Lose a Battle, France 1940* London 1959, p. 159
2. Letter to General Georges, 28 January 1940. Noguères, op. cit. p. 37
3. Baudouin *Neuf mois au gouvernement (Avril–Décembre 1940)* Paris 1948, p. 47
4. Chapman *Why France Collapsed* London 1968. Horne *To Lose a Battle, France 1940* London 1969. John Williams *The Ides of May — The Defeat of France May–June 1940* London 1968
5. Reynaud *In the Thick of the Fight* London 1955, p. 310
6. Churchill *The Second World War* vol. 2 *Their Finest Hour* London 1949, p. 38
7. Baudouin, op. cit. p. 54
8. ibid.
9. Churchill, op. cit. p. 41
10. ibid. p. 42
11. Baudouin, op. cit. p. 56
12. Churchill, op. cit. p. 42
13. *Le Jour - L'Écho de Paris* 19 May 1940
14. ibid. 20 May 1940
15. Baudouin, op. cit. p. 62
16. ibid. p. 71
17. ibid. p. 86. Spears, on the 27th, heard rumours of this attitude of Pétain's. Spears *Assignment to Catastrophe*, vol. 2 *The Fall of France* London 1954, p. 235
18. Baudouin, op. cit. p. 89
19. Churchill, op. cit. pp. 108–9
20. Baudouin, op. cit. p. 90
21. ibid. p. 90
22. ibid. p. 116
23. ibid. p. 118
24. ibid. p. 115
25. ibid. p. 124
26. Chautemps *Cahiers secrets de l'Armistice (1939–1940)* Paris 1963 p. 110
27. ibid. p. 126
28. ibid. p. 110
29. Baudouin, op. cit. p. 127
30. ibid. p. 130
31. ibid. p. 134
32. ibid. p. 136
33. ibid. pp. 140–2
34. Churchill, op. cit. p. 100

35. Spears, op. cit. vol. I, p. 183
36. ibid. vol. 2, p. 84
37. ibid. vol. 1, p. 223
38. ibid, vol. 2, p. 85
39. Churchill, op. cit. pp. 136–7
40. Weygand, *Mémoires* Paris 1950, vol. 3, p. 204
41. Churchill, op. cit. pp. 136–7
42. De Gaulle, *Mémoires de Guerre*, vol. 1 *L'Appel (1940–1942)*, Paris 1954, Livre de poche edition, p. 70
43. Churchill, op. cit. p. 139
44. Aron *Histoire de Vichy, 1940–1944* Paris 1954, vol. 1, p. 19
45. Churchill, op. cit. p. 159
46. ibid. p. 161
47. Quoted in Aron, op. cit. vol. 1, pp. 25–6
48. ibid. p. 15
49. Noguères, op. cit. p. 107
50. Baudouin, op. cit. p. 170
51. De Launay *Le Dossier de Vichy* Paris 1967, pp. 11–12
52. Pétain *Appels aux Français* Paris and Clermont 1940, p. 12
53. Baudouin, op. cit. p. 195
54. Pétain, op. cit. pp. 13–14
55. The best account of the events of these two weeks is in Warner, op. cit. For a full treatment of this subject the reader is referred to that book.
56. Lebrun *Témoignage* Paris 1945, p. 102.
57. Pomaret *Le Dernier Témoin* Paris 1968, p. 242
58. ibid. p. 243
59. Montigny *Toute la vérité sur un mois dramatique de notre histoire* Clermont-Ferrand 1940, p. 61
60. Aron, op. cit. vol. 1, p. 159
61. ibid. p. 168
62. Noguères, op. cit.
63. Claudel, op. cit. 10 July 1940

Chapter 2
1. Quoted in de Launay, op. cit. p. 47
2. Du Moulin de Labarthète, *Le Temps des illusions: souvenirs (juillet 1940–avril 1942)* Geneva 1946
3. Claudel, op. cit. 30 June 1940
4. Paxton, op. cit. p. 59
5. ibid. p. 142
6. *La Nouvelle Guyenne*, June–July 1940. Quoted in Weber, *L'Action Française*, p. 484
7. Claudel, op. cit. 6 July 1940
8. Paxton, op. cit. p. 92
9. See Griffiths, op. cit. and Rémond, op. cit. for studies of these trends.
10. De Launay, op. cit. pp. 263–4. De Launay notes that *Patrie, Famille, Travail* had been one of the slogans of Colonel La Rocque.
11. Montigny, op. cit. p. 129. This book contains the complete text of the *exposé des motifs*.
12. ibid, p. 131
13. ibid.
14. ibid. p. 132
15. Claudel, op. cit. 9 June 1940
16. Pétain *L'Abandon de la vie spirituelle et de l'esprit national*, speech at Metz, 20 November 1938
17. Pétain *Appel du 20 juin 1940*

References

18. Pétain, 'L'Éducation Nationale', *Revue des Deux Mondes* 15 August 1940
19. ibid.
20. *Revue des Deux Mondes* 15 December 1941
21. *Instruction sur l'organisation et l'administration des chantiers de la jeunesse*, Paris, Limoges, Nancy, 1941
22. Olivier de Serres, père de l'agriculture française: *Le Théâtre d'agriculture et mesnage des champs, pages choisies, précédées d'une lettre de M. le Maréchal Pétain, chef de L'État* Paris 1941
23. Paxton, op. cit. p. 194
24. Pétain *Appel du 11 juillet 1940*
25. ibid.
26. Pétain *Discours prononcé le 4 juin 1941 à la séance inaugurale du Comité d'Organisation professionnelle*
27. Pétain *Message du 11 octobre 1940*
28. ibid.
29. ibid.
30. Pétain, *Discours prononcé à St Étienne, le 1 mars 1941*
31. Pétain, *Message du 11 octobre 1940*
32. ibid.
33. ibid.
34. Conversation with René Gillouin
35. Inst. für Zeitgeschichte M.S. Eich. 1381
36. Report of 8 October 1940. Printed in Abetz *Pétain et les Allemands: mémorandum sur les rapports franco-allemands* Paris 1948
37. Documents on German Foreign Policy, Series D, xi, 531, 588 quoted by Paxton, op. cit. p. 171
38. Telegram 1 February 1941. Abetz, op. cit.
39. Report of 23 June 1941. Ibid.
40. Berl *La Fin de la IIIe République* Paris 1968
40. Baudouin, op. cit. p. 339
41. Pétain *Message du 11 octobre 1940*
42. Daudouin, op. cit pp. 378–9
43. Churchill, op. cit. p. 450
44. Pétain *Message du 30 octobre 1940*
45. Claudel *Journal Intime* 30 November 1940
46. Neubronn, 'Als "deutscher General" bei Pétain.' *Vierteljahrshefte für Zeitgeschichte*, 4 Jahrgang 1956 3 Heft/Juli, p. 229
47. Telegram, Abetz to Foreign Minister, No. 1556 18 December 1940. Abetz, op. cit.
48. Aufzeichnung über die Unterredung zwischen den R.A.M. und den japanischen Aussenminister Matsuoka in Berlin am 5 April 1941. Inst. für Zeitgeschichte, PS. 1882
49. Telegram, Richard Hemmen to German Foreign Minister, 16 January 1941, Inst. für Zeitgeschichte, NG.2471

Chapter 3

1. Telegram from Abetz to Ribbentrop, 1 February 1941. Abetz, op. cit.
2. Instruction from Ribbentrop to Abetz, 2 February 1941. ibid.
3. Telegram from Abetz to Ribbentrop, 4 February 1941. ibid.
4. Darlan *L'Amiral Darlan parle* Paris 1952, p. 275
5. Instruction from Ribbentrop to Abetz, 5 February 1941. Abetz, op. cit.
6. Telegram from Abetz to Ribbentrop 19 February 1941. ibid.
7. Schreiben des Chefs der Sicherheitspolizei und des S. D. an den Herrn Reichsaussenminister, August 9, 1941. Inst. für Zeitgeschichte, NG 757
8. Report on the situation in France one year after the armistice, Abetz-Ribbentrop, 23 June 1941. Abetz, op. cit.

9. Pétain, *Message du 15 octobre 1941*
10. Telegram, Abetz to Foreign Minister 6 March 1941 Inst. für Zeitgeschichte, NG 2442
11. Telegram, Abetz to Ribbentrop, 3 April 1941 Inst. für Zeitgeschichte, Eich. 445
12. Pétain *Appel du 11 avril 1941*
13. De Launay, op. cit. p. 154
14. ibid. pp. 156–7. This is the text sent by Darlan to the governors of the French colonies.
15. Pétain *Message du 15 mai 1941*
16. Weygand op. cit.
17. Telegram Paris, 23 August 1941 Inst. für Zeitgeschichte, N.G. 5133
18. Telegram, Abetz to Ribbentrop 25 October 1941 *Inst. für Zeitgeschichte*, NG 4003
19. ibid. 25 October 1941. Inst. für Zeitgeschichte, NG 4003
20. ibid. 25 October 1941 Inst. für Zeitgeschichte, NG 4003
21. ibid. 25 October 1941 Inst. für Zeitgeschichte, NG 4003
22. Abetz, op. cit. p. 118
23. Letter of 27 July 1941. Laure, *Notes politiques et militaires*, p. 141–2. Paillat *L'Echiquier d'Alger* vol. 1, pp. 224–5
24. Laure, op. cit. p. 152. Quoted in Paillat, op. cit. p. 227
25. Weygand, op. cit.
26. Quoted in Manvell and Fraenkel, *Herman Göring* London 1962, pp. 190–1
27. Abetz Memorandum on the Pétain-Göring interview 1 December 1941 Abetz, op. cit.
28. Abetz Letter 11 December 1941 Abetz, op. cit.

Chapter 4

1. Warner, op. cit. p. 282
2. *Le Temps* 22 October 1942
3. Poliakov. Evidence at Eichmann trial. Inst. für Zeitgeschichte, Eich. 1381
4. Telegram 25 September 1942. Office of Chief Counsel for War Crimes, Document NG 1971, Instit. für Zeitgeschichte
5. Claudel, op. cit. Entry for 3 September 1942
6. Telegram Abetz to Ribbentrop 1 June 1942. Abetz, op. cit.
7. Warner, op. cit. p. 313
8. Letter from Pétain to Hitler, Vichy, August 1942
9. Telegram from Auphan to Darlan. Noguères, op. cit. p. 412
10. ibid.
11. Telegram from Schellenberg to Reichsführer S.S. 11 November 1942, 12.50 p.m. Inst für Zeitgeschichte, MA 553
12. ibid. 2.40 p.m. Inst. für Zeitgeschichte, MA 553
13. Darlan op. cit. p. 217
14. Telegram from Dr Knochen to Reichsführer S.S., Paris, 11 November 1942, 10 p.m. Inst. für Zeitgeschichte, MA 553
15. Telegram to Reichsführer S.S., 12 November 1942, 10.05 a.m. Inst. für Zeitgeschichte MA553
16. Telegram, Knochen to Reichsführer S.S., Paris, 14 November 1942. Inst. für Zeitgeschichte, MA 553
17. Knochen to Reichsführer S.S. 14 November 1942. Inst. für Zeitgeschichte, MA 326
18. Aron, op. cit. vol. 2, p. 264

Chapter 5

1. Vercors *La Bataille du silence* Paris 1967, p. 255
2. Warner, op. cit. p. 375
3. Poliakov, op. cit. p. 82. Inst. für Zeitgeschichte, Eich. 1381
4. Roethke report, Paris, 15 August 1943. Inst. für Zeitgeschichte, Eich. 1523
5. ibid.
6. ibid.
7. Quoted in Brissaud, *La Dernière année de Vichy*, Paris 1965, p. 47

8. Roethke report, Paris, 15 August 1943. Inst. für Zeitgeschichte, Eich. 1523
9. ibid.
10. ibid.
11. Roethke note 4 July 1944, quoted in Warner, op. cit.
12. Poliakov, p. 82. Inst. für Zeitgeschichte, Eich. 1523
13. ibid.
14. Letter, Pétain to Brinon, 24 August 1943, quoted in Brissaud, op. cit. p. 48
15. Warner, op. cit. pp. 367–8. Aron, op cit. vol. 2, pp. 331–2
16. Warner, op. cit. p. 379
17. Jeantet *Pétain contre Hitler* Paris 1966, pp. 3–4
18. Auphan's plan, quoted in Annexe A of Jeantet's *Pétain contre Hitler,* p. 270
19. ibid. pp. 278–9
20. ibid. p. 275
21. ibid. p. 275
22. Neubronn, op. cit. pp. 239–40
23. ibid.
24. Nicolle *Cinquante mois d'armistice: Vichy, 2 juillet 1940—26 août 1944, journal d'un témoin,* Paris 1947
25. Jeantet, op. cit. 21–2
26. ibid. p. 23
27. *Notiz für den Führer,* Berlin, 3 December 1943, Inst. für Zeitgeschichte, NG 3013
28. Telegram, Ribbentrop to Abetz, 6 December 1943. Inst. für Zeitgeschichte, NG 5211

Chapter 6

1. See Piétri *Mes Années d'Espagne 1940–8* Paris 1954, pp. 244–9
2. Tournoux, op. cit. (facsimile reproduction among the illustrations)
3. Laval to Abetz, Paris, 17 August 1944
4. See, for example, the document discovered in late 1969, and printed in the *Bulletin de l'amicale des anciens membres des services spéciaux de la Défense Nationale,* No. 63; a document which contains Pétain's proposed declaration for the liberation of Paris.
5. De Gaulle *Mémoires de guerre* vol. 2, pp. 249–50
6. Pétain *Message du 30 octobre 1940*

Conclusion

1. Céline, op. cit. pp. 188–9
2. *Programme minimum*, drawn up in 1960, *O.A.S. parle* Paris 1964, pp. 210–12

Appendix

1. Quoted in Tournoux, op. cit. p. 55
2. Tournoux, op. cit. p. 143
3. Note from Daniel-Rops to Tournoux. Tournoux, op. cit. p. 411
4. Letter from Pétain to publishers Plon, 6 October 1938. Quoted in Tournoux, op. cit. p. 175
5. Letter from Pétain to de Gaulle, 5 September 1938. Quoted in Tournoux, op. cit. p. 174
6. Letter from Pétain to publishers Plon, 6 October 1938. ibid,. p. 175
7. Baudouin, op. cit. p. 130
8. Letter from de Gaulle to Colonel Nachin, 20 June 1929. Quoted in Tournoux, op. cit. p. 134
9. Céline, op. cit. pp. 188–9
10. Report from Gouin to Blum, 11 September 1942. Quoted in Paillat, op. cit. vol 1, p. 348
11. ibid. p. 349
12. ibid. p. 352

Select bibliography

On a subject as controversial as Pétain, a great deal is written which has little value except as a contribution to polemical argument. This bibliography contains only those books which have been of use to the writer; though, in the nature of things, one or two examples of works which illustrate the purely controversial trend are included.

Manuscript sources have on the whole been listed in footnotes at the places where they are used, and have no place here. They include many German sources for the section on the Second World War, and several sources for background material for the earlier sections, including the extensive Lyautey-Terrier correspondence from the Bibliothèque de l'Institut, the Pellé papers from the same library, and such privately-owned documents as Claudel's private diary (quoted by kind permission of Monsieur Pierre Claudel and Madame Renée Nantet), and Governmental documents relating to France's air defences (kindly provided by General Jauneaud).

Much of the other original material results from close persual of the newspapers of the period. Newspaper articles are referred to in footnotes where they occur; as are speeches and articles by Pétain and others. This bibliography is devoted to full-scale published works.

Abetz, Otto *Pétain et les Allemands: Mémorandum sur les rapports franco-allemands* Paris, 1948
Abetz, Otto *Das offene Problem* Köln, 1951
Amouroux, Henri *Pétain avant Vichy—la guerre et l'amour* Paris, 1967
Argenson, Marquis d' *Pétain et le pétinisme* Paris, 1967
Aron, Robert *Histoire de Vichy, 1940–1944* 2 vols. Paris, 1959
Azan, General *Franchet d'Esperey* Paris, 1949

Barnett, Corelli *The Swordbearers: Studies in Supreme Command in the First World War* London, 1963
Barrès, Maurice *Chronique de la Grande Guerre* 14 vols. Paris, 1924–39.
Baudouin, Paul *Neuf mois au gouvernement* Paris, 1948
Beau de Loménie, E *La Mort de la Troisième République* Paris, 1951
Beck, General Ludwig *Studien, hrsg. und eingeleitet von H. Speidel* Stuttgart, 1955
Benjamin, René *Le Maréchal et son peuple* Paris, 1941

Select bibliography

Benoist- Méchin *Lyautey l'Africain, ou le rêve immolé* Lausanne, 1966

Berl, Emmanuel *La Fin de la IIIe République* Paris, 1968

Blond, Georges *Verdun* Paris, 1961

Blond, Georges *Pétain* Paris, 1966

Bolton, John R. G. *Pétain* London, 1957

Bois, Élie *Le Malheur de la France* London, 1941

Bordeaux, Henry *Histoire d'une vie*, vols. 4, 5

Bourget, Pierre *Un Certain Philippe Pétain* Paris, 1966

Bouthillier, Yves *Le Drame de Vichy* Vol. 1, *Face à l'ennemi, face à l'allié* Paris, 1950. Vol 2, *Finances sous la contrainte* Paris, 1951

Bouvard, Commandant H. *Les Leçons militaires de la guerre*, preface by Marshal Pétain Paris, 1920

Brinon, Ferdinand de *Mémoires* Paris, 1949

Brissaud, André *La Dernière Année de Vichy* Paris, 1956

Brissaud, André *Pétain à Sigmaringen* Paris, 1966

Brogan, Denis W. *The Development of Modern France* London, 1940

Buchheit, Gert *Ludwig Beck, ein preussischer General* Munich, 1964

Carcopino, Jérôme *Souvenirs de sept ans* Paris, 1953

Carré, Henri *Les Grandes Heures du maréchal Pétain—1917 et la crise du moral* Paris, 1952

Catroux, General Georges *Dans la bataille de Méditerranée* Paris, 1949

Catroux, General Georges *Lyautey le Marocain* Paris, 1952

Céline, Louis-Ferdinand *D'un château l'autre* Paris, 1957

Chapman, Guy *Why France Collapsed* London, 1968

Charles-Roux, François *Cinq mois tragiques aux Affaires Étrangères* Paris, 1949

Chautemps, Camille *Cahiers secrets de l'Armistice (1939–1940)* Paris, 1963

Chauvineau, General *Une Invasion est-elle encore possible?* Preface by Marshal Pétain. Paris, 1939

Churchill, Winston *The Second World War* vol. 2, *Their Finest Hour* London, 1949

Clemenceau, Georges *Grandeurs et misères d'une victoire* Paris, 1930

Cole, Hubert *Laval: a Biography* London, 1963

Cotta, Michèle *La Collaboration 1940–1944* Paris, 1964

Crawley, Aidan *De Gaulle* London, 1969

Darlan, Alain *L'Amiral Darlan parle* Paris, 1952

Des Vallières, Jean *Au soleil de la cavalerie* Paris, 1962

Du Moulin de Labarthète, Henri *Le Temps des illusions: souvenirs (juillet 1940–avril 1942.)* Geneva, 1946

Fabre-Luce, Alfred *Journal de France 1939–1944* Geneva, 1946

Falkenhayn, Erich von *Die oberste Heeresleitung 1914–1916, in ihren wichtigsten Entschliessungen* Berlin, 1920

Falls, Cyril *Marshal Foch* London, 1939

Select bibliography

Farmer, Paul   *Vichy: Political Dilemma* London, 1955
Fayolle   *Cahiers secrets de la Grande Guerre* Paris, 1964
Feller, Jean   *Le Dossier de l'Armée Française* Paris, 1966
Fernet, Admiral Jean   *Aux côtés du maréchal Pétain. Souvenirs, 1940–44* Paris, 1953
Ferry, Abel   *Carnets secrets, 1914–1918* Paris, 1957
Foch, Marshal   *Mémoires pour servir à l'histoire de la Guerre* Paris, 1931
Furneaux, Rupert   *Abdel Krim — Emir of the Rif* London, 1967

Galliéni, General   *Carnets* Paris, 1932
Gamelin, General Maurice   *Servir.* 3 vols. Paris, 1946–7
Gaulle, Charles de   *Le Fil de l'épée* Paris, 1932
Gaulle, Charles de   *Vers l'armée de métier* Paris, 1934
Gaulle, Charles de   *Vers l'armée de métier* Paris, 1944
Gaulle, Charles de   *La France et son armée* Paris, 1938
Gaulle, Charles de   *Mémoires de Guerre.* vol. 1: *L'Appel* Paris, 1954. vol. 2: *L'Unité* Paris, 1956. vol 3: *Le Salut* Paris, 1959
Geschke, Gunter   *Die deutsche Frankreichpolitik 1940 von Compiègne bis Montoire* Berlin, 1960
Gillouin, René   *J'étais l'ami du maréchal Pétain* Paris, 1966
Girard, Louis-Dominique   *Montoire, Verdun diplomatique: le secret du maréchal* Paris, 1948
Girard, Louis-Dominique   *La Guerre franco-française: le maréchal républicain* Paris, 1950
Göring, Hermann   *Reden und Aufsätze, hrsg von Dr Erich Gritzbach* Munich, 1943
Griffiths, Richard   *The Reactionary Revolution* London, 1966
Guedalla, Philip.   *The Two Marshals: Bazaine, Pétain* London, 1943
Guérard   *Criminel de Paix* Paris, 1953

Hankey, Lord   *The Supreme Command 1914–1918* 2 vols. London, 1961
Hankey, Lord   *The Supreme Control at the Paris Peace Conference 1919* London, 1963
Haig, Douglas, 1st Earl   *The Private Papers of Douglas Haig, 1914–1919,* ed. by Robert Blake. London, 1952
Herbillon, Colonel E.   *Souvenirs d'un officier de liaison auprès de Nivelle et de Pétain* Paris, 1930
Héring   *La Vie exemplaire de Philippe Pétain, chef de guerre, chef d'état, martyr* Paris, 1956
Hervé, Gustave   *C'est Pétain qu'il nous faut* Paris, 1935
Hervé, Gustave   *C'est Pétain qu'il nous faut* Paris, 1937
Horne, Alistair   *The Price of Glory: Verdun 1916* London, 1962
Horne, Alistair   *To Lose a Battle: France 1940* London, 1969
Huddleston, Sisley   *Avec le maréchal* Paris, 1948
Huddleston, Sisley   *Pétain, Patriot or Traitor?* London, 1951

Hytier, Adrienne   *Two years of French Foreign Policy: Vichy, 1940–2* Geneva, 1958

Isorni, Jacques   *Souffrance et mort du maréchal* Paris, 1951
Isorni, Jacques   *C'est un péché de la France* Paris, 1962
Isorni, Jacques   *Pétain a sauvé la France* Paris, 1964
Isorni, Jacques   *Correspondence de l'île d'Yeu* Paris, 1966
Isorni, Jacques, and Lemaire, Jean   *Requête en révision pour Philippe Pétain* Paris, 1950
Isselin, Henri,   *La Ruée allemande — printemps 1918* Paris, 1968

Jeantet, Gabriel   *Pétain contre Hitler* Paris, 1966
Joffre, Marshal Joseph   *Mémoires (1910–1917)* 2 vols. Paris, 1932
Juin, Marshal Alphonse   *Mémoires* vol. 1. Paris, 1959

La Gorce, Paul-Marie de   *The French Army* London, 1963
La Porte du Theil, General de   *Instruction sur l'organisation et l'adminstration des chantiers de jeunesse* Paris, Limoges, Nancy, 1941
Laure, General E.   *La Victoire franco-espagnol dans le Rif* Paris, 1927
Laure, General E., and others   *Pétain* Paris, 1941
Launay, Jacques de   *Le Dossier de Vichy* Paris, 1967
Laurent, Jacques   *Année 40 — Londres — de Gaulle — Vichy* Paris, 1965
Laval, Pierre   *Laval parle: notes et mémoires rédigées par Pierre Laval dans sa cellule* Geneva, 1947
Lebrun, Albert   *Témoignage* Paris, 1945
Lémery, Henri   *D'une république à l'autre* Paris, 1964
Liddell Hart,   Sir Basil   *Reputations* London, 1928
Liddell Hart, Sir Basil   *A History of the World War, 1914–1918* London, 1934
Loucheur, Louis   *Carnets secrets, 1908–1932* Brussels, Paris, 1962
Loustaunau-Lacau   *Mémoires d'un Français rebelle* Paris, 1948
Ludendorff, Erich   *Meine Kriegserinnerungen* Berlin, 1919
Lyautey, Marshal   *Le Rôle social de l'officier* Paris, 1935

Mangin, General Charles   *Lettres de guerre, 1914–1918* Paris, 1950
Manvell, Roger, and Fraenkel, H.   *Hermann Göring* London, 1962
Marcellin, L.   *Politique et politiciens pendant la guerre* Paris, s.d.
Martin du Gard, Maurice   *La Chronique de Vichy (1940–1944)* Paris, 1948
Maurois, André   *Lyautey* Paris, 1931
Michel, Henri   *Vichy: Année 40* Paris, 1966
Michel, Paul-Louis   *Le Procès Pétain* Paris, 1945
Montigny, Jean   *Toute la vérité sur un mois dramatique de notre histoire* Clermont-Ferrand, 1940
Mordacq, General H.   *Pourquoi Arras n'a pas été prise* Paris, 1934
Mordacq, General H.   *Clemenceau au soir de sa vie* Paris, 1933
Mordacq, General H.   *La Vérité sur le commandement unique* Paris, 1934

Naud, Albert *Pourquoi je n'ai pas défendu Pierre Laval* Paris, 1948

Neubronn, Alexander Freiherr von *Als 'deutscher General' bei Pétain* (*Vierteljahrshefte für Zeitgeschichte*, 4 Jahrgang 1956 3 Heft/Juli.)

Nicolle, Pierre *Cinquante mois d'armistice: Vichy, 2 juillet 1940–16 août 1944, journal d'un témoin* 2 vols. Paris, 1947

Nobécourt, Jacques *Une Histoire politique de l'Armée* vol. 1. Paris, 1967

Noguères, Louis *Le véritable Procès du maréchal Pétain* Paris, 1955

O.A.S. parle Paris, 1964

Osgood, Samuel M. *French Royalism under the Third and Fourth Republics* The Hague, 1960

Paillat, Claude *L'Échiquier d'Alger* vol. 1: *Avantage à Vichy* Paris, 1966 vol. 2: *De Gaulle joue et gagne* Paris, 1967

Painlevé, Paul *Comment j'ai nommé Foch et Pétain* Paris, 1924

Pardee, M. A. *Le Maréchal que j'ai connu* Paris, 1952

Paxton, Robert O. *Parades and politics at Vichy: The French Officer Corps under Marshal Pétain* Princeton, 1966

Pershing, John J. *My experiences in the World War* London, 1931

Pétain, Marshal Philippe *La Bataille de Verdun* Paris, 1919

Pétain, Marshal Philippe *Quatre Années au pouvoir* Paris, 1949

Pétain, Marshal Philippe *Une crise morale de la nation française en guerre, 1917* Paris, 1966

Le Procès du maréchal Pétain, compte rendu sténographique 2 vols. Paris, 1945

Après le procès du maréchal Pétain: Documents pour la révision Givors, 1948

Peyrouton, Marcel *Du service public à la prison commune* Paris, 1950

Pierrefeu, Jean de *G.Q.G. Secteur 1, trois ans au Grand Quartier Général* 2 vols. Paris, 1920

Piétri, François *Mes années d'Espagne 1940 8* Paris, 1954

Pitt, Barrie *1918: the Last Act* London, 1962

Poincaré, Raymond *Au Service de la France*, vol. 8: *Verdun* Paris, 1931; vol. 9: *L'Année trouble, 1917* Paris, 1932; vol. 10: *Victoire et Armistice 1918* Paris, 1933

Pomaret, Charles *Le Dernier Témoin* Paris, 1968

Pucheu, Pierre *Ma vie* Paris, 1948

Rémond, René *La Droite en France, de la première Restauration à la Ve. République* Paris, 1968

Ressouches, E. de *Le Chemin de Douaumont* Paris, 1951

Reynaud, Paul *Au coeur de la mêlée, 1930–45* Paris, 1951

Reynaud, Paul (trans. by J. Lambert) *In the Thick of the Fight* London, 1955

Ribot, Alexandre *Journal et correspondances inédites, 1914–1922* Paris, 1936

Rougier, Louis *Les Accords secrets franco-britanniques* Paris, 1954

Rougier, Louis *Mission secrète à Londres* Geneva, 1946

Roy, Jules *The Trial of Marshal Pétain* (tr. by R. Baldick) London, 1968

Select bibliography

Ryan, Stephen *Pétain the Soldier* South Brunswick, 1969

Saint-Paulien (Maurice-Yvan Sicard) *Histoire de la Collaboration* Paris, 1964

Schmitt, G. *Les Accords secrets franco-britanniques de novembre-decembre 1940* Paris, 1957

Serres, Olivier de *Le Théâtre d'agriculture et mesnage des champs, pages choisies, précédées d'une lettre de M. le Maréchal Pétain, chef de l'État* Paris, 1941

Serrigny, *Trente ans avec Pétain* Paris, 1959

Shirer, William *Berlin Diary* London, 1941

Sikorski, General W. *La Guerre moderne, son caractère, ses problèmes*, preface by Marshal Pétain. Paris, 1935

Spears, Sir Edward *Liaison, 1914 . . . the Great Retreat* London, 1930

Spears, Sir Edward *Assignment to Catastrophe*, 2 vols. London, 1954

Spears, Sir Edward *Two men who saved France, Pétain and de Gaulle* London, 1966

Terraine, John *Douglas Haig, the educated soldier* London, 1963

Terraine, John *The Western Front, 1914–1918* London, 1964

Terraine, John *The Great War, 1914–1918, a pictorial history* London, 1965

Thomson, David *Two Frenchmen, Pierre Laval and Charles de Gaulle* London, 1951

Thomson, David *Democracy in France since 1870* London, 1964

Tournoux, J. R. *Pétain et de Gaulle* Paris, 1964

Vercors *La Bataille du silence* Paris, 1967

Warner, Geoffrey *Pierre Laval and the Eclipse of France* London, 1968

Weber, Eugen *L'Action Française*

Weygand, Maxime *Foch* Paris, 1947

Weygand, Maxime *Mémoires* 3 vols. Paris, 1950

Wilhelm, Kronprinz *Meine Erinnerungen aus Deutschlands Heldenkampf* Berlin, 1923

Williams, John *The Ides of May—The Defeat of France May–June 1940* London, 1968

Index